Digital Image Processing and Pattern Recognition

DIGITAL IMAGE PROCESSING AND PATTERN RECOGNITION

MALAY K. PAKHIRA
Professor
Department of Computer Science and Engineering
Kalyani Government Engineering College
Kalyani, West Bengal

PHI Learning Private Limited
Delhi-110092
2021

₹ 995.00

DIGITAL IMAGE PROCESSING AND PATTERN RECOGNITION
Malay K. Pakhira

ISBN-978-81-203-4091-6 (Print Book)
ISBN-978-93-5443-464-8 (e-Book)

Published by Asoke K. Ghosh, PHI Learning Private Limited, Rimjhim House, 111, Patparganj Industrial Estate, Delhi-110092 and Printed by Syndicate Binders, A-20, Hosiery Complex, Noida, Phase-II Extension, Noida-201305 (N.C.R. Delhi).

To

my very first teacher

My Mother

Contents

Preface

Digital image processing and *pattern recognition* are two interrelated subject areas that find many real-life applications which are of utmost importance at present. Both the subjects can be treated as non-separable components of the subject of *artificial intelligence.* A majority of fundamental research in computer science and allied areas involve works on these subjects. Newer processing techniques and applications are being developed and discovered by researchers and scientists almost every day. This book is written keeping in mind the need of making the students conversant with the basic principles and theoretical foundations of the subjects. These subjects got their importance not only due to the fact that they are taught at various levels of academic curriculum of many universities and institutes, but also due to their ever-evolving prospects in fundamental and applied research.

There exist a number of related textbooks in the market, but it is always necessary to write newer ones to incorporate newer developments in relevant areas. Most of the existing texts put importance on either image processing or pattern recognition separately. However, these two areas are very nicely interrelated, and we may visualize image processing to lay down the foundation with its lower level processing techniques while higher level real life-applications are supported by pattern recognition techniques. Hence, in this text, equal importance is given to both the subjects.

There are overall 21 chapters in this book along with one appendix. Chapters 1 through 12 cover image processing concepts, Chapter 13 deals with different image file formats, Chapter 14 forms a bridge for transition from image processing to pattern recognition, and the following 7 chapters include topics of pattern recognition. Besides these, the appendix describes the solution procedure of a specific image processing problem. All the chapters contain sufficient pictorial illustrations, solved problems, easy to read algorithms along with necessary theoretical background. The subject matter is presented in a lucid and student friendly manner. The chapter end questions will help curious students to acquire in-depth knowledge and to build their problem solving skills.

The subject of statistical pattern recognition is comprehensively treated in this book with emphasis on parametric and non-parametric techniques. Unsupervised and supervised learning methodologies are explained with necessary tools and illustrations. However, the concept of syntactical pattern recognition is not covered here.

The figures and illustrations (except sketches) presented here are the results of the author's actual experimentation. There are about 200 such figures and sketches which supplement to the textual material. Sufficient numbers of tables and algorithms are other important features of this book.

The author acknowledges the courtsy of Mathworks Incorporation, USA for using several original images from the MATLAB software package.

The author sincerely acknowledge the contribution of his past and present colleagues at Kalyani Government Engineering College, Kalyani, West Bengal. Their support and encouragement are the driving force behind the fulfilment of this huge project. The author also conveys his thanks to all his family members for their love and assistance. Special thanks are conveyed to all the staff of PHI Learning, New Delhi, for their kind support during the manuscript preperation, editing and publication phases.

Malay K. Pakhira

CHAPTER 1

Introduction

At the very beginning of the cyber age, machines developed by human being were capable of performing numerical computations only. Data or information must be presented in numerical form and the results were obtained again in numerical forms. But historically, human beings knew that a picture is worth ten thousand words (data). But it was also realized that processing of pictorial data is not easy and it requires sophisticated and fast hardware and intelligent software systems. With the development of computing technology and associated theoretical developments, the tasks of processing and decision making based on non-numerical data becomes feasible. Nowadays, using powerful systems we can process billions of data items in a second. With such vast capacity of modern computers, we are now striving to make the computer intelligent like human beings. The subject of machine intelligence is called **artificial intelligence**, which has a large area of common interest and motivation with another subject known as **pattern recognition**. As a major portion of human perceived data and information is visual (pictorial) in nature, processing image data becomes a matter of interest to the researchers for the last few decades, with a target to fulfil the desire of making truly intelligent systems. The processes of receiving, representing, processing and analyzing pictorial informations by digital computers are called **digital image processing**.

Nowadays, we use digital computers to represent images in a digital fashion. Storing and processing of information as digital images are made possible due to the tremendous technological advancements in computing technologies during the last few decades. At present computers are equipped with several Gigabytes of main memory and Terrabytes of secondary storage, also the computing speed is extremely high with the use of improved processors and associated hardware and software. For all the above reasons, we now find it easy and mandatory to process information in pictorial form.

1.1 Development of Digital Image Processing

The history of digital images started possibly for solving the image transmission problems for the newspaper industry during 1920s. Earlier to this, analog images were transported by air or ships or by any other similar means. But this form of communication was found very time consuming and costly. In order to reduce the transmission time, images were being digitized and transmitted via cable electronically. But digitization techniques were found to involve loss of significant image information during reconstruction at the other (receiver) end. Hence, it was needed to develop suitable processes like enhancement, restoration, encoding, compression, etc.

During end of 1960s to early 1970s computerised processing of various medical images, like X-ray images, MRI (Magnetic resonance imaging) images, etc. have been started. For this purpose different areas of medical image processing, like Computerized Axial Tomography (CAT) or Computerized Tomography (CT) are developed. At present many other related areas, like Positron Emission Tomography (PET), etc. have been developed. Also techniques for representing and processing images with other visible and invisible band of the electro magnetic spectrum like gamma rays, ultra-violet (UV) rays, infrared rays, etc. are widely used in many scientific applications, like satellite and remote sensing image processing, astronomical image processing, etc. Processing techniques for images captured in the radio frequency band and microwave band also do exist.

1.2 Components of an Image Processing System

Digital images are used for storing and processing in digital computers. Therefore, an image processing system must have, as one of its basic constituent, a digital computer. The other associated devices are storage devices, display or output devices, etc. As the input of such a system is a digital image, we need either to convert an analog image into a digital one or to capture a digital image directly. Therefore, a sensing and sampling digitizer should also be the part of a digital image processing system. Figure 1.1 illustrates the basic components of such a system.

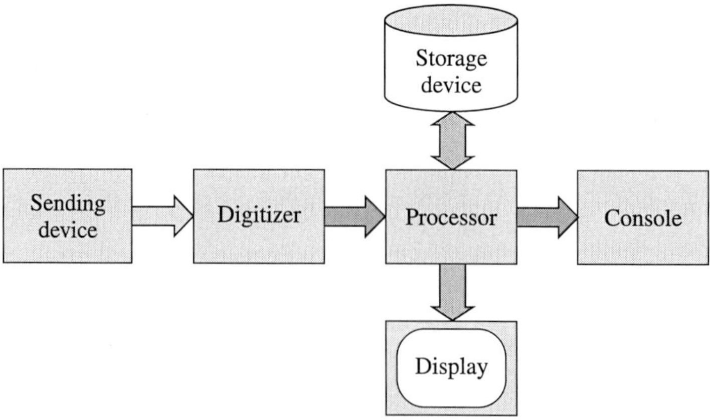

Figure 1.1: Components of an image processing system.

1.3 Different Levels of Processing

Image processing may be performed at several levels of details. At the lowest level, basic image contents are processed to produce another image which is suitable for some applications. This kind of conversion of captured *raw images* into good quality useful ones is called *image enhancement.* Some other relevant processes are image restoration, image registration etc. Images may be represented in various different forms depending on application needs. For example, for the purpose of transmission of images over the internet an encoding technique that may provide a very high compression ratio may be used. This kind of processing is called *image encoding.* Since image encoding processes, in many cases, are combined with encryption (for security) and compression (for packing), the term *image encompression* is commonly used. All the above mentioned techniques constitute what we call low level processing. Low level processing requires very little knowledge of the image contents. Images may be segmented to identify objects and background separately. This process is called *image segmentation.* Sometimes, only the outlines or boundaries of objects are only needed. In such situations *boundary detection* techniques are applied over the input image. These processes are commonly known as *image analysis.*

At the next higher level, the processed images are used for extracting useful information from the images. These are done by feature identification, feature extraction, feature assimilation, etc. Different techniques for identifying different parts of an image exist. In a broad sense, all these techniques constitute a part of the so called *Pattern Recognition* techniques. Identification and extraction are the processes which are also referred to as *Image Analysis.* After identification and extraction of a feature, pattern or object from an image, they are used by other higher level applications for *decision making* in relevant areas. Higher level processing requires human or expert system's knowledge regarding the problem domain. Here, human cognition and decision making power are applied depending on the information contained in the image and the problem concerned.

We shall basically confine ourselves to the lower level processing techniques in the *image processing* part of this book. Some of the higher level decision making techniques will be discussed in the *pattern recognition* part. Some of the basic lower and higher level processing operations of an image processing system are depicted hierarchically in Figure 1.2.

1.4 Lower Level Processing Techniques

As mentioned earlier, lower level processing of images make an image suitable for certain applications, and hence, these are very important. Low level processing techniques are characterized by the fact that both input and output of such a process are images, more specifically, different versions of the same image. We shall mention basic features of some of these processes in brief to have an overview.

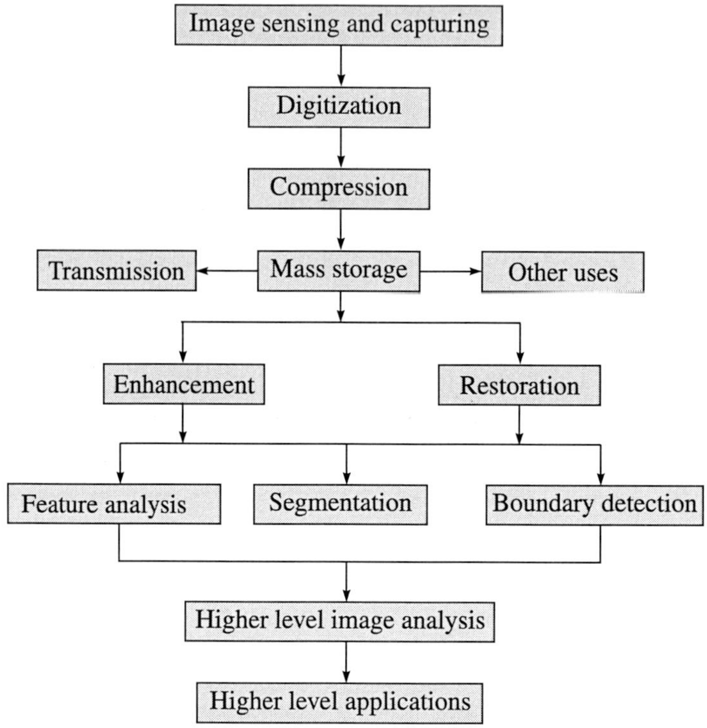

Figure 1.2: Basic steps in an image processing system.

A natural (analog) image is captured by a capturing device. Depending on the mechanism of the device, the captured image may be analog or digital. In classical photographic camera we capture an image as spots of white light, that is reflected from the object surfaces, on a chemical photographic plate. Different areas on the plate react differently depending on the intensity of the incident beam. This image negative is then developed by some other chemical processes to produce a photograph. The image that is produced finally is also analog in nature.

For the purpose of processing an image, it must be converted into a digital or discrete form. The need for digitization is two fold. The first is representability, i.e., to store image in digital media it is compulsory to convert it into a digital form. The second reason is reduction of storage area. Since an analog image is continuous, it contains enormous amount of information (actaully, it is infinite). But for viewing purposes, we need only a very little fraction of this information. Due to inherent limitation of our eyes, we cannot discriminate between small variations in intensity pattern. This concept is successfully employed in image digitization process. The process of conversion of an analog image into a digital image involves the processes of *sampling* and *quantization*. *Sampling* is the process of finding the intensity values at selected image points. In order to maintain appropriate visual or application sensitivity the consecutive sampling points are very close to each other. The sampling frequency is precisely defined by *Shannon's sampling theory.* Generally a rectangular or a hexagonal grid is used for sampling. After sampling, the sampled values need to be fitted within a prespecified range of representable intensity levels. For this reason, the sampled range is divided into a number (equals to the number of prespecified levels) of buckets of equal width. Each bucket is treated as a quantum and the midpoint of each bucket represents the intensity level of that quantum. Thus, we obtain an image with only a limited number of intensity levels. The overall process is called *quantization.*

A digital image can be represented in a number of ways in computer's memory. The difference is due to the use of various types of data structures used to represent it. The most common data structure used in image processing is the square *matrix structure.* Here, image pixels (a sampled point in the image, also called the *picture element*) and the corresponding intensity values are stored in a two dimensional integer array. Although this structure is the most suitable one for many of the image processing tasks, other structures, like *quad tree, topological graph, relational structures* and *pyramid structures* are also used as they are suitable for many applications.

Images captured by capturing devices are in general corrupted by presence of noise. Noise may be inserted in an image for many different reasons, for example, wrong calibration of camera, insufficiency of incident light, malfunctioning of the capturing device, dust and surface roughness on photographic plates, motion of object, wrong focal length, ageing of image, transmission of image, etc. As a result, before applying an image as input to some application, it is necessary to improve the usability of the concerned image in that application. This is done by *image enhancement* techniques. In majority of the cases, enhancement is done by removing noise, smoothing a high contrast image, sharpening a low contrast image, etc. Image enhancement techniques are most appropriately applied when the source and nature of the infiltration is known prior. It is worthwhile to mention that by enhancing we can never improve the quality of an image so as to recover the original true image.

Images can be considered as a two dimensional signal, and hence, it can be represented in either *spatial domain* or *frequency domain.* The process of conversion of images between spatial and frequency domains is called *image transformation.* In frequency domain it is represented in terms of frequencies of component signals. The most common representation is the Fourier series representation. By using reversible Fourier transformation, we can convert an image from its spatial representation to its frequency domain counterpart and vice versa. It is found that almost all the image processing operations can be performed in the frequency domain as well, and in some cases with a better efficiency. There are many other transformations, such as cosine transformation, sine transformation, Hadamard transformation, Slant transformation, etc. All these transformations have their usability for different purposes.

Image restoration is another type of low level processing. Like enhancement techniques, here also we try to improve the appearance of an image. The basic difference between enhancement and restoration is that while image enhancement is subjective, restoration is basically objective. In restoration, we assume suitable models for the image function and the possible degradation function. A succesful model of the degradation process helps us to recover a near approximation of the original undistorted image. On the other hand, enhancement processes rely on subjective human preferences to select a suitable enhancement technique.

Applying the principles of coding theory, an image can be encoded in various different forms. The raw image contains huge amount of data in general. There are different lossy or loss-less compression techniques to reduce image size. Also encryption techniques can be applied along with compression for maintaining security measures. *Image encoding* is therefore, very important from many practical considerations.

Image segmentation is an important process for the purpose of image understanding. By segmenting an image into different intensity regions or patterns we can get sufficient idea about the constituent objects and their structures. There exist different techniques for this purpose. Some of these techniques are edge based, pixel intensity based and region similarity based techniques.

1.5 Applications of Image Processing

The following are very commonly used applications of image processing:

- ***Office Automation:*** Automatic identification of logo icons, optical character recognition, document image analysis, answer script evaluation, biometric authentication, etc.
- ***Industrial automation:*** Automatic control applications, natural resource searching, PCB designing and planning, VLSI floor planning, robotic applications, automatic assembling, etc.
- ***Biomedical applications:*** X-ray, Gamma-ray image processing, MRI, PET, CT image processing, ECG, EEG image processing, Ultrasound testing, and other medical image processing.
- ***Remote sensing:*** Crop estimation, landslide estimation, urban development, costal planning, environment and pollution control, weather forecasting, etc.
- ***Scientific applications:*** High energy physics, gas chamber and bubble chamber image analysis, high energy particle dynamics, etc.
- ***Criminology:*** Finger print identification, face recognition, hand writing style processing, character analysis, etc.
- ***Astronomy and space research:*** Processing of planetary images, restoration of distorted images etc.

- ***Meteorology:*** Weather forecasting, long-term decision making, processing of satellite images, water and gas resource estimation, pollution control, etc.
- ***Information technology:*** Video-conferencing, multimedia document processing and transmission, mobile computing applications, etc.
- ***Entertainment and consumer electronics:*** Multimedia softwares, Embedded systems etc.
- ***Printing and graphics:*** Image formatting, multimedia document preperation, image conversion, colour image processing for printing purposes, etc.
- ***Military applications:*** Target detection, guided missile control, unmanned automatic vehicles, range determination, etc.

1.6 Problems

1. What do you mean by a digital image? Describe the importance of image processing.
2. Draw the block diagram of an image processing system and describe roles of its different parts.
3. Mention some lower level image processing techniques. What are their objectives?
4. Name some common applications of image processing.
5. How can you relate image processing with pattern recognition?
6. Give a physical interpretation of the fact that an image can be considered as a discrete signal.
7. What are the advantages of representing an image as a matrix structure?
8. What are lower level processing and higher level processing of images? What are their significance?
9. What are the differences between grey level and colour images?
10. Describe an application of processing of fingerprint images.
11. What kind of processing of images makes them enabled to be reproduced in different media?

Chapter 2

Image Acquisition

Image acquisition is the process of capturing real images in some media. Generally we capture analog images on photographic plates. This is *photochemical* method of image capturing. The image is recorded on a photographic film by chemical changes on the film. These analog images are then scanned and quantized to get digital images. Real world scenes objects can also be converted to digital images directly using TV cameras. Geo-stationary satellites are used to capture satellite images, whereas, radars are used to capture range images. In such cases, the capturing processes are termed as *photoelectronic* or *remote-sensing*. Only a digital image can be processed by a computer system.

2.1 Capturing Devices

In reality an image is a continuous distribution of intensity or colour values over a bounded 2D space. And a digital image is nothing but a long sequence of 0s and 1s which represent pixels or dots that collectively make up the image. There are two ways to get a digital image:

- A photograph can be taken using a conventional film camera and a printed photograph can be produced. Then using a digital scanner the photograph can be sampled at a certain resolution.
- The reflected beam from the image objects can be directly sampled using a sensory camera.

Different kinds of devices are used to convert a real scene or image into a digital one. Such devices include still camera, TV camera, Charge Coupled Device (CCD) camera, flat-bed scanner, multispectral scanner, etc. In early days of image processing, electro-mechanical devices, like image dissector and microdensitometer were used. Then flying spot scanners and vidicon cameras were used which employed purely electronic technology. Nowadays, the semiconductor devices, like CCD cameras are commonly used. Some of the devices are described here briefly.

2.1.1 Image Dissector

Here, the image is focused directly on the surface of a photosensitive tube whose response is proportional to the incident light pattern. Dissector operates on the principle of electron emission. The image incident on the photosensitive tube produces a beam of electrons. An electromagnet is used to deflect the beam past a pinhole located at the back of the dissector tube which lets through only a small cross-section of the beam, and thus, look at point in the image at a time. Since phosphor or photoemissive materials are very inefficient, the pinhole has to look at the point source for a sufficient time to collect enough electrons. Therefore, dissector is a slow device. Most devices integrate the emission from each point over a time interval before yielding a signal which is proportional to the brightness of the point. Thus, dissectors are useful for applications where very high signal-to-noise ratio is desired. Also since electromagnet and external voltages are applied to deflect the beam into the pinhole, the device is very accurate.

2.1.2 Microdensitometer

This device uses, as its input, a transparency or photograph mounted on a flat bed or wrapped around on a drum. A beam of light is focused on the photograph and the bed is translated, or the drum is rotated for scanning the source. The reflected or transmitted beam is focused on a photodetector which detects the intensity of the beam. This intensity is proportional to the grey level intensity or colour value present on the source. This scanning and detection of intensity produces a digital image. This device is slow, but very accurate due to continuous nature of mechanical translation or rotation.

2.1.3 Flying-spot Scanner

This device works on the principle of focusing a reflected or transmitted beam on a photodetector. Here, the image is kept stationary and a CRT (Cathode Ray Tube) is used as the light source. The object (photograph or photo negative) is placed on the front surface of the tube and the electron beam, deflected by electromagnets, impinges on the fluorescent phosphor surface, produces a tiny spot of light that moves around the face of the tube. The reflected or transmitted beam is measured by the photodetector. A digital image is produced after one complete scanning of the tube surface. It is a very fast and accurate device because of its electronic control.

2.1.4 TV Camera Digitizer

This device employs a vidicon tube which operates on the principle of photoconductivity. The object is focused on the tube surface and a pattern of varying conductivity is produced on the tube surface. This pattern matches the distribution of intensity on the object. The incident electron beam charges points on the photosensitive coating of the tube. This charge then discharges at a rate that is dependent on the amount of incident light. The discharge current is amplified and measured. An independent finely focused electron beam scans the surface of the photoconductive tube, and by charge neutralization, this beam creates a potential difference, and produces, on the collector, a signal proportional to the input brightness pattern. A digital image is obtained by quantizing the signal. This device is somewhat less accurate than the others mentioned above, but, since the process is very fast, it captured digital image on a standard TV monitor.

2.1.5 Filmless Sensory Cameras

The main difference between a digital camera and a film based camera is that the former senses the reflected or refracted beam from the objects and converts it into an electrical signal which is measured for its intensity, and the later directly employ the energy of the reflected beam to perform some chemical reaction on a thin film (negative photographic plate), thereby producing a miniature version of the image.

Image sensors used by most of the sensory cameras fall in two categories: Complementary Metal Oxide Semiconductors (CMOS) and Charge Coupled Devices (CCD). However, since CCDs are most widely used nowadays, we shall describe it in detail.

2.1.6 Charge Coupled Device (CCD) Camera

The CCD is a collection of tiny light-sensitive diodes which convert light into electrical signals. These photosensitive semiconductor diodes act as photosites. At each photosite, a beam of light strikes and the charge accumulated at the photosite becomes proportional to the intensity of the incident beam. These devices are most commonly used due to their simple operation capacity to produce high quality digital images. Here, an array of photosites or semiconductor (MOSFET) cells are used where charge developed by the incident photons (from the scene) are accumulated, and hence, these cells are charged and they act as capacitors. These charges are drained via amplifiers to produce current, proportional to the intensity of the incident beam. This current is then passed through a ADC (Analog to Digital Converter). There are two types of CCDs: Line scan devices and area scan devices (Figures 2.1–2.3).

2.1.7 Flat-bed Scanner

CCD cameras are highly used as flat bed scanners.

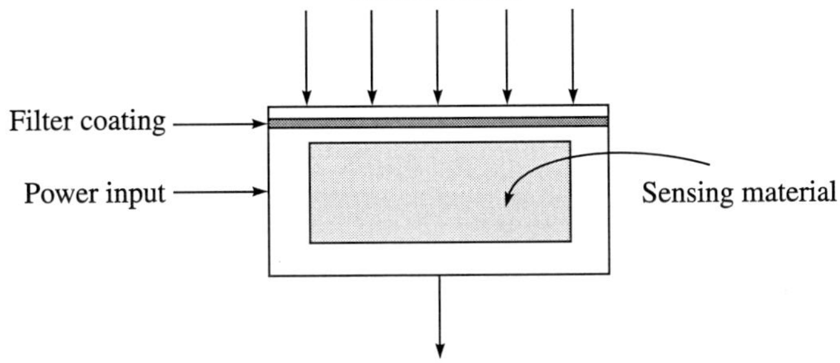

(a) A photosite

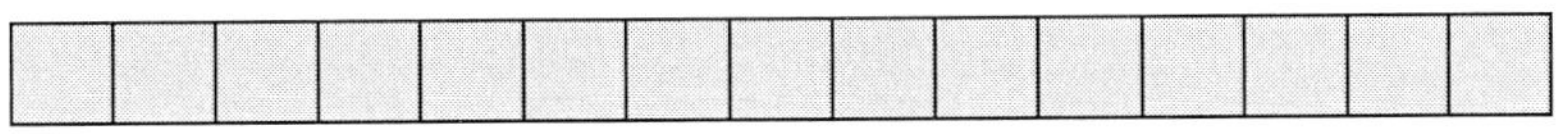

(b) A linear array of photosites

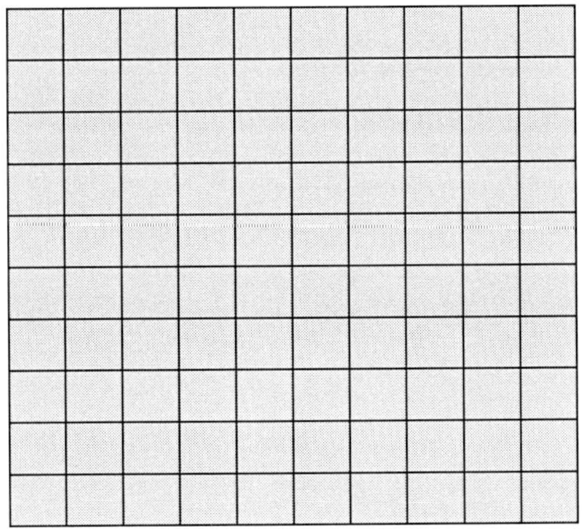

(c) A square array of photosites

Figure 2.1: Components of CCD camera.

2.1.8 Resolution

The amount of image information that the camera can capture per unit area of the captured image is called the *resolution* and it is measured in terms of number of pixels. Some of the commonly used pixel resolutions supported by the commercial digital cameras are: 256×256, 640×640, 1216×912 and 1600×1200 pixels. A particular resolution may be found suitable for a particular application.

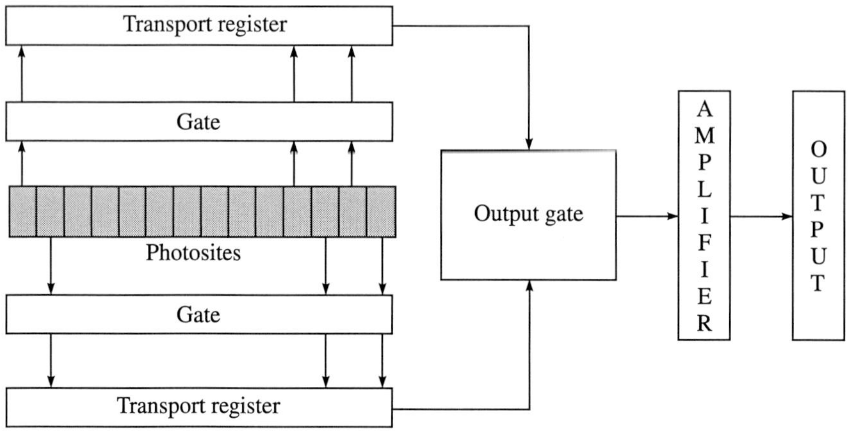

Figure 2.2: A linear array CCD configuration.

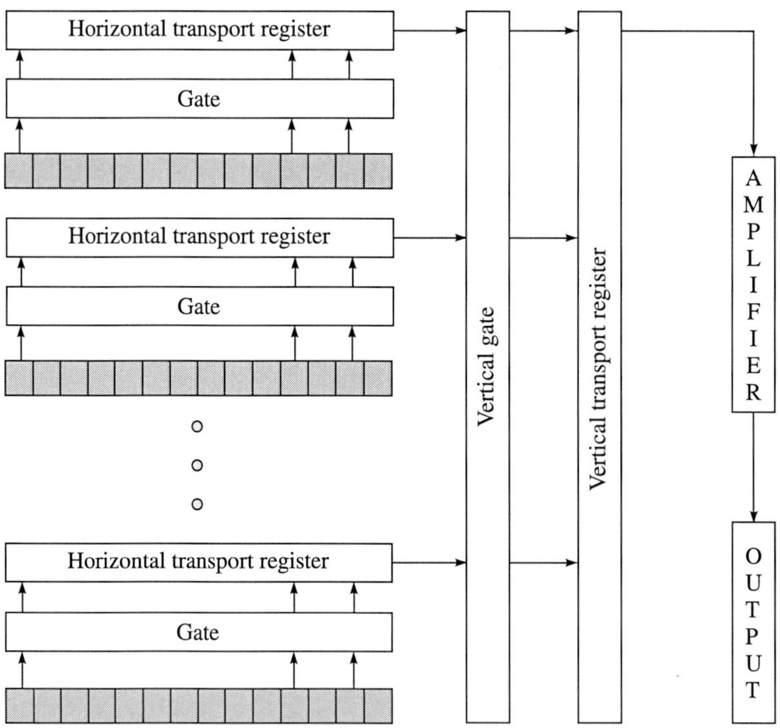

Figure 2.3: A square array CCD configuration.

2.1.9 Capturing Colour Images

The photosites cannot detect colour. They only sense the intensity of the incident beam. However, by using filters we can make light beams of a particular colour to be incident on the photosites. We know that, any colour is essentially a combination of the three basic colours RED, GREEN and BLUE. Hence, we can use three different filters and sense the image thrice to capture three different images.

2.1.10 Other Devices

Generally satellite imagery is done using mechanical scanners. Such devices typically scans six horizontal scan lines at a time. The earth's rotation causes the vertical scanning. A satellite image can cover approximately 100×100 miles with each pixel covering 5×5 metres to 30×30 metres. These types of scanners are placed on surveying satellites, like LANDSAT and ERTS.

Ultrasound radars and laser radars are used to capture images at a relatively shorter distances (compared to satellite images). However, these images are not actually pictorial images, rather they are distance maps, i.e. distances of objects are measured for each pixel position. There are some problems in using ultrasounds in radars. The reflected sound beam may not have sufficient energy to be detected by the receiver. The sound beam may bounce to and fro between the source and the target. The presence of ambient ultrasounds may cause the image noisy. Laser radars are free from such shortcomings.

2.2 Getting Digital Images

The process of converting analog images into computer manageable numerical form is called image digitization. An image captured by a sensor is a continuous function $f(x, y)$ of X and Y coordinate location values in the image plane. The captured image is then sampled in a discrete fashion to produce a matrix of image intensity values. The sampling interval or sampling period and the nature of sampling grid determines the quality of the sampling process in reproducing the image.

After sampling, the image is quantized. It is the process of assigning integer values to the sampled continuous intensity values $f(x, y)$. If the range of intensity values be determined to be limited to $[0, L-1]$, then the range of $f(x, y)$ is divided into L intervals. The larger the value of L, the better will be reproduced image.

2.3 Image Formation and Transformation

The formation of a digital image is a process of mapping 3D Cartesian coordinates onto a 2D plane. The process is called, in general, image coordinate transformation. By this process world coordinates are mapped onto device coordinates. The mapping operation is the so called perspective projection. The schematic of perspective projection of an object point onto the image plane inside the camera are shown in Figures 2.4 and 2.5. Let us consider that the world and device coordinate systems are coincident

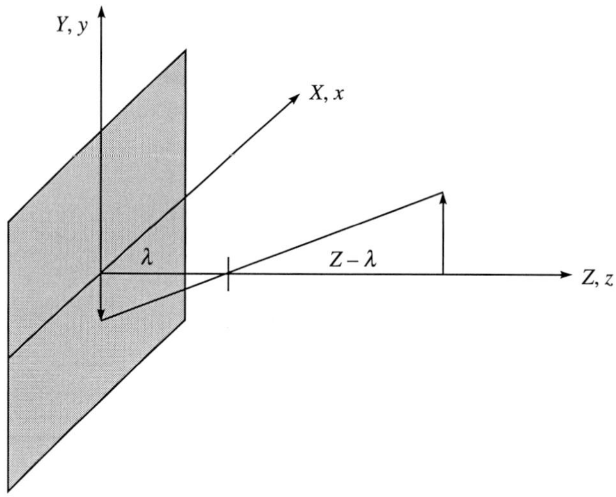

Figure 2.4: Image formation by perspective projection (along Y-axis).

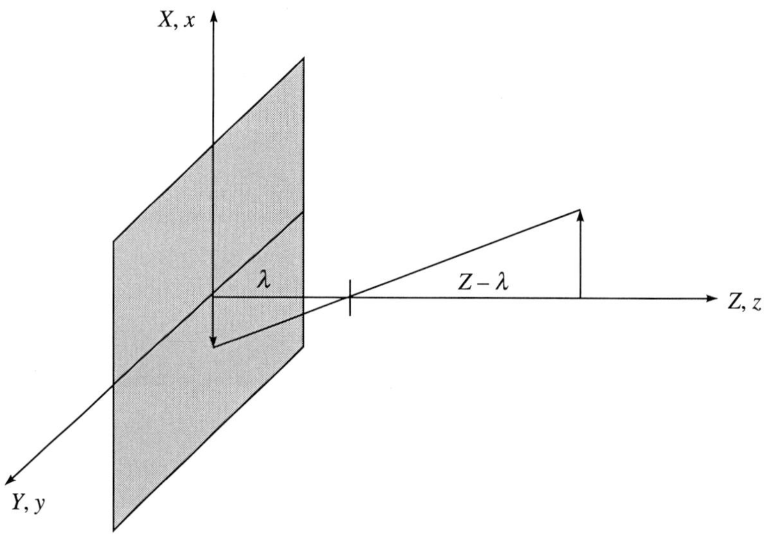

Figure 2.5: Image formation by perspective projection (along X-axis).

and λ is the focal length of the lens of the camera. Then from similarity of triangles, we can write,

$$\begin{aligned} \frac{x}{\lambda} &= \frac{-X}{Z-\lambda} = \frac{X}{\lambda - Z} \\ \frac{y}{\lambda} &= \frac{-Y}{Z-\lambda} = \frac{Y}{\lambda - Z} \end{aligned} \tag{2.1}$$

Thus,

$$x = \frac{-\lambda X}{\lambda - Z}$$
$$y = \frac{-\lambda Y}{\lambda - Z} \tag{2.2}$$

In the *homogeneous coordinate system* we express 2D coordinates as a triple with the help of a constant k. The correspondence between a world coordinate and its homogeneous representation is shown below.

$$\mathbf{w} = \begin{bmatrix} X \\ Y \\ Z \end{bmatrix} \tag{2.3}$$

and

$$\mathbf{w}_h = \begin{bmatrix} kX \\ kY \\ kZ \\ k \end{bmatrix} \tag{2.4}$$

If world coordinate $\mathbf{w}$ is mapped to device coordinate

$$\mathbf{c} = \begin{bmatrix} x \\ y \\ z \end{bmatrix} \tag{2.5}$$

the corresponding homogeneous coordinate representation is:

$$\mathbf{c}_h = \mathbf{P}\mathbf{w}_h = \begin{bmatrix} 1 & 0 & 0 & 0 \\ 0 & 1 & 0 & 0 \\ 0 & 0 & 1 & 0 \\ 0 & 0 & -\frac{1}{\lambda} & 1 \end{bmatrix} \times \begin{bmatrix} kX \\ kY \\ kZ \\ k \end{bmatrix} = \begin{bmatrix} kX \\ kY \\ kZ \\ -\frac{kZ}{\lambda} + k \end{bmatrix} \tag{2.6}$$

where, $\mathbf{P}$ is transformation matrix for perspective projection. Thus,

$$\mathbf{c} = \begin{bmatrix} x \\ y \\ z \end{bmatrix} = \begin{bmatrix} \dfrac{\lambda X}{\lambda - Z} \\ \dfrac{\lambda Y}{\lambda - Z} \\ \dfrac{\lambda Z}{\lambda - Z} \end{bmatrix} \tag{2.7}$$

The above relation can be expressed as

$$x = \frac{\lambda X}{\lambda - Z}, \quad y = \frac{\lambda Y}{\lambda - Z} \quad \text{and} \quad z = \frac{\lambda Z}{\lambda - Z} \tag{2.8}$$

The inverse perspective mapping is done using $\mathbf{P}^{-1}$, i.e.

$$\mathbf{P}^{-1} = \begin{bmatrix} 1 & 0 & 0 & 0 \\ 0 & 1 & 0 & 0 \\ 0 & 0 & 1 & 0 \\ 0 & 0 & \frac{1}{\lambda} & 1 \end{bmatrix} \tag{2.9}$$

It seems that during image formation on the X-Y plane, we do not need the Z-component. However, to reproduce a 3D version, again, we need it. Hence, in inverse transformation we must use this component. Applying Eq. (2.9) we get,

$$\mathbf{w}_h = \mathbf{P}^{-1}\mathbf{c}_h = \begin{bmatrix} 1 & 0 & 0 & 0 \\ 0 & 1 & 0 & 0 \\ 0 & 0 & 1 & 0 \\ 0 & 0 & \frac{1}{\lambda} & 1 \end{bmatrix} \times \begin{bmatrix} lx \\ ly \\ lz \\ l \end{bmatrix} = \begin{bmatrix} lx \\ ly \\ lz \\ \frac{lz}{\lambda} + l \end{bmatrix} \tag{2.10}$$

$$X = \frac{\lambda x}{\lambda + z}, \quad Y = \frac{\lambda y}{\lambda + z} \quad \text{and} \quad Z = \frac{\lambda z}{\lambda + z} \tag{2.11}$$

From Eq. (2.8), we get values of X and Y as

$$X = \frac{x}{\lambda}(\lambda - Z) \quad \text{and} \quad Y = \frac{y}{\lambda}(\lambda - Z) \tag{2.12}$$

Thus, recovering a 3D point from its 2D image by means of inverse perspective projection requires knowledge of at least one of the world coordinates of the point.

2.4 Camera Model

Equation (2.2) constitute the basic mathematical model for an imaging camera. However, this model is based on the assumption that both camera and world coordinate systems are coincident. But generally this is not true, specially, when the camera moves at different locations and orientations. So, before deriving a relation between object and image points, we should make these coordinate systems coincident.

A camera system is shown in Figure 2.6. Here, a world coordinate is $\mathbf{w} = [X\ Y\ Z]^T$ and the corresponding image coordinate is $\mathbf{c} = [x\ y\ z]^T$. Camera is assumed to be mounted on a gimbal which allows 'pan' through an angle θ and 'tilt' through an

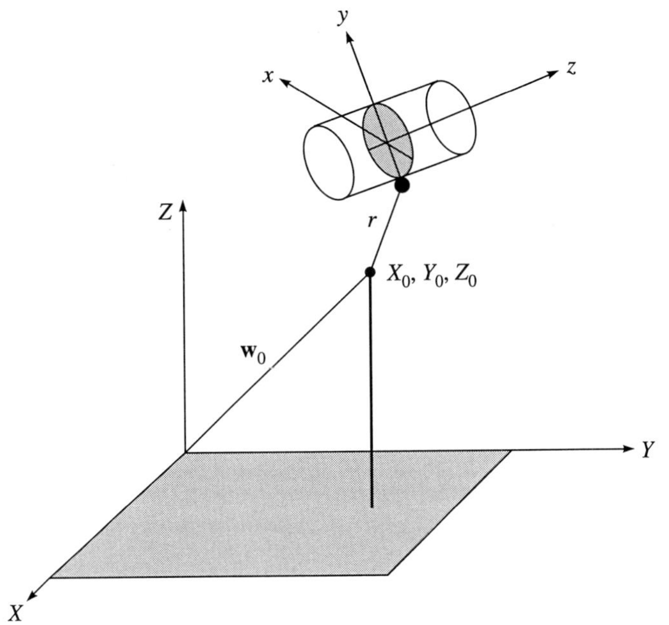

Figure 2.6: Camera and coordinates.

angle α. Pan is the angle between x and X-axes. Tilt is the angle between z and Z-axes. The offset of the centre of the 'gimbal' with respect to the world coordinate origin is denoted by the vector $\mathbf{w}_0$, and the offset of the centre of the imaging plane with respect to the gimbal centre is denoted by the vector $\mathbf{r}$, where $\mathbf{r} = [r_1\ r_2\ r_3]^T$.

Now, we can align the two coordinate systems by means of a set of geometrical transformations. After that we are to apply the projective transformation. Let us assume that initially the camera is in normal position, i.e. the gimbal centre was coincident with origins of the image and world coordinate systems, and all the axes aligned. Now, the required geometric transformations can be achieved in several steps.

1. Translation of gimbal centre from origin.
2. Pan of the X-axis.
3. Tilt of the Z-axis.
4. Translating the image plane from the gimbal centre.

Applying this sequence of transformations, we can obtain an image in its normal position.

Translating the gimbal

Actually this operation corresponds to translating the world coordinate centre to the location of the gimbal centre. The corresponding transformation matrix is

$$\mathbf{G} = \begin{bmatrix} 1 & 0 & 0 & -X_0 \\ 0 & 1 & 0 & -Y_0 \\ 0 & 0 & 1 & -Z_0 \\ 0 & 0 & 0 & 1 \end{bmatrix} \tag{2.13}$$

A world coordinate $\mathbf{w}_h$ will now become $\mathbf{Gw}_h$.

Pan of the X-axis

Now, the X-axis is rotated through the pan angle θ. This is important to keep in mind that when points are rotated clockwise, it indicates that camera is rotated anti-clockwise. The transformation matrix for rotation is

$$\mathbf{R}_\theta = \begin{bmatrix} \cos\theta & \sin\theta & 0 & 0 \\ -\sin\theta & \cos\theta & 0 & 0 \\ 0 & 0 & 1 & 0 \\ 0 & 0 & 0 & 1 \end{bmatrix} \tag{2.14}$$

This $\mathbf{R}_\theta$ is applied to all the points $\mathbf{Gw}_h$.

Tilt of the Z-axis

Now, we are to tilt the camera by angle α. This indicates another rotation about the X-axis. In this case, the rotation matrix is

$$\mathbf{R}_\alpha = \begin{bmatrix} 1 & 0 & 0 & 0 \\ 0 & \cos\alpha & \sin\alpha & 0 \\ 0 & -\sin\alpha & \cos\alpha & 0 \\ 0 & 0 & 0 & 1 \end{bmatrix} \tag{2.15}$$

All points in $\mathbf{R}_\theta\mathbf{Gw}_h$ are transformed by $\mathbf{R}_\alpha$. The two rotation matrices, when combined, produce a resultant matrix

$$\mathbf{R} = \mathbf{R}_\alpha\mathbf{R}_\theta = \begin{bmatrix} \cos\theta & \sin\theta & 0 & 0 \\ -\sin\theta\cos\alpha & \cos\theta\cos\alpha & \sin\alpha & 0 \\ \sin\theta\sin\alpha & -\cos\theta\sin\alpha & \cos\alpha & 0 \\ 0 & 0 & 0 & 1 \end{bmatrix} \tag{2.16}$$

Translation of the image plane

Finally, displacement of the origin of the image plane is done using the following translation matrix

$$\mathbf{C} = \begin{bmatrix} 1 & 0 & 0 & -r_1 \\ 0 & 1 & 0 & -r_2 \\ 0 & 0 & 1 & -r_3 \\ 0 & 0 & 0 & 1 \end{bmatrix} \tag{2.17}$$

So, applying the series of transformations **CRG** to $\mathbf{w}_h$ brings the world and camera coordinate systems into coincidence. The image plane coordinates corresponding to $\mathbf{w}_h$, thus, can be computed as:

$$\mathbf{c}_h = \mathbf{PCRGw}_h \tag{2.18}$$

First and second components of $\mathbf{c}_h$ correspond to image point (x, y) where,

$$x = \lambda \frac{(X - X_0)\cos\theta + (Y - Y_0)\sin\theta - r_1}{-(X - X_0)\sin\theta\sin\alpha + (Y - Y_0)\cos\theta\sin\alpha - (Z - Z_0)\cos\alpha + r_3 + \lambda} \tag{2.19}$$

and

$$y = \lambda \frac{-(X - X_0)\sin\theta\cos\alpha + (Y - Y_0)\cos\theta\cos\alpha + (Z - Z_0)\cos\alpha - r_2}{-(X - X_0)\sin\theta\sin\alpha + (Y - Y_0)\cos\theta\sin\alpha - (Z - Z_0)\cos\alpha + r_3 + \lambda} \tag{2.20}$$

2.5 Automatic Camera Calibration

To establish a correspondence between image coordinate **c** and world coordinate **w**, we need knowledge of focal length, offsets, angles of pan and tilt, etc. These parameters can be measured directly. But measuring one or more of these parameters using the camera itself is more convenient, specially when the camera moves frequently.

Calibration requires a set of image points whose world coordinates are known, and the computational procedure used to obtain the camera parameters using these known points automatic camera calibration.

Let, $\mathbf{A} = \mathbf{PCRG}$, where elements of **A** contains the camera parameters. Now,

$$\mathbf{c}_h = \mathbf{A}\mathbf{w}_h \tag{2.21}$$

Therefore,

$$\begin{bmatrix} c_{h1} \\ c_{h2} \\ c_{h3} \\ c_{h4} \end{bmatrix} = \begin{bmatrix} a_{11} & a_{12} & a_{13} & a_{14} \\ a_{21} & a_{22} & a_{23} & a_{24} \\ a_{31} & a_{32} & a_{33} & a_{34} \\ a_{41} & a_{42} & a_{43} & a_{44} \end{bmatrix} \times \begin{bmatrix} X \\ Y \\ Z \\ 1 \end{bmatrix} \tag{2.22}$$

Here,

$$\mathbf{x} = \frac{c_{h1}}{c_{h4}} \text{ and } \mathbf{y} = \frac{c_{h2}}{c_{h4}}$$

So, we can write,

$$\begin{aligned} xc_{h4} &= a_{11}X + a_{12}Y + a_{13}Z + a_{14} \\ yc_{h4} &= a_{21}X + a_{22}Y + a_{23}Z + a_{24} \\ c_{h4} &= a_{41}X + a_{42}Y + a_{43}Z + a_{44} \end{aligned}$$

The Z coordinate is ignored. Therefore,

$$a_{11}X + a_{12}Y + a_{13}Z - a_{41}xX - a_{42}xY - a_{43}xZ - a_{44}x + a_{14} = 0$$

and

$$a_{21}X + a_{22}Y + a_{23}Z - a_{41}yX - a_{42}yY - a_{43}yZ - a_{44}y + a_{24} = 0 \tag{2.23}$$

There are 12 unknown co-efficients. Calibration is thus, done by using knowledge of correspondence between $m \geq 6$ points in both world and image coordinate systems. The set of 12 simultaneous equations are then solved.

2.6 Stereo Imaging

Mapping a 3D scene onto an image plane is a many-to-one transformation, i.e. an image point does not uniquely determine the location of a corresponding world point. However, the missing depth information can be obtained by using stereoscopic imaging technique. Here, two separate images of the same scene are considered, for which two cameras are used simultaneously. The distance between the centres of the two lenses is called the *baseline*. Say, the object point in world coordinate $\mathbf{P} = (X, Y, Z)$ have image points $\mathbf{P}_1 = (x_1, y_1)$ and $\mathbf{P}_2 = (x_2, y_2)$ [world coordinates are (X_1, Y_1, Z_1) and (X_2, Y_2, Z_2)], in device coordinates of the two cameras (C_1 and C_2), respectively. It is assumed that the camera and world coordinate systems are perfectly aligned. Consider the Figure 2.7(a) and (b) for illustration.

In the world coordinates, $X = 0$ at the midway between the two cameras. Each of the cameras has its own device coordinate system. Let the x-coordinates of the cameras be measured as x_1 and x_2, respectively. At the centres of the left and right cameras $x_1 = 0$ and $x_2 = 0$, respectively. In Figures 2.7(a) and (b), two different situations are depicted. In (a) the object $\mathbf{P}$ is lying on the Z-axis at $X = 0$, when $x_1 = x_2$. And, in (b), $\mathbf{P}$ is located at a different position, while we observe $x_1 \neq x_2$ for the images. In both the above situations, the Z-coordinate of $\mathbf{P}$ is exactly the same for both the camera coordinate systems. Let λ be the focal length of both the cameras.

Let us bring the first camera into coincidence with the world coordinate system. Then, $\mathbf{P}$ lies on the line with coordinates

$$X_1 = \frac{x_1}{\lambda}(\lambda - Z_1) \tag{2.24}$$

If the second coordinate is brought to the origin of the world coordinate system, then $\mathbf{P}$ lies on the line with coordinates

$$X_2 = \frac{x_2}{\lambda}(\lambda - Z_2) \tag{2.25}$$

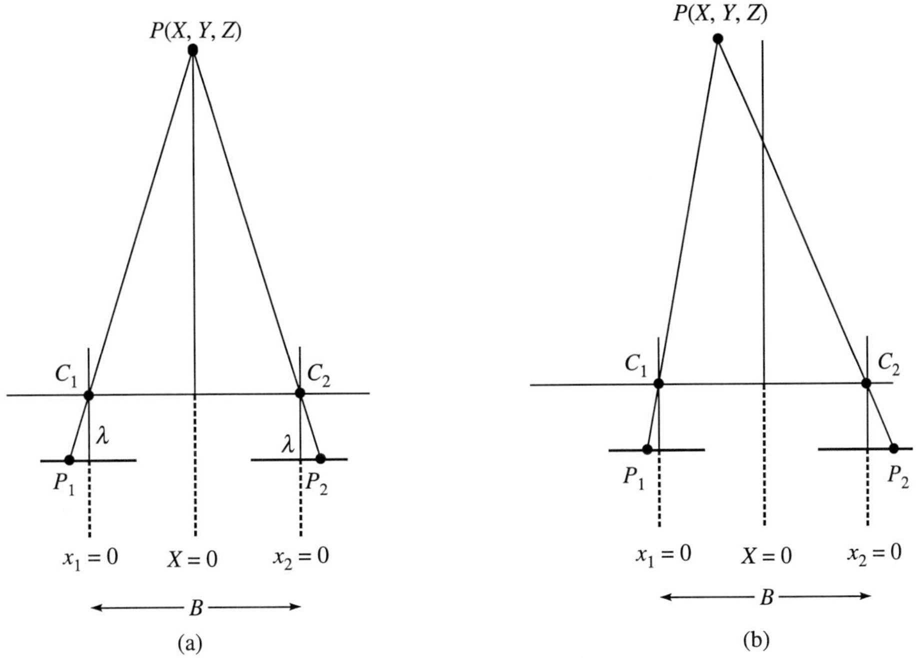

Figure 2.7: Stereo imaging.

But since the Z-coordinate of **P** is the same for both the camera and there is a separation B between the two cameras, we have,

$$X_2 = X_1 + B$$

and

$$Z_2 = Z_1 = Z \tag{2.26}$$

Therefore,

$$X_1 = \frac{x_1}{\lambda}(\lambda - Z)$$

and

$$X_2 = X_1 + B = \frac{x_2}{\lambda}(\lambda - Z) \tag{2.27}$$

Therefore, finally we get,

$$Z = \lambda - \frac{\lambda B}{x_2 - x_1} \tag{2.28}$$

This indicates that, if the difference between the corresponding image x-coordinates, x_2 and x_1, can be determined, and the baseline and focal lengths are known, calculating the depth Z of the object point **P** is a simple matter.

2.7 Problems

1. Name some image acquisition techniques and the corresponding devices.
2. What are world coordinates and device coordinates? How do we make a correspondence between these two.
3. What may be the effect of insufficient ambient light while capturing an image using a photographic camera?
4. What do you mean by camera callibration? What is its significance?
5. Describe configuration and function of a linear CCD camera for image capturing.
6. How 3D scene points can be converted into 2D image points? Show analytically. Is the process reversible?
7. What do you mean by range images? How are they captured?
8. In case of satellite images what may be the range of pixel resolution?
9. A person is observing a lamp post of height 25 feet from a distance of 15 feet. What will be the size of the image formed in his retina? Describe the situation pictorially.
10. What are the mode of operations for linear array and square array CCDs?
11. What kind of sensors are used to capture X-ray images?
12. Draw the schematic diagram of a CCD camera and explain functions of its different components.
13. Explain how stereo imaging helps in recovering depth of 3D objects from 2D images.

CHAPTER 3

Sampling and Digitization

A natural image is a continuous 2D function $f(x, y)$, where $f(x, y)$ is the amplitude of the function at positional coordinate (x, y). This amplitude is a positive value generally describing the intensity or colour of the image at that location. In case of a monochrome image, it is intensity or grey value. In case of colour images, it is the colour value consisting of three basic colours blended at a particular intensity ratio. Thus, $f(x, y)$ is continuous, finite and non-negative, i.e. $0 \leq f(x, y) < \infty$. A digital image, however, possesses all the above properties except that it is discrete.

3.1 Image Formation

Images are formed on the retina of human eye or on the lens of a TV camera by means of plain perspective projection. The surfaces of retina and camera lens are intrinsically 2D and the surrounding world is 3D. So the image formation process is a 3D $\rightarrow$ 2D mapping. Also, since a number of colinear 3D object points are mapped to a single 2D image point, the process may be considered as a many to one mapping. Due to this feature, the reconstruction of original objects from its image becomes ill-posed. The depth information is lost in the captured image.

The detailed process of capturing a 3D scene as a 2D image has been described in Chapter 2. How the 3D points are mapped on a 2D surface has been shown there using the rules of perspective projection. Considering the perspective projection, the length of the image of an object formed on the focal plane of a camera can be calculated.

Example 1: Suppose that a camera is focused at a pillar of height 2 metres and situated at a distance of 10 metres. If the focal length of the camera is 10 mm, what will be the height of the image?

Solution: Here, focal length of the camera is 10 mm, height of the pillar is 2 metres and distance of the pillar from the camera is 10 metres. Therefore, height of the image is

$$h = \frac{2 \times 10}{10} = 2 \text{ mm}.$$

3.2 Image Sampling

After capturing an image using a camera or other sensory devices on a media (like photographic plate, etc.), it becomes a two dimensional distribution of intensity values which is continuous in nature. This is called an analog image. For the purpose of storing and processing by a digital computer, we need to convert the image into a digital (discrete) form. We do this by means of *sampling* the analog image at certain close intervals. Sampled values, in general, are not integral. Since we want the image to consist of a digitally producible integral intensity values, a quantization step follows sampling. By this process, each sampled value is assigned to one of the discrete intensity levels supported by the system. After sampling and necessary quantization processes are applied on an analog image it becomes a digital image.

By the sampling process, a continuous image function $f(x)$ can be sampled or mapped, using a discrete grid of sampling points, into a set of discrete points with integral co-ordinates. The sampling process involves two important parametres (i) sampling interval, and (ii) grid structure. Sampling grid may take many different forms. Some of the very commonly used grid structures are shown in Figure 3.1. Sampling interval determines the quality of the sampled image. As the sampling interval increases, more and more image information will be ignored and we will be unable to reproduce the actual image from the sampled one. On the other hand, if the sampling interval is very small, there may be sufficient overlap between the sampled pixels which eliminates or reduces contrast between nearby pixels or image points. The famous *Shannon's sampling theorem* allows us to set up a limit on the sampling interval for solving the above problems.

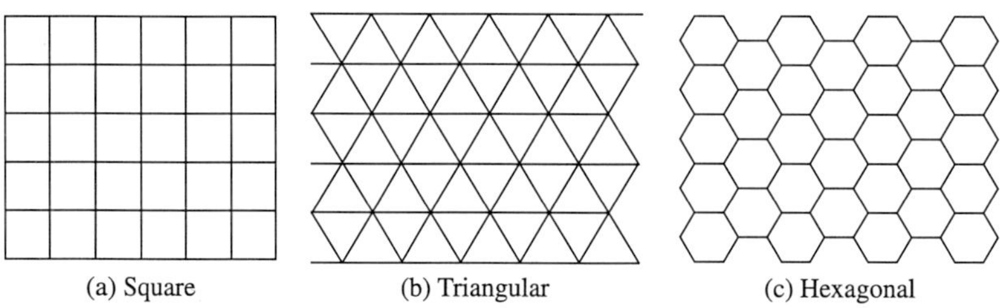

Figure 3.1: Sampling grids.

3.3 Shannon's Sampling Theorem

In digital world sampling of signals plays the most vital role. A naturally occurring signal is generally continuous in time-space. But digital systems cannot deal with continuous signals due to their inherent limitations. Sampling is the process which converts a continuous signal into an approximate discrete form. The processing of sampling is thus referred to as digitization or discretization.

According to the famous Fourier's theorem, a signal can be expressed equivalently in either spatial domain or in frequency domain. In spatial domain representation, a signal is considered to be a plot of amplitude against spatial coordinates. In contrast, in frequency domain, we can represent it as a superposition of infinite number of sine waves with different frequencies and amplitudes. Thus, in both spatial domain and frequency domain, the original signal is continuous in nature. Periodic signals can be represented as a sum of component sine waves whose frequencies are integral multiples of the fundamental frequency. In aperiodic signals, sine waves with all possible frequencies may be present. Although images are generally non-periodic, it is assumed to repeat itself, as a whole; and thereby reduces to a periodic one (at least theoretically).

Fourier Transform is a mathematical tool for converting a signal from one domain to another. Accordingly, there are two different transformations, viz., forward and backward transformations.

Shannon's sampling theorem states that: *A signal can be properly reconstructed from its samples if the sampling frequency is greater than or equal to twice the highest frequency component in the Fourier spectrum of the original signal.* Stated differently, we can say that, if we have a band-limited signal $f(x)$ whose Fourier transform $F(u)$ is zero for $u > u_{\max}$, the signal $f(x)$ can be reconstructed from the sampled signal where sampling interval Δx is such that

$$\Delta x \leq \frac{1}{2u_{\max}} \tag{3.1}$$

or,

$$\frac{1}{\Delta x} \geq 2u_{\max} \tag{3.2}$$

i.e.

$$u_s \geq 2u_{\max} \tag{3.3}$$

where, u_s is the sampling frequency.

An image can be considered as a 2D signal. The detailed shapes of boundaries and corners of the objects present in the image are determined by high frequency components of the constituent signals. The richer the signal is with the high frequency components, the more accurate is the sampled image. For perfect sampling, the number of constituent signals must be infinite, which, in turn, indicates that the sampling frequency must also be infinite. However, in digital world, everything is finite, and hence, to maintain a finite sampling frequency, we must limit the bandwidth of the original signal before sampling. This is done by using a low pass filter. The drawback of this approach is that, the lower the bandwidth of the filtered signal, the lesser it resembles the original one.

3.4 The Sampling Process

The sampling process can be explained by using Dirac's delta function. The delta function may be defined as:

$$\delta(x - x_0) = \begin{cases} 0; & \text{when } x \neq x_0 \\ \infty; & \text{otherwise} \end{cases} \tag{3.4}$$

However,

$$\int_{-\infty}^{\infty} \delta(x - x_0)dx = \int_{x_0^{-1}}^{x_0^{+1}} \delta(x - x_0) = 1 \tag{3.5}$$

So, the function may be viewed as having an unit area in an infinitesimal domain about x_0. Now, we can define a comb function of spacing Δx as

$$\text{comb}(x) = \sum_{r=-\infty}^{\infty} \delta(x - r\Delta x) \tag{3.6}$$

Now, a one dimensional function $f(x)$ can be represented by the samples $f(r\Delta x)$, where r takes on integer values from $-\infty$ to $+\infty$, and Δx is the sampling interval. It is easy to realize that the sampled image $f_s(x)$ is nothing but the product of the continuous image $f(x)$ and the sampling comb function.

$$f_s(x) = f(x)\ \text{comb}(x) = f(x) \sum_{r=-\infty}^{\infty} \delta(x - r\Delta x) \tag{3.7}$$

or equivalently,

$$f_s(x) = f(x)\ \text{comb}(x) = \sum_{r=-\infty}^{\infty} f(r\Delta x)\delta(x - r\Delta x) \tag{3.8}$$

Alternatively, we can say that continuous function $f(x)$ defined over a domain of length $M\Delta x$ can be sampled into a sequence $\{f(0), f(\Delta x), f(2\Delta x), ..., f((M-1)\Delta x)\}$ by taking M samples at Δx intervals apart, and any sample of $f(r\Delta x)$ is given as

$$\int_{-\infty}^{\infty} f(x)\delta(x - r\Delta x)dx \tag{3.9}$$

If we consider unit intervals, i.e. $\Delta x = 1$, then the samples can be represented as periodic with period Δx and can be expanded into a Fourier series, i.e.

$$\sum_{r=-\infty}^{\infty} \delta(x - r\Delta x) = \sum_{m=-\infty}^{\infty} a_m \exp^{i2\pi \frac{mx}{\Delta x}} \tag{3.10}$$

Coefficients of the above expansion can be written as

$$a_m = \frac{1}{\Delta x} \int_{-\frac{\Delta x}{2}}^{\frac{\Delta x}{2}} \sum_{m=-\infty}^{\infty} \delta(x - r\Delta x) \exp^{-i2\pi \frac{mx}{\Delta x}} dx \tag{3.11}$$

Now, in the above sum, the only non-zero term is for $r = 0$, in the range of integration. So, we can write,

$$a_m = \frac{1}{\Delta x} \int_{-\frac{\Delta x}{2}}^{\frac{\Delta x}{2}} \sum_{m=-\infty}^{\infty} \delta(x) \exp^{-i2\pi \frac{mx}{\Delta x}} dx \tag{3.12}$$

The above integral is uniformly one. Therefore,

$$a_m = \frac{1}{\Delta x} \tag{3.13}$$

Thus, as $M \to \infty$, we can write using above value for a_m

$$f_s(x) = f(x) \frac{1}{\Delta x} \sum_{m=-\infty}^{\infty} \exp^{i2\pi \frac{mx}{\Delta x}} \tag{3.14}$$

or

$$f_s(x) = \frac{1}{\Delta x} \sum_{m=-\infty}^{\infty} f(x) \exp^{i2\pi \frac{mx}{\Delta x}} \tag{3.15}$$

In frequency domain,

$$F_s(u) = \frac{1}{\Delta x} \sum_{m=-\infty}^{\infty} \sum_{x=-\infty}^{\infty} f(x) \exp^{i2\pi \frac{mx}{\Delta x}} \exp^{-i2\pi ux} \tag{3.16}$$

or

$$F_s(u) = \frac{1}{\Delta x} \sum_{m=-\infty}^{\infty} \sum_{x=-\infty}^{\infty} f(x) \exp^{-i2\pi x\left(u - \frac{m}{\Delta x}\right)} \tag{3.17}$$

or

$$F_s(u) = \frac{1}{\Delta x} \sum_{m=-\infty}^{\infty} F\left(u - \frac{m}{\Delta x}\right) = \frac{1}{\Delta x} \sum_{r=-\infty}^{\infty} F\left(u - \frac{r}{\Delta x}\right) \tag{3.18}$$

The above equation reveals that the Fourier transform $F_s(u)$ of the sampled function $f(x)$ is nothing but the summation of the shifts of the Fourier transforms $F(u)$ of the continuous function $f(x)$ multiplied by a constant $\frac{1}{\Delta x}$. Again, the shift amount is an integer (constant) multiple of $\frac{1}{\Delta x}$. So in $F_s(u)$, the individual repetitions may overlap around odd multiples of $\frac{1}{2\Delta x}$. Thus, we found that exact reconstruction of $f(x)$ is not possible if $\frac{1}{2\Delta x}$ is less than the highest frequency component in the Fourier expansion of the sample function $f_s(x)$. This is what stated in Shannon's sampling theorem. The sampling process in spatial and frequency domains are depicted in Figures 3.2 and 3.3.

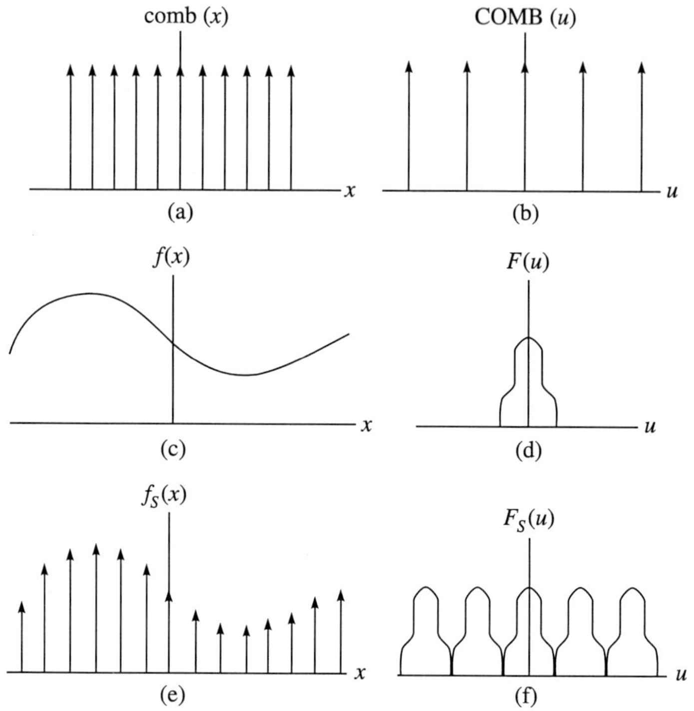

Figure 3.2: The sampling process.

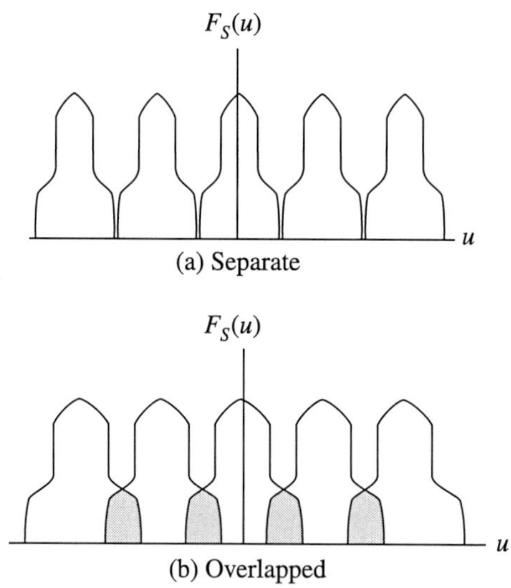

Figure 3.3: Samples in frequency domain.

3.5 The Quantization Process

Values obtained by sampling a continuous image function usually comprises an infinite set of real numbers ranging from a minimum to a maximum. These values must be represented by a finite number of bits usually needed to store and process data. Generally, integral values are stored in computers. So, we need to perform the following mapping:

infinite real numbers $\rightarrow$ finite set of integers

This process of amplitude digitization is called *quantization*. This transformation or mapping is not reversible. The quantization process is shown pictorially in Figure 3.4.

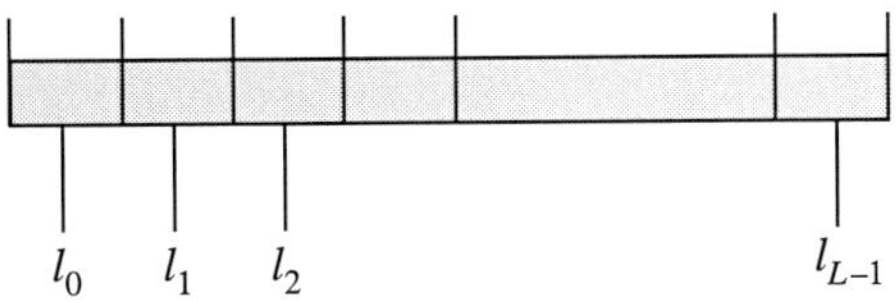

Figure 3.4: The quantization process.

Let, z be a sampled value, and $z_{\min}$ and $z_{\max}$ indicate the range of z. We are to quantize this range into a number of discrete levels. This can be done by dividing the input range into L bins each of width δl and the ith bin centred at l_i.

If the value z be quantized to level l_i then quantization error is:

$$e_q = l_i - z \tag{3.19}$$

Minimum error is 0 and the maximum error can be $\frac{\Delta l}{2}$. Thus, RMS value of the quantization error becomes

$$e_{q\text{rms}} = \sqrt{\sum_{i=0}^{L-1} \int_{\frac{(l_i-\Delta l)}{2}}^{\frac{(l_i+\Delta l)}{2}} (l_i - z)^2 p(z) dz} \tag{3.20}$$

where, $p(z)$ is the probability density of the sampled values, and $z_{\min} = (l_0 - \Delta l)/2$ and $z_{\max} = (l_{L-1} + \Delta l)/2$.

The quantization process introduces noise in the digital image which is called *quantization error*. The signal to noise ratio of a quantized image is

$$\text{SNR} = \frac{\sqrt{\int_{z_{\min}}^{z_{\max}} z^2 p(z) dz}}{\sqrt{\sum_{i=0}^{L-1} \int_{\frac{(l_i-\Delta l)}{2}}^{\frac{(l_i+\Delta l)}{2}} (l_i - z)^2 p(z) dz}} \tag{3.21}$$

In our case, $p(z) = 1$ uniformly. Hence, it can be written as

$$\text{SNR} = \frac{\sqrt{\int_{z_{\min}}^{z_{\max}} z^2 dz}}{\sqrt{\sum_{i=0}^{L-1} \int_{\frac{(l_i-\Delta l)}{2}}^{\frac{(l_i+\Delta l)}{2}} (l_i - z)^2 dz}} \tag{3.22}$$

Main objective of image digitization is to maximize the signal to noise ratio. The discrete version of the above two equations can be written as follows:
Let us consider an image of size $M \times N$. The $e_{q\text{rms}}$ can be computed as

$$e_{q\text{rms}} = \sqrt{\sum_{i=0}^{M-1} \sum_{j=0}^{N-1} {e_{ij}}^2} \tag{3.23}$$

where, e_{ij} is the quantization error inserted at location (i, j).
Therefore, the SNR becomes

$$\text{SNR} = \frac{\sqrt{\sum_{i=0}^{M-1} \sum_{j=0}^{N-1} {z_{ij}}^2}}{\sqrt{\sum_{i=0}^{M-1} \sum_{j=0}^{N-1} {e_{ij}}^2}} \tag{3.24}$$

where, z_{ij} is the intensity value at location (i, j).

Example 2: Consider the scanned image f (in Table 3.1) having grey levels in the range [0 15]. Quantize f into 8 levels from 0 to 7, and compute RMS value of quantization error and signal to noise ratio.

Table 3.1: A Sample Scanned Image

1.4	5.2	13.7	7.8	15.0	14.0	2.4	0.2
1.0	10.3	4.5	9.3	2.3	12.8	3.7	1.2
0.0	7.6	3.9	10.8	4.2	11.9	2.8	0.1
5.5	6.3	14.6	2.5	7.0	12.1	3.2	0.3
6.7	4.5	13.8	3.4	9.5	13.4	5.6	2.3
8.3	3.3	6.9	5.4	14.4	13.5	5.3	4.3
9.3	4.2	7.3	6.2	14.1	14.2	7.3	5.0
1.2	0.5	1.4	1.2	15.0	13.2	9.4	1.6

Solution: Here, the intensity values range from 0 to 15. So each bin has a width of 2.0. If we consider that 8 quantized levels correspond to the midpoints of these bins, they are represented by intensity values 0.5, 2.5, 4.5, 6.5, 8.5, 10.5, 12.5 and 14.5, respectively.

Remaining part of the solution is left as a task for the reader. ♣

3.6 Representation of Sampled Images

After capturing and digitization processes are over, the digital image needs to be stored in computer memory in a suitable form. The basic requirements in this regard are that images should be compact enough (consuming less memory) and can be communicated easily from one machine to another over network or via the internet. Also, in the primary memory, the image should be represented in a manner that facilitate easy processing. Fortunately there exist many data compression techniques which can be applied over digital images as well. For processing purposes, the very common matrix data structure is found to be very suitable. Ofcourse, there exist some other hierarchical data structures that may be suitable at different instances. We shall describe different kinds of representations of a digital image in Chapter 4 in details.

Another important issue in representing a digital image is its contents. Images can be of two types depending on its contents, *intensity image* and *colour image*. In case of intensity images a number of grey shades represent a set of intensity values. The intensity values vary from zero to a certain maximum – zero representing black and the maximum value representing white. Intermediate values represent different shades of black and white (called grey shades). For a binary image only pure black and pure white shades are present. For a colour image, each pixel in the image is represented by a colour triple. When the RGB colour model is used, this triple contains Red, Green and Blue intensity values. So a colour image is three times in size compared to a grey shaded intensity image. Since in a digital image we can use only a limited number of intensity or colour values, and also, since our eyes can discriminate between two consecutive intensity levels with a certain gap between them, we need to select different intensity values very carefully. The very famous Weber's intensity rule helps in this regard. This topic also is discussed in the next chapter comprehensively.

3.7 Problems

1. What do you mean by image sampling and image digitization?
2. Describe the process of conversion of an analog image into a digital image.
3. State and prove Shannon's sampling theorem.
4. Explain in your own words what may the artifacts of digitization caused by lower or higher sampling rates.
5. How can you determine the quantization error present in an image? Explain.
6. What is SNR? What is its importance in image processing? Derive an expression for SNR.
7. During assignment of grey levels to quantization bins how will you determine size of each quanta or bin?

8. Consider the sampled image of Example 2. If additive noise is inserted to each pixel during sampling, as shown in the chart below, compute the SNR of the sampled image.

0.35	0.05	0.05	0.95	0.25	0.25	−0.15	0.05
0.25	0.95	−0.75	−0.65	−0.05	0.95	0.05	0.05
0.25	0.15	−0.15	0.45	−0.55	−0.65	0.95	0.15
0.75	−0.05	−0.95	0.25	−0.25	−0.95	0.55	0.95
−0.45	−0.75	−0.05	0.35	−0.75	−0.15	0.75	−0.05
0.45	0.45	−0.65	0.85	−0.15	0.25	0.95	−0.55
−0.55	−0.45	−0.05	0.05	−0.35	0.05	0.05	0.25
0.05	0.75	−0.15	0.05	0.25	0.05	−0.65	−0.35

Chapter 4

Fundamentals of Digital Images

After capturing and digitization, the obtained digital image is stored in computer memory. As mentioned in earlier chapters, the most common and convenient way is to represent it in the form of a two-dimensional intensity distribution $f(x, y)$, where $f(x, y)$ is the value of the image function at positional coordinate (x, y). This is a discrete integral value describing the intensity or colour of the image at that location. In case of a monochrome image, it is the intensity or grey level. In case of colour images, it is the colour value consisting of three basic *colours* blended at a particular intensity ratio. Thus $f(x, y)$ is discrete, finite and non-negative, i.e. $0 \leq f(x, y) \leq L - 1$, where L is the maximum number of grey levels or colours that can be present in an image.

4.1 Representation of Digital Images

Captured digital images can be represented in computer memory in a number of ways. The most common representation is the matrix notation. Essentially, a digitized image is nothing but an evenly spaced collection of pixels or image elements placed on a 2D surface. Since, it is a common practice to capture, maintain and reproduce rectangular images in the computer world as well as in reality, we can represent them as matrices. Normally, digital images are quantized to discrete integral levels, and hence, elements of the matrix are integer values representing the brightness or intensity or other similar properties of the corresponding pixel.

The matrix representing the image may contain integral intensity values only. In that case we call it to be a grey image. When each pixel value is limited to either 0 or 1, we call it a binary image. For a colour image, we maintain three different matrices of the same size, one each for RED, GREEN and BLUE colour intensities. For a remotely sensed image, generally, information regarding intensities of the image in several spectral bands are maintained. These electromagnetic spectral bands may include both visible and invisible bands. The bands of the spectrum that are commonly used are gamma rays band, hard X-rays band, soft X-rays band, ultraviolet band, visible band (VIBGYOR), infrared band, microwaves band and radio waves band. Since the extreme bands of the above spectrum are not visible, image capturing in those bands cannot be done using ordinary cameras. Special kinds of sensory devices are used for this purpose. Such captured images are often called *multi-spectral images.* Besides, matrix representations, other higher level or abstract representations for images are possible. Some of such notations are pyramids and quad trees. These are commonly called *hierarchical representations.* Besides these, segment description, geometric description, relational description and grammatical description of images are also possible, in specific situations.

4.1.1 Matrix Representation

As mentioned earlier, matrices for sampled and quantized images contain real and integral values in general. By a digital image we commonly understand a fully quantized integral intensity distribution in the form of a rectangular matrix. Let us consider a monochrome grey level intensity image $f(x, y)$ of size $M \times N$. Here, M and N are numbers of rows and columns of the image matrix. $f(x, y)$ is the grey value at location (x, y) in the matrix. Here, both x and y assume only integral values ranging 0 to $M-1$ and 0 to $N-1$, respectively. Of course, these does not mean that the values of x and y correspond to the actual physical locations in the original scene we captured. In general, a finite area of the scene is mapped to a single pixel in the captured image. Using the above matrix notation an $M \times N$ digital image can be written as

$$f(x,y) = \begin{bmatrix} f(0,0) & f(0,1) & \cdots & f(0,N-1) \\ f(1,0) & f(1,1) & \cdots & f(1,N-1) \\ \vdots & \vdots & \vdots & \vdots \\ f(M-1,0) & f(M-1,1) & \cdots & f(M-1,N-1) \end{bmatrix} \tag{4.1}$$

Image digitization needs specifying three parameters. M and N represent the size of the image matrix, and L is the number of grey levels that a pixel can assume. M and N must be positive integers and L is generally a power of 2. Therefore, we can express L as

$$L = 2^k \tag{4.2}$$

where, k is the number of bits needed to code any grey value. The L grey values range from 0 to $L-1$. The look of an image depends on the number of quantized levels. A larger value of L ensures a better look. The total number of bits needed to store a monochrome digital image is $M \times N \times k$.

4.1.2 Pyramid Representation

These are hierarchical data structures. Images can be represented as Matrix pyramids (M-pyramids) and Tree pyramids (T-pyramids). A matrix pyramid is a sequence $(M_K, M_{K-1}, \ldots, M_0)$ of images, where M_K has the same size and dimension as that of the original image, and M_{i-1} is derived from M_i by reducing resolution by one-half. Representing images using this form is useful when the original image is square and dimensions are power of 2. This form uses different degrees of resolution at different levels.

The original image is represented by M_k which has the highest resolution. The next lower level image has resolution reduced by a factor of 4, i.e. the image at level one contains four times less data. Therefore, processing level one image will be four times faster. The user needs to select a desired level of representation according to the need of the resolution accuracy and processing time available. Actually, here we need to store many versions of the same image which together form a hierarchy having different accuracy at different levels.

The M-pyramid allows us to use the image available at a particular level only. The T-pyramid, on the other hand, allows to use multiple levels of images simultaneously. A T-pyramid is defined as:

1. A set of nodes $P = \{P = (k, i, j)$ such that level $k \in (0, K); i, j \in (0, 2^k - 1)\}$.
2. A mapping F between subsequent nodes P_{k-1}, P_k of the pyramid, such that

$$F(k, i, j) = (k - 1, i \text{ div } 2, j \text{ div } 2)$$

   where 'div' indicates integer division.
3. A function V that maps a node of the pyramid P to Z, where Z is the subset of the whole numbers (integers) corresponding to the number of intensity levels, for example, $z = \{0, 1, 2, \ldots, 255\}$.

A T-pyramid contains the elements of an M-pyramid for a certain level k. That is an image $P = \{(k, i, j)\}$ for a particular k constitute an image at the kth level of the pyramid. Every node in the T-pyramid has four children except at the leaf nodes. The leaf nodes contain individual image pixels. Values at the other nodes are either an arithmetic mean of the child elements or they are defined by some coarse approximation (e.g. the maximum value in a block of four pixels, etc.).

If there are K levels in a T-pyramid, the number of pixels in the image (also the number of elements at the leaf nodes) will be 2^{K-1}. The number of image pixels used by an M-pyramid for storing all image matrices can be computed as

$$N^2\left(1 + \frac{1}{4} + \frac{1}{16} + \cdots\right) \approx 1.33N^2 \tag{4.3}$$

where $N \times N$ is the dimension of the original image. The general structure of a T-pyramid is shown in Figure 4.1.

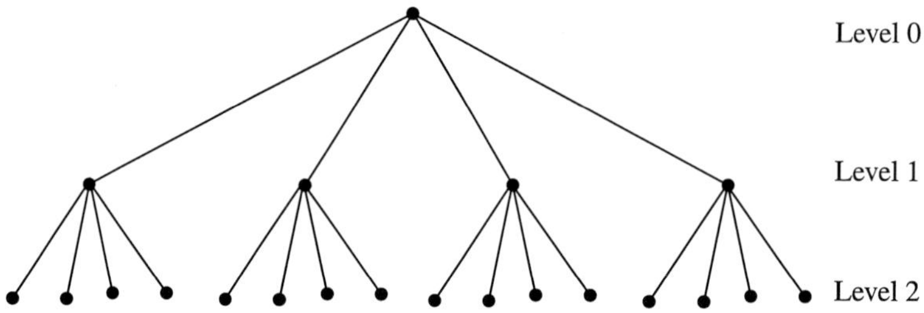

Figure 4.1: T-pyramid representation of an image.

4.1.3 Quad Tree Representation

It is also a form of levelized tree-like structure of an image. In a quad tree, the leaf nodes have at least four children which are the elements of a square 2×2 pixel grid of the image. The combination of these four pixels form a single unit of image information for the next higher level of tree nodes. In a quad tree, it is not necessary to expand all intermediate nodes up to the leaf nodes. We may continue subdividing them as long as there exist sufficient dissimilarity among the elements of a node. Thus, the quad tree may have different heights along different paths.

The quad tree can be formed by successively sub-dividing the image into four quadrants. The root node represents the original image. Therefore, we get images with different resolution at different hierarchy levels. Quad tree allows efficient computation of object areas, object merging, segmentation, etc. One major disadvantage is the dependency on position, orientation and relative size of objects, etc. Two similar images with very little difference between them may have completely different quad tree representations. Therefore, comparing two images in this model is somewhat difficult.

Figure 4.2: Quad tree representation of an image.

4.2 Pixel Geometry

If we represent an image as a function $f(x, y)$, then (x, y) indicates a pixel location whose X-coordinate value is x and Y-coordinate value is y, and $f(.)$ is the intensity value or grey value (for grey level images) of the concerned pixel. In general, a set of contiguous pixels in an image identify an object. In an image there may exist a number of objects and a background. Objects present in an image maintain a particular geometrical or positional relationship amongst themselves. One can identify the position of a particular object in relation to others, the boundary of an object, interior and exterior of an object, shape of an object, etc. using pixel geometry or image geometry. In the following subsection we shall briefly describe some important geometrical properties and measurements that help us in doing the above mentioned image processing tasks.

4.2.1 Neighbourhood and Connectivity

Pixels of a digital image are assumed to occupy integral coordinate locations only. And consecutive pixels are unit distance apart along either X or Y directions. If P be a pixel with coordinate (x, y) we can identify its four neighbour pixels, along X and Y directions, whose coordinates are given by

$$(x-1, y), (x+1, y), (x, y-1) \text{ and } (x, y+1)$$

respectively. The above four neighbours form a neighbourhood set $N_4(P)$ for pixel P.

The diagonal neighbours of pixel P are

$$(x-1, y-1), (x+1, y+1), (x-1, y+1) \text{ and } (x+1, y-1)$$

respectively. The diagonal neighbourhood set for pixel P is represented by $N_d(P)$.

Therefore, we may consider two kinds of neighbourhood or connectivity for any pixel. When diagonal neighbours are not considered, a pixel is called a 4-neighbour pixel, and counting the diagonal pixels as neighbour is called an 8-neighbour pixel. The neighbourhood set of an 8-neighbour pixel P is denoted as $N_8(P)$. Therefore,

$$N_8(P) = N_4(P) \cup N_d(P) \tag{4.4}$$

It should be noted in this context that the neighbourhood size for all the pixels in an image may not be 4 or 8 only. For a pixel lying on the boundary of the image these values are lesser. The pixel neighbourhood is shown in Figure 4.3.

Two pixels are said to be connected if they are neighbours to each other. The concept of connectivity is very useful to determine boundary of an object or to find out regions occupied by an object, etc. Different kinds of pixel connectivity can be defined as follows:

4-connectivity: Two pixels P and Q are said to be 4-connected if either of the following conditions hold

$$Q \in N_4(P) \text{ or } P \in N_4(Q)$$

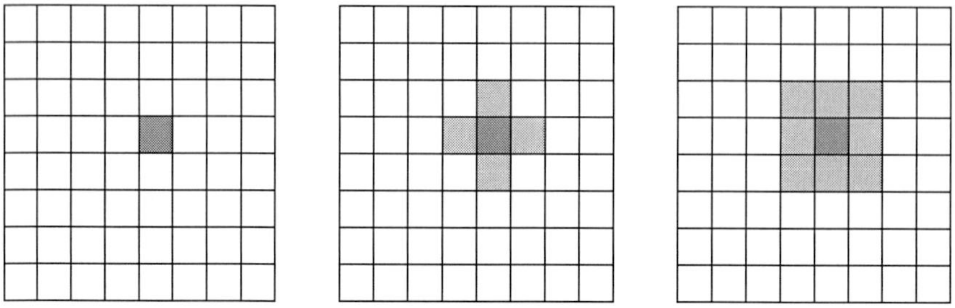

(a) A pixel in image matrix (b) 4-neighbours (c) 8-neighbours

Figure 4.3: Image geometry.

8-connectivity: Two pixels P and Q are said to be 8-connected if either of the following conditions hold

$$Q \in N_8(P) \text{ or } P \in N_8(Q)$$

m-**connectivity**: Two pixels P and Q are said to be m-connected if the following conditions hold

$$Q \in N_m(P) \text{ or } P \in N_m(Q) \text{ and } N_4(P) \cap N_4(Q) = \Phi$$

m-connectivity may be used to eliminate multipath connections that may arise when 8-connectivity is used.

4.2.2 Pixel Adjacency

Two pixels P and Q in an image are said to be *adjacent* if P and Q are connected. Depending on whether 4-connectivity or 8-connectivity or m-connectivity is used, we can define 4-adjacency, 8-adjacency or m-adjacency, respectively. Two regions or pixel subsets in an image are said to be connected if at least one of the pixels from each subset are connected.

4.2.3 Path

A *path* between two pixels P and Q is a sequence of connected pixels between P and Q. For example, there exist a path between pixels (x_1, y_1) and (x_n, y_n), if we have a pixel sequence $(x_1, y_1), (x_2, y_2), (x_3, y_3), \ldots, (x_n, y_n)$ such that (x_i, y_i) is connected to or adjacent to (x_{i-1}, y_{i-1}) and (x_{i+1}, y_{i+1}) for $2 \leq i \leq n-1$.

4.2.4 Pixel Distance

Distance between any two pixels can be computed in many different ways. The most common distance measure is the *Euclidean distance.* Euclidean distance between two pixels (x_1, y_1) and (x_2, y_2) is defined as

$$d_{12} = \sqrt{(x_1 - x_2)^2 + (y_1 - y_2)^2} \tag{4.5}$$

Another well known measure is the *Manhattan distance* (also called city-block distance) defined as

$$d_{12} = |(x_1 - x_2)| + |(y_1 - y_2)| \tag{4.6}$$

The *Minkowski distance* is a generalization of both Euclidean and Manhattan distance measures. It is defined as

$$d_{12} = \{|(x_1 - x_2)|^p + |(y_1 - y_2)|^p\}^{1/p} \tag{4.7}$$

where p is a positive integer. This generalized distance is called L_p norm distance in literature. Hence, the Manhattan and the Euclidean distances are of norms L_1 and L_2, respectively.

4.3 Vector Operations

Algebraic operations based on vectors and matrices are very useful in image manipulation in many cases. In an image, represented as a rectangular matrix, a row or a column may be considered as a row or a column vector, respectively.

A line segment in conventional geometry can be represented as a vector. In an n-dimensional space, a vector is represented as

$$\mathbf{v} = (v_0 \quad v_1 \quad v_2 \quad \cdots \quad v_{n-1}).$$

When written or viewed horizontally, it is called a **row vector**. In vertical representation it is called a column vector. The relation between row and column representation is

$$\mathbf{v} = (v_0 \quad v_1 \quad \cdots \quad v_{n-1})^T = \begin{bmatrix} v_0 \\ v_1 \\ \vdots \\ v_{n-1} \end{bmatrix}$$

Here, the superscript T stands for matrix transposition. A null vector has all its scalar components equal to zero.

4.3.1 Vector Algebra

The *magnitude* of a vector $\mathbf{v}$ is

$$||\mathbf{v}|| = \left(v_0^2 + v_1^2 + \cdots + v_{n-1}^2\right)^{\frac{1}{2}} \tag{4.8}$$

The magnitude is also called the Euclidean norm of a vector. A unit vector has a norm one.

Two vectors **u** and **v** are equal if their corresponding scalar components are equal. That is, $\mathbf{u} = \mathbf{v}$ if $u_0 = v_0, u_1 = v_1, \ldots, u_{n-1} = v_{n-1}$.

Two vectors **u** and **v** can be added or subtracted by adding or subtracting their corresponding scalar components. That is,

$$\mathbf{u} \pm \mathbf{v} = (u_0 \pm v_0 \quad u_1 \pm v_1 \quad \cdots \quad u_{n-1} \pm v_{n-1}) \tag{4.9}$$

A vector can be multiplied by a scalar as follows

$$k\mathbf{v} = [kv_0 \quad kv_1 \quad kv_2 \quad \cdots \quad kv_{n-1}] \tag{4.10}$$

The *inner product* or dot product of two vectors of the same dimension is defined as

$$\mathbf{u} \cdot \mathbf{v} = u_0 v_0 + u_1 v_1 + \cdots + u_{n-1} v_{n-1} \tag{4.11}$$

If **u** and **v** are equal i.e. $\mathbf{u} = \mathbf{v}$, then we have

$$\mathbf{u} \cdot \mathbf{v} = \mathbf{u} \cdot \mathbf{u} = \mathbf{u} \cdot \mathbf{u} = ||\mathbf{u}||^2 = ||\mathbf{v}||^2 \tag{4.12}$$

Vector addition and multiplication operations are commutative, associative and distributive, i.e.

$$\mathbf{u} + \mathbf{v} = \mathbf{v} + \mathbf{u} \text{ and } \mathbf{u} \cdot \mathbf{v} = \mathbf{v} \cdot \mathbf{u} \tag{4.13}$$

$$\mathbf{u} + (\mathbf{v} + \mathbf{w}) = (\mathbf{u} + \mathbf{v}) + \mathbf{w} \tag{4.14}$$

$$\mathbf{u} \cdot (\mathbf{v} + \mathbf{w}) = \mathbf{u} \cdot \mathbf{v} + \mathbf{u} \cdot \mathbf{w} \tag{4.15}$$

4.4 Matrix Operations

The most common representation of an image is in the form of a rectangular matrix containing intensity values as its elements. While a row or a column vector is a linear array, we can consider a matrix as a rectangular array. Matrix manipulation operations are very useful in majority of the image processing tasks. In later chapters we shall see that operations like domain conversion, convolution, correlation, boundary detection, filter design and many enhancement and restoration operations are essentially matrix operations.

It is already shown that the image matrix assumes the following form

$$\mathbf{F} = f(x,y) = \begin{bmatrix} f(0,0) & f(0,1) & \cdots & f(0,N-1) \\ f(1,0) & f(1,1) & \cdots & f(1,N-1) \\ \vdots & \vdots & \vdots & \vdots \\ f(M-1,0) & f(M-1,1) & \cdots & f(M-1,N-1) \end{bmatrix}$$

Here the image is $M \times N$ in size, and $f(i, j)$ is the ijth element of the image matrix. The matrix will be called a Null matrix when $f(i, j) = 0$ for all i, j. If $M = N$, the matrix is a square matrix. A matrix is called a diagonal matrix if its non-diagonal elements are zero. A diagonal matrix becomes a identity matrix if all the diagonal elements are equal to one, and is denoted by **I**.

4.4.1 Matrix Algebra

Two matrices of the same size can be added element wise to form a third matrix. If **F** and **G** are two matrices, each of size $M \times N$, their sum is another matrix **H** of the same size. That is

$$\mathbf{H} = \mathbf{F} + \mathbf{G} \tag{4.16}$$

where, $h(i, j) = f(i, j) + g(i, j)$ for all i, j. Matrix addition is commutative and distributive, i.e.

$$\mathbf{F} + \mathbf{G} = \mathbf{G} + \mathbf{F} \tag{4.17}$$

and

$$\mathbf{F} + (\mathbf{G} + \mathbf{H}) = (\mathbf{F} + \mathbf{G}) + \mathbf{H} \tag{4.18}$$

Two matrices are multiplied if column size of the first matrix is equal to the row size of the second. In other words, two matrices **F** and **G** of sizes $M \times L$ and $L \times N$ can be multiplied to produce a third matrix **H** of size $M \times N$. Elements of the resultant matrix **H** can be given by

$$h(i, j) = \sum_{l=0}^{L-1} f(i, l)g(l, j) \tag{4.19}$$

for all i and j. Matrix multiplication is not commutative, i.e.

$$\mathbf{FG} \neq \mathbf{GF} \tag{4.20}$$

But the distributive law holds in this case, i.e.

$$\mathbf{F}(\mathbf{GH}) = (\mathbf{FG})\mathbf{H} \tag{4.21}$$

and

$$\mathbf{F}(\mathbf{G} + \mathbf{H}) = \mathbf{FG} + \mathbf{FH} \tag{4.22}$$

The *transpose* of a matrix can be obtained by converting its rows into columns and columns into rows. If **G** is the transpose matrix of **F** written as $\mathbf{G} = \mathbf{F}^T$, we have, $g(i, j) = f(j, i)$ for all i and j. When a matrix is exactly equal to its transpose, it is called a symmetric matrix. In this case, $\mathbf{F} = \mathbf{F}^T$.

The *trace* of a matrix is a scalar and is defined as

$$tr(\mathbf{F}) = \sum_{i=0}^{M-1} f(i,i) \tag{4.23}$$

If two matrices **F** and **G** are of the same size then

$$tr(\mathbf{FG}) = tr(\mathbf{GF}) \tag{4.24}$$

The *Euclidean norm* of a matrix **F** is defined as

$$||\mathbf{F}|| = tr(\mathbf{F}^T\mathbf{F}) \tag{4.25}$$

In this connection, the Euclidean norm for a vector **f** can be written as

$$||\mathbf{f}|| = \mathbf{f}^T\mathbf{f} \tag{4.26}$$

And the inner product of two vectors **f** and **g** may be written as

$$\mathbf{fg} = \mathbf{f}^T\mathbf{g} \tag{4.27}$$

The outer product of two vectors **f** and **g**, on the other hand, is a matrix whose size is $M \times N$, where M and N are sizes of vectors **f** and **g**, respectively. The outer product can be expressed as

$$\mathbf{f} \times \mathbf{g} = \mathbf{f}\ \mathbf{g}^T \tag{4.28}$$

The *rank* of a matrix is defined as the number of independent rows or independent columns. A square matrix of size $M \times M$ is said to be **non-singular** if its rank is M. In case its rank is less than M, it is called a **singular** matrix. For every non-singular matrix **F** an *inverse* matrix $\mathbf{F}^{-1}$ can be computed. The product of a matrix with its inverse produces a identity matrix, i.e.

$$\mathbf{FF}^{-1} = \mathbf{F}^{-1}\mathbf{F} = \mathbf{I} \tag{4.29}$$

The *determinant* of a square matrix **F** of size $M \times M$ can be computed from the cofactors of its elements. An example for finding determinant of a 3×3 matrix is shown below.

$$\mathbf{F} = \begin{bmatrix} f_1 & f_2 & f_3 \\ f_4 & f_5 & f_6 \\ f_7 & f_8 & f_9 \end{bmatrix}$$

and

$$\begin{aligned} & f_1 \begin{vmatrix} f_5 & f_6 \\ f_8 & f_9 \end{vmatrix} - f_2 \begin{vmatrix} f_4 & f_6 \\ f_7 & f_9 \end{vmatrix} + f_3 \begin{vmatrix} f_4 & f_5 \\ f_7 & f_8 \end{vmatrix} \\ |\mathbf{F}| \quad = \quad & -f_4 \begin{vmatrix} f_2 & f_3 \\ f_8 & f_9 \end{vmatrix} + f_5 \begin{vmatrix} f_1 & f_3 \\ f_7 & f_9 \end{vmatrix} - f_6 \begin{vmatrix} f_1 & f_2 \\ f_7 & f_8 \end{vmatrix} \\ & +f_7 \begin{vmatrix} f_2 & f_3 \\ f_5 & f_6 \end{vmatrix} - f_8 \begin{vmatrix} f_1 & f_3 \\ f_4 & f_6 \end{vmatrix} + f_9 \begin{vmatrix} f_1 & f_2 \\ f_4 & f_5 \end{vmatrix} \end{aligned}$$

In general, we can express the determinant algebraically as

$$|\mathbf{F}| = \sum \pm f(0,i)f(1,j)\cdots f(M-1,n) \tag{4.30}$$

where, the summation is taken over all permutations $(i,j,\ldots,n)$ of $(0,1,\ldots,M-1)$ with a plus sign if $(i,j,\ldots,n)$ is an even permutation, and with a minus sign if it is an odd permutation. If determinant of a matrix of size $M \times M$ is zero then its rank is less than M and it is called a *singular* matrix.

The concepts of *eigen vector* and *eigen value* are very important in the context of image processing. An eigen vector $\mathbf{v}$ and the corresponding eigen value λ of a matrix $\mathbf{F}$ of size $M \times M$ are related by the following relation

$$\mathbf{F}\mathbf{v} = \lambda\mathbf{v} \tag{4.31}$$

here, λ is a scalar value. Eigen values are the roots of a characteristic polynomial of a matrix given by

$$\mathbf{F} - \lambda\mathbf{I} = 0 \tag{4.32}$$

4.5 Mathematical Morphology

It is a relatively a new concept of set theoretic mathematics that has been found to be very useful for many image processing tasks. The technology deals with the shapes of objects present in an image. Many operations of image pre-processing, segmentation, edge detection, etc. are found to be done in a better and speedier way using morphological operations in comparison to conventional methods.

It is already mentioned that mathematical morphology is applied in situations where shape of objects and speed of processing are involved. One prospective application area is document image analysis, another area is medical image processing. We shall discuss only some very fundamental operations of morphology in order to convey the basic ideas only to the beginners.

The two most basic operations of mathematical morphology are *dilation* and *erosion*. Other operations are different combinations of these basic operations mainly. Ofcourse, dilation and erosion themselves are constituted from more fundamental set theoretic operations, like, *translation*, *union* and *intersection*. Mathematical morphology works with *point sets*, *point connectivity* and *geometrical shapes* present in an image. It needs real images be present as a set of points in any dimension. For planar shapes points are from 2-dimensional Euclidean space. In Mathematical morphology, some basic operations and their symbolic notations are as follows:

Inclusion	$\subset$ *or* $\supset$	Empty set	Φ
Union	$\bigcup$	Set complement	$(\ ^c\ )$
Intersection	$\bigcap$	Set difference	$X - Y = X \bigcap Y^c$

In Euclidean space, a 2D image is formed as a set of integer pairs ($\in Z^2$) for a binary image, where Z is the set of integers. and a set of integer triples ($\in Z^3$) for grey scale images. Thus, a binary image is 2D point set. If object points (points having 1 values) be represented by a set X, then we can represent the background points by the set complement, i.e. X^c. The origin of the object space is represented as a cross ($\times$) mark and has coordinate (0, 0). Other points have 2D coordinate values as usual. In Figure 4.4, the black squares represent the object points (set X). Any point on the object is a vector with respect to the origin (0, 0) denoted by symbol O, and is also called the *representative point.*

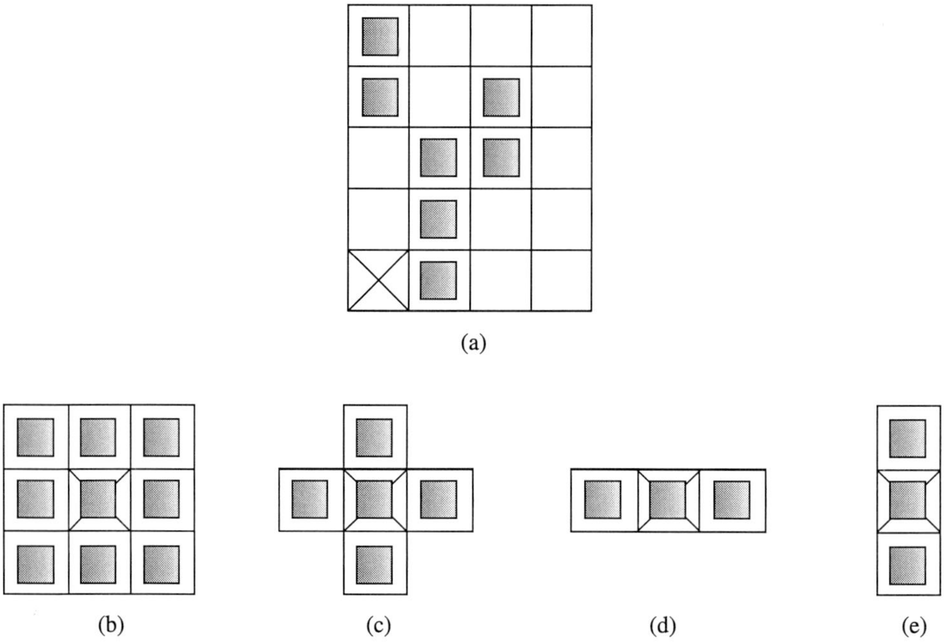

Figure 4.4: (a) Object Point set, (b)–(e) structuring elements.

A morphological operation indicates a relation between two sets: one is the *object point set* and the other is small point set called *structuring element set.* Examples of some simple structuring element are shown in Figure 4.4. A morphological operation is performed by moving an element 'B' over image point set 'X' in a systematic manner. When 'B' is placed at some point on an image, the pixel corresponding to the representative point 'O' of the structuring element is called the *current pixel,* and the result of relation (which is either a 0 or a 1) is stored in the output image in the current pixel location.

Let D be a rectangular domain of the object points and t be a point in the same domain. Then a translation of the point set 'X' by t is denoted as X_t and is expressed as

$$X_t = (p \in D; p = x + t; \text{ for some } x \in X) \tag{4.33}$$

The dilation of X and B, denoted as $X \oplus B$, is defined by

$$X \oplus B = (p \in D;\ p = x + t; \text{ for some } x \in X \text{ and } b \in B) \tag{4.34}$$

Dilation can also be defined as

$$X \oplus B = \bigcup_{b \in B} X_b \tag{4.35}$$

The dilation of X and B, denoted as $X \ominus B$, is defined by

$$X \ominus B = (p \in D; p = x + t; \text{ for some } x \in X \text{ and } b \in B) \tag{4.36}$$

Dilation can also be defined as

$$X \ominus B = \bigcap_{b \in B} X_{-b} \tag{4.37}$$

Dilation and erosion satisfy the following duality property

$$X \ominus B = \left(X^c \oplus \breve{B}\right)^c \tag{4.38}$$

and

$$(X \ominus B)^c = X^c \oplus \breve{B} \tag{4.39}$$

In the above, $\breve{B}$ is the symmetrical set to B (also called transpose or rational set) with respect to the representative point O, i.e.

$$\breve{B} = \{-b : b \in B\} \tag{4.40}$$

For example,

$$B = \{(1,3),(2,3)\}$$
$$\breve{B} = \{(-1,-3),(-2,-3)\}$$

Opening and *closing* are two very important operations in morphology. Erosion followed by dilation constitute the operation of opening, and dilation followed by erosion constitute what is called closing. The operations of *opening* and *closing* are, therefore, defined by

$$X \circ B = (X \ominus B) \oplus B \tag{4.41}$$

and

$$X \bullet B = (X \oplus B) \ominus B \tag{4.42}$$

respectively.

Opening can also be defined as

$$X \circ B = \bigcup_{B_p \subseteq X} X_b \tag{4.43}$$

Opening and closing satisfy the following duality property

$$X \bullet B = \left(X^c \circ \breve{B}\right)^c \tag{4.44}$$

and

$$(X \bullet B)^c = X^c \circ \breve{B} \tag{4.45}$$

Another important morphological operation is *hit-and-miss* transformation. If there are structuring elements B and C such that $B \cap C = \phi$, then hit-and-miss transformation of a set X by B and C is given by

$$A \otimes (B, C) = (X \ominus B) \cap (X^c \ominus C) \tag{4.46}$$

From the above mentioned basic operators, one can derive other relations that may be very useful for many image processing operations. For grey scale images there exist other morphological operators like *top*, *umbra*, etc.

4.6 Visual Preliminaries

In the early days of digital image processing, we could represent images only in black and white. These images were referred to as binary images. With the advancement of computing technology and display devices, we became able to represent, process and produce grey level images. Conventionally, the number of grey values were limited by the number of bit planes used in the frame buffer to store an image. Bi-level, 8-level and 256-level grey images require 1-bit plane, 3-bit planes and 8-bit planes, respectively. At present, we are able to process full colour images using sophisticated hardware and software. Most commonly used image display systems include the following:

- Cathode Ray Tube (CRT)
- Liquid Crystal Display (LCD)
- Light Emitting Diode (LED)
- Plasma Panel Display (PPD)
- Digital Beam Projectors.

Besides the above, image outputs can be obtained using hardcopy devices that includes

- Printer
- Plotter

For colour images, monitor display and hardcopy displays behave differently. Hence different types of colour systems are used for these two types of devices.

In the following section, we shall discuss, requirements of a display system based on human visual properties, different techniques of producing black and white images on output devices.

4.6.1 Human Visual System and Digital Display

The process of displaying digital images on an output device has a very close relationship with the visual characteristics of human eyes. The objective of any such display technology is to maintain the essential attributes of a digital display that are sufficient to satisfy the human perception abilities. The quality of a displayed image depends on its spatial resolution and intensity resolution. The higher the frequency of sampling, the more spatial resolution can be achieved. Intensity resolution increases with number of intensity levels present in the image. These two properties of a digital image are illustrated on a key image (128×128 with 64 intensity levels originally) in Figures 4.5 and 4.6, respectively.

(a) 128×128 (b) 64×64 (c) 32×32

Figure 4.5: Different sampling frequencies produce images with different resolution.

Human eyes work as an analog device during capturing an image. In this sense, abilities of the human eye is always superior than any modern digital camera. Two types of cells: *rods* and *cones*, are responsible for sensing monochrome and colour intensities, respectively. Although the eye can sense a very wide range of intensity spectrum, it cannot simultaneously discriminate between relatively closer intensity levels. This limitation of human eyes allow us to limit the number of intensity levels (quantize), either for grey or colour images, within a reasonable bound for display purposes.

(a) 64 levels (b) 16 levels (b) 2 levels

Figure 4.6: Images with different number of grey levels.

4.6.2 Assigning Intensity Levels to Grey Shades

Digital images are constituted of pixels with discrete intensity values as digital systems are unable to display continuous intensity patterns. However, due to limitation of human eye we cannot differentiate between consecutive intensity levels. Also, human eye perceives different brightness levels for the same object when viewed under different background levels. This effect is called the **Machband effect** and is shown in Figure 4.7 below.

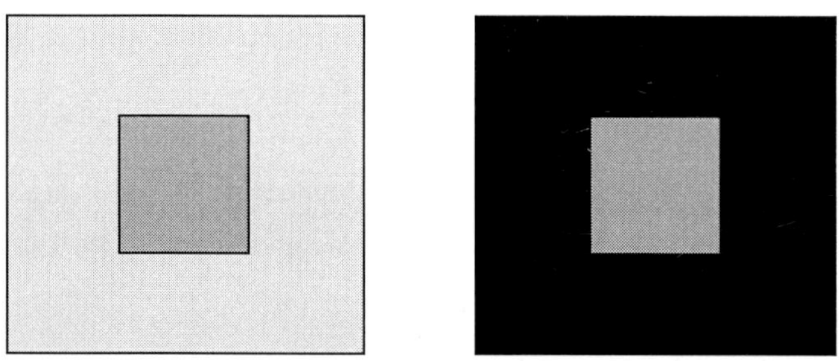

Figure 4.7: The difference in contrast for the same object under different backgrounds.

Therefore, the discriminating power of the eye becomes a very important issue in relation to producing an output image. Here, we must consider the sensitivity of the eye to detect the difference between two different brightness levels or intensities. Our eyes perceive relative light intensities in the same way that our ears perceive sound intensities. This means that relative intensities are detected by human sensory organs on a logarithmic scale. In other words, this means that if the ratio of two intensities is the same as the ratio of two other intensities, we perceive the difference between two pairs of intensities to be the same. So when a number of intensity levels are to be displayed on the monitor, for better perception, the ratio r between any two successive intensities should be constant.

Let us consider a normalized digital picture where intensity values are in the range $(0, 1)$. If we want to produce only L levels $(0, L-1)$ then, each intensity should be r times higher than the preceding intensity, i.e.

$$\frac{I_1}{I_0} = \frac{I_2}{I_1} = \cdots = \frac{I_{L-1}}{I_{L-2}} = r \tag{4.47}$$

or

$$I_0 = I_0, I_1 = rI_0, I_2 = rI_1, \ldots, I_{L-1} = rI_{L-2} = 1 \tag{4.48}$$

Therefore,

$$r = \left(\frac{1}{I_0}\right)^{\frac{1}{L-1}} \tag{4.49}$$

or

$$I_j = r^j I_0 = \left(\frac{1}{I_0}\right)^{\frac{j}{L-1}} I_0 = I_0^{\frac{L-1-j}{L-1}} \tag{4.50}$$

A plot of I_j against j, where $L = 16$, is shown in Figure 4.8.

With 8 intensities (i.e. $L = 8$) and an I_0 of $\frac{1}{128}$ we have, $r = (128)^{\frac{1}{7}}$, i.e. $r = 2$, which gives intensity levels as $\frac{1}{128}, \frac{1}{64}, \frac{1}{32}, \frac{1}{16}, \frac{1}{8}, \frac{1}{4}, \frac{1}{2}, 1$. If the dynamic range of representable intensities is (0–255), i.e. 256 grey levels, then we should select the 8 grey values as: 2, 4, 8, 16, 32, 64, 128, 256 or, without any loss as: 1, 3, 7, 15, 31, 63, 127, 255.

Figure 4.8: Intensity distribution based upon logarithmic scale.

From the above description, it is easy to see that, visual discrimination power of the eye is higher at the lower end of the intensity scale. In actual experimentation, it is observed that, our eyes can differentiate between two intensity levels, I and I', with I' surrounding I, if the difference $\Delta I = I' - I$ between those two intensity levels is such that

$$\frac{\Delta I}{I} \geq 0.02 \tag{4.51}$$

This ratio $\frac{\Delta I}{I}$ is called the *Weber ratio.* Thus, when this ratio is just 0.02, there exists just noticeable difference between the concerned intensity levels. This threshold value of 0.02 is found to be maintained over a wide range of intensity levels. From the Weber's law, we can establish the relationship between two consecutive intensity levels as

$$\frac{I + \Delta I}{I} = 1.02 \tag{4.52}$$

for maintaining just noticeable difference. A set of 16 intensity levels around the upper end of the intensity spectrum is shown in Figure 4.9 which maintain just noticeable difference.

Figure 4.9: Intensity levels with just noticeable difference.

4.6.3 Gamma Correction and Lookup Tables

Video Lookup Tables are very commonly used to store a limited number of colour-intensity combinations required to display an image to serve visual satisfaction as well as to save memory and processing time. However, just like the non-linear response of intensity patterns to human eye, the display monitors also exhibit a form of non-linearity while displaying a linear range of intensity values. This means that the velocity of the electron beam producing illumination on the video monitor are not proportional to the produced intensities. If we plot a curve of displayed intensities against voltage applied to the electron gun, we can observe this non-linear characteristic of the display device (Figure 4.10).

Entries in the video lookup table are thus adjusted to nullify this undesired non-linearity of the voltage-intensity relationship. The monitor response curve can be expressed by an exponential function

$$I = \alpha V^{\gamma} \tag{4.53}$$

Here, I is the displayed intensity and V is the applied input voltage to the electron gun. Parameters *alpha* and γ depends on monitor characteristics. To eliminate this

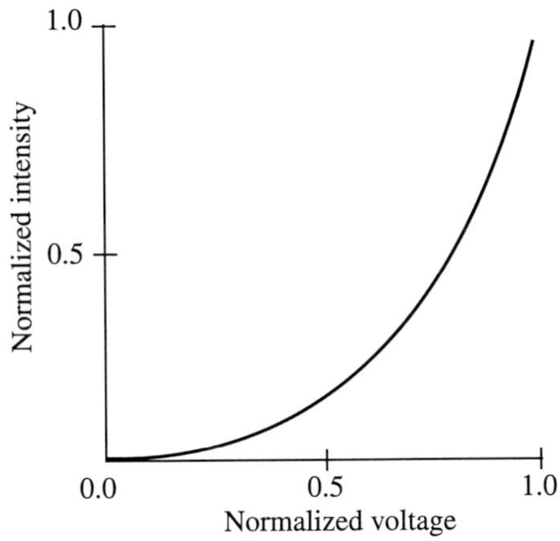

Figure 4.10: Monitor response.

non-linear effect from the output and to produce the correct intensity I, we need to set the voltage level at

$$V = \frac{I^{\frac{1}{\gamma}}}{\alpha} \tag{4.54}$$

This correction applied to the input voltage is called *gamma correction.* It is found that values of γ for different kinds of monitors lie between 2.0 to 3.0. The curve shown in Figure 4.11 represents the required voltage against produced intensity in order to achieve a gamma corrected display.

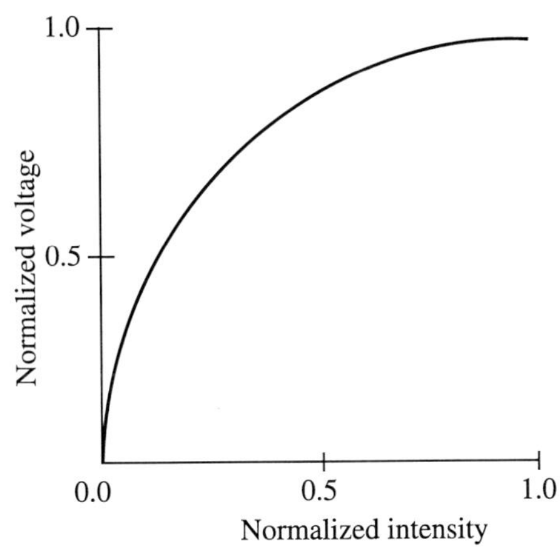

Figure 4.11: Gamma correction.

The above mentioned anomaly factors of human eye and the display monitors can be combined into a single relationship which may be used to determine correct lookup table entries. To produce an intensity level of I, we first identify the nearest value I_j

using Eq. (4.50), then we apply Eq. (4.54) to determine the electron gun voltage as

$$V_j = \left(\frac{I_j}{\alpha}\right)^{\frac{1}{\gamma}} \tag{4.55}$$

Values of V_js are stored in the lookup table to produce I_js.

4.6.4 Creating Grey Shades for Bi-level Displays

In modern computer systems, the output devices are equipped with hardware that can generate a number of different grey or colour levels. However, if we have a bi-level device, with the capacity to produce only either a white or a black pixel, we can create grey shades by using digital halftoning. Halftoning techniques can be classified into patterning and Dithering methods. These methods are described briefly in the following paragraphs.

Patterning

Here, pixels are considered to be formed as matrices of individual dots (a dot means either a black or a white spot on the screen). The matrix of dots is called a pattern grid or simply pattern. Individual locations in this grid are, thus, called dots. Grey levels are created by filling up grid locations with black and white dots. By maintaining an appropriate ratio of black and white dots we can achieve an overall appearance of grey levels. A 2×2 pattern grid and the associated grey-level appearances are shown in Figure 4.12. Here, only five grey levels, including the 0-level can be produced. In general, with an $N \times N$ pattern matrix, we can achieve $N^2 + 1$ number of different grey values.

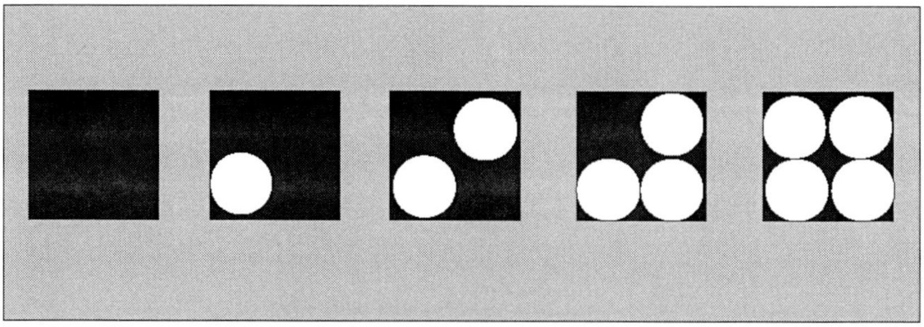

Figure 4.12: Patterns with four dots.

In Figure 4.12, patterns corresponding to 5 different grey levels, that correspond to grey values 0 to 4, are shown. Patterns may be regular or irregular. If for all the occurrences of a certain grey value, the corresponding patterns contain black and white dots at the same positions in the pixel grid, the pattern is called a **regular pattern**. In case of irregular patterns, the individual dot positions are selected randomly at every instance. Regular and irregular patterns have their advantages and disadvantages. Somc of the advantages and disadvantages of regular and irregular patterns are given below.

Advantages of regular patterns:

- Preferred, as they avoid clumps of dots being randomly created.
- Readily available from standard set.
- Useful for printers for storing as font set.

Disadvantages of regular patterns:

- Sometimes produce visible lines in the image which makes it obscure.
- Every time patterns need to be constructed anew.
- Consume much memory area to store the fixed set, specially patterns are large.

Advantages of irregular patterns:

- Avoid generation of visible lines in the image.
- Extra memory is not needed to store patterns.

Disadvantages of irregular patterns:

- Sometimes clumps may be produced in the output image.
- Every time patterns need to be constructed anew.
- Cannot be used as printable fonts due to randomness.
- Makes the system response slower.

Alternative approach

Instead of storing different patterns, we can store only a single integer square matrix whose locations contain integers ranging from 0 to the maximum grey value G. This fixed matrix is called a standard pattern. The grey level corresponding to a particular grey value (g) is created by highlighting only those dot positions whose contents are less than g.

Method for creation of standard patterns

Here, we need to specify the basic patterns of smallest size. Then higher order patterns can be developed using a recurrence relation. For example, patterns of sizes 2×2 and 3×3 can be represented as

$$M_2 = \begin{bmatrix} 3 & 1 \\ 0 & 2 \end{bmatrix} \text{ and } M_3 = \begin{bmatrix} 7 & 2 & 6 \\ 4 & 0 & 1 \\ 3 & 8 & 5 \end{bmatrix}$$

respectively. These basic patterns are created keeping it in mind that consecutive integral values should be placed in the matrix with maximum separation between them.

Now, for a base matrix M_n, the next higher order matrix M_{2n} can be developed as

$$M_{2n} = \begin{bmatrix} 4 \times M_n & 4 \times M_n + 2 \times U_n \\ 4 \times M_n + 3 \times U_n & 4 \times M_n + U_n \end{bmatrix} \tag{4.56}$$

where, U_n is a square matrix of size $2^n \times 2^n$ with all elements equal to 1.

Using this technique the matrix M_4 will be

$$M_4 = \begin{bmatrix} 12 & 4 & 14 & 6 \\ 0 & 8 & 2 & 10 \\ 15 & 7 & 13 & 5 \\ 3 & 11 & 1 & 9 \end{bmatrix}$$

Dithering

Sometimes it is found that the display space is smaller than required for producing an output image with patterning. For patterns of size $n \times n$, the display size must be at least larger than the original image by factors of n along both X and Y directions so that sufficient number of dots per pixel can be produced. If instead, we have a smaller display size where we can produce pixels as $m \times m$ dot arrays where $m < n$, we apply some randomization techniques along with standard patterning. The resulting procedure is called dithering.

To produce a higher number of grey values with a smaller pattern size, dithering is used. The available number of patterns (grey values) are fixed by the pattern size. A dithered pattern is created from a regular pattern by incorporation of some amount of randomness in the distribution of black and white dots. The procedure is as follows:

- Use the pattern creation algorithm to produce a dot array of size, say $n \times n$, sufficient to produce all the colours in the image.
- Scale the image by the factor m along both the directions. This enlargement of the image is done either by interpolation or by simply copying to neighbour locations.
- For each location (x, y) in the enlarged image EI compute

$$i = x \mod n \text{ and } j = y \mod n.$$

- If, $\text{EI}(x, y) > D_n(i, j)$ then produce a dot at (x, y). D_n is $n \times n$ dither matrix.

Example 1: Let us consider the following 2×2 Original Image (OI). A dither pattern (D) of size 4×4 with 16 values, is given. We have an available display space of size 4×4 dots.

Solution: The process and output are described with the help of the following matrices:

- Original Image (OI)
- Dither pattern (D)
- Enlarged Image (EI)
- Dithered Image (DI)

0	10
5	15

Original Image (OI)

0	8	2	10
12	4	14	6
3	11	1	9
15	7	13	5

Dither pattern (D)

0	0	10	10
0	0	10	10
5	5	15	15
5	5	15	15

Enlarged Image (EI)

0	0	1	0
0	0	0	1
1	0	1	1
0	0	1	1

Dithered Image (DI)

In the above, the enlarged image is produced by simply copying grey values from the original image to neighbouring dot locations of size 2×2. If we follow the interpolation technique, we will get a different output. Let us interpolate for intermediate values and extrapolate at the right and bottom of the original image. During extrapolation, resultant grey values are truncated to the minimum (0) and maximum (15) grey values.

0	5	10	15
3	8	13	15
5	10	15	15
7	13	15	15

Enlarged image (EI)

0	0	1	1
0	1	0	1
1	0	1	1
0	1	1	1

Dithered image (DI)

The process of dithering is applied on a grey image called **Lena** having 256 grey levels as shown in Figure 4.13. This image is modified to be reproduced with 8 grey levels, and then dithering is applied over it. Figures 4.14(a) and 4.14(b) depicts the effects of dithering over the *Lena* image.

The above dithering process may produce a very neat and clear image output on bilevel displays. Sometimes a high degree of orderliness of the patterns are visible in the image that is visually unexpected. Also, due to the application of randomness

Figure 4.13: Original *Lena* image with 256 grey levels.

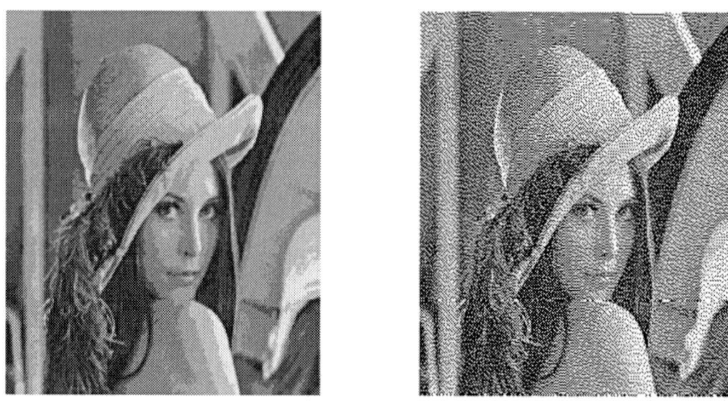

(a) Without dithering (b) With dithering

Figure 4.14: *Lena* image in 16 grey levels.

within the image elements, some amount of noise is likely to be inserted in the dot array. The ordered dither algorithm is presented below. Here, the algorithm is applied over the original image $f(x, y)$ of size $n \times n$ producing a dither image $g(x, y)$.

Ordered dither algorithm

```
begin
    for y = y_max to y_min in step -1 do
    begin
        for x = x_min to x_max do
        begin
            i = (x mod n) + 1
            j = (y mod n) + 1
            begin
            if (f(x, y) < D(i, j))g(x, y) = Black
```

```
            else
                g(x, y) = White
            end
            display g(x, y)
        end
    end
end
```

4.6.5 Floyd-Steinberg Error Diffusion

When we produce a binary image by thresholding, for display purposes, the output image is found to lose finer details at the boundaries of regions with different intensity values. In order to smooth out the effects of the above loss, Floyd and Steinberg proposed an error diffusion algorithm that propagate some amount of errors from each pixel to the neighbor pixels. The algorithm is provided below.

Floyd-Steinberg error diffusion algorithm

```
begin
    Threshold ← (Black+White)/2
    for y = y_max to y_min in step -1 do
    begin
        for x = x_min to x_max do
        begin
            if f(x, y) < Threshold
            begin
                g(x, y) = Black
                error = f(x, y) − Black
            end
            else
            begin
                g(x, y) = White
                error = f(x, y) − White
            end
            display g(x, y)
            f(x + 1, y) = f(x + 1, y) + 7 × Error/16
            f(x + 1, y − 1) = f(x + 1, y − 1) + Error/16
            f(x, y − 1) = f(x, y − 1) + 5 × Error/16
            f(x − 1, y − 1) = f(x − 1, y − 1) + 3 × Error/16
        end
    end
end
```

The above algorithm can be simplified so that errors can be propagated only in the right and downward directions. Therefore, the image can be processed in the scan line order. Here, $\frac{3}{8}$th of the error is propagated toward right, $\frac{3}{8}$th downward, and the remaining $\frac{1}{4}$th diagonally downward. The above algorithm can be modified accordingly. The binary thresholded *Lena* image and its error diffused version are shown Figures 4.15(a) and (b) respectively.

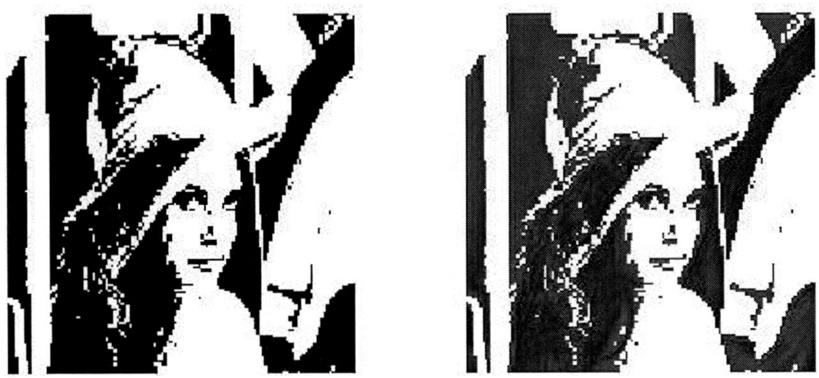

Figure 4.15: *Lena* image (a) with 2 grey levels, (b) after error diffusion

4.7 Problems

1. What are the different possible ways of representing a digital image? Write down relative merits and demerits of these methods.
2. How much memory is needed to store a digital image of size 256×256 having 64 grey levels?
3. How much memory is needed to store a RGB image of size 256×256 having 256 colour triples?
4. Mention some reasons for assigning pseudo colours over grey level images.
5. Write down an algorithm for assignment of pseudo colours in grey level images.
6. What are the different types of pixel connectivity that may be present in a digital image? Illustrate them using suitable diagrams.
7. What are patterning and dithering? In what situations do we need to apply these processes?
8. What are the different ways of measuring between pixel distances? Consider two pixels at locations (2, 3) and (8, 4), respectively. Compute their distance in different techniques you mentioned above.

9. Consider the following 4×4 image (I) having grey level intensities as shown here and a dither pattern (D) having 16 levels only

$I =$

10	12	30	25
10	12	24	28
30	26	12	16
25	23	14	15

$D =$

0	8	2	10
12	4	14	6
3	11	1	9
15	7	13	5

If the available display is limited to 16×16 pixels only, produce a binary image using dithering.

10. What are the advantages and disadvantages of patterning and dithering?
11. Explain the effects of reducing the number of intensity levels keeping the size of the image intact.
12. Write a note on morphological image processing.

Chapter 5

Image Transforms

Image transformation means change of domain of the image elements. In spatial domain, an image is represented as a set of intensity values located at different (x, y) coordinates. Generally, an image is transformed into its frequency domain counterpart. In this new domain, an image is represented by a set of energy spectrum located at different (u, v) values, where u and v represent the frequency components of the underlying waveforms.

We know that a one-dimensional signal can be represented by a series of *orthogonal basis functions.* An example of such representation is Fourier series expansion. Similarly an image can be represented by a series of *basis images.* These basis images can be generated using orthogonal unitary matrices as image transformation operator. The use of unitary matrices as image transforms help us in identifying the basis images. By image transformation, a signal or an image is expanded in the form of a series of waveforms. By series expansion, we get series coefficients which can be used for any further processing of the signal or the image.

5.1 Unitary Transforms

Let us consider a one dimensional signal or a sequence in discrete form:

$$\mathbf{U} = \{u(n)\}, \quad 0 \le n \le N-1$$

Let $\mathbf{A}$ be a unitary transformation matrix. The transformation can be written as:

$$\mathbf{V} = \mathbf{AU} \tag{5.1}$$

i.e.

$$v(k) = \sum_{n=0}^{N-1} a(k,n)u(n), \quad 0 \le k \le N-1 \tag{5.2}$$

Since $\mathbf{A}$ is unitary, we can write $\mathbf{A}^{-1} = \mathbf{A}^{*T}$.
Therefore,

$$\mathbf{U} = \mathbf{A}^{*T}\mathbf{V} \tag{5.3}$$

i.e.

$$u(n) = \sum_{k=0}^{N-1} a^*(k,n)v(k), \quad 0 \le n \le N-1 \tag{5.4}$$

The series coefficients $v(k)$ represent the original signal in the transformed domain.

In case of 2D image data, the transformation can be expressed as:

$$v(k,l) = \sum_{m=0}^{N-1}\sum_{n=0}^{N-1} a_{k,l}(m,n)u(m,n), \quad 0 \le k,l \le N-1 \tag{5.5}$$

and

$$u(m,n) = \sum_{k=0}^{N-1}\sum_{l=0}^{N-1} a^*_{k,l}(m,n)v(k,l), \quad 0 \le m,n \le N-1 \tag{5.6}$$

where, $a_{k,l}(m,n)$ is called the **image transform**.

5.1.1 Separable Unitary Transforms

The number of multiplications and additions required to compute the transform coefficients $v(k,l)$ is $\mathbf{O}(N^4)$. The complexity can be reduced to $\mathbf{O}(N^3)$ when the transform is restricted to be separable, i.e.

$$a_{k,l}(m,n) = a_k(m)b_l(n) = a(k,m)b(l,n) \tag{5.7}$$

where, $a_k(m), k = 0,\ldots,N-1$ and $b_l(n),\ l = 0,\ldots,N-1$ are one-dimensional orthogonal sets of basis vectors. The matrices $\mathbf{A} = a(k,m)$ and $\mathbf{B} = b(l,n)$ should also be unitary matrices themselves. Often one chooses $\mathbf{B}$ to be the same as $\mathbf{A}$.

Now, we can express the transformations as:

$$v(k,l) = \sum_{m=0}^{N-1}\sum_{n=0}^{N-1} a(k,m)u(m,n)a(l,n) \tag{5.8}$$

or

$$v(k,l) = \sum_{m=0}^{N-1} a(k,m) \sum_{n=0}^{N-1} u(m,n)a(l,n) \tag{5.9}$$

i.e. using the vector and matrix notations we can write

$$\mathbf{V} = \mathbf{AUA}^T \tag{5.10}$$

and

$$u(m,n) = \sum_{k=0}^{N-1}\sum_{l=0}^{N-1} a^*(k,m)v(k,l)a^*(l,n) \tag{5.11}$$

or

$$u(m,n) = \sum_{k=0}^{N-1} a^*(k,m) \sum_{l=0}^{N-1} v(k,l) a^*(l,n) \tag{5.12}$$

i.e. using the vector and matrix notations we can write

$$\mathbf{U} = \mathbf{A}^{*T} \mathbf{V} \mathbf{A}^* \tag{5.13}$$

5.1.2 Basis Images

If we denote the kth column of $\mathbf{A}^{*T}$ as a_k^* then the outer products of the columns of this matrix will represent the basis images of the transform, i.e. the products $A_{k,l}^* = a_k^* a_l^{*T}$ will be the basis images. For an image of size $N \times N$, there will be N^2 such basis images. So, now we can represent the image as a series sum of the basis images as:

$$\mathbf{U} = \sum_{k=0}^{N-1} \sum_{l=0}^{N-1} v(k,l) A_{k,l}^* \tag{5.14}$$

Example 1: Let us consider the following 2×2 image and the transformation matrix $\mathbf{A}$. Find out the basis images.

$\mathbf{U} = \begin{bmatrix} 1 & 2 \\ 3 & 4 \end{bmatrix}$ and $\mathbf{A} = \frac{1}{\sqrt{2}} \begin{bmatrix} 1 & 1 \\ 1 & -1 \end{bmatrix}$

Solution: Matrix $\mathbf{A}$ is unitary. Therefore, we have

$$\begin{aligned} \mathbf{V} &= \frac{1}{2} \begin{bmatrix} 1 & 1 \\ 1 & -1 \end{bmatrix} \begin{bmatrix} 1 & 2 \\ 3 & 4 \end{bmatrix} \begin{bmatrix} 1 & 1 \\ 1 & -1 \end{bmatrix} \\ &= \frac{1}{2} \begin{bmatrix} 4 & 6 \\ -2 & -2 \end{bmatrix} \begin{bmatrix} 1 & 1 \\ 1 & -1 \end{bmatrix} \\ &= \begin{bmatrix} 5 & -1 \\ -2 & 0 \end{bmatrix} \end{aligned}$$

here,

$$\mathbf{A}^{*T} = \frac{1}{\sqrt{2}} \begin{bmatrix} 1 & 1 \\ 1 & -1 \end{bmatrix}$$

Therefore,

$$\mathbf{U} = \frac{1}{2}\begin{bmatrix} 1 & 1 \\ 1 & -1 \end{bmatrix}\begin{bmatrix} 5 & -1 \\ -2 & 0 \end{bmatrix}\begin{bmatrix} 1 & 1 \\ 1 & -1 \end{bmatrix}$$

$$= \frac{1}{2}\begin{bmatrix} 3 & -1 \\ 7 & -1 \end{bmatrix}\begin{bmatrix} 1 & 1 \\ 1 & -1 \end{bmatrix}$$

$$= \begin{bmatrix} 1 & 2 \\ 3 & 4 \end{bmatrix}$$

To find the basis images, we calculate the outer product of the columns of $\mathbf{A}^{*T}$

$$A^*_{0,0} = \frac{1}{2}\begin{bmatrix} 1 \\ 1 \end{bmatrix}\begin{bmatrix} 1 & 1 \end{bmatrix} = \frac{1}{2}\begin{bmatrix} 1 & 1 \\ 1 & 1 \end{bmatrix}$$

$$A^*_{0,1} = \frac{1}{2}\begin{bmatrix} 1 \\ 1 \end{bmatrix}\begin{bmatrix} 1 & -1 \end{bmatrix} = \frac{1}{2}\begin{bmatrix} 1 & -1 \\ 1 & -1 \end{bmatrix}$$

$$A^*_{1,0} = \frac{1}{2}\begin{bmatrix} 1 \\ 1 \end{bmatrix}\begin{bmatrix} 1 & -1 \end{bmatrix} = \frac{1}{2}\begin{bmatrix} 1 & 1 \\ -1 & -1 \end{bmatrix}$$

$$A^*_{1,1} = \frac{1}{2}\begin{bmatrix} 1 \\ -1 \end{bmatrix}\begin{bmatrix} 1 & -1 \end{bmatrix} = \frac{1}{2}\begin{bmatrix} 1 & -1 \\ -1 & 1 \end{bmatrix}$$

♣

Example 2: Show that one can construct the original image from its unitary transform coefficients and corresponding basis images (Consider image from Example 1).

Solution: Considering our previous image of size 4×4 and the derived basis images (with the example unitary transform), we can show that the original image is the weighted sum of the transform coefficients and corresponding basis images.

The weighted sum, in our case, can be written as

$$5 \times \frac{1}{2}\begin{bmatrix} 1 & 1 \\ 1 & 1 \end{bmatrix} + (-1) \times \frac{1}{2}\begin{bmatrix} 1 & -1 \\ 1 & -1 \end{bmatrix} + (-2) \times \frac{1}{2}\begin{bmatrix} 1 & 1 \\ -1 & -1 \end{bmatrix} + 0 \times \frac{1}{2}\begin{bmatrix} 1 & -1 \\ -1 & 1 \end{bmatrix}$$

$$= \frac{1}{2}\begin{bmatrix} 2 & 4 \\ 6 & 8 \end{bmatrix} = \begin{bmatrix} 1 & 2 \\ 3 & 4 \end{bmatrix}$$

which is the original image.

♣

5.1.3 Orthogonal Transforms

Orthogonal functions are very useful in image and signal processing applications. Frequency domain processing of images or signals, in general, become useful due to some interesting properties of orthogonal functions. In case of image processing in frequency domain orthogonal and unitary basis functions play a very important role in the design of reversible transforms, modelling different kinds of filters and reducing computational efforts.

A set of continuous periodic functions, real or imaginary, are said to be orthogonal in the interval $[0 \quad N]$ if they satisfy the following criteria.

$$\int_{x=0}^{N-1} \Phi_i(x)\Phi_j(x)dx = \begin{cases} N & \text{if } i = j \\ 0 & \text{otherwise} \end{cases}$$

when $N = 1$, the set of functions $\{\Phi_i(x)\}$ is said to be orthonormal. In discrete notation the above relation can be expressed as

$$\sum_{x=0}^{N-1} \Phi_i(x)\Phi_j(x) = \begin{cases} N & \text{if } i = j \\ 0 & \text{otherwise} \end{cases}$$

The most commonly used orthogonal transform used in image and signal processing is the Fourier transform. In case of discrete Fourier transform the set of orthogonal basis functions is $\left\{\exp\left[-\frac{j2\pi ux}{N}\right], \exp\left[\frac{j2\pi ux}{N}\right]\right\}$, range of x and u being $[0 \quad (N-1)]$ each.

5.1.4 Basic Transformation Theory

A digital image is matrix of integers. Image transforms generally process either the whole image or a subimage of rectangular shape. Images are transformed using symmetric, orthogonal, unitary matrices.

Let an image f be of size $M \times N$ as shown below

$$\mathbf{f} = f(x,y) = \begin{bmatrix} f(0,0) & f(0,1) & \cdots & f(0,N-1) \\ f(1,0) & f(1,1) & \cdots & f(1,N-1) \\ \vdots & \vdots & \vdots & \vdots \\ F(M-1,0) & f(M-1,1) & \cdots & f(M-1,N-1) \end{bmatrix} \tag{5.15}$$

For such an image, the transformation matrices $\mathbf{P}$ and $\mathbf{Q}$ have dimensions of $M \times M$ and $N \times N$ respectively, and they are responsible to produce a transformed image $\mathbf{F}$ such that

$$\mathbf{F} = \mathbf{P}\ \mathbf{f}\ \mathbf{Q}$$

which may also be written as

$$F(u,v) = \sum_{m=0}^{M-1}\sum_{n=0}^{N-1} P(u,m) f(m,n) Q(n,v)$$

for $u = 0, 1, \ldots, M-1$ and $v = 0, 1, \ldots, N-1$.

Here, **P** and **Q** are non-singular and inverse matrices of **P** and **Q**, i.e. $\mathbf{P}^{-1}$ and $\mathbf{Q}^{-1}$ exist.

The inverse transformation can be expressed as

$$f = \mathbf{P}^{-1}\mathbf{F}\ \mathbf{Q}^{-1}$$

Properties of matrices to simplify transformation process are given below.

- **P** is symmetric if $\mathbf{P} = \mathbf{P}^T$.
- **P** is orthogonal if $\mathbf{P}^T\mathbf{P} = \mathbf{I}$.
- If **P** is symmetric, real and orthogonal, $\mathbf{P}^{-1} = \mathbf{P}$.
- A complex matrix **P** is Hermitian if $\mathbf{P}^{*T} = \mathbf{P}$.
- A complex matrix **P** is unitary if $\mathbf{P}^{*T}\mathbf{P} = \mathbf{I}$.
- If **P** is square, complex, Hermitian and unitary, then $\mathbf{P}^{-1} = \mathbf{P}$.
- If both **P** and **Q** are symmetric, real and orthogonal, then

$$\mathbf{F} = \mathbf{P}\ \mathbf{f}\ \mathbf{Q} \text{ and } \mathbf{f} = \mathbf{P}\ \mathbf{F}\ \mathbf{Q}$$

5.2 Fourier Transform

Let $f(x)$ be a continuous function of a real variable x. The Fourier transform of $f(x)$, denoted as $\mathcal{F}\{f(x)\}$ or $F(u)$, is defined by the equation

$$\mathcal{F}\{f(x)\} = \int_{-\infty}^{\infty} f(x) \exp\left[-j2\pi ux\right]dx \tag{5.16}$$

where, $j = \sqrt{-1}$.

The reverse transformation is defined as

$$\mathcal{F}^{-1}\{F(u)\} = \int_{-\infty}^{\infty} F(u) \exp\left[j2\pi ux\right]du \tag{5.17}$$

The Fourier transform of a real function is generally complex, that is,

$$F(u) = R(u) + jI(u) \tag{5.18}$$

where $R(u)$ and $I(u)$, respectively, are the real and imaginary components of $F(u)$. Eq. (5.18) can be expressed in exponent form as,

$$F(u) = |F(u)|e^{\phi(u)} \tag{5.19}$$

where,

$$|F(u)| = [R^2(u) + I^2(u)]^{\frac{1}{2}} \tag{5.20}$$

and

$$\phi(u) = \tan^{-1}\left[\frac{I(u)}{R(u)}\right] \tag{5.21}$$

$|F(u)|$ is called *Fourier spectrum* of $f(x)$ and $\phi(u)$ is its phase angle. The variable u is called the *frequency* variable.

Fourier transform can be easily extended to the 2D situation, where the above relations become:

$$\mathcal{F}\{f(x,y)\} = \int_{-\infty}^{\infty}\int_{-\infty}^{\infty} f(x,y)\ \exp\left[-j2\pi(ux+vy)\right]dx\ dy \tag{5.22}$$

$$\mathcal{F}^{-1}\{F(u,v)\} = \int_{-\infty}^{\infty}\int_{-\infty}^{\infty} F(u,v)\ \exp\left[j2\pi(ux+vy)\right]du\ dv \tag{5.23}$$

$$|F(u,v)| = [R^2(u,v) + I^2(u,v)]^{\frac{1}{2}} \tag{5.24}$$

$$\phi(u,v) = \tan^{-1}\left[\frac{I(u,v)}{R(u,v)}\right] \tag{5.25}$$

Example 3: Find out the Fourier spectrum of a one-dimensional constant function defined as

$$f(x) = C \quad \text{for} \quad 0 \le x \le N-1.$$

Solution: The Fourier transform of $f(x)$ can be written as

$$F(u) = \mathcal{F}\{f(x)\} = \int_{-\infty}^{\infty} f(x)\exp\left[-j2\pi ux\right]dx$$

The above integration can be solved as follows:

$$
\begin{aligned}
F(u) &= \int_{x=0}^{N-1} C \exp[-j2\pi ux]dx \\
&= -\frac{C}{j2\pi u}\{\exp[-j2\pi ux]\}_0^{N-1} \\
&= -\frac{C}{j2\pi u}\{\exp[-j2\pi u(N-1)] - 1\} \\
&= -\frac{C}{j2\pi u}\ \{\exp[-j2\pi u(N-1)][\exp(j2\pi u(N-1)] - \exp[-j2\pi u(N-1)]\} \\
&= \frac{C}{\pi u}\exp[-j2\pi u(N-1)]\left\{\frac{\exp[j2\pi u(N-1)] - \exp[-j2\pi u(N-1)]}{2j}\right\} \\
&= \frac{C}{\pi u}\exp[-j2\pi u(N-1)]\sin[\pi u(N-1)]
\end{aligned}
$$

Therefore, the Fourier spectrum can be expressed as

$$|F(u)| = |C(N-1)| \times |\exp[-j2\pi u(N-1)]| \times \left|\frac{\sin[\pi u(N-1)]}{\pi u(N-1)}\right|$$

or,

$$|F(u)| = |C(N-1)| \times \left|\frac{\sin[\pi u(N-1)]}{\pi u(N-1)}\right|$$

♣

5.3 Discrete Fourier Transform

A continuous function $f(x)$ may be discretized to $f(0), f(1), \ldots, f(N-1)$ corresponding to N uniformly spaced points along X. So, the discrete forms of Fourier transforms can be expressed as

$$\mathcal{F}\{f(x)\} = \sum_{x=0}^{N-1} f(x)\exp\left[\frac{-j2\pi ux}{N}\right] \tag{5.26}$$

for $u = 0, 1, \ldots, N-1$.

$$\mathcal{F}^{-1}\{F(u)\} = \frac{1}{N}\sum_{u=0}^{N-1} F(u)\exp\left[\frac{j2\pi ux}{N}\right] \tag{5.27}$$

for $x = 0, 1, \ldots, N-1$.

In the 2D space,

$$\mathcal{F}\{f(x,y)\} = \sum_{x=0}^{M-1}\sum_{y=0}^{N-1} f(x,y)\ \exp\left[-j2\pi\left(\frac{ux}{M}+\frac{vy}{N}\right)\right] \tag{5.28}$$

for $u = 0, 1, \ldots, M-1$ and $v = 0, 1, \ldots, N-1$

$$\mathcal{F}^{-1}\{F(u,v)\} = \frac{1}{MN}\sum_{u=0}^{M-1}\sum_{v=0}^{N-1} F(u,v)\ \exp\left[j2\pi\left(\frac{ux}{M}+\frac{vy}{N}\right)\right] \tag{5.29}$$

for $x = 0, 1, \ldots, M-1$ and $y = 0, 1, \ldots, N-1$.

The 1D Fourier transformations can be written as

$$F(u) = \sum_{x=0}^{N-1} f(x)W_N^{ux} \tag{5.30}$$

and

$$f(x) = \frac{1}{N}\sum_{x=0}^{N-1} F(u)W_N^{-ux} \tag{5.31}$$

where

$$W_N = \exp\left[\frac{-j2\pi}{N}\right] \tag{5.32}$$

The Fourier transform and its inverse are linear transforms and can be represented in matrix vector notation as

$$\mathbf{F} = \mathbf{W}_N\mathbf{f}$$

and

$$\mathbf{f} = \mathbf{W}_N^{-1}\mathbf{F}$$

$\mathbf{f}$ and $\mathbf{F}$ are N dimensional vectors and $\mathbf{W}_N$ is a $N \times N$ matrix having its elements $W_N(u,x) = W_N^{ux} = \exp[-j2\pi ux/N]$. For example, if $N = 8$, the matrix $\mathbf{W}_8$ looks like

$$\mathbf{W}_8 = \{W_8^{ux}\} = \begin{bmatrix} W_8^0 & W_8^0 & W_8^0 & W_8^0 & W_8^0 & W_8^0 & W_8^0 & W_8^0 \\ W_8^0 & W_8^1 & W_8^2 & W_8^3 & W_8^4 & W_8^5 & W_8^6 & W_8^7 \\ W_8^0 & W_8^2 & W_8^4 & W_8^6 & W_8^0 & W_8^2 & W_8^4 & W_8^6 \\ W_8^0 & W_8^3 & W_8^6 & W_8^1 & W_8^4 & W_8^7 & W_8^2 & W_8^5 \\ W_8^0 & W_8^4 & W_8^0 & W_8^4 & W_8^0 & W_8^4 & W_8^0 & W_8^4 \\ W_8^0 & W_8^5 & W_8^2 & W_8^7 & W_8^4 & W_8^1 & W_8^6 & W_8^3 \\ W_8^0 & W_8^6 & W_8^4 & W_8^2 & W_8^0 & W_8^6 & W_8^4 & W_8^2 \\ W_8^0 & W_8^7 & W_8^6 & W_8^5 & W_8^4 & W_8^3 & W_8^2 & W_8^1 \end{bmatrix}$$

Since, $\mathbf{W}_N$ is unitary and symmetric, $\mathbf{W}_N^{-1} = \frac{1}{N} \times \mathbf{W}_N^*$, where the elements of the matrix $\mathbf{W}_N^*$ are the complex conjugate of that of $\mathbf{W}_N$. So, $\mathbf{W}_N^{-1}$ becomes

$$\mathbf{W}_8^{-1} = \frac{1}{8}\{W_8^{-ux}\}$$

$$= \frac{1}{8}\begin{bmatrix} W_8^0 & W_8^0 & W_8^0 & W_8^0 & W_8^0 & W_8^0 & W_8^0 & W_8^0 \\ W_8^0 & W_8^{-1} & W_8^{-2} & W_8^{-3} & W_8^{-4} & W_8^{-5} & W_8^{-6} & W_8^{-7} \\ W_8^0 & W_8^{-2} & W_8^{-4} & W_8^{-6} & W_8^0 & W_8^{-2} & W_8^{-4} & W_8^{-6} \\ W_8^0 & W_8^{-3} & W_8^{-6} & W_8^{-1} & W_8^{-4} & W_8^{-7} & W_8^{-2} & W_8^{-5} \\ W_8^0 & W_8^{-4} & W_8^0 & W_8^{-4} & W_8^0 & W_8^{-4} & W_8^0 & W_8^{-4} \\ W_8^0 & W_8^{-5} & W_8^{-2} & W_8^{-7} & W_8^{-4} & W_8^{-1} & W_8^{-6} & W_8^{-3} \\ W_8^0 & W_8^{-6} & W_8^{-4} & W_8^{-2} & W_8^0 & W_8^{-6} & W_8^{-4} & W_8^{-2} \\ W_8^0 & W_8^{-7} & W_8^{-6} & W_8^{-5} & W_8^{-4} & W_8^{-3} & W_8^{-2} & W_8^{-1} \end{bmatrix}$$

Example 4: Derive the Fourier transformation matrix for a 4×4 image.

Solution: Here, the transformation relation can be expressed as

$$\mathbf{F} = \mathbf{W}_4\mathbf{f}$$

where, $\mathbf{F}$ and $\mathbf{f}$ are the transformed and the original images, respectively.

Since $N = 4$, the transformation matrix $\mathbf{W}_4$ becomes

$$\mathbf{W}_4 = \{W_4^{ux}\} = \begin{bmatrix} W_4^0 & W_4^0 & W_4^0 & W_4^0 \\ W_4^0 & W_4^1 & W_4^2 & W_4^3 \\ W_4^0 & W_4^2 & W_4^0 & W_4^2 \\ W_4^0 & W_4^3 & W_4^2 & W_4^1 \end{bmatrix} = \begin{bmatrix} 1 & 1 & 1 & 1 \\ 1 & -j & -1 & j \\ 1 & -1 & 1 & -1 \\ 1 & j & -1 & -j \end{bmatrix}$$

Now, we can verify whether it is a unitary matrix as follows:

$$\mathbf{W_4} = \begin{bmatrix} 1 & 1 & 1 & 1 \\ 1 & -j & -1 & j \\ 1 & -1 & 1 & -1 \\ 1 & j & -1 & -j \end{bmatrix}$$

$$\mathbf{W_4^*} = \frac{1}{4} \times \begin{bmatrix} 1 & 1 & 1 & 1 \\ 1 & j & -1 & -j \\ 1 & -1 & 1 & -1 \\ 1 & -j & -1 & j \end{bmatrix}$$

Therefore,

$$\mathbf{W_4}^*\mathbf{W_4} = \frac{1}{4} \times \begin{bmatrix} 1 & 1 & 1 & 1 \\ 1 & j & -1 & -j \\ 1 & -1 & 1 & -1 \\ 1 & -j & -1 & j \end{bmatrix} \times \begin{bmatrix} 1 & 1 & 1 & 1 \\ 1 & -j & -1 & j \\ 1 & -1 & 1 & -1 \\ 1 & j & -1 & -j \end{bmatrix}$$

$$= \frac{1}{4} \times \begin{bmatrix} 4 & 0 & 0 & 0 \\ 0 & 4 & 0 & 0 \\ 0 & 0 & 4 & 0 \\ 0 & 0 & 0 & 4 \end{bmatrix}$$

$$= 1 \times \begin{bmatrix} 1 & 0 & 0 & 0 \\ 0 & 1 & 0 & 0 \\ 0 & 0 & 1 & 0 \\ 0 & 0 & 0 & 1 \end{bmatrix}$$

♣

Example 5: A function $f(x)$ is sampled at four points at $x = 0.50, 0.75, 1.00$ and 1.25, respectively and the sampled values are $f(x) = \{2, 3, 4, 4\}$, respectively. Find out the Fourier transform coefficients for the sampled function.

Solution: Here, the samples are

$$f(x) = \{2, 3, 4, 4\}$$

This can be expressed as a column vector as

$$\mathbf{f} = \begin{bmatrix} 2 \\ 3 \\ 4 \\ 4 \end{bmatrix}$$

Now, applying four point forward transformation matrix, we have

$$\mathbf{F} = \begin{bmatrix} 1 & 1 & 1 & 1 \\ 1 & -j & -1 & j \\ 1 & -1 & 1 & -1 \\ 1 & j & -1 & -j \end{bmatrix} \times \begin{bmatrix} 2 \\ 3 \\ 4 \\ 4 \end{bmatrix}$$

$$= \begin{bmatrix} 13 \\ -2+j \\ -1 \\ -2-j \end{bmatrix}$$

Therefore,

$$F(0) = 13,\ F(1) = -2 + j,\ F(2) = -1,\ F(3) = -2 - j.$$

Now, the coefficients can be found out as the energy values given by

$$|F(0)| = 13,\ |F(1)| = \sqrt{5},\ |F(2)| = 1,\ F(3) = \sqrt{5}.$$

♣

Example 6: Show the inverse transformation for the above example.

Solution: Here, we need to apply the backward Fourier transformation.

$$\mathbf{f} = \frac{1}{4} \times \begin{bmatrix} 1 & 1 & 1 & 1 \\ 1 & j & -1 & -j \\ 1 & -1 & 1 & -1 \\ 1 & -j & -1 & j \end{bmatrix} \times \begin{bmatrix} 13 \\ -2+j \\ -1 \\ -2-j \end{bmatrix}$$

$$= \frac{1}{4} \times \begin{bmatrix} 13 - 2 + j - 1 - 2 - j \\ 13 - 2j - 1 + 1 + 2j - 1 \\ 13 + 2 - j - 1 - 2 + j \\ 13 + 2j + 1 + 1 - 2j + 1 \end{bmatrix} = \begin{bmatrix} 2 \\ 3 \\ 4 \\ 4 \end{bmatrix}$$

♣

Example 7: Prove that $f(x)$ and $F(u)$ as given by Eq. (5.27) and (5.26) are Fourier transforms of each other.

Solution: In discrete notation, the forward transformation is

$$F(u) = \mathcal{F}\{f(x)\} = \sum_{0}^{N-1} f(x) \exp\left(\frac{-j2\pi ux}{N}\right)$$

where, $j = \sqrt{-1}$.

The reverse transformation is defined as

$$f(x) = \mathcal{F}^{-1}\{F(u)\} = \sum_{0}^{N-1} F(u) \exp\left(\frac{j2\pi ux}{N}\right)$$

The basis functions for forward and reverse transformations are $\exp(-j2\pi ux/N)$ and $\exp(j2\pi ux/N)$, respectively. These are orthogonal to each other as they satisfy

$$\sum_{0}^{N-1} \exp\left(\frac{-j2\pi ux}{N}\right) \exp\left(\frac{j2\pi ux}{N}\right) = \begin{cases} N & \text{if } i = j \\ 0 & \text{otherwise} \end{cases}$$

The RHS expression of the forward transformation

$$
\begin{aligned}
&= \sum_{x=0}^{N-1} f(x) \exp\left(\frac{-j2\pi ux}{N}\right) \\
&= \sum_{x=0}^{N-1} \left\{ \sum_{s=0}^{N-1} \left[F(s) \exp\left(\frac{j2\pi sx}{N}\right)\right] \exp\left(\frac{-j2\pi ux}{N}\right)\right\} \\
&= \sum_{s=0}^{N-1} \left[F(s) \sum_{x=0}^{N-1} \exp\left(\frac{j2\pi sx}{N}\right) \exp\left(\frac{-j2\pi ux}{N}\right)\right] \\
&= \sum_{u=0}^{N-1} F(u)N \qquad (\text{when } s = u) \\
&= F(u)
\end{aligned}
$$

♣

5.4 Fourier Transformation in Brief

This is the most important transformation in image processing. The discrete Fourier transformation is analogous to its continuous counterpart. Properties of linearity, shift, separability, convolution, correlation, etc. are similar to the continuous situation.

The Fourier transformation matrices for an $M \times N$ image can be expressed as

$$\mathbf{W}_M = \frac{1}{M} \exp\left(-j\frac{2\pi ux}{M}\right) \qquad \text{for } x, u = 0, 1, \ldots, M-1$$

$$\mathbf{W}_N = \frac{1}{N} \exp\left(-j\frac{2\pi vy}{N}\right) \qquad \text{for } y, v = 0, 1, \ldots, N-1$$

and

$$\mathbf{W}_M^{-1} = \exp\left(j\frac{2\pi ux}{M}\right) \qquad \text{for } x, u = 0, 1, \ldots, M-1$$

$$\mathbf{W}_N^{-1} = \exp\left(j\frac{2\pi vy}{N}\right) \qquad \text{for } y, v = 0, 1, \ldots, N-1$$

respectively.

The forward and backward transformations can, therefore, be expressed as

$$\mathbf{F} = \mathbf{W}_M \mathbf{f}\ \mathbf{W}_N$$

and

$$\mathbf{f} = \mathbf{W}_M^{-1}\mathbf{F}\ \mathbf{W}_N^{-1}$$

respectively.

5.5 Properties of Fourier Transform

The Fourier transform has some interesting and useful properties which are very useful for digital image processing. Some of the very common and useful properties are described here.

5.5.1 Separability

The 2D discrete Fourier transform, as given in Eq. (5.28), is presented here once more.

$$\mathcal{F}\{f(x,y)\} = \frac{1}{MN}\sum_{x=0}^{M-1}\sum_{y=0}^{N-1} f(x,y)\ \exp\left[-j2\pi\left(\frac{ux}{M}+\frac{vy}{N}\right)\right]$$

for $u = 0, 1, \ldots, M-1$ and $v = 0, 1, \ldots, N-1$.

This equation can also be expressed as

$$\mathcal{F}\{f(x,y)\} = \frac{1}{M}\sum_{x=0}^{M-1} F(x,v)\ \exp\left(\frac{-j2\pi ux}{M}\right) \tag{5.33}$$

where,

$$F(x,v) = \frac{1}{N}\sum_{y=0}^{N-1} f(x,y)\ \exp\left(\frac{-j2\pi vy}{N}\right) \tag{5.34}$$

Equations (5.33) and (5.34) are essentially two separate one-dimensional transformations. Cascading these two operations we can get the full effect of the two-dimensional transformation. The first of the two one-dimensional transformations is called a **column transformation**, and the second is a row transformation. In other words, a column transformation followed by a row transformation, or alternatively, a row transformation followed by a column transformation give the effect of a complete transformation. Use of separability to compute a 2D transformation is shown in Figure 5.1.

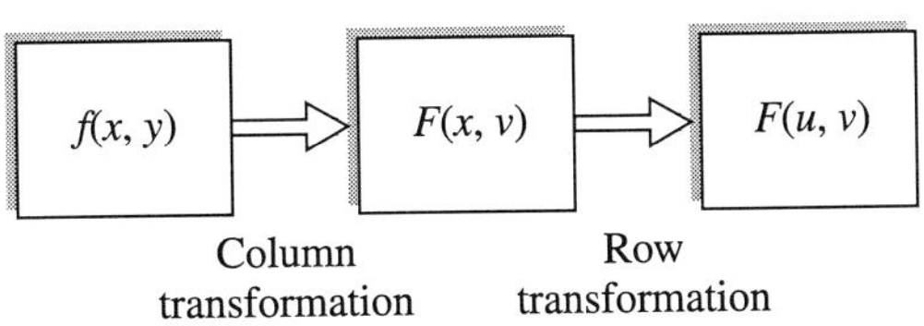

Figure 5.1: Separability of Fourier transform.

5.5.2 Translation

If we plot a DFT with its origin at one corner of the display window, viz. the location $(0,0)$, we can view only one fourth of the complete Fourier spectrum. In order to view the complete we need to shift the centre of the spectrum at another location (u_0, v_0). This can be done by simply multiplying the original image function $f(x, y)$ by an exponential term $\exp[j2\pi(u_0x/M + v_0y/N)]$. Effect of such transformation is shown below.

$$f(x,y)\exp\left[j2\pi\left(\frac{u_0x}{M}+\frac{v_0y}{N}\right)\right] \Rightarrow F(u-u_0, v-v_0) \tag{5.35}$$

In a similar manner, for the reverse transformation, the origin of the spatial image can be shifted to a desired location (x_0, y_0) by multiplying the frequency spectrum $F(u, v)$ by the exponential term $\exp[-j2\pi(ux_0/M + vy_0/N)]$. In this case, the effect on the output is

$$f(x-x_0, y-y_0) \Rightarrow F(u,v)\exp\left[-j2\pi\left(\frac{ux_0}{M}+\frac{vy_0}{N}\right)\right] \tag{5.36}$$

If we substitute, $u_0 = \frac{M}{2}$ and $v_0 = \frac{N}{2}$ in Eq. (5.35), it becomes

$$f(x,y)\exp\left[j\pi\left(\frac{x}{M}+\frac{y}{N}\right)\right] = f(x,y)(-1)^{x+y} \Rightarrow F\left(u-\frac{M}{2}, v-\frac{N}{2}\right)$$

That is, the origin of the concerned Fourier transform of $f(x, y)$ can be moved to the centre by multiplying $f(x, y)$ by $(-1)^{x+y}$. This shifting operation will not affect the magnitude of the Fourier transform in any way. In Figure 5.2 an image of a white square shape is displayed. Fourier transform of the square image and the corresponding shifted transform image are shown in Figures 5.3 and 5.4, respectively. Similarly, for the clown image (Figure 5.5), results are shown in Figures 5.6 and 5.7, respectively.

Figure 5.2: Square image of size 256 × 256.

Figure 5.3: Fourier spectrum of Figure 5.2 without shifting.

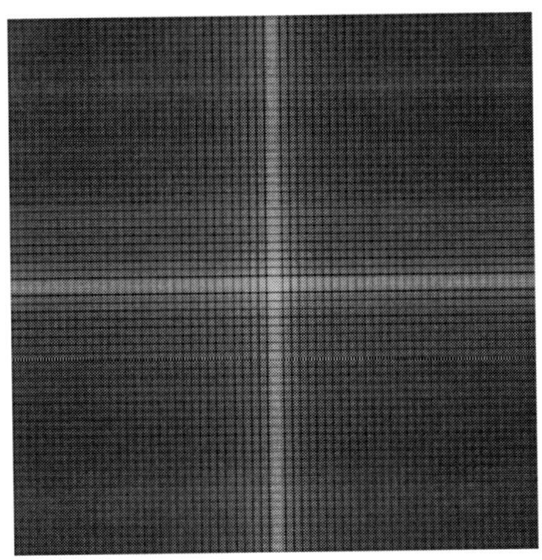

Figure 5.4: Fourier spectrum of Figure 5.2 with shifting.

5.5.3 Periodicity and Conjugate Symmetry

Discrete Fourier transform and its inverse are periodic in nature. Periods along the two dimensions are M and N, respectively. Therefore, we can express the periodicity property as

$$F(u, v) = F(u + M, v) = F(u, v + N) = F(u + M, v + N) \tag{5.37}$$

This periodicity property holds in case of the inverse transformation also. That is according to the Fourier transformation theory, images are periodic themselves. This is however, implied by the fact that we have assumed an image to be a two-dimensional periodic signal for which application of Fourier theorem has been made possible.

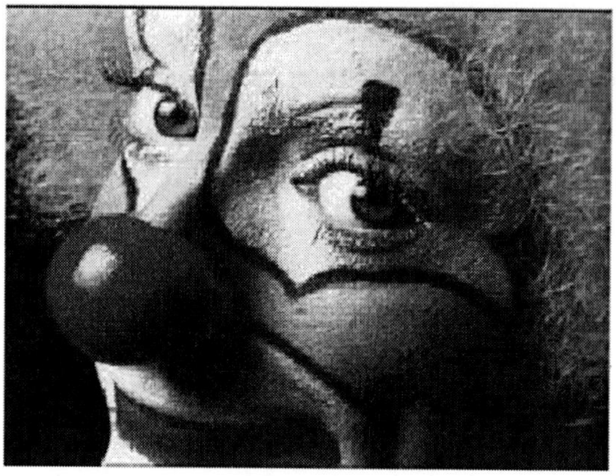

Figure 5.5: Original Clown image.

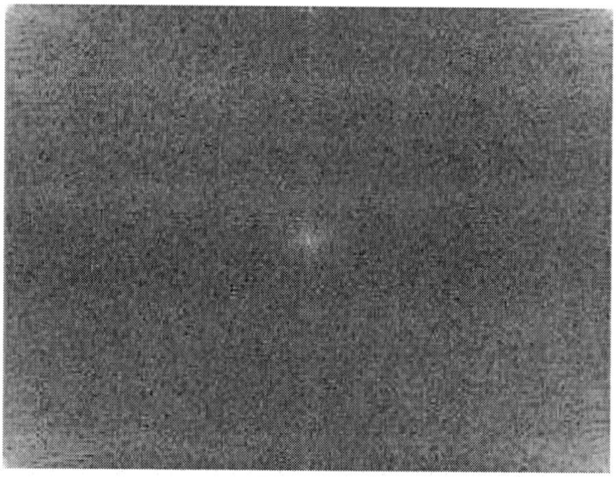

Figure 5.6: Fourier spectrum of Figure 5.5 without shifting.

The Fourier transform also exhibits the conjugate symmetry property, if we consider only real images $f(x, y)$, i.e. if $f(x, y)$ is a real valued matrix. This conjugate symmetry can be expressed as

$$F(u, v) = F^*(-u, -v) \tag{5.38}$$

or

$$|F(u, v)| = |F(-u, -v)| \tag{5.39}$$

Figure 5.7: Fourier spectrum of Figure 5.5 with shifting.

5.5.4 Average Value

The average of a two-dimensional image function can be expressed as

$$\bar{f}(x,y) = \frac{1}{MN}\sum_{x=0}^{M-1}\sum_{y=0}^{N-1} f(x,y)$$

A two-dimensional Fourier transform of the concerned image $f(x,y)$ can be written as

$$F(u,v) = \frac{1}{MN}\sum_{x=0}^{M-1}\sum_{y=0}^{N-1} f(x,y)\ \exp\left[-j2\pi\left(\frac{ux}{M}+\frac{vy}{N}\right)\right]$$

In the above equation, substituting $u = 0$ and $v = 0$, we get

$$F(0,0) = \frac{1}{MN}\sum_{x=0}^{M-1}\sum_{y=0}^{N-1} f(x,y)$$

Therefore, the image average and the corresponding Fourier transform are related as

$$F(0,0) = \bar{f}(x,y) \tag{5.40}$$

5.6 Convolution and Correlation

The convolution and correlation are the means of establishing the correspondences between the spatial domain and frequency domain processing of images. Specifically, the convolution in spatial domain is equivalent to point by point multiplication in frequency domain. This is the famous convolution theorem. But before illustrating the theorem, we need to explain convolution and correlation themselves.

Convolution: The convolution of two continuous one-dimensional functions $f(x)$ and $g(x)$ is defined mathematically as

$$f(x) * g(x) = \int_{-\infty}^{+\infty} f(m)g(x-m)dm \tag{5.41}$$

where α is the variable of integration.

Correlation: The correlation of two continuous one-dimensional functions $f(x)$ and $g(x)$ is defined mathematically as

$$f(x) \circ g(x) = \int_{-\infty}^{+\infty} f^*(m)g(x+m)dm \tag{5.42}$$

where f^* is conjugate complex of f, and m is the variable of integration.

5.7 Convolution in Frequency Domain

Let $f(x)$ and $h(x)$ are two functions, sampled uniformly to form arrays of dimensions A and B, respectively. Here, x is a discrete variable in the range $0, 1, \ldots,$ $A-1$ for $f(x)$ and $0, 1, \ldots, B-1$ for $h(x)$. Generally image size and mask size are not the same. But to apply the concept of convolution in frequency domain, we need both of them to be of the same size. This can be done by zero padding. Let us consider that the image $f(x)$ and the mask $h(x)$ are defined as follows:

$$\{f(0), f(1), \ldots, f(A-1)\}$$
$$\{h(0), h(1), \ldots, h(B-1)\}$$

Here, sizes of $f(x)$ and $h(x)$ are A and B, respectively. To make these functions periodic with the same period M, we can use the following value of M:

$$M \geq A + B - 1$$

so that during convolution operation wraparound error can be eliminated. It is clear that, in this scheme, f is appended with B zeros, and h is appended with A zeros. The extended functions can thus be expressed as

$$f_e(x) = \begin{cases} f(x) & 0 \leq x \leq A-1 \\ 0 & A \leq x \leq M-1 \end{cases}$$

and

$$h_e(x) = \begin{cases} h(x) & 0 \leq x \leq B-1 \\ 0 & B \leq x \leq M-1 \end{cases}$$

After the above extensions, the discrete functions achieve the same period M. We denoted the extended functions as $f_e(x)$ and $h_e(x)$, respectively.

Convolution is not very easy to understand using its mathematical notation. It can be better realized with the assistance of a graphical illustration. Let us consider extended functions $f_e(m)$ and $h_e(m)$, defined for different values of m, where, m specifies the range of function definition, as shown in Figures 5.8 and 5.9, respectively. Again, let us consider computing a convolution of f_e and h_e at different values of location x. For computing convolution at consecutive x values, we initially place the mask function $h_e(m)$ to the left of the image function of $f_e(m)$. Then at each step, we shift the mask towards right and compute convolution products between corresponding points of the image and the mask. Hence, before performing convolution, we convert $h_e(m)$ to $h_e(x-m)$. This is done in two steps. At first we form $h_e(-m)$ by folding $h_e(m)$ about the origin and then we shift the resultant function by a distance of x. Now, for different possible values of x, $f_e(m)$ is multiplied with $h_e(x-m)$, and products are integrated to yield the convolution result at that location.

Example 8: Consider the following function $f_e(m)$ and the mask $h_e(m)$. Compute the convolution of $f_e(m)$ and $h_e(m)$. Show the results pictorially.

$$f_e(m) = \begin{cases} 1 & \text{for } m = 0 \text{ to } 1 \\ 0 & \text{otherwise} \end{cases}$$

and

$$h_e(m) = \begin{cases} \frac{1}{2} & \text{for } m = 0 \text{ to } 1 \\ 0 & \text{otherwise} \end{cases}$$

Solution: It is clear from Figures 5.8 and 5.9 that the product of $f_e(m)$ and $h_e(x-m)$ is zero outside the range $0 \leq x \leq 2$. Within the specified range, the product has a positive value which gets its maximum value of $\frac{1}{2}$ at $x = 1$. The output function can thus be defined as

$$f_e(x) * h_e(x) = \begin{cases} \dfrac{x}{2} & \text{for } x = 0 \text{ to } 1 \\ 1 - \dfrac{x}{2} & \text{for } x = 1 \text{ to } 2 \\ 0 & \text{otherwise} \end{cases}$$

♣

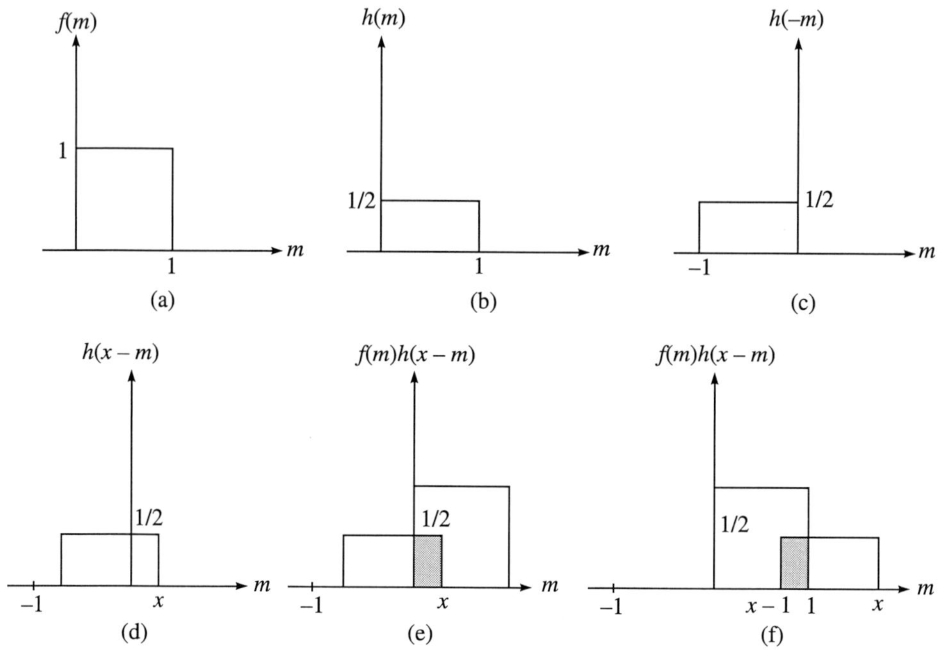

Figure 5.8: Convolution of image and mask of size 1×3.

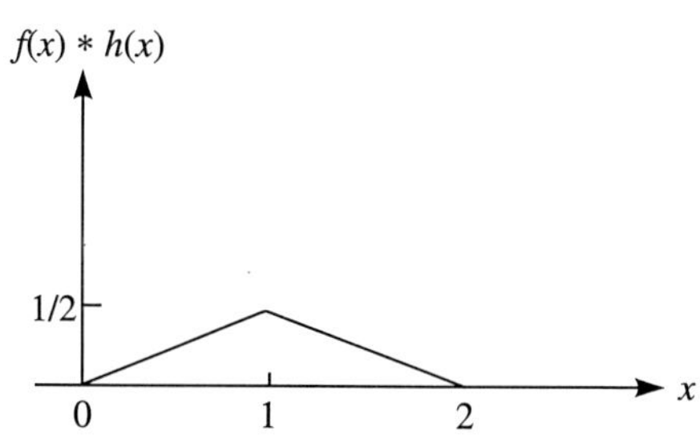

Figure 5.9: Response curve of convolution of image and mask.

One of the important uses of convolution in image processing is to convolve a given image function with the impulse function $\delta(x - x_0)$ which is given in the following equation:

$$\int_{-\infty}^{\infty} f(x)\delta(x - x_0)dx = f(x_0)$$

Convolution in this case is simply copying the value of the image function at the location of the impulse, i.e. $x = x_0$.

Convolution of two discrete functions $f_e(x)$ and $h_e(x)$ is defined as

$$g_e(x) = \sum_{m=0}^{M-1} f_e(m)h_e(x - m) \tag{5.43}$$

for $x = 0, 1, \ldots, M-1$.

The step by step convolution is depicted in Figure 5.10 where both the image (f) and the mask (h) are of size 1×3.

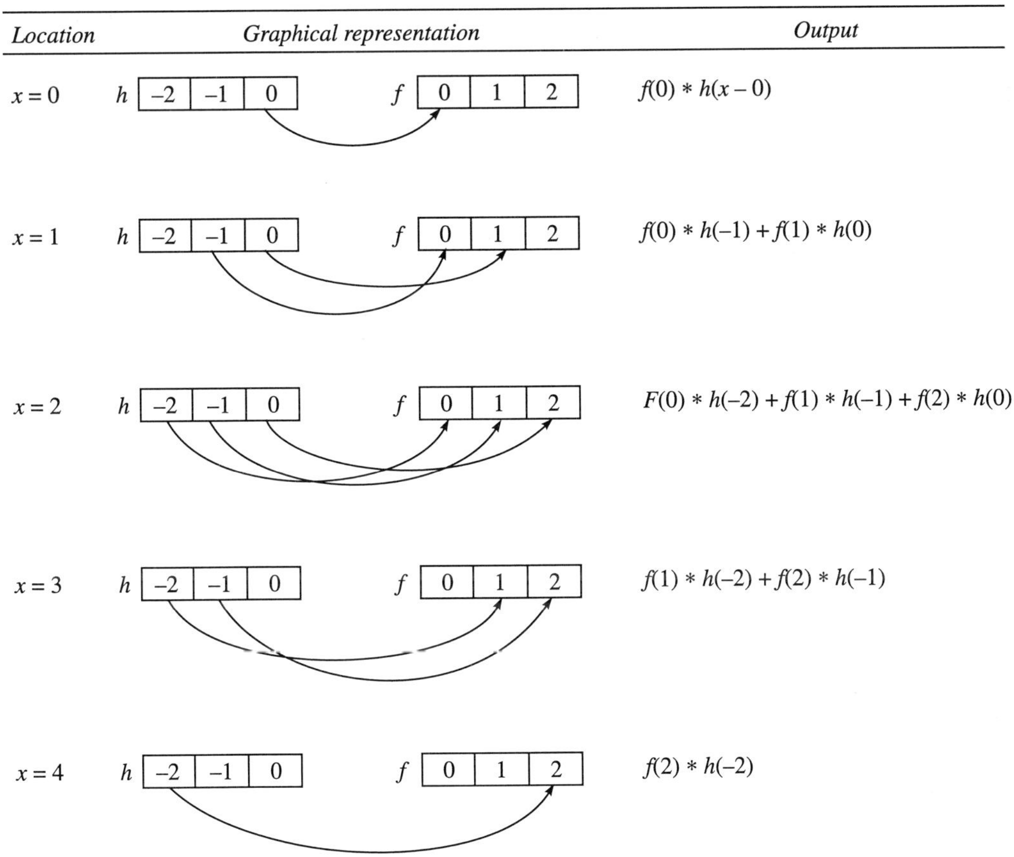

Figure 5.10: Convolution of image and mask of size 1×3.

In matrix notation, we can write,

$$\mathbf{g} = \mathbf{Hf} \tag{5.44}$$

where,

$$\mathbf{f} = \begin{bmatrix} f_e(0) \\ f_e(1) \\ \vdots \\ f_e(M-1) \end{bmatrix}$$

$$\mathbf{g} = \begin{bmatrix} g_e(0) \\ g_e(1) \\ \vdots \\ g_e(M-1) \end{bmatrix}$$

and

$$\mathbf{H} = \begin{bmatrix} h_e(0) & h_e(-1) & h_e(-2) & . & . & . & h_e(-M+1) \\ h_e(1) & h_e(0) & h_e(-1) & . & . & . & h_e(-M+2) \\ h_e(2) & h_e(1) & h_e(0) & . & . & . & h_e(-M+3) \\ & & & & \ddots & & \\ h_e(M-1) & h_e(M-2) & h_e(M-3) & . & . & . & h_e(0) \end{bmatrix}$$

Since $h_e(x)$ is periodic with period M,

$$\mathbf{H} = \begin{bmatrix} h_e(0) & h_e(M-1) & h_e(M-2) & . & . & . & h_e(1) \\ h_e(1) & h_e(0) & h_e(M-1) & . & . & . & h_e(2) \\ h_e(2) & h_e(1) & h_e(0) & . & . & . & h_e(3) \\ & & & & \ddots & & \\ h_e(M-1) & h_e(M-2) & h_e(M-3) & . & . & . & h_e(0) \end{bmatrix}$$

The above matrix is a circulant matrix. Let us define a scalar function $\lambda(k)$ and a vector $\mathbf{w}(k)$ as:

$$\lambda(k) = h_e(0) + h_e(M-1)e^{j\frac{2\pi}{M}k} + h_e(M-2)e^{j\frac{2\pi}{M}2k} + \cdots + h_e(1)e^{j\frac{2\pi}{M}(M-1)k}$$

for $k = 0, 1, \ldots, M-1$
and

$$\mathbf{w}(k) = \begin{bmatrix} 1 \\ e^{j\frac{2\pi}{M}k} \\ e^{j\frac{2\pi}{M}2k} \\ \vdots \\ e^{j\frac{2\pi}{M}(M-1)k} \end{bmatrix}$$

Then we can write the eigen vector equation of the symmetric matrix $\mathbf{H}$ as,

$$\mathbf{H}\mathbf{w}(k) = \lambda(k)\mathbf{w}(k) \tag{5.45}$$

where, $\mathbf{w}(k)$ is the eigen vector of $\mathbf{H}$ and $\lambda(k)$ is its corresponding eigen value. There are M such eigen vectors. Let us form an $M \times M$ matrix $\mathbf{W}$ by using these eigen vectors as columns, i.e.

$$\mathbf{W} = [\mathbf{w}(0)\ \mathbf{w}(1)\ \mathbf{w}(2)\ \cdots\ \mathbf{w}(M-1)]$$

The k ith element of $\mathbf{W}$ is then given by

$$W(k,i) = e^{j\frac{2\pi}{M}k} \quad \text{for} \quad k = 0, 1, \ldots, M-1$$

From the orthogonality property of complex exponentials, we can get the inverse of $\mathbf{W}$, i.e. $\mathbf{W}^{-1}$ whose k ith element is given by

$$W^{-1}(k,i) = \frac{1}{M}e^{-j\frac{2\pi}{M}k} \quad \text{for} \quad k = 0, 1, \ldots, M-1$$

From elementary matrix theory $\mathbf{H}$ can now be expressed as:

$$\mathbf{H} = \mathbf{W}\mathbf{D}\mathbf{W}^{-1}, \quad \text{i.e.} \quad \mathbf{D} = \mathbf{W}^{-1}\mathbf{H}\mathbf{W}$$

where, $\mathbf{D}$ is a diagonal matrix whose elements $D(k,k)$ are the eigen values of $\mathbf{H}$, i.e.

$$D(k,k) = \lambda(k)$$

and

$$D = \begin{pmatrix} \lambda(0) & & \\ & \ddots & \\ & & \lambda(M-1) \end{pmatrix}$$

We know,

$$\mathbf{g} = \mathbf{H}\mathbf{f}$$

Therefore,

$$\mathbf{g} = \mathbf{W}\mathbf{D}\mathbf{W}^{-1}\mathbf{f}$$

or

$$\mathbf{W}^{-1}\mathbf{g} = \mathbf{D}\mathbf{W}^{-1}\mathbf{f}$$

The product $\mathbf{W}^{-1}\mathbf{f}$ is an M-dimensional column vector and its kth element is

$$F(k) = \frac{1}{M}\sum_{i=0}^{M-1} f_e(i)e^{-j\frac{2\pi}{M}ki} \quad \text{for} \quad k = 0, 1, \ldots, M-1$$

This expression is nothing but the Fourier transform of $f_e(x)$. Similarly, $\mathbf{W}^{-1}\mathbf{g}$ yields $G(k)$, i.e. the Fourier transform of $g_e(x)$.

Also since, $e^{j\frac{2\pi}{M}(M-i)k} = e^{-j\frac{2\pi}{M}ik}$ the eigen values can be written as

$$\lambda(k) = h_e(0) + h_e(1)e^{-j\frac{2\pi}{M}k} + h_e(2)e^{-j\frac{2\pi}{M}2k} + \cdots + h_e(1)e^{-j\frac{2\pi}{M}(M-1)k}$$

for $k = 0, 1, \ldots, M-1$
i.e.

$$D(k,k) = \lambda(k) = \sum_{i=0}^{M-1} h_e(i) e^{-j\frac{2\pi}{M}ki}$$

for $k = 0, 1, \ldots, M-1$

Thus, $D(k,k)$ represent the Fourier transform of $h_e(x)$. Therefore,

$$D(k,k) = MH(k)$$

So, finally we can write,

$$G(k) = MH(k)F(k)$$

for $k = 0, 1, \ldots, M-1$

Thus, in the transformed domain, the convolution operation reduces to a term-by-term product. This is the famous convolution theorem.

From the above it is clear that convolution in frequency domain is far more economic. Some necessary considerations need to be kept in mind in this regard are listed below:

- Image and mask sizes need to be the same, i.e. masks must be staffed with zeros initially.
- The image and the mask must first be converted into their frequency domain counterparts.
- Using fast transformation, this conversion time is $\mathcal{O}(n^2 \log_2 n)$.
- The transformation is periodic, i.e. effectively when the mask gets to the edge of the picture it wraps itself around to the other side.
- Transformed image and mask can convolute by simple pointwise multiplication.
- Inverse transformation is needed to put the result into spatial domain again.

Example 9: Consider the following one dimensional image $f(x)$ and the 3×3 mash $h(x)$. Perform convolution of the image with the mask.

$$Image = [2 \;\; 3 \;\; 4 \;\; 6 \;\; 6 \;\; 4 \;\; 3 \;\; 2] \quad \text{and} \quad Mask = [-1 \;\; 0 \;\; 1]$$

***Solution*:** Here, the image and the mask are given by

$$\mathbf{f} = [2 \;\; 3 \;\; 4 \;\; 6 \;\; 6 \;\; 4 \;\; 3 \;\; 2] \quad \text{and} \quad \mathbf{h} = [-1 \;\; 0 \;\; 1]$$

To perform convolution, we may augment the mask with 0's and it becomes

$$\mathbf{h} = [-1 \;\; 0 \;\; 1 \;\; 0 \;\; 0 \;\; 0 \;\; 0 \;\; 0]$$

The processes of linear and circular convolution are depicted below in a stepwise manner. Let us represent convolution result by C.

Linear convolution:

$$
\begin{array}{lll}
x=0 & C=2\times -1 & =-2\\
x=1 & C=2\times 0+3\times -1 & =-3\\
x=2 & C=2\times 1+3\times 0+4\times -1 & =-2\\
x=3 & C=2\times 0+3\times 1+4\times 0+6\times -1 & =-3\\
x=4 & C=2\times 0+3\times 0+4\times 1+6\times 0+6\times -1 & =-2\\
x=5 & C=2\times 0+3\times 0+4\times 0+6\times 1+6\times 0+4\times -1 & =2\\
x=6 & C=2\times 0+3\times 0+4\times 0+6\times 0+6\times 1+4\times 0+3\times -1 & =3\\
x=7 & C=2\times 0+3\times 0+4\times 0+6\times 0+6\times 0+4\times 1+3\times 0+2\times -1 & =2\\
x=8 & C=3\times 0+4\times 0+6\times 0+6\times 0+4\times 0+3\times 1+2\times 0 & =2\\
x=9 & C=4\times 0+6\times 0+6\times 0+4\times 0+3\times 0+2\times 1 & =2\\
x=10 & C=6\times 0+6\times 0+4\times 0+3\times 0+2\times 0 & =0\\
x=11 & C=6\times 0+4\times 0+3\times 0+2\times 0 & =0\\
x=12 & C=4\times 0+3\times 0+2\times 0 & =0\\
x=13 & C=3\times 0+2\times 0 & =0\\
x=14 & C=2\times 0 & =0
\end{array}
$$

Circular convolution:

$$
\begin{array}{lll}
x=0 & C=2\times(-1)+2\times 0+3\times 1+4\times 0+6\times 0+6\times 0+4\times 0+3\times 0 & =1\\
x=1 & C=3\times(-1)+2\times 0+2\times 1+3\times 0+4\times 0+6\times 0+6\times 0+4\times 0 & =-1\\
x=2 & C=4\times(-1)+3\times 0+2\times 1+2\times 0+3\times 0+4\times 0+6\times 0+6\times 0 & =-2\\
x=3 & C=6\times(-1)+4\times 0+3\times 1+2\times 0+2\times 0+3\times 0+4\times 0+6\times 0 & =-3\\
x=4 & C=6\times(-1)+6\times 0+4\times 1+3\times 0+2\times 0+2\times 0+3\times 0+4\times 0 & =-2\\
x=5 & C=4\times(-1)+6\times 0+6\times 1+4\times 0+3\times 0+2\times 0+2\times 0+3\times 0 & =2\\
x=6 & C=3\times(-1)+4\times 0+6\times 1+6\times 0+4\times 0+3\times 0+2\times 0+2\times 0 & =3\\
x=7 & C=2\times(-1)+3\times 0+4\times 1+6\times 0+6\times 0+4\times 0+3\times 0+2\times 0 & =2
\end{array}
$$

♣

5.8 Fast Fourier Transform

The one-dimensional Fourier transformation relations are given in Eqs. (5.26) and (5.27). They are rewritten here for easy reference.

$$F(u) = \frac{1}{N}\sum_{x=0}^{N-1} f(x)\exp\left\{\frac{-j2\pi ux}{N}\right\} \tag{5.46}$$

for $u = 0, 1, \ldots, N-1$

$$f(x) = \frac{1}{N}\sum_{u=0}^{N-1} F(u)\exp\left\{\frac{j2\pi ux}{N}\right\} \tag{5.47}$$

for $x = 0, 1, \ldots, N-1$
Number of complex multiplications required to implement Eq. (5.46) and/or (5.47) is proportional to N^2. Because, for each value of u or x, we are to compute N number of complex multiplications. However, here the computation of $e^{(-j2\pi ux/N)}$ is not considered, as they can be computed and stored in a table for future use.

By properly decomposing Eq. (5.46), we can reduce the multiplication complexity to $O(N \log N)$. The decomposition procedure results Fast Fourier Transform (FFT) algorithm. Equation (5.46) can be written as

$$F(u) = \frac{1}{N}\sum_{x=0}^{N-1} f(x)W_N^{ux}$$

where

$W_N = \exp(-j2\pi/N)$

If $N = 2^n = 2M$ then,

$$F(u) = \frac{1}{2M}\sum_{x=0}^{2M-1} f(x)W_{2M}^{ux}$$

or

$$F(u) = \frac{1}{2}\left\{\frac{1}{M}\sum_{x=0}^{M-1} f(2x)W_{2M}^{u(2x)} + \frac{1}{M}\sum_{x=0}^{M-1} f(2x+1)W_{2M}^{u(2x+1)}\right\}$$

here,

$$W_{2M}^{2ux} = W_M^{ux}$$

so

$$F(u) = \frac{1}{2}\left\{\frac{1}{M}\sum_{x=0}^{M-1} f(2x)W_M^{ux} + \frac{1}{M}\sum_{x=0}^{M-1} f(2x+1)W_M^{ux}W_{2M}^{u}\right\}$$

Let us define,

$$F_{\text{even}}(u) = \frac{1}{M}\sum_{x=0}^{M-1} f(2x)W_M^{ux}$$

for $u = 0, 1, \ldots, M-1$

and

$$F_{\text{odd}}(u) = \frac{1}{M}\sum_{x=0}^{M-1} f(2x+1)W_M^{ux}$$

for $u = 0, 1, \ldots, M-1$
Therefore,

$$F(u) = \frac{1}{2}\left\{F_{\text{even}}(u) + F_{\text{odd}}(u)\right\} \tag{5.48}$$

Also

$$W_M^{u+M} = W_M^u$$

and

$$W_{2M}^{u+M} = -W_{2M}^u$$

Therefore,

$$F(u+M) = \frac{1}{2}\left\{F_{\text{even}}(u) - F_{\text{odd}}(u)W_{2M}^u\right\} \tag{5.49}$$

Here, the N point transformation is divided into two $(N/2)$ point transformations, one for $F_{\text{even}}(u)$ and the other for $F_{\text{odd}}(u)$. Now, to get $F(u)$ for $u = 0, 1, \ldots, N-1$, $F_{\text{even}}(u)$ and $F_{\text{odd}}(u)$ are combined as shown in Eq. (5.48) and (5.49). A scheme for computing FFT in hardware is shown in Figure 5.11. In this figure computation of an 8-point one-dimensional FFT is demonstrated. There are three layers of switch boxes cum computation blocks. At the first layer we use four two-input boxes, at the second layer, two four-input boxes and at the final layer one eight-input box. Before input of a value at any layer, it is multiplied by a precomputed constant term.

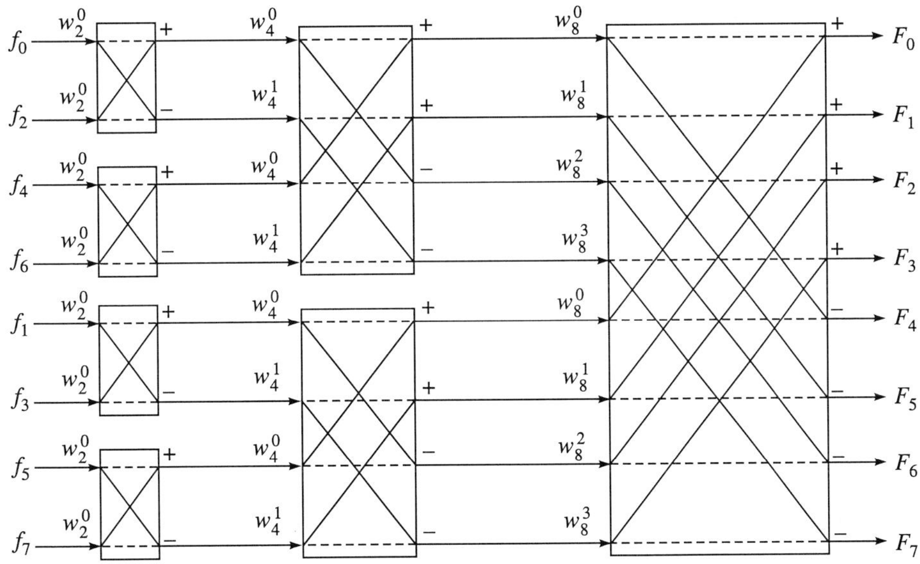

Figure 5.11: Schematic for computing FFT.

5.8.1 Complexity Analysis

Let us denote the number of multiplications and additions needed by an $N = 2^n$ point transformation by $m(n)$ and $a(n)$, respectively.

For $N = 1$, i.e. $n = 0$, the transformation is a single point transformation. Here, $m(0) = 0$ and $a(0) = 0$. Because in this case, the value is its own transform.

For $N = 2$, i.e. $n = 1$, we are to compute $F(0)$ and $F(1)$. Computation of $F(0)$ involves one multiplication and one addition. Computation of $F(1)$ involves one addition (actually subtraction) only.

Therefore,

$$m(1) = 1 \text{ and } a(1) = 2$$

For $N = 4$, i.e. $n = 2$, we are to deal with a four point transformation which can be divided into two two-point transformations. As before, for each partition, we need one multiplication and two additions. Finally, to combine the results, we need two additional multiplications to get $f(0)$ and $f(1)$; and two more additions to get $f(2)$ and $f(3)$.

Therefore, in this case,

$$m(2) = 2m(1) + 2 \text{ and } a(2) = 2a(1) + 4$$

Similarly, for the eight point situation, we get

$$m(3) = 2m(2) + 4 \text{ and } a(3) = 2a(2) + 8$$

In general, we can write,

$$m(n) = 2m(n-1) + 2^{(n-1)} \text{ and } a(n) = 2a(n-1) + 2^n \text{ for } n \geq 1$$

Solving the above equations, we get,

$$m(n) = \frac{1}{2} N \log N \text{ and } a(n) = N \log N$$

Example 10: The following example will illustrate the computational benefit of frequency domain processing of images. Let us consider a digital image of size 1024×1024, and a convolution mask of size 64×64. We shall compute the number of multiplications needed in spatial domain and in frequency domain to perform the convolution operation.

Solution: Image size $= 1024 \times 1024$

Mask size $= 64 \times 64$

Number of multiplication in spatial domain $= 1024 \times 1024 \times 64 \times 64 \approx 4 \times 10^9$.

Number of multiplications to perform the convolution in frequency domain can be computed as follows:

To transform image	$2 \times 1024 \times 1024 \times \log_2 1024$	$= 20,971,520$
To transform mask	$2 \times 1024 \times 1024 \times \log_2 1024$	$= 20,971,520$
To convolute	$4 \times 1024 \times 1024$	$= 04,194,304$
To inverse transform	$2 \times 1024 \times 1024 \times \log_2 1024$	$= 20,971,520$
Total multiplications	$67,108,864$	$\approx 7.0 \times 10^7$

Since each value in the frequency domain is complex, at each point we need to perform four multiplications.

♣

Example 11: Solve the recurrence relation for finding out the multiplication complexity of the one-dimensional Fourier transformation.

Solution: The recurrence relation for the multiplication complexity of FFT with N points can be expressed as

$$m(n) = 2m(n-1) + 2^{(n-1)}$$

where, $N = n^2$. The boundary condition is, $m(1) = 1$.

$$\begin{aligned}
m(n) &= 2m(n-1) + 2^{(n-1)} \\
&= 2[2m(n-2) + 2^{(n-2)}] + 2^{(n-1)} \\
&= 2[2\{2m(n-3) + 2^{(n-3)}\} + 2^{(n-2)}] + 2^{(n-1)} \\
&= \vdots \\
&= 2^{(n-2)} + 2^{(n-3)} + 2^{(n-4)} + \cdots + 2^0 \\
&= 2^{(n-1)} \\
&= \frac{N}{2}
\end{aligned}$$

Therefore, we can write,

$$\begin{aligned}
m(n) &= \frac{N}{2} \\
m(n-1) &= \frac{N}{4} \\
m(n-2) &= \frac{N}{8} \\
&\vdots \\
m(1) &= 1 \\
\hline
T(n) &= m(n) + 2 \times m(n-1) + 4 \times m(n-2) + \cdots + 2^{(n-1)} m(1) \\
&= \frac{N}{2} + 2 \times \frac{N}{4} + 4 \times \frac{N}{8} + \cdots + 2^{(n-1)} \times \frac{N}{N} \\
&= \frac{1}{2} \times N \times \{1 + 1 + \cdots \text{ upto } n \text{ terms}\} \\
&= \frac{1}{2} \times N \times \log_2 N
\end{aligned}$$

♣

5.9 Discrete Cosine Transform

Discrete Cosine Transform (DCT) is a very popular and useful transformation technique for image processing. This is almost similar to the DFT in nature while possessing some useful properties that make it suitable in many image processing operations.

The one-dimensional DCT is defined as

$$F(u) = \alpha(u) \sum_{x=0}^{N-1} f(x) \cos{(2x+1)} \frac{\pi u}{2N} \tag{5.50}$$

for $u = 0, 1, \ldots, N-1$

$$f(x) = \sum_{u=0}^{N-1} \alpha(u) F(u) \cos{(2x+1)} \frac{\pi u}{2N} \tag{5.51}$$

for $x = 0, 1, \ldots, N-1$

The values of $\alpha(u)$ in the above two equations are defined as

$$\alpha(u) = \begin{cases} \sqrt{\dfrac{1}{N}} & \text{for } u = 0 \\ \sqrt{\dfrac{2}{N}} & \text{for } u = 1, 2, \ldots, N-1 \end{cases} \tag{5.52}$$

The two-dimensional DCT expressions are

$$F(u,v) = \alpha(u)\alpha(v) \sum_{x=0}^{M-1} \sum_{y=0}^{N-1} f(x,y) \cos\left[(2x+1)\frac{\pi u}{2M}\right] \cos\left[(2y+1)\frac{\pi u}{2N}\right] \tag{5.53}$$

for $u = 0, 1, \ldots, M-1$ and $v = 0, 1, \ldots, N-1$

$$f(x,y) = \sum_{x=0}^{M-1} \sum_{y=0}^{N-1} \alpha(u)\alpha(v) F(u,v) \cos\left[(2x+1)\frac{\pi u}{2M}\right] \cos\left[(2y+1)\frac{\pi u}{2N}\right] \tag{5.54}$$

for $x = 0, 1, \ldots, M-1$ and $y = 0, 1, \ldots, N-1$.

Using matrix notation a one-dimensional DCT can be expressed as

$$F(u) = \mathbf{C}[f(x)]$$

and

$$f(x) = \mathbf{C}^T[F(u)]$$

where, $\mathbf{C}$ is the transformation matrix given by

$$\mathbf{C} = \sqrt{\frac{1}{N}}[c_{xu}]$$

The elements c_{xu} can be expressed as

$$c_{xu} = \begin{cases} 1 & \text{for } u = 0 \\ \sqrt{2}\cos\left\{\frac{\pi(2x+1)(u)}{2N}\right\} & \text{for } 1 \le u \le N-1 \text{ and } 1 \le x \le N \quad 1 \end{cases}$$

A two-dimensional DCT can be expressed as

$$[F(u,v)] = \mathbf{C}[f(x,y)]\mathbf{C}^T$$

and

$$[f(x,y)] = \mathbf{C}^T[F(u,v)]\mathbf{C}$$

5.10 Properties of DCT

The DCT is a real and orthogonal transformation. Mathematically this can be written as

$$\mathbf{C} = \mathbf{C}^* \;\Rightarrow\; \mathbf{C}^{-1} = \mathbf{C}^T \tag{5.55}$$

DCT is not the real part of a unitary DFT. Actually, DCT of a signal is similar to the corresponding DFT in its symmetric expansion.

DCT is fast transformation technique. For a sequence of N values, the DCT can be calculated in $\mathcal{O}(\mathcal{N} \log \mathcal{N})$ time using a procedure similar to the N-point FFT.

In case of correlated data sequence, like images, DCT shows excellent energy compaction capability. That is DCT can provide higher compression factors than DFT.

5.11 Discrete Sine Transform

Like DCT, a similar type of transform is the Discrete Sine Transform (DST). Just like DCT, the one-dimensional DST can be expressed as

$$[F(u)] = \mathbf{S}[f(x)]$$

and

$$[f(x)] = \mathbf{S}^T[F(u)]$$

where, $\mathbf{S}$ is the transformation matrix given by

$$\mathbf{S} = \sqrt{\frac{2}{N+1}}[s_{xu}]$$

The elements s_{xu} can be expressed as

$$s_{xu} = \sin\left[\frac{\pi(x+1)(u+1)}{N+1}\right]$$

5.12 Discrete Hartley Transform

Discrete Hartley Transform (DHT) is another useful transformation technique for image processing. It is a real-valued frequency transformation using sines and cosines. This is similar to the DFT in many ways and possesses some useful properties that make it suitable in many image processing operations.

The one-dimensional DHT is defined as

$$F(u) = \frac{1}{N}\sum_{x=0}^{N-1} f(x)\ \text{cas}\left\{2\pi\frac{ux}{N}\right\} \tag{5.56}$$

for $u = 0, 1, \ldots, N-1$
The inverse transformation is defined as

$$f(x) = \frac{1}{N}\sum_{u=0}^{N-1} F(u)\ \text{cas}\left\{2\pi\frac{ux}{N}\right\} \tag{5.57}$$

for $x = 0, 1, \ldots, N-1$. In two-dimension, the above transformations can be expressed as

$$F(u, v) = \frac{1}{MN}\sum_{x=0}^{M-1}\sum_{y=0}^{N-1} f(x, y)\ \text{cas}\left\{2\pi\left(\frac{ux}{M} + \frac{vy}{N}\right)\right\} \tag{5.58}$$

for $u = 0, 1, \ldots, M-1$ and $v = 0, 1, \ldots, N-1$

and

$$f(x,y) = \frac{1}{MN} \sum_{u=0}^{M-1} \sum_{v=0}^{N-1} F(u,v) \text{ cas} \left\{ 2\pi \left(\frac{ux}{M} + \frac{vy}{N} \right) \right\} \tag{5.59}$$

for $x = 0, 1, \ldots, M-1$ and $y = 0, 1, \ldots, N-1$.

The value of cas is defined as

$$\text{cas}\theta = \cos\theta + \sin\theta$$

Therefore, expanding the cas function we can rewrite the above expressions as

$$F(u,v) = \frac{1}{MN} \sum_{x=0}^{M-1} \sum_{y=0}^{N-1} f(x,y) \left\{ \cos 2\pi \left(\frac{ux}{M} - \frac{vy}{N} \right) + \sin 2\pi \left(\frac{ux}{M} - \frac{vy}{N} \right) \right\} \tag{5.60}$$

for $u = 0, 1, \ldots, M-1$ and $v = 0, 1, \ldots, N-1$
and

$$f(x,y) = \frac{1}{MN} \sum_{u=0}^{M-1} \sum_{v=0}^{N-1} F(u,v) \left\{ \cos 2\pi \left(\frac{ux}{M} - \frac{vy}{N} \right) + \sin 2\pi \left(\frac{ux}{M} - \frac{vy}{N} \right) \right\} \tag{5.61}$$

While the DFT is complicated due to complex functionals, the DHT is less computation intensive and thus, results in faster transformations, due to the use of real-valued unitary transforms. The cas functions are the kernel of this transformation.

5.12.1 Separability of Hartley Transform

Like the DFT, the DHT maintains the separability property. This is because, the kernel functions in a two-dimensional transform can be divided into two one-dimensional transformations as follows:

$$\begin{aligned}
F(u,v) &= \frac{1}{MN} \sum_{x=0}^{M-1} \sum_{y=0}^{N-1} f(x,y) \text{cas} \left(2\pi \frac{ux}{M} \right) \text{ cas} \left(2\pi \frac{vy}{N} \right) \\
&= \frac{1}{MN} \sum_{y=0}^{N-1} \text{ cas} \left(2\pi \frac{ux}{M} \right) \sum_{x=0}^{M-1} f(x,y) \text{ cas} \left(2\pi \frac{vy}{N} \right) \\
&= \frac{1}{MN} \sum_{y=0}^{N-1} \text{cas} \left(2\pi \frac{ux}{M} \right) F(u,y)
\end{aligned} \tag{5.62}$$

for $u = 0, 1, \ldots, M-1$ and $v = 0, 1, \ldots, N-1$

and

$$f(x,y) = \frac{1}{MN}\sum_{u=0}^{M-1}\sum_{v=0}^{N-1} F(u,v)\text{cas}\left(2\pi\frac{ux}{M}\right)\text{cas}\left(2\pi\frac{vy}{N}\right)$$

$$= \frac{1}{MN}\sum_{v=0}^{N-1}\text{cas}\left(2\pi\frac{ux}{M}\right)\sum_{u=0}^{M-1} F(u,v)\text{cas}\left(2\pi\frac{vy}{N}\right)$$

$$= \frac{1}{MN}\sum_{v=0}^{N-1}\text{cas}\left(2\pi\frac{ux}{M}\right) f(x,v) \tag{5.63}$$

for $x = 0, 1, \ldots, M-1$ and $y = 0, 1, \ldots, N-1$

5.12.2 Fast Hartley Transform

Like the FFT, the DHT has a fast algorithm called the Fast Hartley Transform (FHT). By dividing the input sequence of length $N = 2K$ (in one-dimensional case) into even and odd parts, in a similar fashion like the FFT, the Hartley transform can now be expressed as

$$F(u) = F_{\text{even}}(u) + F_{\text{odd}}(u)\cos 2\pi\left(\frac{u}{K}\right) - F_{\text{even}}(-u)\sin 2\pi\left(\frac{u}{K}\right)$$

and

$$F(-u) = F_{\text{even}}(u) - F_{\text{odd}}(-u)\cos 2\pi\left(\frac{u}{K}\right) - F_{\text{even}}(u)\sin 2\pi\left(\frac{u}{K}\right)$$

In the above relations, we used $F(M+u) = F(-u)$ for convenience.

5.13 Walsh Transform

The Walsh transform contains only two values +1 and –1. The one-dimensional transform of a function $f(x)$ can be expressed as

$$F(u) = \frac{1}{N}\sum_{x=0}^{N-1} f(x)\prod_{i=0}^{n-1}(-1)^{[b_i(x)b_{n-1-i}(u)]} \tag{5.64}$$

where $b_i(x)$ is the ith bit in the binary representation of x and $N = 2^n$.

$$\frac{1}{N}\prod_{i=0}^{n-1}(-1)^{[b_i(x)b_{n-1-i}(u)]}$$

The term is called the kernel of the transformation and is denoted as

$$g(x, u) = \frac{1}{N} \prod_{i=0}^{n-1} (-1)^{[b_i(x) b_{n-1-i}(u)]} \tag{5.65}$$

The transformation matrix for the Walsh transformation is a symmetric one having orthogonal rows and columns.

Walsh transformation is a reversible transformation. For the reverse transformation the kernel is modified as

$$h(x, u) = \prod_{i=0}^{n-1} (-1)^{[b_i(x) b_{n-1-i}(u)]} \tag{5.66}$$

which is exactly the same as $g(x, u)$ except the constant multiplicand $\frac{1}{N}$. Therefore, the inverse transformation can be expressed as

$$f(x) = \sum_{x=0}^{N-1} F(u) \prod_{i=0}^{n-1} (-1)^{[b_i(x) b_{n-1-i}(u)]} \tag{5.67}$$

The Walsh transform consists of a series of expansion of the basis functions whose values are either +1 or –1.

For two-dimensional transformations the forward and reverse transformation kernels become

$$g(x, y, u, v) = \frac{1}{N} \prod_{i=0}^{n-1} (-1)^{[b_i(x) b_{n-1-i}(u) + b_i(y) b_{n-1-i}(v)]} \tag{5.68}$$

and

$$h(x, y, u, v) = \prod_{i=0}^{n-1} (-1)^{[b_i(x) b_{n-1-i}(u) + b_i(y) b_{n-1-i}(v)]} \tag{5.69}$$

The forward and reverse transformations are thus given by

$$F(u, v) = \frac{1}{N} \sum_{x=0}^{N-1} \sum_{y=0}^{N-1} \prod_{i=0}^{n-1} f(x, y) (-1)^{[b_i(x) b_{n-1-i}(u) + b_i(y) b_{n-1-i}(v)]} \tag{5.70}$$

and

$$f(x, y) = \sum_{x=0}^{N-1} \sum_{y=0}^{N-1} \prod_{i=0}^{n-1} F(u, v) (-1)^{[b_i(x) b_{n-1-i}(u) + b_i(y) b_{n-1-i}(v)]} \tag{5.71}$$

The Walsh transform is separable by virtue of its kernel functions. This is shown below.

$$\begin{aligned} g(x, y, u, v) &= g(x, u) \cdot g(y, v) \\ &= h(x, u) \cdot h(y, v) \\ &= \left[\frac{1}{N} \prod_{i=0}^{n-1} (-1)^{[b_i(x) b_{n-1-i}(u)]} \right] \cdot \left[\frac{1}{N} \prod_{i=0}^{n-1} (-1)^{[b_i(y) b_{n-1-i}(v)]} \right] \end{aligned} \tag{5.72}$$

Using $g(x, u)$ and $h(x, u)$ as the elements of the forward and inverse Walsh transformation matrices, we can express a 8-point transformation transformation as

$$\mathbf{W}_8 = \frac{1}{2}\begin{bmatrix} +1 & +1 & +1 & +1 & +1 & +1 & +1 & +1 \\ +1 & +1 & +1 & +1 & -1 & -1 & -1 & -1 \\ +1 & +1 & -1 & -1 & +1 & +1 & -1 & -1 \\ +1 & +1 & -1 & -1 & -1 & -1 & +1 & +1 \\ +1 & -1 & +1 & -1 & +1 & -1 & +1 & -1 \\ +1 & -1 & +1 & -1 & -1 & +1 & -1 & +1 \\ +1 & -1 & -1 & +1 & +1 & -1 & -1 & +1 \\ +1 & -1 & -1 & +1 & -1 & +1 & +1 & -1 \end{bmatrix}$$

A one-dimensional N-point fast Walsh transformation requires N multiplications and $2(N-1)$ additions. The Walsh transform, being an orthogonal transform, is separable in nature and a $M \times N$ point two-dimensional transform can be decomposed as a combination of two one-dimensional ones as given below.

$$[F(u, v)] = \frac{1}{\sqrt{MN}}\mathbf{W}_M[f(x, y)]\mathbf{W}_N$$

and

$$[f(x, y)] = \frac{1}{\sqrt{MN}}\mathbf{W}_M[F(u, v)]\mathbf{W}_N$$

5.14 Hadamard Transform

The Hadamard transform also uses basis functions which assume values of +1 and –1 only. The one-dimensional kernel of the Hadamard transform is given by

$$g(x, u) = \frac{1}{N}(-1)^{\sum_{i=0}^{n-1}[b_i(x)b_i(u)]} \tag{5.73}$$

The one-dimensional transform is given by

$$F(u) = \frac{1}{N}\sum_{i=0}^{n-1} f(x)(-1)^{\sum_{i=0}^{n-1}[b_i(x)b_i(u)]} \tag{5.74}$$

where $N = 2^n$ and $u = 0, 1, \ldots, N-1$.

Since the Hadamard transform is an orthogonal transform, we can define the inverse transform as

$$h(x, u) = (-1)^{\sum_{i=0}^{n-1}[b_i(x)b_i(u)]} \tag{5.75}$$

Hence, the one-dimensional inverse Hadamard transform is given by

$$f(x) = \sum_{i=0}^{n-1} F(u)(-1)^{\sum_{i=0}^{n-1}[b_i(x)b_i(u)]} \tag{5.76}$$

where $x = 0, 1, \ldots, N-1$ and $N = 2^n$.

The two-dimensional kernels can be expressed similarly as

$$g(x, y, u, v) = \frac{1}{N}(-1)^{\sum_{i=0}^{n-1}[b_i(x)b_i(u)+b_i(y)b_i(v)]} \tag{5.77}$$

and

$$h(x, y, u, v) = \frac{1}{N}(-1)^{\sum_{i=0}^{n-1}[b_i(x)b_i(u)+b_i(y)b_i(v)]} \tag{5.78}$$

Therefore, the two-dimensional Hadamard transforms can be expressed as

$$F(u, v) = \frac{1}{N}\sum_{x=0}^{N-1}\sum_{y=0}^{N-1} f(x, y)(-1)^{\sum_{i=0}^{N-1}[b_i(x)b_i(u)+b_i(y)b_i(v)]} \tag{5.79}$$

and

$$f(x, y) = \frac{1}{N}\sum_{x=0}^{N-1}\sum_{y=0}^{N-1} F(u, v)(-1)^{\sum_{i=0}^{N-1}[b_i(x)b_i(u)+b_i(y)b_i(v)]} \tag{5.80}$$

The separability and symmetric properties are satisfied by the Hadamard kernel. These can be expressed as

$$\begin{aligned} g(x, y, u, v) &= g_1(x, u)g_2(y, v) \\ &= h_1(x, u)h_2(y, v) \\ &\left[\frac{1}{\sqrt{N}}(-1)^{\sum_{i=0}^{n-1}[b_i(x)b_i(u)]}\right]\left[\frac{1}{\sqrt{N}}(-1)^{\sum_{i=0}^{n-1}[b_i(y)b_i(v)]}\right] \end{aligned}$$

Since kernels of the Hadamard transforms are separable, the transforms can also be separable and a two-dimensional transform can be decomposed into two one-dimensional transforms.

It is interesting to note that kernels of the Walsh transform and the Hadamard transforms can be obtained from each other. For this reason, in image processing literature, these two transforms are often combinedly termed as Walsh-Hadamard transform. The one-dimensional kernel of Hadamard transform for $N = 8$ is shown below. It is observed that, the Walsh transform kernels can be obtained by simple reordering of columns.

$$\mathbf{HM}_8 = \frac{1}{2}\begin{bmatrix} +1 & +1 & +1 & +1 & +1 & +1 & +1 & +1 \\ +1 & -1 & +1 & -1 & +1 & -1 & +1 & -1 \\ +1 & +1 & -1 & -1 & +1 & +1 & -1 & -1 \\ +1 & -1 & -1 & +1 & +1 & -1 & -1 & +1 \\ +1 & +1 & +1 & +1 & -1 & -1 & -1 & -1 \\ +1 & -1 & +1 & -1 & -1 & +1 & -1 & +1 \\ +1 & +1 & -1 & -1 & -1 & -1 & +1 & +1 \\ +1 & -1 & -1 & +1 & -1 & +1 & +1 & -1 \end{bmatrix}$$

A one-dimensional N-point fast Hadamard transformation requires N multiplications and $2(N-1)$ additions. The Hadamard transform, being an orthogonal transform, is separable in nature and a $M \times N$ point two-dimensional transform can be decomposed as a combination of two one-dimensional ones as given below.

$$[F(u,v)] = \frac{1}{\sqrt{MN}}\mathbf{HM}_M[f(x,y)]\mathbf{HM}_N$$

and

$$[f(x,y)] = \frac{1}{\sqrt{MN}}\mathbf{HM}_M[F(u,v)]\mathbf{HM}_N$$

5.15 Harr Transform

Harr transform is another orthogonal transform found in literature. It is derived from Harr basis functions, $h_k(z)$, defined in the closed continuous interval $z \in [0,1]$ for $k = 0, 1, \ldots, N-1$, where, $N = 2^n$. The Harr transform requires that k be expressed as

$$k = 2^p + q - 1$$

where, $p = 0, 1, \ldots, n-1, q \in 0, 1$ for $p = 0, q \in 1, 2, 4, \ldots, 2^p$ for $p \neq 0$. The following Table 5.1 illustrates the above relationship among k, p and q for $N = 8$.

Table 5.1: Relationship Among k, p and q for $N = 8$

k	0	1	2	3	4	5	6	7
p	0	0	1	1	2	2	2	2
q	0	1	1	2	1	2	3	4

Now, the Harr transform can be defined as

$$h_0(z) \equiv h_{00}(z) = \frac{1}{\sqrt{N}} \text{for } z \in \{0,1\}$$

and

$$h_k(z) \equiv h_{pq}(z) = \begin{cases} \frac{1}{\sqrt{N}} 2^{\frac{p}{2}} & \text{for } \frac{(q-1)}{2^p} \leq z < \frac{\frac{(q-1)}{2}}{2^p} \\ -\frac{1}{\sqrt{N}} 2^{\frac{p}{2}} & \text{for } \frac{\frac{(q-1)}{2}}{2^p} \leq z < \frac{(q)}{2^p} \\ 0 & \text{for } z \in [0,1] \end{cases}$$

We can get a $N \times N$ Harr transform matrix, the ith row of which is represented by the values of $h_i(z)$ for $z = 0, \frac{1}{N}, \frac{2}{N}, \ldots, \frac{N-1}{N}$. If $N = 2$, the Harr matrix will be a 2×2 one. Entries of this matrix are computed as $h_0(z)$ for $z = 0, \frac{1}{2}$, and $h_1(z)$ for $z = 0, \frac{1}{2}$. The matrix is

$$\mathbf{H}_2 = \frac{1}{\sqrt{2}} \begin{bmatrix} 1 & 1 \\ 1 & -1 \end{bmatrix}$$

For $N = 4$ and $N = 8$, we have the following matrices:

$$\mathbf{H}_4 = \frac{1}{2} \begin{bmatrix} 1 & 1 & 1 & 1 \\ 1 & 1 & -1 & -1 \\ -\sqrt{2} & -\sqrt{2} & 0 & 0 \\ 0 & 0 & -\sqrt{2} & -\sqrt{2} \end{bmatrix}$$

$$\mathbf{H}_8 = \frac{1}{2} \begin{bmatrix} 1 & 1 & 1 & 1 & 1 & 1 & 1 & 1 \\ 1 & 1 & 1 & 1 & -1 & -1 & -1 & -1 \\ \sqrt{2} & \sqrt{2} & -\sqrt{2} & -\sqrt{2} & 0 & 0 & 0 & 0 \\ 0 & 0 & 0 & 0 & \sqrt{2} & \sqrt{2} & -\sqrt{2} & -\sqrt{2} \\ 2 & -2 & 0 & 0 & 0 & 0 & 0 & 0 \\ 0 & 0 & 2 & -2 & 0 & 0 & 0 & 0 \\ 0 & 0 & 0 & 0 & 2 & -2 & 0 & 0 \\ 0 & 0 & 0 & 0 & 0 & 0 & 2 & -2 \end{bmatrix}$$

Using Harr transform, in frequency domain, the differential energy in the input signal can be made more localized. It is seen from the above example matrices that the first row of the transform produces the average of the input elements, the second row yields the difference between its first and second halves, etc.

A one-dimensional N-point fast Harr transformation requires N multiplications and $2(N-1)$ additions. The Harr transform, being an orthogonal transform, is separable in nature and a $M \times N$ point two-dimensional transform can be decomposed as a combination of two one-dimensional ones as given below.

$$[F(u,v)] = \frac{1}{\sqrt{MN}} \mathbf{H}_M [f(x,y)] \mathbf{H}_N$$

and

$$[f(x,y)] = \frac{1}{\sqrt{MN}} \mathbf{H}_M [F(u,v)] \mathbf{H}_N$$

5.16 Karhunen–Loeve Transform

This transform (K–L transform) is different from the earlier described ones in the sense that it is not based on the orthogonal basis functions. However, here a discrete signal (uni-dimensional or multi-dimensional) is converted into a sequence of uncorrelated co-efficients based on some statistical properties of the signal. This transform is also known as *Hotelling* transform.

Let us consider a set of n discrete signals as column vectors $\mathbf{f}_0, \mathbf{f}_1, \ldots, \mathbf{f}_{n-1}$, each having M components. The mean vector and the covariance matrix of these vectors are given by

$$\bar{f}(x) = \frac{1}{n}\sum_{i=0}^{n-1} f_i(x)$$

and

$$\Sigma_f(x,y) = \frac{1}{n}\sum_{i=0}^{n-1}\{f_i(x) - \bar{f}(x)\}\{f_i(y) - \bar{f}(y)\}$$

So, we can write

$$\bar{\mathbf{f}} = \frac{1}{n}\sum_{i=0}^{n-1} \mathbf{f}_i$$

and

$$\Sigma_f = \frac{1}{n}\sum_{i=0}^{n-1}(\mathbf{f}_i - \bar{\mathbf{f}})(\mathbf{f}_i - \bar{\mathbf{f}})^T$$

Here, $\bar{\mathbf{f}}$ is a M-dimensional vector and Σ_f is a $M \times M$ matrix. Σ_f is symmetric and we can find out its eigen vectors $\mathbf{w}_j$ and eigenvalues λ_j for $j = 0, 1, \ldots, M-1$.

Now, if we form a matrix $\mathbf{W}$ with the eigen vectors as its rows, i.e.

$$\mathbf{W} = \begin{bmatrix} \mathbf{w}_0 \\ \mathbf{w}_1 \\ \vdots \\ \mathbf{w}_{n-1} \end{bmatrix}$$

we can write, $\mathbf{W}^{-1} = \mathbf{W}^T$, and get the diagonal matrix

$$\mathbf{W}\Sigma_f\mathbf{W}^T = \begin{bmatrix} \lambda_0 & 0 & \cdots & 0 \\ 0 & \lambda_1 & \cdots & 0 \\ & & \ddots & \\ 0 & 0 & \cdots & \lambda_{n-1} \end{bmatrix}$$

Now, the *K–L* transform pair is defined as

$$\mathbf{g}_i = \mathbf{W}(\mathbf{f}_i - \bar{\mathbf{f}}) \tag{5.81}$$

and

$$\mathbf{f}_i = \mathbf{W}^T \; \mathbf{g}_i + \bar{\mathbf{f}} \tag{5.82}$$

Here, $\mathbf{g}$ is the transformed vector corresponding to the input $\mathbf{f}$. Let us now compute the means and covariance matrix for $\mathbf{g}$.

$$\bar{\mathbf{g}} = \frac{1}{n}\sum_{i=0}^{n-1}\mathbf{g}_i = \frac{1}{n}\sum_{i=0}^{n-1}\mathbf{W}(\mathbf{f}_i - \bar{\mathbf{f}}) = \mathbf{W}\left(\frac{1}{n}\sum_{i=0}^{n-1}\mathbf{f}_i - \frac{1}{n}\sum_{i=0}^{n-1}\bar{\mathbf{f}}\right) = 0$$

and

$$\begin{aligned}
\Sigma_g &= \frac{1}{n}\sum_{i=0}^{n-1}(\mathbf{g}_i - \bar{\mathbf{g}})(\mathbf{g}_i - \bar{\mathbf{g}})^T \\
&= \sum_{i=0}^{n-1}\left[\mathbf{W}(\mathbf{f}_i - \bar{\mathbf{f}})\right]\left[\mathbf{W}(\mathbf{f}_i - \bar{\mathbf{f}})\right]^T \\
&= \sum_{i=0}^{n-1}\left[\mathbf{W}(\mathbf{f}_i - \bar{\mathbf{f}})(\mathbf{f}_i - \bar{\mathbf{f}})^T\mathbf{W}^T\right] \\
&= \mathbf{W}\left[\sum_{i=0}^{n-1}(\mathbf{f}_i - \bar{\mathbf{f}})(\mathbf{f}_i - \bar{\mathbf{f}})\right]\mathbf{W}^T \\
&= \mathbf{W}\Sigma_f\mathbf{W}^T
\end{aligned}$$

Therefore, we can write

$$\Sigma_g = \begin{bmatrix} \lambda_0 & 0 & \cdots & 0 \\ 0 & \lambda_1 & \cdots & 0 \\ & & \ddots & \\ 0 & 0 & \cdots & \lambda_{n-1} \end{bmatrix}$$

The covariance matrix of the transformed vectors is diagonal, and hence, elements of transformed vectors $\mathbf{g}_i$ are uncorrelated. Also, $\Sigma_g(x, x) = \lambda_x$ implies that the xth eigen value is equal to the variance of $\mathbf{g}_i(x)$.

5.17 Utility of Image Transforms

Image transformation have simplified representing and processing of digital images to a great extent. Due to the use of separable unitary transformation functions (or matrices) these transformations are reversible in nature and easy to implement either in software or in hardware. Although, in many of the situations, they incur some loss of image information their potential advantages far beyond compensatory. In the following, we point out some of the most common advantages of image transformations.

The Fourier transformations are represented by a set of orthogonal and sinusoidal waveforms. The transformation coefficients are called *frequency components* and the waveforms are ordered by frequency from low to high. Discrete Fourier transforms can be computed efficiently using a fast algorithm called the FFT (Fast Fourier Transform). The first and foremost advantage of this transform is stated by the convolution theorem. Convolution, being so simple in frequency (Fourier) domain, inspired us to develop different kinds of filters for digital images. Filters are used for noise removal, image smoothing, contrast enhancing, etc.

Hartley transformations are represented by real valued unitary basis functions, they are more efficiently computed than the Fourier transforms. This computational advantage comes from the fact here complex coefficients are tactfully avoided.

Hadamard transform consists of square waves represented by Walsh functions. These functions are ordered by their zero-crossings. The frequency domain co-efficients are called the *sequency components*. Since Hadamard transforms of higher order can be defined recursively, a fast transformation algorithm is easy to develop. Basis functions of Hadamard transform are $+1$ and -1, and hence, it is easy to evaluate. Since, lower order zero-crossings indicate sharp changes and higher orders represent minute variations, Hadamard transformation can be used for different kind of filter design.

The Discrete Cosine Transform (DCT) forms the basis of the most commonly used image compression standard, the JPEG. It is due to the fact that the DCT provides a very high compression ratio while maintaining most of the image features.

5.18 Problems

1. What is meant by image transformation? Why is it so important in image processing?

2. Write down the relations for one-dimensional Fourier transformation pair. Show that the imaginary part of Fourier transform of even function is zero.

3. Write down some characteristics of orthogonal transforms.

4. What is the importance of unitary transforms in case of image transformation?

5. Write down a sample unitary 2×2 transformation matrix. Use this transformation matrix to convert the following image into its frequency counterpart:

2	3
1	4

And hence, find the basis images of transformation.

6. Write down the significance of Fourier transformation in image processing. Name some other transformations and mention their utilities.
7. Derive a divide and conquer algorithm for Fourier transformation computation.
8. Follow the algorithm in the above question to compute the Fourier Transform of the following one-dimensional image:

2	3	1	4

9. Write down the convolution theorem and analytically prove it.
10. Two one-dimensional discrete functions are given as

$$f(i) = 4i - 10 \quad \text{for } i = 0, 1, \ldots, 5$$
$$g(i) = 2 - |1 - i| \quad \text{for } i = 0, 1, 2$$

Generate the sequences produced by f and g and compute $f * g$ (convolution).

11. Two matrices **A** and **B** are given below. Convolve **A** with **B**

$$\mathbf{A} = \begin{array}{|c|c|c|}\hline 0 & 1 & 2 \\ \hline 4 & 5 & 6 \\ \hline 1 & 2 & 3 \\ \hline\end{array} \quad \text{and} \quad \mathbf{B} = \begin{array}{|c|c|}\hline 1 & 2 \\ \hline 2 & -1 \\ \hline\end{array}$$

12. Compare the number of multiplications needed to compute the convolution of a 256×256 image with a 8×8 mask in the spatial as weel as in frequency domain.
13. For the above problem, compare the number of additions.
14. A 4×4 image is shown in the following:

0	1	2	3
4	5	6	7
1	2	3	7
8	2	8	1

Compute the DFT of this image.

CHAPTER 6

Image Enhancement

Image enhancement is the process of improving the quality of an image so that it becomes more suitable for some applications. By image enhancement processes appearance of the image can be improved for visual satisfaction also. Actually there is no enhancement technique that can, in general, be applied to all images without regard to their contents. This is because we do not know the exact source or nature of degradation for which the image lacks some specific feature(s) required for a particular application. However, we can always try to modify the image so that the desired features can be highlighted or improved. Naturally, such processes are ad hoc in nature, and by applying them we cannot claim, in any sense, to obtain a better image which is a closer version of the original undegraded one. There are many approaches to do this.

Image enhancement can be performed in either spatial domain or frequency domain. In spatial domain pixel grey values are transformed directly. In majority of the cases, some convolution mask is used for this purpose. Another important tool for spatial domain enhancement is the image histogram. Either local or global enhancement is possible using histogram manipulation techniques. In frequency domain we deal with the Fourier spectrum of the concerned image. This energy spectrum allows us to select, maintain or remove energy contributions of certain specific frequencies. Since frequency domain processing does not involve any convolution operation, computation cost becomes lesser and the processes become simpler.

6.1 Enhancement in Spatial Domain

Basically we an classify the spatial domain enhancement techniques into the following categories:

1. Pixel grey level transformation
    - Linear transformations
        - Image negation
        - Grey level shifting

- Non-linear transformations
    - Logarithmic transformation
    - Exponential transformation
- Grey level slicing
- Bit plane slicing
- Image averaging

2. Mask processing
    - Noise removing filters
    - Smoothing filters
    - Sharpening filters
3. Histogram processing
    - Histogram thresholding
    - Histogram stretching
    - Histogram equalization

Since image processing operations can be performed either in *spatial domain* or in *frequency domain*, enhancement techniques exist for both the domains. We shall discuss some of the spatial domain techniques in the following subsections.

6.2 Pixel Grey Level Transformation

Some transformation functions may be applied to individual pixel grey values directly to enhance the appearance of an image for a particular application. Generally such functions are written as

$$s = T(r) \tag{6.1}$$

where, r and s are original and transformed grey levels, respectively. T is a transformation function. Equation (6.1) can also be expressed as

$$g(x, y) = T[f(x, y)] \tag{6.2}$$

where, $f(x, y)$ and $g(x, y)$ represent input and output images, respectively. If the transformation T is position independent, then Eqs. (6.1) and (6.2) becomes equivalent. In Figure 6.1 one non-linear and one linear transformations are graphically depicted. Some of the commonly used transformation functions are described in following subsections.

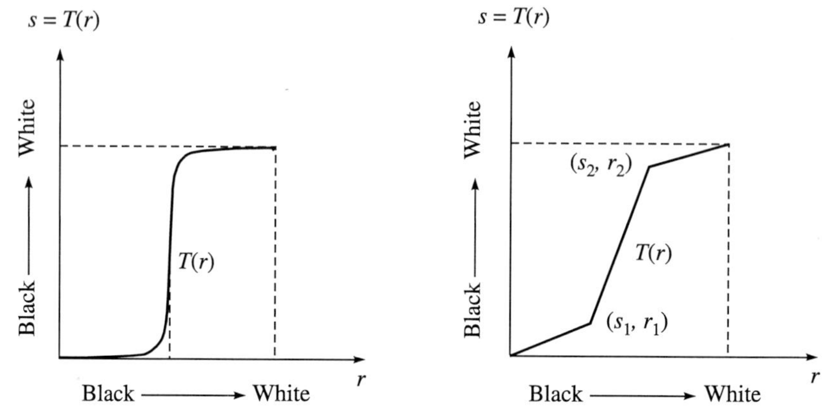

Figure 6.1: Image grey level transformations.

6.2.1 Linear and Non-linear Transformations

Linear grey level transformations are the simplest type of transformations. Here, a linear relationship is maintained between the input and output grey values. Although, in general, grey level transformations may be linear or non-linear, it is found that in many cases the linear transformations are able to provide the desired enhancement in a controllable fashion. Examples of linear and non-linear transformations are shown in Figure 6.2.

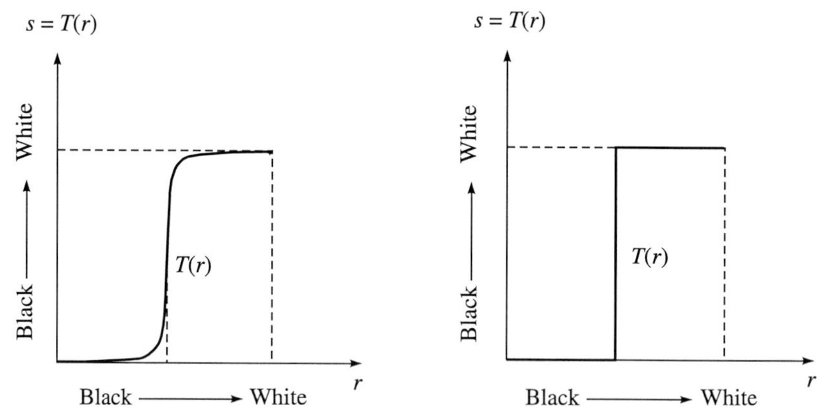

Figure 6.2: Examples of non-linear (log) and linear (step) transformations.

Image negatives

The negative of an image with grey levels in the range $[0, L-1]$ is obtained by using the negative transformation given by the expression:

$$s = L - 1 - r \tag{6.3}$$

Reversing the intensity levels of an image, in this manner, produces the equivalent of a photographic negative. This type of processing is particularly suited for enhancing white or grey details embedded in dark regions of an image, especially when the black areas are dominant in size. The image negation transformation is illustrated in Figure 6.3. Application of the negation transformation on an "eye" image is shown in Figure 6.4.

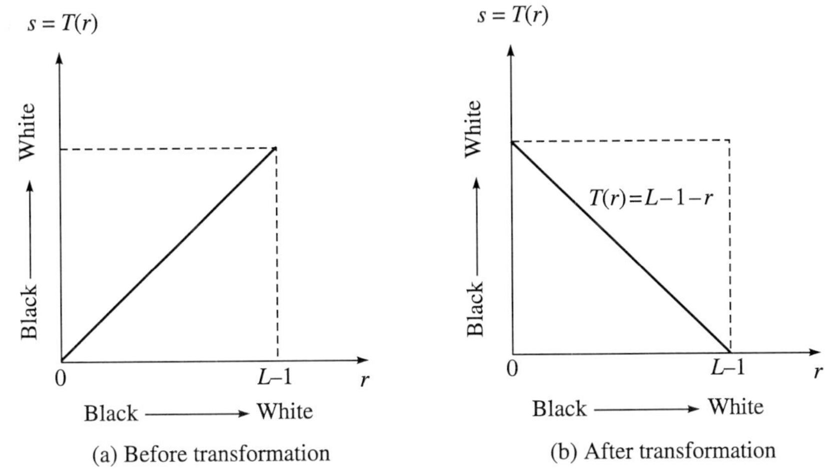

Figure 6.3: Image negation transformation. Input and output grey levels.

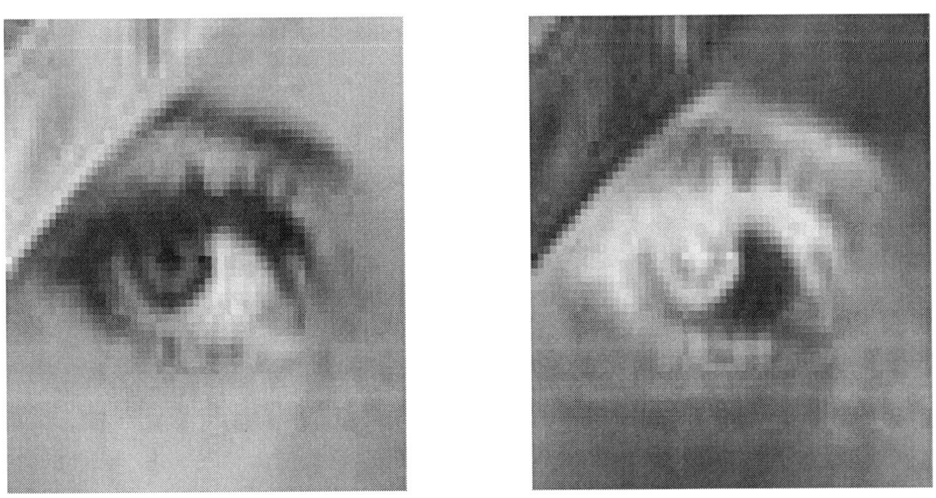

Figure 6.4: Original and negative images.

Grey level shifting

Sometimes we need to highlight a specific range of the input grey values. This has application in understanding image negatives and X-ray images, etc. Here, some constants may be added to a range of desired grey values to shift their levels. In Figure 6.5 two different shifting operations are shown. Figures 6.6 and 6.7 show the effects of applying different shifting operations on the "eye" image.

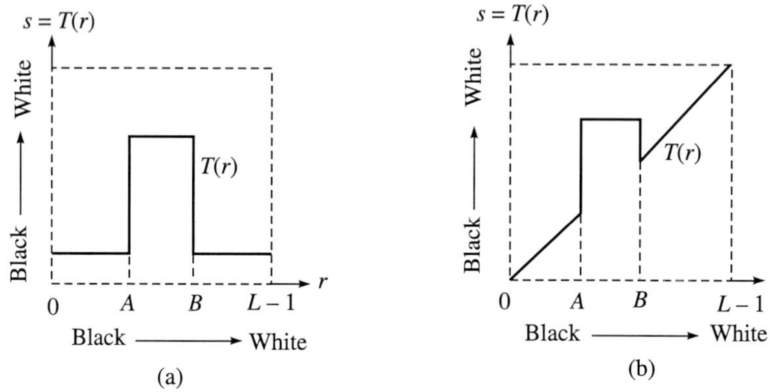

Figure 6.5: Examples of Grey level shifting.

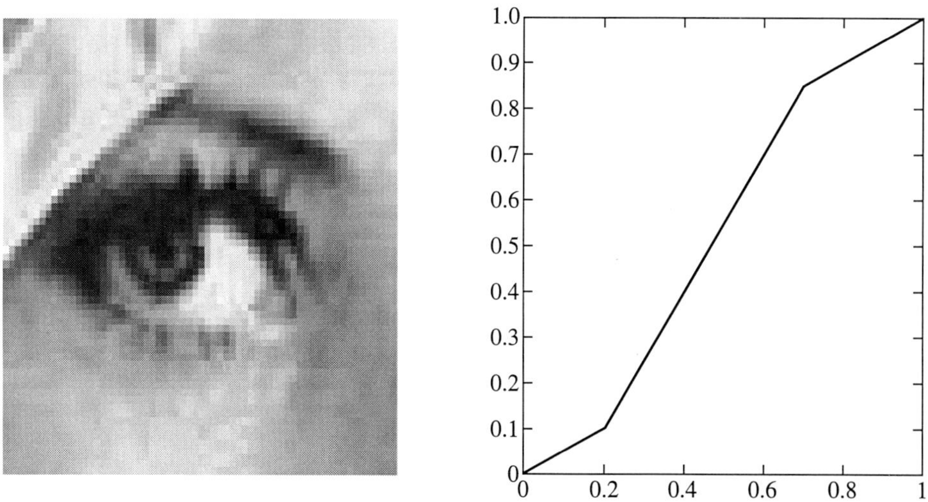

Figure 6.6: Linearly transformed image and the corresponding transformation.

Logarithmic Transformation

The general form of such kind of transformation is given by

$$s = c\log(1 + r)$$

where, c is a scaling constant. This transformation maps a narrow range of input grey levels into a wider range of output values. The opposite is true for higher values of the input grey levels. Of course, in that case the inverse logarithmic transformation

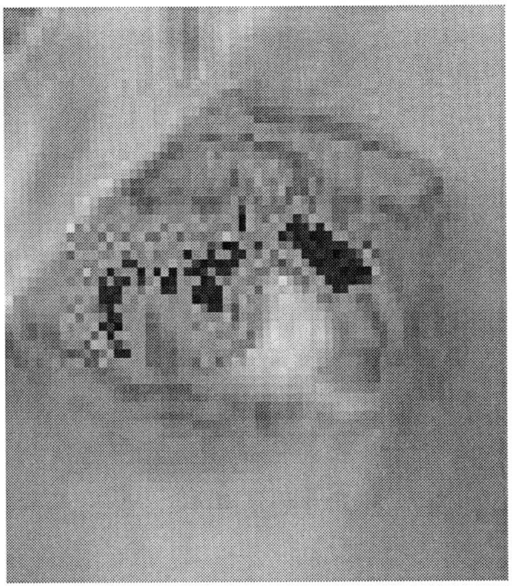
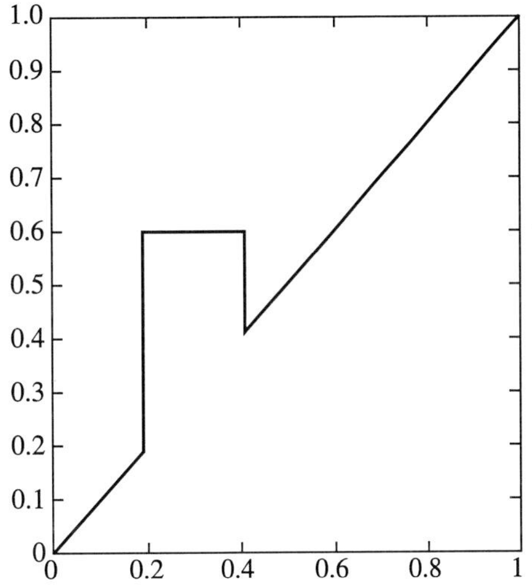

Figure 6.7: Grey-level shifted image and the corresponding transformation.

must be applied. A logarithmic transformation and its effect on the "eye" image have been shown in Figure 6.8.

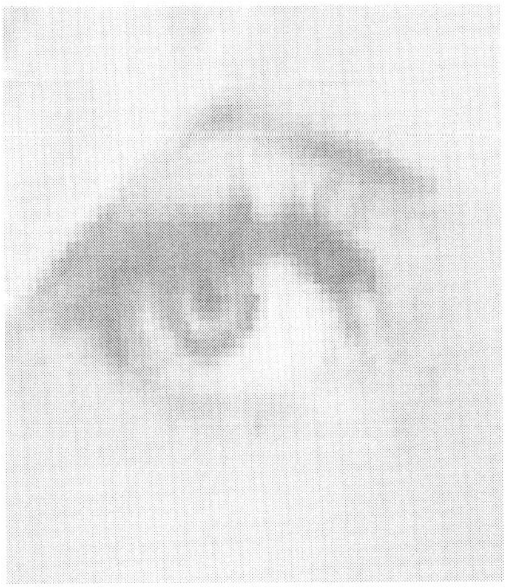
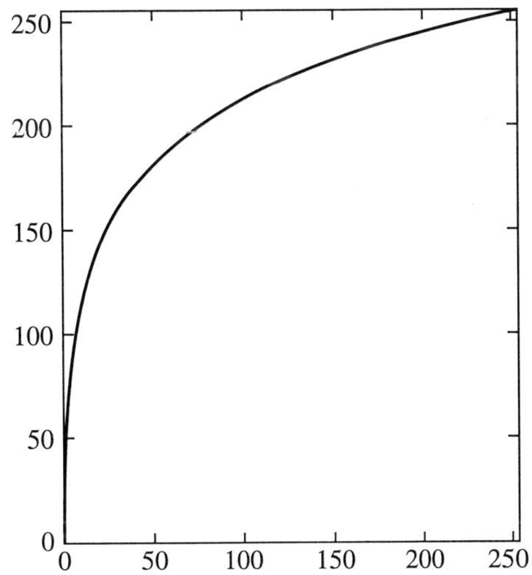

Figure 6.8: Logarithmically transformed image and the corresponding transformation.

6.2.2 Grey Level Slicing

Here, pixels with a certain specific range of grey values are only plotted to produce the output image. Effects of the remaining grey values are ignored. Therefore, objects having the specific range of grey values may be displayed. The discarded grey values, i.e. pixels having outside the range of specified grey values may, however, be plotted by maintaining any of the following principles. If we know the background grey level, then pixels having the out-of-order grey values may be plotted as background pixels. Otherwise, one may plot a binary image using the two classes of pixels, those having the desired grey values and those lacking them.

6.2.3 Bit-plane Slicing

Depending on the allowed range of grey values they can be represented by a fixed number of bit-planes. Each plane contains a single bit for a pixel. For example, in a 256-level image, there are 8 bit-planes (Figure 6.9). Contributions of these bit-planes to the displayed image increases from bit 0 to bit 7. By analyzing the relative importance of different bit-planes, we may drop one or more of them to reduce storage or transmission cost when needed. Contribution of the MSB bit plane and that due to rest of the bit planes for the "eye" image are shown in Figure 6.10.

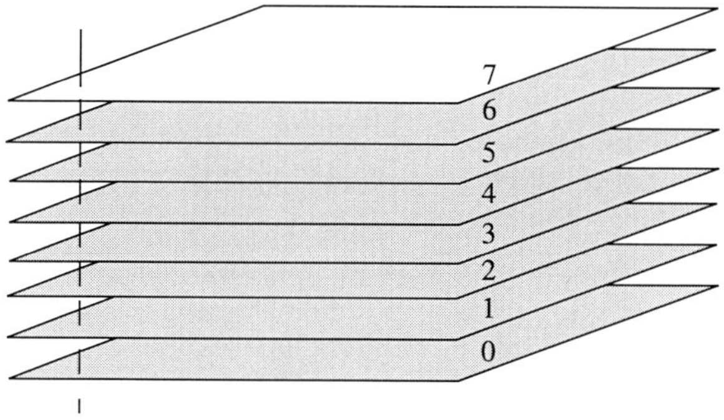

Figure 6.9: Image bit-plane representation.

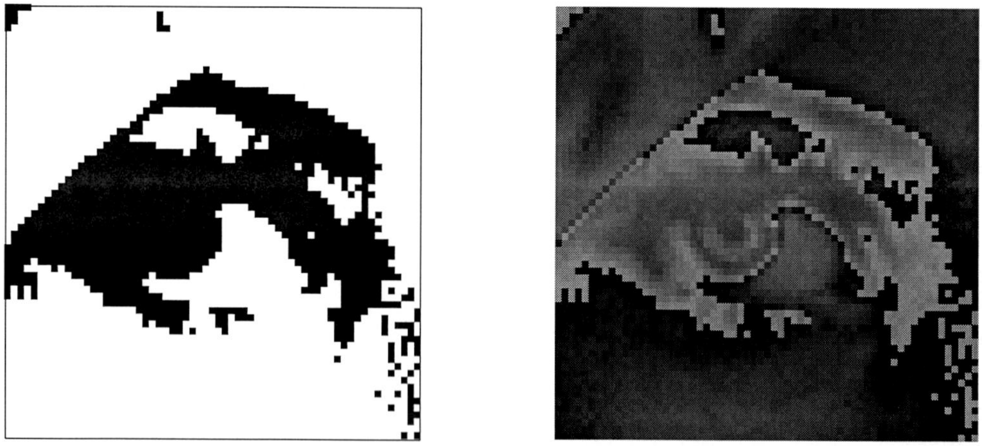

Figure 6.10: Bit-plane sliced images: contribution of the MSB-plane (left) and that of the rest of the bit planes (right).

6.2.4 Image Averaging

Let us consider a number of images of the same object or scene. Generally the image capturing process incorporates some amount of random noise in each of the captured images. That is the captured image $f^c(x, y)$ contains noise $\eta(x, y)$. Therefore, the captured image can be represented as

$$f^c(x, y) = f(x, y) + \eta(x, y) \tag{6.4}$$

where, $f(x, y)$ is the original undegraded image.

Now, if we consider the average of several such degraded image, the error or noise factor can be reduced by significant amount following the principle of statistical averaging. That is, the averaged image becomes

$$f^a(x, y) = \frac{1}{n}\sum_{i=1}^{n} f^c(x, y) = \frac{1}{n}\sum_{i=1}^{n} f(x, y) + \frac{1}{n}\sum_{i=1}^{n} \eta(x, y) \tag{6.5}$$

Since the term representing average noise approaches zero when the number of input images n is large, we can recover a near match of the original image. In Figure 6.11, an input image (top left image), having white and black squares is shown. This image is corrupted using additive Gaussian noise (with 0 mean and 0.005 variance) differently for seven different instances. Average (right bottom image) of the seven corrupted images is found to be almost similar to the original undegraded image.

6.3 Mask Based Processing

Convolution masks are very commonly used to enhance images. These masks are generally very small in size and applied locally to a particular pixel and its neighbours. Some of the important operations performed in this way are smoothing, noise removing, sharpening, etc. In case of noise removal in spatial domain we sometimes call these masks as filters. Different types of filters may be needed according to the nature and distribution of the noise. The schematic of mask operations over an image is shown in Figure 6.12.

Several mask based spatial domain filters are described in the following subsections.

6.3.1 Smoothing Linear Filter

The response of a smoothing spatial linear filter is simply the average of the pixels contained in the neighbourhood of the filter mask. By replacing the values of every pixel in an image by the average of the grey levels in the neighbourhood defined by the filter mask, this process results in an image with a reduction of sharp transitions of grey levels.

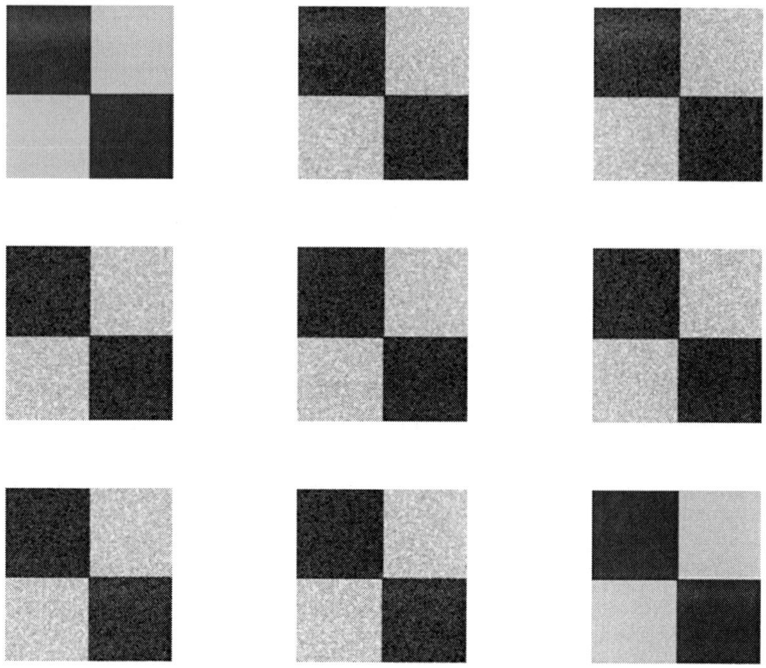

Figure 6.11: Image averaging: original synthetic image, noisy images and average image.

This kind of filter is also called the *mean* filter, because each image grey value is being replaced by the average grey value in its neighbourhood. Let, in a given image, S_{xy} represents the set of coordinates in a rectangular subimage window of size $m \times n$, centred at the point (x, y). The mean filtering process computes the average value of the corrupted image $f(x, y)$ within the area defined by S_{xy}. This can be done as

$$g(x,y) = \frac{1}{mn} \sum_{(s,t)\in S_{xy}} f(s,t) \tag{6.6}$$

Because random noise typically consists of sharp transitions in grey levels, the most obvious application of smoothing is noise reduction. Two such noise reducing masks are shown below where the values of m and n are set as $m = n = 3$. In Figure 6.13, an image of the moon is shown which is degraded by adding additive Gaussian noise and then smoothed by applying the averaging mask as shown here. Another example of smoothing a coarse image is shown in Figure 6.14.

$$\frac{1}{9} \times \begin{array}{|c|c|c|}\hline 1 & 1 & 1 \\ \hline 1 & 1 & 1 \\ \hline 1 & 1 & 1 \\ \hline \end{array} \qquad\qquad \frac{1}{16} \times \begin{array}{|c|c|c|}\hline 1 & 2 & 1 \\ \hline 2 & 4 & 2 \\ \hline 1 & 2 & 1 \\ \hline \end{array}$$

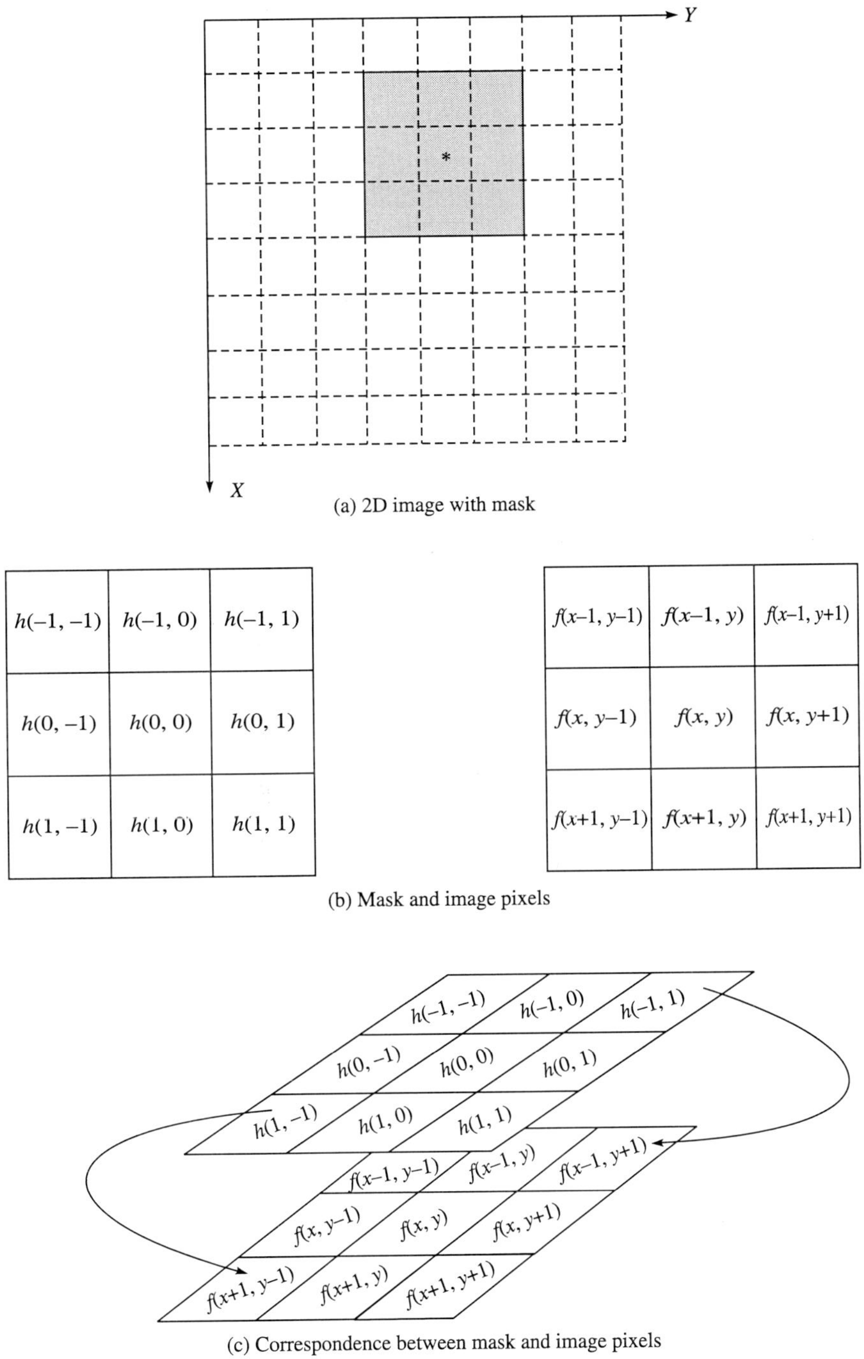

(a) 2D image with mask

(b) Mask and image pixels

(c) Correspondence between mask and image pixels

Figure 6.12: Mask operations over an image.

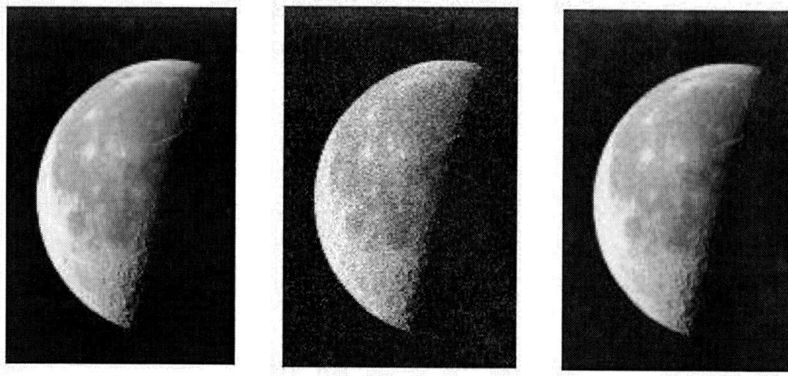

(a) Original image (b) After adding Gussian noise (c) After smoothing

Figure 6.13: Image of moon.

Example 1: Consider the following 4 × 4 image. Apply the above-mentioned linear smoothing masks and find out the smoothed images.

13	5	11	6
15	4	6	7
12	14	4	10
10	12	5	11

Solution: Since, we are to apply a 3 × 3 convolution mask, we need to pad up the image with 0-values at its four boundaries. The 0-padded image is shown below.

0	0	0	0	0	0
0	13	5	11	6	0
0	15	4	6	7	0
0	12	14	4	10	0
0	10	12	5	11	0
0	0	0	0	0	0

Now, applying the first mask, we get

4	6	4	3
7	9	7	5
7	9	4	8
5	6	6	3

The resultant image is fairly smoothed.

♣

Now, let us apply the smoothing mask on a part of the *clown* image. The input image and the resultant smoothed image are shown in Figure 6.14.

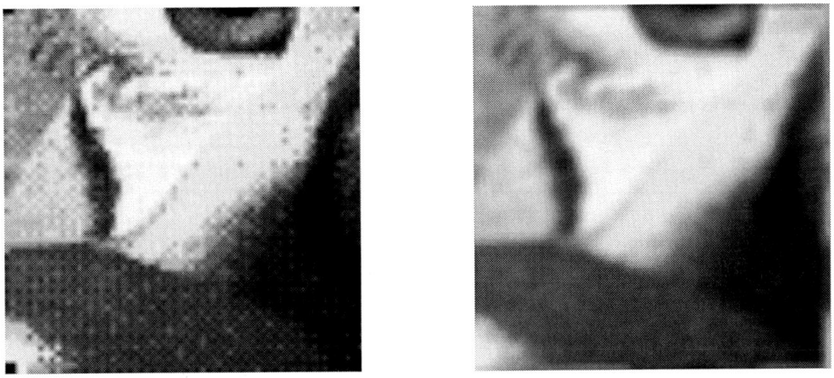

Figure 6.14: Original and smoothed images.

6.3.2 Geometric Mean Filter

An image $f(x, y)$ restored using a geometric mean filter is given by the expression

$$g(x, y) = \left[\prod f(s, t)\right]^{\frac{1}{mn}} \tag{6.7}$$

where (s, t) is in S_{xy}. Here each restored pixel is given by the product of the pixels in the subimage window, raised to the power $\frac{1}{mn}$.

6.3.3 Harmonic Mean Filter

The harmonic mean filter works well for salt noise, but fails for pepper noise. It does well also with other types of noise like Gaussian noise. The harmonic mean filtering operation is given by the expression

$$g(x, y) = \frac{mn}{\sum_{(s,t)\in S_{x\,y}} \frac{1}{f(s, t)}} \tag{6.8}$$

6.3.4 Median Filter

In case of a median filter, each pixel value is replaced by the median of its neighbourhood. If S_{xy} represent the set of coordinates in a rectangular neighbourhood of size $m \times n$, centred at the point (x, y). The median filtering process determines the median value of the subimage of $f(x, y)$ within the area defined by S_{xy}. The process can be described as

$$g(x, y) = \text{median}\,\{f(s, t)|(s, t) \in S_{xy}\} \tag{6.9}$$

The smoothing effect of the median filter is relatively weaker than the mean filter, but it is very effective to remove impulsive noise.

Example 2: Consider the image for Example 1. Apply a 3×3 median filter mask and find out the smoothed images.

Solution: Here, at every pixel location, we need to identify the median grey value. This can be done by arranging all distinct grey values in the neighbourhood, sorting them in ascending order and then selecting the median. Applying this process on the given image, we get the following output:

5	6	5	6
12	11	7	6
10	10	4	7
10	5	10	5

Here, in case of multiple medians, we have selected the lower in magnitude. However, one may arbitrarily select the other median, or the average of the two too.

♣

6.3.5 Max- and Min-Filters

The Max-filter and Min-filter are also statistical filters which can be described as

$$g(x,y) = \max\{f(s,t)|(s,t) \in S_{xy}\} \tag{6.10}$$

and

$$g(x,y) = \min\{f(s,t)|(s,t) \in S_{xy}\} \tag{6.11}$$

Here, each pixel value is replaced by the maximum or minimum of its neighbourhood.

6.3.6 Sharpening Filters

The principal objective of sharpening is to highlight fine detail in an image or to enhance the detail that has been blurred. Sharpening can be accomplished by spatial differentiation. The strength of the response of a derivative operator is proportional to the degree of discontinuity of the image at the point at which the mask is applied. Using a second order differentiation we can sharpen the image discontinuities. The Laplacian operator is defined as

$$\nabla^2 f(x,y) = [f(x,y-1) + f(x-1,y) - 4f(x,y) + f(x,y+1) + f(x+1,y)] \tag{6.12}$$

The above operator is developed considering a neighbourhood of nearest four elements. The corresponding spatial convolution mask may be represented as

0	1	0
1	−4	1
0	1	0

or

0	−1	0
−1	4	−1
0	−1	0

If we consider a neighbourhood of 8 pixels, the diagonal neighbours also contribute to the Laplacian, the convolution mask becomes

1	1	1
1	−8	1
1	1	1

or

−1	−1	−1
−1	8	−1
−1	−1	−1

Application of a Laplacian operator over the *moon* image is shown in Figure 6.15. Here, output of the Laplacian operation is displayed as an intensity image where only sharp variation of intensity patterns in the original image are visible.

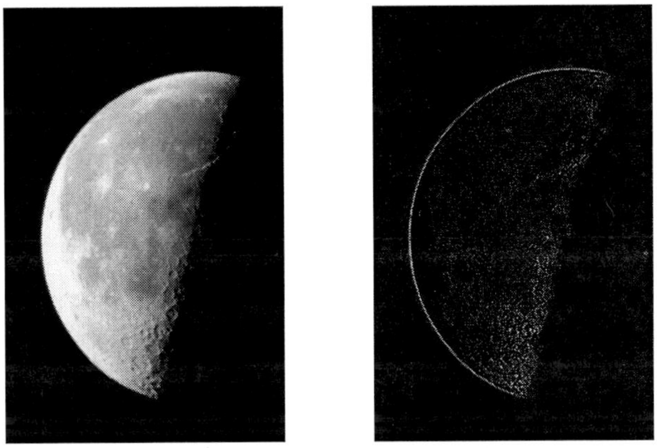

(a) Original operated (b) Laplacian operated

Figure 6.15: Image of moon.

To sharpen the original image, we need to superimpose the Laplacian output with the original one. This can be done by adding or subtracting the Laplacian response with the original image elements. The relations used for this purpose may be written as

$$g(x, y) = \begin{cases} f(x, y) - \nabla^2 f(x, y) \\ f(x, y) + \nabla^2 f(x, y) \end{cases}$$

If the definition of Laplacian uses a negative centre coefficient, we need to subtract, otherwise an addition is needed. Combining these operations (Laplacian followed by add/subtract) we may derive the following sharpening operators:

0	1	0
1	−5	1
0	1	0

or

0	−1	0
−1	5	−1
0	−1	0

or

1	1	1
1	−9	1
1	1	1

or

−1	−1	−1
−1	9	−1
−1	−1	−1

6.3.7 Image Blurring and Deblurring

The inverse process of sharpening is blurring. In most of the case blurring is caused by relative motion between camera and the object during capturing. Besides relative motion between camera and object, image blurring may occur for other reasons also. The process of removing blur from the image different techniques may be employed. One of them is to use sharpening mask. The process of blurring is not an enhancement process, but the reverse process is one. In Figure 6.16, image of a *cameraman* is shown. This image is blurred. Figure 6.17(a) and (b) show a blurred version and sharpened version of the above cameraman image.

Figure 6.16: Original cameraman image.

(a) Blurred image

(b) Sharpened image after blurring

Figure 6.17: Processed Cameraman image.

6.4 Histogram Processing

The histogram of a digital image with grey level in the range $[0, L-1]$ is a discrete function

$$h(r_k) = n_k \tag{6.13}$$

where r_k is the kth grey level and n_k is the number of pixel in the image having grey level r_k. It is common practice to normalize a histogram by dividing each of its value by the total number of pixels in the image denoted by n. Thus, normalized histogram is given by

$$p(r_k) = \frac{n_k}{n} \tag{6.14}$$

for $k = 0, 1, \ldots, L-1$. Loosely speaking, $p(r_k)$ gives an estimate of probability of occurrence of grey level r_k.

Example 3: Consider the following image. Write down the tabular and graphical representations of its histogram.

10	11	12	11	10	11	12	15
12	12	6	5	4	12	13	13
13	12	5	3	5	10	11	12
13	12	4	3	5	11	13	15
12	12	5	4	4	10	10	12
11	11	6	7	5	11	12	15
13	11	7	5	4	12	13	13
13	12	15	13	14	10	11	12

Solution: The tabular histogram of the given image is given below. The problem of drawing the graphical histogram is left for the students.

Grey value	0	1	2	3	4	5	6	7	8	9	10	11	12	13	14	15
No. of pixels	0	0	0	2	5	7	2	2	0	0	6	10	15	10	1	3

♣

6.4.1 Histogram Equalization

Histogram equalization is an automatic contrast enhancement technique where pixels of the entire image are uniformly distributed among all possible grey levels. Let $H(r)$ is the input histogram defined over the grey scale range $[r_0, r_k]$. We want to find a monotonic transform $s = T(r)$ such that the output histogram $G(s)$ is uniform over the output grey scale range $[s_0, s_k]$. One such function is the cumulative distribution function. In continuous domain, with grey level ranges $[0\ 1]$, the transformation function is

$$s = T(r) = \int_0^r p_r(x)dx \tag{6.15}$$

where x is a dummy variable of integration and $p_r(x)$ is the probability density for input grey value x. In discrete domain, the monotonic property of the transformation T implies

$$\sum_{i=0}^{k} G(s_i) = \sum_{i=0}^{k} H(r_i) \tag{6.16}$$

Let the image be of size $N \times N$. The equalized histogram $G(s)$ corresponds to the uniform probability density function f whose function value is a constant

$$f = \frac{N^2}{s_k - s_0} \tag{6.17}$$

Assuming the density function to be continuous, we can write

$$N^2 \int_{s_0}^{s} \frac{1}{s_k - s_0} dz = \frac{N^2(s - s_0)}{s_k - s_0} = \int_{r_0}^{r} H(z)dz \tag{6.18}$$

The desired pixel brightness transformation T can then be written as

$$s = T(r) = \frac{s_k - s_0}{N^2} \int_{r_0}^{r} H(z)dz + s_0 \tag{6.19}$$

Reverting again to the discrete domain,

$$s = T(r) = \frac{s_k - s_0}{N^2} \sum_{i=r_0}^{r} H(i) + s_0 \tag{6.20}$$

Algorithm for histogram equalization

- **Step 1:** For $N \times M$ image of L grey levels create an array H of length L, and initialize it with 0 values.
- **Step 2:** Scan every pixel and increment the relevant member of H. If a pixel has intensity r_p, perform

$$H[r_p] = H[r_p] + 1$$

- **Step 3:** Form the cumulative histogram H_c. Initialize $H_c[0]$ with $H[0]$, i.e. $H_c[0] = H[0]$. Compute the following:

$$H_c[r_p] = H_c[r_p - 1] + H[r_p]$$

for

$$r_p = 1, 2, \ldots, L-1$$

- **Step 4:** Compute the following:

$$T[r_p] = \text{round}\left(\frac{(L-1) \times H_c[r_p]}{N \times M}\right)$$

- **Step 5:** Rescan the image and write an output image with grey levels r_p replaced by new values $T[r_p]$.

Histogram equalization is global technique as pixels are modified by a transformation function based on the grey level content of an entire image. But here we need to enhance details over small areas in an image. We devise transformation functions based on the properties in the neighbourhood of every pixel in the image. All global histogram processing techniques are easily adaptable to local enhancement. The procedure is to define a square or rectangular neighbourhood and move the centre of this area from pixel to pixel. At each location, the histogram of the points in the neighbourhood is computed and the transformation function is obtained. This function is finally used to map the grey level of the pixel centred in the neighbourhood. The centre is then moved to an adjacent pixel location and the procedure is repeated. Since only one new row or column of the neighbourhood changes during a pixel-to-pixel translation of the region, updating the histogram obtained in the previous location with the new data introduced at each motion step is possible.

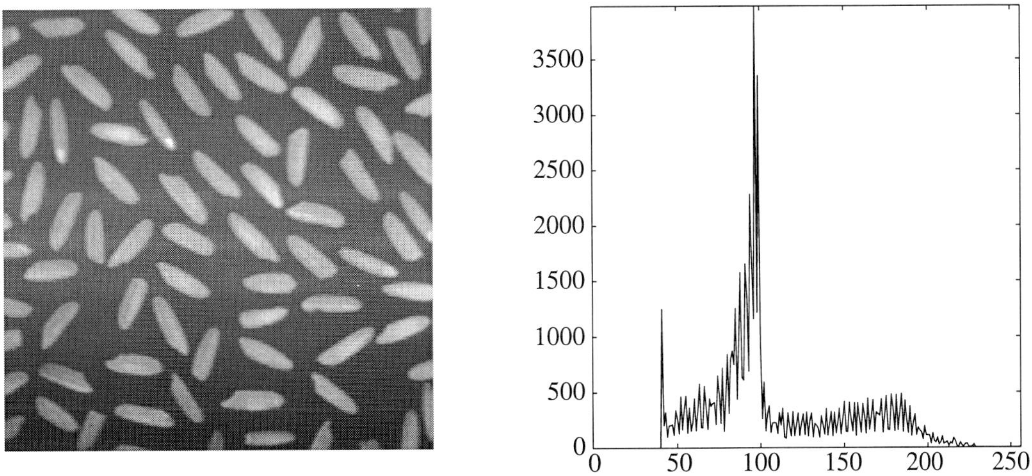

Figure 6.18: Original rice image and its histogram.

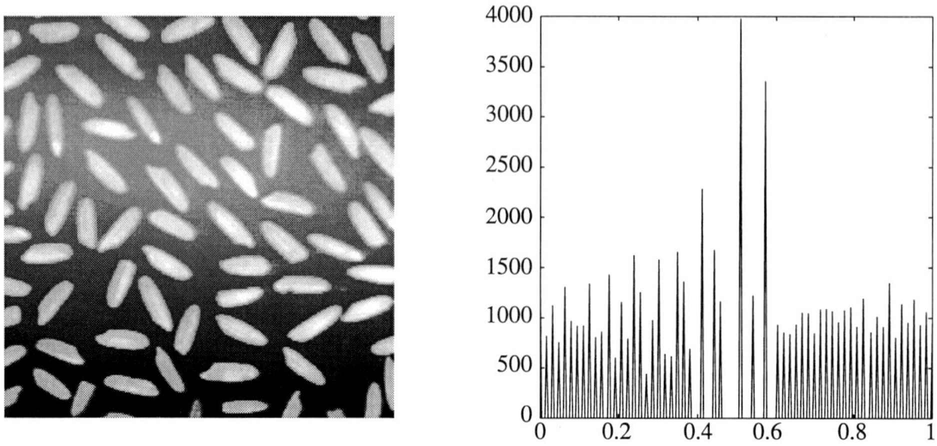

Figure 6.19: Histogram equalized rice image and its histogram.

Example 4: Consider the following 8-level grey image of size 8×8. Show the original histogram of the image. Compute the equalized histogram and display graphically.

$$
\begin{matrix}
0 & 1 & 1 & 0 & 0 & 1 & 1 & 0 \\
0 & 1 & 2 & 3 & 3 & 2 & 1 & 0 \\
0 & 4 & 5 & 3 & 3 & 5 & 4 & 0 \\
0 & 1 & 2 & 7 & 7 & 2 & 1 & 0 \\
0 & 1 & 2 & 6 & 6 & 2 & 1 & 0 \\
0 & 4 & 5 & 3 & 3 & 5 & 4 & 0 \\
0 & 1 & 2 & 3 & 3 & 2 & 1 & 0 \\
0 & 1 & 1 & 0 & 0 & 1 & 1 & 0
\end{matrix}
$$

Solution: The original histogram, cumulative histogram, grey-value transformation and equalized histogram are shown below in tabular and graphical fashion

Original Histogram								
Grey value	0	1	2	3	4	5	6	7
No of pixels	20	16	8	8	4	4	2	2

Cumulative Histogram								
Grey value	0	1	2	3	4	5	6	7
H_c count	20	36	44	52	56	60	62	64

Grey Value Transformation (T)								
Original grey value	0	1	2	3	4	5	6	7
Transformed grey value	2	4	5	6	6	7	7	7

Equalized Histogram								
Grey value	0	1	2	3	4	5	6	7
No. of pixel	0	0	20	0	16	8	12	8

Graphical representations are:

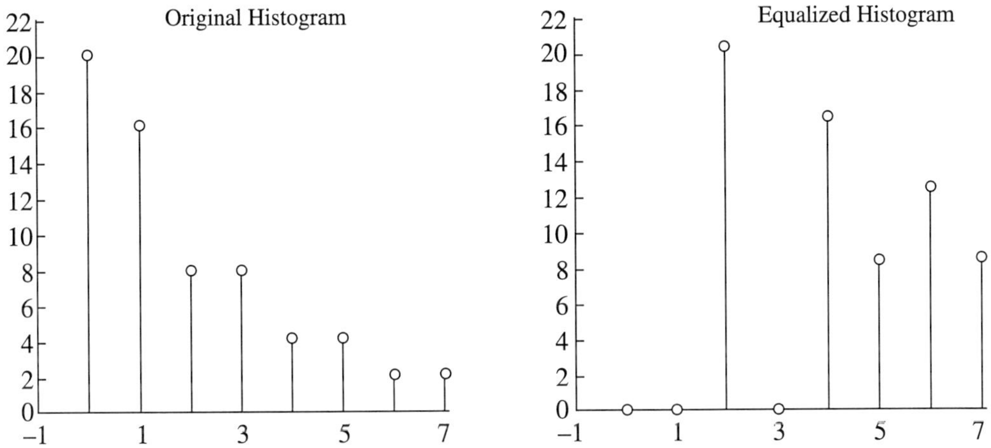

Figure 6.20: Original and equalized histograms for Example 4.

6.4.2 Contrast Stretching

Sometimes it is found that the image histogram tends to be accumulated to one end of the grey scale range. In such situations, objects present in a image cannot be distinguished, in many cases, from the background. One solution is to stretch the histogram and reproduce the image. Stretching can be linear or non-linear. However, all sorts of stretching must maintain the following restrictions:

1. The stretching transformation $s = T(r)$ must be monotonically increasing in the interval $[r_{\min}, r_{\max}]$, i.e.

$$s_{i-1} < s_i < s_{i+1} \quad \text{for} \quad r_{i-1} < r_i < r_{i+1}$$

2. New grey values must lie within the specified range of the output grey levels, i.e.

$$s_{\min} \leq s \leq s_{\max} \quad \text{for} \quad r_{\min} \leq r \leq r_{\max}$$

Linear stretching

Let the input and output grey scale ranges be specified by $(r_{\max}, r_{\min})$ and $(s_{\max}, s_{\min})$, respectively. Let the input grey value r be stretched to the value s in the output grey scale. In this case stretching is linear. So we can write,

$$(s - s_{\min}) \propto (r - r_{\min}) \tag{6.21}$$

i.e.

$$(s - s_{\min}) = k(r - r_{\min}) \tag{6.22}$$

where k is constant of proportionality. Applying boundary conditions (i.e. $s = s_{\min}$ for $r = r_{\min}$ and $s = s_{\max}$ for $r = r_{\max}$), we get

$$k = \frac{s_{\max} - s_{\min}}{r_{\max} - r_{\min}} \tag{6.23}$$

Therefore,

$$s = \frac{(s_{\max} - s_{\min})}{(r_{\max} - r_{\min})} \times (r - r_{\min}) + s_{\min} \tag{6.24}$$

Therefore, the transformation function can be expressed as a straight line having slope $\frac{s_{\max}-s_{\min}}{r_{\max}-r_{\min}}$.

Example 5: Consider the following image having grey values between levels 0 and 15. Stretch the grey values uniformly and linearly within the entire range.

10	11	12	11	10
12	12	13	5	4
13	12	5	3	5
13	12	4	3	5
12	4	5	4	4

Solution: In the given image, different grey values are 3, 4, 5, 10, 11, 12 and 13. Here, we need to use the following relation for stretching.

$$s = \frac{(s_{\max} - s_{\min})}{(r_{\max} - r_{\min})} \times (r - r_{\min}) + s_{\min}$$

Here, $r_{\min} = 3, r_{\max} = 13, s_{\min} = 0$ and $s_{\max} = 15$. The transformation is shown in Table 6.1.

Table 6.1: Linear transformation for Example 1

Input Grey (r)	*Conversion*	*Output Grey* (s)	*Rounded Output*
3	$1.5 \times 0 + 0$	0.0	0
4	$1.5 \times 1 + 0$	1.5	2
5	$1.5 \times 2 + 0$	3.0	3
10	$1.5 \times 7 + 0$	9.5	10
11	$1.5 \times 8 + 0$	12.0	12
12	$1.5 \times 9 + 0$	13.5	14
13	$1.5 \times 10 + 0$	15.0	15

♣

Sometimes, only a portion of the grey level histogram is to be stretched, at the cost of compressing the remaining portion, to facilitate some local features. Suppose, the range (a, b) is to be stretched to the new range of (c, d). Here, c and d be the output grey levels corresponding to a and b respectively. We are to map $(r_{\min}, a)$ to $(r_{\min}, c)$, (a, b) to (c, d) and $(b, r_{\max})$ to $(b, s_{\max})$. Then we get the following condition.

We can write,

$$\frac{(c+d)}{2} = \frac{(a+b)}{2} \tag{6.25}$$

This is because, for uniform stretching along both the directions, the midpoint of the concerned grey scale range remains unchanged. This is shown as follows.

For the range $(r_{\min}, a)$**:**

$$s = \frac{c - s_{\min}}{a - r_{\min}} \times (r - r_{\min}) + s_{\min} \tag{6.26}$$

For the range (a, b)**:**

$$s = \frac{(d-c)}{(b-a)} \times (r - a) + c \tag{6.27}$$

and,

$$s = -\frac{(d-c)}{(b-a)} \times (b - r) + d \tag{6.28}$$

For the range $(b, r_{\max})$:

$$s = \frac{(s_{\max} - d)}{(r_{\max} - b)} \times (r - b) + d \tag{6.29}$$

Now, let us consider the stretching of the range (a, b) by a factor of 2. In this case,

$$\frac{(d-c)}{(b-a)} = 2 \tag{6.30}$$

Solving Eqs. (6.25) and (6.30), $c = \frac{3a-b}{2}$ and $d = \frac{3b-a}{2}$

For the range $(r_{\min}, a)$**:**

From Eq. (6.26), we have

$$s = \frac{3a - b - 2s_{\min}}{2(a - s_{\min})} \times (r - s_{\min}) + s_{\min}$$

since, in this range $s_{\min} = r_{\min}$. Therefore,

$$s = \frac{(3a - b - 2s_{\min})\,m + (b - a)\,s_{\min}}{2\,(a - s_{\min})}$$

For the range (a, b)**:**

Adding Eqs. (6.27) and (6.28), we get

$$2s = \frac{(d - c)}{(b - a)} \times (2r - a - b) + c + d$$

or

$$2s = 2[2r - (a + b)] + (c + d)$$

or

$$s = 2r - (a + b) + \frac{(c + d)}{2} = 2r - (a + b) + \frac{(a + b)}{2} = \frac{4r - a - b}{2}$$

For the range $(b, r_{\max})$**:**

From Eq. (6.29), we get

$$s = \frac{(2s_{\max} - 3b + a)}{2(s_{\max} - b)} \times (r - b) + \frac{3b - a}{2}$$

since in this range $s_{\max} = r_{\max}$. Therefore,

$$s = \frac{(2s_{\max} + a - 3b)r + (b - a)s_{\max}}{2(s_{\max} - b)}$$

Example 6: Consider the image of Example 4 having grey values between levels 0 and 15. Stretch the grey values within the range of (5, 10) linearly and uniformly with a scale factor of 2.

Solution: In the given image, different grey values are 3, 4, 5, 10, 11, 12 and 13. Here, we need to use the following relations for stretching:

$$s = \frac{(3a - b - 2s_{\min})r + (b - a)s_{\min}}{2(a - s_{\min})}$$

$$s = \frac{4r - a - b}{2}$$

and

$$s = \frac{(2s_{\max} + a - 3b)r + (b - a)s_{\max}}{2(s_{\max} - b)}$$

Here, $a = 5, b = 10, c = 2.5$ and $d = 12.5$. The transformation is shown in Table 6.2. Limits in different grey scale ranges are as follows:

$$0 \leq r < 5 \quad r_{\min} = 0, r_{\max} = 5 \quad s_{\min} = 0, s_{\max} = 2.5$$

$$5 \leq r \leq 10 \quad r_{\min} = 5, r_{\max} = 10 \quad s_{\min} = 2.5, s_{\max} = 12.5$$

$$10 < r \leq 15 \quad r_{\min} = 10, r_{\max} = 15 \quad s_{\min} = 12.5, s_{\max} = 15$$

Table 6.2: Linear Transformation for Example 4

Input Range	*Input Grey* (r)	*Conversion*	*Output Grey* (s)	*Rounded Output*
$0 \leq r < 5$	3	$\frac{(15-10-0)\times 3 + 5\times 0}{2\times 5}$	1.5	2
	4	$\frac{(15-10-0)\times 4 + 5\times 0}{2\times 5}$	2.0	2
$5 \leq r \leq 10$	5	$\frac{20-10-5}{2}$	2.5	3
	10	$\frac{40-10-5}{2}$	12.5	13
$10 < r \leq 15$	11	$\frac{(30-5-30)\times 11 + 5\times 15}{2\times 5}$	13.0	13
	12	$\frac{(30-5-30)\times 12 + 5\times 15}{2\times 5}$	13.5	14
	13	$\frac{(30-5-30)\times 13 + 5\times 15}{2\times 5}$	14.0	14

♣

Non-linear stretching

Sometimes exponential or logarithmic stretching is found useful for some situations.

Logarithmic stretching

Sometimes we observe a very high population of pixels in the lower part of the grey scale than in the higher part. The resulting image is thus obscure due to a low contrast factor (Figure 6.21). In such a situation we need to stretch the grey levels with a non-uniform stretching factor having higher values for lower grey values. To stretch the lower grey level zone at the cost of compressing the higher grey level zone we generally use logarithmic transformation functions. This can neutralize the exponential response to the irradiance exhibited by the image sensor.

In this case, we can express the grey level variation on the input and output grey scales as

$$\frac{ds}{dr} \propto \frac{1}{(r - r_{\text{min}}) + 1} \tag{6.31}$$

The 1 in the denominator of Eq. (6.31) is added as an extra, to avoid the chance that the denominator could be zero.
Therefore,

$$\frac{ds}{dr} = k \times \frac{1}{(r - r_{\text{min}}) + 1}$$

where, k is the constant of proportionality. By taking integration on both sides,

$$\int ds = \int \frac{1}{(r - r_{\text{min}}) + 1} dr$$

or

$$s = k \times \ln(r - r_{\text{min}} + 1) + c$$

where, c is the constant of integration. Now, let us apply boundary conditions as: $r = r_{\text{min}} \Rightarrow s = s_{\text{min}}$ and $r = r_{\text{max}} \Rightarrow s = s_{\text{max}}$.
Therefore, we arrive at,

$$s_{\text{max}} = k \times \ln(r_{\text{max}} - r_{\text{min}} + 1) + c$$

and

$$s_{\text{min}} = k \times \ln(1) + c$$

Therefore,

$$s_{\text{max}} = k \times \ln(r_{\text{max}} - r_{\text{min}} + 1) + s_{\text{min}} - \ln(1)$$

Ignoring $\ln(1)$, we get,

$$s_{\text{max}} = k \times \ln(r_{\text{max}} - r_{\text{min}} + 1) + s_{\text{min}}$$

The transformation relation thus becomes,

$$s = (s_{\text{max}} - s_{\text{min}}) \times \frac{\ln(r - r_{\text{min}} + 1)}{\ln(r_{\text{max}} - r_{\text{min}} + 1)} + s_{\text{min}} \tag{6.32}$$

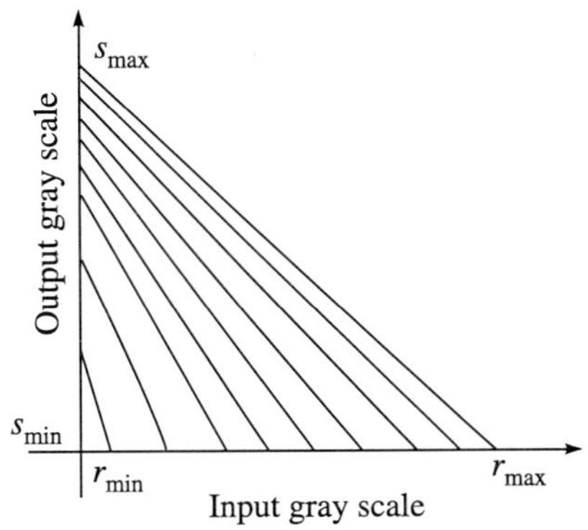

Figure 6.21: Logarithmic contrast stretching.

Exponential stretching

Exponential transformation functions are useful when the grey level histogram shows high population of pixels in the high grey level zone of the grey scale. These functions are also able to cancel the effect of logarithmic response of the image sensor to the irradiance. From Weber's law we know that the just noticeable difference δI in brightness over the brightness I in its neighbourhood is approximately proportional to I.

Let us consider a digital image where intensity values are in the range of $(r_{\min}, r_{\max})$. If we want to produce only L levels within the specified range, each intensity should be k times higher than the preceding intensity, where,

$$\frac{I_1}{I_0} = \frac{I_2}{I_1} = \cdots = \frac{I_{L-1}}{I_{L-2}} = k \tag{6.33}$$

or

$$I_0 = I_0, I_1 = kI_0, I_2 = kI_1, \ldots, I_{L-1} = kI_{L-2} \tag{6.34}$$

or

$$I_0 = I_0, I_1 = kI_0, I_2 = k^2 I_0, \ldots, I_{L-1} = k^{L-1} I_0 \tag{6.35}$$

or

$$k = \left(\frac{I_{L-1}}{I_0}\right)^{\frac{1}{L-1}} \tag{6.36}$$

In our case, $r_{\min} = I_0$ and $r_{\max} = I_{L-1}$. Therefore, the above equation becomes,

$$k = \left(\frac{r_{\max}}{r_{\min}}\right)^{\frac{1}{r_{\max} - r_{\min}}} \tag{6.37}$$

Therefore, any grey value r on the input scale can be expressed as

$$s = s_{\min}\left(\frac{r_{\max}}{r_{\min}}\right)^{\frac{r - r_{\min}}{r_{\max} - r_{\min}}} \tag{6.38}$$

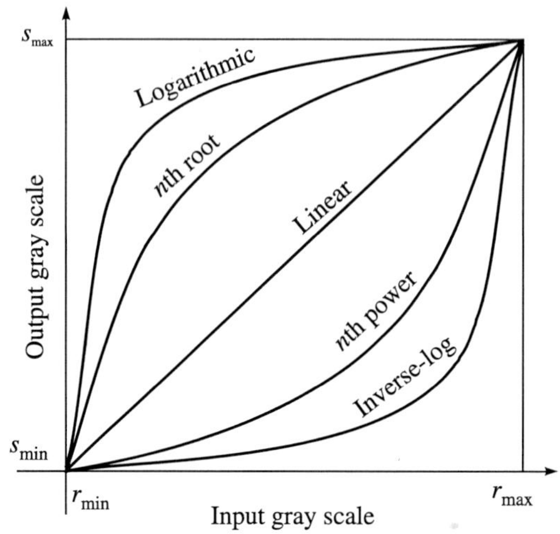

Figure 6.22: General image contrast stretching.

6.5 Enhancement in Frequency Domain

It is already mention in an earlier section that the enhancement process is faster and simpler than their spatial domain counterpart. The advantages in the frequency domain is due to the fact that the convolution operation, here, is replaced by the simple point by point multiplication of the image with a filter transfer function which is binary in nature, in general. Of course, the overhead operations of forward and inverse Fourier transformations are involved here.

The Fourier transform converts an image into a corresponding energy spectrum. Each frequency component is associated to a particular band in the energy spectrum. Therefore, by maintaining or eliminating certain frequency components, we can get a new energy spectrum. When this new spectrum is brought back to the spatial domain, we get a processed image.

The enhancement operators in the frequency domain are called filters or transfer functions. The spatial domain counterpart of this transfer function is the convolution mask. From the convolution theorem, we described earlier in Chapter 5, it is easy to understand that by transforming a spatial mask $h(x, y)$ we can get a corresponding transfer function $H(u, v)$.

The enhancement process in the frequency domain can be expressed mathematically as

$$G(u, v) = H(u, v) \cdot F(u, v) \tag{6.39}$$

where, $F(u, v)$ is the Fourier transform of the original spatial image $f(x, y)$, $H(u, v)$ is the transfer function, and $G(u, v)$ is the transformed (enhanced) image in the frequency domain. The spatial version of the output image can be obtained by an inverse Fourier transform given by

$$g(x, y) = \mathcal{F}^{-1}[G(u, v)] \tag{6.40}$$

Although we mentioned that a transfer function can be obtained from a spatial mask, in reality, it is not that easy. The difficulty lies in the fact the Fourier transformations produce both real and imaginary components. However, we can derive suitable transfer functions by applying common sense and geometrical properties of the frequency spectrum and the filter function.

6.5.1 Ideal Low Pass Filter

A low pass filter is used, in general, to smooth an image. As it is known that the lower frequency spectrum of a Fourier transform contains the average image intensities and high frequency components signify sharp variations, we can develop a low pass filter to eliminate the high frequency components. A suitable threshold is also required to be determined.

An ideal low pass filter transfer function can be described by the following relation

$$H(u, v) = \begin{cases} 1 & \text{if } (u^2 + v^2) \leq D_0 \\ 0 & \text{otherwise} \end{cases} \tag{6.41}$$

where, $D_0 = \sqrt{u_0^2 + v_0^2}$ is the threshold frequency and is representing the distance of the point (u_0, v_0) from the origin of the frequency plane.

The low pass filter described above is shown graphically in Figure 6.23. It is clear that the filter passes all the frequency components inside the circle of radius w_0, while attenuates all other higher frequency components. Therefore, this filter is called the ideal low pass filter.

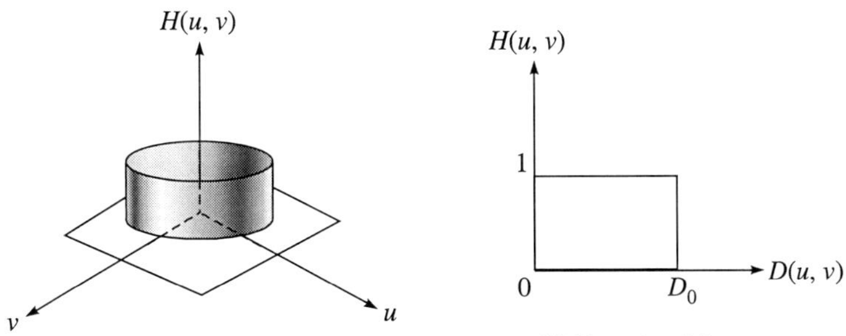

Figure 6.23: Ideal Low pass filter.

6.5.2 Butterworth Low Pass Filter

The ideal low pass filter uses a sharp cut-off that imply hard filtering. If we want to make the filter to allow a part of the energy spectrum at higher frequencies, we may use the Butterworth filter. The response of Butterworth low pass filter of order n is defined as

$$H(u,v) = \frac{1}{1 + \left(\dfrac{D}{D_0}\right)^{2n}} \tag{6.42}$$

where, $D = \sqrt{u^2 + v^2}$ and $D_0 = \sqrt{u_0^2 + v_0^2}$. For this filter, when $D = D_0$, we get the response of the filter as $H(u,v) = 0.5$. This indicates that at the cut-off frequency the response is half of its maximum value (i.e. 50%) (Figure 6.24). If instead of $\frac{1}{2}$, we want to get a cut-off frequency response of $\frac{1}{\sqrt{2}}$, we can use the following relations:

$$H(u,v) = \frac{1}{1 + (\sqrt{2} - 1)\left(\dfrac{D}{D_0}\right)^{2n}} \tag{6.43}$$

or

$$H(u,v) = \frac{1}{1 + 0.414\left(\dfrac{D}{D_0}\right)^{2n}} \tag{6.44}$$

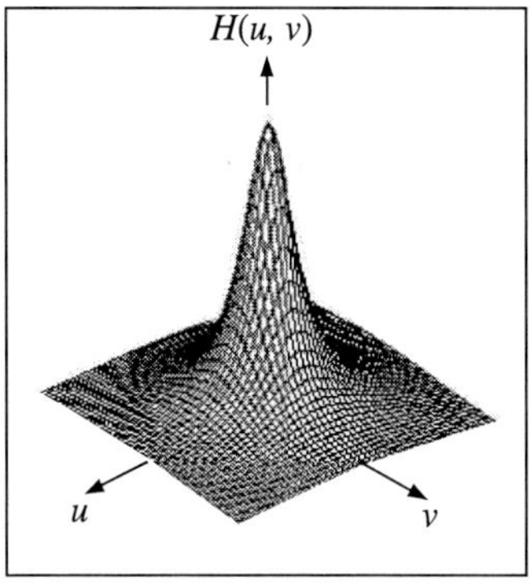

(a) Frequency response

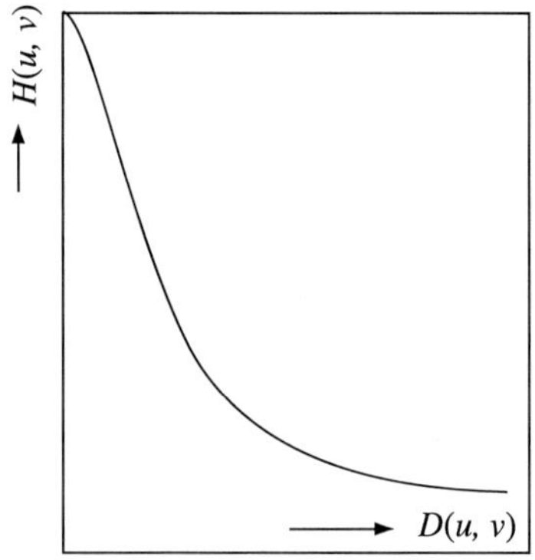

(b) Functional form

Figure 6.24: A typical Butterworth low pass filter.

6.5.3 Ideal High Pass Filter

An ideal high pass filter transfer function can be described by the following relation

$$H(u,v) = \begin{cases} 1 & \text{if } (u^2 + v^2) \geq D_0 \\ 0 & \text{otherwise} \end{cases} \tag{6.45}$$

where, $D_0 = \sqrt{u_0^2 + v_0^2}$ is the threshold frequency and is representing the distance of the point (u_0, v_0) from the origin of the frequency plane.

The high pass filter described above is shown graphically in Figure 6.25. It is clear that the filter passes all the frequency components outside the circle of radius D_0, while attenuates all other lower frequency components. Therefore, this filter is called the ideal high pass filter.

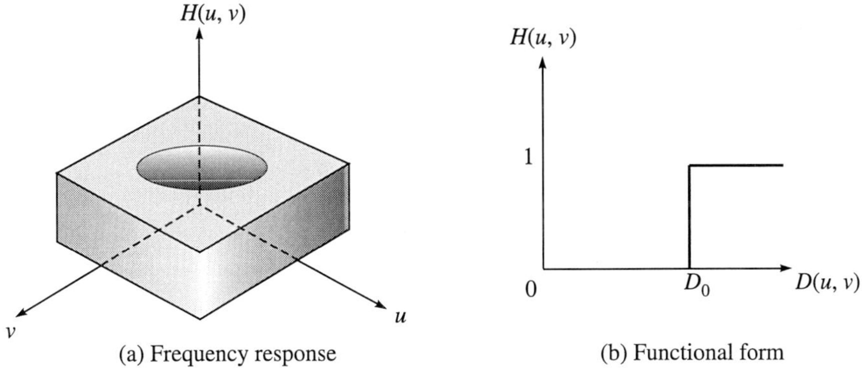

Figure 6.25: Ideal high pass filter.

6.5.4 Butterworth High Pass Filter

The ideal high pass filter uses a sharp cut-off that imply hard filtering. If we want to make the filter to allow a part of the energy spectrum at lower frequencies, we may use the Butterworth filter. The response of Butterworth high pass filter of order n is defined as

$$H(u, v) = \frac{1}{1 + \left(\dfrac{D_0}{D}\right)^{2n}} \tag{6.46}$$

where, $D = \sqrt{u^2 + v^2}$ and $D_0 = \sqrt{u_0^2 + v_0^2}$. For this filter, when $D = D_0$, we get the response of the filter as $H(u, v) = 0.5$. This indicates that at the cut-off frequency the response is half of its maximum value (i.e. 50%) (Figure 6.25). If instead of $\frac{1}{2}$, we want to get a cut-off frequency response of $\frac{1}{\sqrt{2}}$, we can use the following relations.

$$H(u, v) = \frac{1}{1 + (\sqrt{2} - 1)\left(\dfrac{D_0}{D}\right)^{2n}} \tag{6.47}$$

or

$$H(u, v) = \frac{1}{1 + 0.414\left(\dfrac{D_0}{D}\right)^{2n}} \tag{6.48}$$

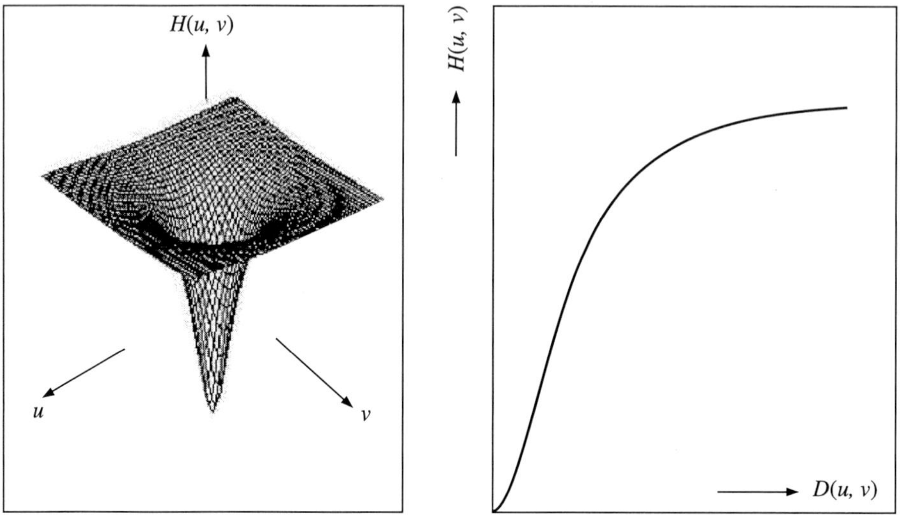

(a) Frequency response (b) Functional form

Figure 6.26: A typical Butterworth high pass filter.

6.5.5 Band Pass Filters

Sometimes another kind of filters are used which maintain features from a specific band of frequencies from the transformed image. These are called **band pass filters**. An ideal band pass filter transfer function can be described by the following relation:

$$H(u,v) = \begin{cases} 1 & \text{if } (u^2+v^2) \geq D_1 \\ 1 & \text{if } (u^2+v^2) \leq D_2 \\ 0 & \text{otherwise} \end{cases} \tag{6.49}$$

where, $D_i = \sqrt{u_i^2 + v_i^2}$, for $i = 1, 2$, are the threshold frequencies and are representing distance of the points (u_i, v_i) from the origin of the frequency plane (Figure 6.27).

6.6 Gaussian Filters

Another kind of filters, based on Gaussian distribution function, are very useful in image processing. These filters, called **Gaussian filters**, have the unique characteristic that the function remain real and Gaussian both in spatial and frequency domains. A Gaussian filter in the frequency domain is represented as

$$G(u) = A\ \exp\left(-\frac{u^2}{2\sigma^2}\right) \tag{6.50}$$

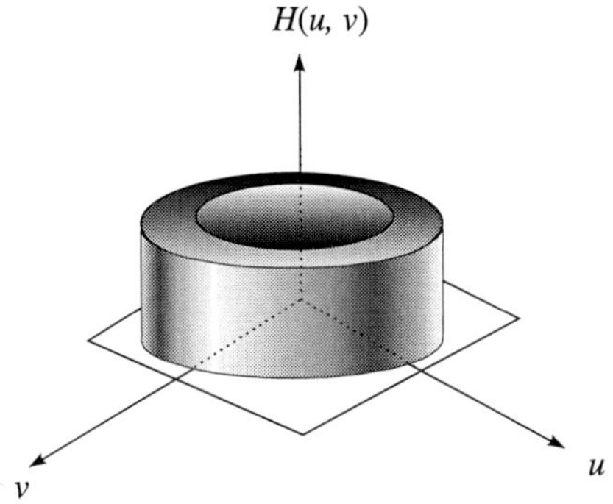

(a) Frequency response

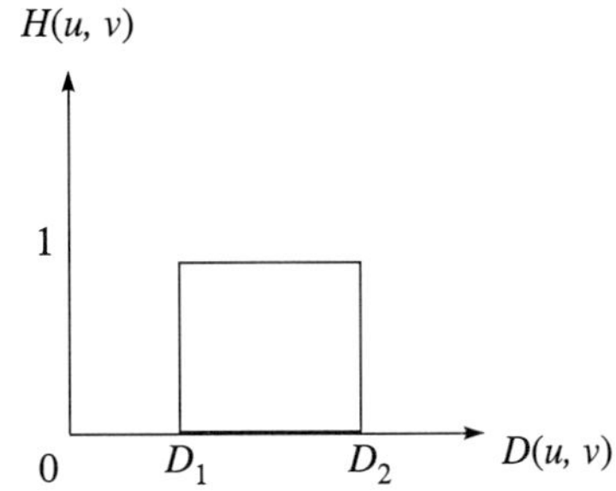

(b) Functional form

Figure 6.27: Ideal band pass filter.

where A is a constant and σ is the standard deviation of the Gaussian function. In spatial domain, it becomes

$$g(x) = \sqrt{2\pi}\sigma A \ \exp\left(-2\pi^2\sigma^2 x^2\right) \tag{6.51}$$

The above two functions constitute a Fourier transform pair that remains real and Gaussian. Gaussian are simple to understand and implement. From observation of the spatial domain functional form of a Gaussian filter we can constitute a real spatial mask filter. For the purpose of implementation, σ can be replaced by the frequency threshold D_0 in Eqs. (6.50) and (6.51).

From the above descriptions, we see that in ideal situations all the filters should operate on the basis of a step thresholding function. Therefore, these may be termed as linear filters also. In practice, to maintain desirable quality factors in the output, we need to consider non-linear filters. Butterworth filters are examples of such non-linear filters. General forms of such non-linear filters are shown in Figure 6.28.

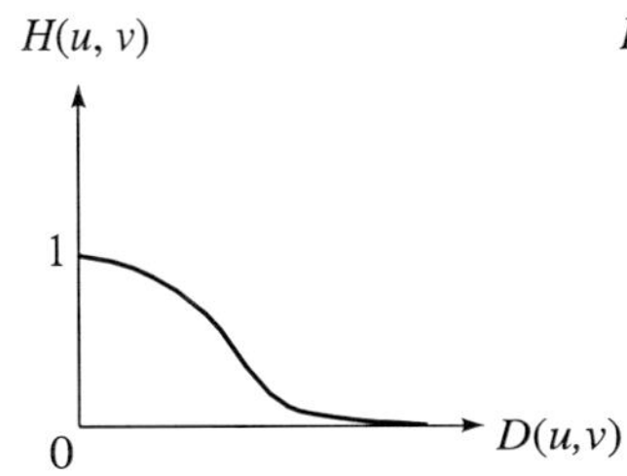

(a) Low pass

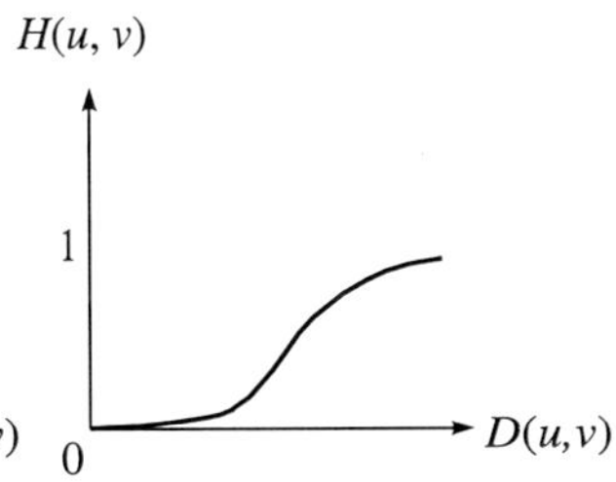

(b) High pass

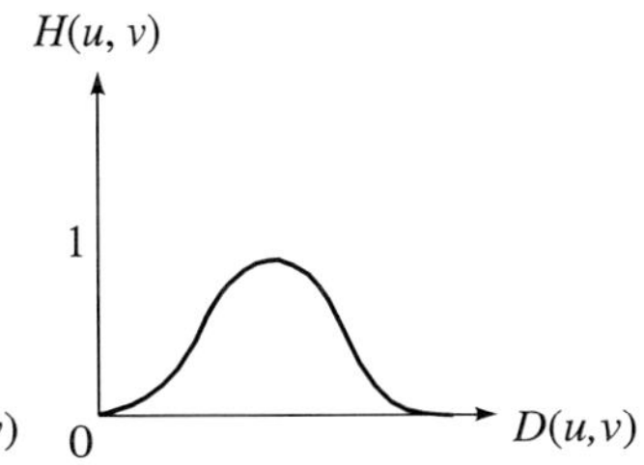

(c) Band pass

Figure 6.28: Non-linear filter.

6.7 Problems

1. What is meant by image enhancement? Do you think that we can achieve a better quality image by such enhancement processes?
2. Classify different types of image enhancement processes. Differentiate between spatial domain and frequency domain techniques of image enhancement.
3. Differentiate between local and global enhancement. Give examples of situations where these two types of enhancements are useful.
4. Mention the assumptions and derive the relations for designing mean and median filters.
5. What are the roles of filters in image processing? How do a spatial domain filter relates itself to its frequency domain counterpart?
6. Mention differences between point processing and histogram processing for enhancement.
7. What is histogram equalization? Briefly discuss the underlying logic behind histogram equalization.
8. A give image has the following histogram:

Grey level	0	1	2	3	4	5	6	7
No. of pixels	123	78	281	1054	417	639	816	688

Compute the probabilities of occurrences of each grey value in the image. Equalize the given histogram, and recompute the grey value probabilities. What difference do you notice in the two sets of probability values?

9. An image is shown in the following:

0	1	2	3	7
4	5	6	7	8
1	2	3	7	5
8	2	8	1	2
6	3	7	2	3

Use a smoothing filter in spatial domain over this image.

10. Apply the mean and median filters over the image in the previous question.
11. Find out a single mask operator whose effect is identical to that of applying

$$\frac{1}{2}\begin{bmatrix}1 & 1\end{bmatrix} \quad \text{and} \quad \frac{1}{2}\begin{bmatrix}1 \\ 1\end{bmatrix}$$

twice each along horizontal and vertical directions, respectively.

12. Consider a mask operator whose sum of elements is equal to zero. What would be the effect of applying this mask on an image with constant elements?

Chapter 7

Colour Image Processing

The colour in an image not only provides a realistic view of its contents but also conveys significant information regarding identification and extraction of an object from within it. Although natural objects contain colours from an infinitely wide spectrum, digital images, by employing limitation of human visual system, contain only a very few of them. Using different levels of colour quantization, different colour images can be produced for the same scene or object. In image processing we deal with either *full colour* or *pseudo colour* processing. Depending on the need of the visual display media or ease of processing, we can employ different colour models for an image. In this chapter, we shall discuss different colour models, their interrelations and uses in colour image processing.

7.1 Concept of Colours

The colour is a property of light. And light is the visible band in the Electromagnetic (EM) spectrum. A broad classification of the EM spectrum is: Hard X-rays, soft X-rays, ultraviolet rays, visible light, infrared rays, micro waves and radio waves. Each of the above bands are characterized by a range of frequencies in the EM spectrum.

The visible band in the spectrum corresponds to the frequency range from 7.5×10^{14} Hz (violet) to 4.3×10^{14} Hz (red). The commonly known colours stay in the visible spectrum in the following order: violet, indigo, blue, green, yellow, orange and red. Although these are dominant colours in the visible spectrum, actually there is no clear boundary between any two colours, because the spectrum is continuous. A source of light, like the sun, generates light beam containing all frequencies within the visible range. When these beams are incident on an object, depending on the optical properties of the object, it absorbs a part of the incident frequency, reflects and transmits others. The combination of frequencies present in the reflected or transmitted beam determines the colour of the object. An object is said to be red, if the reflected beam from the object has a dominant frequency at the red band of the spectrum. The dominant frequency is also called the hue (colour) of the object.

Besides colour, light has other characteristics. One such property is intensity or brightness that is perceived by our eyes. Other perceived characteristic is saturation or purity, which describes how pure or washed out (pale) the colour is. There are infinite number of shades for each colour present in the spectrum. So, it is not possible to use all possible colours in a digital image. Fortunately, it is seen that a finite subset of colours can produce almost all other colours, when mixed in a certain intensity ratio. Such finite set of colours contain what we call primary colours. Red, green, blue, is such a set of primary colours.

7.1.1 Colour Models for Images

Representing images only in grey shades, i.e. by varying intensities of white light, restricts us to a very limited subsection of real world imagery. Most of the objects we see around us are colourful. So, it is not intensity alone, that arouse our visual sensation, colours also play a very important role. Colour of an object is determined by several factors, viz. reflection, absorption and transmission properties of the object surfaces, colour of incident light and properties of the visual system. Again, human visual systems are not equally sensitive to the complete range of the visual spectrum. So processing images with its colour features has enough significance in diverse fields of applications.

The principal factors that motivate us for processing of colour images are:

- Images produced in colours are not only more appealing than its grey counterpart but also they are more natural and realistic.
- In automated image analysis, colour is a powerful descriptor that often simplifies object identification and segmentation of a scene.
- In image analysis performed by human beings, it is seen that, human eyes can discern thousands of colour shades and intensities, compared to about only a few shades of grey.

Two types of colour processings are possible: *true* colour processing and *pseudo* colour processing. True colour images are captured using devices with full colour sensors and then digitized for its colour components separately. Pseudo colour images are artificially produced by assigning a separate colour to a particular grey shade.

A colour space is a model for representing colour numerically in terms of three or more coordinates, e.g. the RGB colour space represents colours in terms of the Red, Green and Blue coordinates. A colour model is an abstract mathematical model describing the way colours can be represented as tuples of numbers, typically as three or four values or colour components (e.g. RGB and CMYK are colour models). However, a colour model with no associated mapping function to a reference colour space is a more or less arbitrary colour system with little connection to the requirements of any given application.

Basically, the colours that human beings perceive in an object are determined by the nature of the light reflected from the object. Visible light is composed of a relatively narrow band of frequencies in the electromagnetic spectrum. A body that reflects light that is relatively balanced in all visible wavelengths appear to the observer. However, a body that favours reflectance in a limited range of the visible spectrum exhibits some shades of the colour. For example, green objects reflect light with wavelengths primarily in the 500 to 570 nm range, while absorbing most of the energy at other wavelengths.

Characterization of light is central to the science of colour. If the light is achromatic (void of colour), its only attribute is its intensity, or amount. For colour to be reproduced in a predictable manner across different devices and materials, it has to be described in a way that is independent of the specific behaviour of the mechanisms and materials used to produce it. For instance, colour CRTs and colour printers use very different mechanisms for producing colour. To address this issue, current methods require that colour to be described using device independent colour coordinates, which are translated into device dependent colour coordinates for each device.

Several different mathematical systems exist which are used to describe colours. This section describes briefly the colour systems most commonly used in the image file formats described in this book. Keep in mind that perception of colour is affected by physiology, experience, and viewing conditions. For these reasons, no system of colour representation has yet been defined, or indeed is likely to be, which is satisfactory under all circumstances. Colours are always represented by numerical values. The most appropriate colour system to use depends upon the type of data contained in the file.

How a colour is created also plays an important role in how it is perceived. Normally, we think of colours as being associated with a single wavelength of light. We know, however, that two or more colours can be mixed together to produce a new colour. An example of this is mixing green and red light to produce yellow light, or mixing yellow and blue pigments to produce green pigment. This mixing of colours can also occur when an object is illuminated by light. The colour of the object will always mix with the colour of the light to produce a third colour. A blue object illuminated by white light appears blue, while the same object illuminated by red light will appear violet in colour.

Classification of colour models

A colour model is an orderly system for creating a whole range of colours from a small set of primary colours. There are two types of colour models, those that are subtractive and those that are additive. Additive colour models use light to display colour while subtractive models use printing inks. Colours perceived in additive models are the result of transmitted light. Colours perceived in subtractive models are the result of reflected light.

The colour systems can be separated into two categories: Additive colour systems and subtractive colour systems. Colours in additive systems are created by adding colours to black, to create new colours. The more colour that is added, the more the resulting colour tends towards white. The presence of all the primary colours in sufficient amounts create pure white, while the absence of all the primary colours create pure black. Additive colour environments are self-luminous. Colour on monitors, for instance, is additive.

The colour subtraction works in the opposite way. Conceptually, primary colours are subtracted from white to create new colours. The more colour that is subtracted, the more the resulting colour tends towards black. Thus, the presence of all the primary colours theoretically creates pure black, while the absence of all primary colour theoretically creates pure white. Another way of looking at this process is that black is the total absorption of all light by colour pigments. Subtractive environments are reflective in nature, and colour is conveyed to us by reflecting light from an external source. Any colour image reproduced on paper is an example of the use of a subtractive colour system.

No colour system is perfect. As an example, in a subtractive colour system the presence of all colours create black, but in real-life printing the inks are not perfect. Mixing all ink colours usually produces a muddy brown rather than black. The blacks we see on paper are only approximations of the mathematical ideal, and likewise for other colours.

Colour management is a term that describes a technology that translates the colours of an object (images, graphics or text) from their current colour space to the colour space of the output devices like monitors, printers, etc. When formally defining a colour space, the usual reference standard is the CIE *Lab* colour space, which was specifically designed to encompass all colours the an average human can see. This is the most accurate colour space, but is too complex for everyday uses.

Since "colour space" is a more specific term for a certain combination of a colour model plus a colour mapping function, the term "colour space" tends to be used to also identify colour models, since identifying a colour space automatically identifies the associated colour model. Informally, the two terms are often used interchangeably, though this is strictly incorrect. For example, although several specific colour spaces are based on the RGB model, there is no such thing as the RGB colour space.

In the generic sense of the definitions above, colour spaces can be defined without the use of a colour model. These spaces, such as Pantone, are in effect a given set of names or numbers, which are defined by the existence of a corresponding set of physical colour swatches. Since any colour space defines colours as a function of the absolute reference frame, colour spaces, along with device profiling, allow reproducible representations of colour, in both analogue and digital representations.

There are several established colour models used in image processing, but the two most common are the RGB model (red, green, blue) for computer display and the CMYK model (cyan, magenta, yellow, black) for printing.

RGB colour

The RGB model forms its gamut from the primary additive colours of red, green and blue. When red, green and blue light is combined it forms white. Computers generally display RGB using 24-bit colour. In the 24-bit RGB colour model there are 256 variations for each of the additive colours of red, green and blue. Therefore, there are 16,777,216 possible colours (256 reds $\times$ 256 greens $\times$ 256 blues) in the 24-bit RGB colour model.

In the RGB colour model, colours are represented by varying intensities of red, green and blue light. The intensity of each of the red, green and blue components are represented on a scale from 0 to 255 with 0 being the least intensity (no light emitted) to 255 (maximum intensity). For example in the above RGB chart the magenta colour would be $R = 255,\ G = 0,\ B = 255$. Black would be $R = 0,\ G = 0, B = 0$ (a total absence of light).

Important features of the RGB colour model are thus:

- Additive colour model
- For computer displays
- Uses light to display colour
- Colours result from transmitted light
- Red + Green + Blue = White

CMYK or "Process Colour"

The CMYK printing method is also known as "four-colour process" or simply "process" colour. All of the colours in the printable portion of the colour spectrum can be achieved by overlapping "tints" of cyan, magenta, yellow and black inks. A tint is a screen of tiny dots appearing as a percentage of a solid colour. When various tints of the four colours are printed in overlapping patterns it gives the illusion of continuous tones—like a photograph.

The CMYK model forms its gamut from the primary subtractive colours of cyan, magenta and yellow. When cyan, magenta and yellow inks are combined it forms black—in theory. However, because of the impurities in ink, when cyan, magenta and yellow inks are combined it produces a muddy brown colour. Black ink is added to this system to compensate for these impurities. Without considering this added black component this colour model is also commonly known as the CMY colour model.

In the CMYK colour model, colours are represented as percentages of cyan, magenta, yellow and black. For example in the above CMYK chart the red colour is composed of 14% cyan, 100% magenta, 99% yellow and 3% black. White would be 0% cyan, 0% magenta, 0% yellow and 0% black (a total absence of ink on white paper).

The RGB model displays a much larger percentage of the visible spectrum than the CMYK model and, as a result, has a wider gamut. Once an image has been converted from RGB to CMYK and brought into printable gamut, the extra RGB data will be lost. One can retain out-of-gamut areas in CMYK images and leave it to the computer to bring the colours into gamut at printing time. However this requires the computer to make the conversion from RGB to CMYK and this does not always work out as well as one might expect. Conversion between colour models is not always a good idea.

Because of this fact, we want to scan or shoot images (with a digital camera) using the appropriate colour model for their primary purpose. If the images will be used primarily for print then use CMYK. If they will be used primarily for screen displays, then we use RGB. We can always convert from RGB to CMYK (or vise-versa), but it is best not to.

If one can afford the time, money and disk space to scan or shoot both versions of an image where both are needed, then this is the best solution. This is especially true if we will be using the same images for both printed material (such as a catalog) and the web (such as an online catalog). A little planning can go a long way here.

But if somebody is not sure, then general recommendation is to save images in RGB mode and create CMYK copies for printed material as needed.

It is important to choose the right colour model for the job. If our images will be printed, then convert them to CMYK and manually bring them into gamut before printing. If our images are to be displayed on a computer, then make sure we use RGB colour so the full gamut will be available for display. Because both models can be available at the same time while using an application, it is easy to make a mistake and choose the wrong palette or set of colour swatches.

Important features of the CMYK colour model are thus as follows:

- They are subtractive colour models
- Used for printed material
- Uses ink to display colour
- Colours result from reflected light
- Cyan + Magenta + Yellow = Black

Additive vs. subtractive colour models

Since additive colour models display colour as a result of light being transmitted (added) the total absence of light would be perceived as black. Subtractive colour models display colour as a result of light being absorbed (subtracted) by the printing inks. As more ink is added, less and less light is reflected. Where there is a total absence of ink the resulting light being reflected (from a white surface) would be perceived as white.

Consider the centres of Figures 7.1 and 7.2, representing RGB and CMYK colour models. In the RGB model, the convergence of the three primary additive colours produces white. In the CMYK model, the convergence of the three primary subtractive colours produces black.

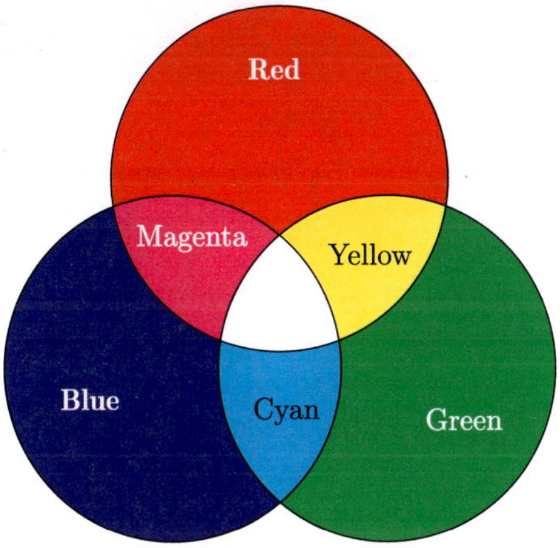

Figure 7.1: Additive colours.

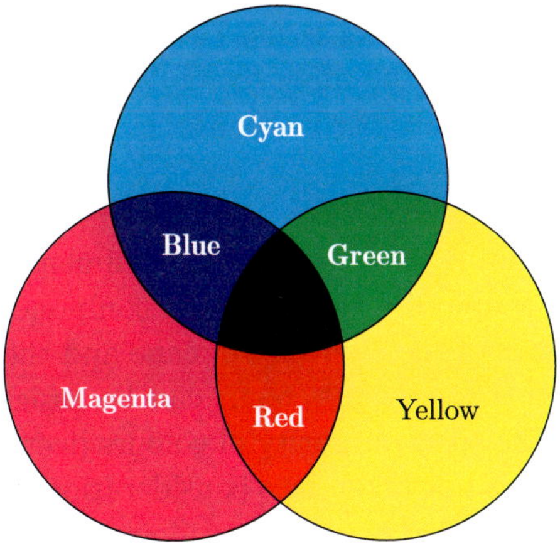

Figure 7.2: Subtractive colours.

In the RGB model notice that the overlapping of additive colours (red, green and blue) results in subtractive colours (cyan, magenta and yellow). In the CMYK model notice that the overlapping of subtractive colours (cyan, magenta and yellow) results in additive colours (red, green and blue) (Figure 7.3).

Also notice that the colours in the RGB model are much brighter than the colours in the CMYK model. It is possible to attain a much larger percentage of the visible spectrum with the RGB model. That is because the RGB model uses transmitted light while the CMYK model uses reflected light. The muted appearance of the CMYK model demonstrates the limitation of printing inks and the nature of reflected light. The colours in this chart appear muted because they are displayed within their printable gamut.

Red Green Blue

Figure 7.3: RGB colour spectrum.

7.2 CIE Colour Standard

Commission Internationale de I'Eclairage (CIE) or International Commission for Colours defined the way how to select three standard primary colours that can produce almost all other colours. Their model is known as the XYZ colour model.

7.2.1 XYZ Colour Model

It is based on the human eye's response to RGB, and designed to accurately represent human colour perception. This model is used to define device-independent colours, which can be reproduced faithfully on any type of devices, such as scanners, monitors, and printers. This model is widely used because it is easy to use on computers and describes a wide range of colours.

In 1931 the CIE developed the XYZ colour system, also called the "norm colour system". This system is often represented as a two-dimensional graphic, which more or less corresponds to the shape of a sail. The red components of a colour are tallied along the X (horizontal) axis of the coordinate plane and the green components along the Y (vertical) axis. In this way every colour can be assigned to a particular point on the coordinate plane. The spectral purity of colours decrease as we move left along the coordinate plane. What is not taken into consideration in this model is brightness.

The three primaries are denoted by X, Y and Z and any arbitrary colour is denoted as

$$C = X\mathbf{X} + Y\mathbf{Y} + Z\mathbf{Z} \tag{7.1}$$

where **X**, **Y** and **Z** represent vectors in a three-dimensional, additive colour space. In the normalized colour space, we can represent the component primary colours as

$$x = \frac{X}{X+Y+Z},\ y = \frac{Y}{X+Y+Z},\ z = \frac{Z}{X+Y+Z} \tag{7.2}$$

where $x + y + z = 1$

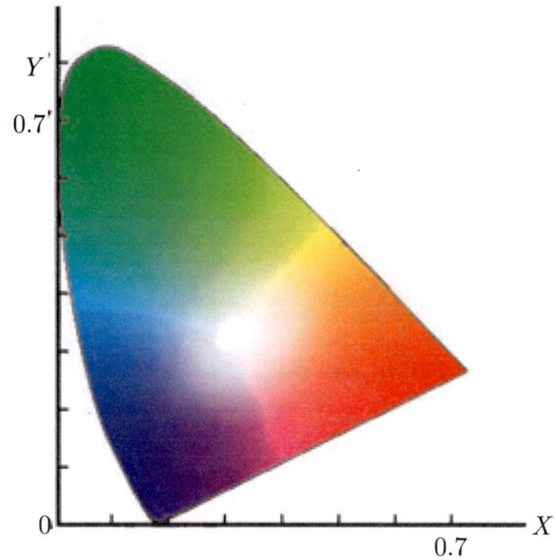

Figure 7.4: XYZ colour space.

7.2.2 RGB Colour Model

As it is seen that in the colour spectrum, the Red, Green and Blue colours causes high response on our retina, these are selected to be the primary colours in the RGB model. Like the XYZ, RGB is an additive colour model, i.e. any other colour is a weighted sum of the primaries. Thus a colour C is

$$C = R\mathbf{R} + G\mathbf{G} + B\mathbf{B} \tag{7.3}$$

The RGB colour space can be represented by a unit cube placed at origin in its standard position. Black is at the origin (0 0 0) and white is at point (1 1 1). The principal diagonal of the cube represents all the grey shades by varying intensities from 0 to 1 (in the normalized scale). Any other colour is just a weighted sum of the R, G and B components and is represented by a point within the cube. The colour space is shown in Figures 7.5 and 7.6.

7.2.3 CMY Colour Model

CMY is a complementary model of the RGB model. It is used to produce colours on hard copy devices. While a pixel is enlightened to produce a colour on the black screen, a colour pigment is spitted on a white paper in case of a hard copy device. In the digital world, Black is represented by zero and white by one. So, intensities of component colours are added to zero to produce a colour in the RGB model. Similarly, the RGB components are subtracted from one to produce a colour in the CMY model (Figure 7.7). Thus, CMY is called a subtractive model. The relations between RGB and CMY colour models thus become as given in Eqs. (7.4) and (7.5).

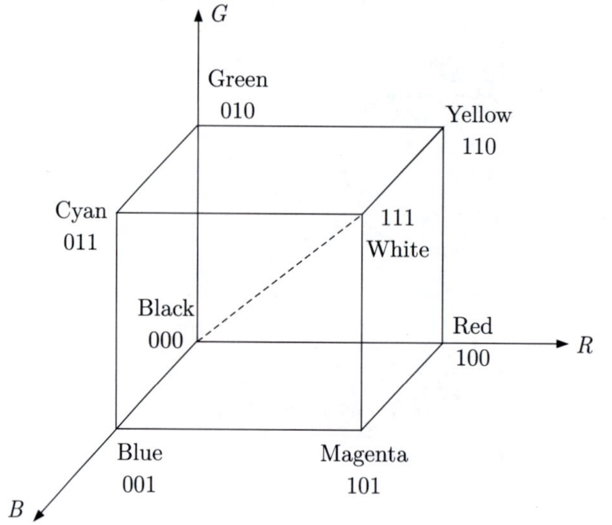

Figure 7.5: RGB colour space.

(a) Original image

(b) Red component

(c) Green component

(d) Blue component

Figure 7.6: An RGB image and its colour components.

$$\begin{bmatrix} C \\ M \\ Y \end{bmatrix} = \begin{bmatrix} 1 \\ 1 \\ 1 \end{bmatrix} - \begin{bmatrix} R \\ G \\ B \end{bmatrix} \tag{7.4}$$

and

$$\begin{bmatrix} R \\ G \\ B \end{bmatrix} = \begin{bmatrix} 1 \\ 1 \\ 1 \end{bmatrix} - \begin{bmatrix} C \\ M \\ Y \end{bmatrix} \tag{7.5}$$

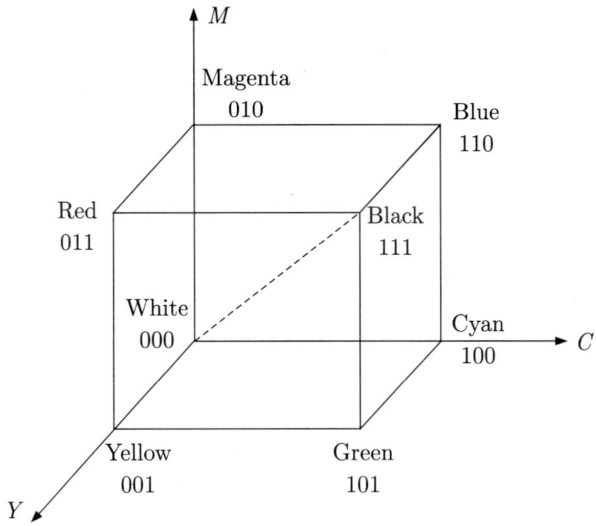

Figure 7.7: CMY colour space.

This model is very popular in TV broadcasting. Using this model, a TV image in the colour space can be easily converted to the grey space, and hence, black and white TVs can also be used as recipient of colour image signals. YIQ (Luminance, In-phase, Quadrature) model is a linear combination of the RGB components as shown in Eq. (7.6):

$$\begin{bmatrix} Y \\ I \\ Q \end{bmatrix} = \begin{bmatrix} 0.300 & 0.587 & 0.144 \\ 0.596 & -0.275 & -0.321 \\ 0.212 & -0.528 & 0.311 \end{bmatrix} \times \begin{bmatrix} R \\ G \\ B \end{bmatrix} \tag{7.6}$$

One similarity among the three colour models described above is that they are best used in specific hardware platforms. RGB is best for monitors, CMY for hard copy devices and YIQ for BW platforms. So these colour models are hardware oriented and their use is thus restricted by properties of the concerned physical devices. However, their are other colour models which are more directly related to the colour perception procedure of the human visual system.

7.2.4 HSV Colour Model

This is one of the most popular intuitive colour models. HSV stands for Hue, saturation and value. Hue deals with the purity of the colour, saturation determines the amount of white light mixed with the original colour, while value gives the intensity of the colour. The compatibility of the HSV model with the human visual perception system is its importance. The colour space of the HSV model is defined as a hex-cone (shown in Figures 7.8 and 7.9) of height unity and apex at the origin. Any point within the hex-cone represents a particular colour. Intensity of any colour is represented by the value component; it is zero at the apex and one on the base of the hex-cone (in normalized scale). Saturation is measured by the distance of the point from the value axis, and it varies from zero to one. Hue varies along a circular path bounding the hex-cone and is measured by the angular distance of the concerned point from red colour in the anticlockwise direction.

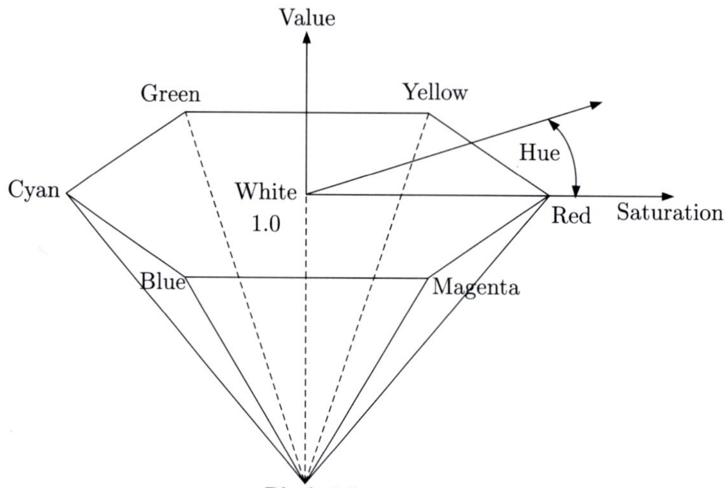

Figure 7.8: HSV colour space.

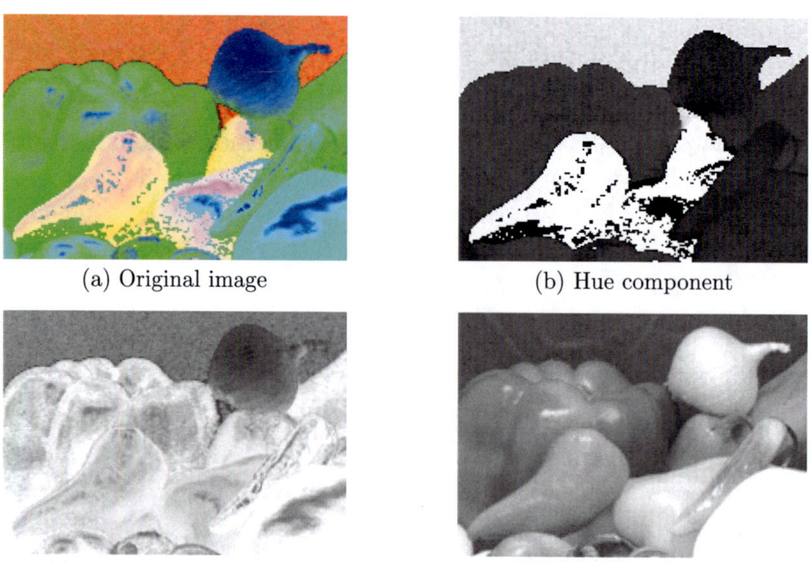

(a) Original image (b) Hue component

(c) Saturation component (d) Value component

Figure 7.9: An HSV image and its colour components.

Let, $M = \max(R, G, B)$ and $N = \min(R, G, B)$. Intensity of a colour is the maximum of its components. Thus, we get, $V = M$. Saturation is measured as $S = \frac{M-N}{M}$ when $M \neq 0$, otherwise it is 0. Now, from Figure 7.8, H can be measured as follows. When red is the dominant colour, $H = 60 \times \frac{G-B}{M-N}$. For green and blue, this become $H = 60 \times 2 + \frac{B-R}{M-N}$ and $H = 60 \times 4 + \frac{R-G}{M-N}$, respectively. Reverse transformations are defined accordingly.

Algorithm for RGB to HSV conversion

begin
  $M = \max(R, G, B)$
  $N = \min(R, G, B)$
  if $(M = 0)$ **then** $S = 0$
    else $S = \frac{M-N}{M}$
  if $(S \neq 0)$ **then**
    begin
      if $(R = M)$ **then** $H = 60 \times \frac{G-B}{M-N}$
      if $(G = M)$ **then** $H = 60 \times \frac{B-R}{M-N}$
      if $(B = M)$ **then** $H = 60 \times \frac{R-G}{M-N}$
    end
  if $(H < 0)$ **then** $H = H + 360$
end

Algorithm for HSV to RGB conversion

begin
  $s = \frac{S}{\max S}$, $v = \frac{V}{\max V}$
  if $(s = 0)$ **then**
  begin
    $r = v, g = v, b = v$
  end
  else
  begin
    if $(H = 360)$ **then** $h = 0$
    else $h = \frac{H}{60}$
    $i = \lfloor h \rfloor$
    $j = h - i$
    $m = v \times (1.0 - s)$
    $n = v \times (1.0 - s \times j)$
    $k = v \times (1.0 - s \times (1.0 - j))$
    if $(i = 0)$ **then**
      begin
        $r = v, g = k, b = m$

```
            end
        if (i = 1) then
            begin
                r = n, g = v, b = m
            end
        if (i = 2) then
            begin
                r = m, g = n, b = v
            end
        if (i = 4) then
            begin
                r = k, g = m, b = v
            end
        if (i = 5) then
            begin
                r = v, g = m, b = n
            end
    end
    R = r × max R, G = g × max G, B = b × max B
end
```

7.2.5 HSI Colour Model

This model is similar to the HSV model. The characteristics generally used to distinguish one colour from another are brightness, hue and saturation. Brightness is a subjective descriptor that is practically impossible to measure. It embodies the chromatic notion of intensity and is one of the key factors in describing colour sensation. Hue is an attribute associated with the dominant wavelength in a mixture of light waves. Thus, hue represents dominant colour as perceived by an observer; when we call an object red, orange, or yellow we are specifying its hue. Saturation refers to relative purity or the amount of white light mixed with a hue. The pure spectrum colours are fully saturated. Colours such as pink (red and white) and lavender (violet and white) are less saturated, with the degree of saturation being inversely proportional to the white light added.

Hue and saturation taken together are called chromaticity, and therefore, a colour may be characterized by its brightness and chromaticity. An image processed in HSI space must be converted back to RGB for display.

The HSI colour space is shown in Figure 7.10. It is a bi-pyramidal shape. Red, green and blue are located at the corners of the base. White and black are at the top and bottom apex, respectively. Hue is measured by the angle with respect to the red axis. Intensity is the vertical distance from the black point. Saturation is the distance from the centre of the base triangle.

For conversion, we use normalized colours, i.e.

$$r = \frac{R}{R+G+B},\ g = \frac{G}{R+G+B},\ b = \frac{B}{R+G+B} \tag{7.7}$$

where, $r + g + b = 1$. Here,

$$I = \frac{R+G+B}{3} \tag{7.8}$$

Here, R, G and B are in the range of [0, 1] i.e. they are individually normalized on the respective scales of isolated colours.

$$H = \cos^{-1}\left\{\frac{1}{2}\left[(R-G)+(R-B)\right]\right\}\left[(R-G)^2+(R-B)(G-B)\right]^2 \tag{7.9}$$

$$S = 1 - \frac{3}{R+G+B} \times [\min(R, G, B)] \tag{7.10}$$

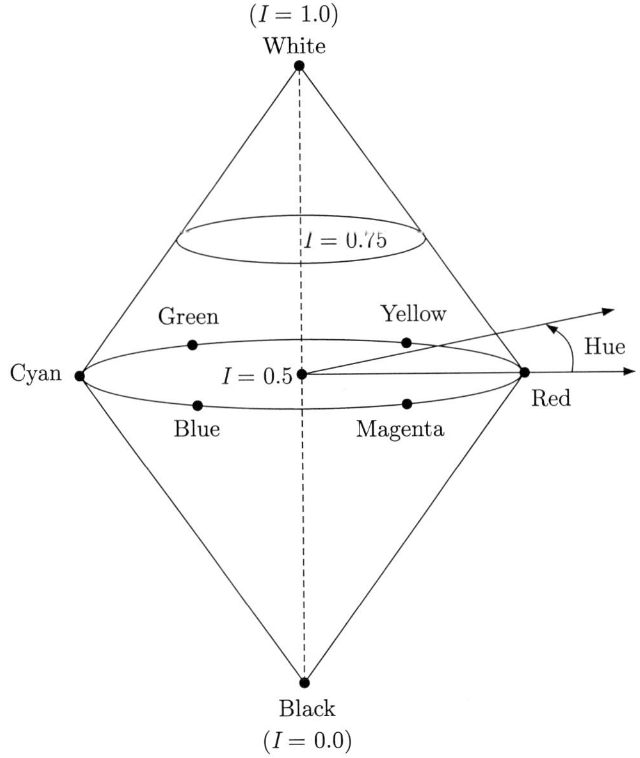

Figure 7.10: HSI colour space.

The inverse transformations are:

$$b = \frac{1}{3}(1-s), r = \frac{1}{3}\left[1 + \frac{S\cos H}{\cos(60-H)}\right] \quad \text{and} \quad g = 1-(r+b) \quad \text{where, } 0 < H \leq 120° \tag{7.11}$$

$$r = \frac{1}{3}(1-s), g = \frac{1}{3}\left[1 + \frac{S\cos H}{\cos(60-H)}\right] \quad \text{and} \quad b = 1-(r+g) \quad \text{where, } 120 < H \leq 240° \tag{7.12}$$

$$g = \frac{1}{3}(1-s), b = \frac{1}{3}\left[1 + \frac{S\cos H}{\cos(60-H)}\right] \quad \text{and} \quad r = 1-(g+b) \quad \text{where, } 240 < H \leq 360° \tag{7.13}$$

The (r, g, b) values are obtained in the normalized scale. The original values are $R = 3Ir$, $G = 3Ig$ and $B = 3Ib$ where, $I = \frac{R+G+B}{3}$ (using R G B values before transformation).

7.2.6 $\mathbf{YC_bC_r}$ Colour Model

In image processing, another colour model consisting of luminance and chrominance factors are often found very useful. This is the YC_bC_r model. It helps to distinguish between different chrominance factors in a better manner, and at the same time can be encoded using a smaller number of bits compared to other colour models.

RGB to $\mathbf{YC_bC_r}$ conversion

The conversion from RGB to YC_bC_r can be done using following: formulas.

$$\begin{aligned} Y &= 0.300 \times R + 0.587 \times G + 0.114 \times B \\ C_b &= -0.169 \times R - 0.331 \times G + 0.500 \times B + 128 \\ C_r &= 0.500 \times R - 0.419 \times G - 0.081 \times B + 128 \end{aligned} \tag{7.14}$$

In matrix notation:

$$\begin{bmatrix} Y \\ C_b \\ C_r \end{bmatrix} = \begin{bmatrix} 0.300 & 0.587 & 0.144 \\ -0.169 & -0.331 & -0.500 \\ 0.500 & -0.419 & -0.081 \end{bmatrix} \times \begin{bmatrix} R \\ G \\ B \end{bmatrix} + \begin{bmatrix} 0 \\ 128 \\ 128 \end{bmatrix} \tag{7.15}$$

The new value of Y is called the **luminance**. It is the value used by the monochrome monitors to represent an RGB colour. Physiologically, it represents the intensity of an RGB colour perceived by the eye. It can be seen that the formula for Y is like a weighted-filter with different weights for each spectral component, the eye is most sensitive to the green component then it follows the red component and the last is the blue component. The values C_b and C_r are called the **chrominance values** and represent 2 coordinates in a system which measures the nuance and saturation of the colour [(Approximately) these values indicate how much blue and how much red is in that colour]. These 2 coordinates are called shortly the **chrominance**.

$[YC_bC_r]$ to [R, G, B] conversion

RGB can be computed directly from YC_bC_r as follows:

$$\begin{aligned} R &= Y + 1.402 \times (C_r - 128) \\ G &= Y - 0.34414 \times (C_b - 128) - 0.71414 \times (C_r - 128) \\ B &= Y + 1.772 \times (C_b - 128) \end{aligned} \tag{7.16}$$

A note relating YC_bC_r to the human visual system

The eye, particularly the retina, has as visual analyzers two kind of cells: cells for night view which perceive only nuances of grey, ranging from intense white to the darkest black and cells for the day view which perceive the colour nuance. The first cells, given an RGB colour, detect a grey level similar to that given by the luminance value. The second cells, responsible for the perception of the colour nuance, are the cells which detects a value related to that of the chrominance. In Figure 7.11 the onion image is shown in different colour models.

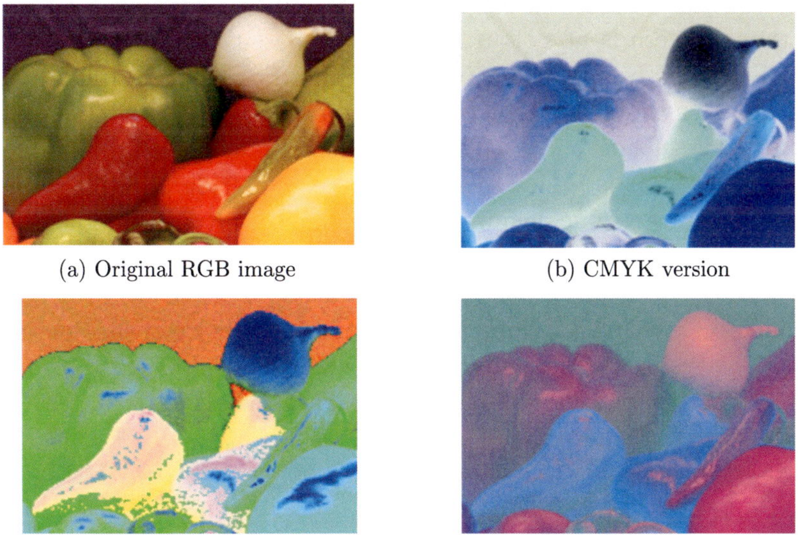

(a) Original RGB image

(b) CMYK version

(c) HSV version

(d) YC_bC_r version

Figure 7.11: The *onion* image and its colour conversions.

7.2.7 YUV Colour Model

What is a colour? A colour is just a particular frequency of light. Our ability to perceive colours derives from three kinds of photo-receptors in our retina which are responsive to three different frequency ranges of light (LMS cones), thus we perceive colour as a decomposition of the light. We can, however, decompose a frequency in any amounts of frequency bands we want, to make it easier to perform certain tasks such as colour reproduction on printers, TV sets and so on. Each colour space has some unique features. In the YUV colour model, in a similar way, the colour is decomposed into three components called respectively

- Y: Luminance
- U: Chroma channel, U axis, blue component
- V: Chroma channel, V axis, red component

with some variations depending on the context. The reasons to use the YUV decomposition are multiple. Firstly, a conversion of an RGB signal (such as the one used on our monitor) to YUV requires just a linear transform, which is really easy to do with analogue circuitry and it is cheap to compute numerically. Secondly, YUV allows separating the colour information from the luminance component (which we perceive as brightness). For this reason YUV is used worldwide for television and motion picture encoding standards such as PAL (commonly used in Europe). In a TV signal the luminance channel is modulated separately, this makes it possible for old TV sets to work even though there is no colour support (that is, the colour information is sent separately). Since the human eye is also much more responsive to luminance, JPEG compresses more heavily the chroma channels which are less likely to cause perceptible differences in the resulting image. The YUV model is a bit different from the other colourimetric models. It is basically a linear transformation of RGB image data and is most widely used to encode colour for use in television transmission. However, this transformation is almost always accompanied by a separate quantization operation, which introduces non-linearities into the conversion. Y specifies grey scale or luminance. Luminance, measured in lumens (lm), gives a measure of the amount of energy an observer perceives from a light source. The U and V components correspond to the chrominance (colour information). The conversion between RGB and YUV is defined by the following sets of equations:

RGB to YUV Conversion

$$\begin{aligned} Y &= 0.257R + 0.504G + 0.098B + 16 \\ U &= 0.493R - 0.368G - 0.071B + 128 \\ V &= -0.148R - 0.291G + 0.439B + 128 \end{aligned} \tag{7.17}$$

In matrix notation:

$$\begin{bmatrix} Y \\ U \\ V \end{bmatrix} = \begin{bmatrix} 0.257 & 0.504 & 0.098 \\ 0.493 & -0.368 & -0.071 \\ -0.148 & -0.291 & 0.439 \end{bmatrix} \times \begin{bmatrix} R \\ G \\ B \end{bmatrix} + \begin{bmatrix} 16 \\ 128 \\ 128 \end{bmatrix} \tag{7.18}$$

YUV to RGB Conversion

$$\begin{aligned} B &= 1.164(Y-16)+2.018(V-128) \\ G &= 1.164(Y-16)-0.813(V-128)-0.391(V-128) \\ R &= 1.164(Y-16)+1.596(V-128) \end{aligned} \tag{7.19}$$

7.2.8 The CIE L∗a∗b Colour Model

The CIE $L*a*b$ Model is an improvement of the CIE XYZ colour model. In this three dimensional model, the colour differences which we perceive correspond to distances when measured colourimetrically. The a axis extends from green $(-a)$ to red $(+a)$ and the b axis from blue $(-b)$ to yellow $(+b)$. The brightness (L) increases from the bottom to the top of the three-dimensional model. Colours are represented by numerical values. In comparison with XYZ, CIE $L*a*b$ colours are more compatible with colours sensed by the human eye. With the CIE $L*a*b$, the colour luminance (L), hue and saturation (a, b) can be revised individually; as a result, the overall colour of the image can be changed without changing the image or its luminance. Because CIE $L*a*b$ is device independent, when RGB is changed to CMYK, or CMYK is changed to RGB, the software requires the change to be first processed via the CIE $L*a*b$ colour model.

7.3 Pseudo Colour Image Processing

Pseudo colour image processing means applying artificially imposed colours to different objects or regions in an image and subsequent analysis. A grey level image is input to the system. False or pseudo colours are assigned to different grey shades present in that image, to convert the monochrome image into a coloured one. One primary reason behind such pseudo colouring is better visualization, understanding and analysis. While naturally coloured images contain infinitely many shades of different colours, human visual system discerns between only a very few number of intensities. This fact is a prime motivation behind pseudo colouring. Pseudo colours may be generated in a number of ways which are described here.

7.3.1 Intensity Slicing

It is a very popular technique for pseudo colouring. Here the grey image is interpreted as a 3D spatial function where intensity values are plotted against 2D spatial coordinates of the image. If the XY-plane contains the image, the colour intensities are plotted along the Z-axis as shown in Figure 7.12.

Now, by placing a horizontal plane at $z = l$, we can slice the intensity space into two levels. A number of such planes at different z-values may be used to slice the intensities into a number of levels. Using $L-2$ number of equidistant planes at

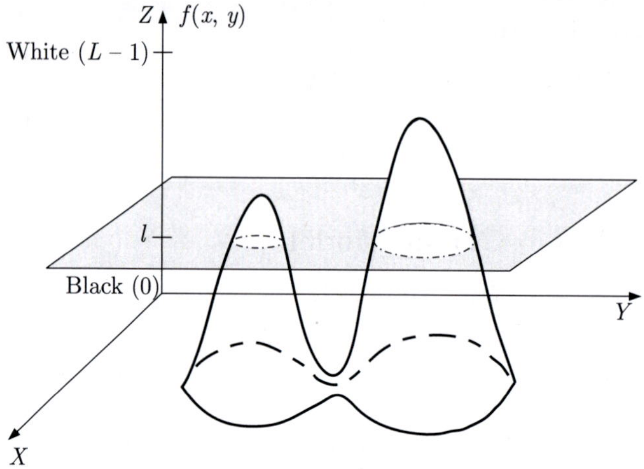

Figure 7.12: Intensity slicing to convert grey image into pseudo colour image.

$z = l_1, l_2, \ldots, l_{L-2}$, we can get L levels between $[0 \quad L-1]$. Now, grey or intensity values in each slice S_k may be replaced by a colour c_k such that,

$$f(x, y) = c_k \quad \text{where,} \quad f(x, y) \in S_k.$$

In Figure 7.13, the grey *Lena* image (a) is converted to a pseudo colour image (b) by slicing of intensity levels.

(a) Original *Lena* image

(b) Result of intensity slicing and assignment of pseudo colour

Figure 7.13: Conversion of grey image into pseudo colour image.

7.3.2 Grey Level to Colour Transformation

In the grey level slicing technique, each slice is assigned a particular colour which has no relation with the contents or significance of the grey shade concerned. A more general technique in this regard is grey level to colour transformation. Here, the grey intensity image is applied separately over red, green and blue transformations, thereby producing three separate intensity images with intensity variations over red, green and blue shades only. This situation is depicted in Figure 7.14.

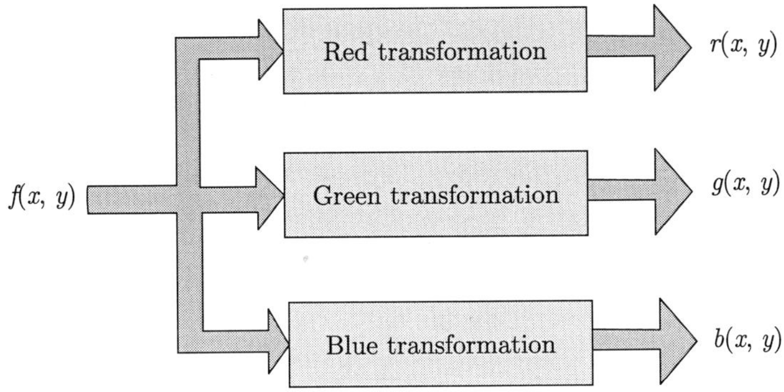

Figure 7.14: Conversion of grey images into pseudo colour image.

Now, these three separate signals (images) are fed to the red, green and blue channels of a colour TV monitor, where by modulation (mix up) of three components a new image is produced. If all the three components are mixed up in the same phase, the original grey image will be the output. However, by incorporating different phase differences between pairs of signals, different pseudo colour images can be produced.

In Figure 7.15, the sinusoidal functions corresponding to red, green and blue components are shown. By varying phase and frequency of individual waveforms we can generate different colour shades of the pseudo colour. If all the three functions are in the same phase and have the same frequency, the output image will be grey.

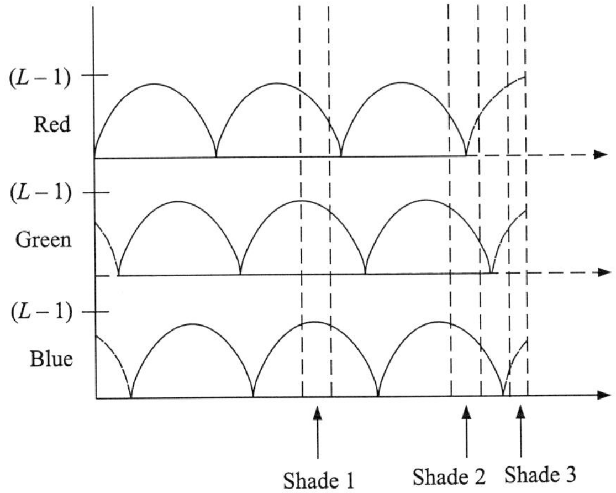

Figure 7.15: Colour transformation functions for producing R, G and B components. Each vertical band represents a particular shade of R, G, and B components.

The approach given deals with a single monochrome image. Sometimes it is necessary to combine more than one images, e.g. in case of multiband satellite images different band-images need to be combined. In such a situation multiple transformation blocks, one per image, are used. The trnasformed images are then combined after some additional processing. This situation is shown in Figure 7.16.

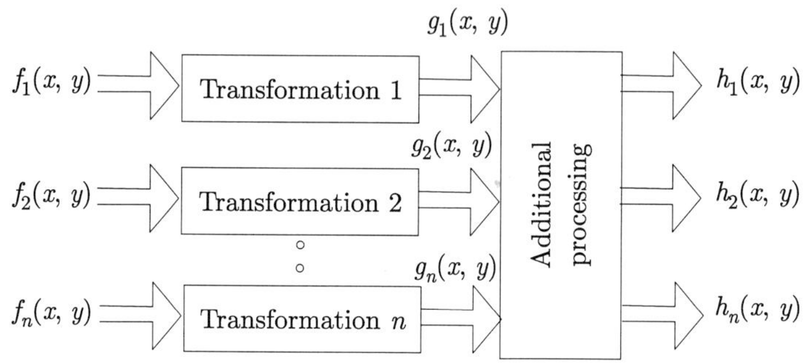

Figure 7.16: Conversion of grey images into pseudo colour image.

7.4 Enhancement of Colour Images

Just like monochrome images, colour images need to be enhanced to improve their suitability for certain applications. Grey level enhancement techniques may be used, in this regard, with or without modification. Enhancement processes in colour domain are also called **colour transformations**. It is different from colour space conversion techniques. Some of the colour transformation techniques are briefly described below.

7.4.1 Colour Complementation

This is similar to grey level negation in monochrome images. Here, if we use a RGB colour image as input, the output will be in the CMY colour space. This is because the negation operations are exactly the same as the colour space conversion relations between the above said colour spaces.

7.4.2 Colour Histogram Processing

Unlike grey level histogram equalization, for colour images, we need to stretch (spread the colour intensities uniformly) the histogram in order to improve the appearance of the image. If we equalize the colour components separately, they may not be matched and can not be exactly combined after the transformation, and the result will be dull.

7.4.3 Colour Image Smoothing

In case of grey images an averaging mask is used as smoothing filter. This concept can be extended for colour images also. If a colour component is represented by $c(x, y)$ (in the image $f(x, y)$), then the neighbourhood averaging can be denoted by

$$\bar{c}(x,y) = \frac{1}{k} \sum_{(x,y)\in S_{xy}} c(x,y)$$

For a RGB colour image, the component transformations can, therefore, be represented as

$$\bar{\mathbf{c}}(x,y) = \begin{bmatrix} \frac{1}{k} \sum_{(x,y)\in S_{xy}} R(x,y) \\ \frac{1}{k} \sum_{(x,y)\in S_{xy}} G(x,y) \\ \frac{1}{k} \sum_{(x,y)\in S_{xy}} B(x,y) \end{bmatrix}$$

where, $\mathbf{c}$ is a RGB colour triple (vector), and S_{xy} is the neighbourhood of size k.

7.4.4 Colour Image Sharpening

For grey scale image, image sharpening is generally done using the Laplacian. Now, since Laplacian of a vector is equal to the Laplacian of its components separately and putted afterwards in a vector form, we can apply Laplacian operator for colour images also. The relations can be expressed as

$$\nabla^2[\mathbf{c}(x,y)] = \begin{bmatrix} \nabla^2 R(x,y) \\ \nabla^2 G(x,y) \\ \nabla^2 B(x,y) \end{bmatrix}$$

7.4.5 Colour Edge Detection

Detection of object boundaries or edges in a colour image can be done in two different ways. One approach is to find out edges from individual colour components, and then adding these edge responses to yield the result. Another strategy is to directly compute the gradients of the colour vectors.

Computing gradients in colour vector space is not easy and it needs to determine partial derivatives of the image function along different directions. Then, the maximum response at each pixel location is thresholded to retain the edge pattern. Instead, to compute the edges from individual colour components is much easier and can provide almost the same output in terms of quality. In Figure 7.17, we have shown the results of edge detection for an *onion* image.

Note that, the edges detected by converting an RGB image into a grey image and then applying an edge detector are not the same with those obtained from the three colour components. Individual colour components convey much more edge information in this regard. In Figure 7.17, the mentioned difference is illustrated.

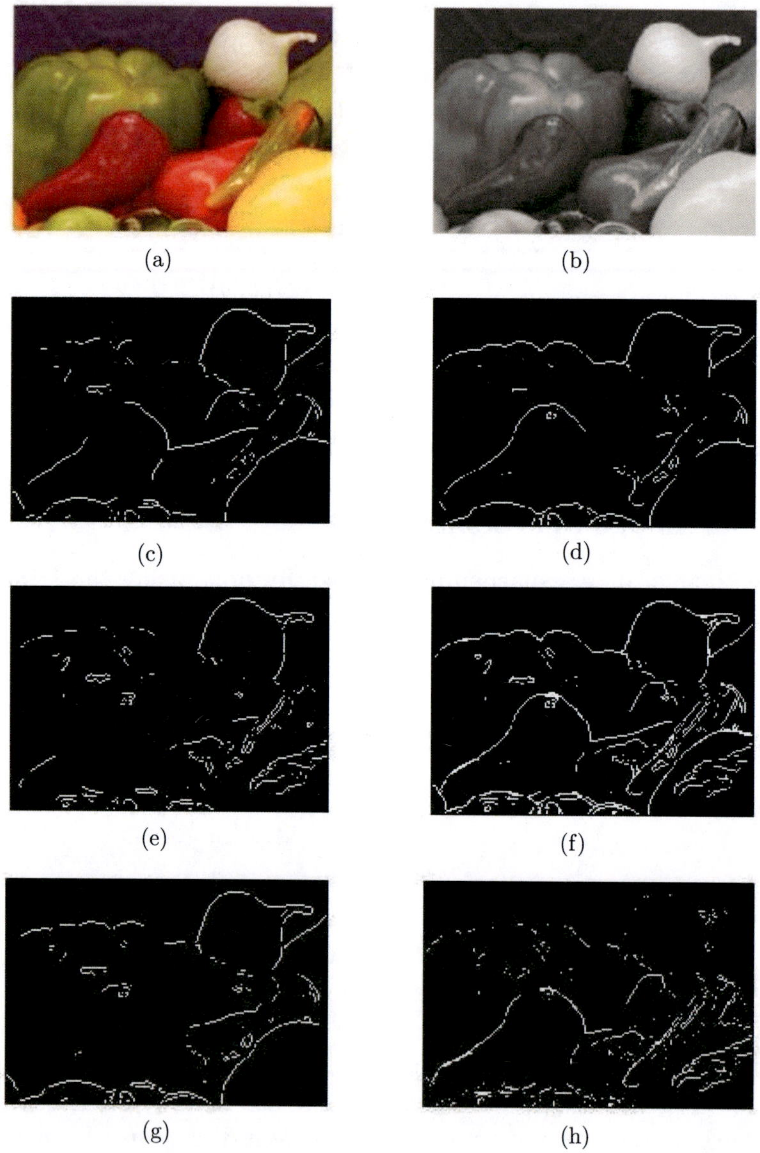

Figure 7.17: The *onion* image and its edges. (a) Original RGB image, (b) Grey counterpart of (a), (c)-(e) Edges extracted from RED, GREEN, and BLUE components, (f) Combination of (c)-(e) above, (g) Edges extracted from grey image (b), and (h) Difference image of (f) and (g).

7.5 Problems

1. What do you mean by hue, saturation and intensity? How are they related to dominant colour, purity and luminance, respectively?
2. Why red, green and blue colours are selected to represent colour objects?
3. What are additive and subtractive colour models? What are their uses?
4. What will be the colour of a red ball in a dark room and why?
5. How many intensity levels in grey shades can be produced by a $n \times n$ dot size pixel, where each dot can have m different intensity settings built into the device?
6. What is the difference between Y in CMY and the Y in YIQ models?
7. What is meant by pseudo colour image processing? How a grey level image can be converted into a pseudo colour image?
8. Describe colour image smoothing and sharpening processes.
9. How can you segment an RGB colour image?

Chapter 8

Image Restoration

Image restoration is a process of recovering the original image by applying the inverse degradation operation. Although the ultimate goal of restoration techniques is to improve a degraded image, one should not mix it up with image enhancement techniques. To further clarify, we can say that "contrast stretching" is an enhancement technique because it is based on the pleasing aspects of the viewer, whereas, "removal of image blur" by using a "deblurring function" is considered a restoration operation. Here the target is to develop a representation of the degraded image which closely resembles the original undegraded image. Most of the available image restoration methods are based on convolution applied globally to the whole image.

8.1 Degradation Model

An image may be degraded by different processes. Some of these are: Non-linearity of electro-optical sensors, graininess of the capturing film, wrong focal length of camera-lenses, relative motion between scene and camera, non-uniform scanning of images, etc.

Image restoration can be performed in two ways: deterministic and stochastic. When the noise present in the image is insignificant and we know the degradation function, we can apply deterministic techniques. At other situations, we apply the stochastic techniques which try to recover the original image by optimizing some objective function such as least squared-error criterion. In such cases, of course, we have to model the process according to the desired objective function.

During restoration, we model the degradation process as a transformation. If this transformation is known and there exists an inverse transformation, we can get back the original image (a near match). The better our knowledge is about the degradation process, the better are the results of restoration. But in reality, in most of the cases, there is very little knowledge about the degradation process. So at first the degradation processes need to be modelled. Estimation of degradation parameters can be done in two ways depending on the information available to us: A priori or a posteriori. A priori knowledge of degradation is known before restoration. For example, if we know that the camera we are using to capture the image is having a wrong lens, we can model the degradation process by studying the effects of the features of a lens on the captured images. A posteriori knowledge of degradation is obtained by analyzing degraded images. In many cases, artificial images of known spectral characteristics are made to degrade by the degrading process; and then the effects of degradation are measured.

Only successful estimation of degradation parameters can lead to a successful restoration. Thus modelling degradation is the most important part of image restoration.

The degradation process is modelled as an operator h, which together with an additive noise term $\eta(x,y)$ operates on an input image $f(x,y)$ to produce a degraded image $g(x,y)$. The degraded image $g(x,y)$ is produced from the original image $f(x,y)$ by a convolution process which can be expressed as

$$g(x,y) = \sum_{\alpha}\sum_{\beta} f(\alpha,\beta)h(x-\alpha, y-\beta) + \eta(x,y) \tag{8.1}$$

or

$$\mathbf{g} = \mathbf{f} * \mathbf{h} + \eta \tag{8.2}$$

In the frequency domain, in absence of noise, the above equation becomes

$$G = HF \tag{8.3}$$

where, F, G and H represent Fourier transforms of the original image, degraded image and the transformation function, respectively. Thus, image restoration is basically an inverse convolution process.

8.1.1 Some Common Degradation Functions

Some common types of degradations can be very easily expressed using mathematical notations. Images degraded by such functions, can thus be restored easily. We illustrate some degradation functions below.

Position dependent brightness variation

In case of ideal and accurate image acquisition, distribution of brightness pattern should be even and uniform in nature. However, in practice, it is found to be distorted by the acquisition and digitization processes. The reasons behind such behaviour may be listed as

- Lenses attenuate light more if it passes farther from the optical axis.
- Photosensitive parts of the sensor device (CCD camera) are not of equal sensitivity.

- Illumination over the object may be uneven, etc.

If degradation is systematic in nature, it can be suppressed by brightness correction. Let, a multiplicative error coefficient $e(x, y)$ describes the change of pixel intensity at location (x, y). Let $f(x, y)$ is the original image and $g(x, y)$ is the degraded image, respectively. Then we can write,

$$g(x, y) = e(x, y) \times f(x, y) \tag{8.4}$$

The error coefficient $e(x, y)$ can be computed if a reference image $f(x, y)$ with known brightness pattern could be captured. In the simplest situation, $f(x, y)$ is an image of constant brightness c. Let, in this case, the degraded result is $g_c(x, y)$. Then

$$e(x, y) = \frac{g_c(x, y)}{c} \tag{8.5}$$

i.e.

$$f(x, y) = \frac{g(x, y)}{e(x, y)} = \frac{c \times g(x, y)}{g_c(x, y)} \tag{8.6}$$

This method can be used only if the degradation process is stable. If we wish to supress this kind of error in the image capturing process, we should perhaps calibrate the device (by finding error coefficients a priori) from time to time.

Relative motion of camera and object

When an image is captured with a camera with a mechanical shutter, the relative motion between the camera an the photographed object during the shutter open time T causes smoothing of the object in the image. Suppose V is the constant speed in the X-direction; the Fourier transform $H(u, v)$ of the degradation caused in time T is given by

$$H(u, v) = \frac{\sin(\pi V T u)}{\pi V u} \tag{8.7}$$

Wrong focal length

If the lens of the camera capturing the image is having imperfect focal length, some kind of smoothing effect may occur in the captured image. This effect can be measured as

$$H(u, v) = \frac{J_1(a\, r)}{a\, r} \tag{8.8}$$

where, $J_1(.)$ is the first order Bessel function, $r = \sqrt{u^2 + v^2}$, and a is the displacement. This model is not space variant.

Atmospheric turbulence

In case of remote sensing satellite images the atmospheric turbulence is found to cause degradation frequently. This is caused by difference in temperature at different atmospheric layers and consequential variation of density in the atmosphere through which light beams pass. The mathematical model of such degradation can be expressed as

$$H(u,v) = \exp\left[-c(u^2+v^2)^{5/6}\right] \tag{8.9}$$

where c is a constant that depends on the type of turbulence which can be computed experimentally. The power $5/6$ may be replaced by 1 for simplicity.

8.1.2 Noise Models for Images

Real images are often degraded by some random errors – this degradation is usually called **noise**. Noise can occur during image capture, processing or transmission, and may be dependent or independent of image contents.

To generate rules to restore degraded images, we generally degrade real and artificial images with different kinds of standard noises. These are called **synthetic noises**. Images with controlled impairment can also be used as test images for investigating noise reducing operators.

Spike noise

This additive noise may include positive and negative spikes and interfere in the image in about the same ratio. The average noise ratio can thus be selected as a measure of noise. Average noise occurrence ratio Q means each Qth image point is noisy. The pseudo code for generating such noise is given below.

1. Select the noise ratio Q (say, $1 < Q < 100$). Select spike height H ($0 \leq H \leq G-1$) where grey level range is $[0, G-1]$.
2. $p_{\text{neg}} = \frac{0.5}{Q}$ and $p_{\text{pos}} = 1 - p_{\text{neg}}$, where p_{neg} and p_{pos} are equal probabilities of occurrences of negative and positive noise, respectively.
3. For each pixel (x,y) of intensity $g(x,y)$ generate a random number r in the range $[0,1]$. Set,

$$\begin{aligned}
f(x,y) &= \max\{0, g(x,y)-H\} && \text{if } r < p_{\text{neg}} \\
f(x,y) &= g(x,y) && \text{if } r \geq p_{\text{neg}} \text{ and } r \leq p_{\text{pos}} \\
f(x,y) &= \min\{G-1, g(x,y)+H\} && \text{if } r > p_{\text{pos}}
\end{aligned}$$

Here, we have set,

$$p_{\text{neg}} = \frac{1}{2Q} \quad \text{and} \quad p_{\text{pos}} = 1 - p_{\text{neg}}.$$

This means that, on the average each $2Q$th image point is effected by a negative noise impulse, and thus, each $2Q$th image point is effected by a positive noise impulse.

Unform noise

The probability density function $p(z)$ of a *uniform noise* is given by

$$p(z) = \begin{cases} \frac{1}{b-a} & \text{if } a \leq z \leq b \\ 0 & \text{otherwise.} \end{cases}$$

The mean of this density function is given by

$$\mu = \frac{a+b}{2}$$

and the variance is given by

$$\sigma^2 = \frac{(b-a)^2}{12}$$

To generate additive uniformly distributed random noise for which we proceed is as follows:

Let, the noise-free and noisy images are represented by $f(x, y)$ and $g(x, y)$, respectively. Let, S be the range of noise, i.e. $0 \leq s \leq \frac{S}{2}$, where s is the noise added to a location (or subtracted from a location). The procedure is as follows:

1. Select the noise range S.
2. For each pixel in the image generate a uniformly distributed random number r_{uniform} in the range $[0, 1]$. Set,

$$g(x, y) = f(x, y) - \frac{S}{2} + S \times r_{\text{uniform}}$$

Gaussian noise

Additive Gaussian noise (normally distributed random noise) is the most commonly used noise model for image degradation. Hence, the generation of such noise is the most important for study and analysis purposes.

A random variable with Gaussian (Normal) distribution has its probability density given by the Gaussian curve. In one dimension, this density function is

$$p(z) = \frac{1}{\sqrt{2\pi}\sigma} \exp\left[\frac{-(z-\mu)^2}{2\sigma^2}\right]$$

where, μ and σ are the mean and standard deviation of the random variable z. The Gaussian noise is a very good approximation to noise that occurs in many practical situations. The procedure for generation of such noise is given as follows.

1. Select a value for σ; low values to generate less noise effects.
2. If the image grey level range is $[0, G-1]$, calculate

$$p[i] = \frac{1}{\sqrt{2\pi}\sigma} \exp\left[\frac{-i^2}{2\sigma^2}\right]$$

   for $i = 0, 1, \ldots, G-1$.
3. For each pixel (x, y) in the image having intensity $f(x, y)$, generate a uniformly distributed random number r in the range [0, 1], and determine

$$j = \text{argmin}_i (r - p[i])$$

4. Generate a random number s (for sign) from the set $\{-1, 1\}$, and set

$$h(x, y) = f(x, y) + s \times j$$

5. Set,

$$\begin{aligned} f(x,y) &= 0 && \text{if } \ h(x,y) < 0 \\ f(x,y) &= G-1 && \text{if } \ h(x,y) > G-1 \\ f(x,y) &= h(x,y) && \text{otherwise} \end{aligned}$$

6. Go to step 3 until all pixels have been scanned.

Besides the above there exists some other commonly used noises one of which is the *impulse noise*. This is described below.

Impulse noise

This type of noise is characterized by white spots in dark regions and black spots in bright regions. The probability density function of the *impulse noise* (also called **salt and pepper noise**) is given by

$$p(z) = \begin{cases} p_a & \text{if } \ z = a \\ p_b & \text{if } \ z = b \\ 0 & \text{otherwise.} \end{cases}$$

where, a and b are grey levels of the image with $a < b$. If either p_a or p_b is zero, then the impulse noise is said to be *unipolar*.

8.1.3 Signal-to-Noise Ratio

When an image $f(x, y)$ is impaired by an additive noise $\eta(x, y)$, the impaired becomes

$$g(x, y) = f(x, y) + \eta(x, y)$$

The squared value of the noise contribution is

$$E = \sum_{x, y} \eta^2(x, y)$$

The squared value of the observed image signal is

$$F = \sum_{x, y} f^2(x, y)$$

The signal-to-noise ratio is then defined as

$$\text{SNR} = \frac{F}{E}$$

The SNR is a measure of relative goodness of the corrupted image.

8.2 Image Restoration Models

Image restoration may be viewed as the process of obtaining an approximation to the original image **f**, given the degraded image **g** and a knowledge of the degradation in the form of an operator **H** which is the Fourier transform of the operator **h**.

The input-output relationship is expressed as

$$g(x, y) = H[f(x, y)] + \eta(x, y) \tag{8.10}$$

Let us assume that $\eta(x, y) = \{0\}$, so that

$$g(x, y) = H[f(x, y)] \tag{8.11}$$

Now, the operator H is linear if

$$H[k_1 f_1(x, y) + k_2 f_2(x, y)] = k_1 H[f_1(x, y)] + k_2 H[f_2(x, y)] \tag{8.12}$$

where k_1 and k_2 are constants and $f_1(x, y)$ and $f_2(x, y)$ are two input images. If $k_1 = k_2 = 1$, then the above equation becomes

$$H[f_1(x, y) + f_2(x, y)] = H[f_1(x, y)] + H[f_2(x, y)] \tag{8.13}$$

which is called the property of "additivity", i.e. if H is a linear operator, its response to a sum of two inputs is equal to the sum of its two responses when applied to the two inputs separately.

When

$$f_2(x, y) = \{0\}$$

we get,

$$H\left[k_1 f_1(x, y)\right] = k_1 H\left[f_1(x, y)\right] \tag{8.14}$$

which is called the property of "homogeneity". Therefore, a linear operator possesses both the properties of additivity and homogeneity.

An operator having an input-output relationship $g(x, y) = H\left[f(x, y)\right]$ is said to be position invariant if

$$H\left[f(x-\alpha, y-\beta)\right] = g(x-\alpha, y-\beta) \tag{8.15}$$

for any $f(x, y)$ and α and β. In this case, the response at any point in the image depends on the value of the input at that point and not the position of that point.

8.2.1 Degradation Model for Continuous Functions

Making a slight change in the notation in the definition of the impulse function, $f(x, y)$ can be expressed in the form

$$f(x, y) = \int_{\infty}^{\infty}\int_{\infty}^{\infty} f(\alpha, \beta)\delta(x-\alpha, y-\beta)\, d\alpha\, d\beta \tag{8.16}$$

If $\eta(x, y) = \{0\}$, then

$$g(x, y) = H\left[f(x, y)\right] = H\left[\int_{\infty}^{\infty}\int_{\infty}^{\infty} f(\alpha, \beta)\delta(x-\alpha, y-\beta)\, d\alpha\, d\beta\right] \tag{8.17}$$

If H is a linear operator, then

$$g(x, y) = \int_{\infty}^{\infty}\int_{\infty}^{\infty} H\left[f(\alpha, \beta)\delta(x-\alpha, y-\beta)\right] d\alpha\, d\beta \tag{8.18}$$

Since $f(\alpha, \beta)$ is independent of x and y, then

$$g(x, y) = \int_{\infty}^{\infty}\int_{\infty}^{\infty} f(\alpha, \beta) H\left[\delta(x-\alpha, y-\beta)\right] d\alpha\, d\beta \tag{8.19}$$

The term $h(x, \alpha, y, \beta) = H\left[\delta(x-\alpha, y-\beta)\right]$ is called the **impulse response** of H. If $\eta(x, y) = \{0\}$, then $h(x, \alpha, y, \beta)$ is the response of H to an impulse of strength 1 at coordinate (α, β).

Substituting the value of
$h(x, \alpha, y, \beta)$ in the above equation, we get

$$g(x, y) = \int_{\infty}^{\infty} \int_{\infty}^{\infty} f(\alpha, \beta) h(x, \alpha, y, \beta) \, d\alpha \, d\beta \tag{8.20}$$

or

$$g(x, y) = \int_{\infty}^{\infty} \int_{\infty}^{\infty} f(\alpha, \beta) h(x - \alpha, y - \beta) \, d\alpha \, d\beta \tag{8.21}$$

which is called the **superposition integral** of the first kind.

8.2.2 Discrete Formation

Let us simplify the development of a discrete, space invariant degradation model by starting with 1D case and temporarily neglecting the noise term. Let $f(x)$ and $h(x)$ are two functions sampled uniformly to form arrays of dimensions A and B, respectively. x is a discrete variable in the range $0, 1, \ldots, A-1$ for $f(x)$ and $0, 1, \ldots, B-1$ for $h(x)$. Let us assume that these discrete functions are periodic with period M. So let us extend the range of x for both $f(x)$ and $h(x)$ to be equal to $0, 1, \ldots, M - 1$ such that $M \geq A + B - 1$. We now denote the extended functions as $f_e(x)$ and $h_e(x)$, respectively. Convolution of these two discrete functions is defined as

$$g_e(x) = \sum_{m=0}^{M-1} f_e(m) h_e(x - m) \tag{8.22}$$

for $x = 0, 1, \ldots, M - 1$. In matrix notation, we can write,

$$\mathbf{g} = \mathbf{Hf} \tag{8.23}$$

8.2.3 Unconstrained Least Square Error Restoration

The noise term in degradation model is

$$\eta = \mathbf{g} - \mathbf{Hf} \tag{8.24}$$

In absence of any knowledge about η, a meaningful "criterion function" is to seek an image $\mathbf{f}'$ such that $\mathbf{Hf}'$ approximates $\mathbf{g}$ in a least squares sense by assuming that the norm of the noise term is as small as possible. In other words, we want to find an $\mathbf{f}'$ such that

$$||\eta||^2 = ||\mathbf{g} - \mathbf{Hf}'||^2 \tag{8.25}$$

is minimum, where,by definition, $||\eta||^2 = \eta^T \eta$, i.e. $||\mathbf{g} - \mathbf{Hf}'||^2 = (\mathbf{g} - \mathbf{Hf}'^T) \cdot (\mathbf{g} - \mathbf{Hf}')$.

The equivalent view of this problem is one of minimizing the criterion function

$$J(\mathbf{f}') = ||\mathbf{g} - \mathbf{H}\mathbf{f}'||^2 \tag{8.26}$$

We simply differentiate J with respect to $\mathbf{f}'$ and set the result to zero, i.e.

$$\frac{\delta J(\mathbf{f}')}{\delta(\mathbf{f}')} = 0 = -2\mathbf{H}^T(\mathbf{g} - \mathbf{H}\mathbf{f}') \tag{8.27}$$

By solving the above equation for $\mathbf{f}'$, we get

$$\mathbf{f}' = \mathbf{H}^{-1}(\mathbf{H}^{\mathbf{T}})^{-1}\mathbf{H}^{\mathbf{T}}\mathbf{g} \tag{8.28}$$

or

$$\mathbf{f}' = \mathbf{H}^{-1}\mathbf{g} \tag{8.29}$$

8.2.4 Inverse Filtering

The relation for unconstrained restoration is derived in Eq. (8.24). Now, if we replace the expression for H in that equation, we get

$$\mathbf{f}' = (\mathbf{W}\mathbf{D}\mathbf{W}^{-1})^{-1}\mathbf{g} \tag{8.30}$$

or

$$\mathbf{f}' = (\mathbf{W}\mathbf{D}^{-1}\mathbf{W}^{-1})\mathbf{g} \tag{8.31}$$

Multiplying both sides by W^{-1}, we get

$$W^{-1}\mathbf{f}' = (\mathbf{D}^{-1}\mathbf{W}^{-1})\mathbf{g} \tag{8.32}$$

Now, applying Fourier transformation relations the above relation becomes

$$F'(u,v) = \frac{G(u,v)}{H(u,v)} \quad \text{for } u,v = 0,1,\ldots,N-1 \tag{8.33}$$

In Eq. (8.33), $F'(u,v)$ represents the Fourier transform of the recovered image $\mathbf{f}'$. Therefore, a pointwise division of $G(u,v)$ by $H(u,v)$ followed by an inverse transform yields the restored image.

In Figure 8.1, the *cameraman* image is blurred by using a Gaussian spread function, and then it is deblurred using inverse filtering process. This kind of recovering of image is also called **deconvolution**.

In the inverse filtering process, we may face a problem of division by zero. This is because of the fact that the $H(u,v)$ may have very small values (zero or near zero)

(a) Original image (b) Blurred image (c) Deblurred image

Figure 8.1: Image deblurring.

in the region of interest in the uv-plane. We may eliminate this problem by removing the zero values in $H(u,v)$ by some fixed and finite values.

When we consider degradation in presence of noise, the degradation model can be expressed as

$$G(u,v) = H(u,v) \cdot F(u,v) + N(u,v) \tag{8.34}$$

In this case, we get

$$F^{'}(u,v) = \frac{G(u,v)}{H(u,v)} = F(u,v) + \frac{N(u,v)}{H(u,v)} \tag{8.35}$$

This is clearly a more hazardous situation, because in this case the term $\frac{N(u,v)}{H(u,v)}$ may dominate over $F(u,v)$. Fortunately, like any other function, the Fourier spectrum of $H(u,v)$ also falls of gradually from the origin of the uv-plane to the boundaries. So, it is a better practice to limit the region of interest of the restored image only surrounding the origin of the uv-plane, and to ignore the rest.

8.2.5 Constrained Least Square Error Filtering

In constrained restoration, we define a measure of image quality as $||\mathbf{Qf}^{'}||^2$ which is to be minimized subject to the constraint $||\mathbf{g} - \mathbf{Hf}^{'}||^2 = ||\eta||^2$.

Let the auto-correlation matrices of the image f and the noise η be defined as

$$\mathbf{C}_f = E\{ff^T\}$$

and

$$\mathbf{C}_\eta = E\{\eta\eta^T\}$$

respectively.

The correlation between ith and jth element of the image be defined as $E\{f_i f_j\}$. This is also true for the noise. For real values of f and η we have $E\{f_i f_j\} = E\{f_j f_i\}$

and $E\{\eta_i\eta_j\} = E\{\eta_j\eta_i\}$, i.e. $\mathbf{C}_f$ and $\mathbf{C}_\eta$ are symmetric real-valued matrices. Hence, $\mathbf{C}_f$ and $\mathbf{C}_\eta$ can be approximated by block circulant matrices and can be diagonalized by the matrix W. If the diagonal matrices are represented by $\mathbf{A}$ and $\mathbf{B}$ then we can write,

$$\mathbf{C}_f = \mathbf{WAW}^{-1}$$

and

$$\mathbf{C}_\eta = \mathbf{WBW}^{-1}$$

where elements $\mathbf{A}$ and $\mathbf{B}$ are diagonal forms of the auto-correlation matrices $\mathbf{C}_f$ and $\mathbf{C}_\eta$, respectively.

To handle the condition of quality constraint by minimization, we need to employ the method of Lagrange multiplier (λ), when the constraint can be expressed as,

$$J(\mathbf{f}') = ||\mathbf{Qf}'||^2 + \lambda(||\mathbf{g} - \mathbf{Hf}'||^2 - ||\eta||^2) \tag{8.36}$$

or

$$J(\mathbf{f}') = \mathbf{f}'^{\mathbf{T}}\mathbf{Q}^{\mathbf{T}}\mathbf{Qf}' + \lambda(\mathbf{g}^T\mathbf{g} - \mathbf{g}^T\mathbf{Hf}' - \mathbf{f}'^T\mathbf{Hg} + \mathbf{f}'^T\mathbf{H}^T\mathbf{Hf}' - \eta^T\eta) \tag{8.37}$$

Differentiating the above equation with respect to $\mathbf{f}'$ and equating to zero, we get

$$\frac{\delta J(\mathbf{f}')}{\delta(\mathbf{f}')} = 0 = 2\mathbf{Q}^{\mathbf{T}}\mathbf{Qf}' + 2\lambda(-\mathbf{H}^T\mathbf{g} + \mathbf{H}^T\mathbf{Hf}') \tag{8.38}$$

The solution of the above equation becomes

$$\mathbf{f}' = (\mathbf{H}^T\mathbf{H} + \gamma\mathbf{Q}^{\mathbf{T}}\mathbf{Q})^{-1}\mathbf{H}^T\mathbf{g} \tag{8.39}$$

where, $\gamma = \frac{1}{\lambda}$. Converting to the Fourier domain, we get

$$F'(u,v) = \frac{H^*(u,v)}{H^*(u,v)H(u,v) + \gamma Q^*(u,v)Q(u,v)}G(u,v) \tag{8.40}$$

for $u = 0, 1, \ldots, N-1$ and for $v = 0, 1, \ldots, N-1$.

The above is a general derivation. Now, depending on the specified quality criteria we may obtain different results. If we wish to minimize the *signal-to-noise* ratio, then $\mathbf{Q}^{\mathbf{T}}\mathbf{Q} = \mathbf{C}_f^{-1}\mathbf{C}_\eta$. Therefore, in Fourier domain, the estimated image becomes

$$F'(u,v) = \frac{H^*(u,v)}{H^*(u,v)H(u,v) + \gamma\frac{C_\eta(u,v)}{C_f(u,v)}}G(u,v) \tag{8.41}$$

for $u = 0, 1, \ldots, N-1$ and for $v = 0, 1, \ldots, N-1$.

8.2.6 Least Mean Square Error Filtering

Here, an estimate $\mathbf{f}'$ of the original image $\mathbf{f}$ is derived such that the mean squared error between them becomes the minimum. The error term is defined as

$$\text{err}^2 = E\{(f - f')^2\} \tag{8.42}$$

where $E\{.\}$ represents the expected value of the argument. It is assumed that both the image and the noise are uncorrelated random processes, with the noise having a zero mean.

The block circulant matrix H can be diagonalized using relation

$$\mathbf{D} = \mathbf{WHW}^{-1} \tag{8.43}$$

The relation for constrained restoration (Eq. 8.39) is

$$\mathbf{f}' = (\mathbf{H}^T\mathbf{H} + \gamma\mathbf{Q}^\mathbf{T}\mathbf{Q})^{-1}\mathbf{H}^T\mathbf{g}$$

From Eq. (8.43), we get

$$\mathbf{H}^T = \mathbf{WDW}^{-1} \tag{8.44}$$

Now, relation for constrained restoration becomes

$$\mathbf{f}' = (\mathbf{WDDW}^{-1} + \gamma\mathbf{WA}^{-1}\mathbf{BW}^{-1})^{-1}\mathbf{WDW}^{-1}\mathbf{g} \tag{8.45}$$

Multiplying both sides by $\mathbf{W^{-1}}$ and simplifying, we get

$$\mathbf{W}^{-1}\mathbf{f}' = (\mathbf{DD} + \gamma\mathbf{A}^{-1}\mathbf{B})^{-1}\mathbf{DW}^{-1}\mathbf{g} \tag{8.46}$$

Therefore, in Fourier domain, the estimated image becomes

$$F'(u,v) = \frac{H(u,v)}{|H(u,v)|^2 + \gamma\frac{C_\eta(u,v)}{C_f(u,v)}}G(u,v) \tag{8.47}$$

for $u = 0, 1, \ldots, N-1$ and for $v = 0, 1, \ldots, N-1$.

In Eq. (8.47) the factor γ is a variable. When $\gamma = 1$, we call this restoring filter as the *Wiener filter* and with variable γ it is called a *pametric Wiener filter*. In absence of the noise factor, Wiener filter reduces to the ideal inverse filter (Figure 8.2).

(a) Original (b) With Gaussian noise (c) After Wiener filtering

Figure 8.2: Image of Saturn.

8.3 Problems

1. Write the differences between image enhancement and image restoration.
2. What is meant by image degradation? Is it caused by noise present in an image?
3. Mention some common ways of incorporation of degradation in an image. How can you recover the original image from such degradations?
4. Mention different kinds of noise that may be present in an image. Wirte down a procedure to generate Gaussian noise of zero mean and standard deviation 0.05 in image having grey levels in the range [0 63].
5. What is the importance of artificially generated noise in image processing?
6. Develop restoration procedures using mean square filtering and Wiener filtering. What are the similarities and differences between these two filters?
7. Consider an image having grey levels in the range [0 63]. Corrupt it using Gaussian noise of zero mean and standard deviation 0.05. Recover the original image using constrained least square estimation.

Chapter 9

Image Registration

Image registration is the process of establishing correspondence between two or more related images. In case of satellite imaging, often a number of images, corresponding to different band in the electromagnetic spectrum are captured at different instances. Now to get a combined view of the image, all these spectral components need to be fused keeping a perfect point-to-point correspondence among image elements. This process of information fusion establishing correspondence between features of different image components is called image registration. In this process, pixels of one or more images are geometrically transformed to occupy new locations. We shall describe some of the common techniques generally used in image registration in the following sections.

9.1 Geometrical Transformations

In image processing, we often need the operation of geometrical mappings of a given image. Image values at some locations may have to be modified as a consequence of such mapping operations. These operations are mainly translation, scaling, rotation and geometrical matching of two images. A certain amount of image value correction or fitting is often a partial task within the scope of such mappings.

A coordinate transformation defines a geometrical operator with respect to the image point mappings. If f and g represent the input and output images and T is a one-to-one coordinate transformation operator, the following relation holds:

$$g(x, y) = T(f(x, y)) \tag{9.1}$$

For such kind of geometrical transformations, for all image points (x, y) in the resultant image g, at first the coordinate transformation is performed for (x, y), and then the value $g(x, y)$ is computed, based on the value of $f(x, y)$, at the transformed location. This approach is called the **backward coordinate transformation**. The method ensures that all the image points (x, y) in g are assigned appropriate image values.

9.1.1 Basic Transformations

In this section, we deal with the development of a unified representation for the transformation operators. We shall restrict ourselves to 2D images only. For the sake of unification, we represent a Cartesian coordinate point (x, y) in homogeneous coordinate system as (x, y, w) where, $w = 1$ for 2D cases.

Translation

Here we need to translate a point with coordinate (x_1, y_1) to a new location by using displacements (dx, dy). The translation operation can be performed easily by using the following equations:

$$x_2 = x_1 + dx$$
$$y_2 = y_1 + dy$$

where, (x_2, y_2) is the new coordinate of the point. The above relations can be represented (using homogeneous coordinate system) in matrix notation as:

$$\begin{bmatrix} x_2 \\ y_2 \\ 1 \end{bmatrix} = \begin{bmatrix} 1 & 0 & dx \\ 0 & 1 & dy \\ 0 & 0 & 1 \end{bmatrix} \begin{bmatrix} x_1 \\ y_1 \\ 1 \end{bmatrix} \tag{9.2}$$

Equation (9.2) can be put as a vector product

$$\mathbf{v}_2 = \mathbf{T}\mathbf{v}_1 \tag{9.3}$$

where,

$$\mathbf{v}_1 = \begin{bmatrix} x_1 \\ y_1 \\ 1 \end{bmatrix} \qquad \mathbf{v}_2 = \begin{bmatrix} x_2 \\ y_2 \\ 1 \end{bmatrix} \qquad \mathbf{T} = \begin{bmatrix} 1 & 0 & dx \\ 0 & 1 & dy \\ 0 & 0 & 1 \end{bmatrix}$$

Scaling

Scaling by scale factors s_x and s_y along X and Y directions are given by the transformation matrix

$$\mathbf{S} = \begin{bmatrix} s_x & 0 & 0 \\ 0 & s_y & 0 \\ 0 & 0 & 1 \end{bmatrix} \tag{9.4}$$

Rotation

Rotation can be performed in anticlockwise or clockwise directions. The axis of rotation may be the X-axis, the Y-axis or any arbitrary line on the X-Y plane.

For rotation about the X-axis and by an angle θ in the anticlockwise direction, the transformation matrix is

$$\mathbf{R}_\theta = \begin{bmatrix} \cos\theta & -\sin\theta & 0 \\ \sin\theta & \cos\theta & 0 \\ 0 & 0 & 1 \end{bmatrix} \tag{9.5}$$

For a clockwise rotation the matrix becomes

$$\mathbf{R}_{-\theta} = \begin{bmatrix} \cos\theta & \sin\theta & 0 \\ -\sin\theta & \cos\theta & 0 \\ 0 & 0 & 1 \end{bmatrix} \tag{9.6}$$

9.1.2 Application of Geometrical Transformations

In the above discussion, the transformations have been applied on a single isolated point on the $X-Y$ plane. In an image, however, there is a large number of pixels. The idea of matrix multiplication allows us to transform a set of n points simultaneously by using a single transformation. Let, $\mathbf{v_1}, \mathbf{v_2}, \ldots, \mathbf{v}_n$ represent the coordinates of n points. Each $\mathbf{v_i}$ represent a 3×1 vector. Using these n vectors as columns, we can form a $3 \times n$ matrix $\mathbf{V}$. Now, if $\mathbf{A}$ represent a 3×3 transformation matrix then the simultaneous transformations can be denoted as

$$\mathbf{V_t} = \mathbf{AV} \tag{9.7}$$

where, $\mathbf{V}$ and $\mathbf{V_t}$ contain the input coordinates and the transformed coordinates, respectively.

Products of transformation matrices

Let us consider two basic transformations $\mathbf{A}$ and $\mathbf{B}$ given by their homogeneous transformation matrices. These transformations are to be carried out in a certain order in the image plane. Multiplying two transformation matrices, we get the resultant transformation matrix $\mathbf{C}$. The resultant transformation is given by

$$\mathbf{C} = \mathbf{A} \times \mathbf{B} \tag{9.8}$$

It is to be noted that matrix multiplication is not commutative.

A backward transformation matrix $\mathbf{A}^{-1}$ uniquely corresponds to a forward transformation matrix $\mathbf{A}$, and vice versa. Thus, the resulting matrix product $\mathbf{C}$ can be mapped into the corresponding forward transformation matrix by means of a matrix inversion.

Combined transformation

In some cases, a number of transformations need to be applied on an object in sequence. Suppose we are to apply scaling immediately after translation. In this case, the combined transformation matrix is developed first, and then it is applied to object coordinates. The above process of combined transformation is very useful for the following purposes:

- ***Computational efficiency:*** In case of a combined transformation, we can achieve a significant amount of computational time benefits, specially when the resultant transformation matrix needs to be applied to a large number of coordinate points. Let us consider the application of translation, scaling and rotation operations serially on the coordinates of an object. If the object is a single point (a triple in homogeneous coordinate representation), then the number of multiplications needed can be computed as follows. For independent application of transformation matrices separately, the number of multiplications will be $9 + 9 + 9 = 27$. If, on the other hand, at first we compute the combined transformation matrix, then the number of multiplications will be $54 + 9 = 63$. It seems apparently that using the combined transformation method we need more number of multiplications. However, an object normally contains many more points. For illustration consider an object with 5 points only. In this case, without using combined transformation the number of multiplications will be $5 \times 27 = 135$, while using combined transformation this number will reduce to $54 + 5 \times 9 = 99$ only. In general, for an n pixel transformation, where m number of individual transformations are applied, number of multiplications, in two different situations, are $m \times n \times 9$ and $(m - 1) \times 27 + n \times 9$, respectively.
- ***Visual reality:*** Besides computational efficiency, as mentioned above, we can also achieve benefits form the combined technique in respect of visual presentation of the resultant object. It might be the case that after applying some of the component transformations the new object or part of it falls outside the visible range of coordinates. Since a graphical system always limits coordinate values, it tries to truncate to put everything within limit. Thus, the following transformations may not produce the correct result. In case of combined transformations this situation will not arise.

9.2 Image Mapping

Image mapping is a technique for establishing correspondence between related image pairs. Generalized image mapping can be performed by means of a generalized transformation which stems from the above mentioned ideas of matrix multiplication and commonly known as **affine Transformations**. Very often affine transformations are used for *image registration.* Image registration involves establishing feature based correspondence between a pair of related images. As mentioned earlier, in case of satellite imagery, two photographs of the same landscape may be captured from two different locations or on two different days. Now, it may be needed to make a point-by-point correspondence between these two images before some image processing applications (say, image averaging). Establishing correspondence means matching of identical shapes in the related image pair. This requires transformation of one image into the other, in sense of geometrical distribution of pixels in the 2D Cartesian space.

In case of affine transformation we consider only backward transformations. It is a linear mapping $T(x, y) = (x_t, y_t)$, i.e. here we map image coordinates (x, y) from image g onto the image coordinates (x_t, y_t) in image f.

In general, the computed coordinates (x_t, y_t) are not necessarily integers, and also not necessarily within the $M \times N$ image domain. Therefore, after transforming the g coordinates, a one-to-one mapping of the real point coordinates onto integer image coordinates of the image f must be performed.

While establishing correspondence between image pairs using affine transformation, we need the following:

- Determining a set of corresponding points from ground information or landmarks by means of inspection, and
- Computing the transformation matrix for establishing correspondence among the landmark points.

9.2.1 Determining a Set of Landmarks

For the purpose of establishing a correspondence between image pairs it is extremely important to identify a set of points on both the images which are highly stable and each pair refers to the same physical location or object point. This statement can be clarified with the help of a suitable example. Let us consider a triangle and its deviated counterpart. Although, the object triangle may have many pixels defining it, three of them are clearly stable in both the forms. These are the vertices of the triangle. Vertices of a triangle must always be stable and always correspond physically. Actually, the landmark points satisfy the concept invariance, i.e. they always remain intact in the related image pairs. One other important characteristic of the landmark points is that they must be easily identifiable within the image.

9.2.2 Image Transformation Matrices

To convert one image into another is called **image transformation**. There exist many situations where we need to perform such conversion. One very common example is that of transforming a real world scene into a captured image. Here, a 2D image is obtained from a 3D scene by means of projective transformation. A *plane projective* transformation from one space to another space, in general, can be defined by a 3×3 matrix in homogeneous coordinates. A general form of such a transformation is

$$\begin{bmatrix} x_2 \\ y_2 \\ z_2 \end{bmatrix} = \begin{bmatrix} a_{11} & a_{12} & a_{13} \\ a_{21} & a_{22} & a_{23} \\ a_{31} & a_{32} & a_{33} \end{bmatrix} \times \begin{bmatrix} x_1 \\ y_1 \\ z_1 \end{bmatrix} \tag{9.9}$$

or

$$\mathbf{P}_2 = \mathbf{A} \times \mathbf{P}_1$$

where, the transformation $\mathbf{A}$, between points $\mathbf{P}_1$ and $\mathbf{P}_2$, has eight degrees of freedom because, in case of homogeneous coordinate system only eight ratios out of the nine elements of the matrix $\mathbf{A}$ are significant. The ninth element reduces to a constant (1) in homogeneous notation.

A special case of the plane projective transformation is the *plane affine* transformation. In this case, the transformation reduces to a form

$$\mathbf{A} = \begin{bmatrix} a_{11} & a_{12} & a_{13} \\ a_{21} & a_{22} & a_{23} \\ 0 & 0 & a_{33} \end{bmatrix} \tag{9.10}$$

The corresponding transformation has six degrees of freedom. This form is a combined general form of basic geometrical transformations like translation, scaling, rotation, etc. In the following subsection we shall show that we really need to find out values of six transformation coefficients (corresponding to six degrees of freedom) when we try to affinely map one image onto another. When ratio of division by the ninth element is considered, the above transformation is reduced to the following form:

$$\mathbf{A} = \begin{bmatrix} a_{11} & a_{12} & a_{13} \\ a_{21} & a_{22} & a_{23} \\ 0 & 0 & 1 \end{bmatrix} \tag{9.11}$$

9.2.3 Computing Transformation Coefficients

The task consists of performing a geometrical fitting for two $M \times N$ images f_1 and f_2. More exactly, an input image f_1 has to be affinely transformed into a resultant image g such that the image g and the template image f_2 are geometrically fitted (as much as possible) after the transformation. The task consists in computing the homogeneous transformation matrix of this affine transformation.

As mentioned earlier, in homogeneous notation, the affine transformation can be expressed as

$$\mathbf{A} = \begin{bmatrix} a_{11} & a_{12} & a_{13} \\ a_{21} & a_{22} & a_{23} \\ 0 & 0 & 1 \end{bmatrix}$$

and the transformation between two corresponding points $\mathbf{P}_1 = (x_1, y_1)$ and $\mathbf{P}_2 = (x_2, y_2)$ can be written as

$$\mathbf{P}_2 = \mathbf{A} \times \mathbf{P}_1 \tag{9.12}$$

or

$$\begin{bmatrix} x_2 \\ y_2 \\ 1 \end{bmatrix} = \begin{bmatrix} a_{11} & a_{12} & a_{13} \\ a_{21} & a_{22} & a_{23} \\ 0 & 0 & 1 \end{bmatrix} \times \begin{bmatrix} x_1 \\ y_1 \\ 1 \end{bmatrix} \tag{9.13}$$

Initially three fitted corresponding point pairs (p_{1k}, p_{2k}) for $k = 1, 2, 3$, are selected as inputs. The point $p_{2k} = (x_{2k}, y_{2k})$ are located in the image f_2. The geometrical fitting operation must map a point p_{1k} in f_1 onto the corresponding point p_{2k} in f_2, for each pair $k = 1, 2, 3$. These three point pairs can be determined by inspection, i.e. by means of an interactive corresponding point selection process or by an analytic coordinate transformation, e.g. for selecting size reductions or magnifications of arbitrary scaling factors. The basic transformations given in the earlier section are special affine transformations, i.e. they can be determined by three point pairs in each case.

An affine transformation is uniquely characterized by six transformation parameters $a_{11}, a_{12}, a_{13}, a_{21}, a_{22}, a_{23}$ defining its homogeneous transformation matrix. These parameters and three pairs of fitted points satisfy the following two linear equation systems.

$$\begin{aligned} x_{21} &= a_{11} \cdot x_{11} + a_{12} \cdot y_{11} + a_{13} \\ x_{22} &= a_{11} \cdot x_{12} + a_{12} \cdot y_{12} + a_{13} \\ x_{23} &= a_{11} \cdot x_{13} + a_{12} \cdot y_{13} + a_{13} \end{aligned}$$

and

$$\begin{aligned} y_{21} &= a_{21} \cdot x_{11} + a_{22} \cdot y_{11} + a_{23} \\ y_{22} &= a_{21} \cdot x_{12} + a_{22} \cdot y_{12} + a_{23} \\ y_{23} &= a_{21} \cdot x_{13} + a_{22} \cdot y_{13} + a_{23} \end{aligned}$$

By solving these linear equation systems one can find out the desired transformation parameters. However, if the three points in f_1 are colinear, i.e. on a straight line, they will not be usable. An affine transformation sufficient if three pairs of fitted points are given.

$$\sum_{k=1,2,3} \left[(a_{11}.x_{1k} + a_{12}.y_{1k} + a_{13} - x_{2k})^2 + (a_{21}.x_{1k} + a_{22}.y_{1k} + a_{23} - y_{2k})^2 \right]$$

A *least-square error optimization* of the sum is a possible approach in situations with more than three pairs of fitted points.

Example 1: Let us consider a simple example of a polygon. Let the polygon be defined by its vertices $\mathbf{A}(1, 1)$, $\mathbf{B}(7, 1)$, $\mathbf{C}(6, 5)$, and $\mathbf{D}(2, 5)$. This polygon is distorted by two known transformations of scaling with factors $s_x = 2$, $s_y = 3$ and anticlockwise rotation by an angle of 30° (both about the origin). Derive the affine transformation matrix that reverts the distorted polygon to its original one.

Solution: The vertices of the polygon ABCD can be represented by

$$\mathbf{P} = \begin{bmatrix} 1 & 7 & 6 & 2 \\ 1 & 1 & 5 & 5 \\ 1 & 1 & 1 & 1 \end{bmatrix}$$

The scaling and rotation matrices are

$$\mathbf{S} = \begin{bmatrix} 2 & 0 & 0 \\ 0 & 3 & 0 \\ 0 & 0 & 1 \end{bmatrix} \quad \text{and} \quad \mathbf{R} = \begin{bmatrix} 0.866 & 0.500 & 0 \\ -0.500 & 0.866 & 0 \\ 0 & 0 & 1.000 \end{bmatrix},$$

respectively.

The combined transformation matrix is

$$\mathbf{T} = \mathbf{R} \times \mathbf{S} = \begin{bmatrix} 1.732 & -1.500 & 0 \\ 1.000 & 2.598 & 0 \\ 0 & 0 & 1.000 \end{bmatrix}$$

Transformed vertices are $Q = \{\mathbf{A}', \mathbf{B}', \mathbf{C}' \text{ and } \mathbf{D}'\}$ such that

$$\mathbf{Q} = \mathbf{T} \times \mathbf{P} = \begin{bmatrix} 1.732 & -1.500 & 0 \\ 1.000 & 2.598 & 0 \\ 0 & 0 & 1.000 \end{bmatrix} \times \begin{bmatrix} 1 & 7 & 6 & 2 \\ 1 & 1 & 5 & 5 \\ 1 & 1 & 1 & 1 \end{bmatrix}$$

Therefore, we get,

$$\mathbf{Q} = \begin{bmatrix} 0.23 & 10.62 & 2.89 & -4.04 \\ 3.60 & 9.60 & 18.99 & 14.99 \\ 0 & 0 & 0 & 1.00 \end{bmatrix}$$

In order to find the affine transformation matrix, let us consider that $\{\mathbf{A}', \mathbf{B}', \mathbf{C}'\}$ represent the input set of 3 vertices, and $\{\mathbf{A}, \mathbf{B}, \mathbf{C}\}$ represent the base or reference set of 3 vertices.

Therefore, the set of equations to be solved to determine the affine co-efficients

$$\begin{aligned}
x_{21} &= a_{11} \cdot x_{11} + a_{12} \cdot y_{11} + a_{13} \\
x_{22} &= a_{11} \cdot x_{12} + a_{12} \cdot y_{12} + a_{13} \\
x_{23} &= a_{11} \cdot x_{13} + a_{12} \cdot y_{13} + a_{13} \\
y_{21} &= a_{21} \cdot x_{11} + a_{22} \cdot y_{11} + a_{23} \\
y_{22} &= a_{21} \cdot x_{12} + a_{22} \cdot y_{12} + a_{23} \\
y_{23} &= a_{21} \cdot x_{13} + a_{22} \cdot y_{13} + a_{23}
\end{aligned}$$

becomes

$$
\begin{aligned}
a_{11} \times x_{11} + a_{12} \times y_{11} + a_{13} &= 1.0 \\
a_{11} \times x_{12} + a_{12} \times y_{12} + a_{13} &= 1.0 \\
a_{11} \times x_{13} + a_{12} \times y_{13} + a_{13} &= 7.0 \\
a_{21} \times x_{11} + a_{22} \times y_{11} + a_{23} &= 1.0 \\
a_{21} \times x_{12} + a_{22} \times y_{12} + a_{23} &= 6.0 \\
a_{21} \times x_{13} + a_{22} \times y_{13} + a_{23} &= 5.0
\end{aligned}
$$

Solving this set of equations, we arrive at the affine transformation matrix as

$$
\mathbf{A} = \begin{bmatrix} 0.4331 & 0.2500 & 0.0004 \\ -0.1667 & 0.2887 & -0.0010 \\ 0 & 0 & 1.0000 \end{bmatrix}
$$

Now, to verify whether this affine matrix is correct or not we shall apply it over the fourth vertex, i.e. $\mathbf{D}$ and $\mathbf{D}'$. And we arrive at,

$$
\mathbf{A} \times \mathbf{D}' = \begin{bmatrix} 0.4331 & 0.2500 & 0.0004 \\ -0.1667 & 0.2887 & -0.0010 \\ 0 & 0 & 1.0000 \end{bmatrix} \times \begin{bmatrix} -4.04 \\ 14.99 \\ 1.00 \end{bmatrix} = \begin{bmatrix} 1.9982 \\ 5.0001 \\ 1.0000 \end{bmatrix} \approx \mathbf{D}
$$

That is original $\mathbf{D}$ vertex is arrived at.

♣

It is notable that, in case of the above example we could have directly arrived at the desired reverse transformation matrix (affine transformation matrix) by simply taking inverse of matrix $\mathbf{T}$. In this case we arrive at

$$
\mathbf{T}^{-1} = \begin{bmatrix} 0.4330 & 0.2500 & 0.0000 \\ -0.1667 & 0.2887 & -0.0000 \\ 0 & 0 & 1.0000 \end{bmatrix}
$$

which is the same as the one derived earlier. This inverse technique is, however, possible to apply here only because of the fact that the deforming transformations and their forms are known a priori. In case of any arbitrary, complex and unknown type of transformations, we must derive the affine transformation matrix.

An application of the above technique over the distorted *Cameraman* image is shown in Figure 9.1. Here, the original is scaled by a scale factor of 0.6 along both sides, and then rotated by 30° in anticlockwise direction. The registered image by applying affine transformation is found almost similar to the original one. The difference between the original image and the registered image is somewhat significant here, because we have selected input and reference set of points manually which is erroneous. Note that, here we have used the original image itself as the target image.

Figure 9.1: Image restoration: (a) original *Cameraman* image, (b) Distorted image, (c) Recovered image and (d) Difference between (a) and (c). (Reference and base points are shown in circles.)

9.3 Problems of Transforming Digital Images

In the above process of image transformation, we try to map each pixel from the source (input) image to a corresponding pixel in the destination (output). In case of digital images all coordinate locations are integral, but transformation results are not discrete (integral) always. That is, while the input coordinates are always integers, the outputs may not. Hence, we may follow a rounding process for computing appropriate integral coordinates.

9.3.1 Direct Mapping

Since the rounding process cannot guarantee to produce strictly monotonic outputs [i.e. for $x_1 < x_2$, round($x_1 <$ round(x_2) is not ensured], we may face situations where

- some locations exist in the output image where no input pixel is mapped, and
- some locations exist in the output image where multiple pixels of the source image are mapped.

That is in the direct mapping method, there are possibilities of existence of holes (pixel locations having no intensity value assigned to it), and pixel locations where a number of intensity values compete for occupation while receiving only the last assigned value.

9.3.2 Reverse Mapping

Instead of mapping source locations onto destination locations, we can compute destination coordinates from source coordinates also. Here, the source coordinates always have integral values, but not the destination coordinates. Hence, use of rounding operation may lead to situations where

- some locations exist in the source image which are not mapped to any destination pixel, and
- some locations exist in the source image which are mapped to multiple source pixels.

To overcome above problems in mapping or reverse mapping processes, we need to apply a grey level interpolation technique.

9.3.3 Grey Level Interpolation

Let, an image $g(u, v)$ is obtained from another image $f(p, q)$ by applying some transformation. Now we have to calculate the grey values in the destination image g. We can do this by applying reverse transformation over g to get corresponding location in original image f. For the reverse transformation g is the source and f is the destination image respectively. Let, the transformation is applied over source image g for mapping its pixels onto those of the destination image f. Applying the transformation on a pixel located at (u, v) in g, suppose, we get the destination location (x, y) of the original source image f. If the resultant co-ordinate values x and y are integral then the intensity value at (x, y) in f is directly substituted at location (u, v) in the destination image g. Otherwise, intensity of the non-integral co-ordinate (x, y) in f is calculated by interpolating intensities of neighbor pixels of (x, y) and transferred to the destination image at location (u, v). The above process is repeated for each location (u, v) in g.

The simplest interpolation technique, in this regard, is the linear interpolation. Let us consider the situation depicted in Figure 9.2. Here, we need to find out interpolated intensity value at non-integral pixel location (x, y) having integral neighbour locations (p, q), $(p, q + 1)$, $(p + 1, q)$ and $(p + 1, q + 1)$. Here, p and q represent integer parts of x and y, respectively. Now, let us define $d_x = x - p$ and $d_y = y - q$, respectively such that $0 \leq d_x, d_y \leq 1$. We can also use $p = \lfloor x \rfloor$ and $q = \lfloor y \rfloor$, i.e. $d_x = x - p = x - \lfloor x \rfloor$ and $d_y = y - q = y - \lfloor y \rfloor$. In this case, using linear interpolation, we can find out the destination intensity as

$$\begin{aligned} f(x,y) &= (1 - d_y)\left[(1 - d_x)\ f(p,q) + d_x\ f(p,q+1)\right] \\ &\quad + d_y\left[(1 - d_x)\ f(p+1,q) + d_x\ f(p+1,q+1)\right] \end{aligned} \tag{9.14}$$

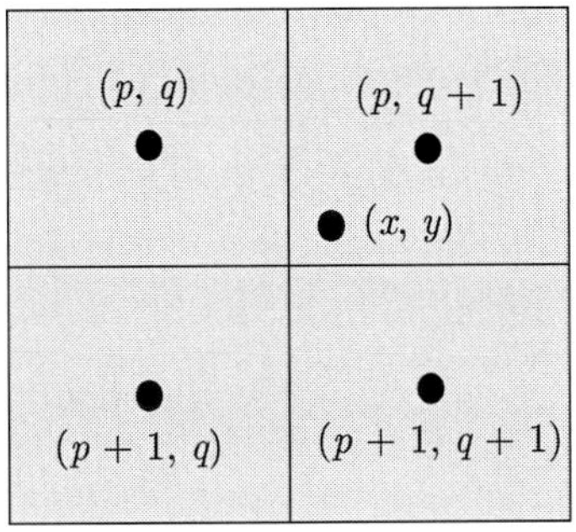

Figure 9.2: Determining intensity value at non-integral pixel location (x, y) by interpolation.

The complexity of the bilinear interpolation can be avoided by using another technique. Here, instead of interpolation, we can simply use the following relations:

$$x = \text{round}(x) \quad \text{and} \quad y = \text{round}(y).$$

This scheme is called the **nearest neighbour** mapping.

Application of such intensity mapping procedures may not be applicable for binary images. Because in that case a value between 0 and 1 may be generated which is useless.

An application of the above mentioned bilinear interpolation technique is shown in Figure 9.3. Here, the *Lena* image is rotated by 300°. The rotated image (Figure 9.3(b)) is found to have many gaps within it. This effect of direct mapping is removed by using interpolation technique as shown in Figure 9.3(c).

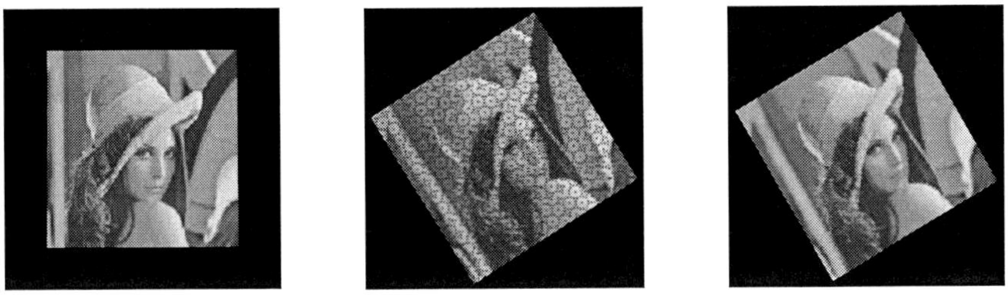

(a) (b) (c)

Figure 9.3: Rotation of the *Lena* image and its reconstruction by interpolation.

9.4 Problems

1. What is image registration and why is it needed?
2. Find out similarities between plane projective transformation and affine transformation.

3. What is homogeneous transformation? What is its significance in image geometry transformation?
4. Write an algorithm to perform any type of geometrical transformations (either basic or composite) using calls to translation, scaling and rotation routines and a matrix multiplication routine.
5. A rectangular polygon with vertices at (x_1, y_1), (x_2, y_1), (x_2, y_2) and (x_1, y_2) is to be scaled to quadruple its area without changing its centroid. Write down the sequence of basic transformation matrices needed to do this.
6. Derive the transformation matrix to rotate an object by 30° about the origin. What will be the effect of applying this matrix operator on the point $P(2, -6)$?
7. Perform a 45° rotation in the anticlockwise direction of the triangle $A(0,0)$, $B(1,1)$, $C(5,2)$ about (a) the origin, and (b) the point $(-1,-1)$.
8. Magnify the triangle with vertices at $A(0,0)$, $B(1,1)$ and $C(5,2)$ to twice its size while keeping $C(5,2)$ fixed.
9. Reflect the polygon with vertices $A(-1,0)$, $B(0,2)$, $C(1,0)$ and $D(0,2)$ about (a) the horizontal line $y = 2$, (b) the vertical line $x = 2$ and (c) the line $y = x+2$.
10. Prove that a $2D$ transformation matrix is always of the form:

$$\begin{bmatrix} a & b & c \\ d & e & f \\ 0 & 0 & 1 \end{bmatrix}$$

11. Establish the logic for making correspondence between two images of the same objects captured differently.
12. Apply scaling ($s_x = 2, s_y = 2$) and rotation (30°) transformations over an input image of size 64×64. Apply the combined transformation on the same image. Compute the advantage gained in the later method.
13. Explain the role of interpolation in transforming a grey image properly.
14. An image is rotated by 30° in anticlockwise direction and then scaled down by a factor of 0.5 along both axes. Deduce the reverse mapping matrix.

Chapter 10

Edge Detection

Although a digital image contains a huge amount of information regarding the intensity or colour of each and every pixel of its constituent objects and the background, the most important of them is lying at the boundaries of objects and background. The outer shape of an object is the most valuable information to the human visual system for its recognition and shape of an object is most clearly defined by its boundaries or edges. In many applications, related to image analysis and understanding, detected edges are the principal inputs. Detection of edges allows us to store structural information of the objects present in an image in a very small storage area. Thus, detection of edges or boundaries allows us to

- preserve structural information of objects and background,
- save storage, and
- reduce communication overhead.

10.1 Objective of Edge Detection

Edge detection process identifies all the lines (straight or curved) that form outline of the objects present in the image. The performance criteria for any edge detector is described by the following factors.

Good detection: Low probability of failing to mark real edge points and low probability of falsely marking non-edge points.

Good localization: Edge points detected should be as close as possible to the real edge points.

Single response to single edge point: In some cases, more than one response of the edge detector is found for the same edge pattern. It will elude the viewer regarding the presence of thin structures which are really non-existent.

However, the edge detectors rarely satisfy the above criteria. There are many difficulties for the edge detectors to fulfill their objectives. Some of the major problems of edge detection procedures are mentioned as follows.

- Poor lighting or poor capture devices often cause edges at places where they are really not. Thus, spurious edge patterns may be produced by the detectors.
- Object boundaries are often found to be incomplete or broken because at some positions in the images the background is too similar to the foreground. Thus, edge detectors fail in many cases to detect occurrences of such edge patterns.
- Ill definition of edges—Edge patterns, i.e. changes in grey shades may take different forms. Some of the common edge patterns are perfect step edge, roof edge, noisy step edge, spike edge, spike with step, etc. as shown in Figure 10.1. No edge detector can detect all sorts of edge patterns with the same perfection.
- Ill-posed nature of differentiation—Almost all image data are noisy. Due to imperfect capturing processes or for other reasons noises inevitably corrupt captured images. It is found that the differentiation processes are not robust against noise. Even a small amount of noise may disrupt the differentiation process. For example, let us consider the image $f(x)$ and the corrupted image $g(x)$. We also assume the presence of a source of periodic noise of the form $c\ \sin(wx)$, such that

  $$g(x) = f(x) + c\ \sin(wx)$$

  Now, $g(x) = f(x)$, if $c \to 0$. But, $g'(x)$ is quite different from $f'(x)$ if w is large. So the problem of differentiation is an ill posed one.
- Uncertainty of detection and localization—It can be mathematically verified that using the finite difference edge detectors, the detection and localization precesses are contradictory to each other. That is, good detection may lead to bad localization and vice versa.

Edges are not existing physically in an image. These are the positions of strong variations in intensity levels between consecutive pixel areas. This difference in intensity or brightness levels is detected by human visual system as presence of boundaries at those positions. So, we can say that edges are the positions of discontinuity of the image intensity function. Apart from object boundaries, false edges may also be produced by the uneven distribution of a particular incident light, shades of objects, transparency of objects, etc. The process of edge detection is, therefore, a challenging task. For a binary (two level) image, detection of edges is straightforward. A simple thresholding operation is sufficient for this purpose. The process becomes complex when we consider a grey level or a continuous tone colour image. In such cases, abrupt changes in the intensity patterns are not always found, even in the boundary areas. Thus, detection and localization of edge patterns become complicated. As in mathematics, we determine functional discontinuities by using difference or derivative operators, a number of derivative operators are applied for boundary detection also. Commonly used operators are the first and second order derivatives and their combinations. After the preliminary detection of edges, they, in most cases, seem to be discontinuous and fragmented. Hence, some other operation is applied to link these otherwise isolated parts. Also, existence of spurious edge patterns, generally produced by existence of noise in the image or limitations of the derivative operator, are eliminated by some thresholding operations.

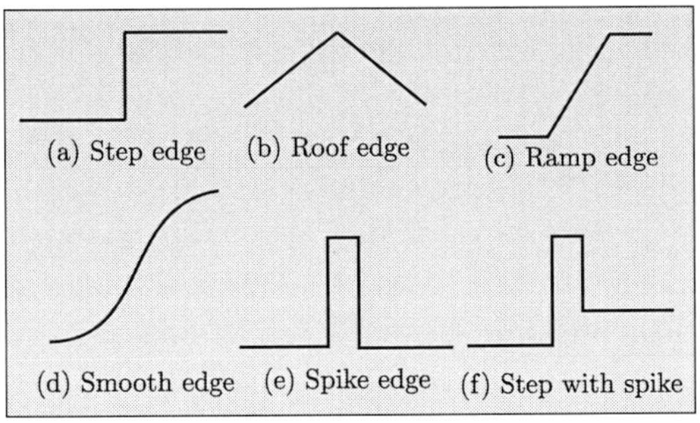

Figure 10.1: Edge patterns.

10.2 General Techniques for Edge Detection

In edge detection we actually detect discontinuity or abrupt changes in grey levels. So, the implementation of edge detectors involve computing derivatives in the 2D intensity images. Differences of first and second orders are commonly used. First order detectors are generally called **gradient operators**, and the second order detectors are termed Laplacian operators. Some edge images, their graphical form and response of first and second order operators are shown in Figures 10.3 and 10.4.

10.2.1 Gradient Edge Detectors

A 3×3 image matrix can be written as

$f(x-1, y-1)$	$f(x, y-1)$	$f(x+1, y-1)$
$f(x-1, y)$	$f(x, y)$	$f(x+1, y)$
$f(x-1, y+1)$	$f(x+1, y)$	$f(x+1, y+1)$

Gradients can be computed in both X and Y directions. Using mathematical symbols gradient vector can be written as

$$\nabla f = \begin{bmatrix} \nabla_x f \\ \nabla_y f \end{bmatrix} = \begin{bmatrix} \dfrac{\delta f}{\delta x} \\ \dfrac{\delta f}{\delta y} \end{bmatrix} \tag{10.1}$$

where,

$$\begin{aligned} \nabla_x f &= \frac{\delta f}{\delta x} &= f(x,y) - f(x-1,y) \\ \nabla_y f &= \frac{\delta f}{\delta y} &= f(x,y) - f(x,y-1) \end{aligned}$$

When put in a mask form, we get

$$\nabla_x f = \begin{bmatrix} -1 & 1 \end{bmatrix} \qquad \text{and} \qquad \nabla_y f = \begin{bmatrix} -1 \\ 1 \end{bmatrix}$$

Example 1: Let us apply the above detectors for a binary image given below.

$$\begin{bmatrix} 1 & 1 & 1 & 1 & 1 \\ 1 & 1 & 1 & 1 & 1 \\ 1 & 1 & 1 & 0 & 0 \\ 1 & 1 & 0 & 0 & 0 \\ 1 & 1 & 0 & 0 & 0 \end{bmatrix}$$

Applying ∇_x and ∇_y, we get the following intermediate edge patterns:

$$\begin{bmatrix} 0 & 0 & 0 & 0 & * \\ 0 & 0 & 0 & 0 & * \\ 0 & 0 & -1 & 0 & * \\ 0 & -1 & 0 & 0 & * \\ 0 & -1 & 0 & 0 & * \end{bmatrix} \text{ and } \begin{bmatrix} 0 & 0 & 0 & 0 & 0 \\ 0 & 0 & 0 & 1 & 1 \\ 0 & 0 & 1 & 0 & 0 \\ 0 & 0 & 0 & 0 & 0 \\ * & * & * & * & * \end{bmatrix}$$

The symbol '*' in the above edge patterns indicates indeterminate values. We can find these values by zero-padding the original image to the right and bottom. Actual edge patterns are found out by merging these two intermediate patterns. The result is given below.

$$\begin{bmatrix} 0 & 0 & 0 & 0 & 0 \\ 0 & 0 & 0 & 1 & 1 \\ 0 & 0 & 1 & 0 & 0 \\ 0 & 1 & 0 & 0 & 0 \\ 0 & 1 & 0 & 0 & 0 \end{bmatrix}$$

We can also write the gradient operators as

$$\nabla_x f = f(x, y) - f(x-1, y) \tag{10.2}$$

and

$$\nabla_y f = f(x, y) - f(x, y-1) \tag{10.3}$$

Putting in a 2 × 2 mask form, we get

$$\nabla_x f = \begin{bmatrix} 0 & 0 \\ -1 & 1 \end{bmatrix} \quad \text{and} \quad \nabla_y f = \begin{bmatrix} 0 & -1 \\ 0 & 1 \end{bmatrix}$$

The above masks are called **ordinary operators**. Roberts developed another operator, considering diagonally oriented masks, which are given by

$$\nabla_x f = f(x, y) - f(x-1, y-1) \tag{10.4}$$

and

$$\nabla_y f = f(x, y-1) - f(x-1, y) \tag{10.5}$$

Putting in a 2 × 2 mask form we get,

$$\nabla_x f = \begin{bmatrix} -1 & 0 \\ 0 & 1 \end{bmatrix} \quad \text{and} \quad \nabla_y f = \begin{bmatrix} 0 & 1 \\ -1 & 0 \end{bmatrix}$$

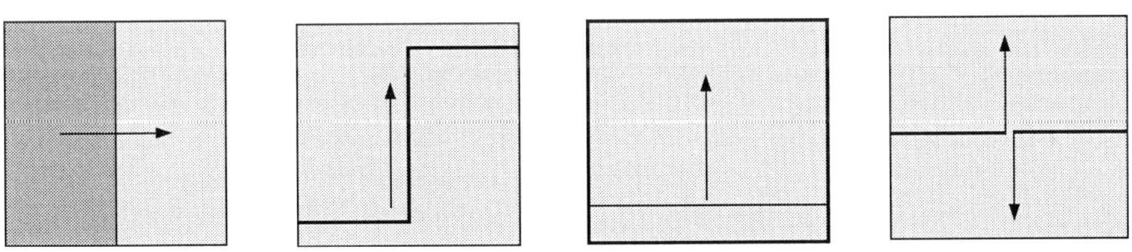

(a) Input image (b) Graphical form (c) First difference (d) Second difference

Figure 10.2: Step edge.

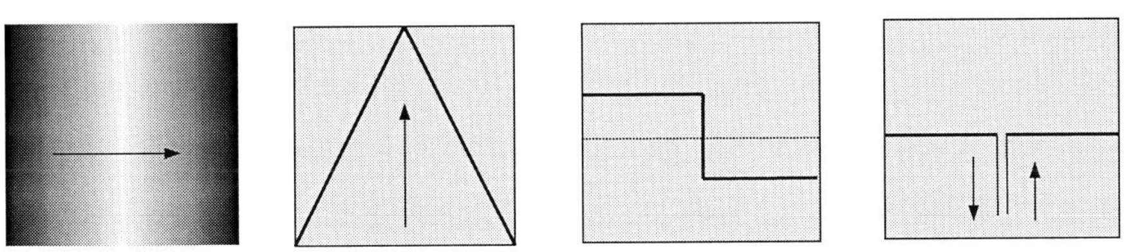

(a) Input image (b) Graphical form (c) First difference (d) Second difference

Figure 10.3: Roof edge.

Chaudhury and Chanda have developed a 3 × 3 4-neighbour operator given by

$$\nabla_x f = \begin{bmatrix} 0 & 0 & 0 \\ -1 & 0 & 1 \\ 0 & 0 & 0 \end{bmatrix} \quad \text{and} \quad \nabla_y f = \begin{bmatrix} 0 & -1 & 0 \\ 0 & 0 & 0 \\ 0 & 1 & 0 \end{bmatrix}$$

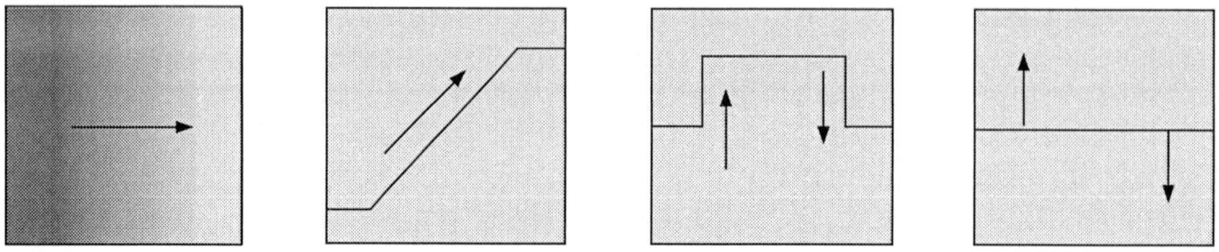

(a) Input image (b) Graphical form (c) First difference (d) Second difference

Figure 10.4: Ramp edge.

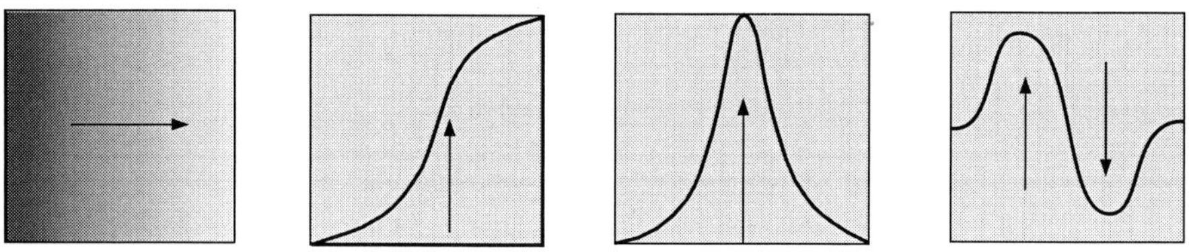

(a) Input image (b) Graphical form (c) First difference (d) Second difference

Figure 10.5: Smooth edge.

∇_x can also be written as

$$\nabla_x f = \frac{\delta f}{\delta x} = f(x+1, y) - f(x, y) \tag{10.6}$$

Therefore, adding Eqs. (10.2) and (10.6) we get,

$$2\nabla_x f = -f(x-1, y) + f(x, y) \tag{10.7}$$

and

$$2\nabla_y f = -f(x, y-1) + f(x, y+1) \tag{10.8}$$

Putting in a 3×3 mask form,

$$\nabla_x f = \begin{bmatrix} -1 & 0 & 1 \end{bmatrix} \quad \text{and} \quad \nabla_y f = \begin{bmatrix} -1 \\ 0 \\ 1 \end{bmatrix}$$

Here, we have eliminated the constant factor of 2. A 3×3 mask can be formed as

$$\nabla_x f = \begin{bmatrix} -1 & 0 & 1 \\ -1 & 0 & 1 \\ -1 & 0 & 1 \end{bmatrix} \quad \text{and} \quad \nabla_y f = \begin{bmatrix} -1 & -1 & -1 \\ 0 & 0 & 0 \\ 1 & 1 & 1 \end{bmatrix}$$

The above is the 'Prewitt operator' for edge detection. Adding weights at the centre of the above masks we get the 'Sobel operator' as

$$\nabla_x f = \begin{bmatrix} -1 & 0 & 1 \\ -2 & 0 & 2 \\ -1 & 0 & 1 \end{bmatrix} \quad \text{and} \quad \nabla_y f = \begin{bmatrix} -1 & -2 & -1 \\ 0 & 0 & 0 \\ 1 & 2 & 1 \end{bmatrix}$$

Edge detectors based on first derivative of the image function are also called **compass operators** because of their ability to find gradient direction.

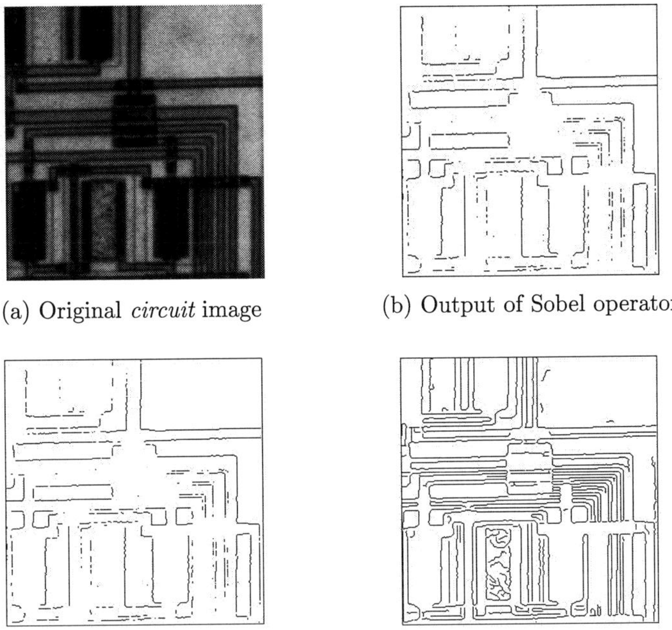

(a) Original *circuit* image (b) Output of Sobel operator

(c) Output of Prewitt operator (d) Output of Canny operator

Figure 10.6: Detected boundaries.

10.2.2 Laplacian Edge Detectors

Laplacian is the second derivative. Taking derivative of the gradient, we get

$$\nabla^2 f = \frac{\delta^2 f}{\delta x^2} + \frac{\delta^2 f}{\delta y^2} \tag{10.9}$$

Here,

$$\begin{aligned} \frac{\delta^2 f}{\delta x^2} &= \frac{f(x,y) - f(x-1,y)}{\delta x} \\ &= \frac{\delta f(x,y)}{\delta x} - \frac{\delta f(x-1,y)}{\delta x} \\ &= f(x,y) - f(x-1,y) - f(x-1,y) + f(x-2,y) \\ &= f(x,y) - 2f(x-1,y) + f(x-2,y) \end{aligned} \tag{10.10}$$

Since the above relation is position independent, we can write

$$\begin{aligned} \frac{\delta^2 f}{\delta x^2} &= f(x+1,y) - 2f(x,y) + f(x-1,y) \\ &= f(x-1,y) - 2f(x,y) + f(x+1,y) \end{aligned} \tag{10.11}$$

Similarly,

$$\frac{\delta^2 f}{\delta y^2} = f(x, y-1) - 2f(x, y) + f(x, y+1) \tag{10.12}$$

Combining the Eqs. (10.11) and (10.12)

$$\nabla^2 f = f(x-1, y) + f(x-1, y) - 4f(x, y) + f(x, y-1) + f(x, y+1) \tag{10.13}$$

which can be represented as a 3×3 mask

$$L = \begin{bmatrix} 0 & 1 & 0 \\ 1 & -4 & 1 \\ 0 & 1 & 0 \end{bmatrix} \quad \text{or} \quad L = \begin{bmatrix} 0 & -1 & 0 \\ -1 & 4 & -1 \\ 0 & -1 & 0 \end{bmatrix}$$

Again adding higher weight (putting more stress) at the central pixel we get a modified mask

$$L = \begin{bmatrix} 0 & 1 & 0 \\ 1 & -8 & 1 \\ 0 & 1 & 0 \end{bmatrix} \quad \text{or} \quad L = \begin{bmatrix} 0 & -1 & 0 \\ -1 & 8 & -1 \\ 0 & -1 & 0 \end{bmatrix}$$

Also, exchanging 1s and 0s, we get

$$L = \begin{bmatrix} 1 & 0 & 1 \\ 0 & -4 & 0 \\ 1 & 0 & 1 \end{bmatrix} \quad \text{or} \quad L = \begin{bmatrix} -1 & 0 & -1 \\ 0 & 4 & 0 \\ -1 & 0 & -1 \end{bmatrix}$$

All the above second derivative masks are called 4-neighbourhood Laplacian masks. Combining two 4-neighbourhood masks (before and after exchanging 1s and 0s), we get 8-neighbourhood masks as

$$L = \begin{bmatrix} 1 & 1 & 1 \\ 1 & -8 & 1 \\ 1 & 1 & 1 \end{bmatrix} \quad \text{or} \quad L = \begin{bmatrix} -1 & -1 & -1 \\ -1 & 8 & -1 \\ -1 & -1 & -1 \end{bmatrix}$$

One major disadvantage of the Laplacian detector is that it may respond doubly to some edge patterns present in the image. Laplacians are unable to determine gradient direction, they compute gradient magnitudes only.

10.3 Difference between First and Second Order Detectors

In the above section, it has been shown that a second order operator is obtained by repeated application of a first order operator. While first order operators determine difference in grey values in the image, second order operators find out difference of gradients. In case of step like edges in the image, the first derivative have a maxima or a minima at the position of the edge, while the second derivative corresponds to a zero crossing at this position. Hence, the location of the true edge can be easily identified using a second derivative. There are situations when intensity variations are smooth, but a hidden abrupt variation of the gradient exists. In such situations second order operators become more useful. The following examples will clarify the matter.

Example 2: The input image indicates a constant variation of grey levels.

$$\begin{bmatrix} 1 & 2 & 3 & 4 & 5 & 6 & 7 & 8 & 9 \\ 1 & 2 & 3 & 4 & 5 & 6 & 7 & 8 & 9 \\ 1 & 2 & 3 & 4 & 5 & 6 & 7 & 8 & 9 \\ 1 & 2 & 3 & 4 & 5 & 6 & 7 & 8 & 9 \\ 1 & 2 & 3 & 4 & 5 & 6 & 7 & 8 & 9 \end{bmatrix}$$

Applying the Sobel operator (First order detector) in the following form.

$$S = \begin{bmatrix} -1 & 0 & 1 \\ -2 & 0 & 2 \\ -1 & 0 & 1 \end{bmatrix}$$

we get the output as

$$\begin{bmatrix} 8 & 8 & 8 & 8 & 8 & 8 & 8 \\ 8 & 8 & 8 & 8 & 8 & 8 & 8 \\ 8 & 8 & 8 & 8 & 8 & 8 & 8 \end{bmatrix}$$

i.e. an all 8 grey value image. Now, if we consider 5 to be the threshold for edge detection, all the output pixels become edge pixels, which is incorrect. Applying the same operator produces a row of zeros only which looks like

$$\begin{bmatrix} 0 & 0 & 0 & 0 & 0 \end{bmatrix}$$

So, in this case, repeated application of a first order detector produces a zero response at all the image locations.

The same result can be obtained by a single application of the second order laplacian operator of the form

$$L = \begin{bmatrix} -1 & 0 & -1 \\ 0 & 4 & 0 \\ -1 & 0 & -1 \end{bmatrix}$$

Here, the result becomes

$$\begin{bmatrix} 0 & 0 & 0 & 0 & 0 & 0 & 0 \end{bmatrix}$$

Sometimes, images come with smooth variation of intensity or colours along them. One side of such an image contains lighter shades which gradually changes to a darker shade on the other side. A proper edge between these two regions (lighter and darker) can be hardly found using a gradient (first operator). A second order operator can, in many cases, effectively find out a proper boundary in such cases.

It is also notable that while the first order operators produce directional gradients, the outputs of second order operators are non-directional, and hence, they possess good localization characteristics.

Example 3: The input image indicates a smooth variation of grey levels.

$$\begin{bmatrix} 1 & 2 & 4 & 7 & 10 & 12 & 13 \\ 1 & 2 & 4 & 7 & 10 & 12 & 13 \\ 1 & 2 & 4 & 7 & 10 & 12 & 13 \\ 1 & 2 & 4 & 7 & 10 & 12 & 13 \\ 1 & 2 & 4 & 7 & 10 & 12 & 13 \end{bmatrix}$$

Applying the above first order operator, we get

$$\begin{bmatrix} 12 & 20 & 24 & 20 & 12 \\ 12 & 20 & 24 & 20 & 12 \\ 12 & 20 & 24 & 20 & 12 \end{bmatrix}$$

Here, although an edge detection is possible using a high threshold, it is very difficult to determine the threshold.

Again, applying the Laplacian, we get

$$\begin{bmatrix} -2 & -2 & 0 & 2 & 2 \\ -2 & -2 & 0 & 2 & 2 \\ -2 & -2 & 0 & 2 & 2 \end{bmatrix}$$

It is seen from the above result that the edge is clearly lying at the second order zero-crossing of the Laplacian. Hence, detection is easier in this case.

From the above examples, it is clear that the Laplacian operators are able to effectively determine an edge structure when the input image contains smooth or continuous variation of intensity or colours between objects and background. Actually, the Laplacian enhances and highlight regions of more discrete variations within the image and ignores minor variations. Since Laplacian is very sensitive to noise in an image, sometimes it is useful to apply some kind of Gaussian smoothing before applying laplacian. This kind of operators are called Laplacian-of-Gaussian (LoG). Use of such LoG operators helps eliminating spurious and noisy edge responses. The algorith for Laplacian-of-Gaussian edge detector is given below.

1. Smooth the original image $f(x, y)$ using a Gaussian smoothing mask.
2. Apply the laplacian mask operator over the smoothed image.
3. Determine the zero-crossings in the output of the laplacian operator.

10.4 Uncertainty of Detection and Localization

It is already mentioned that there exist an uncertainty principle relating detection and localization of noisy edges, and there is direct trade-off between these two. To get an analytical verification of the above statement, let us assume that the image is composed of the edge pattern with white Gaussian noise added to it.

Let the edge detector function be represented by $e(x)$ and the edge image itself by $g(x)$. We also assume that the edge is centred at $x = 0$. Then the response of the detector to the edge at its centre h_g can be defined as a convolution integral

$$h_g = \int_{-w}^{+w} g(-x)e(x)dx$$

The root mean square response to the noise $n(x)$ only will be

$$h_n = n_0 \times \left\{ \int_{-w}^{+w} e^2(x)dx \right\}^{1/2}$$

where n_0^2 is the mean-squared noise amplitude per unit length. The output signal-to-noise ratio (SNR) is thus given by

$$\text{SNR} = \frac{\| \int_{-w}^{+w} g(-x)e(x)dx \|}{n_0 \times \left\{ \int_{-w}^{+w} e^2(x)dx \right\}^{\frac{1}{2}}} \tag{10.14}$$

For the localization criterion, we need some measures that increase localization improves, and we shall use the reciprocal of the root-mean-square distance from the centre of the true edge. We want to select edge pixels at the local maxima in the response of the operator $e(x)$. Therefore, the first derivative of the response will be zero at these points. Since the edges are created at $x = 0$, in absence of noise, there will be a local maxima in the total response at the point at $x = 0$.

As already mentioned, $h_n(x)$ is the response of the detector to the noise only, and $h_g(x)$ is that for the edge only. If there is a local maxima in the total response $h_g(x) + h_n(x)$ at $x = x_0$, we can write

$$h'_g(x_0) + h'_n(x_0) = 0$$

Taylor series expansion of $h'_g(x_0)$ about the origin can be expressed as

$$h'_g(x_0) = h'_g(0) + h''_g(0) \times x_0 + \mathcal{O}(x_0^2)$$

Here, $h'_g(0) = 0$, i.e. the response of the operator in absence of noise has a maximum at the origin, so the first term in the above expression can be ignored. The displacement

x_0 of the actual maxima is assumed to be small, so we can ignore the quadratic and other higher order terms. It can be shown that if the edge is either or antisymmetric, all even terms in the expansion will vanish. Therefore, we arrive at

$$h''_g(0) \times x_0 = -h'_n(x_0) \tag{10.15}$$

Now, $h'_n(x_0)$ is a Gaussian random quantity whose variance is the mean squared value of $h'_n(x_0)$ and is given by Eq. (10.16)

$$E[h'_n(x_0)^2] = n_0^2 \int_{-w}^{+w} e'^2(x)dx \tag{10.16}$$

So, combining this result with Eq. (10.15) and substituting for $h''_g(0)$, we get

$$E[x_0^2] = \frac{n_0^2 \times \left\{\int_{-w}^{+w} e'^2(x)dx\right\}}{\left\{\int_{-w}^{+w} g'(-x)e'(x)dx\right\}^2} = \delta x_0{}^2$$

where δx_0 is an approximation to the standard deviation of x_0. The localization is defined as the reciprocal of δx_0, i.e.

$$\text{Localization} = \frac{\| \int_{-w}^{+w} g'(-x)e'(x)dx \|}{n_0 \times \left\{\int_{-w}^{+w} e'^2(x)dx\right\}^{1/2}} \tag{10.17}$$

Equations (10.14) and (10.17) are mathematical forms for the criteria for detection and localization, respectively. Design of an optimal edge detector requires the maximization of both of these expressions, simultaneously. But, it is not possible to find a function $e(x)$ that satisfies these criteria, simultaneously.

10.5 Some Other Finite Difference Edge Detectors

Besides the first and second edge detectors described in above sections, there exist some other common edge detectors that combine selective and specific features of different first, second or third order differences. These are found to be very useful for many applications. Canny has developed a difference operator using directional gradients. The details of the operator is included in the following subsection. It is notable that considering directional gradients we can improve the performance of the finite difference edge detectors to a great extent. The Canny's algorithm reports boundaries at peaks of the first difference in the gradient direction. The other edge detectors we shall describe here are the Boie–Cox and Marr–Hildreth edge detectors.

10.5.1 Canny's Algorithm

Canny's algorithm marks boundaries at the maximum of image gradient magnitude in the direction of the gradient. Actually, here the edge direction is reduced to one of the four possible directions. A mask is considered to compute the gradient magnitude along these directions. Then by following a non-maximal suppression procedure the edge strength along the proper direction is maintained. Canny applied a double thresholding technique commonly known as hysteresis. The upper and lower thresholds are determined by the user. Actually selection of threshold is application dependent. Originally Canny used the following masks:

−1	1
−1	1

and

−1	−1
1	1

to compute the X and Y components of the gradient. However, this method creates a symmetric bias in the boundary locations. Hence, instead of using the above masks, a modified implementation with masks

−1	0	1
0	0	0
−1	0	1

and

−1	0	−1
0	0	0
1	0	1

or

$$[-1\ 0\ 1] \quad \text{and} \quad [-1\ 0\ 1]^T$$

are used to compute first differences in the four directions, viz., *horizontal*(H), *vertical*(V), and *diagonal directions*$(D_1$ and $D_2)$, respectively. The X and Y components of the gradient are computed by projecting the diagonal differences onto the axes as

$$X = H + \frac{(D_1 + D_2)}{2}$$

$$Y = V + \frac{(D_1 - D_2)}{2}$$

If we consider the original masks, the above gradient components can be expressed as

$$H = \frac{1}{2} \times [-f(x,y) + f(x,y+1) - f(x+1,y) - f(x+1,y+1)]$$

$$V = \frac{1}{2} \times [-f(x,y) + f(x+1,y) - f(x,y+1) - f(x+1,y+1)]$$

$$D_1 = -f(x+1,y) + f(x,y+1)$$

$$D_2 = -f(x,y) + f(x+1,y+1)$$

Using modified masks, these differences will become

$$H = \frac{1}{2} \times [-f(x-1, y-1) + f(x-1, y+1) - f(x+1, y-1) - f(x+1, y+1)]$$

$$V = \frac{1}{2} \times [-f(x-1, y-1) + f(x+1, y-1) - f(x-1, y+1) - f(x+1, y+1)]$$

$$D_1 = -f(x+1, y-1) + f(x-1, y+1)$$

$$D_2 = -f(x-1, y-1) + f(x+1, y+1)$$

The amplitude of the gradient is then

$$A = \sqrt{X^2 + Y^2}.$$

At each cell, a value is then interpolated for a pseudo cell in the gradient direction. Values are extracted from the two neighbouring cells closest to the gradient direction: one from a horizontal or vertical direction (A_{hv}), and the other from a diagonal neighbour (A_d). Let, B be larger of the magnitudes of X and Y, and S be the smaller. The pseudo cell value is then

$$A_g = \frac{((B - S)A_{hv} + SA_d)}{B}$$

A value A_{-g} for a pseudo cell in the opposite direction is computed in the same way. A cell (x, y) is a boundary if $A(x, y)$ is greater than a threshold T_1 (we can consider this value to be 3.0), $A(x, y) \geq A_g(x, y)$ and $A(x, y) \leq A_{-g}(x, y)$.

The output of the real image may found to be noisy. Boundaries may be wobble and there may be spurious boundaries on the slopes. In such a situation, threshold T_1 may be set to higher values to disguish these problems, but they actually reflect some flaws in Canny's design.

These problems can be eliminated with a better peak detector. Just adding a threshold to Canny's peak detector eliminated real boundaries if they lie approximately halfway between the two cells. Instead, the new implementation interpolates two additional pseudo cell values A_{2g} and A_{-2g} using values of two cells from the starting locations. A cell (x, y) is then marked as a boundary if

$$A(x, y) \geq T_1$$

$$A_g(x, y) - A(x, y) \leq T_2$$

$$A_{-g}(x, y) - A(x, y) \leq T_2$$

$$A(x, y) - A_{2g}(x, y) > T_3$$

$$A(x, y) - A_{-2g}(x, y) > T_3$$

In the above T_2 and T_3 are two other user determined thresholds. Values of T_2 and T_3 are set to 3.75 and 5.1, respectively.

10.5.2 Boie–Cox Algorithm

Boie and Cox have proposed an algorithm similar to Canny's algorithm, but they replace the peak detector with second difference zero crossings and the gradient direction with the direction of the maximum first difference.

The new code computes the first and second differences in four directions, using the following masks:

$$[-1\ 0\ 1] \quad \text{and} \quad [-1\ \ 1\ \ 1\ -1]$$

Let, M be the magnitude of the maximum first difference, F and S are the first and second difference values in some direction, and (dx, dy) is a one pixel displacement in the same direction. For a cell (x, y) to be marked as a boundary in this direction, the first difference must be non-trivial and close to the maximum, i.e.

$$\|F(x,y)\| > T_1 \text{ and } M(x,y) - \|F(x,y)\| \leq T_2$$

The cell must also be a second order zero crossing, i.e. one of the following, or one of the similar expressions with '<' and '>' reserved must hold.

- $S(x+\frac{dx}{2}, y+\frac{dy}{2}) > T_3$ and $S(x-\frac{dx}{2}, y-\frac{dy}{2}) < -T_3$
- $\|S(x+\frac{dx}{2}, y+\frac{dy}{2})\| \leq T_3, S(x+\frac{3dx}{2}, y+\frac{3dy}{2}) < -T_3$ and $S(x-\frac{dx}{2}, y-\frac{dy}{2}) > T_3$
- $\|S(x-\frac{dx}{2}, y-\frac{dy}{2})\| \leq T_3, S(x+\frac{dx}{2}, y+\frac{dy}{2}) > T_3$ and $S(x-\frac{3dx}{2}, y-\frac{3dy}{2}) > T_3$

For majority of applications, the values of T_1, T_2 and T_3 can be set to 1.95, 1.95 and 2.25, respectively. In Boie–Cox's original design T_3 was set to 0. Just like the *missing threshold* on 'Canny's peak detector', this causes wobbly boundaries and spurious boundaries on slopes. Boie and Cox set T_1 to a higher value to compensate these effects.

This edge founder produces rings around junctions of four or more regions, like Canny's algorithm. It breaks only at a few sharp corners, but others have short spines sticking out of them.

10.5.3 Marr–Hildreth Algorithm

The Marr and Hildreth Algorithm locates boundaries at the zero crossings of the Laplacian, while also checks the sign of the first difference in the direction of the Laplacian's gradient. Therefore, here 3 different thresholds T_1, T_2 and T_3 are used corresponding to first, second and third order differences. The Laplacian is the sum of the directional second differences in all directions. The Laplacian is computed here using the following mask

$\frac{1}{\sqrt{2}}$	1	$\frac{1}{\sqrt{2}}$
1	$-4-\frac{2}{\sqrt{2}}$	1
$\frac{1}{\sqrt{2}}$	1	$\frac{1}{\sqrt{2}}$

Laplacian responses below a noise threshold T_2 are reset to zero. In majority of the situations a value of $T_2 = 3.85$ is found to produce good results. The Laplacian is well suited to localizing boundaries, but not to detecting them. First, some zero crossings of the Laplacian do not correspond to sharp changes in the intensity. Second, the Laplacian amplitude often drops below T_2 in the middle of the boundary. Sometimes, for multiple cells, if the boundary is blurred, it is difficult to distinguish these zero crossings in the middle of uniform intensity regions.

The direction map here is obtained by computing the directional first and third differences in four directions using masks

$$[-1 \;\; 0 \;\; 1] \quad \text{and} \quad [-1 \;\; -2 \;\; 0 \;\; 2 \;\; 1]$$

Values below T_1 and T_3 are reset to zeros. The values of $T_1 = 1.95$ and $T_3 = 3.05$ are useful in many situations. The detector responds if there is some direction in which the first and third differences have opposite non-zero signs.

10.6 Problems in Difference Edge Detectors

From the above discussion, it is clear that all of the finite difference edge detectors have their shortfalls. Most of the problems are related to detection and localization of appropriate boundary pixels. Besides these, most of the algorithms are found to produce several unwanted artifacts, like

- Biasing towards a direction.
- Spurious and unstable boundaries on slopes.
- Spurious, but stable boundaries in staircase patterns or near the edges of slopes.
- Gaps or spines at sharp corners.
- Small deformations at sharp corners.
- Rings at junctions.
- Gaps and small distortions at junctions.

Which artifacts seems most obstrusive will depend on the intended application. However, all these algorithms are easy to implement, run quickly and produce fair outputs. For an output oriented comparison, we have used a box image as shown in

Figure 10.7(a), and executed some finite difference edge detectors. The outputs obtained with Sobel, Prewitt, Canny, Boie–Cox and Marr–Hildreth algorithms are presented in Figures 10.7(b)-(f). These results clearly depicts the presence of different kinds of artifacts as discussed previously.

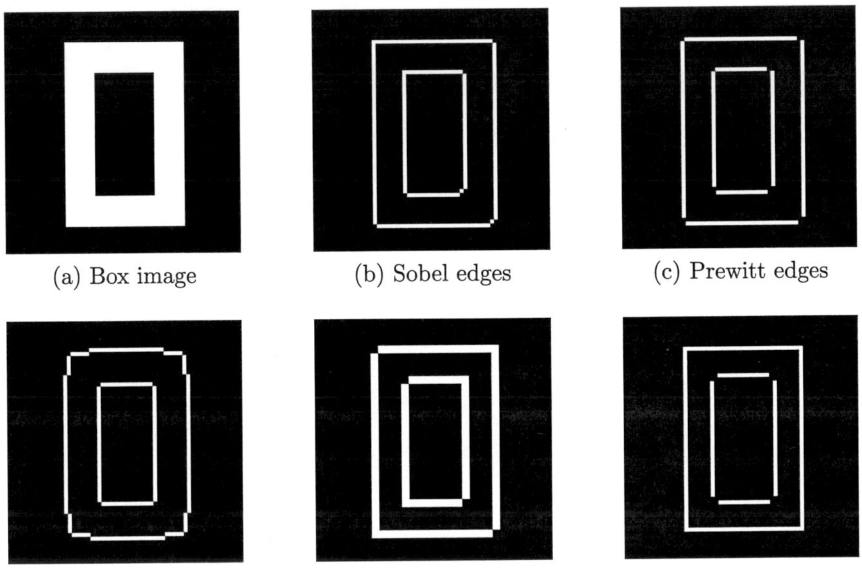

(a) Box image (b) Sobel edges (c) Prewitt edges

(d) Canny edges (e) Boie-Cox edges (f) Marr-Hildreth edges

Figure 10.7: Images and edge patterns.

Besides the finite difference detectors, there exist other kinds of simple edge detectors in literature which include edge linking, edge following, pyramid edge detectors, etc.

10.7 Problems

1. What are the motivations behind boundary detection?
2. Can we say that image smoothing and edge detection have conflicting objectives? Explain.
3. Explain the roles of first and second order difference operators in detection and localization of boundaries of an image. Use suitable examples for illustration.
4. Write down potential problems of boundary detection.
5. Develop a mask for first order gradient edge detector using differences in pixel values within a 2×2 pixel grid.
6. Develop the Laplacian edge detector based mask operator.

7. Consider the following image:

$$\begin{bmatrix} 1 & 0 & 1 & 1 & 1 & 1 & 4 & 5 \\ 1 & 0 & 1 & 1 & 3 & 2 & 4 & 3 \\ 1 & 0 & 2 & 4 & 5 & 5 & 5 & 4 \\ 1 & 0 & 0 & 4 & 5 & 6 & 4 & 6 \\ 1 & 1 & 2 & 4 & 5 & 6 & 5 & 4 \\ 0 & 1 & 1 & 5 & 6 & 6 & 1 & 2 \\ 1 & 2 & 1 & 6 & 5 & 5 & 2 & 2 \\ 0 & 2 & 3 & 5 & 6 & 6 & 1 & 3 \end{bmatrix}$$

   Apply Sobel and Prewitt edge detectors over this image with threshold value of 10. And also find out the difference of the two edge images.
8. List some artifacts that may be present in an edge detector output. Mention the reason behind this briefly.
9. Show that the Prewitt edge detector can be developed by convolving an image with mask [1 1 1] followed by $[-1\ 0\ 1]^T$ and then scaling the result by $\frac{1}{3}$.
10. Do you think that prior application of equalization will improve an edge detector performance? Explain.
11. Write down the roles of gradient directions in edge detection w.r.t. Canny's algorithm.
12. What kind of grey level variations are detected by a Laplacian edge detector: sharp changes or minor changes, and why?
13. Explain why addition or subtraction, whichever is applicable, of the Laplacian output to or from the original image has the effect of image sharpening.
14. Why LoG operator may be considered a better edge detector compared to the Laplacian operator?
15. What are hysteresis and non-maximal supression in Canny's edge detection algorithm? What are their importance?
16. List qualitative factors to determine an edge detector performance.

CHAPTER 11

Image Segmentation

Image segmentation is the process of partitioning the image into a set of objects and background. Identifying a particular object within an image is an important task in some applications. Let us consider the case of military application. An automatic air-to-ground target acquisition system, one of the interests is to identify an enemy-tank on the ground surface. The landcover may contain a combination of jungle, river, field, road, etc. Now, if the tank moves on the ground, the first task is to segment the field portion from the remaining parts of the image and then to segment the contents over the field into discrete objects of probable shape and sizes. Then using some matching criteria or recognition scheme, the tank may be identified and located appropriately. Thus, segmentation techniques basically divides the digital image into meaningful parts or regions. There may be number of different objects in the scene which have been isolated by the segmentation process. But only one or some of the objets might convey some meaning to the user of the system. So the problem of segmentation is more that of psycho-physical one. Since the object of interest must be associated with it some meaning to be conveyed, they are very hard to be defined mathematically. It is due to this reason, that there exists no general purpose segmentation algorithm. But, a number of different ad-hoc methods do exist in literature, some of which are applicable in some cases and some for others. The success of a segmentation process mostly depends on the appropriate choice of algorithm for a particular segmentation task. Also images of different category, such as, photographs, infra-red images, X-ray images or satellite images, etc. may need different types of segmentation criteria.

For monochrome images, segmentation algorithms are developed based on the two fundamental properties of the grey-level values. These properties are:

1. Discontinuity or abrupt changes in grey level between objects.
2. Similarity or homogeneity of grey levels over a region.

The first approach is to partition the image based on abrupt changes in the grey levels. The main idea behind these techniques is to identify boundaries or edges of an object, or identifying lines, circles or other known patterns within the image. These techniques can be categorized as *edge detection* techniques. The second approach is based on thresholding, region splitting and region merging, and are categorized under the heading of *region extraction*.

11.1 Measuring Discontinuities

There are generally three basic types of discontinuities present in a digital image. These are points, lines and edges. The most common approach to measure discontinuities is to use a square mask. The mask is moved over the image, at each image point computing the sum of products of the mask coefficients with the corresponding image grey values.

If we consider a mask of size 3×3, as shown below, the response of the mask at any point in the image is

$$R = w_1 f_1 + w_2 f_2 + \cdots + w_9 f_9 = \sum_{i=1}^{9} w_i f_i \tag{11.1}$$

w_1	w_2	w_3
w_4	w_5	w_6
w_7	w_8	w_9

where, f_i is the grey value of the pixel under the mask coefficient w_i. The response of the mask is defined with respect to the centre of the mask. When the mask in centred on a boundary pixel, image grey values corresponding to the cells of the mask that fall outside the image are considered to be zeros.

11.1.1 Point Detection Using Mask

Isolated points in an image are those points which have abruptly different grey values than those of its surrounding points. Thus, formation of a mask for point detection involves the idea of highlighting this grey value difference. An example of such a mask is shown below. For this mask, the response of the mask is zero when it is placed over a region having same grey values for all the pixels. However, if the central pixel contains a different grey value, the response of the mask is 8 times of the difference (in grey values). Here, our aim is to detect isolated points. So, a high response of the mask indicates a different central grey value and the presence of an isolated point. Thus, the criteria for selection of an isolated point can be formulated as

$$|R| > T \tag{11.2}$$

where, T is a non-negative threshold and R is the response of the mask.

One example of point detection 3×3 mask is as given below:

−1	−1	−1
−1	8	−1
−1	−1	−1

11.1.2 Line Detection Using Mask

The presence of straight line segments in an image can be determined by the use of specially designed masks. We may be interested in detecting all lines in a specified direction. We would use the mask associated in that direction and threshold the output. If we are interested in detecting all the lines in an image in the direction defined by the mask given, we simply run the mask along the image and threshold the absolute value of the result. The masks for determining lines of horizontal, vertical and diagonal orientations are shown below.

−1	−1	−1
2	2	2
−1	−1	−1

(a) Horizontal

−1	2	−1
−1	2	−1
−1	2	−1

(b) Vertical

−1	−1	2
−1	2	−1
2	−1	−1

(c) Diagonal-1

2	−1	−1
−1	2	−1
−1	−1	2

(d) Diagonal-2

The technique for determining line segments is similar to that of determining points, i.e. a high response of the mask indicates the presence of a line segment. To determine the orientation of the line segment, we apply all the four masks at the same point in the image. The mask whose response is higher will then determine the orientation of the line.

11.2 Detection of Known Shapes Using Hough Transform

The identification of known geometrical shapes in an image can be considered to be a part of the segmentation process. The Hough transform is very useful for this purpose. generally this transform is applied for known figures like line, circle, ellipses, etc., but with parameterization of any general curve pattern can be detected. However, in case of a curve of complicated nature the amount of processor memory needed by this method would be very high, and thus, the process becomes less interesting. For basic shapes, specially for lines and circles this method is very much useful.

11.2.1 Line Detection

A straight line is a sequence of points (pixels) connected linearly. The general equation of a line is

$$y = mx + c \tag{11.3}$$

where m is the inclination of the line about the positive X-axis and c is the Y-intercept.

The line passes through a number of points (x, y) for a particular value of m and c. The original line is represented in the $2D$ Cartesian space, i.e. in the X-Y plane.

The Hough transform converts it into a line in a new space. In fact, it transforms each significant edge pixel in X-Y space into a straight line in the new space. When this has been done for all the pixels, the intersecting points of these lines in the new space will indicate the existence of a real line segment in the original X-Y space.

We can rewrite Eq. (11.3) of a straight line as:

$$c = (-x)m + y \tag{11.4}$$

It is also the equation of a line in the M-C space having slope $-x$ and c-intercept y. As in the X-Y space, each value of the pair M-C indicate a line, similarly here, each X-Y value indicates a straight line.

We need to store the set of lines in an array called the *accumulator array.* This array is considered in the M-C space. The points in the M-C space that correspond to a point X-Y in the original space are incremented. So, after the first point in the X-Y space has been processed, there will be a line of 1s in the M-C array. Bresenham's algorithm can be used to determine the points on the line in the M-C space.

At the end of processing all the X-Y pixels, the highest value in the accumulator array indicates that a large number of lines cross in the array at some position (m', c'). The value in this element corresponds to the same number of pixels being on the same line in the X-Y space and the equation of line in the X-Y space will be

$$y = m'x + c' \tag{11.5}$$

Problems: For horizontal and vertical lines m may properly vary from $-\infty$ to $+\infty$ and the other for lines with $-1 < \frac{1}{m} < 1$.

Example: Let us consider the following line in the X-Y space.

$$x + y = 4$$

The line is shown in Figure 11.1(a). Let us investigate the conversion of each point (x, y) into a line segment in the M-C space. Table 11.1 shows this conversion process.

Table 11.1: Lines in the X-Y and M-C Space

x	y	*Line Equation in X-Y Space*	*Line Equation in M-C Space*
0	4	$4 = m.0 + c$	$c = 0.m + 4$
1	3	$3 = m.1 + c$	$c = -1.m + 3$
2	2	$2 = m.2 + c$	$c = -2.m + 2$
3	1	$1 = m.3 + c$	$c = -3.m + 1$
4	0	$0 = m.4 + c$	$c = -4.m + 0$

The lines in the accumulator array are shown in Figure 11.1(b).

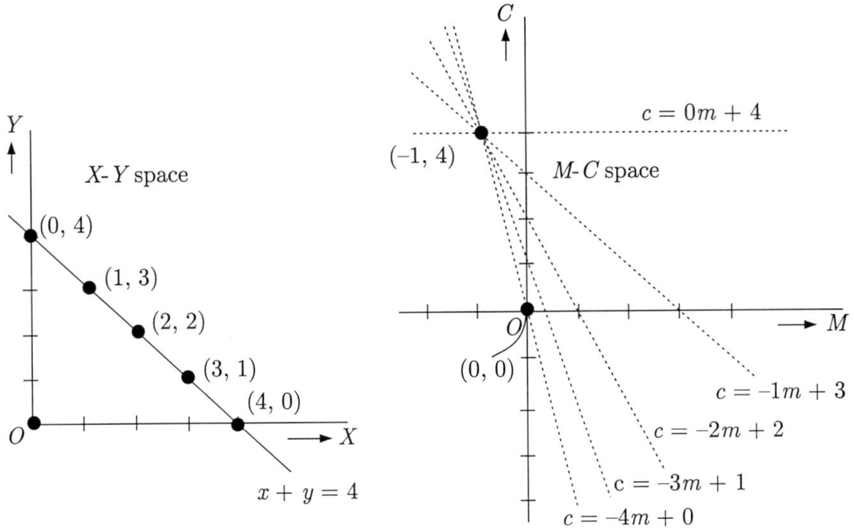

(a) Original line in the X-Y space (b) Corresponding lines in the M-C space

Figure 11.1: Hough method for line detection.

11.2.2 Circle Detection

The equation of a circle centred at the point (a, b) and having radius R is

$$(x - a)^2 + (y - b)^2 = R^2 \tag{11.6}$$

Our problem is to devise a method that will detect the presence of a circle of radius R in an edge detected image. For this purpose, we convert the circle from X-Y space to A-B space. The equation of the circle in the new space is the same as before. If we draw circles of radius R in the A-B space considering each pixel on a circle in the X-Y space as centre then all of them will intersect each other at a point (a, b) in the A-B space. As before (in the case of lines) we draw circles by incrementing the values in the accumulator array. So the point (a, b) will attain the maximum value. This point will be the centre of a possible circle of radius R in the X-Y space. Circles in the accumulator array can be drawn using Bresenham's circle drawing algorithm. Applying this method, it is also possible to determine the existence of circles of different radii.

In Figure 11.2, an example of Hough method for circle detection is illustrated. Here, in the X-Y space (original image) a circle of unit radius with centre at coordinate location (2, 3) is present. In the A-B space we need to draw a circle for each point over the parameter of the original circle considering the point as centre. Four such circles are shown in Figure 11.2(b).

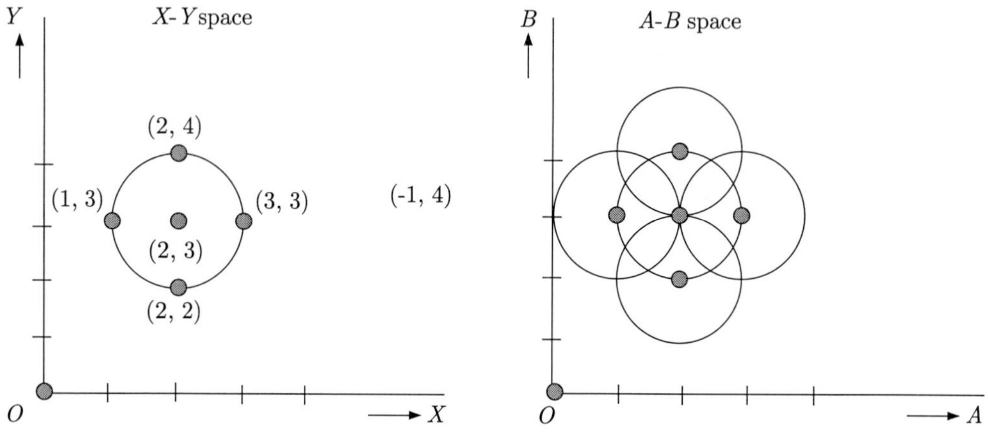

(a) Original circle in the X-Y space (b) Corresponding circles in the A-B space

Figure 11.2: Hough method for circle detection.

All these circles pass through the centre of the original circle in the A-B space. Therefore, when we use an accumulator array in the A-B space, one location of the array will contain a large value compared to others. This coordinate of this location (expressed in the original X-Y space) is the centre of the original image. The pictorial view of an accumulator array is shown in Figure 11.3.

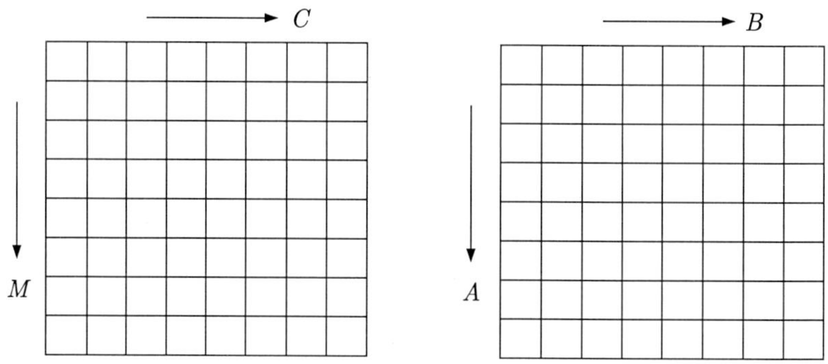

(a) For line in M-C space (b) For circle in A-B space

Figure 11.3: Accumulator array in Hough transform.

The above process can be verified by executing it on a real image. In Figure 11.4 one such real example is shown. In this figure (a) represents the original 128×128 image of a coin. The corresponding edge image is shown in (b). Figures (c) and (d) are accumulator images for thresholds 10 and 20, respectively. (e) using threshold of 150 we can locate the centre of the circle (perimeter of the coin) at a location where the highest value of 183 is accumulated. Figure 11.4(f) shows the original coin image superimposed with the detected circular perimeter.

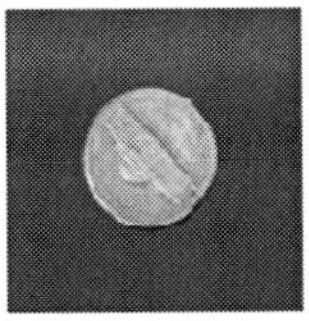

(a) Original 128 × 128 coin image

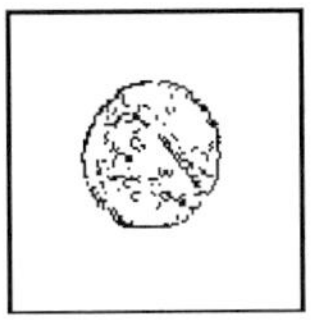

(b) Detected edge image

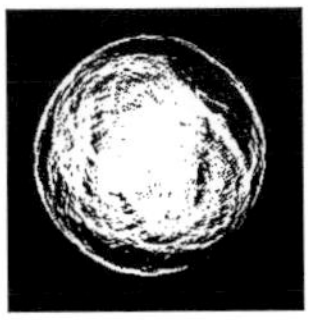

(c) Image of the accumulator array for threshold 10

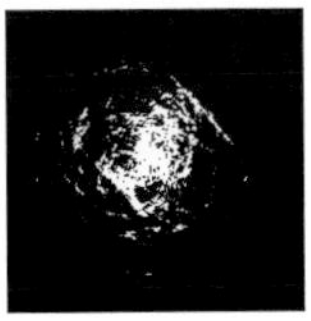

(d) Image of the accumulator array for threshold 20

(e) Location of centre with threshold 150

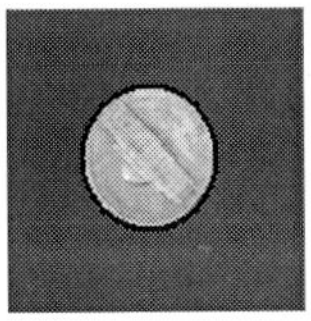

(f) Circle superimposed on the original image

Figure 11.4: Output of Hough circle detection.

11.3 Thresholding

Grey-level thresholding is the simplest approach to image segmentation. A brightness threshold may be selected to segment the image into objects and background. This approach is computationally inexpensive and fast. Also, thresholding can be done in real time using special hardware.

Thresholding process generates a binary image g from a given input image f. The process is,

$$g(i,j) \quad = \begin{cases} 1 & \text{if } f(i,j) \geq T \\ 0 & \text{otherwise} \end{cases} \tag{11.7}$$

Here, T is a predefined threshold. The selection of threshold is very crucial in segmentation process. Its value can be determined by an interactive fashion or it can be the result of automatic threshold selection method. A single global threshold partitions the image into objects and background. But this segmentation may be satisfactory in many cases. Objects may have different characteristic grey values. In such cases, multiple threshold values are needed which can be applied over different areas of the image. Threshold values in such cases are called local thresholds and the process of thresholding is called multilevel thresholding. Use of multiple threshold may help us detecting different objects in an image separately. Let, there are two different objects.

If we can identify two thresholds T_1 and T_2 such that,

$$\begin{array}{ll} T_1 \leq f(x,y) \leq T_2 & \text{for one object} \\ f(x,y) > T_2 & \text{for the other object, and} \\ f(x,y) \leq T_1 & \text{for the background} \end{array}$$

then thresholding can become more meaningful and informative in sense of segmentation. However, determining multiple thresholds is a non-trivial task, and results of such thresholding are generally less reliable than its single-threshold counterpart.

In general, thresholding may be viewed as an operation that involves tests against a function T of the form

$$T = T[x, y, p(x, y), f(x, y)] \tag{11.8}$$

where, $f(x, y)$ is the grey value at point (x, y), and $p(x, y)$ is some local property of this point. When T depends only on $f(x, y)$, the threshold is called *global.* If T depends on both $f(x, y)$ and $p(x, y)$, the threshold is called **local**. If T is also dependent on the spatial coordinates x and y, the threshold is called **dynamic**.

11.3.1 Histogram Based Thresholding

Generally thresholds are determined using the grey level histogram of an image. There are different techniques by which thresholds are selected from a histogram. Some of these are simple global thresholding, weighted valley thresholding, p-tile thresholding, etc.

Let us consider that $f(x, y)$ be an image of size $M \times N$ having two regions R_1 and R_2. The grey levels are $l = 0, 1, \ldots, L-1$, i.e. the maximum grey level is $L-1$ and there are L levels. The grey level histogram of this image can be denoted as

$$\sum_{l=0}^{L-1} n_l = M \times N \tag{11.9}$$

where, n_l is the number of pixels with grey level l.

The image information present in the grey level histogram can be used to determine a suitable threshold for segmentation. A familiar approach is the p-tile method. This method can applied only when we have some prior knowledge about distribution of pixels in regions R_1 and R_2. Let, number of pixels in region R_2 is about $p\%$ of the total number of pixels present in the image. Then threshold T can be selected by using the following relation

$$\sum_{i=T+1}^{L-1} n_i = \frac{p \times M \times N}{100} \tag{11.10}$$

Another method is based on histogram *modes*. In this method, if there are two peaks in the histogram separated by a valley, then the threshold can be selected at the middle of the valley. The problem here is that the histogram must be bimodal.

Let the two peaks (corresponding to the two regions) be represented by the grey levels $l = l_1$ and $l = l_2$. Then we can determine the thresholding position in the valley as

$$l = l_m = \frac{l_1 + l_2}{2}$$

Bimodality of the image can be determined by following a method due to Chanda (Chanda, 1988).

Let, m_1 and m_2 be the slopes of the two lines joining the valley and the two peaks, i.e.

$$m_1 = \left| \frac{n_{l_1} - n_{l_m}}{l_1 - l_m} \right| \text{ and } m_2 = \left| \frac{n_{l_2} - n_{l_m}}{l_2 - l_m} \right|$$

Now, the histogram can be said to be bimodal if

$$m_1 > T \qquad \text{and} \qquad m_2 > T$$

where, T is a predetermined threshold. If the histogram is such that the following relations hold

$$m_1 > T \qquad \text{and} \qquad m_2 \leq T$$

it is said to have peak and shoulder. A flat histogram, on the otherhand, satisfy the following criteria

$$m_1 \leq T \qquad \text{and} \qquad m_2 \leq T.$$

It should be clear that for a strongly bimodal histogram, an image can be easily segmented into background and foreground easily.

In Figure 11.5(a) An image of a bunch of keys is shown. The size of the image is 128×128, and it contains a maximum of 64 grey levels varying in the range $[0 - 63]$. The histogram of this image (Figure 11.5(b)) is found to contain a strong peak which represent the background of the image. This histogram is of the peak and shoulder type. The histogram shows that the background is constituted mainly by grey level range [35-50] (as majority of the pixels are covered by them). Also shades of the keys may be assumed to be covered by the range [25-35]. Hence, by eliminating contribution of the grey levels [25-50], we can extract (segment) the keys from the image. Segmented keys are shown in Figure 11.5(c).

11.3.2 Optimal Thresholding

Here we approximate the histogram of an image using a weighted sum of two or more probability densities with normal distribution. The threshold is set as the closest grey

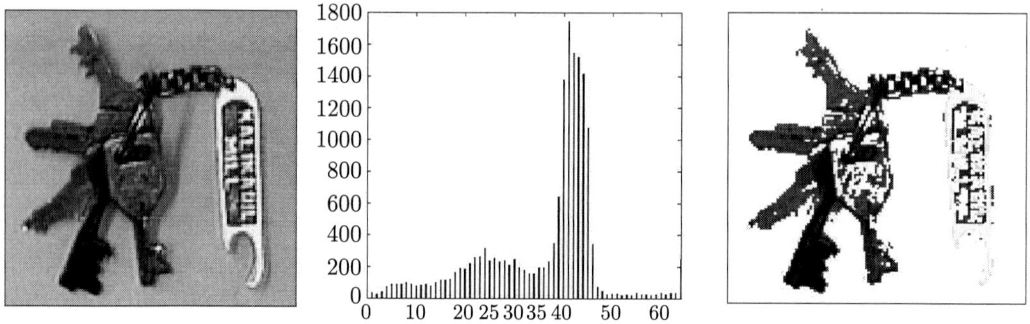

(a) Original 'keys' image (b) Histogram of 'keys' (c) Extracted 'keys' using histogram sementation

Figure 11.5: Histogram based segmentation.

level corresponding to the minimum probability between the maxima of two or more normal distributions, which results in the minimum error segmentation.

Let us consider that there are two different normal distributions present in the image, one corresponding to the objects and the other corresponding to the background. Thus, the image contains two regions R_1 and R_2 with mean grey values μ_1 and μ_2, respectively. σ_1 and σ_2 are standard deviations about the means in the two regions. The a priori probability that a pixel belongs to region R_1 or R_2 is P_1 and P_2, respectively. So, here $P_1 + P_2 = 1$.

Let, the grey level in the image be denoted by z. The probability density functions of grey values in R_1 and R_2 are given by

$$p_1(z) = \frac{1}{\sqrt{2\pi}\sigma_1} \exp\left[\frac{-(z-\mu_1)^2}{2\sigma_1^2}\right] \tag{11.11}$$

and

$$p_2(z) = \frac{1}{\sqrt{2\pi}\sigma_2} \exp\left[\frac{-(z-\mu_2)^2}{2\sigma_2^2}\right] \tag{11.12}$$

Therefore, the mixture probability density function of the image is given by

$$p(z) = P_1 \times p_1(z) + P_2 \times p_2(z) \tag{11.13}$$

or

$$p(z) = \frac{1}{\sqrt{2\pi}\sigma_1} \exp\left[\frac{-(z-\mu_1)^2}{2\sigma_1^2}\right] + \frac{1}{\sqrt{2\pi}\sigma_2} \exp\left[\frac{-(z-\mu_2)^2}{2\sigma_2^2}\right] \tag{11.14}$$

If the darker region corresponds to the background and the brighter region corresponds to the objects, then $\mu_1 < \mu_2$. Now, a threshold T should be such that a pixel will belong to R_1 if $z \le T$ and belong to R_2 if $z > T$. Here R_1 and R_2 represent objects and background, respectively.

The probability that an object point be misclassified as a background point is

$$E_1(T) = \int_{-\infty}^{T} p_2(z)dz$$

And the probability that a background point be misclassified as an object point is

$$E_2(T) = \int_{T}^{\infty} p_1(z)dz$$

Thus, total error probability due to misclassification is

$$E(T) = P_2 \times E_1(T) + P_1 \times E_2(T)$$

The optimal threshold will correspond to minimal total error and can be obtained by differentiating $E(T)$ with respect to T and equating the result to 0, i.e.

$$\frac{d}{dT}\left(P_2 \int_{-\infty}^{T} p_2(z)dz\right) + \frac{d}{dT}\left(P_1 \int_{T}^{\infty} p_1(z)dz\right) = 0$$

or

$$\frac{d}{dT}\left(P_2 \int_{-\infty}^{T} p_2(z)dz\right) + \frac{d}{dT}\left[P_1\left(1 - \int_{-\infty}^{T} p_1(z)dz\right)\right] = 0$$

or

$$P_2 \times p_2(T) = P_1 \times p_1(T) \tag{11.15}$$

or

$$P_2 \frac{1}{\sqrt{2\pi}\sigma_2} \exp\left[\frac{-(T-\mu_2)^2}{2\sigma_2^2}\right] = P_1 \frac{1}{\sqrt{2\pi}\sigma_1} \exp\left[\frac{-(T-\mu_1)^2}{2\sigma_1^2}\right]$$

or

$$\frac{P_2}{P_1}\frac{\sigma_1}{\sigma_2} \exp\left[\frac{-(T-\mu_2)^2}{2\sigma_2^2}\right] = \exp\left[\frac{-(T-\mu_1)^2}{2\sigma_1^2}\right]$$

Taking logarithms on both sides, we get

$$\ln \frac{P_2\sigma_1}{P_1\sigma_2} - \frac{(T-\mu_2)^2}{2\sigma_2^2} = -\frac{(T-\mu_1)^2}{2\sigma_1^2}$$

Now, if we assume that $\sigma_1 = \sigma_2 = \sigma$, we get

$$\ln \frac{P_2}{P_1} - \frac{(T-\mu_2)^2}{2\sigma^2} = -\frac{(T-\mu_1)^2}{2\sigma^2}$$

or

$$2\sigma^2 \ln \frac{P_2}{P_1} = (T-\mu_2)^2 - (T-\mu_1)^2$$

or

$$2\sigma^2 \ln \frac{P_2}{P_1} = -2T\mu_2 + \mu_2^2 + 2T\mu_1 + \mu_1^2$$

or

$$2\sigma^2 \ln \frac{P_2}{P_1} = 2T(\mu_1 - \mu_2) - (\mu_1 + \mu_2)(\mu_1 - \mu_2)$$

or

$$\frac{2\sigma^2}{\mu_1 - \mu_2} \ln \frac{P_2}{P_1} = 2T - (\mu_1 + \mu_2)$$

Hence, the optimal threshold is,

$$T = \frac{\mu_1 + \mu_2}{2} + \frac{2\sigma^2}{\mu_1 - \mu_2} \ln \frac{P_2}{P_1} \tag{11.16}$$

If the priori probabilities are equal, i.e. $P_1 = P_2$, the optimal threshold is the average of the means.

Iterative method for selecting optimal threshold

- Select two subsets of background and foreground pixels B and F, respectively by inspection.
- Determine mean grey levels $\mu_B^{(t)}$ and $\mu_F^{(t)}$ for B and F. Use the following relations for $\mu_B^{(t)}$ and $\mu_F^{(t)}$.

$$\mu_B^{(t)} = \frac{\sum\limits_{(i,j)\in B} f(i,j)}{|B|}$$

and,

$$\mu_F^{(t)} = \frac{\sum\limits_{(i,j)\in F} f(i,j)}{|F|}$$

- Compute the new threshold as

$$T^{(t+1)} = \frac{\mu_B^{(t)} + \mu_F^{(t)}}{2}$$

- If $T^{(t+1)} = T^{(t)}$, then exit, otherwise use $T^{(t+1)}$ to segment the image into B and F and continue until threshold T is stable.

11.4 Region Based Segmentation

In case of histogram based thresholding approaches, the pixels are classified into objects and background based on statistical measure of some homogeniety property. All the pixels are considered simultaneously to construct a histogram and the segmentation is obtained as a result of thresholding the histogram. Thus, the processes do not consider the location of any individual pixel, and hence, the segmented image contains several regions which are identified by the process to be the same region. In region-based techniques, we construct the regions by associating or dissociating neighbour pixels, and hence, the detected regions can be labelled separately. The underlying algorithms are iterative in nature.

11.5 Segmentation Based on Region Similarity

The objective of image segmentation is to partition the image into regions of similar properties. The methods discussed in earlier sections are based on detection of grey level discontinuities. Here, we shall try to find out homogeneous regions within the image.

11.5.1 Definition of a Region

Let us denote the entire image to a region R. This image may be thought to be composed of n disjoint subregions, $R_1, R_2, \ldots, R_n$, such that the following relations are satisfied:

1. $\bigcup_{i=1}^{n} R_i = R$,
2. $R_i \cap R_j = \phi$ for $i \neq j$,
3. $\text{Prop}(R_i) = \text{TRUE}$ for $i = 1, 2, \ldots, n$,
4. $\text{Prop}(R_i \cup R_j) = \text{FALSE}$ for $i \neq j$

where, $\text{Prop}(R_i)$ is a property defined in terms of feature values over region R_i. As an example of property, we can say that pixels within a region must have grey values between g_1 and g_2. From the above conditions, it is clear that, regions must be connected, disjoint and homogeneous in nature.

11.5.2 Region Growing

In this approach pixels in a region are labelled with a unique label which is different from the labels of other regions. The process starts by selecting a *seed* pixel within the image. The seed is assigned a label. Now each of the neighbour pixels are labelled recursively using a similarity measure or a homogeniety property. When no more pixels can be labelled with the same label, the first region is found. In the next step, another seed pixel is selected out of the yet to label pixels. The same labelling process is followed. The overall process is repeated until no more pixels remain unlabelled. For determining neighbours, the concepts of 4-connected or 8-connected pixel windows may be considered. The following algorithm describes the process in a better manner.

Region growing algorithm

```
begin
    set label l = 0
    repeat
        begin
        select a seed pixel (x_s, y_s), label it with label l
        push all the unlabelled neighbours of (x_s, y_s) onto a stack
        while the stack is not empty do
            begin
                pop a pixel (x_s, y_s) from the stack
                if it satisfies the homogeniety property
                begin
                    label (x_s, y_s) with label l
                    push all the unlabelled neighbours onto the stack
                end
            end
            set label l = l + 1
        end
    until all the pixels are labelled
end
```

To execute the above procedure, a suitable homogeniety metric should be determined beforehand. Generally, a homogeneous region within an image should exhibit the spatial coherence property, i.e. pixels within the same region should have nearly equal grey values (if not the same). Therefore, to define a metric, one may assume that the variance of grey levels of the pixels within a region should be within a limit (small value). Therefore, the homegeniety metric can be defined as

$$\text{Prop}(R): \; M_H(R) = \frac{1}{|R|} \sum_{(x,y) \in R} \{f(x,y) - \bar{f}(x,y)\} \leq T \tag{11.17}$$

where, $|R|$ represents the size of region R in number of pixels, and T is the limit or threshold. $\bar{f}$ is the average grey value within R given by

$$\bar{f}(x,y) = \frac{1}{|R|} \sum_{(x,y) \in R} \{f(x,y)\} \tag{11.18}$$

It is clear that the above metric is defined over a region of a certain size. This region size increases as more and more pixels are included in a region. The value of the threshold T have a significant effect on the outcome of the procedure. Small values of T results in a large number of tiny regions, while larger values identify a small number of large areas.

The homogeniety metric can be defined in many different ways. A simple and computationally efficient homogeniety property can be defined as

$$\text{Prop}(R): \ M_H(R) = \max\{f(x,y)\} - \min\{f(x,y)\} \leq T \tag{11.19}$$

where T is a predefined threshold. Here the maximum and the minimum are defined over the region concerned. An example of usage of this criteria is shown in the Figure 11.6. Here, (a) is the original image matrix, (b) represents the segmented image when a threshold of 3 is considered. Encircled pixels are seed pixels. Depending on the order of processing of the neighbour pixels, one may have a different result as is shown in (c). The result is also dependent and sensitive to selection of the seed pixels. In (d) the second seed is considered to be 7 instead of 3.

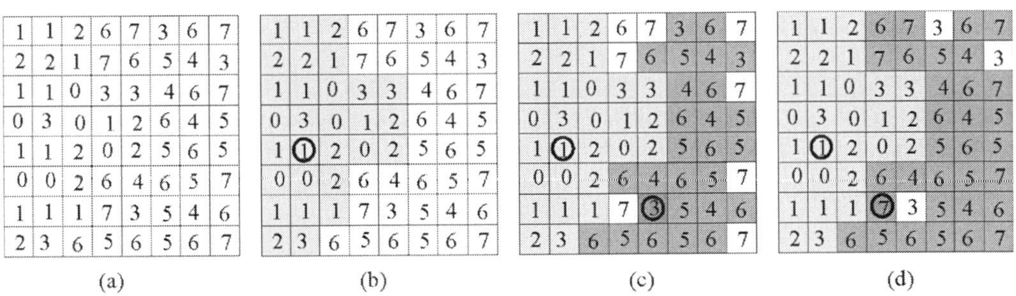

Figure 11.6: Example of region growing based segmentation.

11.5.3 Region Splitting

In this method, the image is divided into smaller and smaller disjoint regions until all the regions satisfy the homogeniety property. To simplify the process, we consider an image whose width (M) and height (N) are assumed to be some powers of 2. Initially, the image is considered to be a single region. Then, at each split step we divide the image into four regions. If we maintain a quad tree structure to store the fragments, the process will become easier. At the root node of the tree, there is the complete image represented by region R. It is divided into four fragments R_1, R_2, R_3 and R_4 and the fragments are placed at the child nodes. Now, we need to check whether all the regions satisfy the homogeniety property. If any region does not satisfy, it is again fragmented as before. The process is then repeated until all the leaf nodes of the quad tree satisfy the homogeniety property given by Eq. (11.19). An example of the fragmented image and the corresponding quad tree, using threshold 3, are shown in Figure 11.7.

Region splitting algorithm

begin
  define a homogeneity condition
  form a quad tree with the image at the root node
  repeat
    begin
      for each leaf node of the quad tree **do**
      begin
        if (homogeniety condition = false)
          split the node into four child-regions and place in the quad tree
      end
    end
  until no more splitting is possible
end

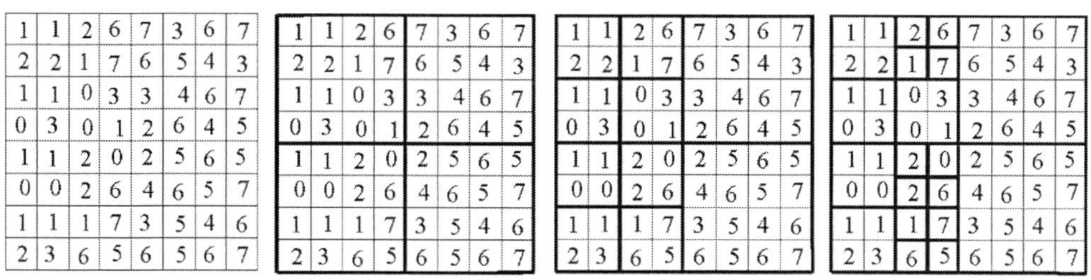

(a) (b) (c) (d)

Figure 11.7: Example of region splitting based segmentation.

11.5.4 Region Merging

This method is just the opposite of the splitting method. In this case, we start each pixel as a distinct region. So, initially regions are of size 1×1 pixel, and we are at the lowest level of the complete quad tree. Now, at each step, we consider four adjacent regions to check whether they satisfy the homogeniety property. If 'true', we merge the four regions and place the result in the next higher level node in the quad tree, and remove the childs. After all leaf nodes are considered, we go to the next higher level of the quad tree and repeat the overall process. We stop when we reach the root node of the tree with the complete image as a single region. Here also, each of the leaf nodes of the quad tree represents a rectangular homogeneous region. An example of region merging is shown in Figure 11.8. Here we have used a threshold value of 3 again. It should be noted here that region splitting and region merging processes may produce very coarse outputs in case of real images. Hence some form of post-processing in generally applied over the actual outputs to smoothout local abrupt changes or discontinuities.

Region merging algorithm

begin
  define a homogeneity condition
  form a quad tree with individual pixels at the leaf nodes
  repeat
    begin
      for each group of four neighbour leaf nodes **do**
      begin
        if (homogeniety condition = true)
          merge the nodes into a parent-regions and place in the quad tree
      end
    end
  until no more merging is possible
end

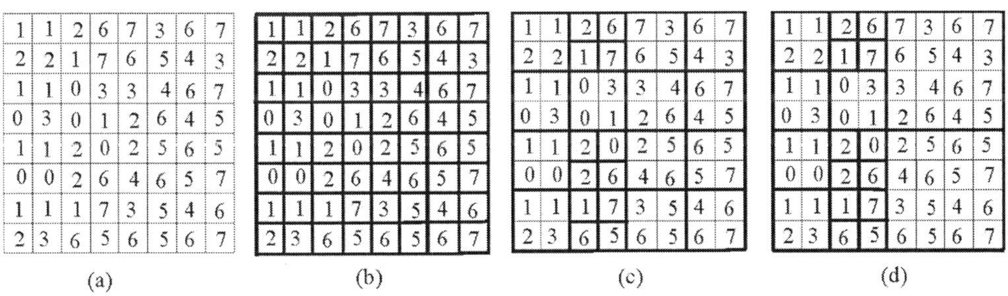

Figure 11.8: Example of region merging based segmentation.

11.5.5 Split and Merge Process

The above mentioned region splitting and merging can be performed simultaneously within the same algorithm. The resulting algorithm will be a hybrid of the split and the merge processes. This hybrid split and merge algorithm is outlined below.

Split and merge algorithm

begin
  define a homogeniety condition
  create a pyramid data structure for the image
  form a quad tree with level numbers and fragment numbers at nodes
  repeat

```
        begin
            for each node of the quad tree do
            begin
                if (homogeneity condition = false)
                    split the node into four child-regions
            end
            for each group of four neighbour with the same parent do
            begin
                if (homogeneity condition = true)
                    merge the nodes
            end
        end
    until no more splitting or merging is possible
end
```

Unlike region splitting or merging techniques, the hybrid split-merge process starts at any intermediate level of the quad tree (of the image). If we start with two consecutive nodes (regions) of size $m \times m$, a true split condition will split them into four quadrants each of size $\frac{m}{2} \times \frac{m}{2}$; and a true merge condition will produce a region of size $(2m) \times (2m)$. The process stops when no more split or merge are possible.

11.6 Problems

1. What do you mean by image segmentation and why is it used?

2. Name two basic approaches of image segmentation and mention their differences.

3. What is an image histogram? How can it help in image segmentation? What are bimodal and multimodal histogram?

4. For classifying an image into foreground and background, what is the optimal threshold? Derive the expression analytically.

5. How can you decide optimal thresholds when the image contains a background and several foreground objects? Write down a corresponding algorithm.

6. Write down the region growing algorithm. What are its advantages and disadvantages?

7. Consider the following 8×8 image having 8 grey levels.

8	7	5	6	7	7	8	8
7	7	2	3	7	6	7	8
8	6	3	4	8	6	5	8
6	7	2	2	7	7	8	7
8	7	9	5	2	2	1	3
8	6	5	6	4	3	3	2
8	8	7	7	1	3	1	3
8	7	5	6	2	2	8	4

Use the region splitting algorithm to segment the image. Consider a threshold of 3, and use a homogeniety property as is given in Eq. (11.18). Select arbitrary seeds.

8. Use the above image for segmentation by region merging. Consider 4 neighbour seeds at each step. Decide your own homogeniety property and threshold.
9. Use the image matrix in problem 7 to produce a histogram and then to segment into two regions. What is the threshold grey value found?
10. Consider an image with an object(R_1) and a background(R_2), where R_1 and R_2 have prior probabilities of 0.3 and 0.7, respectively. Let mean and standard deviations in the two regions are 2 and 10, and 1 and 2, respectively. Compute the optimal threshold.
11. Use the image matrix in problem 7. From the information available by histogram based segmentation (Problem 9) compute the means and standard deviations. Then compute the optimal threshold.

CHAPTER 12

Image Compression

Representing digital images in computers requires large volume of data. The more the resolution of the image is, the more will be the storage requirement. Present day computing systems are able to process high resolution images quite efficiently. Hence, to ensure quality factors in processed images, digital computers need to be equipped with very large storage space. Also, transmission of such huge data requires sufficient amount of transfer time over communication networks. Since space and time are two most valuable computing resources, we need to reduce image data size without compromising its information content. In many applications, like satellite image processing or medical image processing, etc. we need a large number of very high quality images. There are many other applications like facsimile transmission, remote sensing, weather forecasting, video conferencing, document image analysis, guided missile control, geographical information processing, etc.

12.1 Image Compression Fundamentals

Fortunately, it has been observed that an image contains a large amount of redundant data which are absolutely unnecessary for storage and communication purposes. Thus, image data compression is a process of reducing the amount of image data while at the same time to maintain a prespecified image quality. In other words, we need to maintain essential image information only by elimination of redundant data. Data contents of an image is not equal to its information contents. More data does not always ensure more information, and the same information may be represented using different amount of data. So, the essential objective behind image compression is to find out the minimum possible amount of data to represent a certain image.

In brief, we can say that

- Digital images, either still or video, contain huge amount of data.
- Compression of such data yields a compact digital representation of them.
- Compressed data consumes less storage area.
- Compressed data can be easily transmitted over a communication network.

From the above image processing requirements, the necessity of image compression is very clear. For better understanding, we can illustrate the scenario with proper examples. Two situations are described below.

Situation 1: During facsimile transmission, generally, the document is scanned and digitized. Typically, an 8.5 × 11 inch page is scanned at 200 dpi, thus, resulting in 3.74 Mbits. Transmitting this data over a low cost 14.4 kbits/s modem would require 5.62 minutes. With compression, the transmission time can be reduced to 17 seconds. This results in substantial savings in transmission costs.

Situation 2: Let us consider a video-based CD-ROM application. Full-motion video, at 30 frames per second and at 720×480 resolution, generates data at 20.736 Mbytes/s. At this rate, only 31 seconds of video can be stored on a 650 Mbyte CD-ROM. Compression technology can increase the storage capacity to 74 minutes, for VHS-grade video quality.

The above two examples are only two instances of many applications that benefit from data compression technology. For multimedia data, i.e. image, video and audio signals, compression is an obvious choice due to the following factors:

- There is considerable statistical redundancy in the signal.
- There is considerable information in the signal that is irrelevant from a perceptual point of view.
- Some data tend to have high-level features that are redundant across space and time, i.e. the data is of a fractal nature.

12.1.1 Data Redundancy

As mentioned earlier, an image may contain a sufficient amount of redundant information, and also an image can be encoded in many possible ways. Hence, any two different representation of the same image contains different amount of redundancy. A measure of comparative data redundancy may help us to estimate the actual information content of a digital image.

Let us consider two digital representations of an image. Size of these two representations, in terms of number of bytes, be m_1 and m_2, respectively. Then the relative **data redundancy** d_r of the first representation over the second may be expressed as

$$d_r = 1 - \frac{1}{c_r} \tag{12.1}$$

where c_r is called the **compression ratio** and is defined as

$$c_r = \frac{m_1}{m_2} \tag{12.2}$$

The following conditions may arise:

- If $m_1 = m_2$, then $d_r = 0$. This means both the representations contain the same amount of redundancy.
- If $m_1 > m_2$, then $0 < d_r < 1$, meaning the first representation contains more redundancy. When, $c_r \to \infty$ then $d_r \to 1$.
- If $m_1 < m_2$, then $d_r < 0$, meaning the second representation contains more redundancy. When, $c_r \to 0$ then $d_r \to -\infty$.

Three different types of redundancies are important in case of image compression. These are:

- Coding redundancy,
- Inter-pixel redundancy, and
- Psycho-visual redundancy.

In practice, image compression processes try to reduce or eliminate one or more of the above redundancies and at the same time maintain some objective fidelity criteria as per requirements.

Coding redundancy

Each pixel in an image is generally represented by 8 bits (using grey levels 0 to 255 for a grey image). Thus, an $M \times N$ grey image contains $M \times N \times 8$ bits of data. We can compute the average number of bits needed to represent these grey values.

Let us consider that the number of grey levels be L where each pixel is encoded using $b_{\max}$ number of bits, and number of pixels having grey value g_k be n_k. Then the average number of bits per pixel becomes

$$b_{\text{avg}} = \sum_{k=0}^{L-1} b_{g_k} \times p_{g_k} \tag{12.3}$$

where, p_{g_k} is the probability of occurrence of grey level g_k, and b_{g_k} is the number of bits needed to represent g_k. Therefore, total number of bits needed to encode the image is $M \times N \times b_{\text{avg}}$. In such a case of L level grey image, the amount of redundant bits can be expressed as

$$\text{Number of redundant bits} = M \times N \times (b_{\max} - b_{\text{avg}}) \tag{12.4}$$

In a later section, we shall describe the use of frequency dependent encoding techniques which can effectively reduce data contents of an image by avoiding fixed length codes.

Inter-pixel redundancy

We have already mentioned that, in general images contain huge amount of spatial coherence. This means that grey values of neighbour pixels are highly correlated and can be predicted from each other. The more coherent the pixels are, in an image, the more will be the spatial redundancy. That is values of more pixels can be predicted from the others. Inter-pixel redundancy is another term used to describe spatial redundancy. We can, therefore, conclude that the more predictable the pixel values are, the more will be the inter-pixel redundancy and the less will be the information content of the image. Hence, lesser number of bits are needed to represent such images, even if histograms of competing images are exactly the same. Images with high inter-pixel redundancy can be most effectively encoded as difference images.

Formation of difference image may be considered as a reversible linear mapping. Let us consider a one-dimensional image $f(x)$ and a mapping defined as

$$\begin{bmatrix} g(1) \\ g(2) \\ \vdots \\ g(n) \end{bmatrix} = \begin{bmatrix} a_{11} & a_{12} & \cdots & a_{1n} \\ a_{21} & a_{22} & \cdots & a_{2n} \\ & \ddots & & \\ a_{n1} & a_{n2} & \cdots & a_{nn} \end{bmatrix} \times \begin{bmatrix} f(1) \\ f(2) \\ \vdots \\ f(n) \end{bmatrix} \tag{12.5}$$

or

$$\mathbf{g} = A\mathbf{f} \tag{12.6}$$

In case of the difference mapping, A takes the form

$$\begin{bmatrix} 1 & 0 & 0 & 0 & \cdots & 0 & 0 & 0 & 0 \\ 1 & -1 & 0 & 0 & \cdots & 0 & 0 & 0 & 0 \\ 0 & 1 & -1 & 0 & \cdots & 0 & 0 & 0 & 0 \\ & & & & \ddots & & & & \\ 0 & 0 & 0 & 0 & \cdots & 0 & 1 & -1 & 0 \\ 0 & 0 & 0 & 0 & \cdots & 0 & 0 & 1 & -1 \end{bmatrix}$$

In this case, the first element of g becomes $g(1) = f(1)$, but all the subsequent difference coefficients are given by $g(i) = f(i-1) - f(i)$. The more similar the adjacent pixels of f are, the less will be the differences $g(i) = f(i-1) - f(i)$, and the less number of bits will be needed to encode the difference coefficients. Note that the above transform is reversible.

Psycho-visual redundancy

This kind of redundancy is related to the visual sensitivity of human eye to perceive consecutive grey levels or intensities. Our eyes are not able to respond to very close intensities separately. This means that presence of consecutive pixels with almost same grey values cause yet another kind of redundancy in images. We refer to this as the psycho-visual redundancy. To eliminate such psycho-visual redundancy we need to quantize the grey scale range suitably so that the image can be represented using lesser number of grey levels, causing a significant amount of image data reduction.

12.1.2 Concept of Amount of Information

According to information theory, the less likely the message, the more information it conveys. So measuring information content must be related to uncertainty, the uncertainty of the user as to what the message will be.

A fine example, in this regard, is found in literature (Carlson 1986). During planning a trip to a distant city, to determine what clothes to pack, you telephone the weather bureau and hear one of the following forecasts:

- The sun will rise.
- There will be scattered rainstorms.
- There will be a tornado.

The first message conveys virtually no information since you are quite sure in advance that the sun will rise. The second, however, provides more information not previously available to you. The third forecast gives you more information, tornados being rare and unexpected events. You might even decide to cancel the trip.

As probability is a measure of uncertainty, it should be evident that measurement of information involves the probability of occurrence of the message. If x_i is an arbitrary message and $P(x_i) = p_i$ is its probability, the amount of information associated with x_i should be some function of p_i.

Shannon specifically defined the information content by the following function:

$$I_i = -\log_b p_i = \log_b \frac{1}{p_i} \tag{12.7}$$

I_i is the self-information of message x_i. From Eq. (12.7), we can see that the following necessary conditions are also satisfied:

$$\begin{array}{lll} I_i \geq 0 & \text{for} & 0 \leq p_i \leq 1 \\ I_i \to 0 & \text{for} & p_i \to 1 \\ I_i > I_j & \text{for} & p_i < p_j \end{array} \tag{12.8}$$

Also, if x_i and x_j are two independent messages with joint probability $P(x_i, x_j)$ $= p_{ij}$, then

$$I_{ij} = \log_b \frac{1}{p_i p_j} = \log_b \frac{1}{p_i} + \log_b \frac{1}{p_j} = I_i + I_j \tag{12.9}$$

So the total information equals the sum of the individual message contributions. Shannon's information measure $\log_b \frac{1}{p_i}$ is the only function that satisfies all the above properties given in Eqs. (12.8) and (12.9).

Specifying the logarithmic base b determines the unit of information, the standard convention of information theory takes $b = 2$ and the corresponding unit is a *bit*.

12.1.3 Average Information, Entropy

Let there are M different and independent messages $m_1, m_2, \ldots, m_M$ with probabilities $p_1, p_2, \ldots, p_M$. We have a message generating system which can generate any of these messages randomly. Suppose during a long interval of time L messages have been generated. Since L is very large, we can assume that the message m_i has been generated $p_i L$ number of times.

Thus, total information of all the messages is

$$I_{\text{total}} = L \sum_{i=1}^{M} p_i \log_b \frac{1}{p_i} \tag{12.10}$$

and the average information or entropy per message is

$$H = \frac{I_{\text{total}}}{L} = \sum_{i=1}^{M} p_i \log_b \frac{1}{p_i} \tag{12.11}$$

To show the dependence of H on the probability p_i, we consider a simple case of only two messages with probability p and $1 - p$. In this case

$$H = p \log_2 \frac{1}{p} + (1 - p) \log_2 \frac{1}{1 - p}$$

The maximum value of H can be obtained by setting $\frac{dH}{dp}$ to zero. This maximum occurs at $p = \frac{1}{2}$, i.e. when the two messages are equally likely. The corresponding H is

$$H_{\max} = \tfrac{1}{2} \log_2 2 + \tfrac{1}{2} \log_2 2 = \log_2 2 = 1 \text{ bit/message}$$

When there are M messages, it may likewise be proved that H becomes a maximum when all the messages are equally likely, i.e. all have equal probability $p_i = \frac{1}{M}$ for $i = 1, 2, \ldots, M$, and then,

$$H_{\max} = \sum \tfrac{1}{M} \log_2 M - \log_2 M$$

From information theory, if the symbols or messages are distinct, then the average number of bits needed to encode them is always bounded by their entropy. In practice, the entropy of a source is in general unknown, and the estimates for the entropy depend on the probability model we adopt for the structure of the symbols.

For example, consider the following sequence of symbols:

$$4\ 5\ 8\ 6\ 4\ 7\ 8\ 9\ 4\ 8$$

In one probability model, we can assume that our source generates six distinct symbols ($s_1 = 4, s_2 = 5, s_3 = 6, s_4 = 7, s_5 = 8, s_6 = 9$) and that each symbol is generated with equal probability, i.e. $p_i = \frac{1}{6}$, for $i = 1, 2, \ldots, 6$. From the definition of entropy

$$H = 6 \times \frac{1}{6} \log_2 6 = 2.585 \tag{12.12}$$

In other words, using this model, we cannot find a coding scheme for this sequence that can code better than 2.585 bits per symbol.

In a different model, we can assume that the probability of each symbol corresponds to the number of occurrences of that symbol in our sequence. Then, for the symbols defined before, $p_1 = p_3 = \frac{3}{10}$, and $p_2 = p_4 = p_5 = p_6 = \frac{1}{10}$. Using this model $H = 2.371$.

The general model of a lossless compression scheme is as depicted in Figure 12.1. Given a set of input symbols, a model generates an estimate of the probability distribution of the input symbols. This probability model is then used to map symbols into codewords. The combination of the modelling and the symbol-to-codeword mapping function is usually referred to as *entropy encoding*. In entropy encoding, the higher frequency symbols are coded with lesser number of bits. Decompression is performed by reversing the flow of operations shown in Figure 12.2. This decompression process is usually referred to as *entropy decoding*.

Example 1: Find out the information content of the following 4×4 image.

5	10	15	15
10	15	20	20
20	20	25	30
25	25	30	30

Different grey values and their frequencies of occurrences in the given image are shown in the following chart:

Grey value	5	10	15	20	25	30
Frequency	1	2	3	4	3	3

Hence, probabilities of occurrence are:

Grey value	5	10	15	20	25	30
Probability	$\frac{1}{16}$	$\frac{1}{8}$	$\frac{3}{16}$	$\frac{1}{4}$	$\frac{3}{16}$	$\frac{3}{16}$

The entropy is computed as

$$\begin{aligned} H &= \sum_{i=1}^{6} p_i \log_2 p_i \\ &= \frac{1}{16}\log_2\frac{1}{16} + \frac{1}{8}\log_2\frac{1}{8} + \frac{1}{4}\log_2\frac{1}{4} + 3\times\frac{3}{16}\log_2\frac{3}{16} \\ &= 2.4835 \end{aligned}$$

Therefore, the average information content of the image is 2.4835 bits/symbols. And the total information content is $16 \times 2.4835 = 39.736$ bits.

12.1.4 Fidelity Criteria

Image compression processes may lead to loss of a certain amount of image information during encoding and decoding stages. In other words, errors may be inserted into the image contents during such processes. In many cases, some amount of errors in the reconstructed (decoded) images can be tolerated. A measure of quality (criteria) of the reconstructed image may be the rms signal-to-noise ratio as explained below.

Input image	$f(x, y);\ x, y = 0, 1, \ldots, N-1$	m-bit grey values
Output image	$g(x, y);\ x, y = 0, 1, \ldots, N-1$	m-bit grey values

For any (x, y), the error term is

$$e(x, y) = g(x, y) - f(x, y)$$

The mean square error is

$$\begin{aligned} \bar{e^2} &= \frac{1}{N^2}\sum_x\sum_y e^2(x, y) \\ &= \frac{1}{N^2}\sum_x\sum_y \{g(x, y) - f(x, y)\}^2 \end{aligned}$$

Now, the rms error is defined as

$$e_{\text{rms}} = \sqrt{\bar{e^2}}$$

This error may be treated as noise in the output image, i.e.

$$g(x, y) = f(x, y) + e(x, y)$$

The rms signal-to-noise ratio $(\text{SNR})_{\text{rms}}$ then becomes

$$(\text{SNR})_{\text{rms}} = \left[\frac{\sum_x \sum_y g^2(x, y)}{\sum_x \sum_y \{g(x, y) - f(x, y)\}^2} \right]^{\frac{1}{2}}$$

Depending on the value of SNR, the output image may be termed as excellent, fine, passable, marginal, inferior, etc.

12.2 Image Compression Models

The block diagram of a generic compression process is depicted in Figure 12.1 and source encoding-deconding model in Figure 12.2. The core of the system is the source encoder. The performance of the source coder is measured by *compression ratio*, denoted by c_r. An intuitive definition of c_r is

$$c_r = \frac{\text{Source coder input size}}{\text{Source coder output size}} \tag{12.13}$$

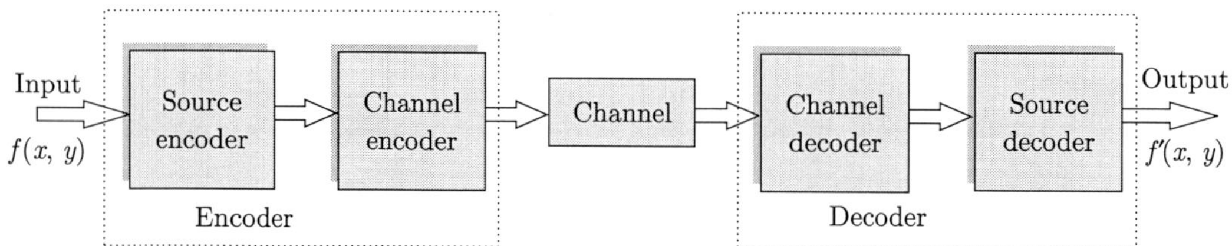

Figure 12.1: General compression model.

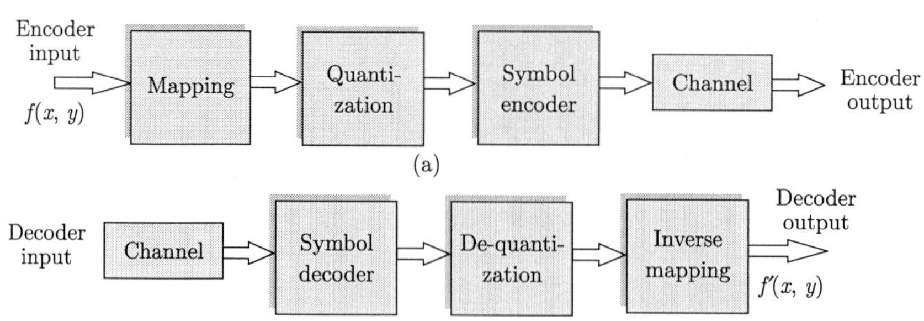

(a)

(b)

Figure 12.2: Source encoding-decoding model.

12.2.1 Types of Compression

Generally there are two types of compression techniques: Lossless and Lossy. In case of lossless compression, the reconstructed data from the decoder and the original input to the encoder must be identical. But many applications are there that do not require that the original data and the reconstructed data be identical. In such cases, some amount of loss is permitted in their constructed data. A compression system that produce non-identical decoder output is referred to as lossy compression process. Since lossy compression techniques enjoy additional degree of freedom than the lossless ones, they can yield higher compression ratios.

In lossless compression, the choice of a compression method involves a tradeoff among the following factors: Coding efficiency, coding complexity and coding delay. For lossy compression, there is one more factor, viz. signal quality. Although there is no universally accepted measure for signal quality, one measure that is often cited is the Signal-to-Noise-Ratio (SNR), which can be expressed as

$$\text{SNR} = 10 \log_{10} \frac{\text{Encoder input signal energy}}{\text{Noise signal energy}} \tag{12.14}$$

The noise signal energy is defined as the energy measured for a hypothetical signal that is the difference between the encoder input and the decoder output signals. Note that the SNR is expressed here in units of decibels (DB). In case of images or video, PSNR (Peak Signal-to-Noise-Ratio) is used instead of SNR. The calculations are essentially the same as in the case of SNR; however, in the numerator, instead of using the encoder input signal, one uses a hypothetical signal with a maximum signal strength (e.g. 255 in case of a 8-bit pixel). It should be remembered that high SNR or PSNR values do not always correspond to perceptual high quality.

12.3 LossLess Coding Techniques

There exist several image compression techniques that do not incorporate any distortion of image information. These techniques are error-free in nature, and called **lossless encoding techniques**. We shall describe several such lossless techniques in the following subsections.

12.3.1 Run Length Encoding

The grey values present along a row in an image are nothing but a sequence of integers. In general, a run of the same grey value is observed frequently. If we find a run of length n_i for grey value g_i, we can encode this run by an ordered pair (g_i, n_i). For example, let a row of an 8-level grey image be

000000222222222255555555555555555577777777777111111111100000000

We can encode it as

$$(0,6),(2,10),(5,18),(7,11),(1,11),(0,8)$$

Therefore, instead of 64 integers, we need to store only 12 integers. To implement this scheme, we need to define the maximum length of a run to encode. Let in the above example, this maximum length be 32. Hence, we need 3 bits per grey value and 5 bits for a run, i.e. a total of 8 bits for each pair. Thus, total number of bits to encode the row becomes $6 \times 8 = 48$ bits. While the original data could be encoded using $3 \times 64 = 192$ bits. In general, the total number of grey levels is L and the maximum number of pixels per run is N, then we need $\log_2 L + \log_2 N$ bits for each ordered pair. This encoding scheme is very commonly used with other encoding techniques and many variations are also available.

12.3.2 Differential Encoding

Another preprocessing technique that improves the compression ratio is differential coding. Differential coding skews the symbol statistics so that the resulting distribution is more amenable to compression. Image data tend to have strong inter-pixel correlation. If say, the pixels in the image are in the order $x_1, x_2, \ldots, x_n$, then instead of compressing these pixels, one might process the sequence of differentials $y_i = x_i - x_{i-1}$, where $i = 1, 2, \ldots, N$, and $x_0 = 0$. In compression terminology, y_i is referred to as the *prediction residual* of x_i. The notion of compressing the prediction residuals instead of x_i is used in all image and video compression standards. One method for image subtraction is already described in earlier sections.

12.3.3 Shannon–Fano Coding

Shannon–Fano coding generates an efficient code in which the word length increases as the message probability decreases. This algorithm provides a tree code structure to ensure unique decipherability. Let us consider an example where we want to encode 8 different symbols with specific probabilities. The procedure and results are summarized the Table 12.1.

12.3.4 Huffman Encoding

This encoding technique can be used to perform lossless compression. It is a frequency dependent code. Initially the frequency of occurrence of each individual symbols determined from a statistical analysis. Then this frequency becomes the probability of occurrence also. To produce Huffman code we arrange the symbols along with their probabilities in arbitrary order. Now, a tree is formed by adding two smallest probabilities at each level. In this tree each edge is marked with a zero or one following a conversion (here left edge is 0 and right edge is 1). Now, we trace back the tree starting at the root node and the code obtained to reach a symbol will be its Huffman

Table 12.1: Example of Shannon–Fano Encoding Scheme

x_i	p_i	Coding Steps						*Code word*
		1	2	3	4	5	6	
A	0.50	0						0
B	0.15	1	0	0				100
C	0.15	1	0	1				101
D	0.08	1	1	0				110
E	0.08	1	1	1	0			1110
F	0.02	1	1	1	1	0		11110
G	0.01	1	1	1	1	1	0	11110
H	0.01	1	1	1	1	1	1	11111

code. The order in which the symbols are arranged initially is unimportant. Hence, various different code forms may arise. However, in all the cases the highest frequency symbol will be assigned the smallest length code. Once a set of code is constructed, coding and/or decoding is accomplished in a simple table look-up manner. Huffman coding involves the following hierarchical procedure. For our example symbols, the hierarchy is shown in Figure 12.3.

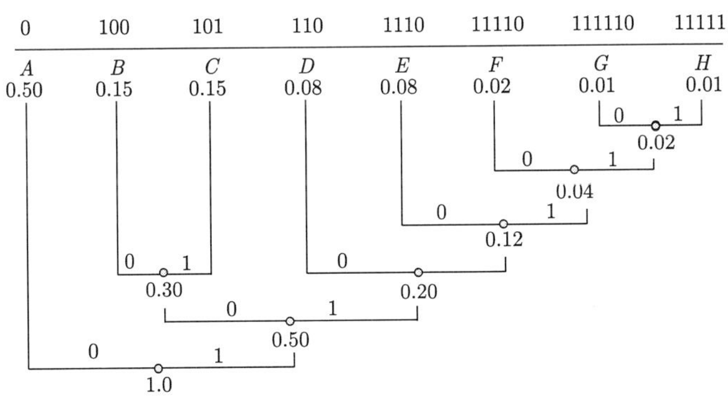

Figure 12.3: Huffman encoding.

1. Write down the symbols together with the associated probability of occurrences, in some order, at the leaf node positions of an inverted tree.
2. Connect the two lowest probability nodes by edges to a next higher level node. Mark this new node with the sum of the above two probabilities.
3. Repeat step 2 until we reach the root node with probability label of value 1.
4. Starting at the root node find the path to a leaf node. While moving along the left edge mark it with a 0, and while moving along the right edge mark it with a 1. The bit sequence labelling the edges from root to a leaf node is the codeword for the corresponding symbol.

In Tables 12.2 and 12.3 two schemes of Huffman encoding are shown for the above example. In both the cases, we encode the symbols starting with the LSB and moving to the MSB in a step by syep fashion. At each step, we merge two subsets of symbols, one is a left subset (encoded with a 0 bit) and the other is a right subset (encoded with 1 a bit). In Tables 12.2 and 12.3 symbols are arranged according to their descending probability values. The two lowest probability symbols G and H are merged first while $\{G\}$ is considered as the left subset and $\{H\}$ as the right subset. In the next step, the subset $\{G, H\}$ is merged with $\{F\}$ in a similar fashion.

Table 12.2: Tabular Representation of Huffman Encoding: Scheme 1

		Coding Steps							
x_i	p_i	1	2	3	4	5	6	7	*Code word*
A	0.50	0.50	0.50	0.50	0.50	0.50	**0.50**	1.00	0
B	0.15	0.15	0.15	0.15	**0.15**	**0.30**	**0.50**		100
C	0.15	0.15	0.15	0.15	**0.15**				101
D	0.08	0.08	0.08	**0.08**	0.20	**0.20**			110
E	0.08	0.08	**0.08**	**0.12**					1110
F	0.02	**0.02**	**0.04**						11110
G	**0.01**	**0.02**							111110
H	**0.01**								111111

Table 12.3: Tabular Representation of Huffman Encoding: Scheme 2

		Coding Steps						
x_i	p_i	1	2	3	4	5	6	*Code word*
A	0.50						0	0
B	0.15				0	0	1	100
C	0.15				1	0	1	101
D	0.08				0	1	1	110
E	0.08			0	1	1	1	1110
F	0.02		0	1	1	1	1	11110
G	0.01	0	1	1	1	1	1	111110
H	0.01	1	1	1	1	1	1	111111

Huffman decoding procedure is somewhat more complex than the corresponding coding procedure. Two approaches are possible.

Bit serial decoding

Let the tree representing symbol to code word mapping is known to both the encoder and decoder. Now, the decoding process involves the following steps:

1. Read the input compressed stream bit by bit and traverse the tree until a leaf node is reached.
2. As each bit in the input stream is read, it is discarded. When the leaf node is reached, the decoder outputs the symbol at the leaf node.
3. Repeat steps 1 and 2 until the input stream is finished.

Lookup-table-based decoding

This is a relatively easy decoding technique. Here, a lookup table is formed by the decoder with 2^L entries where, L is the maximum code word length. For a particular symbol s_i with code word length l_i lookup table entries are as follows:

1. Let c_i be the code word for s_i. An L bit address is formed for s_i with c_i at the most significant l_i bit positions followed by $L - l_i$ number of bits which can take all possible combinations of 0 and 1. So, for each symbol s_i there will be 2^{L-l_i} addresses.
2. At each entry, we form a 2-tuple (s_i, l_i).

Now, the decoding process can be listed as:

1. L bits are read from the input compressed bit stream into a buffer.
2. The buffer points to a location in the lookup table containing a symbol, say, s_k with code word length l_k. Thus, one symbol is decoded.
3. First l_k bits are discarded from the buffer and next l_k bits from the input stream are appended there.
4. Repeat steps 2 to 3 until all of the symbols have been decoded.

The primary advantage of this technique is that it takes constant amount of time to decode any of the symbols. It is easy to implement. However, it is somewhat memory consuming. And, since each symbol must be encoded with integral number of bits, the theoretically maximum coding efficiency is unreachable. This problem is tried to be eliminated in arithmetic encoding where we try to encode a number of symbols at a time.

12.3.5 Arithmetic Coding

In this coding, there is no one-to-one correspondence between symbols and code words. An entire sequence of source symbols is assigned a single code. The code word itself defines an interval of real numbers between 0 and 1. As the number of symbols in the message increases, the interval used to represent it becomes smaller and the number of information units (say, bits) required to represent the interval becomes larger. Each symbol of the message reduces the size of the interval in accordance with its probability of occurrence.

Arithmetic encoding is different from other conventional lossless encoding schemes in that, here we encode a string of symbols as a real value (a fraction between 0 and 1). While, other approaches try to encode each individual symbol of an alphabet separately with an objective to represent the symbol under consideration with the minimum possible number of bits, arithmetic encoding try to encode a word or a group of symbols at a time. Hence, it is quite likely that the arithmetic scheme can provide a higher compression ratio compared to the other methods. However, with larger input size (in terms of number of symbols in an input string) this real encoding may demand sufficient number of bits in order to maintain required precision. The arithmetic encoding process is described in the following paragraph.

The encoding process

1. Initially the string is assumed to be in the half-open interval $[0, 1]$. This interval is split into a number of subintervals, one subinterval for each symbol in the alphabet. Length of each subinterval is proportional to the probability of occurrence of the concerned symbol. The upper limit of each subinterval is the cumulative probability up to and including the corresponding symbol. The lower limit is the cumulative probability up to but not including the symbol.
2. Upon encountering the first symbol in the input string, we select the corresponding subinterval and make it the new current interval. This interval is then divided into subintervals as before.
3. A new subinterval is determined by the second symbol in the message. This subinterval is made the current interval. This interval is then divided into subintervals as before.
4. Step 3 is repeated until there is no more symbol in the input string. The process of encoding, thus, proceeds by narrowing down the length of the subinterval obtained in the immediate earlier step.
5. The final subinterval corresponds to the specified range for the input string. Any value within the lower and upper bounds of the final subinterval can represent the input string. We are free to choose any suitable value within this interval that can be appropriately (minimally) coded in binary.

The above process starts with a table for the alphabet under consideration where each table entry (a row) represents an input symbol and its probability of occurrence. The arithmetic coding process is illustrated, in decimal notation, with the following two examples.

Example 2: Let an alphabet contains four symbols a, b, c and d having their probabilities of occurrences $0.2, 0.2, 0.4$ and 0.2, respectively. We are to encode the string *cbcad* using arithmetic technique.

For encoding using arithmetic encoding approach, we need to map the probabilities of individual symbols on a scale having values between 0 and 1. Here, let us perform this mapping as shown in Table 12.4.

Now, the first symbol in our input string is c. Hence, we select the range $[0.2 \;\; 0.6]$ on the scale and subdivide this range to accommodate the next input symbol (This

Table 12.4: Symbol Table for Alphabet in Example 2

Symbol Index (i)	*Symbol*	*Probability* (p_i)	*Initial Subintervals*	
			Low	*High*
1	a	0.20	0.80	1.00
2	b	0.20	0.60	0.80
3	c	0.40	0.20	0.60
4	d	0.20	0.00	0.20

subdivision is shown in Figure 12.4). The next symbol b falls in the range [0.44 0.52]. Proceeding in a similar manner for the rest of the input symbol, we see that the string *cbcad* can be specified by any value in the range [0.4688 0.4694].

Therefore, the input string can be encoded as a decimal fraction in the range [0.4688 0.4694]. A suitable value in this range can now be converted into binary, and can be stored or transmitted as per requirement of the concerned application.

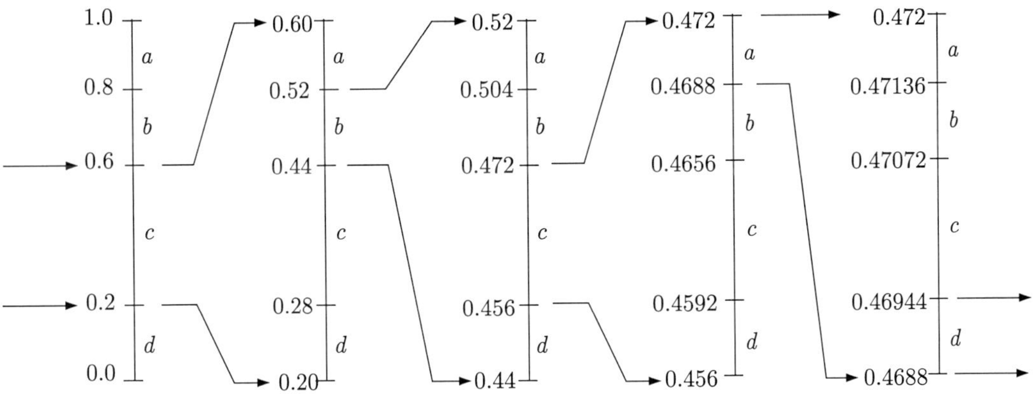

Figure 12.4: Arithmetic encoding (Example 2).

In the above example, we have initially formed a decimal code for an input string by applying a graphical approach, and then converted it into binary. The process, however, can be automatized using the arithmetic encoding algorithm given earlier. Let us consider Example 3 below.

Example 3: We consider a four symbol alphabet with probabilities for the individual symbols as $a_1(0.50), a_2(0.20), a_3(0.10), a_4(0.15)$ and $*$ (0.05). Let the alphabet and its symbols are as shown in Table 12.5. Here, the column *probability* contains the probabilities of occurrences of individual symbols. We have considered a special symbol ('*') as delimeter for each input string. We are to encode the string $a_2a_1a_4$.

The symbol table for the given alphabet is shown in Table 12.5. We shall now apply the arithmetic encoding algorithm to encode $a_2a_1a_4$.

Table 12.5: Symbol Table for Alphabet in Example 3

Symbol Index (i)	*Symbol*	*Probability (p_i)*	*Initial Subintervals*	
			Low	*High*
1	a_1	0.50	0.00	0.50
2	a_2	0.20	0.50	0.70
3	a_3	0.10	0.70	0.80
4	a_4	0.15	0.80	0.95
5	$*$	0.05	0.95	1.00

Our input string is $a_2a_1a_4*$ considering the delimeter '*' as the terminal symbol. The following Table 12.6 illustrates the encoding procedure in a stepwise fashion. In this table, we start with the initial range of the scale [0 1]. Then depending on incoming input symbols we identify the appropriate subrange on the scale at each step. With every encounter with a new symbol in the input string this process is performed, and finally a narrow subrange, specifying the input string, is found out. The encoding process is shown pictorially in Figure 12.5.

Table 12.6: Encoding Steps for the Input String $a_2a_1a_4*$

Old_low	*Old_high*	*Range*	*Symbol*	*Subinterval*	*New_low*	*New_high*
0.00	1.00	1.00	a_2	(0.50 – 0.70)	0.50	0.70
0.50	0.70	0.20	a_1	(0.00 – 0.50)	0.50	0.60
0.50	0.60	0.10	a_4	(0.80 – 0.95)	0.58	0.595
0.58	0.595	0.015	$*$	(0.95 – 1.00)	0.59425	0.595

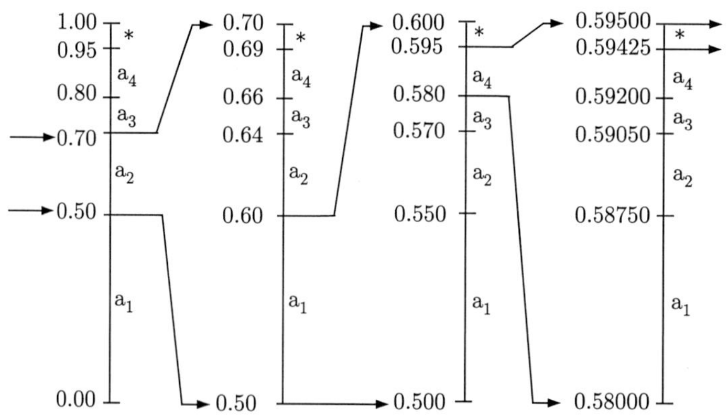

Figure 12.5: Arithmetic encoding (Example 3).

It is clear from the Table 12.6 that we can encode the input string as a fractional value between 0.59425 and 0.59500.

Direct binary encoding

Using a suitable algorithm, we can readily contain the encoded value as a binary string. In this case, all the probability values are initially converted to binary. A pseudocode for the encoding process, in binary, is given below.

Arithmetic Encoding Algorithm:

```
begin
    input the desired string (s)
    create the initial interval as
        lower ← 0
        upper ← 1
        range ← upper − lower
    for each new symbol i in the string s do
    begin
        assign lower and upper limits of subintervals for the symbol as
            lower ← lower + range * subinterval_low_i
            upper ← lower + range * subinterval_high_i
            range ← upper − lower
        set L =binary equivalent of lower as u_k.2^(-k)
        set R =binary equivalent of lower as v_k.2^(-k)
        output equal bits in u and v starting with u_i = v_i
            and stop when u_j ≠ v_j for any j > i
    end
end
```

Example 4: Let us consider a four symbol alphabet with probabilities for the individual symbols as given here. $a_1(0.5), a_2(0.25), a_3(0.125)$ and $a_4(0.125)$.

Encoding process

Initially each symbol is alloted a subinterval within 0 to 1 which is equal to its probability.

- $a_l \rightarrow 0$ to 0.5 (binary 0.0 to 0.1)
- $a_2 \rightarrow 0.5$ to 0.75 (binary 0.1 to 0.11)
- $a_3 \rightarrow 0.75$ to 0.875 (binary 0.11 to 0.111)
- $a_4 \rightarrow 0.875$ to 1.0 (binary 0.111 to 1.0)

Let us now try to derive a code for the sequence $a_2a_1a_3$.

1. For the first symbol a_2,

$$\begin{array}{lll} \text{left boundary} & L = 0.10 & = \sum u_k.2^{-k} \text{ (say)} \\ \text{right boundary} & R = 0.11 & = \sum v_k.2^{-k} \text{ (say)} \\ \text{and} & u_l = v_l = 1 & \text{output } a_1. \end{array}$$

Here, $u_2 = 0, v_2 = 1$, so read next symbol (a_1).

2. Divide the current interval (0.5–0.75) into four subintervals. a_1a_2 corresponds to the subinterval (0.5–0.625). Here,

$$\begin{array}{lll} \text{left boundary} & L = 0.100 & = \sum u_k.2^{-k} \text{ (say)} \\ \text{right boundary} & R = 0.101 & = \sum v_k.2^{-k} \text{ (say)} \\ \text{and} & u_2 = v_2 = 0 & \Rightarrow \text{output } a_0. \end{array}$$

Here, $u_3 = 0, v_3 = 1$, so read next symbol(a_3).

3. Divide the current interval (0.5–0.625). $a_2a_1a_3$ corresponds to the subinterval (0.59375–0.609375). Here,

$$\begin{array}{lll} \text{left boundary} & L = 0.100110 & = \sum u_k.2^{-k}(say) \\ \text{right boundary} & R = 0.100111 & = \sum v_k.2^{-k}(say) \\ \text{and} & u_3 = v_3 = 0 & \Rightarrow \text{output } a_0 \\ & u_4 = v_4 = 1 & \Rightarrow \text{output } a_1 \\ & u_5 = v_5 = 1 & \Rightarrow \text{output } a_1 \end{array}$$

Now, $u_6 = 0, v_6 = 1$, so finish as there is no more symbol.

Therefore, the code for $a_2a_1a_3$ is 10011.

The decoding process

Since, the encoding process produces a single real fraction for an input string of arbitrary length, the decoder has no way to determine the length of the input sequence. Hence, it is absolutely necessary to use a specific delimeter symbol for each input string. This delimeter must also be a member of the symbol alphabet.

A second requirement for the decoding process is to maintain a symbol table which is all the same as the one used in the encoding process, but an extra column augmented to it containing cumulative probabilities for each of the symbols in order.

Arithmetic decoding algorithm

begin
  input the encoded value (v)
  create the initial interval as
    $lower \leftarrow 0$
    $upper \leftarrow 1$
    $range \leftarrow upper - lower$
  repeat
    begin
    for $i = 1$ **to** *alphabet_size* **do**

```
        if (cum_prob_i ≤ (v−lower)/range < cum_prob_{i−1})
            exit the for loop
        output the ith symbol on the output stream
        lower ← lower + range * cum_prob_{i−1}
        upper ← lower + range * cum_prob_i
        range ← upper − lower
    end
  until (symbol decoded ≠ delimeter)
end
```

Let us consider that in the earlier encoding example, the value 0.5945 is used to represent the input string. Now we apply the decoding algorithm to decode this value. The decoder uses an augmented version of the symbol table. This augmented table is shown in Table 12.7. The stepwise description of the decoding process is presented in Table 12.8.

Table 12.7: Augmented Symbol Table for Decoding

Symbol Index (i)	*Symbol*	*Probability* (p_i)	*Cumulative Probability*	*Initial Subintervals*	
				Low	*High*
5	a_1	0.50	0.00	0.00	0.50
4	a_2	0.20	0.50	0.50	0.70
3	a_3	0.10	0.70	0.70	0.80
2	a_4	0.15	0.80	0.80	0.95
1	$*$	0.05	0.95	0.95	1.00
0	–	0.00	1.00	–	–

Table 12.8: Decoding Steps for the Encoded Value $v = 0.60$

Low	*High*	*Range*	*Cum_Prob*$_i$	$\frac{Value-Low}{Range}$	*Cum_Prob*$_{i-1}$	*Symbol*
0.00	1.00	1.00	0.50	0.5945	0.70	a_2
0.50	0.70	0.20	0.00	0.4745	0.50	a_1
0.50	0.60	0.10	0.80	0.9450	0.95	a_4
0.58	0.595	0.015	0.95	0.9670	1.00	‘*’

Therefore the decoded sequence is $a_2a_1a_4*$.

Alternative Approach

Arithmetic decoding algorithm

```
begin
    input the encoded value (v)
```

```
    create the initial interval as
        lower ← 0
        upper ← 1
        range ← upper − lower
    repeat
        begin
        for i = 1 to alphabet_size do
            if (cum_prob_i ≤ (v−lower)/range < cum_prob_{i+1})
                exit the for loop
            output the ith symbol on the output stream
            lower ← lower + range * cum_prob_i
            upper ← lower + range * cum_prob_{i+1}
            range ← upper − lower
        end
    until (symbol decoded ≠ delimeter)
end
```

Table 12.9: Augmented Symbol Table for Decoding

Symbol Index (i)	*Symbol*	*Probability* (p_i)	*Cumulative – Probability*	*Initial Subintervals*	
				Low	*High*
1	a_1	0.50	0.00	0.00	0.50
2	a_2	0.20	0.50	0.50	0.70
3	a_3	0.10	0.70	0.70	0.80
4	a_4	0.15	0.80	0.80	0.95
5	$*$	0.05	0.95	0.95	1.00
6	–	0.00	1.00	–	–

Table 12.10: Decoding Steps for the Encoded Value $v = 0.60$

Low	*High*	*Range*	Cum_Prob_i	$\frac{Value-Low}{Range}$	Cum_Prob_{i+1}	*Symbol*
0.00	1.00	1.00	0.50	0.5945	0.70	a_2
0.50	0.70	0.20	0.00	0.4745	0.50	a_1
0.50	0.60	0.10	0.80	0.9450	0.95	a_4
0.58	0.595	0.015	0.95	0.9670	1.00	'*'

Therefore the decoded sequence is $a_2a_1a_4*$.

12.3.6 LZW Coding

The LZW coding technique is named after its inventors viz. Lempel, Ziv and Welch. It is one of the few compression techniques that reduces redundancy in image data while at the same time maintains image information error-free. It has the capability to reduce coding redundancy and inter-pixel redundancy, simultaneously. Many graphic image file formats use the LZW compression standard as an integrated tool. Graphic Interchange Format (GIF), Tagged Image File Format (TIFF), Portable Document Format (PDF) are some of the image formats that fall under this category.

Conceptually the LZW coding is simple. The process works in a lookup table fashion. Initially a codebook for all possible symbols is created. In case of grey level image files with 256 levels, 256 different symbols are needed. So, there are 256 entries in the codebook initially which are assigned to locations 0 to 255 with location 0 containing 0, location 1 containing 1 and so on. The remaining locations of the codebook are reserved for different sequences of input symbols. Now, let a sequence of two consecutive white pixels are encountered in the input stream of the encoder. The encoder will place this sequence at the next available location in the codebook, i.e. location 256, and transmit the address 256 on the output stream to represent the sequence '255–255'. Thus, instead of sending $8 + 8 = 16$ bits, we can send only 9 bits on the output stream. In this way other sequences are also stored in the codebook. However, the size of the codebook is very important in this coding scheme. If the size is very small (< 256), we cannot encode all input symbols. If the size is equal to the number of different symbols, no benefit is available. If the size is very large, size of the codebook and code words will degrade the performance of the scheme.

Example 5: Let us consider the following 4×4 image.

20	20	50	50
20	20	50	50
20	20	50	50
20	20	50	50

We need to encode this image in LZW scheme with a maximum sequence size of 2. We consider that the grey value range is 0 to 255, and a codebook of 512 entries is used. The initial codebook is given in Table 12.11.

Table 12.11: The Initial Codebook

Location	*Entry*
0	0
1	1
⋮	⋮
255	255
256	–
⋮	⋮
511	–

The process of encoding is shown in a stepwise fashion in Table 12.12 below.

Table 12.12: Sample Run of the LZW Coding Scheme

Current Sequence	*Current Symbol*	*Dictionary Location*	*Dictionary Entry*	*Encoded Output*
–	20	–	–	–
20	20	256	20–20	20
20	50	257	20–50	20
50	50	258	50–50	50
50	20	259	50–20	50
20	20	–	–	–
20–20	50	–	–	256
50	50	–	–	–
50–50	20	–	–	258
20	20	–	–	–
20–20	50	–	–	256
50	50	–	–	–
50–50	20	–	–	258
20	20	–	–	–
20–20	50	–	–	256
50	50	–	–	–
50	50	–	–	258

Besides the above, there exist many other encoding schemes that includes block encoding, quad tree encoding, contour encoding, etc. which may be useful for certain kinds of images.

12.4 Predictive Coding Techniques

In predictive encoding, the value at particular location in the encoded image is computed as some local statistics of neighbour pixels.

12.4.1 LossLess Predictive Encoding

This method is based on eliminating the interpixel redundancies of closely spaced pixels by extracting and encoding only the new information in each pixel. The new information is defined as the difference between the actual and predicted value of that pixel.

In Figure 12.6, the basic components of a lossless predictive encoding system are shown. Here, both the encoder and the decoder contain an identical predictor.

For each successive input pixel values f_n, the predictor generates an anticipated value based on the past input values. The predictor output, denoted by $\hat{f}_n$, is rounded

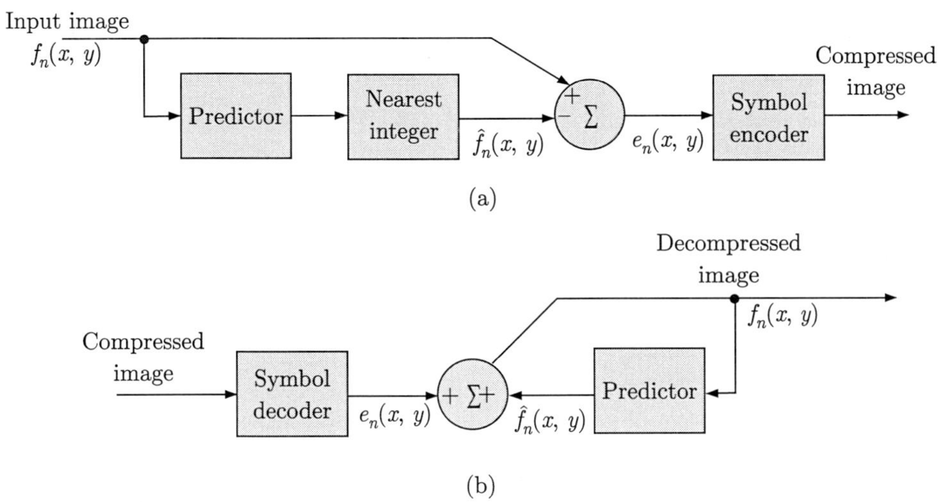

Figure 12.6: LossLess predictive compression model.

and used to form the prediction error

$$e_n = f_n - \hat{f}_n \tag{12.15}$$

The decoder reconstructs e_n from the received code and performs the inverse operation

$$f_n = e_n + \hat{f}_n \tag{12.16}$$

Various local, global and adaptive methods are used to generate $\hat{f}_n$. In many cases, the prediction is performed by a linear combination of m previous pixels, i.e.

$$\hat{f}_n = \text{round}\left[\sum_{i=1}^{m} w_i f_{n-i}\right] \tag{12.17}$$

w_i's are called prediction coefficients.

12.4.2 Lossy Predictive Encoding

In this case, we add a quantizer to the predictive model and examine the resulting trade-off between reconstruction accuracy and compression efficiency. A quantizer, which absorbs the nearest integer function of the error-free encoder is inserted between the symbol encoder and the point where the prediction error is formed. It maps the prediction error into a limited range of outputs, denoted by $\dot{e}_n$, which establishes the amount of compression and distortion associated with lossy predictive coding (Figure 12.7).

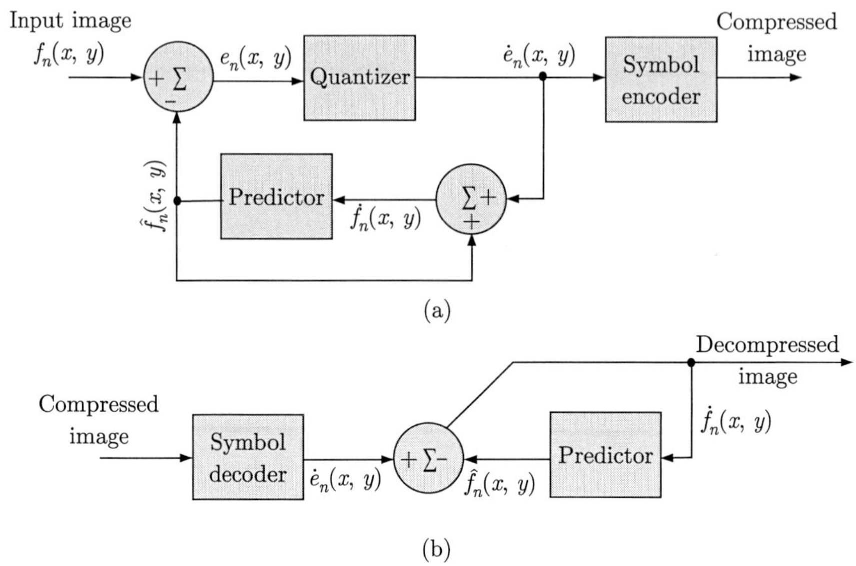

Figure 12.7: Lossy predictive compression model.

The input to the predictor, denoted by $\dot{f}_n$, is generated as a function of past predictions and the corresponding quantized errors. That is

$$\dot{f}_n = \dot{e}_n + \hat{f}_n \tag{12.18}$$

where $\hat{f}_n$ is the rounded predictor output. This closed loop configuration prevents error buildup at the decoder's output.

Sample based coding

Here, images are compressed on a sample-by-sample basis. This can be done either in spatial or in frequency domain. A very simple technique is the DPCM (Differential Pulse Code Modulation) method. This is very similar to lossless JPEG coding, except that quantization is done here. It is basically a predictive coding scheme. For each input sample $f(x, y)$, an error signal $e(x, y)$ is produced using the prediction signal $\hat{f}(x, y)$. $\hat{f}(x, y)$ is a weighted sum of three to four previously decoded pixels near $f(x, y)$, where,

$$\dot{f}(x, y) = \hat{f}(x, y) + \dot{e}(x, y) \tag{12.19}$$

denotes the decoder's estimate for $f(x, y)$. Here, $\dot{e}(x, y)$ is the quantized output sample.

A sample prediction mask w and the corresponding image fragment $\dot{f}$ are shown below. Here, the predictor is:

$$\hat{f}(x, y) = w_1\dot{f}(x-1, y-1) + w_2\dot{f}(x-1, y) + w_3\dot{f}(x, y-1) \tag{12.20}$$

$$w = \begin{array}{|c|c|}\hline w_1 & w_2 \\ \hline w_3 & * \\ \hline \end{array} \quad \text{and} \quad f = \begin{array}{|c|c|}\hline (x-1,y-1) & (x-1,y) \\ \hline (x,y-1) & (x,y) \\ \hline \end{array}$$

where w_1, w_2 and w_3 are weights that sum to one. The same predictor function must be used in both encoder and decoder.

If the image is highly correlated, $\hat{f}(x, y)$ will be comparable to $f(x, y)$, and hence, prediction error $e(x, y)$ will be small. Generally a uniform quantizer is used to quantize the error signal.

Block-based coding

Instead of coding individual samples separately, here, a block of input samples is considered at a time. Common methods are Vector Quantization (VQ) and transform coding. In the spatial domain VQ methods are used. VQ needs more processing in the encoder than in the decoder. In transform coding, the basis functions commonly used are Discrete Fourier Transform (DFT), Discrete Cosine Transform (DCT), Discrete Sine Transform (DST), Discrete Hartley transform (DHT) and Karhunen–Loeve Transform (KLT). Of these, the KLT is found to produce the highest compression ratio and the DHT the poorest compression ratio. The KLT has several drawbacks also. For example, the basis function, here, depends on the image itself. Out of the other transforms, the DCT produces results closer to the KLT.

12.5 Lossy Transform Coding

Transform based coding techniques fall in the category of lossy image compression. Here, a reversible transformation is applied over the input spatial image to obtain its frequency domain counterpart. In fact, in this process, a set of transform coefficients are derived in this transformation process. These transform coefficients hide image information within themselves. It has been found that in case of DFT or DCT, lower frequency components contain average image properties, while higher frequency components contain finer image details or sharp image properties. All the transform coding techniques are basically block based coding techniques also. Here, the complete image is broken into pieces or blocks of suitable sizes, and the transformation is applied over each block separately.

An $N \times N$ image can be subdivided into $\left(\frac{N}{n}\right)^2$ number of sub-images of size $n \times n$. Generally, most of the image informations are found to be correlated in a small number of transform coefficients around the origin of the frequency axes. Therefore, during encoding we need to maintain only a few transform coefficients which are assumed to contain essential image information. The remaining coefficients have small or negligible effect on reconstruct of the image applying inverse transformation.

By breaking the image into sub-images, we can ensure

- reduction of processing cost, and
- a better output.

The most common choice is subdivision into 8×8 sub-images. Applying forward transformation and maintaining atmost 50% transform coefficients we can safely store or transmit an image.

DCT based coding

DCT based image encoding forms a standard for still and video image compression. Here, the image is divided into blocks of size $n \times n$ in the spatial domain. In the DCT standard n is taken to be 8. DCT is performed on each block separately. A quantization step eliminates all insignificant values. The remaining frequency domain coefficients are entropy encoded to get the final coded form. DCT based compression technique comes out to be a standard because of the following properties:

- For highly correlated image data (which is very often the case) the performance of compression is nearly equal to the theoretical maximum.
- Due to its orthogonality property, the DCT is a reversible process. This means that the same computations are needed for forward and backward transformations.
- Two-dimensional DCT is linearly separable and can be performed as a sequence of two one-dimensional transforms.
- Like fast Fourier transform, a fast DCT algorithm exist which allows efficient implementation of encoding and decoding processes.
- Since the basis transformation matrices for DCT are independent of image contents, they need not be recomputed for each image differently.

A DCT (transform) based compression system works in the following manner. The encoder transforms each 8×8 block of the image using DCT. The DCT coefficients, thus obtained, are quantized to eliminate non-significant ones. This process of quantization is thus losing information which is irrecoverable. However, besides quantization errors, the process of computing DCT itself may cause loss of information due to its level of accuracy. After quantization the non-zero coefficients are zig-zag coded. The resulting sequence is then fed to an entropy encoder. Sometimes a run length encoder is concatenated with the entropy encoder.

An example of a DCT based encoding is shown below. Here, the input image is considered to be a 8×8 matrix of intensity values

$$X = \begin{bmatrix} 60 & 57 & 55 & 61 & 63 & 71 & 72 & 70 \\ 55 & 53 & 65 & 79 & 99 & 87 & 77 & 71 \\ 57 & 56 & 98 & 103 & 120 & 124 & 67 & 65 \\ 55 & 66 & 98 & 122 & 125 & 121 & 66 & 75 \\ 64 & 67 & 89 & 117 & 122 & 121 & 76 & 70 \\ 67 & 65 & 98 & 103 & 113 & 123 & 63 & 65 \\ 63 & 67 & 65 & 61 & 63 & 64 & 73 & 67 \\ 65 & 65 & 67 & 69 & 89 & 87 & 72 & 69 \end{bmatrix}$$

After level shifting (subtracting 128 from each value), we get

$$Y = \begin{bmatrix} -68 & -71 & -73 & -67 & -65 & -57 & -56 & -58 \\ -73 & -75 & -63 & -49 & -29 & -41 & -51 & -57 \\ -71 & -72 & -30 & -25 & -8 & -4 & -61 & -63 \\ -73 & -62 & -30 & -6 & -3 & -7 & -62 & -53 \\ -64 & -61 & -39 & -11 & -6 & -7 & -52 & -58 \\ -61 & -63 & -30 & -25 & -15 & -5 & -65 & -63 \\ -65 & -61 & -63 & -67 & -65 & -64 & -55 & -61 \\ -63 & -63 & -61 & -59 & -39 & -41 & -56 & -59 \end{bmatrix}$$

Applying forward DCT the following matrix is obtained

$$Z = \begin{bmatrix} -394 & -40 & -102 & 29 & 7 & -12 & 29 & -6 \\ -4 & -14 & -9 & 0 & 5 & 3 & 1 & 0 \\ -78 & 1 & 75 & -3 & -7 & 5 & -23 & 12 \\ -12 & 6 & 18 & -1 & -2 & 6 & -4 & -5 \\ 6 & -2 & 1 & -1 & 5 & -1 & -6 & -7 \\ -18 & 8 & 16 & -14 & -6 & 2 & 0 & -3 \\ 21 & 4 & -23 & 9 & -4 & -4 & 21 & -3 \\ -10 & 1 & 12 & 1 & -5 & 6 & -5 & 1 \end{bmatrix}$$

The following quantization matrix is used for point by point division to get quantized image.

$$T = \begin{bmatrix} 16 & 11 & 10 & 16 & 24 & 40 & 51 & 61 \\ 12 & 12 & 14 & 19 & 26 & 58 & 60 & 55 \\ 14 & 13 & 16 & 24 & 40 & 57 & 69 & 56 \\ 14 & 17 & 22 & 29 & 51 & 87 & 80 & 62 \\ 18 & 22 & 37 & 56 & 68 & 109 & 103 & 77 \\ 24 & 35 & 55 & 64 & 81 & 104 & 113 & 92 \\ 49 & 64 & 78 & 87 & 103 & 121 & 120 & 101 \\ 72 & 92 & 95 & 98 & 112 & 100 & 103 & 99 \end{bmatrix}$$

This quantization process is also called non-maximal supression. After quantization and rounding, we get

$$W = \begin{bmatrix} -25 & -4 & -10 & 2 & 0 & 0 & 1 & 0 \\ 0 & -1 & -1 & 0 & 0 & 0 & 0 & 0 \\ -6 & 0 & 5 & 0 & 0 & 0 & 0 & 0 \\ -1 & 0 & 1 & 0 & 0 & 0 & 0 & 0 \\ 0 & 0 & 0 & 0 & 0 & 0 & 0 & 0 \\ -1 & 0 & 0 & 0 & 0 & 0 & 0 & 0 \\ 0 & 0 & 0 & 0 & 0 & 0 & 0 & 0 \\ 0 & 0 & 0 & 0 & 0 & 0 & 0 & 0 \end{bmatrix}$$

The above matrix contains mostly zero valued elements in its lower diagonal part. Hence, we can use zig-zag encoding process to store this, and thereby attain atleast 50% savings of storage area. The encoded version, here, becomes

$$-25\ -4\ 0\ -6\ -1\ -10\ 2\ -1\ 0\ -1\ 0\ 0\ 5\ 0\ 0\ 0\ 0\ 0\ 1\ 0\ -1\ 0\ 0\ 0\ 0\ 0\ 0\ 1.$$

It may be noted that by keeping lesser number of transform coefficients we can achieve higher compression ratio. The process of zig-zag encoding is illustrated in a later section.

To decompress the above encoded image, we follow the reverse processes in order. Applying pointwise multiplication with T (inverse quantization), we get

$$V = \begin{bmatrix} -400 & -44 & -100 & 32 & 0 & 0 & 51 & 0 \\ 0 & -12 & -14 & 0 & 0 & 0 & 0 & 0 \\ -84 & 0 & 80 & 0 & 0 & 0 & 0 & 0 \\ -14 & 0 & 22 & 0 & 0 & 0 & 0 & 0 \\ 0 & 0 & 0 & 0 & 0 & 0 & 0 & 0 \\ -24 & 0 & 0 & 0 & 0 & 0 & 0 & 0 \\ 0 & 0 & 0 & 0 & 0 & 0 & 0 & 0 \\ 0 & 0 & 0 & 0 & 0 & 0 & 0 & 0 \end{bmatrix}$$

Applying inverse DCT, we get

$$U = \begin{bmatrix} -69 & -86 & -72 & -79 & -68 & -49 & -66 & -57 \\ -66 & -74 & -49 & -47 & -36 & -26 & -55 & -55 \\ -74 & -73 & -33 & -21 & -11 & -11 & -55 & -65 \\ -75 & -70 & -25 & -10 & 0 & -5 & -54 & -68 \\ -63 & -62 & -23 & -12 & -3 & -4 & -48 & -58 \\ -60 & -67 & -40 & -37 & -28 & -22 & -55 & -58 \\ -63 & -76 & -58 & -62 & -54 & -41 & -65 & -62 \\ -56 & -73 & -59 & -67 & -58 & -43 & -63 & -56 \end{bmatrix}$$

The output image is obtained by adding 128 to each element as

$$O = \begin{bmatrix} 59 & 42 & 56 & 49 & 60 & 79 & 62 & 71 \\ 62 & 54 & 79 & 81 & 92 & 102 & 73 & 73 \\ 54 & 55 & 95 & 107 & 117 & 117 & 73 & 63 \\ 53 & 58 & 103 & 118 & 128 & 123 & 74 & 60 \\ 65 & 66 & 105 & 116 & 125 & 124 & 80 & 70 \\ 68 & 61 & 88 & 91 & 100 & 106 & 73 & 70 \\ 65 & 52 & 70 & 66 & 74 & 87 & 63 & 66 \\ 72 & 55 & 69 & 61 & 70 & 85 & 65 & 72 \end{bmatrix}$$

The difference image between input and output becomes

$$DI = \begin{bmatrix} 1 & 15 & -1 & 12 & 3 & -8 & 10 & -1 \\ -7 & -1 & -14 & -2 & 7 & -15 & 4 & -2 \\ 3 & 1 & 3 & -4 & 3 & 7 & -6 & 2 \\ 2 & 8 & -5 & 4 & -3 & -2 & -8 & 15 \\ -1 & 1 & -16 & 1 & -3 & -3 & -4 & 0 \\ -1 & 4 & 10 & 12 & 13 & 17 & -10 & -5 \\ -2 & 15 & -5 & -5 & -11 & -23 & 10 & 1 \\ -7 & 10 & -2 & 8 & 19 & 2 & 7 & -3 \end{bmatrix}$$

12.6 Image Compression Standards

As already mentioned, digital images are important components of a multimedia document or applications. Images may come in colour or black and white modes. Since images contain huge amount of data, they must be put into a compressed form before using them in some multimedia application. From the presentation point of view images may be of two types—still image and moving image. Therefore, two kinds of compression standards exist. In Chapter 13, we shall discuss the formats of representation of different types of images used in different computer applications. Here, a brief introduction on image compression standards are provided.

12.6.1 Compression Standard for Still Images

The JPEG (Joint Photographic Expert Group of ISO/CCITT) standard is taken to be the de-facto standard for still images. It works for both monochrome (grey) and colour images and supports a variety of applications. This is the first international standard for continuous tone still images. To satisfy the needs of different applications, JPEG developed two different standards. A DCT (Discrete Cosine Transform) based lossy compression standard, and a predictive lossless compression standard.

LossLess JPEG compression

Commonly, we know JPEG (Joint Photographic Expert Group) as a lossy compression standard that uses transformation coding. However, JPEG suggested a lossless compression standards also. It performs differential coding to produce prediction residuals which are categorized according to the exact number of bits to represent them. These categories are specified in a prediction table which is available to both the encoder and the decoder. Predicted value y for a pixel with value x can be determined by using any of the following functions:

$$y = \begin{cases} 0 \\ a \\ b \\ c \\ a+b-c \\ a+\dfrac{b-c}{2} \\ b+\dfrac{a-c}{2} \\ \dfrac{a+b}{2} \end{cases} \tag{12.21}$$

where, the prediction kernel is a 2×2 pixel grid as shown below.

c	b
a	$*$

Here, * indicates the position of predicted value. The particular choice of the prediction function is communicated to the decoder as a part of the input stream header.

Example 6: Consider a pixel grid with $a = 120$, $b = 64$, $c = 100$ and $x = 75$ as shown below. The problem is to encode the value of $x = 75$.

100	64
120	75

Answer: Let $y = a + \frac{b-c}{2}$ be the prediction function. Thus $y = 102$ and the prediction residual is $r = y - x = 102 - 75 = 27$. Now from Table 12.13, 27 falls in the category of 5. Binary equivalent of 27 in 5 bits is 11011. So 27 is encoded as the pair (Huffman code of 5, 11011). It is notable that only the indices of the prediction table (categories) are entropy encoded. The residue is presented in one's complement form. In the decoder, the category code (i.e. 5) is extracted first, and hence, the next 5 bits are the magnitude of the residual. Values of a, b and c are already decoded by the decoder. So, $y = 102$ as before and x can be evaluated as $x = y - r = 102 - 27 = 75$. If, we consider that Huffman code for 5 is of length 4 bits, then, to code 75 we need only 9 bits instead of 16 bits as usual (if 16-bit intensity values are considered).

Table 12.13: Categorical Prediction Residual Table for LossLess JPEG

Category	*Prediction Residual*
0	0
1	$-1, 1$
2	$-3, -2, 2, 3$
3	$-7, \ldots, -4, 4, \ldots, 7$
4	$-15, \ldots, -8, 8, \ldots, 15$
5	$-31, \ldots, -16, 16, \ldots, 31$
6	$-63, \ldots, -32, 32, \ldots, 63$
7	$-127, \ldots, -64, 64, \ldots, 127$
8	$-255, \ldots, -128, 128, \ldots, 255$
9	$-511, \ldots, -256, 256, \ldots, 511$
10	$-1023, \ldots, -512, 512, \ldots, 1023$
11	$-2047, \ldots, -1024, 1024, \ldots, 2047$
12	$-4095, \ldots, -2048, 2048, \ldots, 4095$
13	$-8191, \ldots, -4096, 4096, \ldots, 8191$
14	$-16383, \ldots, -8192, 8192, \ldots, 16383$
15	$-32767, \ldots, -16384, 16384, \ldots, 32767$
16	32768

Lossy JPEG compression

There are different kinds of lossy compression standards developed by the JPEG. Of these the very commonly used kinds are

- ***Sequential DCT-based compression:*** This is the default JPEG standard. Here grey levels or colour components are encoded in a single left-to-right and top-to-bottom fashion.
- ***Progressive DCT-based compression:*** Here multiple scan over the image are needed. The first scan encodes an low resolution version of the image using a small number of bits. Subsequent scans provide more bits per pixel information to reach a picture quality as indicated in the quantization table. The number of scans, thus, determines the output image quality. For online applications (web, etc.) the image after the first scan only may be used.
- ***Hierarchical DCT-based compression:*** A pyramidal or hierarchical encoding technique is followed here. Encoded blocks at each level of the hierarchy differ in resolution by a factor of 2 in either horizontal or vertical dimensions or both. The image at the root of the hierarchy is with the lowest resolution, and it is actually a compressed low-pass filtered image. Images at successive levels provide more details.

In lossless compression standards, the compression ration can hardly be around 3. But in case of lossy compression standards we can achieve a value as high as 15 whilst maintaining a very good output image quality.

The sequential JPEG compression applies the following processes in sequence: a forward DCT, zig-zag reordering, quantization, zero run length coding and entropy encoding. The decompression involves entropy decoding, run length decoding, de-quantization, reverse zig-zag ordering and a reverse DCT in that order. The encoding steps are briefly described here.

The 8×8 Discrete Cosine Transform (DCT)

The image breaks into 8×8 blocks of pixels, then for each 8×8 block, is applied the DCT transform. Note that if the X dimension of the original image is not divisible by 8, the encoder should make it divisible by completing the remaining right columns (until X becomes a multiple of 8) with the right-most column of the original image. Similar, if the Y dimension is not divisible by 8, the encoder should complete the remaining lines with the bottom-most line of the original image. The 8×8 blocks are processed from left to right and from top to bottom. Since a pixel in the 8×8 block has 3 components, the DCT is applied separately to 3 blocks of 8×8.

The zig-zag reordering of the 64 DCT coefficients

So, after we performed the DCT transform over a block of 8×8 values, we have a new 8×8 block. Then, this 8×8 block is traversed in zig-zag like this (The numbers in the 8×8 block indicate the order in which we traverse the bi-dimensional 8×8 matrix). The zig-zag sequence is shown in Figure 12.8.

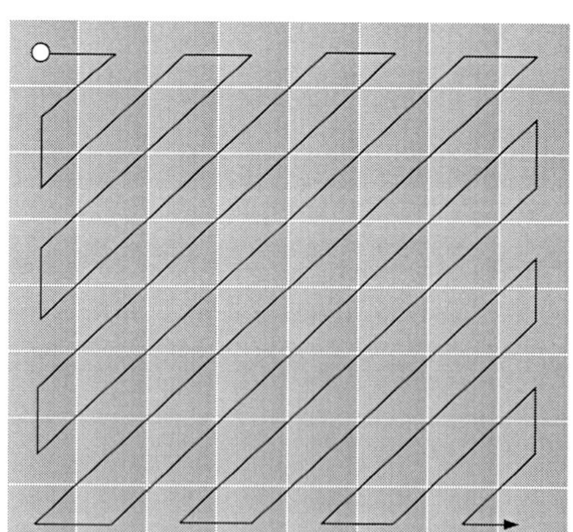

Figure 12.8: Zig-zag ordering sequence in JPEG.

Quantization

At this stage, we have a sorted vector with 64 values corresponding to the amplitudes of the 64 spatial frequencies present in the 8×8 block. These 64 values are quantized: Each value is divided by a dividend specified in a vector with 64 values—the quantization table, then it is rounded to the nearest integer.

$$\text{for}(i = 0; i \leq 63; i++)\text{vector}[i] = (\text{int})\left(\frac{\text{vector}[i]}{\text{quantization\_table}[i]} + 0.5\right)$$

This table is based upon "psycho visual thresholding," it has "been used with good results on 8-bit per sample luminance and chrominance images". Most existing encoders use simple multiples of this example, but the values are not claimed to be optimal (An encoder can use ANY OTHER quantization table). The table is specified in the JPEG file with the DQT (Define Quantization Table) marker. Most commonly there is one table for Y, and another one for the chrominance (C_b and C_r). The quantization process has the key role in the JPEG compression. It is the process which removes the high frequencies present in the original image—in consequence the high detail. We do this because of the fact that the eye is much more sensitive to lower spatial frequencies than to higher frequencies, so we can remove, with very little visual loss, higher frequencies. This is done by dividing values at high indexes in the vector (the amplitudes of higher frequencies) with larger values than the values by which are divided the amplitudes of lower frequencies. The bigger the values in the quantization table are, the bigger is the error (in consequence of the visual error) introduced by this lossy process, and the smaller is the visual quality. Another important fact is that in most images the colour varies slow from one pixel to another, so most images will have a small quantity of high detail $\rightarrow$ a small amount (small amplitudes) of high spatial frequencies—but they have a lot of image information contained in the low spatial frequencies. In consequence in the new quantized vector, at high spatial frequencies, we will have a lot of consecutive zeroes.

The zero Run Length Coding (RLC)

The basic concept of the run length coding is to code the consecutive 0's encountering right of the scan of a number by its length.

The Huffman coding

This is final step in the encoding process. A standard table of codewords is used for this purpose.

The overall JPEG encoding and decoding processes are shown in Figure 12.9.

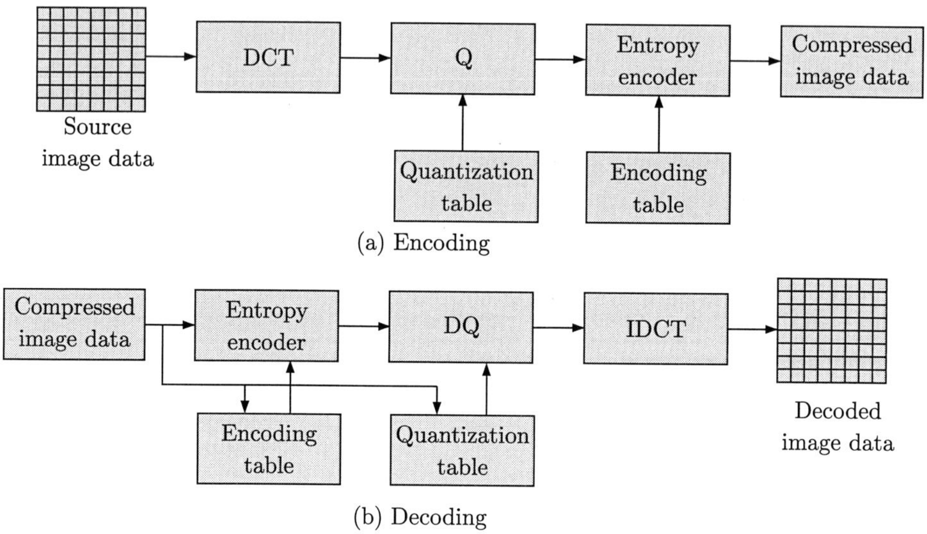

Figure 12.9: JPEG encoding and decoding.

12.7 Problems

1. Define the following terms: (i) image entropy, (ii) image redundancy, and (iii) compression ratio.
2. What do you mean by image compression? Derive an expression for compression ratio.
3. Explain the significance of image compression.
4. What do you mean by compression ratio? Do you consider that lower compression ratio ensures better images upon reproduction?
5. Mention different kinds of redundancies normally present in an image. Name some techniques to eliminate or reduce such redundancies.
6. Draw a block diagram of an image compression system and explain roles of its different components.
7. You want to use variable length encoding in images. You are given one image and its histogram equalized version. For which image your compression ratio will be higher?
8. A grey level image involves two bits per pixel. Probabilities of the four grey levels $\{0, 1, 2, 3\}$ are $P_0 = 0.1, P_1 = 0.3, P_2 = 0.5, P_3 = 0.1$. Determine the entropy of the image, amount of information redundancy, achievable compression ratio.

9. How can achievable compression ratio be determined from image histogram?
10. Derive frequency dependent prefix codes for symbols **a**, **b**, **c** and **d** having probabilities of 0.15, 0.30, 0.50 and 0.05, respectively.
11. What is meant by entropy of some message? How can you compute it?
12. An alphabet and its symbol probabilities are given as

Symbol	a_1	a_2	a_3	a_4	a_5	a_6	a_7	a_8
Probability	0.19	0.25	0.21	0.16	0.08	0.06	0.03	0.02

Find out entropy of the source.

13. For the symbols in the alphabet in Question 12, construct the Huffman tree and find out Huffman codes.
14. Consider the following 4 grey image:

10	10	15	15
15	15	50	50
25	25	25	50
15	15	50	50

Find out the entropy of the image.

15. For the image given in Question 14, find out the Huffman code and arithmetic code, and compare efficiencies of the two strategies (for arithmetic coding consider each row of the image as a string).
16. Consider three symbols and their probabilities as shown in table below.

Symbol	*Probability*	*Subinterval*
a_1	0.2	[0.0 0.2]
a_2	0.4	[0.2 0.6]
a_3	0.4	[0.6 1.0]

Find out the arithmetic code of the string "$a_2a_1a_1a_3$" in binary.

17. For the symbol table given in Question 16, find out the string whose arithmetic code value is 0.076.
18. Find a set of code words and average word length using Huffman coding scheme for a set of input symbols with probabilities given in Table below.

Symbol	a_1	a_2	a_3	a_4	a_5	a_6	a_7	a_8
Probability	0.02	0.15	0.03	0.15	0.05	0.20	0.10	0.30

Find out the lowest possible average number of bits per code word to represent these symbols.

19. Mention the steps of lossy and lossless JPEG compression.

CHAPTER 13

Image File Formats

In earlier chapters, we have described several commonly used image processing techniques. Images are part and parcel of any graphical software, user interfaces and multimedia documents. In order to maintain portability and to help graphical and multimedia application developers, a number of image representation standards have been developed. In this chapter, we shall study some of the common image file formats which help us accessing, processing and converting image data as per requirements.

13.1 Image Formats

In different commercial packages images are produced in many different forms. A particular representation may be suitable for some specific applications, while other forms stand for some others. Accordingly a number of image representation standards are used in practice. Some of the key features of such image representation standards are:

- Easy editing (modification)
- Easy interchange among formats
- Fast transmission
- Low storage consumption (after compression)
- High visual resolution
- Applicability for animation
- Multiple image support

We shall discuss some of the common image formats.

Most commonly used device independent raster image formats: are

- BMP - BitMaP format
- GIF - Graphics Interchange Format
- JPEG - JPEG File Interchange Format (JFIF)
- MIX - Microsoft Image eXtension format

- PNG - Portable Network Graphics format
- TIFF - Tagged Image File Format

Most of the raster formats have specific headers and an image reader must know this information before accessing the actual data. Most of the sophisticated formats also contain many other meta data regarding the organization of the image data.

13.1.1 Raster Formats

BMP, GIF, JPEG, MIX, PNG, and TIFF are raster image formats. A raster image is also known as a bitmap and is created from rows of small dots called pixels ("picture elements") or "bits". In the monochrome era, pixels were represented by a single bit denoting either black or white.

Because a raster format uses a fixed method of specifying an image, the image cannot always be immediately rescaled without losing definition.

13.1.2 Bitmap (BMP) Format

The Microsoft Windows BMP format (.bmp file extension) can display millions of colours. It contains raw uncompressed (in some cases lossless compression) data in most of the cases. Hence, images can be edited easily. Because it is supported by several programs, it is an extremely practical file format to use when you are providing an image to someone who may not have the program in which you created the image. However, it does not support transparency and animation.

13.1.3 Graphics Interchange Format (GIF)

The GIF format (.gif file extension) is one of the two most common file formats for images on the world wide web (www), since it is supported by almost all web browsers. Because this format can only display a maximum of 256 colours, it is best used for black-and-white line drawings, colour clip art, and pictures with large blocks of solid colours. The GIF89a format also supports both transparency and animation.

13.1.4 Joint Photographic Experts Group (JPEG)

The JPEG format (.jpg) is the most common file format for images on the web. It can be used to display high-quality photographs, or pictures containing millions of colours. It can efficiently compress large, high-quality photos into very compact files, so it is very useful for inclusion in e-mails. However, the more the reduction in the image's file size (or modify and re-save the image), the more image information is discarded and quality is decreased. Moreover, this format does not support transparency or animation.

13.1.5 Tagged Image File Format (TIFF)

The TIFF format (.tif or .tiff file extension) produces very high quality images and is therefore used in publishing quite often. It can display millions of colours (although greyscale images are limited to 256 colours or shades), and typically results in larger image files than the GIF or JPEG formats. If one plans to edit an image in a program other than the one in which it is created, saving it in this format is helpful, since it is widely recognized by various programs.

13.1.6 Microsoft Image Extensions (MIX)

The MIX format (.mix file extension) is the Microsoft PhotoDraw native file format and can display millions of colours. It maintains all the objects in the image separately, allowing us to edit the individual objects when we reopen the file. (Other file formats "flatten" all the objects into a single object.) Currently, it is only supported by PhotoDraw, but one can save to other file formats.

13.1.7 Portable Network Graphics (PNG)

The PNG format (.png file extension) can display millions of colours. Being a new format, fewer browsers currently support it (although it is quickly gaining support). Images saved in this format will not degrade in quality, even if the file is modified, compressed and saved many times. It supports transparency, but it does not support animation, since it cannot contain multiple images. Table 13.1 shows a comparison of different image formats.

Table 13.1: Comparison among Different Image Formats

Action	*BMP*	*GIF*	*JPG*	*MIX*	*PNG*	*TIFF*
Post image on web page		X	X			
Export easily to other programs	X					X
Compress a large image for e-mail			X			
Use transparent areas in images	X			X		
Create animation files		X				
Decompress images without loss	X		X			
Create highest quality images					X	
Edit individual objects in an image				X		
Display millions of colours	X	X		X	X	X
Retain image quality	X	X		X	X	

13.2 BMP Format

Device-Independent Bitmap (DIB) format allows us to display the bitmap on any type of display device, i.e. the bitmap specifies pixel colour in a form independent of the method used by a display to represent colour. In windows the default file name extension for DIB file is .BMP. As it is supported by several programs, it is an extremely useful portable image format (Figure 13.1).

Typical BMP file contains four sections of data :
File Header
Bitmap Header
Colour Palette
Bitmap Data
Os2 Bmp file header is 14 bytes in length

```
typedef struct_Os2BmpFileHeader
    {
        WORDFileType;              /* File type identifier */
        DWORDFileSize;             /* Size of the file in bytes */
        WORDXHotSpot;              /* X coordinate of hotspot */
        WORDYHotSpot;              /* Y coordinate of hotspot */
        DWORDBitmapOffset;         /* Starting position of image data */
    }   OS2BMPFILEHEADER;
```

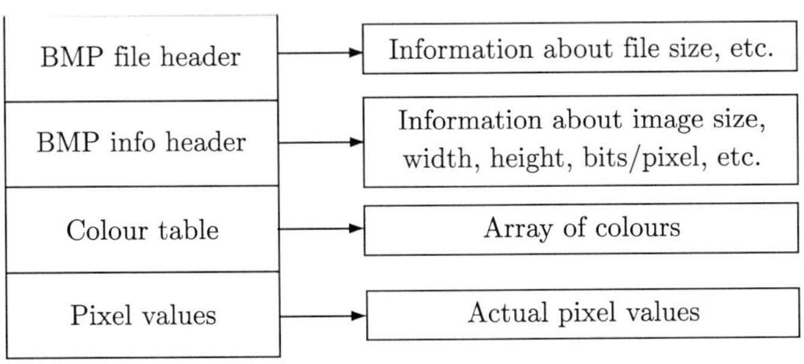

Figure 13.1: General BMP file format.

FileType holds a 2-byte magic value used to identify the file type. This value is 4D42h (or "BM" in ASCII) for a single bitmap, 4142h ("BA") for a bitmap array, 4349h ("IC") for an icon, 4943h ("CI") for a colour icon, 5450h ("PT") for a pointer, and 5043h ("CP") for a colour pointer. Size is the combined size of the file header plus the bitmap header in bytes. This value is typically zero in many BMP files. XHotSpot and YHotSpot store the coordinates of the central point of the hotspot on the bitmap for icons and pointers. These coordinates are relative to the lower-left corner of the bitmap. If there is no hotspot, then these values will be zero. These values are not used in bitmap and bitmap array BMP files. BitmapOffset is the offset, in bytes, from the beginning of the file to the pixel data that corresponds to this header.

BMP version 1.x (IBM OS/2 1.x)

Following the file header in v1.x BMP files is a second header called the **bitmap header**. This header contains information specific to the bitmap data. This header is 12 bytes in length and has the following format:

```
typedef struct_Os21x Bitmap Header
    {
    DWORD Size;             /* Size of this header in bytes */
    WORD Width;             /* Image width in pixels */
    WORD Height;            /* Image height in pixels */
    WORD NumPlanes;         /* Number of colour planes */
    WORD BitsPerPixel;      /* Number of bits per pixel */
    }   OS2 1x BITMAPHEADER;
```

Following is the header of the colour palette data. The colour palette is present if the image supports 1, 4 and 8-bit data. 24-bit data never uses a palette.

```
Typedef struct_OS21x Palette Element
    {
        BYTEBlue;
        BYTEGreen;
        BYTERed;
    }   OS21xPaletteElement;
```

Each component ranges from 0 to 255.

```
typedef struct_Os22x Bitmap Header(Size = 64bytes)
    {
        DWORD Size;                 /* Size of this structure in bytes */
        DWORD Width;                /* Bitmap width in pixels */
        DWORD Height;               /* Bitmap height in pixel */
        WORD NumPlanes;             /* Number of bit planes (colour depth) */
        WORD BitsPerPixel;          /* Number of bits per pixel per plane */
                                    /* Fields added for OS/2 2.x follow this line */
        DWORD Compression;          /* Bitmap compression scheme */
        DWORD ImageDataSize;        /* Size of bitmap data in bytes */
        DWORD XResolution;          /* X resolution of display device */
        DWORD YResolution;          /* Y resolution of display device */
        DWORD ColoursUsed;          /* Number of colour table indices used */
        DWORD ColoursImportant;     /* Number of important colour indices */
```

```
    WORD Units;                 /* Type of units used to measure resolution */
    WORD Reserved;              /* Pad structure to 4-byte boundary */
    WORD Recording;             /* Recording algorithm */
    WORD Rendering;             /* Halftoning algorithm used */
    DWORD Size1;                /* Reserved for use by halftoning algorithm */
    DWORD Size2;                /* Reserved for use by halftoning algorithm */
    DWORD ColourEncoding;       /* Colour model used in bitmap */
    DWORD Identifier;           /* Reserved for application use */
} OS2 2x BITMAPHEADER;
```

The colour palette definition is almost the same as that for version 1.x.

```
Typedefstruct_OS22x Palette Element
{
    BYTE Blue;
    BYTE Green;
    BYTE Red;
    BYTE Reserved; /* for padding upto even-byte boundary */
} OS2 2x PaletteElement;
```

BMP colour palette is an array of structures that specify B, G, R intensity values. However, in the bitmap we always store the index of a colour palette entry. FileType holds a 2-byte magic value used to identify the file type. This value is 4D42h (or "BM" in ASCII) for a single bitmap. Uncompressed data is a series of values representing either colour palette indices or actual RGB colour values. Monochrome bitmaps contain one bit per pixel, eight pixels per byte (with the most significant bit being the leftmost pixel), and have a 2-element colour palette. If a BMP reader chooses to ignore the colour palette, all "one" bits are set to the display's foreground colour and all "zero" bits are set to the background colour.

4-bit pixels are packed two per byte with the most significant nibble being the leftmost pixel. 8-bit pixels are stored one per byte. Both 4- and 8-bit pixel values are indices into colour palettes 16 and 256 elements in size, respectively. The OS/2 BMP format supports a simple Run Length encoded (RLE) compression scheme for compressing 4-, 8-, and 24-bit bitmap data. 1-bit monochrome data may be compressed using the Huffman 1D algorithm common to facsimile transmission applications. A two-value RLE scheme is used: 1st contains the run length and the 2nd contains pixel value.

In addition to encoded runs, there are unencoded runs, delta markers, end-of-scan-line markers, and an end-of-RLE data marker. An unencoded run may contain from 3 to 255 pixel values. The first byte of an unencoded run is always zero. This makes it possible to tell the difference between the start of an encoded and the start of an unencoded run. The second byte value is the number of unencoded pixel values that follow. If the number of pixels is odd, then a 00 padding value also follows. This padding value is not the part of the original pixel data and should not be written to the decoded data stream.

Table 13.2: Examples of Encoding and Decoding

Encoded Bytes:	05 10
Decoded Bytes:	10 10 10 10 10
Encoded Bytes:	00 05 23 65 34 56 45 00
Decoded Bytes:	23 65 34 56 45
Encoded Bytes:	0*A* 0*A*
Decoded Bytes:	0*A* 0*A* 0*A* 0*A* 0*A* 0*A* 0*A* 0*A* 0*A* 0*A*
Encoded Bytes:	00 04 46 57 68 79
Decoded Bytes:	46 57 68 79

Three marker values may also be found in the RLE data. Each of these markers also begins with a zero-byte value. The second byte value indicates the type of marker. These markers specify positional information relating to the decoded bitmap data. The first is the end-of-scan-line marker identified by two byte values 00 and 00. This indicates the end of data for the current scan line. Encoded data occurring after this marker is decoded starting at the beginning of the next scan line. If an end-of-scan-line marker is not present, then the pixels will automatically wrap from the end of one scan line to the start of the next.

This marker is only used if we want to force the decoding of a scan line to end at a particular place. If the end-of-line marker occurs in the middle of a scan line, all remaining pixels in the decoded bitmap for the line are ignored. This "short scan line" technique is used to omit undesired portions of scan lines. Most often, it is found in icon and pointer BMP files. The next marker is the end of RLE data marker. It is identified by the two byte values 00 and 01. This marker occurs only as the last two bytes of the RLE data. This marker is an indication that the reader should stop decoding data.

The last marker is the run offset marker, also called a **delta** or **vector** code. This is of four bytes in size: first two bytes being the values 00 and 02, and the last two specify a pixel address using X and Y values as an offset from the current bitmap cursor position. The X value is the number of pixels across the scan line, and the Y value is the number of rows forward in the bitmap. This marker indicates the location, in the bitmap, of the next decoded run of pixels. For example, a run offset marker value of 00 02 05 03 would indicate that the offset of the bitmap cursor should move five pixels down the scan line, three rows forward, and write out the next run.

The 4-bit RLE algorithm (RLE4) stores repeating pixel values in a very similar manner to RLE8. All of the markers are the same. The only real difference is that two pixel values are packed per byte, and these pixel values alternate when decoded. For example, an RLE4-encoded data stream of 07 48 would decode to seven pixels, alternating in value as 04 08 04 08 04 08 04.

Runs of identical pixel values may be encoded by RLE4 as well. For example, a run of twelve pixels, all of the value 9, would be RLE4-encoded as 0C 99 and would decode to the run 09 09 09 09 09 09 09 09 09 09 09 09.

Padding is added to unencoded pixel runs that are an odd number of bytes, rather than pixels, in length. And an unused final nibble in odd-length runs is set to zero. For example, the six pixel values 1 3 5 7 9 0 would be stored as the unencoded run 00 06 13 57 90 00, while the five pixel values 1 3 5 7 9 would be stored as the unencoded run 00 05 13 57 90 00.

An example of decoding a 4-bit data stream is given in Table 13.3. Each of the values is a 4-bit index value into the colour palette, not an actual colour value.

Table 13.3: Encoding and Decoding of 4-bit Colour-index Values

Encoded Bytes:	04 16
Decoding Description:	Four alternating 1 and 6
Decoded Bytes:	1 6 1 6
Encoded Bytes:	08 44
Decoding Description:	Eight alternating 4 and 4
Decoded Bytes:	4 4 4 4 4 4 4 4
Encoded Bytes:	00 00
Decoding Description:	End of scan line
Decoded Bytes:	None
Encoded Bytes:	00 02 04 02
Decoding Description:	Move to offset four pixels forward and two rows up
Decoded Bytes:	None
Encoded Bytes:	03 E4
Decoding Description:	Three values alternating E and 4
Decoded Bytes:	E 4 E
Encoded Bytes:	00 06 12 A4 46 00
Decoding Description:	Six values of unencoded data
Decoded Bytes:	1 2 A 4 4 6
Encoded Bytes:	00 00
Decoding Description:	End of scan line
Decoded Bytes:	None
Encoded Bytes:	00 01
Decoding Description:	End of RLE data
Decoded Bytes:	None

The 24-bit RLE algorithm (RLE24) encodes pixel values using nearly the same algorithm as RLE4 and RLE8. The only difference is that run values encoded are three bytes in size (one byte per RGB colour component), rather than four or eight bits in size.

An example of decoding a 24-bit data stream is shown in Table 13.4. Each of the values is an actual colour value found in the bitmap data. Run length values must be a multiple of three, and odd-length encoded runs are padded with a final zero byte, which is not part of the decoded data.

Table 13.4: Encoding and Decoding of 24-bit True-colour Values

Encoded Bytes:	04 16 D4 6F
Decoding Description:	Four pixels of value 16, D4, 6F
Decoded Bytes:	16 D4 6F 16 D4 6F 16 D4 6F 16 D4 6F
Encoded Bytes:	02 00 00 00
Decoding Description:	Two pixels of value 0, 0, 0
Decoded Bytes:	00 00 00 00 00 00
Encoded Bytes:	00 00
Decoding Description:	End of scan line
Decoded Bytes:	None
Encoded Bytes:	00 02 09 0C
Decoding Description:	Move to offset nine pixels forward and twelve rows up
Decoded Bytes:	None
Encoded Bytes:	03 E4 E4 E4
Decoding Description:	Three pixels of value E4, E4, E4
Decoded Bytes:	E4 E4 E4 E4 E4 E4 E4 E4 E4
Encoded Bytes:	00 01 12 A4 46 00
Decoding Description:	One pixel of unencoded data
Decoded Bytes:	12 A4 46
Encoded Bytes:	00 00
Decoding Description:	End of scan line
Decoded Bytes:	None
Encoded Bytes:	00 01
Decoding Description:	End of RLE data
Decoded Bytes:	None

13.2.1 BMP Formats in Brief

Black and White bitmap is monochrome and the colour table contains two entries. Each bit in the bitmap array represents a pixel. If the bit is clear, the pixel is displayed with the colour of the first entry in the colour table. If the bit is set, the pixel has the colour of the second entry in the table. 4-bit bitmap has a maximum of 16 colours. Each pixel in the bitmap is represented by a 4-bit index into the colour table array. The first pixel contains the colour in the second table entry, and the second pixel contains the colour in the sixteenth table entry. 8-bit bitmap has a maximum of 256 colours. Each pixel in the bitmap is represented by a 1-byte index into the colour table.

24-bit bitmap has a maximum of 2^{24} colours. Each pixel is a 3-byte sequence in the bitmap array represents the relative intensities of red, green, and blue.

13.2.2 Bitmap Compression

Windows versions 3.0 and later support Run Length Encoded (RLE) formats for compressing bitmaps that use 4 bits per pixel and 8 bits per pixel.

Compression of 8-bits-per-pixel bitmaps the DIB is compressed using a run length encoded format for a 256-colour bitmap. This format uses two modes: Encoded mode and absolute mode. Both modes can occur anywhere throughout a single bitmap.

Compression of 4-bits-per-pixel bitmaps the DIB is compressed using a run length encoded format for a 16-colour bitmap. This format uses two modes: Encoded mode and absolute mode. These are different than the 8-bit methods.

13.3 JPEG and JFIF Format

- JPEG: Joint Photographic Expert Group
- JFIF: JPEG File Interchange Format
- JPEG includes a series of specifications
  - (Baseline) Sequential JPG
  - Progressive JPG
  - Hierarchical JPG

Since sequential JPG is most commonly used, we describe this format only.

13.3.1 JPEG Encoding Steps

The process of encoding a raw image in JPEG format involves a sequence of steps. These are described below.

Transformation in colour space

$$[R\ G\ B] \to [Y\ C_b\ C_r]$$

(It is defined in the CCIR Recommendation 601)

$$\begin{bmatrix} Y \\ C_b \\ C_r \end{bmatrix} = \begin{bmatrix} 0.2990 & 0.5870 & 0.1140 \\ -0.1687 & -0.3313 & 0.5000 \\ 0.5000 & -0.4187 & -0.0813 \end{bmatrix} \times \begin{bmatrix} R \\ G \\ B \end{bmatrix} + \begin{bmatrix} 0 \\ 128 \\ 128 \end{bmatrix}$$

Y is called the **luminance**. It is the value used by the monochrome monitors to represent an RGB colour. Physiologically, it represents the intensity of an RGB colour perceived by the eye.

C_b, C_r are called the **chrominance values** and represent 2 coordinates in a system which measures the nuance and saturation of the colour [(approximately), these values indicate how much blue and how much red is in that colour]. These 2 coordinates are called shortly the **chrominance**. RGB can be computed directly from $\mathrm{YC_bC_r}$ (8-bit unsigned values) as follows:

$$R = Y + 1.402(C_r - 128)$$

$$G = Y - 0.34414(C_b - 128) - 0.71414(C_r - 128)$$

$$B = Y + 1.772(C_b - 128)$$

The eye, particularly the retina, has as visual analyzers two kind of cells: Cells for night view which perceive only nuances of grey ranging from intense white to the darkest black and cells for the day view which perceive the colour nuance. The first cells, given an RGB colour, detect a grey level similar to that given by the luminance value. The second cells, responsible for the perception of the colour nuance, are the cells which detect a value related to that of the chrominance.

Sampling

The JPEG standard takes into account the fact that the eye seems to be more sensitive at the luminance of a colour than at the nuance of that colour (the white-black view cells have more influence than the day view cells). So, on most JPG, luminance is taken in every pixel while the chrominance is taken as a median value for a 2×2 block of pixels (Note that it is not necessity). It could be taken in every pixel, but good compression results are achieved this way, with almost no loss in visual perception of the new sampled image.

Level shift

All 8-bit unsigned values (Y, C_b, C_r) in the image are "level shifted": They are converted to an 8-bit signed representation, by subtracting 128 from their values.

The 8×8 Discrete Cosine Transform (DCT)

The image is divided into 8×8 blocks of pixels. For each 8×8 block the DCT transform is applied. Note that if any of the X and Y dimensions of the original image is not divisible by 8, the encoder should make it divisible by completing the remaining right columns and bottom rows in the original image. The 8×8 blocks are processed from left to right and from top to bottom.

Since a pixel in the 8×8 block has 3 components (Y, C_b, C_r) the DCT is applied separately to 3 blocks of size 8×8. The first 8×8 block is the block which contains the luminance of the pixels in the original 8×8 block. The second and third 8×8 blocks correspond to the C_b and C_r values of the pixels in the original 8×8 block. The purpose of the DCT transform is that instead of processing the original samples, you work with the spatial frequencies present in the original image. These spatial frequencies are very related to the level of detail present in an image. High spatial frequencies corresponds to high levels of detail.

Zig-zag reordering of 64 DCT coefficients

After DCT transform over a block of 8×8 values, we have a new 8×8 block. Then, this 8×8 block is traversed in zig-zag as shown in Table 13.5: (The numbers in the 8×8 block indicate the order of traversal.

Table 13.5: Zig-zag Ordering Sequence

0	1	5	6	14	15	27	28
2	4	7	13	16	26	29	42
3	8	12	17	25	30	41	43
9	11	18	24	31	40	44	53
10	19	23	32	39	45	52	54
20	22	33	38	46	51	55	60
21	34	37	47	50	56	59	61
35	36	48	49	57	58	62	63

First the upper-left corner (0, 0), then the value at (0, 1), then (1, 0) then (2, 0), (1, 1), (0,2), (0, 3), (1, 2), (2, 1), (3, 0), etc.

Quantization

At this stage, we have a sorted vector with 64 values corresponding to the amplitudes of the 64 spatial frequencies present in the 8×8 block. These 64 values are quantized: Each value is divided by a dividend specified in a vector with 64 values — the quantization table, then it is rounded to the nearest integer.

$$\text{for}(i = 0; i \leq 63; i++)$$
$$\text{vector}[i] = (\text{int})(\text{vector}[i]/\text{quantization\_table}[i] + 0.5)$$

Quantization tables are formed on the basis of some psychovisual experiments. We shall present two such tables developed by Lohscheller, on the basis of his experiments on visibility thresholds for 2D DCT basis functions. These tables yield compressed images with a good compression factor and decompressed images with a very good quality factor. However, the use of these tables is optional in JPEG standard and one can uniformly quantize the corresponding supports.

Lohscheller's quantization table for luminance (Y) provided in a JPEG standard (It is given in a form of an 8×8 block; in order to obtain a 64 vector it should be zig-zag reordered). This quantization table is shown in Table 13.6.

Table 13.6: Quantization Table I

16	11	10	16	24	40	51	61
12	12	14	19	26	58	60	55
14	13	16	24	40	57	69	56
14	17	22	29	51	87	80	62
18	22	37	56	68	109	103	77
24	35	55	64	81	104	113	92
49	64	78	87	103	121	120	101
72	92	95	98	112	100	103	99

Another quantization table for highlighting chrominance values is shown in Table 13.7.

Table 13.7: Quantization Table II

17	18	24	47	99	99	99	99
18	21	26	66	99	99	99	99
24	26	56	99	99	99	99	99
47	66	99	99	99	99	99	99
99	99	99	99	99	99	99	99
99	99	99	99	99	99	99	99
99	99	99	99	99	99	99	99
99	99	99	99	99	99	99	99

The quantization process has the key role in the JPEG compression. It is the process which removes the high frequencies present in the original image—in consequence the high detail. We do this because of the fact that the eye is much more sensitive to lower spatial frequencies than to higher frequencies, so we can remove, with very little visual loss, higher frequencies. This is done by dividing values at higher indexes with larger values. The bigger the values in the quantization table are, the bigger is the error (visual error) introduced by this lossy process, and the smaller is the visual quality.

Another important fact is that in most images the colour varies slow from one pixel to another, so most images will have a small quantity of high detail → a small amount (small amplitudes) of high spatial frequencies, but they have a lot of image information contained in the low spatial frequencies.

In consequence of the new quantized vector, at high spatial frequencies, we will have a lot of consecutive zeroes.

The zero run length coding (RLC)

Now, we have the quantized vector with a lot of consecutive zeroes. We can exploit this by run length coding the consecutive zeroes. IMPORTANT: Here we skip the encoding of the first coefficient of the vector (the *DC* coefficient) which is coded a bit different. Let us consider the original 64 vector a 63 vector (it is the 64 vector without the first coefficient).

Say, we have 57, 45, 0, 0, 0, 0, 23, 0, –30, –16, 0, 0, 1, 0, 0, 0, 0, 0, 0, ..., 0 RLC JPEG compression is done as follows: (0, 57); (0, 45); (4, 23); (1, –30); (0, –16); (2, 1); EOB.

We encode each value, other than 0, by a pair, the number of consecutive zeroes preceding that value, followed by the value itself.

EOB is the short form for End of Block, it is a special coded value (a marker). If we have reached in a position in the vector from which we have till the end of the vector only zeroes, we will mark that position with EOB and finish the RLC compression of the quantized vector. [Note that if the quantized vector does not finish with zeroes (has the last element not 0) we will not have the EOB marker.] Actually, EOB has as an equivalent (0, 0) and it will be (later) Huffman coded like (0, 0), so we will encode: (0, 57); (0, 45); (4, 23); (1, –30); (0, –16); (2, 1); (0, 0). Another major thing: Say that somewhere in the quantized vector we have: 57, eighteeen zeroes, 3, 0, 0, 0, 0, 2, thirty-three zeroes, 895, EOB.

The JPG Huffman coding makes the restriction that the number of previous 0's to be coded as a 4-bit value, so it can not overpass the value 15 ($0 \times F$).

So, the previous example would be coded as: (0, 57); (15, 0) (2, 3); (4, 2); (15, 0) (15, 0) (1, 895), (0, 0)

(15, 0) is a special coded value which indicates that there follows 16 consecutive zeroes. Note: 16 zeroes not 15 zeroes.

The final step → Huffman coding

Instead of storing the actual value, the JPEG standard specifies that we store the minimum size in bits in which we can keep that value (it's called the category of that value) and then a bit-coded representation of that value like what is presented in Table 13.8:

Table 13.8: Category and Code-bits Used in Huffman Encoding

Values	*Category*	*Bits for the Value*
0	0	–
$-1, 1$	1	$0, 1$
$-3, -2, 2, 3$	2	$00, 01, 10, 11$
$-7, -6, -5, -4, 4, 5, 6, 7$	3	$000, 001, 010, 011, 100, 101, 110, 111$
$-15, \ldots, -8, 8, \ldots, 15$	4	$0000, \ldots, 0111, 1000, \ldots, 1111$
$-31, \ldots, -16, 16, \ldots, 31$	5	$00000, \ldots, 01111, 10000, \ldots, 11111$
$-63, \ldots, -32, 32, \ldots, 63$	6	.
$-127, \ldots, -64, 64, \ldots, 127$	7	.
$-255, \ldots, -128, 128, \ldots, 255$	8	.
$-511, \ldots, -256, 256, \ldots, 511$	9	.
$-1023, \ldots, -512, 512, \ldots, 1023$	10	.
$-2047, \ldots, -1024, 1024, \ldots, 2047$	11	.
$-4095, \ldots, -2048, 2048, \ldots, 4095$	12	.
$-8191, \ldots, -4096, 4096, \ldots, 8191$	13	.
$-16383, \ldots, -8192, 8192, \ldots, 16383$	14	.
$-32767, \ldots, -16384, 16384, \ldots, 32767$	15	.

In consequence for the previous example:

(0, 57); (0, 45); (4, 23); (1, –30); (0, –8); (2, 1); (0, 0)

Let us encode ONLY the right value of these pairs, except the pairs that are special markers like (0, 0) or (if we would have) (15, 0).

57 is in the category 6 and it is bit-coded 111001, so we will encode it like (6, 111001) and similarly the following codes can be derived:

$$45 \to (6, 101101)$$

$$23 \to (5, 10111)$$

$$-30 \to (5, 00001)$$

$$-8 \to (4, 0111)$$

$$1 \to (1, 1)$$

Now, we will write the string of pairs: (0, 6), 111001; (0, 6), 101101; (4, 5), 10111; (1, 5), 00001; (0, 4), 0111; (2, 1), 1; (0, 0).

The pairs of 2 values enclosed in bracket parentheses, can be represented on a byte because of the fact that each of the 2 values can be represented on a nibble [the counter of previous zeroes is always smaller than 15 and so it is the category of the numbers

(numbers encoded in a JPG file are in range $-32767, \ldots, 32767$)]. In this byte, the high nibble represents the number of previous 0s, and the lower nibble is the category of the new value different by 0.

The final step of the encoding consists in Huffman encoding this byte, and then writing in the JPG file, as a stream of bits, the Huffman code of this byte, followed by the remaining bit-representation of that number.

For example, let us say that for byte 6 [the equivalent of (0,6)] we have a Huffman code = 111000; for byte 69 = (4, 5) (for example) we have 1111111110011001. Similarly,

$$21 \to (1,5) \to 11111110110$$
$$4 \to (0,4) \to 1011$$
$$33 \to (2,1) \to 11011$$
$$0 \to EOB \to (0,0) \to 1010$$

The final stream of bits written in the JPG file on disk for the previous example of 63 coefficients is 111000 111001 111000 101101 1111111110011001 10111 11111110110 00001 1011 0111 11011 1 1010 (Note that we have skipped the first coefficient called the *DC* **coefficient**)

Since there is a very close connection between the *DC* coefficient of consecutive blocks, we can encode the difference between the *DC*s of consecutive 8×8 blocks of the same image component, Y, C_b or C_r.

$$\text{Diff} = DC_i - DC_{i-1}$$

So *DC* of the current block (DC_i) will be equal to:

$$DC_i = DC_{i-1} + \text{Diff}$$

And in JPG decoding we start from 0, i.e. the first *DC* coefficient $= 0$; $DC = 0$. And then we can add to the current value the value decoded from the JPG (the Diff value). So, in the JPG file, the first coefficient, the *DC* coefficient, is actually the difference, and it is Huffman encoded differently from the encoding of *AC* coefficients.

Here is how it is done: (Remember, we now code the Diff value) Diff corresponds as you have seen before to a representation made by category and it is bit coded representation. In the JPG file it will be Huffman encoded only the category value, like this: Diff = (category, bit-coded representation). Then Diff will be coded as Huffman_code(category), bit-coded representation. For example, if Diff is equal to -511, then Diff corresponds to (9, 000000000) Say that 9 has a Huffman code = 1111110 (In the JPG file, there are 2 Huffman tables for an image component: one for *DC* and one for *AC*). In the JPG file, the bits corresponding to the *DC* coefficient will be: 1111110 000000000.

Applied to our example of DC and to the previous example of ACs, for this vector with 64 coefficients, The final stream of bits written in the JPG file will be:

1111110 000000000 111000 111001 111000 101101 1111111110011001 10111 11111110110 00001 1011 0111 11011 1 1010

(In the JPG file, at first there is the encoded DC followed by ACs).

In brief the JPEG coding steps are:

- Colour space transform
- Sampling
- Level shifting
- DCT transformation
- Quantization
- Zig-zag encoding
- Run length encoding
- Frequency encoding

13.3.2 JFIF Format

What we have discussed so far is a standard compression technique only. JFIF is one of the standard file formats. It includes file and table headers as well. At the start of the image we have SOI = Start Of Image = 'FFD8' marker. At the end of a JFIF file there is EOI = End Of Image = 'FFD9' marker. A lot of other markers and tables are also maintained (we shall not discuss them here).

13.4 GIF Format

GIF (Graphics Interchange Format) allows high-quality, high-resolution graphics to be displayed on a variety of graphics hardware and is intended as an exchange and display mechanism for graphics images. The image format is designed to support current and future image technology and will in addition serve as a basis for future graphics products. The GIF file structure is shown in Figure 13.2.

GIF signature

The following GIF Signature identifies the data following as a valid GIF image stream. It consists of the following six characters: G I F 8 7 a. The last three characters '87a' may be viewed as a version number for this particular GIF definition and will be used in general as a reference in documents regarding GIF that address any version dependencies.

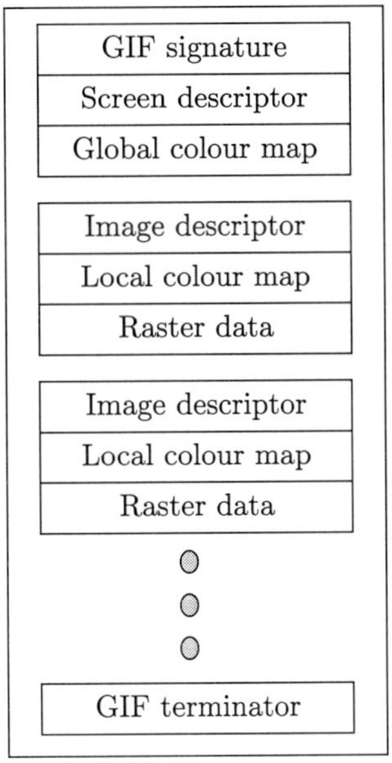

Figure 13.2: General GIF file format.

Screen descriptor

The Screen Descriptor describes the overall parameters for all GIF images following. It defines the overall dimensions of the image space or logical screen required, the existance of colour mapping information, background screen colour, and colour depth information. This information is stored in a series of 8-bit bytes as described below.

The logical screen width and height can both be larger than the physical display. How images larger than the physical display are handled is implementation dependent and can take advantage of hardware characteristics (e.g. Macintosh scrolling windows). Otherwise images can be clipped to the edges of the display. The value of 'pixel' also defines the maximum number of colours within an image. The range of values for 'pixel' is 0 to 7 which represents 1 to 8 bits. This translates to a range of 2 (B/W) to 256 colours. Bit 3 of word 5 is reserved for future definition and must be zero. The GIF image descriptor is shown in Figure 13.3.

Global colour map

The global colour map is optional, but recommended for images where accurate colour rendition is desired. The existence of this colour map is indicated in the 'M' field of byte 5 of the screen descriptor. A colour map can also be associated with each image in a GIF file as described later. However, this global map will normally be used because of hardware restrictions in equipment available today. In the individual image descriptors the 'M' flag will normally be zero. If the global colour map is present, its definition

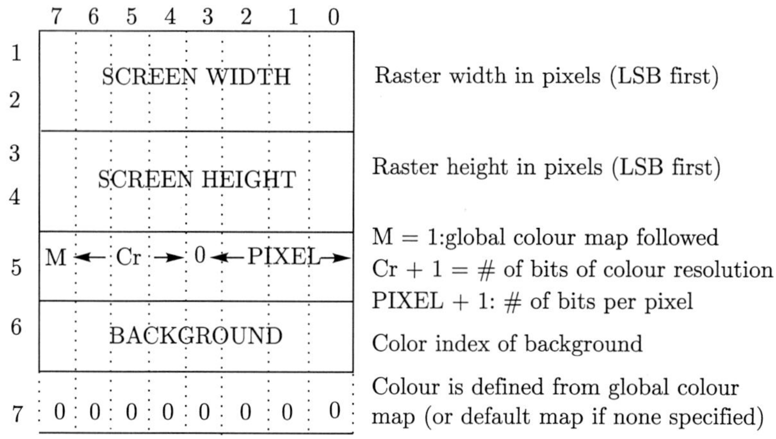

Figure 13.3: Screen descriptor in GIF.

immediately follows the screen descriptor. The number of colour map entries following a screen descriptor is equal to $2^{\#\text{ of bits per pixel}}$, where each entry consists of three byte values representing the relative intensities of red, green and blue, respectively.

Each image pixel value received will be displayed according to its closest match with an available colour of the display based on this colour map. The colour components represent a fractional intensity value from none (0) to full (255). White would be represented as (255, 255, 255), black as (0, 0, 0) and medium yellow as $(180, 180, 0)$. If the display device supports fewer than 8 bits per colour component, the higher order bits of each component are used. In the creation of a GIF colour map entry with hardware supporting fewer than 8 bits per component, the component values for the hardware should be converted to the 8-bit format with the following calculation:

$$\text{map\_value} = \frac{\text{component\_value} \times 255}{(2^{n\text{ bits}} - 1)}$$

This assures accurate translation of colours for all displays. In the cases of creating GIF images from hardware without colour palette capability, a fixed palette should be created based on the available display colours for that hardware. If no global colour map is indicated, a default colour map is generated internally which maps each possible incoming colour index to the hardware colour index = incoming colour index modulo $< n >$, where $< n >$ is the number of available hardware colours. The GIF colour map structure is shown in Figure 13.4.

Image descriptor

The image descriptor (see Figure 13.5) defines the actual placement and extents of the following image within the space defined in the screen descriptor. Also defined are flags to indicate the presence of a local colour lookup map, and to define the

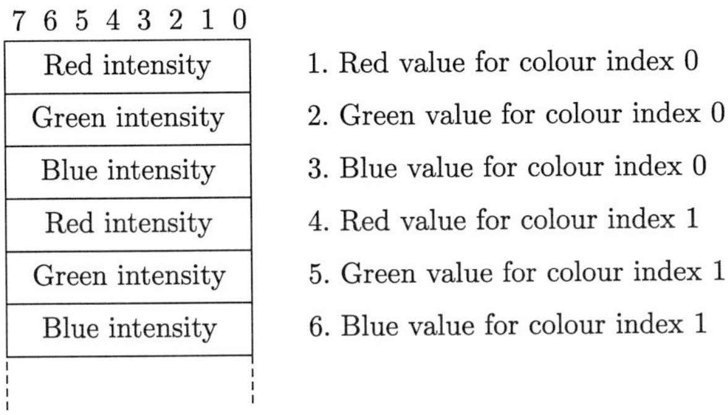

Figure 13.4: Global colour map in GIF.

pixel display sequence. Each image descriptor is introduced by an image separator character. The role of the image separator is simply to provide a synchronization character to introduce an Image Descriptor. This is desirable if a GIF file happens to contain more than one image. This character is defined as $0 \times 2C$ hex or ',' (comma). When this character is encountered between images, the image descriptor will follow immediately. Any characters encountered between the end of a previous image and the image separator character are to be ignored. This allows future GIF enhancements to be present in newer image formats and yet ignored safely by older software decoders.

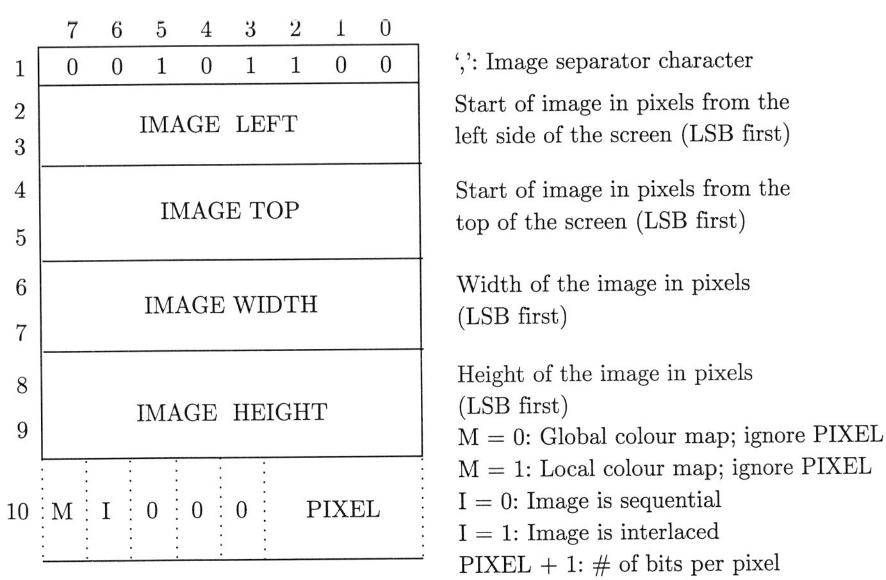

Figure 13.5: Image descriptor in GIF.

Local colour map

A local colour map is optional and defined here for future use. If the 'M' bit of byte 10 of the image descriptor is set, then a colour map follows the image descriptor that applies only to the following image. At the end of the image, the colour map will revert to that defined after the screen descriptor. Note that the 'pixel' field of byte 10 of the image descriptor is used only if a Local colour map is indicated. This defines the parameters not only for the image pixel size, but determines the number of colour map entries that follow. The bits per pixel value will also revert to the value specified in the screen descriptor when processing of the image is complete.

Raster data

The format of the actual image is defined as the series of pixel colour index values that make up the image. The pixels are stored left to right sequentially for an image row. By default each image row is written sequentially, top to bottom. In the case that the interlace or 'I' bit is set in byte 10 of the image descriptor then the row order of the image display follows a four-pass process in which the image is filled in by widely spaced rows. The first pass writes every 8th row, starting with the top row of the image window. The second pass writes every 8th row starting at the fifth row from the top. The third pass writes every 4th row starting at the third row from the top. The fourth pass completes the image, writing every other row, starting at the second row from the top. A tabular description of this process is shown in Table 13.9.

Table 13.9: Interlacing Pattern for GIF Data

Image Row	*Pass 1*	*Pass 2*	*Pass 3*	*Pass 4*	*Results*
0	1*a*				1*a*
1				4*a*	4*a*
1			3*a*		3*a*
1				4*b*	4*b*
1		2*a*			2*a*
1				4*c*	4*c*
1			3*b*		3*b*
1				4*d*	4*d*
1	1*b*				1*b*
1				4*e*	4*e*
1			3*c*		3*c*
1				4*f*	4*f*
1		2*b*			2*b*
1			⋮		

The image pixel values are processed as a series of colour indices which map into the existing colour map. The resulting colour value from the map is what is actually displayed. This series of pixel indices the number which is equal to image-width*image-height pixels, are passed to the GIF image data stream one value per pixel, compressed and packaged according to a version of the LZW compression algorithm.

GIF terminator

In order to provide a synchronization for the termination of a GIF image file, a GIF decoder will process the end of GIF mode when the character $0 \times 3B$ hex or ';' is found after an image has been processed. By convention the decoding software will pause and wait for an action indicating that the user is ready to continue. This may be a carriage return entered at the keyboard or a mouse click. For interactive applications this user action must be passed on to the host as a carriage return character so that the host application can continue. The decoding software will then typically leave graphics mode and resume any previous process.

13.4.1 GIF Extension Blocks

To provide for orderly extension of the GIF definition, a mechanism for defining the packaging of extensions within a GIF data stream is necessary. Specific GIF extensions are to be defined and documented by CompuServe in order to provide a controlled enhancement path.

GIF extension blocks are packaged in a manner similar to that used by the raster data though not compressed (Figure 13.6).

A GIF extension block may immediately preceed any image descriptor or occur before the GIF terminator. All GIF decoders must be able to recognize the existence of GIF extension blocks and read past them if unable to process the function code. This ensures that older decoders will be able to process extended GIF image files in the future, though without the additional functionality.

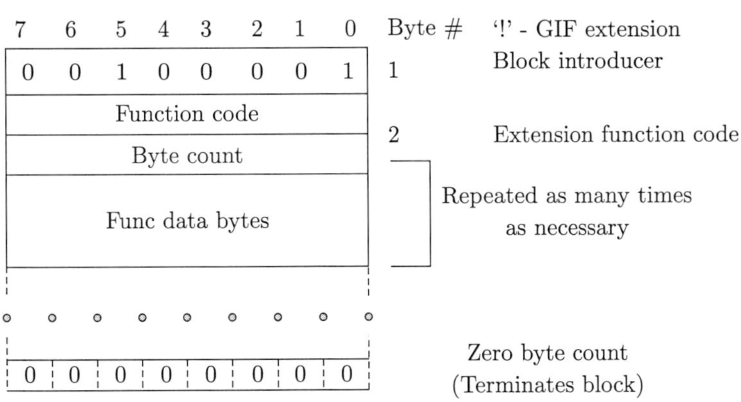

Figure 13.6: GIF extension block.

13.4.2 Image Packaging and Compression

The raster data stream that represents the actual output image (in GIF format) can be represented as shown in Figure 13.7. The conversion of the image from a series of pixel values to a transmitted or stored character stream involves the following steps:

1. ***Establish code size:*** Define the number of bits needed to represent the actual data.
2. ***Compress the data:*** Compress the series of image pixels to a series of compression codes.
3. ***Build a series of bytes:*** Convert a set of compression codes into a string of 8-bit bytes.
4. ***Package the bytes:*** Package the bytes into blocks preceded by character counts and output.

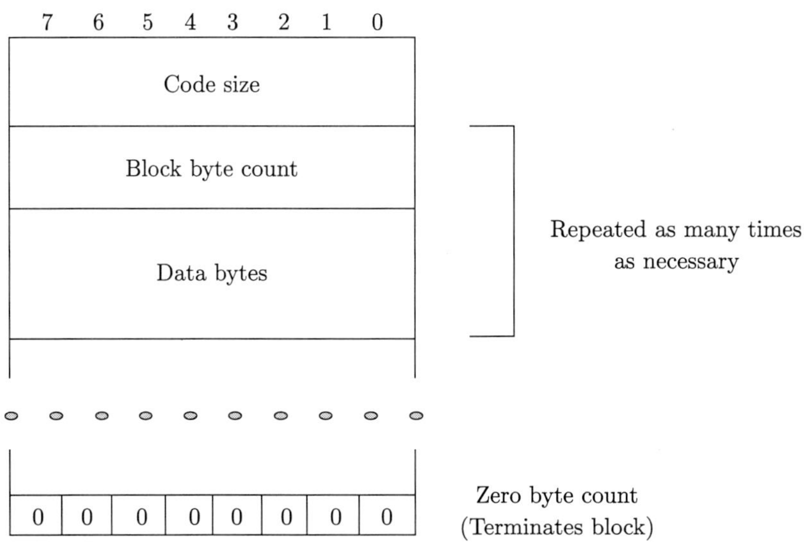

Figure 13.7: Packaged GIF data.

The following paragraphs describe how GIF images are compressed and packed for the purpose of communication and storage.

Compression

The LZW algorithm converts a series of data values into a series of codes which may be raw values or a code designating a series of values. Using text characters as an analogy, the output code consists of a character or a code representing a string of characters. The LZW algorithm used in GIF matches algorithmically with the standard LZW algorithm with the following differences:

1. A special *Clear_code* is defined which resets all compression/decompression parameters and tables to a start-up state. The value of this code is 2^{code_size}. For example if the code size indicated was 4 (image was 4 bits per pixel) the clear code value would be 16 (10000 in binary). The clear code can appear at any point in the image data stream, and therefore, requires the LZW algorithm to process succeeding codes as if a new data stream was starting. Encoders should output a clear code as the first code of each image data stream.
2. An end of information code is defined that explicitly indicates the end of the image data stream. LZW processing terminates when this code is encountered. It must be the last code output by the encoder for an image. The value of this code is $Clear\_code + 1$.
3. The first available compression code value is $Clear\_code + 2$.
4. The output codes are of variable length, starting at <code size>+1 bits per code, up to 12 bits per code. This defines a maximum code value of 4095 (hex FFF). Whenever the LZW code value would exceed the current code length, the code length is increased by one. The packing/unpacking of these codes must then be altered to reflect the new code length.

Building 8-bit bytes

Because the LZW compression used for GIF creates a series of variable length codes, of between 3 and 12 bits each, these codes must be reformed into a series of 8-bit bytes that will be the characters actually stored or transmitted. This provides additional compression of the image. The codes are formed into a stream of bits as if they were packed right to left and then picked off 8 bits at a time to be output. Assuming a character array of 8 bits per character and using 5-bit codes to be packed, an example layout would be similar to as shown in Figure 13.8.

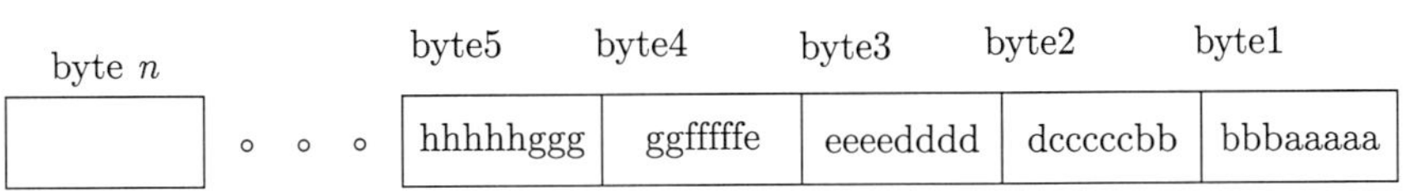

Figure 13.8: Packaging in 8-bit bytes.

Note that the physical packing arrangement will change as the number of bits per compression code changes, but the concept remains the same.

Packaging the bytes

Once the bytes have been created, they are grouped into blocks for output by preceeding each block of 0 to 255 bytes with a character count byte. A block with a zero byte count terminates the raster data stream for a given image. These blocks are what are actually output for the GIF image. This block format has the side effect of allowing a decoding program the ability to read past the actual image data if necessary by reading block counts and then skipping over the data.

13.4.3 Multiple Image Processing

Since a GIF data stream can contain multiple images, it is necessary to describe processing and display of such a file. Because the image descriptor allows for placement of the image within the logical screen, it is possible to define a sequence of images that may each be a partial screen, but in total fill the entire screen. The guidelines for handling the multiple image situation are:

1. There is no pause between images. Each is processed immediately as seen by the decoder.
2. Each image explicitly overwrites any image already on the screen inside of its window. The only screen clears are at the beginning and end of the GIF image process.

13.5 TIFF Format

TIFF is the abbreviation for Tagged Image File Format. It is a file consisting of a sequence of 8-bit bytes, where the bytes are numbered from 0 to N. The largest possible TIFF file is 2**32 bytes in length.

A TIFF file begins with an 8-byte image file header that points to an Image File Directory (IFD). An image file directory contains information about the image, as well as points to the actual image data.

TIFF file header

The TIFF file header, contains the following information: Bytes 0–1: The byte order used within the file. Legal values are: "II" (4949.H) "MM" (4D4D.H) In the "II" format, byte order is always from the least significant byte to the most significant byte, for both 16-bit and 32-bit integers. This is called **little-endian byte order**. In the "MM" format, byte order is always from most significant to least significant, for both 16-bit and 32-bit integers. This is called **big-endian byte order**. An Image File Directory (IFD) consists of a 2-byte count of the number of directory entries (i.e. the number of fields), followed by a sequence of 12-byte directory entries, followed by a 4-byte offset of the next IFD (or 0 if none).

Bytes 2–3 are arbitrary, but carefully chosen number (42) that further identifies the file as a TIFF file. The byte order depends on the value of bytes 0–1.

Bytes 4–7 are the offset (in bytes) of the first IFD. The directory may be at any location in the file after the header, but must begin on a word boundary. In particular, an image file directory may follow the image data it describes. We must follow the pointers wherever they may lead.

The term byte offset always refers to a location with respect to the beginning of the TIFF file TIFF format TIFF format. The 4 bytes offset of the last IFD are all 0s.

There must be at least 1 IFD in a TIFF file and each IFD must have at least one entry.

IFD entry

Each 12-byte IFD entry has the following format: Bytes 0–1 are the Tags that identify the field. Bytes 2–3 are the field Type. Bytes 4–7 are the number of values, count of the indicated type. Bytes 8–11 are the value offset, the file offset (in bytes) of the value for the field. The value is expected to begin on a word boundary; the corresponding value offset will thus be an even number. This file offset may point anywhere in the file, even after the image data.

The TIFF file data structure is shown in Figure 13.9.

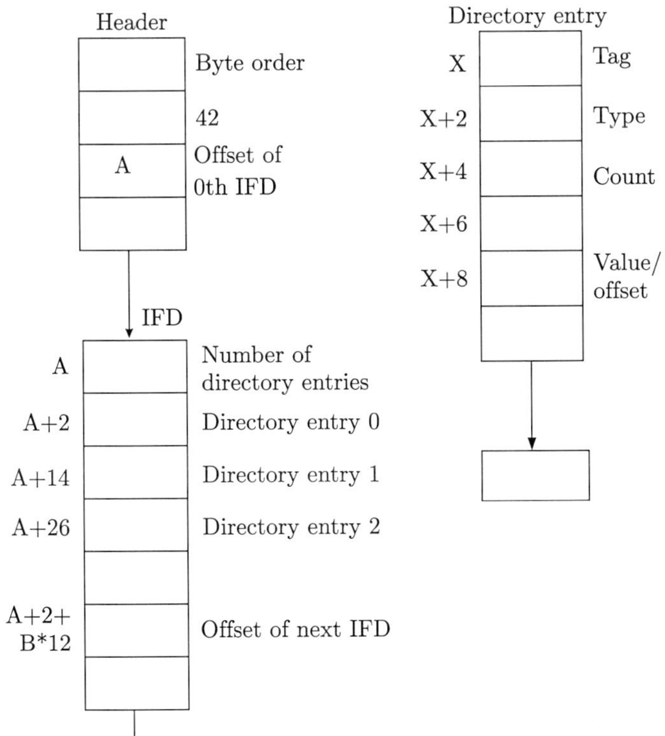

Figure 13.9: TIFF file data structure.

IFD terminology

A TIFF field is a logical entity consisting of TIFF tag and its value. This logical concept is implemented as an IFD entry, plus the actual value if it does not fit into the value/offset part, the last 4 bytes of the IFD entry. The terms TIFF field and IFD entry indicate the same item. Sort order the entries in an IFD must be sorted in ascending order by the tag. The values to which directory entries point need not be in any particular order in the file.

Value/Offset

To save time and space the value offset contains the value instead of pointing to the value if and only if the value fits into 4 bytes. If the value is shorter than 4 bytes, it is left-justified within the 4-byte value offset, i.e. stored in the lower-numbered bytes. Whether the value fits within 4 bytes is determined by the type and count of the field.

Count

Count called length in previous versions of the specification is the number of values. Note that count is not the total number of bytes. For example, a single 16-bit word (SHORT) has a count of 1; not 2.

Types

Types of different data items and their sizes are mentioned in Table 13.10.

Table 13.10: Types of different data items and their sizes

Field Types	*Sizes*
1 = BYTE	8-bit unsigned integer
2 = ASCII	8-bit byte that contains a 7-bit ASCII code the last byte must be NUL (binary zero)
3 = SHORT	16-bit (2-byte) unsigned integer
4 = LONG	32-bit (4-byte) unsigned integer
5 = RATIONAL	Two LONGs: the first represents the numerator of a fraction; the second, the denominator. The value of the count part of an ASCII field entry includes the NUL.

Multiple images per TIFF file

There may be more than one IFD in a TIFF file. Each IFD defines a subfile. One potential use of subfiles is to describe related images, such as the pages of a facsimile transmission. A Baseline TIFF reader is not required to read any IFDs beyond the first one.

Bilevel images

The overall TIFF structure has been described above. We can now move on to filling the structure with actual fields (tags and values) that describe raster image data. To simplify matters, we discuss the organization for the (out of four baseline TIFF image types) bilevel image only (Others are grey scale, palette-colour, and full-colour images). A bilevel image contains two colours black and white. TIFF allows an application to write out bilevel data in either a white-is-zero or black-is-zero format. The field that records this information is called **photometric interpretation**.

Photometric interpretation

Tag = 262 (106.H), Type = SHORT, Values: 0 = WhiteIsZero. For bilevel and greyscale images: 0 is imaged as white. The maximum value is imaged as black. This is the normal value for Compression = 2. 1 = BlackIsZero. For bilevel and greyscale images: 0 is imaged as black. The maximum value is imaged as white. If this value is specified for Compression = 2, the image should display and print reversed.

Data can be stored either compressed or uncompressed. Compression: Tag = 259 (103.H), Type = SHORT, Values: 1 = No compression, but pack data into bytes as tightly as possible, leaving no unused bits (except at the end of a row). The component values are stored as an array of type BYTE. Each scan line (row) is padded to the next BYTE boundary. 2 = CCITT Group 3: One-dimensional modified Huffman run length encoding. 32773 = PackBits compression, a simple byte-oriented run length scheme. Data compression applies only to raster image data. All other TIFF fields are unaffected. Baseline TIFF readers must handle all three compression schemes.

Rows and columns

An image is organized as a rectangular array of pixels. The dimensions of this array are stored in the following fields: ImageLength Tag = 257 (101.H), Type = SHORT or LONG. The number of rows (sometimes described as scanlines) in the image. ImageWidth Tag = 256 (100.H), Type = SHORT or LONG. The number of columns in the image, i.e. the number of pixels per scanline.

Physical dimensions

Applications often want to know the size of the picture represented by an image. This information can be calculated from ImageWidth and ImageLength given the following resolution data: ResolutionUnit Tag = 296 (128.H), Type = SHORT Values: 1 = No absolute unit of measurement. Used for images, that may have a non-square aspect ratio, but no meaningful absolute dimensions. 2 = Inch, 3 = Centimetre, Default = 2 (inch).

Xresolution

Tag = 282 (11A.H), Type = RATIONAL. The number of pixels per ResolutionUnit in the ImageWidth (typically, horizontal —see orientation) direction.

Yresolution

Tag = 283 (11B.H), Type = RATIONAL. The number of pixels per ResolutionUnit in the ImageLength (typically, vertical) direction.

Location of the data

Compressed or uncompressed image data can be stored almost anywhere in a TIFF file. TIFF also supports breaking an image into separate strips for increased editing flexibility and efficient I/O buffering. The location and size of each strip is given by the following fields: RowsPerStrip Tag = 278 (116.H), Type = SHORT or LONG. The number of rows in each strip (except possibly the last strip.) For example, if ImageLength is 24, and RowsPerStrip is 10, then there are 3 strips, with 10 rows in the first strip, 10 rows in the second strip, and 4 rows in the third strip. (The data in the last strip is not padded with 6 extra rows of dummy data.)

StripOffsets

Tag = 273 (111.H), Type = SHORT or LONG. For each strip, the byte offset of that strip. StripByteCounts Tag = 279 (117.H), Type = SHORT or LONG. For each strip, the number of bytes in that strip after any compression. Putting it all together (along with a couple of less-important fields that are discussed later), a sample bilevel image file might contain the following fields: address, offset and value.

A sample TIFF file is shown in Table 13.11. Here, the rows of the table contain address in memory, a description of the code, offset addresses in Hex code and the Hex value. The memory references are resolved the codes shown in the lines below the Table.

Table 13.11: A Sample TIFF File for Demonstration

Address	*Description*	*Offset (Hex)*	*Value (Hex)*
Header:			
0000	Byte Order	4D4D	
0002	42	002A	
0004	1st IFD offset	00000014	
IFD:			
0014	No. of Directory Entries	000C	
0016	NewSubfileType	00FE	0004 00000001 00000000
0022	ImageWidth	0100	0004 00000001 000007D0
002E	ImageLength	0101	0004 00000001 00000BB8
003A	Compression	0103	0003 00000001 8005 0000
0046	PhotometricInterpret.	0106	0003 00000001 0001 0000
0052	StripOffsets	0111	0004 000000BC 000000B6
005E	RowsPerStrip	0116	0004 00000001 00000010
006A	StripByteCounts	0117	0003 000000BC 000003A6
0076	XResolution	011A	0005 00000001 00000696
0082	YResolution	011B	0005 00000001 0000069E
008E	Software	0131	0002 0000000E 000006A6
009A	DateTime	0132	0002 00000014 000006B6
00A6	Next IFD offset	00000000	

Values longer than 4 bytes:

00B6 StripOffsets	Offset0, Offset1, ... Offset187
03A6 StripByteCounts	Count0, Count1, ... Count187
0696 XResolution	0000012C 00000001
069E Yresolution	0000012C 00000001
06A6 Software	"PageMaker 4.0"
06B6 DateTime	"1988:02:1813:59:59"

Image Data:	
00000700	Compressed data for strip 10
xxxxxxxx	Compressed data for strip 179
xxxxxxxx	Compressed data for strip 53
xxxxxxxx	Compressed data for strip 160

⋮

End of example

13.6 Problems

1. Explain the significance of the following file formats: (i) *.bmp (ii) *.gif (iii) *.tiff
2. Describe the compression technique of JPEG images.
3. What do you mean by zig-zag encoding? Briefly illustrate.
4. What are the differences between lossy and lossless JPEG compression?
5. If the same image be encoded in JPEG and GIF formats, which one will be of larger size?
6. Explain the importance of GIF and TIFF image formats.
7. How can you vary the compression ration in JPEG format?
8. Why entropy encoding is used in JPEG technique?

Chapter 14

Feature Extraction and Representation

In the earlier chapters, we have discussed lower level image processing techniques like modifying and recovering images by means of enhancement, registration, restoration, etc. We also have studied techniques like edge detection, segmentation, etc. which are some of important image analysis techniques. By edge detection we can extract the information of shapes of the objects present in an image. Similarly, by applying segmentation techniques, we can identify the number of different objects present in an image. The information extracted by above mentioned processes are incomplete in consideration to a proper and application oriented abstract representation of an image. Image abstraction can be done using many other higher level processes which we already referred to as higher level image analysis techniques. In this chapter, we shall deal with some more techniques that can be applied to either extract or assist in extraction of features like size, shape, orientation, texture or colour of objects. These features are generally used, by representing them in a suitable form, as pattern inputs for classification processes.

14.1 Image Features

Our primary objective is to identify and extract features from images that can be used in a pattern classification (or recognition) process. It must be said here that the classical lower level processing techniques can inherently provide many such features. Some of these are:

- Image histogram: Helps quantitative measurement of grey level distribution in images.
- Image transformation: Helps in finding out transformation co-efficients, which are important components of abstract image or object representation.
- Edge detection: Helps in detection of object skeleton. When detected edge patterns are represented as approximate polygonal shapes they can be stored

using geometrical parametres like length, angle, number of segments, direction of segments, etc.

- Image segmentation: Helps in finding number of distinct regions. Each distinct region can further be quantitatively measured for their relative shape, size, shade, etc.
- Hough transform: Helps in identifying known shapes. Identification of standard shapes like line, circles, etc. helps in geometrical description of an underlying object.

The above processes have been discussed in details in earlier chapters. The application programmer can easily identify suitable attribute (feature) values from the outcome of all the above mentioned processes.

14.1.1 Image Histogram

The histogram of an image is a plot of the number of pixels with a certain grey value against the grey value. Histogram can be expressed in graphical as well as in tabular form. For a very large histogram one may consider a cumulated histogram also. Now, how to extract features from a histogram for analysis purposes?

Let us consider we have a number of photographs of different flowers and their digital forms. We need to extract features from these images in order to generate input patterns to a classification system. In this case, we can proceed as follows:

1. Scale the digital images to enclose each of the flowers within a certain bounding box.
2. Create histogram of each of the flower images separately.
3. Count pixels with different shades (colours) for each image separately.
4. Count pixels with specific shades (colours) for each image separately.

From the scale factors, we can have relative size information for the flowers. From the histogram, we can extract colour information for the flowers. A number of size features and a number of colour features can be measured. Using a subset of all these features, we can form a flower pattern suitable for classification purposes.

14.1.2 Image Transformation

Image transformation processes present us with a number of transformation co-efficients. Each of these co-efficients carry a specific significant measure regarding the image contents. For example, the zeroth co-efficient of Fourier transform contains the average grey value for a grey shade image. It is also known that higher frequency co-efficients lose their significance and drop down to zero quickly. Hence, we can use only a few co-efficients as significant features.

14.1.3 Edge Detection

Detected edges provide not only the visual shape of the object, but also a number of characteristic points and primitive structures present in it. These primitive structures may be line segments and their lengths, a curve with a certain curvature, a junction with a certain angle, etc. By measuring these features geometrically we can form a suitable pattern representing the concerned object.

14.1.4 Image Segmentation

The segmented images provide a clue for number of distinct regions (objects), their colours (shades), relative size, shape, etc.

14.1.5 Hough Transforms

These techniques are used mainly to identify the presence and location of a number of specific shapes present in an image. Generally, an edge detected image is used for this purpose. This will reduce the complexity of the underlying process significantly.

14.2 Feature Representation

Image features may be determined and extracted by a number of different approaches. These features may include pixel information, boundary information, region information, texture information etc. However, we need to represent these extracted information in a standard compact form so that they become considerably more useful for higher level computation. This section provides descriptions of some common techniques in this regard.

14.2.1 Chain Code Representation

Once boundary of an object is determined, it can be represented (abstracted) as a sequence of connected line segments with specification for segment length and direction. Two different approaches may be followed for representing direction of a line segment. These are (i) 4-directional chain coding (*mod*-4) and (ii) 8-directional chain coding (*mod*-8). These two schemes are depicted in Figure 14.1.

We can consider a grid of pixels over which an edge image is placed. The end points of line segments constituting the image are at integral locations of the 2D grid. Following an anti-clockwise convention for direction of line segments we can represent the edge image as a sequence of *length* and *direction* pair (l, d). In many cases, when the image is very large, the number of pairs representing it become very large and awkward. To eliminate this problem we can resample the edge image using larger

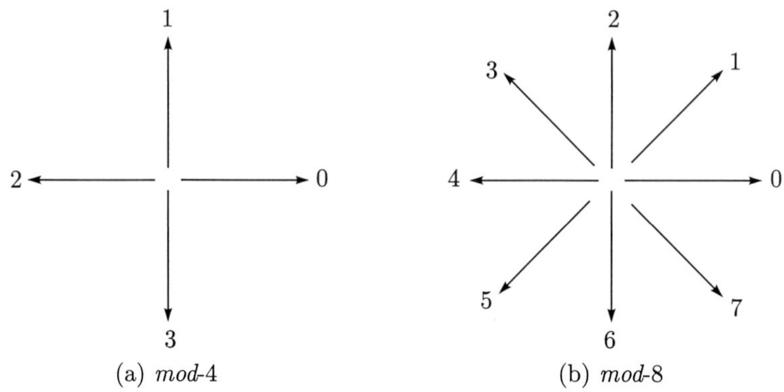

Figure 14.1: Two different boundary representation schemes.

grid size and edge image is presented in a more compact and more abstract form. An example of this process is shown in Figure 14.2.

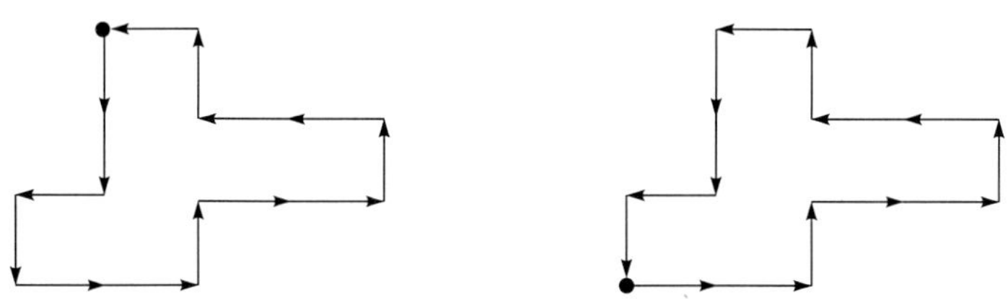

Figure 14.2: Two different codes for the same boundary.

The chain code representation of a boundary can be depending on the starting point. However, the code can be normalized w.r.t. the starting point in a straightforward fashion. The chain code is actually a circular sequence, because the starting point is normally the ending point also (for closed boundaries). We can normalize the direction sequence by choosing a starting point so that the resulting sequence becomes an integer with the smallest magnitude. For example, the boundary in Figure 14.2 can have two different chain codes as

$$3\ 3\ 2\ 3\ 0\ 0\ 1\ 0\ 0\ 1\ 2\ 2\ 1\ 2$$

and

$$0\ 0\ 1\ 0\ 0\ 1\ 2\ 2\ 1\ 2\ 3\ 3\ 2\ 3$$

The minimum magnitude code, i.e. the second representation, may be accepted as the normalized one.

If we consider only four directions we get a *mod-4* code. If instead eight directions are considered, a *mod-8* code is obtained.

14.2.2 Polygonal Approximation

If the pixel grid is very finely drawn, a digital boundary can be very cleanly approximated by a polygonal representation using the grid pixels over the boundary. The main objective in this technique is to represent the boundary with as few polygon edges as possible. This process is not very simple and may be very computation-intensive depending on the solution procedure. A number of techniques are available for this, some of which are:

Minimum perimeter polygon: The polygonal apprixation technique for representing an object boundary requires finding out the minimum perimeter polygonal. In case of non-straight and small irregular curvy shapes it can be done by partial replacement with straight line segment. For example, the boundary shown in Figure 14.3(a) can be represented by the polygonal approximation shown in Figure 14.3(b).

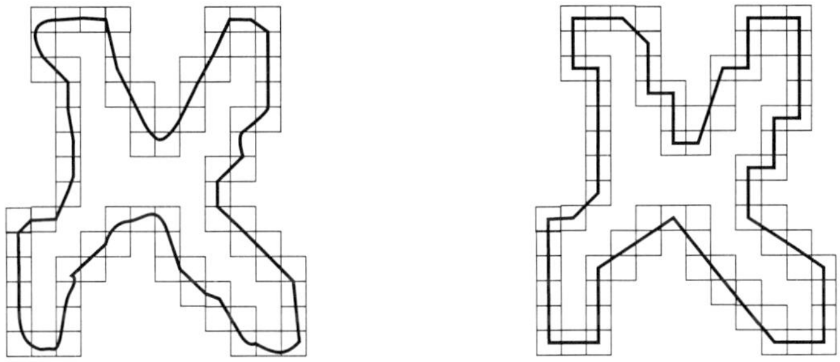

(a) Object boundary within cell (b) Polygon representation of (a)

Figure 14.3: Polygonal approximation.

Merging: In this case, consecutive pixels on the boundary are tried to be merged into a straight line segment. The process continues until, for a particular line segment, the **error factor** exceeds a certain tolerance value. The *error* in this case arises due to the fact that we select pixels which are not actually on the boundary but very near to them. The deviation or difference in distance values are summed up, for a curve segment, to count the error value.

Splitting: This approach is the reverse procedure of merging. Here, a larger segment is tried to be divided into a number of smaller nearly linear fragments such that a prespecified error criterion is minimized.

14.2.3 Boundary Segments

For representing a boundary in a proper form it is often found to be very useful to decompose it into segments. If a closed boundary contains some concave parts within it, the concept of *convex hull* is very useful to decompose it. A closed boundary B

and its convex hull H are shown in Figure 14.4. The convex hull of a closed region is the smallest convex set enclosing the region. The set difference $H - B$ is called the *convex deficiency* D of the set B. Figure 14.4 shows a closed boundary (set B) and its convex deficiency (set D).

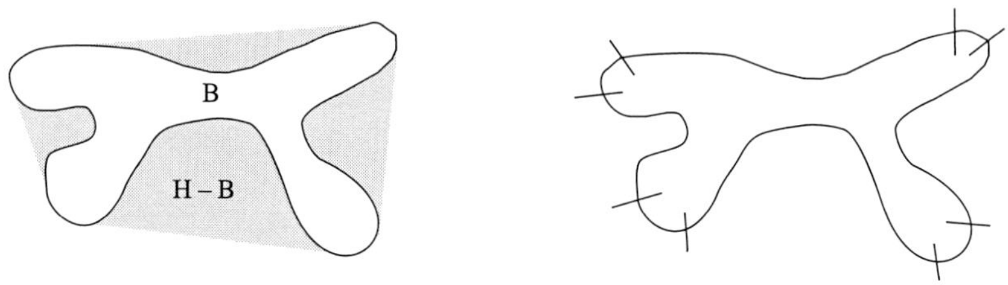

(a) A region and its convex deficiency set (b) Partitioned boundary

Figure 14.4: Convex set approximation.

Digital boundaries are rough and noisy in shape in many cases. So prior to segmentation, it is useful to try to smooth out such portions by postprocessing. After smoothing (to a continuous smooth curve), nearly linear fragments may be extracted for their length, orientation, etc. The boundary can be segmented into curve segments also, where the fragments can be represented by simple second order polynomials such as circular, elliptic, parabolic, etc. All these segments are considered as primitives for syntactic shape representation procedures. Concepts of convex hull and its deficiency may also be used to describe an entire region in a similar manner. The area and relative positions of such regions may be determined.

14.2.4 Approximation Curve

Boundary can be represented by piecewise continuous polynomial approximation curves such as B-splines. B-spline curves describe boundary shapes which have close resemblance to their control polygons—a sequence of control vertices yield a polygonal representation of the curve segment. Third order B-spline curves can be used for this purpose.

14.2.5 Different Measurements

Once the boundary of an object is suitably represented, different features of it can be measured to obtain compact mathematical form for future processing. Some of the features and their measurement techniques are briefly mentioned here.

Boundary length: The length of a boundary can be computed from the pixel geometry of the boundary. Two consecutive pixels, on a boundary, lying on a horizontal or vertical line have a distance of 1. In a *mod-4* code for boundary, only unit distances are countable. In case of *mod-8* code representation, diagonal directions impart a distance of $\sqrt{2}$. Length of closed boundary, i.e. perimeter length can be computed in this method. It should be clear that boundary length increases with pixel resolution of the display device.

A run of chain code is a maximal subsequence of the sequence of codes such that in the subsequence the value of the code does not change. The number of codes in a run is called the *run-length*. Thus, run-length coded chain code of an object is a sequence of ordered pairs $\{(l_i, n_i)|i = 0, 1, 2, \ldots, m-1\}$, where n_i is the value of chain code in the ith run and $n_i \in \{0, 1, 2, 3\}$, and l_i is the run-length and is cyclic, i.e. $(l_{m+i}, c_{m+i}) = (l_i, c_i)$. So n_i is a member of *mod-4* code. In case of *mod-8* code $n_i \in \{0, 1, 2, 3, 4, 5, 6, 7\}$ and the boundary will be called 8-connected boundary. The value of chain code in a sequence changes at a corner of the boundary. It may be observed that evan and odd code values generally occur alternatively. With the above notation, the perimeter P of an object, i.e. length of boundary, for *mod-4* code, can be defined as

$$P = \sum_{i=0}^{m-1} l_i + (\sqrt{2} - 2)n_d$$

where n_d is the number of occurrences of code pairs (0, 1), (1, 2), (2, 3) and (3, 0). For *mod-8* code

$$P = \text{sum of all } l_i (\text{if } n_i \text{ is even}) + \sqrt{2} \times \text{sum of all } l_i (\text{if } n_i \text{ is odd})$$

Diameter of enclosing circle: An object can be enclosed by a circle and the diameter of this circle can be defined as the largest distance between any two pixels of the object. Let, s_i denotes the sequence of pixels in the ith run, i.e. $s_i =< s_{i,1}, s_{i,2}, \ldots, s_{i,l_i} >$. Thus, $s_{i,k}$ is the kth pixel of the sequence. Then we can write,

- The distance $d(p, s_{i,k})$ between any arbitrary pixel p and any pixel $s_{i,k}$ of a run s_i is the maximum if $k = 1$ or $k = l_i$.
- The maximum distance between any two pixels of the sequence can thus be given by

  $$\max\{\max_j(r_j + c_j) - \min_j(r_j + c_j), \max(r_j - c_j) - \min(r_j - c_j)\}$$

  where $\{r_i, c_j)|j = 1, 2, \ldots\}$ is a sequence of pixels.

From the above discussion, it is clear that, only corner pixels are used to compute diameter, and only sum of difference of coordinate values of the corner pixels is sufficient to compute maximum distance or diameter.

Object area: The area under a closed curve can be required as a special feature in many applications. Actual area computation may be computed by multiplying the total number of pixels under the curve by the true area of each individual pixel. However, for practical purposes, the total number of pixels may simply be used as such a measure. Computing number of pixels under a rectangular polygon is easy to compute which is not the case for arbitrary shaped curves. Also in case of quadtree representation of the image it is further difficult.

Computing areas in quadtrees: The following algorithm may be used for this purpose:

1. Set all region area variables to 0, and determine the global quadtree depth H. For example, for a 256×256 image the global quadtree depth is 8.
2. Upon searching the tree, if a leaf node at depth h has a non-zero label, go to step 3.
3. Compute: $area[region\_label] \quad = \quad area[region\_label] \; + \; 4^{(H-4)}$.
4. Region areas are stored in variables $area[region\_label]$.

For a n-vertex polygon having vertices (x_i, y_i) for $i = 1, 2, \ldots, n-1$ and $(x_n, y_n) = (x_0, y_0)$, the area can be written as

$$Area = \frac{1}{2}|\sum_{k=0}^{(n-1)} (k_k y_{k+1} - x_{k+1} y_k)|$$

Computing areas in 4-connected chain code representation: When Freeman's 4-connected chain code is used represent a boundary the area can be computed using the following method. In 4-connected chain code representation direction codes are 0, 1, 2 and 3.

1. Set $area \rightarrow 0$.
2. Set the starting point x-coordinate to the variable *vertical_position.*
3. For each element in the chain code do steps 4 through 7.
4. If $(code = 0)$ $area \rightarrow area - vertical\_position$.
5. If $(code = 1)$ $vertical\_position \rightarrow vertical\_position + 1$.
6. If $(code = 2)$ $area \rightarrow area + vertical\_position$.
7. If $(code = 3)$ $vertical\_position \rightarrow vertical\_position - 1$.
8. When all boundary elements are processed *area* contains the region area.

Slope and boundary curvature: A finite set of 8-connected pixels form an open digital arc. Each point on this arc has two neighbour pixels except the two end point pixels which have only one neighbour. A slope at any pixel p_i of the digital arc is defined as the slope of the line segment between pixels p_i and p_{i+1}. Therefore, value of the slope is an integral multiple of 90° for 4-connected pixels, and integral multiples of 45° for 8-connected pixels. Slope at any pixel, θ may be considered in $[-180°, 180°]$. For 8-connected pixel situation the slope s_i at pixel p_i may be given by

$$s_i = \begin{cases} 45n_i & \text{if } n_i \leq 4 \\ 45(n_i - 8) & \text{otherwise} \end{cases}$$

Curvature is the rate of change of slope on a boundary. This definition works in continuous domain. In discrete domain, the curves are not smooth.

Elongatedness: It is the ratio between length and width of the rectangle of minimum area bounding a region of concern. This method can be applied only for nearly polygonal shaped areas. For highly curved areas other approaches may be applicable. Examples of such areas are shown in Figures 14.5(a) and (b) respectively. For curved areas elongatedness can be measured as the ratio of region area and the square of its thickness. The maximum area thickness can be measured as the number of erosion steps (needed to erode the area) applied before the area totally disappears. Therefore, if the number of erosion steps be d, then elongatedness is

$$\text{Elongatedness} = \frac{\text{Area}}{(2d)^2}$$

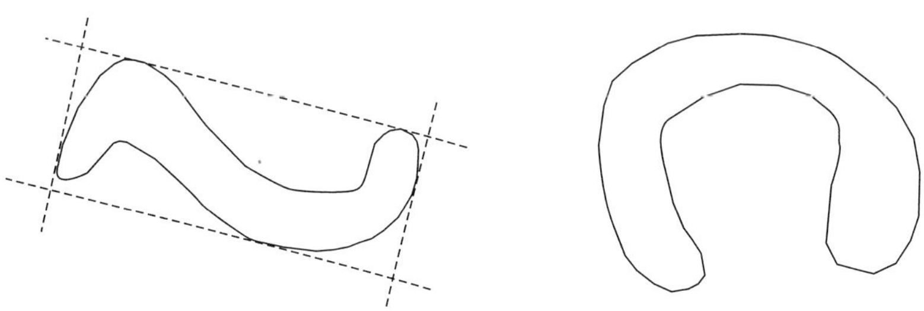

(a) Length of bounding rectangle gives result

(b) Bounding rectangle method is inappropriate

Figure 14.5: Elongatedness.

Direction: The direction makes sense only in case of an elongated object. It is the direction of the longest side of a minimum bounding rectangle. If the shape moments are known earlier, the direction can be calculated as

$$\theta = \frac{1}{2}\tan^{(-1)}\left(\frac{2\mu_{11}}{\mu_{20} - \mu_{02}}\right)$$

It is important to note that rectangularity and direction are independent of basic geometrical transformations, i.e. translation, scaling and rotation. Mutual direction of two rotating objects is rotation invariant also.

Compactness: Compactness of an object or shape is a very important and useful feature. It is independent of linear transformations, and is given by

$$\text{Compactness} = \frac{(\text{Length of closed boundary})^2}{\text{Area}}$$

In 2D Euclidean space the most compact object is a circle. Compactness feature has a value in the range $[1, \infty)$.

14.2.6 Some Other Shape Descriptors

Two-dimensional curved shapes can be described by many other techniques. A few of them are mentioned here.

Hough transform: Standard geometrical shapes can be detected and represented suitably using this technique. General curve shapes can also be detected using generalized Hough transforms.

Mathematical morphology: This technique can be used for shape description. The main idea here is to apply a thinning procedure to extract a shape or skeleton of some objects. Elements on a skeleton can be accompanied with other information like actual distance from object boundary, etc. so that the object shape can be properly described.

Neural networks: Artificial neural networks can be used to train boundary shapes extracted from a family of objects. After training the network can recognize any arbitrary input shape based on close resemblance.

14.3 Measuring Moments

For a two-dimensional function $f(x, y)$, moment of order $(p + q)$ is defined as

$$m_{pq} = \int_{-\infty}^{\infty} \int_{-\infty}^{\infty} x^p y^q f(x, y) dx dy \tag{14.1}$$

for $p, q = 0, 1, \ldots$. The famous Papoulis theorem states that, if $f(x, y)$ is piece-wise continuous and has non-zero values only in a finite part of the XY-plane, moments of all orders can exist, and the moment sequence (m_{pq}) is uniquely determined by $f(x, y)$. The reverse is also true, i.e. (m_{pq}) can uniquely determine $f(x, y)$.

The central moments are defined as

$$\mu_{pq} = \int_{-\infty}^{\infty} \int_{-\infty}^{\infty} (x - \bar{x})^p (y - \bar{y})^q f(x, y) dx dy \tag{14.2}$$

where,

$$\bar{x} = \frac{m_{10}}{m_{00}} \quad \text{and} \quad \bar{y} = \frac{m_{01}}{m_{00}}$$

If we consider $f(x, y)$ to be a digital image then, Eq. 14.2 becomes

$$\mu_{pq} = \sum_x \sum_y (x - \bar{x})^p (y - \bar{y})^q f(x, y) \tag{14.3}$$

Central moments of up to order three are defined as

$$\begin{aligned}
\mu_{00} &= \sum_x \sum_y (x - \bar{x})^0 (y - \bar{y})^0 f(x, y) \\
&= \sum_x \sum_y f(x, y) \\
&= m_{00} \\
\mu_{10} &= \sum_x \sum_y (x - \bar{x})^1 (y - \bar{y})^0 f(x, y) \\
&= \sum_x \sum_y (x - \bar{x}) f(x, y) \\
&= m_{10} - \frac{m_{01}}{m_{00}}(m_{00}) \\
&= 0 \\
\mu_{01} &= \sum_x \sum_y (x - \bar{x})^0 (y - \bar{y})^1 f(x, y) \\
&= \sum_x \sum_y (y - \bar{y}) f(x, y) \\
&= m_{01} - \frac{m_{01}}{m_{00}}(m_{00}) \\
&= 0 \\
\mu_{11} &= \sum_x \sum_y (x - \bar{x})^1 (y - \bar{y})^1 f(x, y) \\
&= \sum_x \sum_y (x - \bar{x})(y - \bar{y}) f(x, y) \\
&= m_{11} - \frac{m_{10} m_{01}}{m_{00}} \\
&= m_{11} - \bar{x} m_{01} = m_{11} - \bar{y} m_{10} \\
\mu_{20} &= \sum_x \sum_y (x - \bar{x})^2 (y - \bar{y})^0 f(x, y) \\
&= m_{20} - \frac{2m_{10}^2}{m_{00}} + \frac{m_{10}^2}{m_{00}} \\
&= m_{20} - \frac{m_{10}^2}{m_{00}} \\
&= m_{20} - \bar{x} m_{10}
\end{aligned}$$

$$\begin{aligned}
\mu_{02} &= \sum_x \sum_y (x-\bar{x})^0 (y-\bar{y})^2 f(x,y) \\
&= m_{02} - \frac{m_{01}^2}{m_{00}} = m_{02} - \bar{y} m_{01} \\
\mu_{21} &= \sum_x \sum_y (x-\bar{x})^2 (y-\bar{y})^1 f(x,y) \\
&= m_{21} - 2\bar{x} m_{11} - \bar{y} m_{20} + 2\bar{x}^2 m_{01} \\
\mu_{12} &= \sum_x \sum_y (x-\bar{x})^1 (y-\bar{y})^2 f(x,y) \\
&= m_{12} - 2\bar{y} m_{11} - \bar{x} m_{02} + 2\bar{y}^2 m_{10} \\
\mu_{30} &= \sum_x \sum_y (x-\bar{x})^3 (y-\bar{y})^0 f(x,y) \\
&= m_{30} - 3\bar{x} m_{20} + 2\bar{x}^2 m_{10} \\
\mu_{03} &= \sum_x \sum_y (x-\bar{x})^0 (y-\bar{y})^3 f(x,y) \\
&= m_{03} - 3\bar{y} m_{02} + 2\bar{y}^2 m_{01}
\end{aligned}$$

Normalized central moments are defined as

$$\eta_{pq} = \frac{\mu_{pq}}{\mu_{00}{}^{\gamma}} \tag{14.4}$$

where,

$$\gamma = \frac{p+q}{2} + 1 \tag{14.5}$$

for $p + q = 1, 2, \ldots$.

A set of seven *invariant moments* can be derived from the second and third order moments. These are given by

$$\begin{aligned}
\phi_1 &= \eta_{20} + \eta_{02} \\
\phi_2 &= (\eta_{20} - \eta_{02})^2 + 4\eta_{11}{}^2 \\
\phi_3 &= (\eta_{30} - 3\eta_{12})^2 + (3\eta_{21} - \eta_{03})^2 \\
\phi_4 &= (\eta_{30} + \eta_{12})^2 + (\eta_{21} + \eta_{03})^2 \\
\phi_5 &= (\eta_{30} - 3\eta_{12})(\eta_{30} + \eta_{12})[(\eta_{30} + \eta_{12})^2 - 3(\eta_{21} + \eta_{03})^2] + (3\eta_{21} - \eta_{03})(\eta_{21} + \eta_{03}) \\
&\quad [3(\eta_{30} + \eta_{12})^2 - (\eta_{21} + \eta_{03})^2] \\
\phi_6 &= (\eta_{20} - \eta_{02})[(\eta_{30} + \eta_{12})^2 - (\eta_{21} + \eta_{03})^2] + 4\eta_{11}(\eta_{30} + \eta_{12})(\eta_{21} + \eta_{03}) \\
\phi_7 &= (3\eta_{21} - \eta_{03})(\eta_{30} + \eta_{12})[(\eta_{30} + \eta_{12})^2 - 3(\eta_{21} + \eta_{03})^2] + (3\eta_{12} - \eta_{30})(\eta_{21} + \eta_{03}) \\
&\quad [3(\eta_{30} + \eta_{12})^2 - (\eta_{21} + \eta_{03})^2].
\end{aligned}$$

The above moments are invariant to geometrical translation, rotation and scaling operations. Due to this inavariace property these moments are very useful for extracting different image features. Very common applications are, therefore, hand written character recognition, object shape detection, etc.

Example 1: For the 3×3 image given below compute the first and second order moments.

$f(x,y)$	$y=1$	$y=2$	$y=3$
$x=1$	3	2	1
$x=2$	2	1	3
$x=3$	3	3	2

Solution: The stepwise computation of central moments is described here.

$$
\begin{aligned}
\mu_{00} &= \sum_x \sum_y (x-\bar{x})^0 (y-\bar{y})^0 f(x,y) \\
&= \sum_x \sum_y f(x,y) \\
&= 3+2+1+2+1+3+3+3+2 = 20 \\
\mu_{10} &= \sum_x \sum_y (x-\bar{x})^1 (y-\bar{y})^0 f(x,y) \\
&= \sum_x \sum_y (x-\bar{x}) f(x,y) \\
&= \sum_x (x-\bar{x}) \sum_y f(x,y) \\
&= -1 \times 6 - 0 \times 6 + 1 \times 6 = 0 \\
\mu_{01} &= \sum_x \sum_y (x-\bar{x})^0 (y-\bar{y})^1 f(x,y) \\
&= \sum_x \sum_y (y-\bar{y}) f(x,y) \\
&= \sum_y (y-\bar{y}) \sum_x f(x,y) \\
&= -1 \times 8 - 0 \times 8 + 1 \times 8 = 0 \\
\mu_{11} &= \sum_x \sum_y (x-\bar{x})^1 (y-\bar{y})^1 f(x,y) \\
&= \sum_x \sum_y (x-\bar{x})(y-\bar{y}) f(x,y) \\
&= (-1) \times (-1) \times 3 + (-1) \times 0 \times 2 + (-1) \times 1 \times 1 \\
& \quad 0 \times (-1) \times 2 + 0 \times 0 \times 1 + 0 \times 1 \times 3 \\
& \quad 1 \times (-1) \times 3 + 1 \times 0 \times 3 + 1 \times 1 \times 2 \\
&= 3+0-1+0+0+0-3+0+2 = 1
\end{aligned}
$$

Computation of second order moments is left as a task for the students.

14.4 Principal Components

In a colour image each pixel involves three component intensity values corresponding to Red, Green and Blue colours. In case of a multispectral image there are n such components. Each pixel in such images can be represented as a vector $\mathbf{x}$, where

$$\begin{bmatrix} x_1 \\ x_2 \\ x_3 \end{bmatrix}$$

or

$$\begin{bmatrix} x_1 \\ x_2 \\ \vdots \\ x_n \end{bmatrix}$$

The total image is a combination of $K = M \times N$ number of such vector. The *mean vector* and *covariance matrix* of all the vectors are defined as

$$\mathbf{m_x} = E\{\mathbf{x}\} \tag{14.6}$$

where $E\{.\}$ is the expected value of the argument and the subscript of $\mathbf{m}$ indicates that the mean is taken over a population of $\mathbf{x}$ vectors.

The covariance matrix of the vector population is

$$\mathbf{C_x} = E\{(\mathbf{x} - \mathbf{m_x})(\mathbf{x} - \mathbf{m_x})^T\} \tag{14.7}$$

If $\mathbf{x}$ is n-dimensional, $\mathbf{C_x}$ matrix is of size $n \times n$. Elements x_{ii} of $\mathbf{C_x}$ are the auto covariance for the elements x_i, and x_{ij} are the covariance between elements, x_i and x_j. If x_i and x_j are uncorrelated then their covariance is zero, i.e. $c_{ij} = cji = 0$.

For a vector population of size K, the mean vector is

$$\mathbf{m_x} = \frac{1}{K}\sum_{k=1}^{K} \mathbf{x}_k \tag{14.8}$$

The covariance matrix can also be approximated as

$$\mathbf{C_x} = \frac{1}{K}\sum_{k=1}^{K} \mathbf{x}_k\mathbf{x}_k^T - \mathbf{m_x}\mathbf{m_x}^T \tag{14.9}$$

Since $\mathbf{C_x}$ is real and symmetric, we can find out a set of n orthonormal eigenvectors. Let, $\mathbf{e}_i$ and λ_i for $i = 1, 2, \ldots, n$ be eigenvectors and corresponding eigenvalues of $\mathbf{C_x}$, arranged in descending order, for convenience, so that $\lambda_i \geq \lambda_{i+1}$ for $i = 1, 2, \ldots, n-1$.

If we form a matrix $\mathbf{A}$ whose rows correspond to the eigenvectors, ordered so that the first row corresponds to the highest eigenvalue and the last row corresponds to the lowest eigenvalue.

Now, let us assume that $\mathbf{A}$ is a transformation matrix that maps $\mathbf{x}$'s into $\mathbf{y}$'s, as follows:

$$\mathbf{y} = \mathbf{A}(\mathbf{x} - \mathbf{m_x}) \tag{14.10}$$

The above expression is the *Hotelling transformation.* Following this transformation, we can show that the mean value of $\mathbf{y}$ is zero, i.e.

$$\mathbf{m_y} = E\{\mathbf{y}\} = 0 \tag{14.11}$$

We can also write

$$\mathbf{C_y} = \mathbf{A}\mathbf{C_x}\mathbf{A}^T \tag{14.12}$$

Here, $\mathbf{C_y}$ is a diagonal matrix whose main diagonal elements are the eigenvalues of $\mathbf{C_x}$.

$$\mathbf{C_y} = \begin{bmatrix} \lambda_1 & 0 & \cdots & 0 \\ 0 & \lambda_2 & \cdots & 0 \\ & & \ddots & \\ 0 & 0 & \cdots & \lambda_n \end{bmatrix} \tag{14.13}$$

Since the off-diagonal elements are 0, $\mathbf{y}$ vectors are uncorrelated. So, $\mathbf{C_x}$ and $\mathbf{C_y}$ have same eigenvalues and eigenvectors.

The Hotelling transform also allows us to reconstruct $\mathbf{x}$ from $\mathbf{y}$ using the following relation

$$\mathbf{x} = \mathbf{A}^T + \mathbf{m_x} \tag{14.14}$$

Now, if instead of all eigenvectors of $\mathbf{C_x}$ we form a matrix $\mathbf{A}_k$ using k largest eigenvalue vectors, then we get transformation matrix of size $k \times n$. Vectors reconstructed by this matrix $\mathbf{A}_k$ will be

$$\hat{\mathbf{x}} = \mathbf{A}_k^T + \mathbf{m_x} \tag{14.15}$$

The mean square error between $\mathbf{x}$ and $\hat{\mathbf{x}}$ is given by

$$e_{ms} = \sum_{j=1}^{n} \lambda_j - \sum_{j=1}^{k} \lambda_j = \sum_{j=k+1}^{n} \lambda_j \tag{14.16}$$

The above equation indicates that the error is zero if $k = n$ (when all eigenvectors are used). Now, since λ_i's decrease monotonically, it also shows that the error can be minimized by selecting k eigenvectors associated with the largest eigenvalues. The Hotelling transform, thus, helps in minimizing the error between $\mathbf{x}$ and its approximation $\hat{\mathbf{x}}$. Due to this property the Hotelling transform is also known as the *principal components* transform.

14.5 Boundary Thinning

In many cases detected boundary of an object is found to be unnecessarily thick (i.e. more than one-pixel wide). For proper representation and further measurements it is necessary to reduce the thickness. Several techniques are available for image thinning. One simple approach is described below.

The process of boundary thinning essentially involved with finding out and removing excess boundary pixels such that

- Connectivity of boundary is not changed, and
- Length of the curve or boundary segment is not reduced.

If we eliminate an end point pixel from a curve its length will be reduced. And the pixels whose elimination causes segmentation of the curve into pieces are called *critical pixels*. We may consider a 3×3 binary window whose central location indicates a boundary pixel. The boundary image is considered to be a binary image. Now, we can move the window over the image by placing the central location on each image pixel sequentially. Several such boundary portions falling within the window are shown in Figure 14.6. It is observed that, centre pixels of windows (b), (c) and (d) are critical pixels, but those in (a), (e), (f) and (g) are not. Also centre pixels in windows (f) and (g) are end point pixels. Therefore, we can delete the centre pixels in (a) and (e) without affecting local connectivity. Here, we must take into accout as to which of two coding systems ($mod-4$ or $mod-8$ connected) have been used for representing the boundary. In case of 4-connected boundary the central pixel in (a) is a critical pixel which is not the case in (b).

0	1	1
0	1	1
0	1	0

(a)

0	1	1
0	1	1
1	0	0

(b)

0	1	0
0	1	0
0	1	0

(c)

0	1	0
0	1	0
0	0	1

(d)

0	1	0
0	1	1
0	0	0

(e)

0	0	0
0	1	1
0	0	0

(f)

0	0	0
0	1	0
0	0	1

(g)

0	0	0
0	1	0
1	0	0

(h)

Figure 14.6: Some edge patterns and corresponding thinning windows.

14.6 Measuring Textures

Textures are created due to regular or random variation in grey level or colour in an image. By measuring variations of smoothness, coarseness and regularity of grey level occurrence we can quantify different types of textures differently. Therefore, texture features are very useful in automatic recognition of objects.

14.6.1 Using Statistical Moments

Statistical moments can be used to measure texture properties. The grey level histogram of the image can be used for this purpose. Let, grey levels can be described by a random variable z and its distribution in the histogram be $p(z_i)$ for $i = 0, 1, \ldots, L-1$, where L is the number of grey levels present in the image. Now, the nth moment of the variable z about its mean m is defined as

$$\mu_n(z) = \sum_{i=0}^{L-1} (z_i - m)^n p(z_i) \tag{14.17}$$

The mean m is defined as

$$m = \sum_{i=0}^{L-1} z_i p(z_i) \tag{14.18}$$

From Eq. 14.17, we see that $\mu_0(z) = 1$ and $\mu_1(z) = 0$. The second moment, the variance $\sigma^2(z) = \mu_2(z)$, is very significant in describing texture properties. It is a measure of grey-level contrast and can be used to define as relative smoothness as

$$R = 1 - \frac{1}{1 + \sigma^2(z)} \tag{14.19}$$

R has a value of 0 in areas of constant intensity (and the variance is also 0 there). Higher values of R occur (maximum value is 1) with higher variance. The standard deviation $\sigma(z)$ is also used as an important measure of texture. The third moment is

$$\mu_n(z) = \sum_{i=0}^{L-1} (z_i - m)^3 p(z_i) \tag{14.20}$$

It is a measure of skewness of the histogram, and the fourth moment is a measure of its relative flatness. Although higher order moments are not very significantly sensitive to histograms, they may also be used in certain situations.

Uniformity of the histogram can be measured as

$$U(z) = \sum_{i-0}^{L-1} p^2(z_i) \tag{14.21}$$

and the average entropy of the histogram is measured as

$$e(z) = -\sum_{i=0}^{L-1} p(z_i \log_2 p(z_i) \tag{14.22}$$

Entropy is a measure of variability or coarseness of the image grey-levels.

One major problem with histogram based measurement of texture features is that the histogram displays the number of occurrences of a particular intensity in the image ignoring its location. However, location information is very important regarding texture property evaluation. One way to associate the position information with the histogram is to use the *grey-level cooccurrence matrix.* This matrix consists of counts of grey-level occurrences in the vicinity of a certain pixel location, and therefore, can provide information regarding periodicity or repetition of texture patterns within a small region.

Let us denote the grey-level cooccurrence matrix by $\mathbf{C} = [c_{i,j}]$, where, $c_{i,j}$, the ijth element of the matrix, is the count of number of occurrences that a pair of points in a predefined local area R have grey values z_i and z_j, respectively, with $0 \le z_i, z_j \le L-1$ for an L-level image. Values of $c_{i,j}$ depends on the size of area R. Therefore, we need to use a suitable position operator P for measuring texture properties.

Let $\mathbf{C}$ be a $k \times k$ matrix with elements c_{ij} denoting the number of times the grey-value pair z_i, z_j occur in prespecified relative positions for $0 \le i, j \le k-1$. For example, let us consider the following image matrix $\mathbf{I}$ with three grey values $z_0 = 0, z_1 = 1$ and $z_2 = 2$.

$$\mathbf{I} = \begin{bmatrix} 1 & 1 & 0 & 0 & 0 \\ 2 & 2 & 0 & 2 & 2 \\ 1 & 1 & 2 & 1 & 1 \\ 1 & 2 & 2 & 0 & 0 \\ 1 & 1 & 1 & 2 & 2 \end{bmatrix}$$

If the position operator P is defined as "one position towards right and one position below" we can get the following cooccurrence matrix $\mathbf{C}$.

$$\mathbf{C} = \begin{bmatrix} 0 & 2 & 1 \\ 0 & 1 & 3 \\ 3 & 3 & 2 \end{bmatrix}$$

Here, the first entry $c_{00} = 0$ indicates that there is no of occurrence of grey-value 0 at specified relative position P for a pixel with grey-value 0. And, the last entry $c_{22} = 2$ indicates that there are two occurrences of grey-value 2 at specified relative position P for a pixel with grey-value 2.

We can obtain a joint probability of occurrences, of a grey-value pair (z_i, z_j) that satisfy the positional operator P, by dividing each element of $\mathbf{C}$ by the sum total of individual values in the matrix $\mathbf{C}$. In our example, this sum is $n = 15$. Some statistical measures that are commonly used for texture analysis are given below.

1. Maximum probability: $\max_{i,j}(c_{ij})$
2. Uniformity: $\sum_i \sum_j (c_{ij}^2)$
3. Energy: $\sum_{i=0}^{L-1} \sum_{j=0}^{L-1} (c_{ij}^2)$
4. Entropy: $-\sum_i \sum_j c_{ij} \log_2 c_{ij}$
5. Contrast: $\sum_{i=0}^{L-1} \sum_{j=0}^{L-1} (i-j)^2 c_{ij}$
6. (m, n)-th Moment: $\sum_{i=0}^{L-1} \sum_{j=0}^{L-1} i^m j^n c_{ij}$
7. Homogeneity: $\sum_{i=0}^{L-1} \sum_{j=0}^{L-1} \frac{c_{ij}}{1+|i-j|}$
8. Difference Moment(order k): $\sum_i \sum_j c_{ij}(i-j)^k$
9. Inverse Difference Moment(order k): $\sum_i \sum_j \frac{c_{ij}}{(i-j)^k}$

The above mentioned features can be used to measure different kind of variations in grey levels within a texture image. They describe different properties of the concerned texture pattern. For example, *entropy* is a measure of randomness; a high value of entropy indicates that elements of $\mathbf{C}$ are mostly random, and it is not easy to find a regular pattern.

14.6.2 Structural Approach

Structural description of texture patterns is possible by using a set of rules. Frequent patterns found in a texture image can be represented by a definite rule. For example, the rule $S \rightarrow aS$ a premitive pattern a appears in a series of a certain length. By using other useful rules we can get a complete set of rules that can describe all possible types of texture patterns. These rules will determine how textures are formed from different primitives and their ordered combinations.

14.6.3 Spectral Approach

The Fourier spectrum can also be used to determine and analyse the occurrences of periodic patterns in an image. While global texture patterns are easy to distinguish in this approach, local and minute variations are difficult to detect. Strong peaks in the Fourier spectrum determines the direction of texture pattern. Position of the peaks determine the frequency or period of the pattern occurrences.

14.7 Biometric Features

Recently biometric features like fingerprints, face geometry, hand geometry, etc. are being used for automatic authentication purposes. In such situations, we need to extract sufficient features from the corresponding images. Biometric authentication technology is mainly used in ID cards, voter ID cards, driving license, ATM cards, computer login IDs, e-commerce, net banking, smart cards, criminal investigation, missing person identification, etc.

Biometric recognition is a very difficult problem to solve. We need to deal with a very lerge number of patterns and pattern classes. We need to differentiate between intra-class variability and inter-class similarity also. Biometric images are captured in noisy state in many cases, deformation and alignment problems are almost unavoidable. Biometric systems are always exposed to attacks. Face images of different persons may seem similar due to orientation, bad lighting, pose, expression, etc. Fingerprints suffer from the problem of temporal variation due to aging. This is also true for hand and finger geometry. Segmentation of objects from its surrounding background is also a difficult problem. Almost all biometric systems render a certain error rate which is significant.

14.7.1 Fingerprint Recognition

Among several various commercially available biometric recognition techniques such as face, fingerprint, iris, etc. fingerprint based techniques form the most popular and useful family of recognition systems. Fingerprints are imprints or impression of patterns formed by friction ridges of the skin in the fingers and thumbs.

Fingerprints may be broadly classified into several classes like: Plain arch, tented arch, right loop, left loop, accidental, pocket whorl, plain whorl, double loop, etc. These classifications are based on the presence of such patterns in the fingerprint images. Fingerprints are evaluated for different features like types of ridge ending, ridge bifurcation, etc. Also many other minutiae may be used for measurements. These minutiae may include: angle formed by the ridges with horizontal axis, finding gradient direction perpendicular to the ridge direction, local variation of grey levels in the fingerprint area, ridge ending, delta, core, etc. Ending is the point at which a ridge stops. Bifurcation is the point at which one ridge divides into two. Several different types of fingerprints are shown in Figure 14.7(a).

To determine minutiae, fingerprint image of a person is captured using a sensor. This image is then digitized and converted into a grey image. Now, by finding out the number of neighbour pixels at a certain location we can measure a minutiae. For example, in case of a bifurcation, there are three neighbour pixels at the point of bifurcation. For a ridge end, there is only one neighbour pixel. These situations are shown in Figure 14.7(b). It can be said here that, ridge ends and bifurcations are two most popular minutiae used for fingerprint based authentication and identification.

(a) Different types of fingerprints

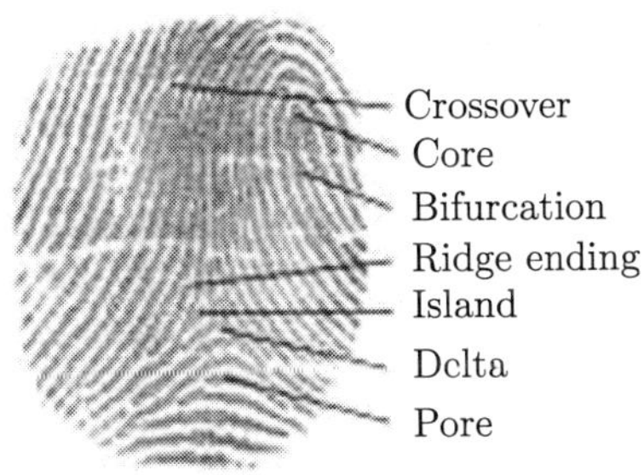

(b) Minutiae of fingerprints

Figure 14.7: Fingerprint recognition.

Many algorithms exist to extract ridges, remove holes and speckles from the fingerprint images, connect ridges, remove spikes and minutiae matching. After all these preprocessings, the base and target patterns are aligned and matching scores are computed.

14.8 Handwritten Script

Optical character recognition has long been a matter of interest among the scientists. Character recognition processes form two broad categories. One for typed characters and the other for handwritten characters. Definitely the later is more challenging than the former. For different languages different recognition schemes are used. However, almost all the processes follow the general steps of preprocessing, feature extraction and classification in this sequence for recognizing a character.

In the preprocessing phase, generally some kind of normalization of the character image is performed. This may be scaling the character to a predefined fixed geometrical size. So the normalization process includes geometrical transformations like translation, scaling, rotation and slanting, etc. Another preprocessing requirement, commonly in practice, is to perform thinning of the character image.

Feature extraction is a measurement on a population of entities that will be classified. This assists the classification stage by looking for features that allow fairly easy to distinguish between different classes. Several features may be used for classification. A number of selective features, for a character, encode the character in a pattern vector. The pattern vectors for all possible characters are then fed into a classifier for classification purpose. Very commonly a neural network based training-testing system is used for recognition.

14.9 Conclusion

In the above sections we have described several common approaches to extract image information from grey level images and their representation techniques. Image information are commonly available in object boundary and object region forms. Boundaries may be linear, polygonal shaped or curves. In case of curve boundaries they can be segmented into smaller nearly linear sections, and then using a suitable coding technique the boundary shape can be represented for further processing. Object regions can be extracted by applying different region segmentation techniques. Extracted objects may need further conversion like skeletonization, such that a suitable mathematical description and representation of the object shape can be obtained. While object descriptors are generally statistical in nature, boundary descriptors have syntactic descriptions in many cases. Therefore, syntactic and statistical analysis processes are applied for recognition purposes. This kind of higher level analysis of images produces higher level image descriptions that constitute a part of the so called image understanding.

14.10 Problems

1. What are the prerequisite and importance of shape description?
2. In what ways you can represent a boundary and what are their differences?
3. Define boundary representation using 4-connected and 8-connected chain coding schemes.
4. Define the following border description schemes:
    - Boundary length
    - Boundary curvature
    - Elongatedness

5. Define the following shape description schemes:
   - Area
   - Direction
   - Elongatedness
   - Compactness
   - Rectangularity
6. Write down a boundary thinning algorithm.
7. What are geometrical moments and what are their importance in image analysis?
8. Describe how can you use moments to measure image symmetry.
9. For the following 3×3 image compute geometrical moments up to 2nd order:

$f(x,y)$	$y=1$	$y=2$	$y=3$
$x=1$	3	1	2
$x=2$	2	0	3
$x=3$	3	3	1

   Compute both regular and central moments.

Chapter 15

Pattern Recognition

Pattern recognition is a very important subject in the fields of Artificial Intelligence (AI) and machine learning. Recognition, classification, and grouping of patterns are important problems in fields like computer vision, remote sensing, biology, psychology, medicine, marketing, etc. patterns encapsulate significant information about some objects or events. Objects can be classified and recognized by processing of patterns. In general, information may be available in pictorial or other non-numerical forms. As most often, human experts are needed to extract information from such sources and to process them, machines may also be employed for this task, with higher speed and possibly greater accuracy. Pattern recognition is the study of how machines can observe the environment, extract information from natural representation of objects to create patterns, learn to classify patterns, and make sound and reasonable decision about categories of patterns.

15.1 Recognition and Learning

Recognition is one of the very basic attributes of human beings and other living beings. It is a process by which we can identify objects in our daily lives. any object we recognize can be represented by a pattern. So pattern is something that distinguishes an object from others of different kinds. Thus, we can define pattern as any distinguishable interrelation of data, events or concepts.

We perform the task of pattern recognition at every instant of our daily lives. We can recognize a friend by looking at his/her face or by hearing his/her voice over telephone; we can read books by distinguishing one character from the others; we can identify somebody by looking at his/her handwriting or signature or by analyzing his/her fingerprint; we are also able to distinguish between gestures of happiness from that of anger. All the above processes involve some human decision making ability. This ability of human being cannot be taken as granted, but they learn from observation and experience. The more are the number of observed patterns, the better is the decision.

15.1.1 Human Learning

The process of recognition by computers is similar to that of human being. Actually the human brain can be considered to be a super processor which possesses a superior pattern recognition capability. But this capability was not with him right from birth. A new born baby learns how to recognize its mother, father and other objects or patterns in the surrounding. The very basic step of learning is attaining the ability to make a difference. This ability is attained by psycho-physiological processes that make a copy of each pattern receive via. physical stimulus into brain memory cells. As more and more patterns are perceived by a child, initially it tries to identify all of them as separate entities. But from experience it comes to knows that some objects are of a certain category and some others are different. Then it tries to categorize them into classes and refines the recognition process by storing a replica of each category. This process is called **learning**.

Thus, although at the very beginning any particular object has no specific meaning to a child and the world is absolutely fuzzy, a sense of learning arise in it gradually; and it then attempts to categorize objects. Each new object is tried to be associated with one of the already formed statistical populations in the brain. Thus the problem of pattern recognition may be regarded as one of discriminating the input data, not between individual patterns, but between populations. These populations are searched for a match with the new object with the help of its attributes or features. In pattern recognition terminology, these populations are called **clusters** and each object is given a machine representation in the form of a feature vector.

15.1.2 Machine Learning

The idea of the learning process mentioned above has been imitated in the field of statistical pattern recognition. Here each pattern consisting of d features is modelled as a vector of dimension d. So each pattern of feature vector is an instance of a point in a d-dimensional space. The objective is to categorize patterns into classes so that patterns belonging to different classes are well separated. The process may start with or without any knowledge of the feature space. Accordingly there are two categories of classification schemes. When we have prior information regarding the class of a subset of the data, the classification scheme is called **supervised classification** or **simply classification**; and when nothing is known a priori, the scheme is called **unsupervised classification** or **clustering**. In case of supervised classification, the labelled subset of data is called the training data. Given a set of training patterns the objective is to determine the decision boundaries in the feature space which separate patterns belonging to different classes. In some cases, it becomes absolutely impossible to label data items from ground informations. In such situations, emphasis is given to identify relatively high density regions in the feature space and then trying to minimize the squared-error objective function of clustering by possible rearrangements of patterns between regions.

By pattern recognition, we mean recognition of patterns (representing different objects) by machines. Automatic recognition of patterns, classification and grouping of patterns into coherent and contrasted groups are considered to be important problems in a variety of engineering and scientific disciplines. At present, this topic is being highly utilized in disciplines like medical sciences, computer vision, data mining and remote sensing.

15.2 Recognition by Machines

The idea of building intelligent computers by constructing an artificial brain or neural network has been proposed by many researchers. For example, it has been suggested (Singh, 1966) that "the search for synthetic intelligence must begin with an inquiry into the origin of natural intelligence, i.e. into the working of our own brain." There are two major obstacles in a general simulation of brain. Firstly, we do not know the detailed structure of the brain, and secondly, we do not have computers with enough capabilities to simulate the brain, even if we did know the details of its structure. This is because, the human brain comprises at least 2×10^{10} neurons, each possessing about 10,000 synapses distributed over each dendrite tree. Therefore, it is almost practically infeasible to simulate the behaviour of human brain in its entirety and it is wise to settle for models that mimic specific and limited human behaviour. But, even this is found to be quite difficult due to the lack of complete understanding of the process behind specific behaviours. In practice, therefore, the objective is to construct programs that learn to imitate a class of input/output behaviours resulting in intelligent computer systems.

According to Haykin (1994), *Learning is the process by which the states (parameters) of the system are adapted through a continuing process of simulation by the environment in which the system is embedded.* This definition presupposes the following sequence of events: the system interacts with an environment, undergoes changes as a result of interaction, and responds in a new way because of the change that has occurred. That is, a learning model consists of a learning system interacting with an unknown environment. The interaction includes the learning system responding to a certain input from the environment and getting a feedback for this response from the environment. The learning system tries to find a suitable response (action) for each input from the environment based on the favourability of the feedback. In general, a learning system improves its behaviour with time by moving towards a goal.

The learning models can be classified into three categories depending on the type of interaction between the learner and the environment. In *supervised learning*, the environment provides the desired action from the learning system as the feedback. The objective of the learning system is to emulate the environment, i.e. the system has to learn a representation such that it outputs actions that are same as those provided by the environment for the respective inputs. In *unsupervised learning*, there is no feedback from the environment, but the system works towards an internally generated goal. The system has to learn a representation (internal state) that optimizes a measure of representation which is defined in terms of inputs it receives from the environment. We discuss more on unsupervised learning models in a later section. A model that lies between the above two models is the *reinforcement learning model*. In this model, the feedback is indicative of the relative effectiveness of different actions and need not explicitly give the best action. Because of this, reinforcement learning is also termed *learning with a critic*. The reinforcement feedback provides less information than the supervised learning model, and is often stochastic.

Pattern recognition processes may involve either *deterministic* or *statistical* models. Deterministic approaches do not make any assumption regarding the statistical properties of the pattern classes (such as statistical distribution characteristic of patterns). On the other hand, statistical approaches assumes such statistical properties like distribution of patterns and density function, etc. A very important tool in statistical decision making is the Bayes theorem. This theorem forms the basis of many unsupervised learning systems. In case of supervised learning, we need to train the recognition system about patterns whose classes are already determined by means of expert observation. The process of training, as already mentioned, mimics the human learning process. Since, we have sufficient information regarding pattern classes, in this case, we do not assort to any assumption regarding statistical properties; and hence, deterministic decision making is applied here. A very convenient tool for this purpose is the Artificial Neural Network (ANN). In deterministic techniques like minimum distance classifier, nearest neighbour classifier, etc. different kind of distance measurements are commonly used. Besides these distance based classifiers, there exists techniques that use linear discriminating functions, template matching, etc.

Recently many statistical decision making processes are being boosted using the search capabilities of non-deterministic methods like evolutionary algorithms, simulated annealing, etc. Accordingly many derivatives of conventional classifiers have been developed. Evolutionary computation or Evolutionary Algorithms (EAs) are a class of stochastic search and optimization tools that are based on the mechanisms of natural (evolutionary) systems. There are mainly three techniques within this computing paradigm. Genetic Algorithms (GAs), Evolution Strategies (ES), and Evolutionary Programming (EP). EAs work with a population of solutions. New solutions are created by randomly changing the existing solutions. Each solution is associated with an objective measure of performance that reflect the fitness of the solution. A selection mechanism determines the solution to be maintained in the subsequent generations.

The differences between various EAs are characterized by the types of random changes and the methods employed in selection. Simulated Annealing (SA) is also a search and optimization technique which is based on the metallurgical cooling process. One basic difference of SA with EAs is that unlike EAs, SA starts with a single solution and develops a new solution at each iteration by means of a random, but local search. It is, thus a faster process than EAs, but having lesser search capability.

In this book, we shall discuss development of some unsupervised pattern classification techniques that use searching capabilities of evolutionary algorithms and simulated annealing. The basic principle behind using these techniques lies in appropriately encoding the solutions in a solution space that suits for such random searches.

15.3 Overview of Pattern Recognition

A typical pattern recognition system consists of three phases as shown in Figure 15.1. These phases are *data acquisition*, *feature extraction* and *classification*. In the data acquisition phase, data regarding objects are collected from the environment using different kinds of sensory devices. After this, the gathered data is passed through the feature extraction phase where only significant components of the data are retained and others are rejected. This phase is very important because eliminating unnecessary data not only reduces processing time but also significantly influences the performance of the entire recognition system. This kind of selection of relevant features from gathered data is also called *reduction of dimensionality*. The selected features are then passed through the classification stage where a mapping function is executed between the features and the classes.

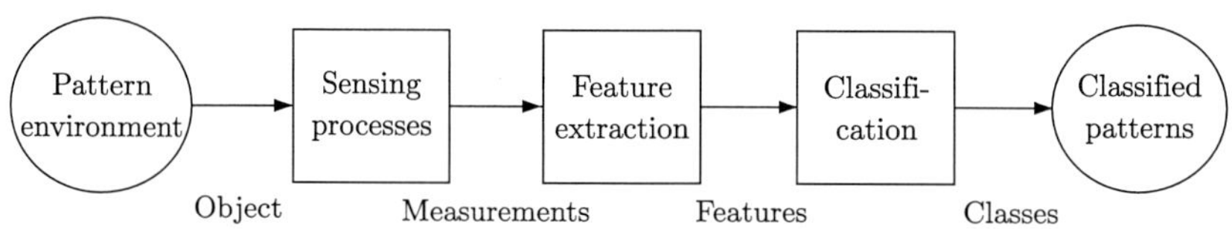

Figure 15.1: A pattern recognition system.

In general, the classification process may be of two types—supervised and unsupervised. In supervised classification, some preclassified data, also called **training data**, are used for designing the classifier. Bayes rule, nearest neighbour rule, linear discriminant functions, perceptron rules are some of the widely used supervised classification rules. The resulting classifiers are known as the Bayes maximum likelihood classifier, nearest Neighbour (NN) and k-NN classifier, linear discriminant classifier, single and multilayer perceptron.

When no labelled data is available, then the process of classification is referred to as unsupervised classification or clustering. In clustering, the purpose is to extract the inherent structure present in the data. Here, data is grouped into partitions, which may or may not be disjoint, such that points within a group are more similar to each other in some sense, than they are to points in different groups.

Clustering is considered to be an important component of *exploratory data analysis.* Many clustering algorithms and their variations exist in the literature. Some of them are the k-means algorithm, the *ISODATA* algorithm, the fuzzy c-means algorithm, single linkage method, minimum spanning tree based techniques, etc. We have used Simulated Annealing (SA) and different kinds of evolutionary algorithms (EAs) and their hybrids for developing some clustering algorithms in this book. In one of the following sections, we elaborate the definition of a cluster and describe a few clustering techniques. But before that we shall briefly describe the processes of data acquisition and feature selection.

15.3.1 Acquisition and Representation of Patterns

A pattern recognition system, at first, needs a suitable representation of data measured from the objects to be recognized. Such data items are constituent of what we call patterns. Each of the measured entities represent a particular attribute or characteristic of the concerned object. An aggregation of all such attribute values form a pattern. Now, if we assume that all the attributes (say, n in number) have scalar values then we can put these values in the form of a pattern vector

$$\mathbf{x} = \begin{pmatrix} x_1 \\ x_2 \\ \vdots \\ x_n \end{pmatrix} = \begin{bmatrix} x_1 & x_2 & \cdots & x_n \end{bmatrix}^T \tag{15.1}$$

The above equation shows an n-dimensional pattern consisting of n features or attribute values. A pattern recognition system may be described by the block diagram shown in Figure 15.1. Here, the input is some representation of the input object, e.g. a scanned photograph, an MRI image, a database record, etc. The first phase analyzes the input to extract essential features, i.e. features of interests to construct an n-dimensional pattern vector $\mathbf{x}$. This task is called **feature selection**. If the input data is in the form of a wave signal, as shown in Figure 15.2, which may be represented as a continuous function of some variable t, then the function can be sampled at n discrete points $t_1, t_2, \ldots, t_n$, to get individual components of the feature vector as $x_1 = f(t_1), x_2 = f(t_2), \ldots, x_n = f(t_n)$.

Pattern recognition techniques are applicable in a wide domain, where the data may be qualitative, quantitative, or both; they may be numerical, linguistic, pictorial, or any combination of them. The *object data* used in a pattern recognition system are sets of numerical vectors having d features. These are represented by $\mathbf{X} = \mathbf{x}_1, \mathbf{x}_2, \ldots, \mathbf{x}_N$, a set of N pattern vectors in the d-dimensional measurement space Ω_X. The ith object,

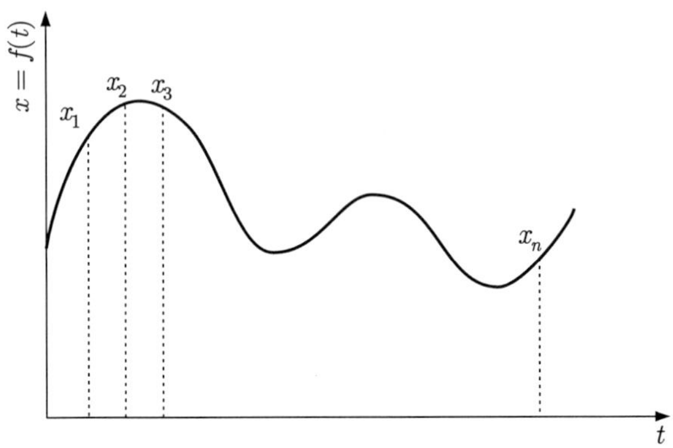

Figure 15.2: Feature measurement.

$i = 1, 2, \ldots, N$, observed in the process has vector $\mathbf{x}_i$ as its numerical representation; x_{ij} is the jth feature associated with the object i.

Relational data is a set of t^2 numerical relationship, say $r_{ii'}$, between pairs of objects. In other words, $r_{ii'}$ represents the extent to which object i and i' are related in the sense of some binary relationship ρ. If the objects that are pair wise related by ρ are called $\mathbf{O} = o_1, o_2, \ldots, o_t$, then $\rho : \mathbf{O} \times \mathbf{O} \rightarrow R$.

Sometimes, data acquisition phase includes some preprocessing tasks like noise reduction, filtering, encoding, enhancement for extracting pattern vectors. For example, if the input pattern is an image, these preprocessing operations play a crucial role for extracting salient features for its recognition.

15.3.2 Feature Selection

Feature selection is one of the major task in any automatic pattern recognition system. Since a pattern may contain many features, most of which are relatively unimportant, they may unduly complicate the classification and decision making processes. Hence, before applying classification techniques, patterns may need to be preprocessed for selection of significant features and elimination of the others. This preprocessing step is called *feature selection.*

The main objective of *feature selection* is to retain the optimum salient characteristics necessary for the recognition process and to reduce the dimensionality of the measurement space Ω_X so that effective and easily computable algorithms can be devised for efficient classification. The problem of feature selection has two aspects. The formulation of suitable criterion to evaluate the goodness of a feature and the selection of optimal subset from the available features.

The major mathematical measures so far devised for the estimation of feature quality are mostly statistical in nature, and can be broadly classified into following two categories:

- Feature selection in the measurement space.
- Feature extraction in the transformed space.

The techniques in the first category generally reduce the dimensionality of the feature set by discarding redundant information carrying features. On the other hand, those in the second category utilize all the information contained in the pattern vectors, and reduce higher dimensional pattern vector to a lower dimensional one.

Feature selection is the process of selecting a map of the form $X' = f(X)$, by which a sample $\mathbf{x} = (x_1, x_2, \ldots, x_n)$ in an n-dimensional measurement space Ω_X is transformed into a point $\mathbf{x}' = (x_1, x_2, \ldots, x_d)$ in a d-dimensional feature space $\Omega_{X'}$, where $d < n$.

For successful implementation of a pattern recognition system, it is necessary to find out important features from the collected or extracted pattern vectors. In majority of the cases, it is found that many of the features are either correlated or unnecessary or unimportant. There presence may not only complicate the process of classification, but can degrade the accuracy and quality of the decision making processes.

An object or pattern can be recognized by its categorization to a specific class by using a number of discriminatory properties of its features. Hence, the very first step of the recognition process is to select a limited number of discriminatory features by applying suitable methodologies. The feature selection or extraction process is also known as *reduction of dimensionality* in literature. There exist many techniques for feature selection including feature ordering, entropy minimization, orthogonal expansion, pioneering research on feature selection, mostly deals with statistical tools. Later, the thrust of the research shifted to the development of various other approaches to feature selection, including fuzzy and neural approaches.

15.3.3 Pattern Classification

After feature selection and formation of patterns, a classifier is needed to group patterns according to some similarity properties. A classifier can be designed using many different approaches.

If a distance based similarity measure or metric is used to minimize classification error, a *nearest neighbour* or a *nearest mean* approach is very useful in many situations. In case of a nearest mean classifier, a single prototype (the mean vector) represents a class. The classifier works as a vector quantizer or learning vector quantizer. In nearest neighbour classifier decisions are made based on class of the closest training pattern.

Classifiers can be designed using Bayes probability theorem. Here, a pattern is assigned to a class with the maximum posterior probability. When the class conditional probabilities are known *a priori* the Bayes classifier produces the optimum results. In such a situation, Bayes rule and the maximum likelihood rule coincides. These classifiers are based on parameter values of the concerned distribution, viz. mean, covariance and probabilities.

Decision boundaries can be constructed between classes by optimizing some error criteria. In general, Minimization of Squared Error (MSE) between predefined output and the observed value leads to generation of a decision boundary. Decision boundaries can be linear or non-linear in nature. This technique is used in neural network based classifiers.

Pattern classification can also be done using a decision tree. The tree is trained by using different features as splitting attributes for obtaining a minimum entropy hierarchy. During classification, the input vector is classified by following a suitable path in the tree based on the splitting attribute and predicate values. It is the only classifier where decision can be made based on individual features.

Pattern classification techniques are of two types: supervised and unsupervised. If we have a set of training patterns, i.e. a set of already labelled data, we can use them to find decision boundaries between different classes by means of training. Therefore, this kind of classification techniques are also called **supervised classification**. In case of clustering, no pre-labelled data are available, and we try to group unlabelled data into a number of coherent clusters. The, concerned techniques, thus, are referred to as unsupervised classification or clustering. Any classification process attempts to organize data points in multidimensional space (also called **feature vectors**) into *natural groups* or *clusters* such that data points within the same cluster are similar in some sense and those belonging to different clusters are dissimilar in the same sense.

15.4 Applications of Pattern Recognition

Automatic pattern recognition is needed to process and analyze data and information originated from the interaction between human society, science and technology. As already mentioned, in order to make machines more intelligent and human like, it must posses automatic pattern recognition capability. Some of the application areas of pattern recognition are:

Bioinformatics: Protein sequence analysis, gene pattern classification

Data mining: Searching for meaningful patterns, rule generation

Medicine and surgery: Medical diagnosis, disease classification, analysis of MRI images

Man-machine communication: Automatic speech recognition, natural language processing, image processing, script recognition

Natural resource study and estimation: Agriculture, forestry, geology, environment

Vehicular control: Automobile, airplane train, boat controllers

Defense services: Automatic target detection, guidance, control

Police and detective: Criminal detection from analysis of photographs, fingerprint, handwriting and speech recognition

Remote sensing: Detection of man-made objects, estimation of natural resources

Industry automation: CAD, CAM, product testing, assembly, inspection, quality control

Domestic systems: Household appliances, device controllers.

15.5 Pattern Recognition Strategies

Although there exist a number of different approaches for recognizing patterns, with one superior to the others in certain applications, we can broadly identify two specific approaches. These are statistical pattern recognition and syntactic pattern recognition.

15.5.1 Statistical Pattern Recognition

In statistical approach, each pattern is represented as a d-dimensional vector having d feature values from some measurement domain. The primary goal is to classify patterns into compact and disjoint regions in d-dimensional feature space. In statistical decision theoretic approach, similar patterns are tried to be separated from dissimilar ones by decision boundaries. These decision boundaries are generated using the statistical properties of the distribution of patterns in different categories. These properties must either be known *a priori* or they may be learned. Very commonly patterns in a set are found to follow Gaussian distribution. This type of distributions are characterized by features by *mean*, *standard deviation*, *variance* and *probability density function*. Other kinds of distributions are also possible like Poisson distribution, Cauchy distribution, uniform distribution, etc.

15.5.2 Syntactic Pattern Recognition

In many situations, recognition problems may involve very complex type of patterns which are difficult to process statistically. Such patterns, in general, involve a number of sub-patterns and thereby form a hierarchy of patterns. In other words, these patterns form themselves using simpler sub-patterns. Therefore, these patterns can be better processed if we consider some hierarchical representation and manipulation techniques. In syntactic pattern recognition, a formal analogy is drawn between the structure of patterns and the syntax of some language. Patterns are viewed as sentences of a language, primitives are viewed as alphabets, and sentences are considered to be generated from a grammar or set of rules. The grammar for each pattern class must be inferred from the available training samples. Syntactic recognition is intuitively more appealing because, in addition to classification, this approach provides a description of the given pattern, is constructed from the primitives.

15.5.3 Other Approaches

Besides the above two major approaches, there exist some other techniques like *template matching* and *neural network* based techniques. Template matching is one of the simplest and earliest techniques. Some similarity measure like *correlation coefficient* are computed between a reference pattern and the given input. Sometimes the reference pattern is learned from the training set.

Neural networks may be considered as massively parallel computing systems consisting of a large number of simple processors with many connections. These networks can be learned in a systematic way by following a suitable learning rule and a set of training patterns. They can adapt to different types of classification problems.

15.6 Optimization Methods Used for Pattern Recognition

A number of optimization techniques are commonly used for the purposes of pattern recognition and image processing. Some of these methods are simulated annealing, genetic algorithm, evolutionary programming, annealing evolution, etc. We shall describe these methods briefly in the following sections.

15.6.1 Overview of Simulated Annealing

Simulated Annealing (SA) (Kirkpatrik et al. 1983) is a recent technique for finding good solutions to a wide variety of combinatorial optimization problems. Simulated annealing may be suitable for NP-complete optimization problems. Although it does not guarantee that the global optimum is found, the solution is always a near optimal one. Simulated annealing combines two basic optimization principles, *divide and conquer* and *iterative hill climbing.* This combination avoids getting stuck in local optima. A strong connection between statistical mechanics or thermodynamics, and multivariate or combinatorial optimization is the basis for annealing optimization.

It mimics the principles of the annealing procedure which is a physical process where a crystal is cooled down from the liquid to the solid phase. In statistical mechanics, only the most probable change of state of a system in thermal equilibrium at a given temperature is observed in experiments; each configuration (state) defined by the set of atomic position x_i of the system is weighted by its Boltzmann probability factor, $\exp(-\frac{-E(x_i)}{k_\beta T})$, where T and k_β represent the temperature and Boltzmann's constant, respectively.

The physical model of the process starts with heating the solid until it melts; then the resulting liquid is cooled down slowly to keep the quasi-equilibrium. The cooling algorithm consists of repeated random displacements (state changes) of atoms in the matter, and the energy change ΔE is evaluated after each state change. If $\Delta E \leq 0$, the state change is accepted, and the new state is used as the starting state of the next step. If $\Delta E > 0$, the state is accepted with probability $P(\Delta E) = \exp(-\frac{-\Delta E}{k_\beta T})$.

To apply this physical model to an optimization problem, the temperature T must be decreased in a controlled manner during optimization. The random part of the algorithm can be implemented by generating random numbers uniformly distributed in the interval (0, 1); one such random number is selected and compared with $P(\Delta E)$. The simulated annealing algorithm is given below.

The simulated annealing optimization algorithm

begin
    initialize temperature T
    select a vector $\mathbf{x}$ of optimization parameters
    compute the value of the objective function or energy function $E(\mathbf{x})$
    termination_condition = *false*
    while (NOT *termination_condition*) do
        begin
            perturb the parameter vector $\mathbf{x}$ slightly, creating the new vector $\mathbf{x}'$
            evaluate $E(\mathbf{x}'$generate a random number $r \in (0, 1)$, form a uniform distribution in the interval $(0, 1)$
            if $r < \exp\left[-\frac{E(\mathbf{x}' - E(\mathbf{x})}{k_\beta T}\right]$ then
                begin
                    assign $\mathbf{x} = \mathbf{x}'$
                    assign $E(\mathbf{x}) = E(\mathbf{x}')$
                end
            lower T
        end
end

Simulated annealing is a robust search and optimization technique that mimics the thermo-dynamical cooling process used in metallurgy. The ability of the process to overcome local minima barriers and to reach a near global solution makes it useful for various applications. Annealing has been applied to many optimization problems, including image processing, pattern recognition, graph partitioning, and many others

In the field of image processing and pattern recognition, many problems have been successfully tackled by this algorithm.

15.6.2 Overview of Evolutionary Algorithms

Evolutionary algorithms are randomized search and optimization tools that mimic natural and biological evolution strategies to solve complex optimization problems. When Darwin proposed the laws of *biological evolution* and *natural selection* scientists realized that these rules can be used as a robust search and optimization mechanism, and they have tried to develop powerful algorithms using the same idea. A series of different algorithms have been developed all of which constitute what is known as Evolutionary Algorithms (EA). There are mainly three classes of evolutionary algorithms: Genetic algorithm by Holland (1975), evolution strategies by Schwefel (1981) and Rechenberg (1973), and evolutionary programming by Fogel. All the evolutionary algorithms use some form of several basic genetic operators. These operators include reproduction and evolution. Generally a particular *selection* operator is used for reproduction. The evolution operators, commonly considered, are *crossover* and *mutation*. The physical processes of reproduction and evolution are generally stochastic in nature. EAs use a population of solutions, each of which represent an instant in the search space. Once an initial population is available, EAs iterate through a loop of reproductive and evolution operators. Each iteration is called a **generation**. During each generation, new solutions are created by applying genetic operators over the solutions in the current population. Each solution in a population is associated with some figure of merit or fitness depending on the function to be optimized. The selection operator decides the solutions to be maintained in the population of the next generation depending on their fitness values. EAs differ from each other in their use of operators. Brief descriptions of these algorithms are provided in the subsequent subsections. We shall describe genetic algorithm, evolutionary programming and annealing evolution programs mainly.

15.6.3 Genetic Algorithms

Genetic algorithms (Holland 1975 and Goldberg 1989), use natural evolution mechanisms to search for the maximum or minimum of an objective function; as with any optimization technique, they can be used in recognition and machine learning.

Genetic algorithms do not guarantee that a global solution will be found, but empirical results from many applications show that the results are always very close to the global optimum one. In case of image understanding, matching and pattern recognition genetic algorithms are considered as a useful tool.

Genetic algorithms differ substantially from other optimization methods in the following ways:

1. GAs work with a coding of the parameters and the parameters themselves. The natural parameters of the problem are converted into the form of a string over some finite alphabets. Binary strings are very often used. But other symbolic representations are possible.
2. GAs search from a finite set of population of the solution strings and not from a single instance of the solution. The population of solutions is modified during each iteration. So, they can search at different places in the search space simultaneously. This gives a better chance of finding the global solution.
3. GAs use the objective function directly for optimization, i.e. merit of a solution is determined by corresponding value of the objective function only.
4. GAs use probabilistic transition rule and not deterministic rules. Transition from current population of solutions to a new population is guided by the rules of natural selection rule of Darwin. The survival of the fittest and the death of the poor solution strings is achieved by three basic operations: *reproduction*, *crossover* and *mutation*.

Chromosome initialization

GAs start with a pool of randomly generated solution strings called chromosomes. Chromosomes are nothing but an encoded representation of the problem variables. Individual variables may be encoded in binary, real or symbolic codes. In the basic GA only binary representation is allowed. For example, let us consider minimization of the following two variable functions:

$$f(x, y) = (x - y)^2 - 5xy$$

Here, the chromosome is normally represented as a sequence 'xy' of the concerned variables in binary code. If 8-bit binary code is used for both 'x' and 'y', we get a 16-bit chromosome. A certain instance of the values of 'x' and 'y' may be as follows

$$x = 01000101 \qquad\qquad y = 11010011$$

Therefore, the chromosome becomes

0100010111010011

Let another chromosome in the pool is given by the code

0110110101010110

In a similar fashion, a number (population size) of chromosomes are maintained in the pool.

Reproduction operation

The reproduction operator is responsible for the survival of the fittest and the death of the poor solution strings based on a probabilistic treatment. Different selection mechanisms are there. Some commonly used techniques are the proportionate selection or the *roulette-wheel* selection, the *tournament* selection, etc. This process results in a set of solution strings where some strings of higher fitness may be copied more than once into the next population. The total number of strings in any population usually remains unchanged.

Crossover operation

The crossover operation can be performed in a number of ways. The crossover may be single point or multipoint one. Also the position of crossover may be fixed or variable. However, its aim is to generate diversity in the pool of solution strings. Let us consider an instance of the crossover operation with our sample chromosomes. Let the fifth bit from the left be the position of crossover. Before the operation, the chromosomes are called parent chromosomes; after the operation they will produce two child chromosomes.

Parent Chromosomes		*Child Chromosomes*
0100010111010011		0100110101010110
	⇒	
0110110101010110		0110010111010011

Notice the difference between parent and child chromosomes. Child chromosomes share parts of parent chromosomes.

Mutation operation

The mutation operator plays only a secondary role in GAs. Its principle is randomly to change the character of some string of the population from time to time. The rate of mutation is generally kept very low, for example one bit out of one thousand bits may be mutated during some execution. The main reason for mutation is the fact that some local configurations of characters in strings of the population can be totally lost as a result of reproduction and crossover operations. Mutation protects GAs against such irrecoverable loss of good solution features.

With our example chromosome 'x', the mutation operation is shown below (considering the seventh bit from the left as the location of mutation.

Before Mutation		*After Mutation*
0100010111010011	⇒	0100011111010011

The basic form of the genetic algorithm is given below. This general form may be used to implement GA for any specific problem area with necessary minor modifications.

The Basic Genetic Algorithm

```
begin
    g = 0
    initialize P(g)
    evaluate P(g) using fitness function
    termination_condition = false
    while (NOT termination_condition) do
        begin
            g = g + 1
            select parents from P(g)
            crossover
            mutation
            evaluate P(g + 1) using fitness function
        end
end
```

In the above algorithm, g stands for *generation number* and $P(g)$ represents population at generation g. It is to be noted that reproduction, crossover and mutation operations are done probabilistically, i.e. for reproduction, each string attains a certain probability to be reproduced and there are certain probabilities with which crossover and mutation operations are performed. The success of a GA procedure for a particular problem depends on: (i) The coding used for representing the solutions, (ii) The fitness function that evaluates each solution, and (iii) The form of the genetic operators used to manipulate solution strings or chromosomes. Recently, it has been shown that GAs that maintain the best discovered solution at each generation asymptotically converge to the global optimum. Since a large variation of these genetic operators is possible, GAs can take different forms depending upon application. Experiments on GAs show that use of different kinds of other operators or modified genetic operators may become effective in many situations. Davis strongly suggested the use of other optimization techniques along with GA models for developing hybrid GAs which assume some of the best features of the original algorithms.

Unlike conventional search methods, GAs deal with multiple solutions simultaneously and compute the fitness function values for these candidate solutions. GAs are theoretically and empirically found to provide near globally optimal solutions for various complex optimization problems in the field of operations research, VLSI design, pattern recognition, image processing, machine learning, etc.

15.6.4 Evolutionary Programming

As in the case GAs, EPs also start with a set of initial solutions, called parents, generated randomly in the search space. The solution strings are evaluated for their fitnesses and the strings of relatively higher merits are selected for the next generation. In EPs no crossover is generally used. Optimization by EPs can be summarized into two major steps:

1. Mutate the solutions in the current population;
2. Select the next generation from the mutated and the current solutions.

In a canonical GA, generally the *roulette-wheel* or *proportionate* selection scheme is used. This selection operator chooses individuals with a probability proportional to their relative fitness, but this may lead to premature convergence when coupled with a strong reliance on crossover. In this case, the selection operator strongly constrains the convergence velocity of evolutionary algorithms. To avoid these problems, in EPs, other selection operators like rank selection or tournament selection are used. The crossover operation is abolished and emphasis is given on a more powerful mutation operation.

In the mutation phase of the evolution process, the gene positions of the solution strings are altered by adding small quantities generated by either Gaussian or Cauchy distribution function. These mutation schemes are described elaborately by Yao et al. 1999.

In case of genetic algorithms, we generally code the solution strings or chromosomes in binary, but in EPs, floating point or other complex representation of the chromosomes (solution strings) may be maintained, and non-uniform mutation is commonly used. In case of functional optimization using conventional EPs, we can code the chromosomes as a sequence of functional parameter values. Let $\{x_1, x_2, \ldots, x_k, \ldots, x_m\}$ be a chromosome, and the element x_k has been selected for mutation. The result will be a vector $\{x_1, x_2, \ldots, x_k^{'}, \ldots, x_m\}$. In Classical Evolutionary Programming (CEP) Gaussian mutation is commonly used. The mutation operations are self-adaptive in nature. Description of self-adaptive and non-adaptive mutation strategies and their merits and demerits may be found in literature.

It is found that, after some generations, the Gaussian mutation cannot generate offsprings which are substantially further away from their parents. This is due to long flat tails of the Gaussian distribution. As a result, the searching ability of the algorithm becomes limited within a local neighbourhood. But the Cauchy mutation is more likely to generate offsprings further away from its parents than the Gaussian mutation, because it is expected to have a higher probability of escaping from a local optima or moving away from a plateau, especially when the "basin of attraction" of the local optimum is large relative to the mean step size. On the other hand, the smaller hill around the centre of a Cauchy distribution indicates than Cauchy mutation spends less time in exploiting a local neighbourhood, and thus, have a weaker fine-tuning ability than the Gaussian mutation.

Gaussian mutation requires two parameters: A mean value and a standard deviation. Generally, mutation in this approach was achieved by transforming the component x_i of a vector X into $x_i^{'}$ by the following relation:

$$x_i^{'} = x_i + \eta_i(j)N_j(0,1) \tag{15.2}$$

$$\eta_i^{'}(j) = \eta_i(j)\exp\left(\tau^{'}N(0,1) + \tau N_j(0,1)\right) \tag{15.3}$$

where η_i's are standard deviations for Gaussian mutations. $N(0,1)$ denotes a normally distributed one-dimensional random number with mean zero and standard deviation one. $N_j(0,1)$ indicates that the random number is generated anew for each value of j. The factors τ and $\tau^{'}$ are commonly set to $\left(\sqrt{2\sqrt{n}}\right)^{-1}$ and $\left(\sqrt{2n}\right)^{-1}$, respectively, where n represents the length of a chromosome.

Yao et al. (1999) have shown that the Cauchy mutation function performs better than the Gaussian mutation function for most of the benchmark problems used for EPs. Cauchy mutation can perform longer jumps at a high probability, and hence, its search step size is considerably large than the Gaussian one.

The Cauchy distribution function is given by $F_t(x) = \frac{1}{2} + \frac{1}{\pi}$ arc tan $\left(\frac{x}{t}\right)$. where $t > 0$ is a scale parameter.

The Cauchy mutation follows the following relation:

$$x_i^{'} = x_i + \eta_i(j)\delta_j \tag{15.4}$$

where, $\delta_j = t.\tan\left[\pi\left(F_t - \frac{1}{2}\right)\right]$. Generally t is taken to be 1. δ_j is computed for each j anew. The relation for changing η remains same as in the case of Gaussian mutation and is given by Eq. (21.40).

15.6.5 Annealing Evolution

The annealing evolution is one kind of evolutionary algorithm. Here, the basic evolution program is used along with some features of simulated annealing. In annealing evolution the mutation operation of an evolution program is modified using the Boltzmann distribution function used in simulated annealing.

The SA algorithm starts from a random initial configuration at high temperature. It then proceeds by generating new candidates states and accepting/rejecting them according to a probability which is a function of the current temperature and energy difference. The temperature is gradually decreased towards a minimum value, while the system settles down to a stable low energy state. One major drawback of SA is its slow cooling. Also SA knows very little about whether a region in the configuration space has been explored or whether a region is a good place to search.

In order to improve the search abilities of the SA, it can be supplied with the information regarding the goodness of a search area from within the framework of an evolution program. Evolutionary Programming (EP) is a very recent technique for solving very large scale optimization problems. The most important feature of an EP is its parallel searching ability. An EP starts with a population of randomly generated configurations and proceeds towards a better solution by applying rules of natural selection and biological evolution, i.e. mutation.

15.7 Problems

1. What are the basic steps of pattern recognition? Show them clearly using a block diagram.
2. What is meant by a pattern? Explain how patterns can represent real life objects or entity.
3. Explain differences between statistical and syntactic pattern recognition.
4. Name some common pattern classification techniques.
5. Explain how can you relate image processing with pattern recognition.
6. How patterns can be constructed from the outputs of some sensory devices?
7. Explain the processes of feature selection and dimensionality reduction.
8. What, in your opinion, will be problems if patterns contain a large number of attributes.
9. How can you categorize pattern classification processes?
10. What are statistical and syntactic pattern recognition?
11. What is the role of a temperature schedule in SA?
12. Find out similarities and dissimilarities between SA and GA.
13. Write down an algorithm for pattern classification using the basic GA.
14. In what way use of optimization algorithms help in the process of pattern recognition?

Chapter 16

Classification and Decision Making

Pattern classification is a technique for classifying pattern vectors (or simply patterns) into different possible categories based on past experiences. In Artificial Intelligence (AI) this technique is very often referred to as machine learning. To predict the future based on past information or knowledge has always been recognized as a superior human expert quality. For making accurate predictions, machines are being employed in machine learning methodologies. Classification techniques are considered as integral components of machine learning algorithms where machines are made to learn how to classify patterns using samples or training patterns having predefined class labels. In the field of pattern recognition, problems like optical character recognition, speech recognition, hand written script recognition, etc. can be successfully handled by classification algorithms. Out of many classification algorithms some very well known and popular ones are: Decision tree algorithm, Naive Bayes algorithm, Bayesian belief network, k-nearest neighbour algorithm and Neural network algorithms. Some of these techniques will be discussed in the forthcoming chapters. In this chapter, we shall focus mainly on the role of decision functions in pattern classification.

16.1 Decision Making

The most important function of a pattern recognition system is to make decision regarding class membership of patterns. Therefore, we need to establish some rules for decision making. The corresponding mathematical functions are called **decision functions** or discriminating functions. Patterns in some space or domain are naturally separated in groups or classes by class boundaries which may be linear or non-linear in nature. In the following subsection we shall consider simple situations of linear class boundaries only.

16.1.1 Linear Functions

Here, the pattern classes can be separated from each other by using linear boundaries only. Hence, development of linear decision functions will solve the problem of classification. Linear decision boundaries may be of different natures depending on the distribution of pattern classes, some of which are discussed here.

Boundary separating individual classes

Let us consider a simple situation with two groups of two-dimensional patterns as shown in Figure 16.1. As shown in this figure, patterns can be separated by a straight line segment

$$d(\mathbf{x}) = w_1x_1 + w_2x_2 + w_3 = 0 \tag{16.1}$$

in Euclidean space having coordinates x_1 and x_2. Here, w_1, w_2 and x_3 are decision parameter values. A two class classifier needs to determine the values of these decision parameter values.

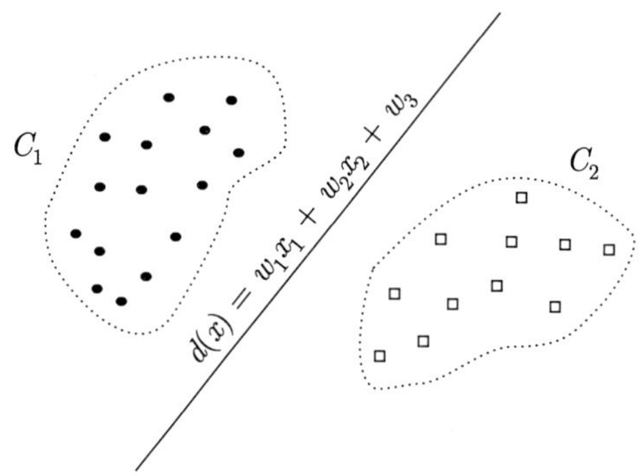

Figure 16.1: Linear decision boundary separating two classes.

Any pattern $\mathbf{x}$ having features x_1 and x_2 will yield either a positive or a negative value of the decision function $d(\mathbf{x})$ when replaced in Eq. (16.1). So, we can say that,

$$\begin{aligned} d(\mathbf{x}) < 0 &\Rightarrow \mathbf{x} \text{ belongs to class } C_1 \\ d(\mathbf{x}) > 0 &\Rightarrow \mathbf{x} \text{ belongs to class } C_2 \end{aligned} \tag{16.2}$$

If a pattern $\mathbf{x}$ lies on the boundary itself then $d(\mathbf{x}) = 0$.

From the above example it is clear that two convex shaped 2-dimensional pattern classes can be separated by a linear boundary. For more number of classes more linear decision boundaries are needed. Non-linear boundaries may be more general and more effective for this purpose. However, these are hard to realize and define.

The above two-dimension function can be easily extended for n-dimensional Euclidean spaces also. The general form of the equation then can be written as

$$d(\mathbf{x}) = w_1x_1 + w_2x_2 + \cdots + w_nx_n + w_{n+1} = \mathbf{w}^T\mathbf{x} + w_{n+1} \tag{16.3}$$

where, $\mathbf{w} = (w_1, w_2, \ldots, w_n)^T$ and $\mathbf{x} = (x_1, x_2, \ldots, x_n)^T$. To represent using suitable matrix notation, in general, a1 is appended with each pattern vector, i.e. we write

$\mathbf{x} = (x_1, x_2, \ldots, x_n, 1)^T$. With this notation, the above equation becomes

$$d(\mathbf{x}) = \mathbf{w}^T\mathbf{x} \tag{16.4}$$

where, $\mathbf{w} = (w_1, w_2, \ldots, w_{n+1})^T$ and $\mathbf{x} = (x_1, x_2, \ldots, x_n, 1)^T$. In the above, $\mathbf{x}$ is the pattern vector or simply pattern, and $\mathbf{w}$ is the weight vector. Therefore, a two class decision function $d(\mathbf{x})$ can be written as

$$d(\mathbf{x}) = \mathbf{w}^T\mathbf{x} \begin{cases} < 0 & \text{iff } \mathbf{x} \in C_1 \\ > 0 & \text{iff } \mathbf{x} \in C_2 \end{cases} \tag{16.5}$$

A multiclass (> 2) decision problem can be represented as a series of decision functions

$$d_i(\mathbf{x}) = \mathbf{w}_i^T\mathbf{x} \begin{cases} < 0 & \text{iff } \mathbf{x} \in C_i \\ > 0 & \text{otherwise} \end{cases} \tag{16.6}$$

where, $\mathbf{w}_i = (w_{i,1}, w_{i,2}, \ldots, w_{i,n+1})^T$ is the weight vector associated with the ith decision function.

Example 1: Let us consider a situation where each of the 3 classes is separate from others by a single decision boundary. How can we determine class membership of a pattern to any of these three classes?

Solution: Here the three classes C_1, C_2 and C_3 are separated by three decision boundaries (Figure 16.2)

$$d_i(\mathbf{x}) = \begin{cases} -x_1 - x_2 + 5 = 0 & \text{for } i = 1 \\ x_2 - 2 = 0 & \text{for } i = 3 \\ x_1 - 2x_2 - 2 = 0 & \text{for } i = 3 \end{cases}$$

Now, since a decision functions will attain value > 0 on one side and a value < 0 on the other side, any pattern $\mathbf{x}$ can be classified as

$$\begin{aligned} d_1(\mathbf{x}) > 0,\ d_2(\mathbf{x}) < 0,\ d_3(\mathbf{x}) < 0 &\Rightarrow \mathbf{x} \in C_1 \\ d_2(\mathbf{x}) > 0,\ d_1(\mathbf{x}) < 0,\ d_3(\mathbf{x}) < 0 &\Rightarrow \mathbf{x} \in C_2 \\ d_3(\mathbf{x}) > 0,\ d_1(\mathbf{x}) < 0,\ d_2(\mathbf{x}) < 0 &\Rightarrow \mathbf{x} \in C_3 \end{aligned}$$

For example, let us consider the pattern vector $\mathbf{x} = (5, 3)$. For this pattern we get,

$$\begin{aligned} d_1(\mathbf{x}) &= -x_1 - x_2 + 5 = -5 - 3 + 5 = -3 &\Rightarrow \mathbf{x} \notin C_1 \\ d_2(\mathbf{x}) &= x_2 - 2 = 3 - 2 = 1 &\Rightarrow \mathbf{x} \in C_2 \\ d_3(\mathbf{x}) &= x_1 - 2x_2 - 2 = 5 - 6 - 2 = -3 &\Rightarrow \mathbf{x} \notin C_3 \end{aligned}$$

Therefore, the pattern vector $\mathbf{x} = (5, 3)$ belongs to class C_2. The decision boundaries and the decision regions for the given classes are shown pictorially in Figures 16.2 and 16.3, respectively.

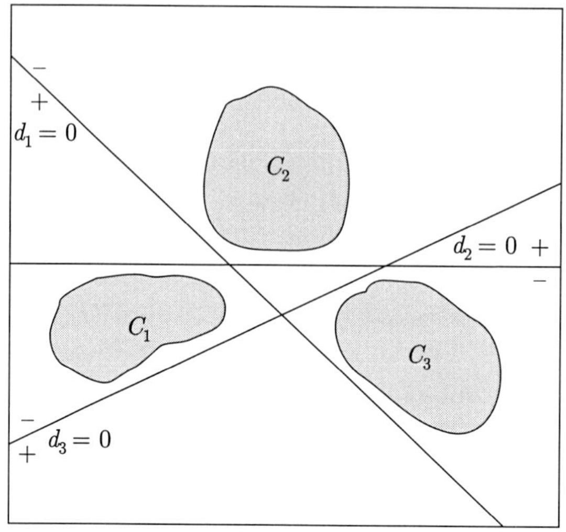

Figure 16.2: Decision boundaries separating individual classes.

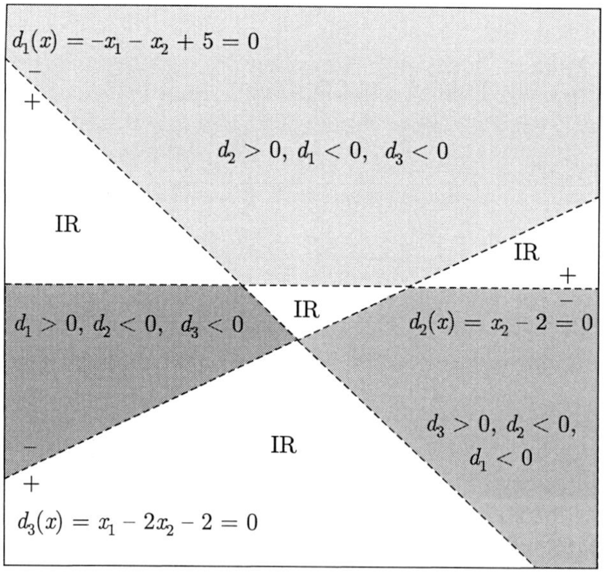

Figure 16.3: Decision regions separating individual classes.

Example 2: Can we determine class membership of a pattern $\mathbf{x} = (9, 3)$ to any of the three classes?

Solution: Simply using three decision boundaries we cannot solve the classification problem completely. This is because any of the decision functions may have positive (> 0) or negative (< 0) values for more than one region. In our example, the decision space is divided into seven different regions separated by the boundaries. There are four intermediate regions for which decision functions given in Eq. (16.8) not be able to classify patterns.

For the pattern vector $\mathbf{x} = (9, 3)$, we get

$$\begin{aligned} d_1(\mathbf{x}) &= -x_1 - x_2 + 5 = -9 - 3 + 5 = -7 && \Rightarrow \mathbf{x} \notin C_1 \\ d_2(\mathbf{x}) &= x_2 - 2 = 3 - 2 = 1 && \Rightarrow \mathbf{x} \in C_2 \\ d_3(\mathbf{x}) &= x_1 - 2x_2 - 2 = 9 - 6 - 2 = 1 && \Rightarrow \mathbf{x} \in C_3 \end{aligned}$$

Here, two of the decision conditions have been satisfied simultaneously, and hence, we are unable to classify pattern vector $\mathbf{x} = (9, 3)$.

Example 3: Can we determine class membership of a pattern $\mathbf{x} = (8, 3)$ to any of the three classes?

Solution: We cannot solve the classification problem when a pattern falls directly on a certain boundary. This is because the concerned decision function will yield a zero (0) value for the pattern. In our example, the decision function $d_2(\mathbf{x})$ will become zero which is neither (> 0) nor (< 0). In such cases both the concerned regions will have claim for membership of the input pattern.

For the pattern vector $\mathbf{x} = (8, 3)$, we get

$$\begin{aligned} d_1(\mathbf{x}) &= -x_1 - x_2 + 5 = -8 - 3 + 5 = -6 && \Rightarrow \mathbf{x} \notin C_1 \\ d_2(\mathbf{x}) &= x_2 - 2 = 8 - 2 = 6 && \Rightarrow \mathbf{x} \in C_2 \\ d_3(\mathbf{x}) &= x_1 - 2x_2 - 2 = 8 - 6 - 2 = 0 && \Rightarrow \mathbf{x} \notin C_3 \end{aligned}$$

Here, the decision condition seems to be favourable for class C_2, but the pattern is lying on the boundary line $d_3(\mathbf{x})$, and hence, we are unable to reach a decision for the pattern vector $\mathbf{x} = (8, 3)$.

Boundary separating class pairs

Let us consider a situation where each pattern class is separable from every other class by a distinct decision boundary. With such a linear decision function pattern classes are pairwise separable. This means that if we have n classes then a total of $\frac{n(n-1)}{2}$ number of decision functions. These decision boundaries are of the form

$$d_{ij}(\mathbf{x}) = \mathbf{w}_{ij}^T \mathbf{x} \tag{16.7}$$

and if the pattern $\mathbf{x}$ belongs to class C_i, then we have

$$d_{ij}(\mathbf{x}) > 0 \text{ for all } i \neq j \tag{16.8}$$

It is also intuitive that, $d_{ij}(\mathbf{x}) = -d_{ji}(\mathbf{x})$.

Example 4: Consider position of pattern classes C_1, C_2 and C_3 as shown in Figure 16.4. Using the concept of decision boundaries between class pairs, find out the decision regions.

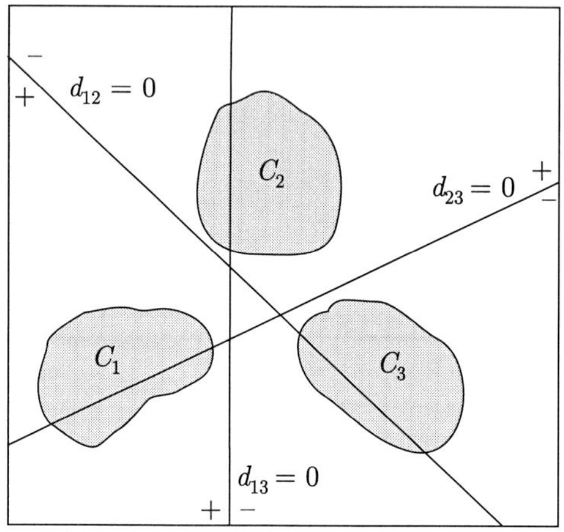

Figure 16.4: Decision boundaries separating pair of classes.

Solution: Here, no pattern class is separable from the others by a single decision boundary. However, each boundary is capable of separating any two of the classes C_1, C_2 and C_3. In Figure 16.4, the following lines are used as decision boundaries.

$$\begin{aligned} d_{12}(\mathbf{x}) &= x_1 + x_2 - 5 = 0 \\ d_{23}(\mathbf{x}) &= x_1 - 2x_2 - 2 = 0 \\ d_{13}(\mathbf{x}) &= -x_1 + 4 = 0 \end{aligned}$$

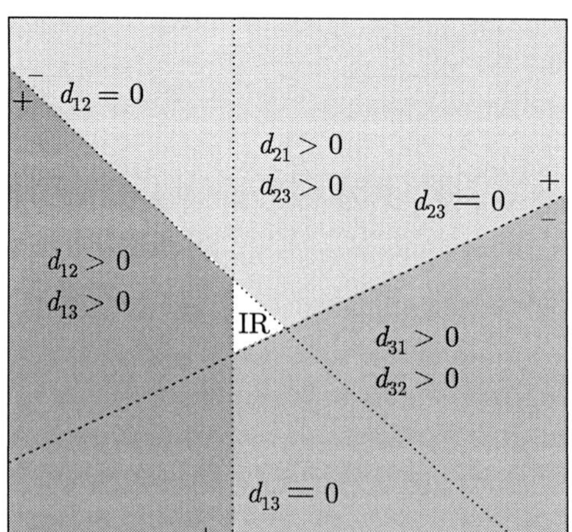

Figure 16.5: Decision regions separating pair of classes

We see that each of the decision boundaries now separate exactly two classes without regard to the position of remaining classes. Specifically $d_{ij}(\mathbf{x})$ separates classes C_i and C_j only. If $d_{ij}(\mathbf{x}) > 0$ then $\mathbf{x} \in C_i$, and if $d_{ij}(\mathbf{x}) < 0$ then $\mathbf{x} \in C_j$. However, in this representation of decision functions also, we cannot overcome the problem of indeterminate regions fully. This is because the three decision boundaries do not intersect at a single point.

Boundary separating classes and class pairs

In this case also, we can use n number of decision boundaries to separate each of the n classes from the others. Here, we shall order the decision function values for each new pattern $\mathbf{x}$, and assign it to the class whose function yields the highest.

In other words, there exist n decision functions $d_1(\mathbf{x}), d_2(\mathbf{x}), \ldots, d_n(\mathbf{x})$ and a pattern $\mathbf{x}$ is assigned to the class C_i iff

$$d_i(\mathbf{x}) > d_j(\mathbf{x}) \quad \text{for all} \quad j \neq i$$

A decision boundary between classes C_i and C_j can be written as

$$\begin{aligned} d_{ij}(\mathbf{x}) &= d_i(\mathbf{x}) - d_j(\mathbf{x}) \\ &= (\mathbf{w}_i - \mathbf{w}_j)^T\mathbf{x} \\ &= \mathbf{w}_{ij}^T\mathbf{x} \end{aligned} \tag{16.9}$$

The above equation indicates that, if the pattern $\mathbf{x}$ belongs to class C_i, then we have

$$d_{ij}(\mathbf{x}) > 0 \text{ for all } i \neq j \tag{16.10}$$

Example 5: Illustrate Example 1, using the above boundary concept (Figure 16.6).

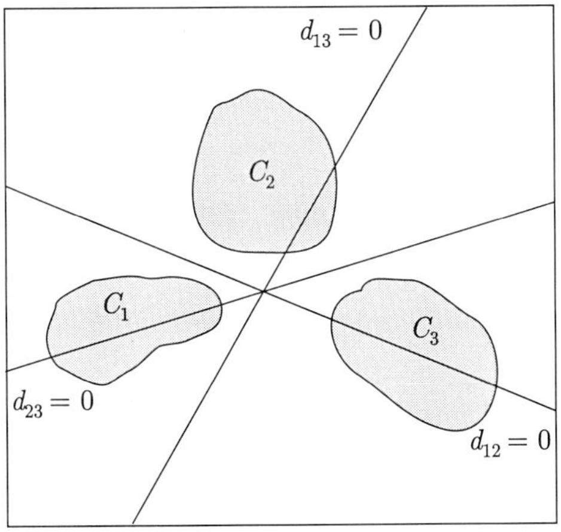

Figure 16.6: Decision boundaries separating classes and class pairs.

Solution: The initial boundary definitions, we started with, were

$$d_i(\mathbf{x}) = \begin{cases} -x_1 - x_2 + 5 = 0 & \text{for } i = 1 \\ x_2 - 2 = 0 & \text{for } i = 3 \\ x_1 - 2x_2 - 2 = 0 & \text{for } i = 3 \end{cases}$$

If a pattern $\mathbf{x}$ falls in class C_1, then we must have

$$d_1(\mathbf{x}) > d_2(\mathbf{x}) \text{ and } d_1(\mathbf{x}) > d_3(\mathbf{x})$$

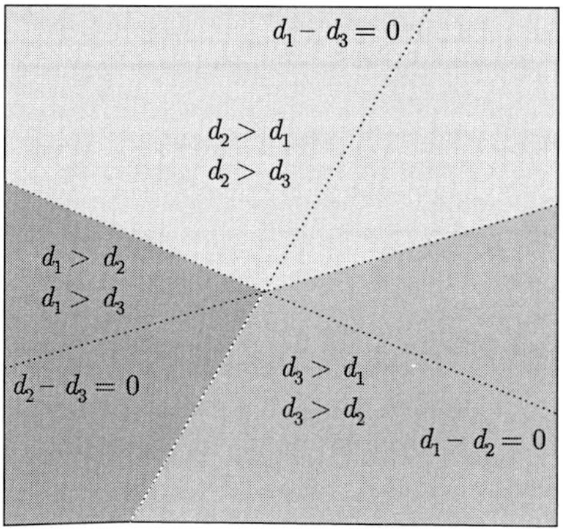

Figure 16.7: Decision regions separating classes and class pairs.

In other words, the pattern must lie on positive sides of surfaces (boundaries)

$$d_1(\mathbf{x}) - d_2(\mathbf{x}) = 0 \text{ and } d_1(\mathbf{x}) - d_3(\mathbf{x}) = 0$$

In general, the concerned pattern class C_i must lie on the positive sides of surfaces

$$d_i(\mathbf{x}) - d_j(\mathbf{x}) = 0 \text{ for all } j = 1, 2, \ldots, n, \; j \neq i$$

Here, the decision surfaces (boundaries) can be redefined as

$$\begin{aligned} d_1(\mathbf{x}) - d_2(\mathbf{x}) &= -x_1 - 2x_2 + 7 = 0 \\ d_2(\mathbf{x}) - d_3(\mathbf{x}) &= -2x_1 + x_2 + 7 = 0 \\ d_1(\mathbf{x}) - d_3(\mathbf{x}) &= -x_1 + 3x_2 = 0 \end{aligned}$$

Region for class C_1 is defined by relations

$$d_1(\mathbf{x}) > d_2(\mathbf{x}) \text{ and } d_1(\mathbf{x}) > d_3(\mathbf{x})$$

In other words, the region is on the positive sides of lines $-3x_3+3=0$ and $x_1-x_2-4 = 0$. Similarly, region for class C_2 is on the positive sides of lines $3x_2-3=0$ and $x_1+2x_2-7=0$, and that for class C_3 is on the positive sides of lines $-x_1+x_2+4=0$ and $-x_1-2x_2+7=0$, respectively.

Note that in this kind of boundary definition, there is no indeterminate decision region left over the decision space. Only uncertainty prevails on the boundary lines themselves.

16.1.2 Non-linear Separability

It may not always be the case that a number of classes are linearly separable. Two classes having non-convex shapes may be linearly non-separable. A number of classes may have distribution of patterns that prohibit them from being linearly separable. In such situations, we require non-linear decision functions to be developed (Figure 16.8).

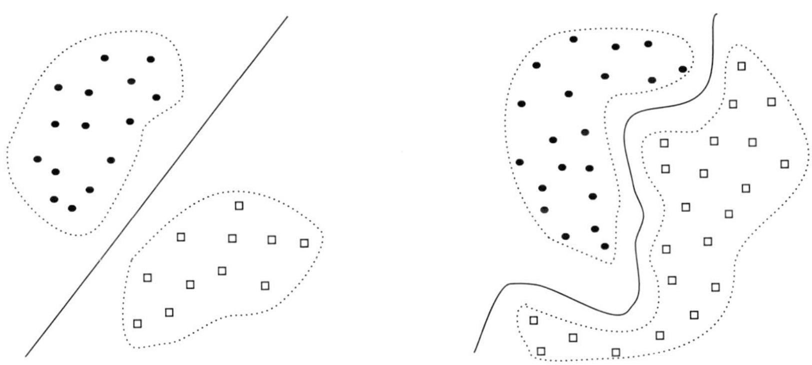

(a) Linearly separable (b) Non-linearly separable

Figure 16.8: Linearly and non-linearly separable classes.

16.2 Generation of Decision Functions

If pattern classes are separable by a linear decision function they are said to be linearly separable. A linear decision function can be represented as

$$y = w_1x_1 + w_2x_2 + \cdots + w_nx_n + w_{n+1}$$

where n is the dimension of the feature space. Once the decision functions are specified, using initial values of coefficients (w's), it is necessary to find out their final values. This can be done by training or learning.

Decision functions can be generated from close observations of the representative pattern classes. In other words, if we have prior knowledge of the class membership of some sample patterns, we can develop decision functions by observation. It is easy to say that the larger the sample sizes for representative classes the more accurate will be the decision function generated. This kind of formulation of decision functions is also called generation by training. Using this trainability property, pattern classifiers of different types may be developed.

Once a general functional form of the decision functions has been chosen, their coefficients can be computed using a priori information about classification of patterns, provided that such information is available. In this approach, design of a classifier can be based entirely on the computation of decision boundaries as derived from patterns and their membership in classes. Once a type of decision functions has been assumed, a training or learning algorithm should produce the initially unknown coefficients iteratively, provided that the training patterns are separable by the decision functions. By this approach we can develop adaptable and trainable classifiers. The following assumptions are made in this regard:

- A set of labelled training patterns are available for supervision.
- Discriminant functions are linear and their coefficients can be adjusted iteratively during the training phase.

Using the above assumptions, a trainable classifier can be implemented that learns by example. The classification problem is then reduced to the problem of finding a set of suitable decision boundaries (lines or surfaces). A simple decision boundary algorithm is presented below.

Decision Boundary Algorithm

begin
    for $i \leftarrow 1$ **to** $n+1$ **do**
        initialize weights w_i
    repeat
    for $p \leftarrow 1$ **to** T_N **do**
        begin
            input training pattern $\mathbf{x}_p$ with class l
            calculate $d = w_1 x_{p1} + w_2 x_{p2} + \cdots + w_n x_{pn} + w_{n+1}$
            calculate the signum function value, $l' = sgn(d)$
            if $l' \neq l$ **then**
                update weight as $w_i \leftarrow w_i + c\ l\ x_{pi}$
        end
    until weights are stable
end

In the above algorithm T_N is the size of training set, $sgn(d)$ is the signum function whose output is either $+1$ or -1 (in other words, $sgn(d) = +1$ if $d \geq 0$, and -1

otherwise) indicating one side or other of the decision boundary, and $class(\mathbf{x}_p) = l$ (which is also having values either $+1$ or -1) is the predefined class of the training pattern $\mathbf{x}_p$. c is a small random number.

16.3 Generalized Decision Functions

It is already mentioned that linear decision boundaries may not be always sufficient for classifying patterns. Non-linear surfaces may be needed for separating for arbitrary shaped classes. Although generation of non-linear decision boundaries may be time costly and may not be technically supporting, they can be represented mathematically in a similar manner as their linear counterparts. One approach is to use a generalized linear decision boundary concept. In this concept decision functions may assume the following form:

$$d(\mathbf{x}) = w_1 f(\mathbf{x}_1) + w_2 f(\mathbf{x}_2) + \cdots + w_n f(\mathbf{x}_n) + w_{n+1} = \sum_{i=1}^{n+1} w_i f_i(\mathbf{x}) \tag{16.11}$$

where, $\{f_i(\mathbf{x})\}$ for $i = 1, 2, \ldots, n$, are real valued functions of the pattern $\mathbf{x}$, $f_{n+1}(\mathbf{x}) = 1$, and $n = 1$ is the number of terms used in the expansion. By varying the nature of $\{f_i(\mathbf{x})\}$ infinitely different types of decision functions can be generated. Equation (16.11) may also be written as

$$d(\mathbf{x}) = \mathbf{w}^T\mathbf{x} \tag{16.12}$$

where, $\mathbf{w} = (w_1, w_2, \ldots, w_{n+1})^T$ and $\mathbf{x} = [f(\mathbf{x}_1), f(\mathbf{x}_2), \ldots, f(\mathbf{x}_n), 1]^T$. The Eq. (16.12) is a linear function with respect to new patterns.

16.4 Distance Based Classifier

One of the simplest and the earliest approaches of pattern classification is to use distance functions. If the pattern classes are separable by proximity concepts then use of distance function may be very effective and efficient in many situations. However, in many cases classes do not exhibit this property fully. Even then distance based functions may be able to determine approximate class boundaries efficiently (Figure 16.9).

When pattern vectors in each class are very close to each other (for members of the same class) minimum distance based classifiers may be very useful technique for classification. Let, there exist K classes, and their representative patterns be $\mathbf{z}_1, \mathbf{z}_2, \ldots, \mathbf{z}_K$. The Euclidean distance between an arbitrary vector $\mathbf{x}$ and the ith prototype $\mathbf{z}_i$ is given by

$$d_i = ||\mathbf{x} - \mathbf{z}_i|| = \sqrt{(\mathbf{x} - \mathbf{z}_i)^T(\mathbf{x} - \mathbf{z}_i)} \tag{16.13}$$

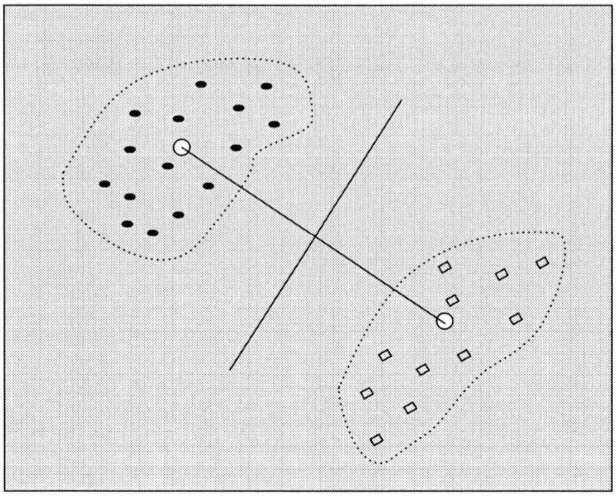

Figure 16.9: Distance based decision boundary between two pattern classes.

A minimum distance classifier computes the distance from a pattern $\mathbf{x}$ to the prototype of a class, and assigns the pattern to the closest class. The Eq. (16.13) can be written as

$$\begin{aligned} d_i^2 &= ||\mathbf{x} - \mathbf{z}_i||^2 \\ &= (\mathbf{x} - \mathbf{z}_i)^T(\mathbf{x} - \mathbf{z}_i) \\ &= \mathbf{x}^T\mathbf{x} - 2\mathbf{x}^T\mathbf{z}_i + \mathbf{z}_i^T\mathbf{z}_i \\ &= \mathbf{x}^T\mathbf{x} - 2(\mathbf{x}^T\mathbf{z}_i - \tfrac{1}{2}\mathbf{z}_i^T\mathbf{z}_i) \end{aligned} \tag{16.14}$$

Since all distances are positive, minimum distance d_i is obtained for minimum d_i^2. From Eq. (16.14), minimum d_i^2 is equivalent to the maximum of $\mathbf{x}^T\mathbf{z}_i - \frac{1}{2}\mathbf{z}_i^T\mathbf{z}_i$. Therefore, we can arrive at the decision function

$$d_i(\mathbf{x}) = \mathbf{x}^T\mathbf{z}_i - \frac{1}{2}\mathbf{z}_i^T\mathbf{z}_i \text{ for } i = 1, 2, \ldots, K \tag{16.15}$$

It is notable that $d_i(\mathbf{x})$ is a linear decision function, i.e. if z_{ij} for $j = 1, 2, \ldots, n$, are the components of $\mathbf{z}_i$, and we let

$$w_{ij} = z_{ij} \text{ for } j = 1, 2, \ldots, n, \quad w_{i,n+1} = -\frac{1}{2}\mathbf{z}_i^T\mathbf{z}_i$$

and also if $\mathbf{x} = (x_1, x_2, \ldots, x_n, 1)^T$, then we may express Eq. (16.15) in the linear form

$$d_i(\mathbf{x}) = \mathbf{w}_i^T\mathbf{x} \quad \text{for } i = 1, 2, \ldots, K \tag{16.16}$$

where $\mathbf{w}_i = (w_{i1}, w_{i2}, \ldots, w_{i(n+1)})^T$.

When the problem is to classify patterns into two classes, it is seen that the decision boundary (line or plane) lies perpendicular to the line joining the two corresponding prototypes. Therefore, minimum distance classifiers are special cases of linear boundaries where the decision boundaries are determined by satisfying the minimum distance criteria.

16.5 Problems

1. What do you mean by supervised classification?
2. Explain the role of decision functions in pattern classification.
3. How can you find out a two class discriminating function using training patterns?
4. Consider a set of the following 2-dimensional patterns: $(20\ \ 20)^T$, $(20\ \ 100)^T$ and $(100\ \ 20)^T$. Using Euclidean distance norm find out a discriminating function for classifying the patterns into two classes.
5. Find out a decision boundary between two classes with the following training set

Pattern	*Features*	*Class*
$\mathbf{x}_1$	$(1,2)$	1
$\mathbf{x}_2$	$(5,4)$	2

6. Consider the following training patterns

Pattern	*Features*	*Class*
$\mathbf{x}_1$	$(3,0)$	1
$\mathbf{x}_2$	$(4,1)$	1
$\mathbf{x}_3$	$(3,2)$	1
$\mathbf{x}_4$	$(1,-1)$	2
$\mathbf{x}_5$	$(1,-2)$	2

   Classify the input pattern $\mathbf{x} = (1,\ 1)$.

7. Show that distance based classifiers can be represented as linear ones.

Chapter 17

Statistical Decision Making

The process of pattern classification always involves some sort of decision making techniques. Decisions are generated by studying the geometrical and statistical properties of the set of patterns under consideration. When we do not have sufficient information regarding the distribution of patterns, pattern density, etc. we must follow a non-parametric decision making algorithm. On the other hand, when such information is available, we can use parametric decision making algorithms. In many situations such information is only available as an optimistic assumption and no measures of such parameters are available initially. Thus we need to estimate, the values of parameters like mean and variance, etc. before applying the algorithm. In discrete domains, these parameters are estimated as probability values from a set of known training patterns. Hence, the concerned algorithms actually compute the probability of a pattern to belong to a certain class.

17.1 Bayes Theorem for Decision Making

Given a set of data items (samples) and the number of classes the samples may belong to, the Bayes theorem helps us to calculate the probabilities of the class membership for a sample to a particular class.

Let us consider two events: Existence of a sample x in the data set X, and the existence of a cluster C in X. Let, $P(x)$ be the probability of occurrence of the item x in the entire set X, and $P(C)$ is the prior probability of class C, i.e., the probability that an arbitrary random sample belongs to class C. Also, let $P(x|C)$ be the conditional probability of obtaining a sample with value x given that it comes from class C. Now, we are to calculate the conditional probability that a sample belongs to class C given that it has a feature value of x, i.e. $P(C|x)$.

Here, we are dealing with two sets, the set of samples X and the set of samples in class C. We can draw a Venn diagram to describe the relation amongst X, C and x.

For any arbitrary sample x and class C the following four different combinations may arise.

$x \in X, x \notin C$	x is found in X but C is not found	(x and $\bar{C}$)
$x \notin X, x \in C$	x is not found in X but C is found	($\bar{x}$ and C)

$x \in X, x \in C$	x is found in X and C is found	(x and C)
$x \notin X, x \notin C$	x is not found in X and C is not found	($\bar{x}$ and $\bar{C}$)

The above description of class membership of patterns into classes is pictorially depicted in Figure 17.1.

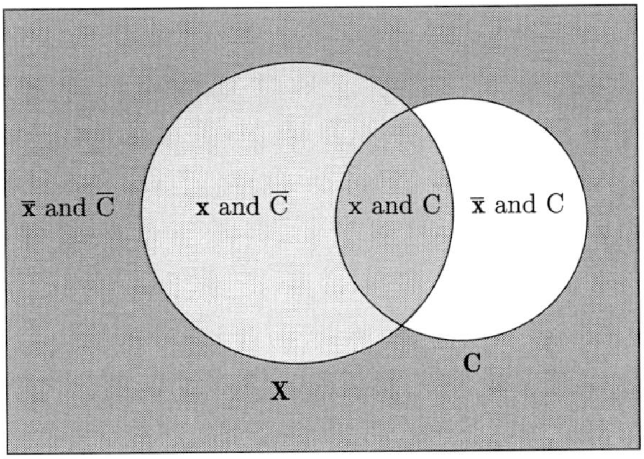

Figure 17.1: Venn diagram describing class membership.

Now, the probability that x is found such that class C contains x, i.e. $P(x|C)$ is a fraction of the situations such that C is found. Therefore

$$P(x|C) = \frac{P(x \text{ and } C)}{P(C)}$$

Similarly, the probability that C is found such that x is a member of C, i.e. $P(C|x)$ is fraction of the situations such that x is found in X. Thus

$$P(C|x) = \frac{P(x \text{ and } C)}{P(x)}$$

Therefore, we can write,

$$P(x|C)\ P(C) = P(C|x)\ P(x) \Rightarrow P(C|x) = \frac{P(C)\ P(x|C)}{P(x)} \tag{17.1}$$

This is Bayes decision rule.
Now, if there are K different classes $\{C_1, C_2, \ldots, C_K\}$, then we can express $P(x)$ as

$$P(x) = \sum_{k=1}^{K} P(C_k)\ P(x|C_k)$$

where, $\sum_{k=1}^{K} P(x|C_k) = 1$. Therefore, we have

$$P(C_i|x) = \frac{P(C_i)\ P(x|C_i)}{\sum_{k=1}^{K} P(C_k)\ P(x|C_k)} \tag{17.2}$$

In the above expression, $P(C_i)$ are called **prior probabilities** because these are the probabilities of classes in the population of samples when actual values of x are unknown. $P(C_i|x)$ are called **posterior probabilities** because they signify probabilities of classes after we have observed values of samples x. Thus, Bayes theorem allows us to calculate posterior probabilities from an approximate knowledge of prior probabilities. In other words, Bayes theorem plays the role of a foundation stone of probabilistic reasoning with partial knowledge or partial beliefs.

Example 1: Three factories manufacture Integrated Circuit Chips (IC). Let the share of manufacture of the three factories $F_1, F_2,$ and F_3 are 20%, 30% and 50%, respectively. Also let the above factories produce 2%, 3% and 5% defective ICs. For an arbitrarily picked up defective IC, what is the probability that it is manufactured by F_1, F_2 or F_3.

Solution: Let $E_1, E_2,$ and E_3 be the events that an IC be picked form factories $F_1, F_2,$ and F_3, respectively, and condition D indicates that an IC is defective. Therefore, the prior probabilities are

$$P(E_1) = 0.2$$
$$P(E_2) = 0.3$$
$$P(E_3) = 0.5$$

and

$$P(D|E_1) = 0.02$$
$$P(D|E_2) = 0.03$$
$$P(D|E_3) = 0.05$$

The posterior probabilities can now be computed as:

$$\begin{aligned} P(E_1|D) &= \frac{P(E_1)\ P(D|E_1)}{\sum_{i=1}^{3} P(E_i)\ P(D|E_i)} \\ &= \frac{0.2 \times 0.02}{0.2 \times 0.02 + 0.3 \times 0.03 + 0.5 \times 0.05} \\ &= 0.105 \end{aligned}$$

$$\begin{aligned} P(E_2|D) &= \frac{P(E_2)\ P(D|E_2)}{\sum_{i=1}^{3} P(E_i)\ P(D|E_i)} \\ &= \frac{0.3 \times 0.03}{0.2 \times 0.02 + 0.3 \times 0.03 + 0.5 \times 0.05} \\ &= 0.237 \end{aligned}$$

$$\begin{aligned} P(E_3|D) &= \frac{P(E_3)\ P(D|E_3)}{\sum_{i=1}^{3} P(E_i)\ P(D|E_i)} \\ &= \frac{0.5 \times 0.05}{0.2 \times 0.02 + 0.3 \times 0.03 + 0.5 \times 0.05} \\ &= 0.658 \end{aligned}$$

♣

17.2 Simple Bayes Classification

Bayes classification rules estimate probabilities of occurrence of different attribute values for different classes in a training pattern set. These probabilities are then used to classify unknown patterns.

Let, the patterns have set of attributes $A = \{A_1, A_2, \ldots, A_M\}$. And, $P(A)$ be the probability that a training pattern have attributes A, regardless of its class. Let there exist K classes of patterns $C_1, C_2, \ldots, C_K$.

To classify an unknown pattern with an attribute set A, we assign it to the most probable class satisfied by A. That is, we assign it to a class k $(1 \leq k \leq K)$ with the maximum posterior probability $P(C_k|A)$.

According to Bayes rule

$$P(C_k|A) = \frac{P(C_k)\ P(A|C_k)}{P(A)} \tag{17.3}$$

Now, since the denominator of the right hand side of the above equation is a constant, to maximize $P(C_k|A)$, we need to maximize only $P(C_k)\ P(A|C_k)$.

For simplifying matters, we assume that attributes are conditionally independent. Therefore,

$$P(A|C_k) = \prod_{i=1}^{M} P(A_i|C_k) \tag{17.4}$$

With the above assumption, the classifier is called a **Naive Bayes classifier**, based on the attribute probabilities only we can classify patterns by maximizing

$$P(C_k) \prod_{i=1}^{M} P(A_i|C_k) \tag{17.5}$$

17.3 Probability and Expected Values

In Baye's theorem, we used several kinds of probabilities. Thus, we need to compute different prior probabilities. Let us consider a data set X in which data are assumed to be distributed in K classes $C_1, C_2, \ldots, C_K$ with class C_i having n_i number of patterns in it. Then prior probability of class C_i is given by

$$P(C_i) = \frac{n_i}{\sum_{j=1}^{K} n_j} \tag{17.6}$$

Conventionally, the above probability is called a **maximum likelihood estimate.**

An alternative estimation, called the **Bayesian estimation** is given by

$$P(C_i) = \frac{n_i + 1}{\sum_{j=1}^{K} n_j + K} \tag{17.7}$$

Thus, in Bayesian estimation, we assume one more element in each class. In general, classes contain huge amount of patterns, so adding one extra does not change any statistical property of the distribution significantly. Moreover, since in Bayesian estimation the probability can never be zero, it is very useful in many situations. Note that the sum of probabilities is unity, i.e. $\sum_{j=1}^{K} P(C_j) = 1$, in both the cases.

The *expected* value of a random sample x is denoted by $E(x)$ and is given by

$$E(x) = \sum_{i=1}^{n} x_i P(x_i) = \mu_x$$

Thus expected value of x is the mean of a distribution μ_x. If x is a continuous variable then, using probability density function $p(x)$ instead of probabilities, we have

$$E(x) = \int_{-\infty}^{+\infty} x p(x) dx = \mu_x$$

If $f(x)$ is a discrete function of x, then its expected value is given by

$$E\{f(x)\} = \sum_{i=1}^{n} f(x_i) P(x_i)$$

This is the sum of all possible values of $f(x)$ weighted by its probability of occurrence. In the continuous domain, we use integration

$$E\{f(x)\} = \int_{-\infty}^{+\infty} f(x) p(x) dx$$

The *variance* of a random variable x is defined as

$$\sigma_x^2 = E\left[(x - E(x))^2\right] = E\left[(x - \mu_x)^2\right]$$

Thus, variance of x is the expected squared deviation of x from its mean and describes the spread of the values of the random variable x from their mean. The advantage of using the squared spread is that the values always become positive. This is very important for statistical computation purposes. To get a measure of the deviation in the linear norm, we should use the *standard deviation*, σ_x which is nothing but the square root of the variance.

One interesting property of the expectation operator $E(.)$ is that it is linear in nature. That is, if x can be expressed as weighted sum of x_1 and x_2 like $w_1x_1 + w_2x_2$, then, we can write

$$E(x) = E(w_1x_1 + w_2x_2) = w_1E(x_1) + w_2E(x_2)$$

Using the above linearity property, we can express variance in yet another form

$$\begin{aligned}\sigma_x^2 &= E\left[(x - E(x))^2\right] \\ &= E\left[x^2 - 2xE(x) + E(x)^2\right] \\ &= E\left[x^2\right] - 2E\left[xE(x)\right] + E\left[E(x)^2\right]\end{aligned}$$

Now,

$$E\left[xE(x)\right] = E(x\mu_x) = \mu_x E(x) = \mu_x^2$$

Therefore,

$$\sigma_x^2 = E(x^2) - 2\mu_x^2 + \mu_x^2$$

Example 2: Let us consider a pattern set consisting of two classes of patterns. The patterns, their attributes and classes are given in Table 17.1.

Table 17.1: Training Patterns, Attribute Values and Class

Pattern	*Features*			*Class*
	Fiber(F)	*Weight(W)*	*Cost(C)*	
P_1	Cotton	Heavy	Medium	Winter dress
P_2	Woolen	Heavy	High	Winter dress
P_3	Cotton	Light	High	Summer dress
P_4	Cotton	Light	Low	Summer dress
P_5	Jeans	Heavy	High	Summer dress
P_6	Woolen	Light	Low	Winter dress
P_7	Cotton	Heavy	Medium	Winter dress
P_8	Jeans	Light	Medium	Summer dress

Now, the problem is to find out the class or category of the following patterns as shown in Table 17.2.

Solution: In the above dress-material training data set patterns belong to two different classes: Winter Dress (WD) and Summer Dress (SD), four samples in each category. Here, $n = 2$. Therefore, the maximum likelihood of winter dress = Maximum likelihood of summer dress $= \frac{4}{4+4} = \frac{1}{2}$ each.

Table 17.2: Unknown Patterns with Attribute Values

Pattern	*Features*			*Class*
	Fiber(F)	*Weight(W)*	*Cost(C)*	
P_9	Cotton	Light	Medium	?
P_{10}	Jeans	Heavy	Low	?
P_{11}	Cotton	Heavy	High	?
P_{12}	Woolen	Light	Medium	?

Now, let us compute the maximum likelihood estimates for unknown patterns from Naive Bayes relations. For the first unknown pattern P_9, using Eq. 17.6, we have

$$
\begin{aligned}
P(WD) \times P[(F = \text{Cotton})|WD] \times P[(W = \text{Light})|WD] \times P[(C = \text{Medium})|WD]&\\
&= \frac{1}{2} \times \frac{2}{4} \times \frac{1}{4} \times \frac{2}{4}\\
&= \frac{2}{4 \times 4 \times 4}\\
&= \frac{1}{32}
\end{aligned}
$$

and

$$
\begin{aligned}
P(SD) \times P[(F = \text{Cotton})|SD] \times P[(W = \text{Light})|SD] \times P[(C = \text{Medium})|SD]&\\
&= \frac{1}{2} \times \frac{2}{4} \times \frac{3}{4} \times \frac{1}{4}\\
&= \frac{3}{4 \times 4 \times 4}\\
&= \frac{3}{64}
\end{aligned}
$$

Therefore, pattern P_9 belongs to the category of summer dress. The above values are computed using Eq. (17.6). We can also use Eq. (17.7) in this regard. The later is very useful in cases where no training pattern is available with a certain attribute value (always a non-zero probability is generated). Let us recompute the probabilities for unknown pattern P_9 using Eq. (17.7).

$$
\begin{aligned}
P(WD) \times P[(F = \text{Cotton})|WD] \times P[(W = \text{Light})|WD] \times P[(C = \text{Medium})|WD]&\\
&= \frac{1}{2} \times \frac{2+1}{4+3} \times \frac{1+1}{4+2} \times \frac{2+1}{4+3}\\
&= \frac{1}{2} \times \frac{3}{7} \times \frac{2}{6} \times \frac{3}{7}\\
&= \frac{3 \times 2 \times 3}{2 \times 7 \times 6 \times 7}\\
&= \frac{3}{98}
\end{aligned}
$$

and

$$\begin{aligned}
P(SD) \times P[(F = \text{Cotton})|SD] \times P[(W = \text{Light})|SD] \times P[(C = \text{Medium})|SD] \\
&= \frac{1}{2} \times \frac{2+1}{4+3} \times \frac{3+1}{4+2} \times \frac{1+1}{4+3} \\
&= \frac{1}{2} \times \frac{3}{7} \times \frac{4}{6} \times \frac{2}{7} \\
&= \frac{3 \times 4 \times 2}{2 \times 7 \times 6 \times 7} \\
&= \frac{2}{49}
\end{aligned}$$

Table 17.3 summarizes the estimates of prior and conditional probabilities for the dress material training data set.

Table 17.3: Likelihood and Bayesian Estimates of Probability Values

	Estimates	
Probability	*Likelihood*	*Bayesian*
P(SD)	4/8	5/10
P(F = Cotton|SD)	2/4	3/7
P(F = Woolen|SD)	0/4	1/7
P(F = Jeans|SD)	2/4	3/7
P(W = Heavy|SD)	1/4	2/6
P(W = Light|SD)	3/4	4/6
P(C = High|SD)	2/4	3/7
P(C = Medium|SD)	1/4	2/7
P(C = Low|SD)	1/4	2/7
P(WD)	4/8	5/10
P(F=Cotton|WD)	2/4	3/7
P(F = Woolen|WD)	2/4	3/7
P(F = Jeans|WD)	0/4	1/7
P(W = Heavy|WD)	3/4	4/6
P(W = Light|WD)	1/4	2/6
P(C = High|WD)	1/4	2/7
P(C = Medium|WD)	2/4	3/7
P(C = Low|WD)	1/4	2/7

♣

17.4 Likelihood Estimation

In a particular distribution of data, different classes will have different posterior probability values. The class with the maximum probability for a particular sample will be the winner of that sample. From this concept, we can derive a likelihood estimation L which is found very important in statistical decision making. Let us consider a situation with two classes C_i and C_j only. The likelihood ratio is given by

$$L = \frac{P(C_i)\ P(x|C_i)}{P(C_j)\ P(x|C_j)} \tag{17.8}$$

If $L > 1$, then class C_i is the most likely class for sample x, otherwise, if $L < 1$, we should assign x to class C_j.

17.5 Decision Regions and Decision Boundaries

Computing the likelihood function is a possible approach for decision making in a two class problem. Another approach is to compare posterior probabilities of the concerned classes is to compute the decision regions and decision boundaries. Decision regions are specified by the range of values along all the dimensions. Each decision region is associated with a class. A boundary between the two regions or classes is a decision boundary.

Let us consider a monovariate two class decision making problem. Here, the classes are C_1 and C_2 and the regions are R_1 and R_2, respectively. Now, a decision boundary between the two regions or classes is characterized by that value of the variable x such that x is equally probable in either C_1 or C_2. Therefore, by equating the posterior probabilities, we have

$$P(C_1|x) = P(C_2|x)$$

Applying Bayes theorem, we get

$$P(C_1)\ P(x|C_1) = P(C_2)\ P(x|C_2) \tag{17.9}$$

at the optimal decision boundary. In case of a continuous pattern space we can write

$$P(C_1)\ p(x|C_1) = P(C_2)\ p(x|C_2) \tag{17.10}$$

where $p(x|C_1)$ and $p(x|C_2)$ are probability density functions.

Now, if we consider a normal distribution of samples in each of the classes, the above equation becomes

$$P(C_1)\frac{1}{\sqrt{2\pi}\sigma_1}\exp\left[\frac{-(x-\mu_1)^2}{2\sigma_1^2}\right] = P(C_2)\frac{1}{\sqrt{2\pi}\sigma_2}\exp\left[\frac{-(x-\mu_2)^2}{2\sigma_2^2}\right]$$

Taking natural logarithm on both the sides

$$-2\ln\left(\frac{P(C_1)}{\sigma_1}\right)+\left(\frac{x-\mu_1}{\sigma_1}\right)^2=-2\ln\left(\frac{P(C_2)}{\sigma_2}\right)+\left(\frac{x-\mu_2}{\sigma_2}\right)^2$$

Therefore, we can write the decision or discrimination function as

$$d=-2\ln\left(\frac{P(C_1)}{\sigma_1}\right)+\left(\frac{x-\mu_1}{\sigma_1}\right)^2+2\ln\left(\frac{P(C_2)}{\sigma_2}\right)-\left(\frac{x-\mu_2}{\sigma_2}\right)^2 \tag{17.11}$$

It is clear that,

$$d=\begin{cases}\text{positive} & \text{if } C_2 \text{ is the most likely class}\\ 0 & \text{on the decision boundary}\\ \text{negative} & \text{if } C_1 \text{ is the most likely class}\end{cases}$$

Example 3: Let us consider a monovariate two class problem. Prior probabilities of the two classes are 0.8 and 0.2, respectively. Their mean and variances are 26, 22 and 2, 3, respectively. Find out a suitable decision boundary to partition the feature space.

Solution: Here, the following statistical information is provided:

$$P(C_1)=0.8$$

$$P(C_2)=0.2$$

$$\mu_1=26$$

$$\mu_2=22$$

$$\sigma_1=2$$

$$\sigma_2=3$$

Therefore, the discrimination function can be computed as

$$\begin{aligned}d&=-2\ln\left(\frac{P(C_1)}{\sigma_1}\right)+\left(\frac{x-\mu_1}{\sigma_1}\right)^2+2\ln\left(\frac{P(C_2)}{\sigma_2}\right)-\left(\frac{x-\mu_2}{\sigma_2}\right)^2\\&=-2\ln\left(\frac{0.8}{2.0}\right)+\left(\frac{x-26.0}{2.0}\right)^2+2\ln\left(\frac{0.2}{3.0}\right)-\left(\frac{x-22.0}{3.0}\right)^2\end{aligned}$$

Simplifying and equating to zero, we get

$$5x^2-292x+4018.99=0$$

This quadratic equation can be solved to produce values

$$x=22.2 \quad \text{and} \quad x=36.2$$

Thus, here we get two decision boundaries, corresponding to each of the above values of x. However, since the value 22.2 is in between the two means, and the value 36.2 is away from both, we may consider the former to yield the required decision boundary.

17.6 Multivariate Decision Making

The decision function developed above is applicable only to monovariate problems. But, in practice we need to deal with multivariate problems, i.e. problem domains contain samples or data items in multidimensional vector forms, i.e. feature vectors. Fortunately, in this case also, the Bayesian probability expressions are almost similar to the univariate case. Here, we shall replace the sample x by the corresponding feature vector $\mathbf{x}$. For discrete classification into K classes, we get

$$P(C_i|\mathbf{x}) = \frac{P(C_i)\ P(\mathbf{x}|C_i)}{\sum_{k=1}^{K} P(C_k)\ P(\mathbf{x}|C_k)} \tag{17.12}$$

In case of continuous feature space, the above equation modifies itself as

$$p(C_i|\mathbf{x}) = \frac{P(C_i)\ p(\mathbf{x}|C_i)}{\sum_{k=1}^{K} P(C_k)\ p(\mathbf{x}|C_k)} \tag{17.13}$$

by using the density functions instead of probabilities.

The multivariate probability distributions (Gaussian) functions are expressed using vector notations. For a d-dimensional feature space a distribution with mean μ and co-variance matrix $\mathbf{\Sigma}$, the normal density function can be expressed as

$$p(\mathbf{x}) = \frac{1}{\sqrt{(2\pi)^d|\mathbf{\Sigma}|}} \exp\left[-\frac{1}{2}(\mathbf{x}-\mu)^T\mathbf{\Sigma}^{-1}(\mathbf{x}-\mu)\right] \tag{17.14}$$

In the above equation $\mathbf{x}$ is the feature vector or sample vector given by

$$\mathbf{x} = \begin{pmatrix} x_1 \\ x_2 \\ \vdots \\ x_d \end{pmatrix} \tag{17.15}$$

The mean vector μ is given by

$$\mu = \begin{pmatrix} \mu_1 \\ \mu_2 \\ \vdots \\ \mu_d \end{pmatrix} \tag{17.16}$$

The symmetric covariance matrix is given by

$$\mathbf{\Sigma} = \begin{pmatrix} \sigma_{11} & \sigma_{12} & \cdots & \sigma_{1d} \\ \sigma_{21} & \sigma_{22} & \cdots & \sigma_{2d} \\ \vdots & \vdots & \ddots & \vdots \\ \sigma_{d1} & \sigma_{d2} & \cdots & \sigma_{dd} \end{pmatrix} = \begin{pmatrix} \sigma_1^2 & \sigma_{12} & \cdots & \sigma_{1d} \\ \sigma_{12} & \sigma_2^2 & \cdots & \sigma_{2d} \\ \vdots & \vdots & \ddots & \vdots \\ \sigma_{1d} & \sigma_{2d} & \cdots & \sigma_d^2 \end{pmatrix} \tag{17.17}$$

$|\mathbf{\Sigma}|$ is the determinant of $\mathbf{\Sigma}$ and $\mathbf{\Sigma}^{-1}$ is the inverse of $\mathbf{\Sigma}$.

To realize the significance of the covariance matrix, let us consider a bivariate situation. The exponent on the RHS of the multivariate distribution function can be expressed as

$$-\frac{1}{2}\sum_{ij}(x_i - \mu_i)c_{ij}(x_j - \mu_j) \tag{17.18}$$

Here, c_{ij} is the ijth component of Σ^{-1}. When a bivariate situation is considered we can write

$$\mathbf{x} = \begin{pmatrix} x \\ y \end{pmatrix}$$

$$\mu = \begin{pmatrix} \mu_x \\ \mu_y \end{pmatrix}$$

and

$$\begin{pmatrix} \sigma_x^2 & \sigma_{xy} \\ \sigma_{xy} & \sigma_y^2 \end{pmatrix} = \begin{pmatrix} \sigma_x^2 & \rho_{xy}\sigma_x\sigma_y \\ \rho_{xy}\sigma_x\sigma_y & \sigma_y^2 \end{pmatrix}$$

Here, $\sigma_{xy} = E\left[(x - \mu_x)(y - \mu_y)\right]$ is the covariance of x and y. For any two individual samples x_1 and y_1, the term $(x - \mu_x)(y - \mu_y)$ gives a measure of combined deviation of x_1 and y_1 from their respective means, which we call covariance. For the purpose of normalization, we divide the term by the two individual standard deviations and get the correlation between x and y as

$$\rho_{xy} = \frac{\sigma_{xy}}{\sigma_x\sigma_y} = E\left[\left(\frac{x - \mu_x}{\sigma_x}\right)\left(\frac{y - \mu_y}{\sigma_y}\right)\right] \tag{17.19}$$

The value of ρ varies as

$$-1 \le \rho \le 1$$

It is clear that

$$\rho_{xy} = \begin{cases} 1 & \text{when } x \text{ and } y \text{ are perfectly correlated} \\ 0 & \text{when } x \text{ and } y \text{ are uncorrelated} \\ -1 & \text{when } x \text{ and } y \text{ are anti-correlated} \end{cases}$$

The bivariate normal density distribution is given by

$$p(x, y) = \frac{1}{2\pi\sigma_x\sigma_y\sqrt{(1-\rho_{xy}^2)}}$$
$$\exp\left\{-\frac{1}{2(1-\rho_{xy}{}^2)}\left[\left(\frac{x-\mu_x}{\sigma_x}\right)^2 - \frac{2\rho_{xy}(x-\mu_x)(y-\mu_y)}{\sigma_x\sigma_y} + \left(\frac{y-\mu_y}{\sigma_y}\right)^2\right]\right\} \tag{17.20}$$

Let us now turn back to the general multivariate situation. The likelihood ratio between two classes in this case is

$$L = \frac{P(\mathbf{x}|C_i)}{P(\mathbf{x}|C_j)} = \frac{P(C_i)\ P(x|C_i)}{P(C_j)\ P(x|C_j)} \tag{17.21}$$

or

$$L = \frac{P(\mathbf{x}|C_i)}{P(\mathbf{x}|C_j)} = \exp\left[-\frac{1}{2}(\mathbf{x}-\mu_i)^T\mathbf{\Sigma}^{-1}(\mathbf{x}-\mu_i) - (\mathbf{x}-\mu_j)^T\mathbf{\Sigma}^{-1}(\mathbf{x}-\mu_j)\right] \tag{17.22}$$

Since the covariance matrix is symmetrical, the class conditional probability ratio becomes

$$L = \frac{P(\mathbf{x}|C_i)}{P(\mathbf{x}|C_j)} = \exp\left[\mathbf{x}^T\mathbf{\Sigma}^{-1}(\mu_i-\mu_j) - \frac{1}{2}(\mu_i+\mu_j)^T\mathbf{\Sigma}^{-1}(\mu_i-\mu_j)\right] \tag{17.23}$$

The decision function can now be obtained by taking natural logarithm on both sides

$$d_{ij} = \ln\frac{P(\mathbf{x}|C_i)}{P(\mathbf{x}|C_j)} \tag{17.24}$$

or

$$d_{ij} = \mathbf{x}^T\mathbf{\Sigma}^{-1}(\mu_i-\mu_j) - \frac{1}{2}(\mu_i+\mu_j)^T\mathbf{\Sigma}^{-1}(\mu_i-\mu_j) \tag{17.25}$$

The above discriminating parameter d_{ij} can have $K(K-1)$ different values, one each for a particular combination of (i, j) such that $(i \neq j)$. The largest of these values determines the class of $\mathbf{x}$.

As in the case of monovariate problem, discussed earlier, here also we can get the decision boundary as the hyperplane at $d_{ij} = 0$, for a two class conflict.

$$d_{ij} = \begin{cases} \text{positive} & \text{if } \mathbf{x} \in C_i \\ 0 & \text{if } \mathbf{x} \text{ is on the decision boundary} \\ \text{negative} & \text{if } \mathbf{x} \in C_j \end{cases}$$

17.7 Estimation of Error Rates

Once the probability density function and the decision functions are found the *probability of errors* or the *error rate* of the classifier can be estimated.

The probability that a sample $\mathbf{x}$ is correctly classified for class C_i in region R_i is given by

$$P(C|C_i) = \sum_{x \in R_i} P(\mathbf{x}|C_i) \tag{17.26}$$

and the probability or error or misclassification is

$$P(E|C_i) = \sum_{x \notin R_i} P(\mathbf{x}|C_i) \tag{17.27}$$

The overall probability of a correct decision is

$$P(C) = \sum_{i=1}^{K} P(C_i)\ P(C|C_i) = \sum_{i=1}^{K} P(C|C_i) \sum_{x \in R_i} P(\mathbf{x}|C_i) \tag{17.28}$$

and the overall probability of error is

$$P(E) = 1 - P(C) = 1 - \sum_{i=1}^{K} P(C|C_i) \sum_{x \in R_i} P(\mathbf{x}|C_i) = \sum_{i=1}^{K} P(C|C_i) \sum_{x \notin R_i} P(\mathbf{x}|C_i) \tag{17.29}$$

The probability of error can be accurately determined if the distribution is exactly known.

17.8 Minimizing Risk Factor

During classification, we want to minimize the probability of misclassifying patterns. But, there is always a chance for misclassification which may be fatal in many applications. For example, in case of medical image segmentation using probabilistic models, we may misclassify a tumor cell to be a normal cell, as there is always a chance. To minimize this chance factor, we need to minimize some well defined penalty or loss functions.

Let us assume that x is a discrete random variable under consideration. A very commonly used classification error estimation function is the *squared error function*, where the loss or penalty of misclassification is proportional to the square of the actual error terms as given by

$$L(x, x_d) = (x - x_d)^2 \tag{17.30}$$

Here, x_d is the predicted value of an observation and x is the actual outcome. Therefore, the risk associated to the prediction is

$$R(x_d) = E\left[L(x, x_d)\right] = E\left[(x - x_d)^2\right] \tag{17.31}$$

As x is a discrete random variable we can write,

$$R(x_d) = \sum_{i=1}^{N} (x_i - x_d)^2 P(x_i) \tag{17.32}$$

The minimum risk condition can be obtained by differentiation and subsequent equalization to zero. i.e.

$$\frac{dR}{dx_d} = -2\sum_{i=1}^{N} (x_i - x_d) P(x_i) = 0$$

or

$$\sum_{i=1}^{N} x_i P(x_i) = x_d \sum_{i=1}^{N} P(x_i)$$

Now, since $\sum_{i=1}^{N} P(x_i) = 1$ and $\sum_{i=1}^{N} x_i P(x_i) = E(x)$, we have

$$x_d = E(x) = \mu_x \tag{17.33}$$

Therefore, we arrive at the conclusion that the squared error loss function leads to the mean μ_x as the minimum risk prediction for the next outcome of x.

If we consider the loss to be proportional to the absolute value of the actual error then

$$L(x, x_d) = |x - x_d| \tag{17.34}$$

The risk factor is

$$R(x_d) = E\left[L(x, x_d)\right] = E\left[|x - x_d|\right] \tag{17.35}$$

Now, since $|x - x_d|$ can be positive, negative or zero, we should express the above equation in the following form:

$$R(x_d) = \sum_{x_i > x_d} (x_i - x_d) P(x_i) + \sum_{x_i < x_d} (x_i - x_d) P(x_i) + \sum_{x_i = x_d} (x_i - x_d) P(x_i) \tag{17.36}$$

Differentiating and equating to zero, we get

$$\frac{dR}{dx_d} = -\sum_{x_i > x_d} P(x_i) + \sum_{x_i < x_d} P(x_i) = 0.$$

From the above expression it is clear that the sufficient condition for minimizing the risk factor is to select x_d such that probability of $x_i > x_d$ becomes equal to that of $x_i < x_d$. This is a necessary condition for a symmetric distribution only; for an asymmetric distribution the above condition may not be true.

Now, let us consider a general continuous situation. We want to estimate the loss or a risk measure for classifying patterns into classes. Let, L_{kj} represent the loss or error associated to misclassifying a pattern $\mathbf{x}$ to class C_j when the actual class should be C_k. Summing over all the patterns coming from class C_k, the expected or average loss becomes

$$R_k = \sum_{j=1}^{K} L_{kj} \int_{\mathcal{R}_j} p(C_k|\mathbf{x})d\mathbf{x} \tag{17.37}$$

Therefore, the overall risk factor for patterns of all the classes is

$$R = \sum_{k=1}^{K} R_k P(C_k) = \sum_{k=1}^{K} \int_{\mathcal{R}_j} \{L_{kj} p(C_k|\mathbf{x})\} \, d\mathbf{x} \tag{17.38}$$

Therefore, it is clear that the integrand of the RHS of the above equation should be minimized. This minimum risk can be obtained when,

$$\sum_{k=1}^{K} L_{kj} p(\mathbf{x}|C_k) < \sum_{k=1}^{K} L_{ki} p(C_k|\mathbf{x}) \tag{17.39}$$

for all $i \neq j$. Now, if we assume that the loss of misclassification is 1 and that for correct classification is 0, then according to Bayes theorem, the above expression reduces to

$$p(\mathbf{x}|C_k)P(C_k) > p(\mathbf{x}|C_j)P(C_j) \tag{17.40}$$

for all $j \neq k$. The above is nothing but the rule for minimizing the probability of misclassification.

17.9 Problems

1. What do you mean by statistical decision making?
2. What are the differences between parametric and non-parametric decision making?
3. State Bayes theorem. Explain the Bayes theorem in decision making.
4. Define the following terms: prior probability, Posterior probability, likelihood ratio.
5. Explain how class membership of patterns can be determined by likelihood ratio.
6. Under what condition Bayes probability measures reduce to Naive Bayes ones?

7. In a two class recognition problem classes are represented by mean vector and covariance matrices as given below

$$\text{Class 1:} \quad \mu_1 = \begin{bmatrix} 20 \\ 30 \end{bmatrix} \quad \Sigma_1 = \begin{bmatrix} 5 & 0 \\ 0 & 10 \end{bmatrix}$$

$$\text{Class 2:} \quad \mu_2 = \begin{bmatrix} 50 \\ 80 \end{bmatrix} \quad \Sigma_2 = \begin{bmatrix} 8 & 0 \\ 0 & 20 \end{bmatrix}$$

Find out a decision function between the classes using Mahalanobis distance.

8. Determine the optimal decision boundary between two bivariate normal classes where the features are independent within each class. The parameters of the two distributions are as follows:

$$\text{Class 1:} \quad \mu_x = 0 \quad \mu_y = 0 \quad \sigma_x = 1 \quad \sigma_y = 1 \quad \rho_{xy} = 0$$

$$\text{Class 2:} \quad \mu_x = 2 \quad \mu_y = 0 \quad \sigma_x = 1 \quad \sigma_y = 2 \quad \rho_{xy} = 0$$

9. Show that for two class classification the maximum likelihood ratio can be expressed as

$$L = \frac{P(C_1)\ P(x|C_1)}{P(C_2)\ P(x|C_2)}$$

Chapter 18

Nearest Neighbour Classifier

In reality neighbourhood is defined by some proximity and similarity characteristics. For example, in society we observe neighbourhoodness among poor and among rich separately. In general a mixup between a poor and a rich is rare in existence. If a rich person lives in a slum, among many poor, he may be treated as an *outlier*. In pattern classification also, we consider neighbouring patterns to belong the same class. This similarity between patterns can, therefore, be measured as a distance between them. It is believed that neighbour patterns are closer to each other compared to non-neighbour patterns. Using the above concept, an elegant distance based classification technique has been developed which is termed as the k-nearest neighbour classifier.

18.1 Distance Based Classification

In classification, we try to find out the class of an unknown incoming sample. The number of classes (K) are already defined on the basis of some historical training data. Since the training database is already classified, we have K distinct groups of training data and (possibly) their prototypes (representatives). When an unknown sample is input to the classifier, it tries to allocate the incumbent to the most appropriate class. In a multidimensional numeric feature space, very commonly, the Euclidean distance measure is used as the determining factor. If $\mathbf{x}$ and $\mathbf{y}$ are two sample patterns in n-dimensional space R^n, then Euclidean distance between $\mathbf{x}$ and $\mathbf{y}$, i.e. d_{xy} is defined as

$$d_{xy} = \sqrt{\sum_{i=0}^{n-1} (\mathbf{x}_i - \mathbf{y}_i)^2} \tag{18.1}$$

For patterns with numeric attributes only, we can measure the distance values using the above Euclidean norm or any other existing distance norms. For patterns with non-numeric attributes one may use the Hamming distance or other suitable norms.

18.2 The Nearest Neighbour Classifier

This is the most basic instance-based learning method. This algorithm is very commonly used as a non-parametric classification techniques. Here, a new sample (instance) is classified on the basis of its nearest distance from the elements of a set of randomly chosen training samples. This process is intuitively very simple and fast. But it has the disadvantage of insertion of outliers in a class, i.e. misclassification rate may be very high. An *outlier* may be considered to be a pattern that is in some way dissimilar to other patterns in the concerned class. In the nearest neighbour classification technique, the randomly chosen training samples are assumed to be neighbours of the input sample. The task is to find out the nearest neighbour out of all the neighbours. The nearest neighbour algorithm is generally termed as the k-NN algorithm, where k is the number of training samples compared. The algorithm is given below.

The nearest neighbour algorithm

```
begin
    input the unknown sample x
    for i = 0 to T_N - 1 do
        compute the Euclidean distance d_i between x and x_i
    heuristically choose the value of k
    NN={Φ}

    for j = 0 to k - 1 do
        begin
            d_min = large_value
            for i = 0 to T_N - 1 - j do
                if (d_i < d_min)  d_min = d_i
            S = S - {x_i}
            NN = NN ∪ {x_i}
        end

    label ← = class label of data in NN with lowest distance
    set class label of x ← label
end
```

Here, S is the set of training patterns, and T_N is the number of available training patterns. NN is the set of selected nearest neighbours. It is seen that if the nearest neighbour is an outlier, then the input sample is likely to be misclassified. When $k = 1$, the algorithm is called the 1-NN algorithm. It is clear that higher values of k indicates better classification, but slower execution. To reduce the error rate, the following modification can be incorporated in the algorithm. The modification is simply to assign the incumbent a class that is most frequent among its k nearest neighbours.

Here, k is a design choice from the user. One may try out with different values of k and select the value that gives the best result. To obtain a value of k heuristically, we can start with an integer approximation of the square root of the number of training patterns in the class that contains the fewest training patterns.

In Figure 18.1, an example for nearest neighbour classification is shown. Here $k = 3$ is assumed. The three nearest neighbours of the unknown sample $\mathbf{x}$ come from three different classes of which the neighbour from class 1 is the closest. Hence, $\mathbf{x}$ is classified in class 1.

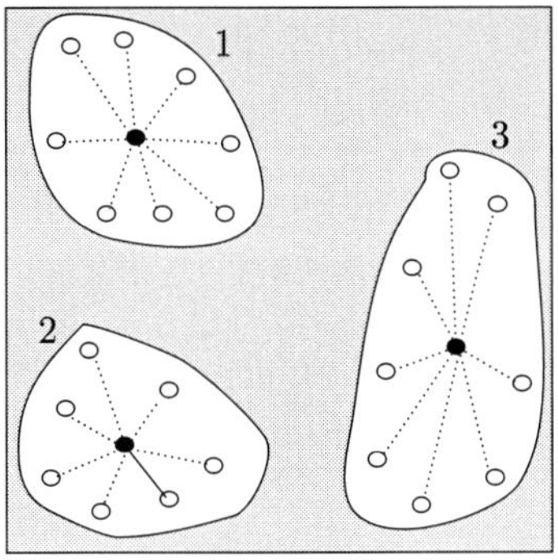

(a) Training classes

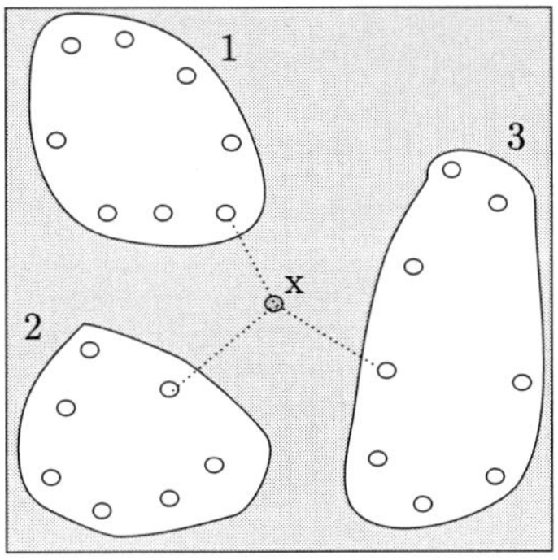

(b) Classifying sample $\mathbf{x}$

Figure 18.1: Example of k-NN classification.

Example 1: Consider the following 2-dimensional training set having 12 elements as shown in Table 18.1. Apply the k-NN algorithm using 3 neighbours and determine the class label for the data item $\mathbf{x} = (5, 5)$.

Table 18.1: Labelled Training Data

Data Item	*Data Value*	*Class Label*
$\mathbf{x}_1$	(1, 1)	1
$\mathbf{x}_2$	(1, 2)	1
$\mathbf{x}_3$	(3, 1)	1
$\mathbf{x}_4$	(2, 2)	1
$\mathbf{x}_5$	(3, 4)	2
$\mathbf{x}_6$	(4, 4)	2
$\mathbf{x}_7$	(4, 5)	2
$\mathbf{x}_8$	(5, 3)	2
$\mathbf{x}_9$	(6, 5)	3
$\mathbf{x}_{10}$	(7, 2)	3
$\mathbf{x}_{11}$	(7, 3)	3
$\mathbf{x}_{12}$	(8, 3)	3

Solution: The training data and then distance matrix are shown in Tables 18.1 and 18.2, respectively.

Table 18.2: Distance matrix for the data set

Training Data	1	2	3	4	5	6	7	8	9	10	11	12
Distance	5.66	5.00	4.47	4.24	2.24	1.41	1.00	2.00	1.00	3.61	2.83	3.61

From Table 18.2, the three nearest neighbours of $\mathbf{x}$ are found to be $\mathbf{x}_6, \mathbf{x}_7$ and $\mathbf{x}_9$. Out of these three nearest neighbours, $\mathbf{x}$ is nearest to $\mathbf{x}_7$ and $\mathbf{x}_9$ which are members of class 2 and class 3, respectively. Hence, the new pattern $\mathbf{x}$ may be classified to either of class 2 or class 3.

Modified nearest neighbour algorithm

```
begin
    input the unknown sample x
    for i = 0 to T_N − 1 do
        compute the Euclidean distance d_i between x and x_i
    heuristically choose the value of k
    NN={Φ}

    for j = 0 to k − 1 do
        begin
            d_min = large_value
            for i = 0 to T_N − 1 − j do
                if (d_i < d_min) d_min = d_i
            S = S − {x_i}
            NN = NN ⋃ {x_i}
            label_j ← class label of x_i
        end

    label ← class label of data in NN with highest frequency
    set class label of x ← label
end
```

Example 2: Consider the 2-dimensional training set as shown in Table 18.1. Apply the modified k-NN algorithm using 3 neighbours and determine the class label for the data item $\mathbf{x} = (5,\ 5)$.

Solution: In this case, the training set and the distance matrix remain the same as in the case of Example 1. Since it is found that out of the three nearest neighbours, $\mathbf{x}_6, \mathbf{x}_7$ and $\mathbf{x}_9$, the first two belong to class 2 and the other belongs to class 3, we can classify $\mathbf{x}$ to be a member of class 2 unambiguously.

18.3 Nearest Neighbour Error Rate

The Bayesian classification technique always classifies a pattern to its most likely class and the corresponding error rate is given by

$$P(E|\mathbf{x})_{\text{Bayes}} = 1 - P(C_m|\mathbf{x}) \tag{18.2}$$

where C_m is the most likely class for pattern $\mathbf{x}$. The nearest neighbour probability for x is correct if it is equal to that of its neighbour in the same class C_m, or $P(C_i|\mathbf{x})^2$, summed over all i. The total probability of error is therefore,

$$\begin{aligned} P(E|\mathbf{x})_{NN} &= 1 - \sum_{i=1}^{K} P(C_i|\mathbf{x})^2 \\ &= 1 - P(C_m|\mathbf{x})^2 - \sum_{i \notin m} P(C_i|\mathbf{x})^2 \end{aligned} \tag{18.3}$$

Using above two equations, we get

$$\begin{aligned} P(E|\mathbf{x})_{NN} &= 1 - (1 - P(E|\mathbf{x})_{\text{Bayes}})^2 - \sum_{i \notin m} P(C_i|\mathbf{x})^2 \\ &= 2P(E|\mathbf{x})_{\text{Bayes}} - P(E|\mathbf{x})^2_{\text{Bayes}} - \sum_{i \notin m} P(C_i|\mathbf{x})^2 \\ &\leq 2P(E|\mathbf{x})_{\text{Bayes}} - P(E|\mathbf{x})^2_{\text{Bayes}} \end{aligned} \tag{18.4}$$

Therefore, the nearest neighbour error rate will never be larger than twice the Bayesian error rate minus its square.

18.4 Performance of Nearest Neighbour Classifier

Performance of nearest neighbour classifier can be measured by the proportion of misclassified data patterns. It is a proved fact that the k-NN error rate can never be greater than twice the Bayes error rate. The NN error rate approaches the Bayes error rate in either of the following situations:

- When the Bayes error rate approaches either 0 or 1.
- When $k \to \infty$ and $\dfrac{\text{number of training patterns}}{k} \to \infty$.

However, the NN classifier may be assumed to perform well when we have a lot of training patterns. But increase in training pattern size involves more distance computation, and hence, more computational complexity, thereby slow down the process.

18.5 NN Learning in Discrete and Continuous Domains

The nearest neighbour learning method has a target function defined on either a discrete or a continuous real-valued domain. The above mentioned classification algorithm is an example of a discrete target function.

When the target function is discrete we can represent it as

$$f : R^n \rightarrow v \tag{18.5}$$

where, v is a finite set of discrete values $\{v_0, v_1, \ldots, v_{s-1}\}$. When the NN algorithm is used for approximating a discrete target function, it can be described as follows:

---

k-NN Algorithm with discrete target function

begin
  input the unknown instance $\mathbf{x}$
  find k training instances $\mathbf{x}_0, \mathbf{x}_1, \ldots, \mathbf{x}_{k-1}$
    that are nearest to $\mathbf{x}$
  calculate $r \leftarrow argmax \sum_{i=0}^{k-1} \delta(v, f(\mathbf{x}_i))$
  return r
end

Here,

$$\delta(a, b) = \begin{cases} 1 & \text{if } a = b \\ 0 & \text{otherwise} \end{cases}$$

The value r returned by the algorithm is an estimate of $f(\mathbf{x})$ and is the most common value of $f(.)$ among the k training instances nearest to $\mathbf{x}$.

The algorithm can be adapted to an approximate continuous valued target function by calculating the mean value of the target function arising out of the k nearest training samples. Therefore, the return value in this case is

$$r = f(\mathbf{x}) \leftarrow \frac{1}{k} \sum_{i=0}^{k-1} f(\mathbf{x}_i) \tag{18.6}$$

18.6 Some Important Features of the NN Algorithm

Instead of Euclidean distance measures, other measures like Manhattan distance (city block distance) or Mahalanobis distance, etc. can also be used as the proximity measures.

When the patterns have a very large number of irrelevant attributes, then their contributions toward the proximity measure may significantly affect the accuracy of the algorithm. This phenomena is called the **curse of dimensionality**. There are two approaches to avoid this situation:

- By using weighted attributes during computation of proximity measures, and
- By eliminating irrelevant attributes a priori.

A significant overhead of this process is computation of a large number of distance measures for each new sample. Also, all other processing must be delayed by this distance computation step. Hence, it may seem to be very slow.

NN method can be a local method or a global method. When a subset of the training patterns (k in number) are used for classification, it is called a **local method**. If all the training patterns are used then it becomes a global method.

18.7 Modification for Non-Numeric Attributes

When the attributes of patterns are non-numeric in nature, we cannot calculate the Euclidean or other numeric distance measures. In such a situation, the proximity measures between the input sample and the reference training patterns are computed differently depending on the domain of patterns. A very common domain-independent approach is to use the Hamming distance. It is defined as the number of attributes for which the two patterns have different values.

For mixed type attributes (numeric and non-numeric both) conventional distance measures (Euclidean, etc.) can be used only for numeric attributes, and Hamming distance for the non-numeric or categorical attributes separately. Then, a weighted sum of these two measures can be used as a final measure. A weighted version of the NN algorithm is given below:

Weighted k-NN algorithm

begin
  input the unknown instance $\mathbf{x}$
  find k training instances $\mathbf{x}_0, \mathbf{x}_1, \ldots, \mathbf{x}_{k-1}$
    that are nearest to $\mathbf{x}$
  calculate $r \leftarrow argmax \sum_{i=0}^{k-1} w_i \delta(v, f(\mathbf{x}_i))$
  return r
end

Here, w_i is the weight associated with the ith nearest neighbour. If applied only with numeric patterns, generally, weights for nearest neighbours are adjusted according to their distance from the input sample giving higher weight to closer neighbours. A possible formulation for the weights can thus be written as

$$w_i = \frac{1}{d(\mathbf{x}, \mathbf{x}_i)^2} = \frac{1}{{d_i}^2} \tag{18.7}$$

18.8 Problems

1. Describe the advantages and disadvantages of k-NN algorithm.
2. What is the role of number of neighbours in k-NN algorithm?
3. Consider the training set as given in the following chart

Name	*Gender*	*Height*	*Class*
Kousik	Male	1.6 m	Short
Shyama	Female	2.0 m	Tall
Soma	Female	1.9 m	Medium
Sourav	Male	1.7 m	Medium
Rathin	Male	1.6 m	Short
Anup	Male	2.2 m	Tall
Tanmoy	Male	2.1 m	Tall
Manas	Male	1.5 m	Short
Gopa	Female	1.8 m	Medium
Manju	Female	1.4 m	Short

   Find out the class of pattern (Sikha, Female, 1.95) using k-NN algorithm with $k = 5$.

4. Will there be any difference in the above classification problem if instead of Euclidean distances Mahalanobis distances are used?
5. Find out an expression for complexity of the k-NN algorithm.
6. Show that NN-classifier error rate is always greater than Bayes error rate.
7. Under what condition do NN-classifier error and Bayes error become equal?

CHAPTER 19

Decision Tree Learning

A Decision Tree is a very popular classification technique that yields a hierarchical structure where each internal node denotes a test on some attribute value and each branch represents an outcome of the test. The leaves represent the classes identified by range of attribute values along the paths from the root node. The tree is built by learning from a set of training patterns, where internal nodes indicate rules and leaf nodes represent decisions or classes. A decision tree algorithm follows a predictive model and graphically organize patterns into classes.

19.1 Tree

A *tree* is a hierarchical data structure with one or more nodes. In every tree, there is a *root* node, a number of *intermediate* nodes and a number of *leaf* nodes. Root and the intermediate nodes are also called **internal** nodes in together. The most common form of a tree is a *binary tree*. In a binary tree, each node, except the leaf nodes can have at most two descendants which are called the **left** and **right child** of the concerned (parent) node. In general an internal node may have any number of children nodes. For m children nodes, the tree is called **m–ary tree**. All the children nodes of an internal node are *siblings* of each other. Leaf nodes do not have any children.

19.1.1 Decision Tree

A *decision tree* is a kind of tree where, the leaf nodes represent classes of patterns, and all other nodes, including the root node, represent predicates (nodes labelled with a question). Arcs emanating from each node represent possible answer to the associated question. Leaf nodes represent solutions of the concerned classification problem.

In machine learning, the decision tree is formed using the training pattern set in the training phase. The training subset of patterns are assumed to be already classified into appropriate groups. In the testing phase, this decision tree is used to classify unknown patterns. For the same set of training patterns, decision trees may have different structures. This depends on the topological ordering and relevance of the predicate nodes used in the decision making process.

As mentioned earlier, each internal node of a decision tree is labelled with a *predictor attribute*, called the *splitting attribute*, and each leaf node is labelled with a class label. Each arc originating from an internal node is labelled with a *splitting condition* that involves the node's splitting attribute values only. The splitting predicates have the property that any record will follow a unique path from the root to exactly one leaf node. Splitting attributes and splitting predicate pair at a node constitute what is called **splitting criteria**.

19.1.2 Example of a Decision Tree

Let us consider an example of pattern classification using decision tree. Let our objective is to classify records of members of a society based on their educational qualification and their income. We can consider records (patterns) consisting of attributes (*Name, Qualification, Income*), for simplicity. In general, during formation of a decision tree, we like to select a predicate at the root node which have a small number of values. Here, we may choose *Degree* to be at the root because it can have the following possible values: Non-graduate, graduate, post-graduate and doctorate. The next level attribute is *Income*. Since income is a continuous attribute, we need to quantize it into a spectrum of finite bands like:

$$\text{poor } (<20 \text{ K}); \quad \text{mediocre } (>20 \text{ K}, <50 \text{ K}); \quad \text{rich } (>50 \text{ K})$$

It should be noted here that different classification algorithms use different ways of choosing predicate attributes at different levels to make a partition at each node. In general different branches of the tree could grow up to different levels and different nodes at the same level may use different partitioning attributes also.

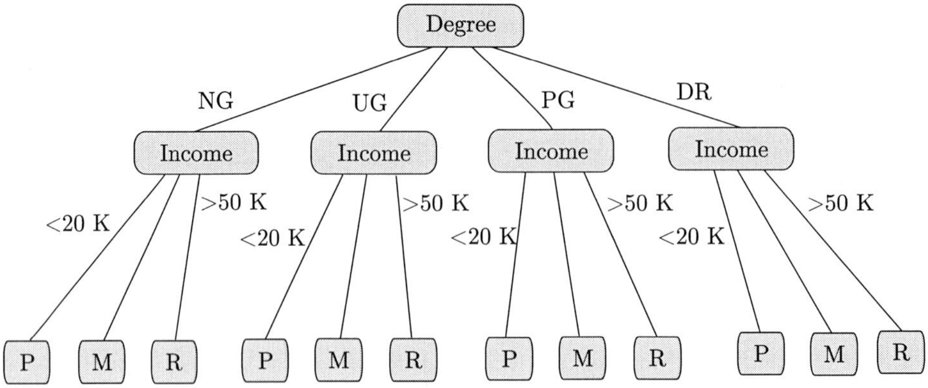

P: Poor M: Mediocre R: Rich

Figure 19.1: A sample decision tree.

19.2 Decision Tree Construction and Learning

One possible approach to construct a decision tree is to apply the *breadth-first* technique. Here, all the nodes at a particular level are generated before proceeding to the next level. We start with generating the root node at first. Then all the first level nodes are generated, then all the second level nodes, and so on. An iterative algorithm is described below.

19.2.1 Iterative Learning Algorithm

We need to maintain two lists called **OPEN** and **CLOSED**. At any instance during the construction of the tree, a node of the tree is expanded to the next level by taking nodes from the list **OPEN**. And the already expanded nodes are placed in the list **CLOSED**, indicating that they are no more available for expansion. During an expansion, we generate children of an internal node by taking nodes from the **OPEN** list and then put these nodes in the **CLOSED** list as well. In our notation all internal nodes will be found in the list **OPEN**, and all leaf nodes in list **CLOSED**.

Let the set containing training patterns be represented by V. Training patterns must have at least one attribute, and each attribute must have at least two possible values, the number of classes should be $K \geq 1$, and each pattern must belong to exactly one class.

Decision tree building algorithm

begin
    if $(K = 1)$ then create a single node N, label N with the class
        label and exit from procedure;
    else
        begin
            initialize lists OPEN = CLOSED = ϕ;
            $i = 0$;
            create a root node N_i and associate the training set V_i
                with it put N_i in OPEN;
            while OPEN $\in \phi$ **do**
                begin
                    remove the frontmost node N_i from OPEN ;
                    create a candidate set of attributes for N_i, where
                        the attributes have not been checked for splitting
                            at any earlier level (if any);
                    select an attribute A from the candidate set for
                        checking at node N_i;
                    if $(i = 0)$, put node N_i at the back of list CLOSED
                        together with the attribute A being examined at
                            N_i (leaf node);

```
                else
                   put node Ni at the back of list CLOSED
                       together with the attribute A being examined at
                           Ni and the label of the arc from its parent
                              node (non-leaf node);
                if attribute A has n possible values v_0, v_1,
                   ..., v_{n-1} expand Ni to generate its n
                           children N_{i0}, N_{i1}, ..., N_{i(n-1)};
                for j = 0 to n - 1 do
                   begin
                       leaf = FALSE;
                       label the arc from N_i to N_ij with attribute
                           value v_j;
                       associate the set V_ij ⊆ V_i with N_ij
                           such that the value of attribute A for the
                              patterns in V_ij is v_j ;
                           if V_ij = φ, label node N_ij with #
                              indicating a rejection, i.e., unable to classify a
                                 pattern, and set leaf = TRUE;
                           if patterns in set V_ij belong to only one class
                              label node N_ij with the name of the single
                                 class, and set leaf = TRUE;
                           if patterns in set V_ij belong to more than one
                              class and all the attributes have been checked
                                 from the root to N_i label node N_ij with #
                                   indicating a rejection, and set leaf = TRUE;
                           if (leaf = TRUE)
                              put node N_ij at the back of list CLOSED
                                 together with the label of the arc from N_i to
                                   N_ij (leaf node);
                           else
                              put node N_ij at the back of list OPEN
                                 together with the label of the arc from N_i to
                                 N_ij (non-leaf node);
                   end
            end
       end
end
```

The basic algorithm learns the decision trees by constructing them in a top-down fashion, starting with the question *which attribute should be tested at the root node?* To answer this question, each attribute is evaluated using a statistical test to determine how well alone classifies the training examples. The best attribute is selected and used as the test attribute at the root node of the tree. A descendant of the root node is then created for each possible value of the attribute, and the training patterns are allocated (stored) at the appropriate descendant nodes. The entire process is then repeated using the training patterns associated with each descendant node to select the best attribute to test at that point in the tree. The overall process is essentially a greedy technique to construct an acceptable decision tree and there is no chance to backtrack along the arcs to reconsider any earlier choice.

19.2.2 Recursive Learning Algorithm

There exists a number of different implementations of the decision tree learning algorithm. But all of them maintain a basic framework. A recursive routine, that generalizes the common framework, is given below. In this framework, a *main* routine invokes the initial call to the *decision_tree* procedure which then proceeds recursively. The input to main procedure is the training data set D, and the output is a Decision Tree DT. For the *decision_tree* procedure, during each call, a sub-tree T is produced.

Recursive decision tree learning algorithm

procedure *decision_tree*(D, N)

begin
    $T = \{N\}$
    determine the splitting attribute(s) for node N
    consider N to be the root node and label it with the splitting attribute(s)
    generate child nodes for each split predicate and assign labels for arcs
    for each child node N_i **do**
    begin
        create a subset D_i of the training set D using split predicate
        if N_i is a leaf node, label it with appropriate class
        else call procedure *decision_tree*(D_i, N_i)
        return the subtree T produced above
    end
end

procedure *main*()

begin
    $D \leftarrow$ training data set
    $DT = \{\Phi\}$
    generate a node N
    call procedure *decision_tree*(D, N)
    $DT = DT \bigcup T$
end

In the above decision tree algorithm, we have used some of the attributes of the training patterns as *splitting attributes* around which divisions of the training data space are performed. The predicates by which the arcs of the tree are labelled are termed as *splitting predicates*. The recursive algorithm presented here builds the decision tree in a *top-down* fashion. The quality of a decision tree mainly depends on the selection criteria of the splitting attributes at different levels. This criteria differentiate among the family of decision tree learning algorithms. Also, these algorithms, generally, differ in choosing a *stopping criteria*. One simple but sound criteria for stopping is to stop when all the samples in the reduced training set belongs to the same class. This class may then be assigned to label the leaf node created.

19.3 Performance of Decision Tree Learning

Some of the major performance criteria of a decision tree algorithm are briefly described below:

Selecting splitting attributes: It is necessary to determine the importance of different attributes of the training set for optimizing the performance of the decision tree algorithm. Any arbitrary selection may yield a very bad performance.

Ordering splitting attributes: After finding out splitting attributes, they need to be sorted according to decreasing order of merit or importance. It is essential that the most important attribute is used for splitting at the root node, and the next in the rank for the immediate descendants of the root, and so on.

Number of splits: It is found that for some attributes the domain is relatively larger than other attributes. If we use such attribute for splitting at top level nodes, the number of splits (subtrees) will also be larger.

Stopping criteria: The decision tree building and learning processes are simultaneous. Therefore, when learning all the training patterns (labelling them) is complete, the tree formation process must also be completed. It is possible to stop the tree formation process at any level of the decision tree. This will enable us to stop the learning process at any desired level of classification accuracy also.

Size of training set: The decision tree learning process is significantly affected if the training data set size is very small. On the other hand, a huge training set may introduce over fitting of the tree.

In view of the above observation, we may follow some protective measures like:

- Maintaining a moderate training data size.
- Maintaining a height balance tree structure with a moderate number of levels.
- Maintaining a provision for heuristically improving the classification accuracy by adding or removing subtrees at the lowest level.

19.4 Determining the Best Splitting Attribute

It is already mentioned that the performance of a decision tree depends, among other reasons, on the proper selection of a sequence of splitting attributes for different levels in the hierarchy. Decision regarding selection of a proper splitting attribute depends on statistical properties of the values in the domain of the attribute under consideration. Hence, we need to apply information theoretical concepts in attribute selection procedure.

19.4.1 Information Content of a Set

The selection process should be guided by the amount of information that can be provided by a splitting attribute. The more the information, the better is the underlying attribute for splitting. The information theoretic approach to quantify information is to measure *entropy*. The *entropy* is defined to be the amount of uncertainty or randomness present in a set of data. Intuitively, for a data subset that perfectly describe a class entropy should be the minimum, i.e. zero. Now, the objective of decision tree classification is to partition the training data set into subsets where elements in a particular subset belong to the same class. In other words, we want to minimize the entropy.

Let there are n different values $v_0, v_1, \ldots, v_{n-1}$ of an attribute with probabilities of occurrences $p_0, p_1, \ldots, p_{n-1}$. We have a generating system which can generate any of these values randomly. Suppose in a database there exists L records. Since L is very large, we can assume that the value v_i occurs $p_i \times L$ number of times.

Here, total information of all the values is

$$I_{\text{total}} = L \sum_{i=0}^{n-1} p_i \log_2 \frac{1}{p_i} \tag{19.1}$$

and the average information or entropy per record is

$$H = H(p_0, p_1, \ldots, p_{n-1}) = \frac{I_{\text{total}}}{L} = \sum_{i=0}^{n-1} p_i \log_2 \frac{1}{p_i} \tag{19.2}$$

To show the dependence of H on the probability p_i, we consider a simple case of only two values with probabilities p and $1-p$. In this case

$$H = p \log_2 \frac{1}{p} + (1-p) \log_2 \frac{1}{1-p}$$

The maximum value of H can be obtained by setting $\frac{dH}{dp}$ to zero. This maximum occurs at $p = \frac{1}{2}$, i.e. when the two values are equally likely. The corresponding H is

$$H_{\max} = \frac{1}{2}\log_2 2 + \frac{1}{2}\log_2 2 = \log_2 2 = 1 \ \text{ bit/value}$$

When there are n values, it may likewise be proved that H becomes a maximum when all the values are equally likely, i.e. have equal probability $p_i = \frac{1}{n}$ for $i = 0, 1, \ldots, (n-1)$. That is,

$$H_{\max} = \sum \frac{1}{n}\log_2 n = \log_2 n \tag{19.3}$$

From information theory, if the symbols or values are distinct, then the average number of bits needed to encode them is always bounded by their entropy. In practice, the entropy of a source is in general unknown, and the estimates for the entropy depend on the probability model we adopt for the structure of the symbols.

Example 1: Let us consider generation of binary digits. In a sequence 14 binary digits are generated of which there are 9(nine) 1's and 5(five) 0's. Find out the entropy of the sequence.

Solution: In the sequence, there are two classes of values, 1's and 0's. probabilities of occurrences of these two classes are $p = \frac{9}{14}$ and $1 - p = \frac{5}{14}$, respectively. The entropy related to classification becomes

$$H = p\log_2\frac{1}{p} + (1-p)\log_2\frac{1}{1-p} = 0.940$$

Note that, the entropy would be zero if all the digits belong to the same class. In that case, $p = 1$ and $(1-p) = 0$ (say). And therefore, the entropy becomes

$$H = -p\log_2 p - (1-p)\log_2(1-p) = 0$$

The above is true for any number of attribute values also.

♣

19.4.2 Information Gain

Information Gain (IG) is defined as the reduction in entropy due to partitioning using the splitting attribute. For a training set D and splitting attribute A, the information gain $IG(D, A)$ can be expressed as

$$IG(D, A) = H(D) - \sum_{i=0}^{k-1} p(D_i)H(D_i) \tag{19.4}$$

where, k is the number of subsets, $p(D_i)$ is the probability of subset D_i and $H(D_i)$ is its entropy. In the above expression, the probability $p(D_i)$ can be computed as

$$p(D_i) = \frac{\text{Number of elements in} D_i}{\text{Number of elements in} D} = \frac{|D_i|}{|D|} \tag{19.5}$$

In Eq. (19.4), the first term on the RHS is the entropy of the set D, and the second term is the expected value of the entropy after D is partitioned into k subsets by the splitting attribute A.

We can define *Information Gain*(IG), *Information Content*(IC) and *Information Gain Ratio*(IGR) of a split as

$$IG\left(D, \{D_0, D_1, \ldots, D_{k-1}\}\right) = Entropy(\{D\}) - Entropy\left(\{D_0, D_1, \ldots, D_{k-1}\}\right) \quad (19.6)$$

and

$$IC(D, \{D_0, D_1, \ldots, D_{k-1}\}) = \sum_{i=0}^{k-1} \frac{|D_i|}{|D|} \log_2 \frac{|D_i|}{|D|} \quad (19.7)$$

Therefore,

$$\begin{aligned} IGR(D, \{D_0, D_1, \ldots, D_{k-1}\}) &= \frac{IG\left(D, \{D_0, D_1, \ldots, D_{k-1}\}\right)}{IC\left(D, \{D_0, D_1, \ldots, D_{k-1}\}\right)} \\ &= \frac{IG\left(D, \{D_0, D_1, \ldots, D_{k-1}\}\right)}{H\left(\frac{|D_1|}{|D|}, \frac{|D_2|}{|D|}, \ldots, \frac{|D_{k-1}|}{|D|}\right)} \end{aligned}$$

The best split for an attribute is the one that gives the maximum information gain ratio.

Example 2: Consider a training data set containing records of persons with their gender and annual income.

Name	*Gender*	*Income*	*I-Status*
Kousik	Male	6.0 m	Rich
Shyama	Female	2.1 m	Poor
Soma	Female	1.9 m	Poor
Sourav	Male	4.8 m	Rich
Rathin	Male	5.6 m	Rich
Anup	Male	2.2 m	Poor
Tanmoy	Male	2.1 m	Poor
Manas	Male	1.5 m	Poor
Gopa	Female	6.8 m	Rich
Manju	Female	2.5 m	Poor

Calculate the gain ratio for splitting the complete training set considering gender as the first splitting attribute.

Solution: This training set has two classes male and female according to gender. Therefore, entropy of the training set is

$$H = \frac{4}{10} \log_2 \left(\frac{10}{4}\right) + \frac{6}{10} \log_2 \left(\frac{10}{6}\right) = 0.9710$$

Considering gender as the splitting attribute, there are three rich and three poor among males, and one rich and three poor among females. Therefore, entropy of the subsets separately after the split are

$$H_m = \frac{3}{6}\log_2\left(\frac{6}{3}\right) + \frac{3}{6}\log_2\left(\frac{6}{3}\right) = 1.0000$$

and

$$H_f = \frac{1}{4}\log_2\left(\frac{4}{1}\right) + \frac{3}{4}\log_2\left(\frac{4}{3}\right) = 0.8113$$

Weighted sum of the entropies is

$$H' = \frac{6}{10} \times H_m + \frac{4}{10} \times H_f = 0.6 \times 1.0 + 0.4 \times 0.8113 = 0.3245$$

The information gain by using the Gender attribute is

$$IG = H - H' = 0.9710 - 0.3245 = 0.5465$$

Now, to calculate the gain ratio for split using Gender, we find the entropy associated with the split ignoring classes as,

$$H\left(\frac{4}{10}, \frac{6}{10}\right) = \frac{4}{10}\log_2\left(\frac{10}{4}\right) + \frac{6}{10}\log_2\left(\frac{10}{6}\right) = 0.9710$$

Therefore,

$$\text{Gain ratio} = \frac{IG}{H\left(\frac{4}{10}, \frac{6}{10}\right)} = \frac{0.5465}{0.9710} = 0.5628.$$

♣

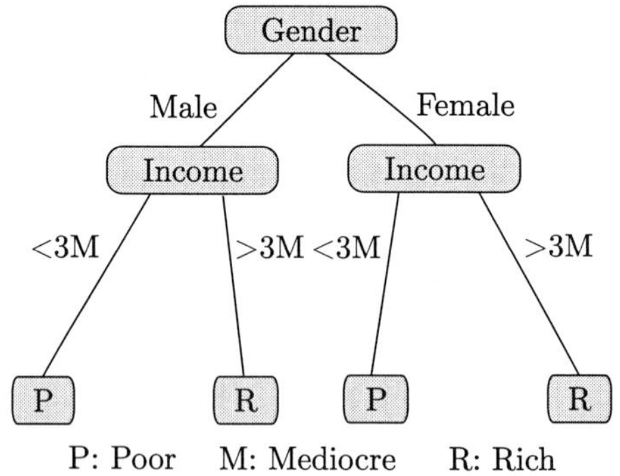

Figure 19.2: Decision tree for Example 2.

Example 3: Let us consider our earlier example of generation of binary attribute values. If the attribute represents the day temperature and if we decide that a 1 means a hot day and a 0 means a cold day, then within a period of 2 weeks (14 days) we observed 9 hot days and 5 cold days. Let another attribute is rainfall and out of the 14 days of observation 7 are rainy days and 7 are dry days, such that depending on temperature attribute we have the following classifications: {5 rainy days, 4 dry days} and {2 rainy days, 3 dry days}. And based on rainfall, we have {6 hot days, 1 cold days} and {3 hot days, 4 cold days}. Find out the better splitting attribute to maximize gain.

Solution: Here, D can be split into D_1 and D_2 in two different ways depending on the attribute selected. When *temperature* is the splitting attribute, we get

$$D_{\text{hot}} = \{5 \text{ rainy days}, 4 \text{ dry days}\} \text{ and } D_{\text{cold}} = \{2 \text{ rainy days}, 3 \text{ dry days}\}$$

and

$$\begin{aligned} IG(D, \text{temperature}) &= H(D) + \frac{9}{14} \times \left(\frac{5}{9}\log_2\frac{5}{9} + \frac{4}{9}\log_2\frac{4}{9}\right) + \frac{5}{14} \times \left(\frac{3}{5}\log_2\frac{3}{5} + \frac{2}{5}\log_2\frac{2}{5}\right) \\ &= -\frac{9}{14}\log_2\frac{9}{14} - \frac{5}{14}\log_2\frac{5}{14} - \frac{9}{14} \times \left(\frac{5}{9}\log_2\frac{5}{9} - \frac{4}{9}\log_2\frac{4}{9}\right) \\ &\quad - \frac{5}{14} \times \left(\frac{3}{5}\log_2\frac{3}{5} - \frac{2}{5}\log_2\frac{2}{5}\right) \\ &= 1.9242 \end{aligned}$$

And when *rainfall* is the splitting attribute, we get

$$D_{\text{rainy}} = \{6 \text{ hot days}, 1 \text{ cold days}\} \text{ and } D_{\text{dry}} = \{3 \text{ hot days}, 4 \text{ cold days}\}$$

and

$$\begin{aligned} IG(D, \text{rain}) &= H(D) - \frac{7}{14} \times \left(\frac{6}{7}\log_2\frac{6}{7} - \frac{1}{7}\log_2\frac{1}{7}\right) - \frac{7}{14} \times \left(\frac{3}{7}\log_2\frac{3}{7} - \frac{4}{7}\log_2\frac{4}{5}\right) \\ &= -\frac{7}{14}\log_2\frac{7}{14} - \frac{7}{14}\log_2\frac{7}{14} - \frac{7}{14} \times \left(\frac{6}{7}\log_2\frac{6}{7} - \frac{1}{7}\log_2\frac{1}{7}\right) \\ &\quad - \frac{7}{14} \times \left(\frac{3}{7}\log_2\frac{3}{7} - \frac{4}{7}\log_2\frac{4}{5}\right) \\ &= 1.7885 \end{aligned}$$

Therefore, it is observed that using *temperature* as the splitting attribute will yield higher information gain than that when *rainfall* is used as the splitting attribute.

♣

19.5 Some Common Decision Tree Algorithms

In the above sections we have discussed the general process of formation of a decision tree and studied some of its basic properties. There exists some well known and powerful decision tree learning algorithms in literature. Two of these algorithms are ID3 and C4.5. In the following subsections we shall try to briefly sketch these two algorithms.

19.5.1 The ID3 Decision Tree Algorithm

The ID3 algorithm builds a decision tree based on the largest information gain. A training data set $D = \{\mathbf{x}_1, \mathbf{x}_2, \ldots, \mathbf{x}_n\}$ is already classified based on feature values. At each node of the tree ID3 chooses an attribute that most effectively splits the attribute values yielding the maximum gain. The other attributes are then treated in a similar and recursive manner. The basic steps of the ID3 are, therefore, as follows:

1. Select an attribute for the root node to ensure the maximum information gain.
2. Create branches for subranges of attribute values.
3. Split attribute values according to branches.
4. Recurse the overall process for other attributes considering each branch as a root.

After completion of the process, each leaf node will represent patterns of a single class only, i.e. no more splitting attributes are available for splitting a node that has objects of more than one class.

19.5.2 The C4.5 Decision Tree Algorithm

The C4.5 algorithm builds a decision tree from the training data based on the largest information gain ratio. A training data set $D = \{\mathbf{x}_1, \mathbf{x}_2, \ldots, \mathbf{x}_n\}$ is already classified based on feature values. At each node of the tree C4.5 chooses an attribute that most effectively splits the attribute values yielding the maximum gain ratio. The other attributes are then treated in a similar and recursive manner. The basic steps of the C4.5 are, therefore, as follows:

1. Select an attribute for the root node to ensure maximum gain ratio.
2. Create branches for subranges of attribute values.
3. Split attribute values according to branches.
4. Recurse the overall process for other attributes considering each branch as a root.

After completion of the process, each leaf node will represent patterns of a single class only, i.e. no more splitting attributes are available for splitting a node that has objects of more than one class.

19.6 Problems

1. What do you mean by a decision tree? Explain its importance in pattern classification.
2. Explain the selection and ordering of splitting attributes in a decision tree.
3. How can you measure the information gain from a decision tree.
4. Consider the training set as given in the following chart

Name	*Gender*	*Height*	*Class*
Kousik	Male	1.6 m	Short
Shyama	Female	2.0 m	Tall
Soma	Female	1.9 m	Medium
Sourav	Male	1.8 m	Medium
Rathin	Male	1.6 m	Short
Anup	Male	2.2 m	Tall
Tanmoy	Male	2.1 m	Tall
Manas	Male	1.5 m	Short
Gopa	Female	1.8 m	Medium
Manju	Female	1.5 m	Short

   Calculate the entropy of the complete training set without considering gender.
5. For the above problem, calculate the entropies of male and female subsets. What will be the gain in information if gender is used as the first splitting attribute? Hence, compute the gain ratio.
6. For the above problem, what will be the gain ratio if height is used as the first splitting attribute.

Chapter 20

Recognition and Artificial Neural Networks

Artificial Neural Networks (ANN) are a kind of soft computing tools that help us recognizing patterns besides allowing us to accomplish a lot of other tasks. The essential idea of learning by an ANN is borrowed from the neural learning system of human being. The recognition capability of human being is due to the potential of nerve cells to store and propagate information. Keen observations over the biological neuro system enables us with the insight of the learning process. This knowledge has been applied in the design of ANN that work in a manner similar to the biological system. It is not that the ANN must resemble the above said biological system, but the major learning steps can be reliably imitated.

In this chapter, we shall describe the formation of different types of neural networks, their working principles and also the logic behind applying them in different real life situations.

20.1 Human Recognition System

The recognition capability of human being was not with him from the very time of birth. A new born baby learns how to recognize its mother, father and other objects or patterns surrounding him. The very basic step of learning is attaining the ability to make a difference. This ability is attained by psycho-physiological processes that make a copy of each pattern received via physical stimulus into brain memory cells. As more and more patterns are perceived by a child, initially it tries to identify all of them as separate entities. But from experience it comes to know that some of the objects are of a certain category and some others are of different category and so on. Then it tries to categorize them into classes and refines the recognition process by storing a replica of each category in its brain memory cells. This process is called **learning**. When we perceive a pattern, we try to make an inference by associating this perception with some concept that has been developed in memory from past experiences. So, human recognition system tries to associate each input pattern to a set of statistical population whose nature depends on past experience. Thus, the problem of pattern ecognition may be regarded as the process of discriminating the input data or pattern nong populations, a process made possible by search of common features among the embers of a population.

Let us now briefly look at the human neuro-physiological aspects of recognition. 1 human neural system, a major component is a typical nerve cell or neuron. Neuron as a cell body called **soma**, and a number of irregularly shaped filaments called **dendrites**, and one relatively thick elongated object called **axon**. A membrane separates ne intracellular plasma from the interstitial fluid external to the cell. The cell is able) maintain a potential difference between these two kinds of liquids separated by the nembrane. The electrical charge that cause the potential difference comes from the ansmission of some ionic species through the membrane. Specifically, this process ivolves the transmission of sodium ions out of the cell and potassium ions into the ell. Of course, there exist other inorganic (basically chloride ions) and organic ions lso.

The axon, attached to each neuron, is covered by a mylene sheath at certain itervals of its body. The gaps are called **nodes of Ranvier**. At the electronic quilibrium there occurs a potential difference across the cell membrane, causing a elatively negative charge inside the body of the cell. Excitatory inputs to the cell educe the potential difference. The resulting depolarization at the axon hillock causes arge sodium ions to enter the cell, contributing further to the polarization.

The transmission of action potential is due to a sequence of depolarizations at the odes of Ranvier. Once the action potential passes through a given point, the point ecomes incapable of being reexited for about 1 millisecond, while it is restored to ts resting potential. This phenomena limits the propagation frequency to about 1000 ulses per second.

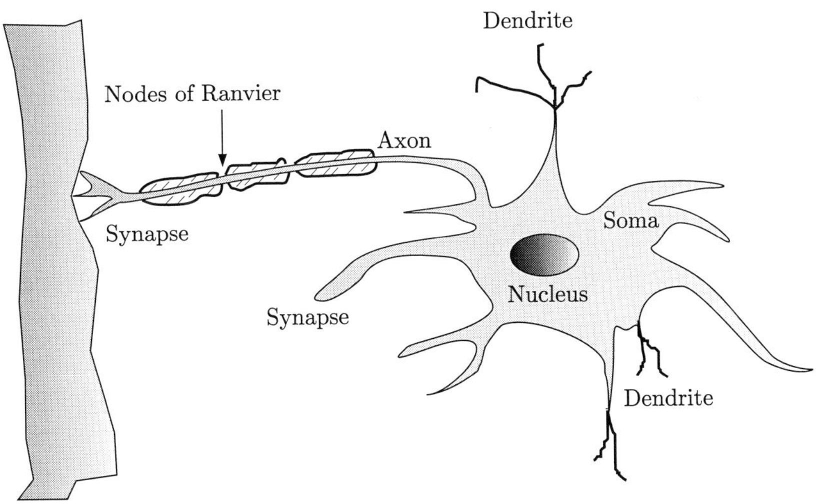

Figure 20.1: Structure of a human neuron cell.

Two neurons are connected at the *synapse* or *synaptic junction*. Synapses may have variable size and areas. A synapse with a higher area possesses higher efficiency in activating other neurons. The presynaptic cell, called the neurotransmitter sends pulses to the postsynaptic cell. After receiving the pulses from the transmitter, the postsynaptic cell becomes activated via depolarization and now acts as the transmitter in a chain of cells. It is to be noted here that, at some receptory positions of a neuron, several presynaptic cells cause activation. When the sum total of all such activations cross some threshold, the receiver becomes activated. In a neuron, dendrites act as input channels, and the axon acts as the output channel. The structure of a neuron is illustrated in Figure 20.1. Information received by sensory organs are transmitted as signals via neurons and stored in brain memory cells for future reference. For different kinds of input patterns (as sensed by the sensory organs), signals of different strengths and types are generated, and different brain memory locations are used for storing information. The complete process of sensing, activation, transmission and storage of signals (information) constitutes what is called **human recognition system**.

20.2 Machine Recognition

The above mechanism of human neuro cells is simulated in a computer based learning system. The discrimination, that is done in human brain memory cells, is tried to be imitated. Of course this does not mean that machines are as much capable of recognizing things as human being are. Each recognition system has its limitations and generally it is applicable to a certain specific domain of patterns. For example, a recognizer that is designed for identification of English characters may not work fine for identification of flowers from their machine representations. In any case, classification of patterns can be considered as a major step in the pattern recognition process. This classification depends on the statistical distribution of patterns in the relevant domain.

For recognition of a pattern by machine we must give the pattern a machine understandable form. This form comes out to be a vector consisting of numerical measures (in general) of the significant features of the entity concerned. Thus it is very crucial to identify the features which will constitute the pattern vectors. Too few or too poorly selected features may not characterize the patterns in question. On the other hand, too many features may unnecessarily complicate the processing involved, and in many cases, may produce undesired results. The extraction of effective features from input data is a very important task and in technical literature this is called **preprocessing of feature vectors** or **reduction of dimensionality**.

20.3 Artificial Neural Networks

The above mentioned activation and propagation of neuronal signals through a chain of neuro cell, is the foundation of McCulloch and Pitts theory (1943) of artificial eurons. From their observations over the human nervous system, they have modelled n artificial neuronal system based upon the following assumptions:

- The activity of a neuron is an all-or-none process.
- A certain fixed number of synapse (> 1) must be excited within a specific period to active a neuron.
- The only significant delay within the nervous system is the synaptic delay.
- The activity of any inhibitory synapse absolutely prevents excitation of the neuron at that time.
- The structure of the interconnection network does not change with time.

rtificial neurons are the basic building blocks of an artificial neural network.

0.3.1 The Basic Neuron

very simple mathematical model of a neuron was first presented by McCulloch and 'itts. In their model, there are n input nodes $I_1, I_2, \ldots, I_n$, and one output node O. he operation of the neuron is as follows:

- An n-vector $\mathbf{x}$ is applied at the input nodes, with one component to each of the input nodes.
- A weight vector $\mathbf{w}$ of size n is randomly generated and applied to the net connectors such that weight vector component w_i is assigned as the connection weight between input node I_i and the output node O.
- A summation unit computes the weighted sum of the input pattern vector and the corresponding weight, $y = \sum_{i=1}^{n} w_i x_i$.
- A predetermined threshold T is stalled at the output node.
- y is thresholded against T. If $y \geq T$, output is set to 1, otherwise it is 0.

The summation and thresholding operations are done in between input and output. The input nodes only receive external inputs, and hence, their role is trivial. In neural network terminology, the output nodes are assumed to perform the summation and hresholding operations. Hence, the output nodes are the actual **nodes** in neural networks. A single node, therefore, have n inputs and one output.

Weights may be positive or negative. Inputs with positive weights are called **excitatory** and those with negative weights are called **inhibitory**.

Functionally, a node can be described by the following relations.

Net weighted input or **activation** to a node is

$$y = w_1 x_1 + w_2 x_2 + \cdots + w_n x_n = \mathbf{w}^T \mathbf{x} \tag{20.1}$$

In the above equation, **w** and **x** are *weight vector* and *input vector* respectively. Let us now define a threshold function $\mathcal{F}$ and a threshold value T, such that output of the concerned node becomes

$$o = \mathcal{F}(y) = \begin{cases} 1; & \text{if } y \geq T \\ 0; & \text{if } y < T \end{cases} \tag{20.2}$$

For convenience, we can rewrite Eq. (20.2), as

$$o = \mathcal{F}(y - T) = \begin{cases} 1; & \text{if } y \geq T \\ 0; & \text{if } y < T \end{cases} \tag{20.3}$$

Since the threshold plays an important role in many ANN models, we generally include it in the network as the weight of an extra connection with an extra input. This extra input is always set to 1. By adding this extra input, we actually get an augmented network. Now, by letting $w_0 = -T$ and $x_0 = 1$, we can have an augmentation of Eq. (20.1) as

$$y' = w_0x_0 + w_1x_1 + w_2x_2 + \cdots + w_nx_n \tag{20.4}$$

and this will further simplify Eq. (20.3) as:

$$o' = \mathcal{F}(y') = \begin{cases} 1; & \text{if } y' \geq 0 \\ 0; & \text{if } y' < 0 \end{cases} \tag{20.5}$$

Here, x_0 is considered to be an extra input, used only for simplifying expressions. The extra input is also called a **bias input** and the corresponding weight w_0 is a **bias weight**. y' and o' correspond to the values of y and o for the augmented network, respectively. Neuron with a bias input is shown in Figure 20.2. Without a bias input it looks like Figure 20.3.

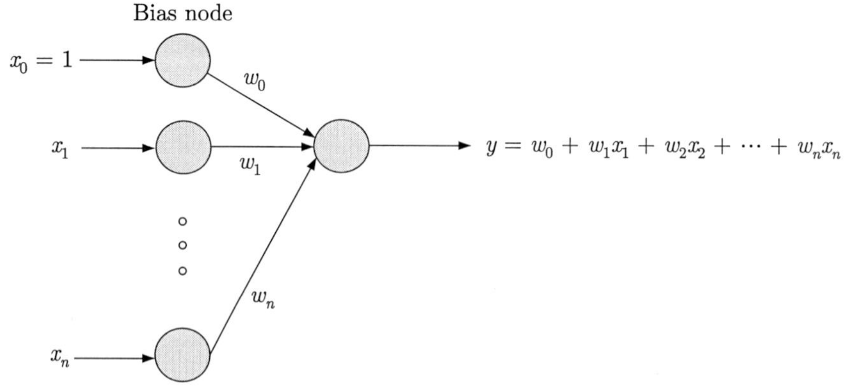

Figure 20.2: Neuron with a bias input.

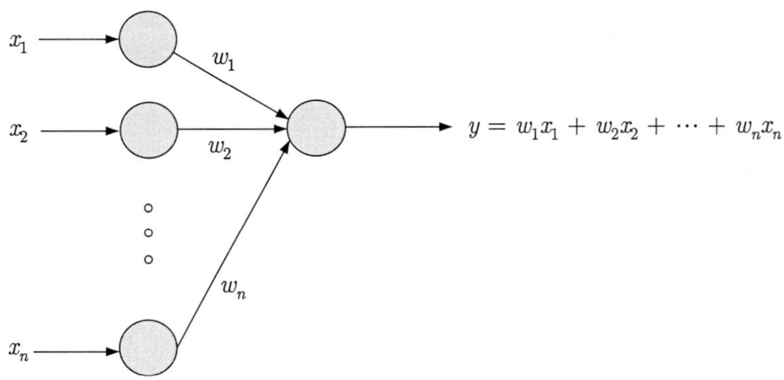

Figure 20.3: Neuron without any bias input.

Neural networks are constituted using one or more neurons. Network with a single node is nothing but a neuron. A number of neurons with separate output nodes but using the same inputs is a general single layer neural network. Figures 20.4(a) and 20.4(b) show single layer single output node and single layer multiple output nodes neural networks respectively. It should be noted here that, for multiple output nodes, the corresponding weight vectors are different, in general. If there are m output nodes $o_1, o_2, \ldots, o_m$, we label the weight between input x_i and output node o_j as w_{ij}. Now, the output values can form an output vector as

$$\mathbf{o} = [o_1 \ o_2 \ \cdots \ o_m]^T$$

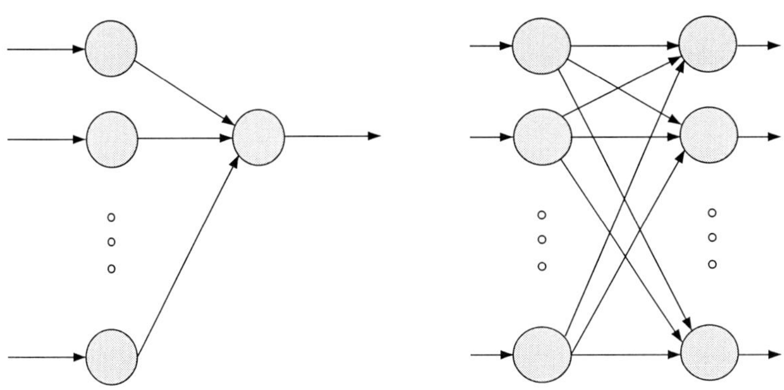

Figure 20.4: Single and multiple output nodes in single layer network.

20.3.2 Activation Functions

Activation plays an important role in ANNs. These functions are called **activation functions** as they decide the amount and nature of activation needed to stimulate the next neuron in sequence or to generate a particular output. Activation functions are also known as *filters*, *transfer functions* or *squash functions* that generate outputs.

Step function: This is a very commonly used activation function. Here, the weighted sum is compared with a fixed threshold value T. The transfer function or activation function is expressed as

$$o = \mathcal{F}(y)$$

If the sum y is greater than T, then output is 1, else it is 0. The above equation, therefore, can also be expressed as

$$o = \mathcal{F}(y - T)$$

Here, the step function F is known as **Heaviside function**, and it can be logically represented as

$$\mathcal{F}(y) = \begin{cases} 1; & \text{if } \ y \geq T \\ 0; & \text{if } \ y < T \end{cases}$$

Figure 20.5(a) illustrates the step function.

Signum function: This is also known as the **quantizer function**, and is defined as

$$\mathcal{F}(y) = \begin{cases} +1; & \text{if } \ y \geq T \\ -1; & \text{if } \ y < T \end{cases}$$

Figure 20.5(b) illustrates the Signum function.

Sigmoid function: This is a continuous function that varies asymptotically between 0 and 1, and is defined as

$$\mathcal{F}(y) = \frac{1}{1 + e^{-\alpha y}}$$

where, α is the slope parameter. These, sigmoidal functions, being continuous, create a spectrum of activation values. Figure 20.5(c) illustrates the Sigmoidal function.

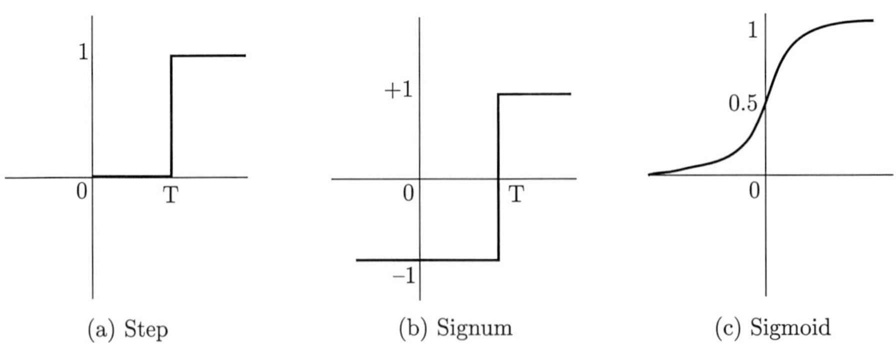

Figure 20.5: Different kinds of activation functions.

20.4 Different Models of ANN

Depending on the arrangements, interconnections and direction and nature of information flow within a network we can categorize an ANN into several major classes. Some of these are introduced here briefly.

20.4.1 Feedforward Network

Let us consider a general form of neuronal arrangements having n inputs and m output nodes. The input and output vectors of this network can, therefore, be described by

$$\mathbf{x} = [x_1 \; x_2 \; \cdots \; x_n] \text{ and } \mathbf{o} = [o_1 \; o_2 \; \cdots \; o_m]^T$$

respectively. As mentioned earlier, w_{ij} is the weight between input x_i and output o_j.

We can compute the activation value for the jth neuron as

$$y_j = \sum_{i=1}^{n} w_{ij} x_i, \quad \text{for} \quad j = 1, 2, \ldots, m$$

The output from the jth neuron is a non-linear function of y_j expressed as

$$o_j = \mathcal{F}\left(\sum_{i=1}^{n} w_{ij} x_i\right) = \mathcal{F}\left(\mathbf{w}_j{}^T \mathbf{x}\right)$$

where weight vector $\mathbf{w}_j$ contains weights leading to the jth output node and is defined as

$$\mathbf{w}_j = [w_{1j} \; w_{2j} \; \cdots \; w_{nj}]^T$$

Outputs of the complete network can be expressed as

$$\mathbf{o} = \mathcal{F}(\mathbf{W}\mathbf{x})$$

where, the *weight matrix* or the *connection matrix* $\mathbf{W}$ is defined as

$$\mathbf{W} = \begin{bmatrix} w_{11} & w_{21} & \cdots & w_{n1} \\ w_{12} & w_{22} & \cdots & w_{n2} \\ \vdots & \vdots & \ddots & \vdots \\ w_{1m} & w_{2m} & \cdots & w_{nm} \end{bmatrix}$$

and the component wise activation function matrix ($\mathcal{F}$) can be expressed as

$$\mathcal{F} = \begin{bmatrix} f(.) & 0 & \cdots & 0 \\ 0 & f(.) & \cdots & 0 \\ \vdots & \vdots & \ddots & \vdots \\ 0 & 0 & \cdots & f(.) \end{bmatrix}$$

Here, individual activation values are scalar products of an input vectors with the corresponding weight vectors.

The basic perceptron is an example of a single layer feedforward network.

During the learning phase, the perceptron is trained for its weight parameters as follows:

$$w_{ij}^{(k+1)} = w_{ij}^{(k)}; \text{ if the actual output matches the desired one}$$

$$w_{ij}^{(k+1)} = w_{ij}^{(k)} \pm \beta x_i; \text{ if the actual output does not match the desired one}$$

where, β is a learning rate related factor. Plus sign is used actual output is 0 and a 1 is desired. In the reverse situation, a minus sign is used. The superscripts indicate iteration numbers.

Schematic diagrams for single layer and multilayer feedforward networks are shown in Figure 20.6.

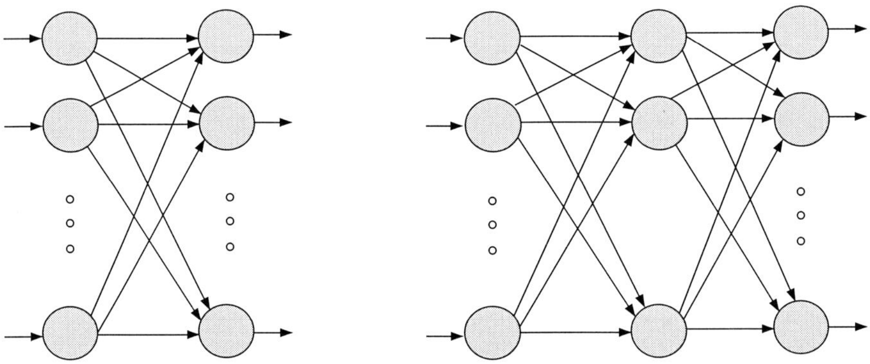

(a) (b)

Figure 20.6: Single and multilayer feedforward network.

20.4.2 Feedback Network

A feedback network is obtained by associating feedback connections from output nodes to input nodes of the network. This type of feedback connection enables us to control temporal outputs. That is, in this case, outputs are time dependent and the present output $\mathbf{o}(t)$ controls or determines the next output $\mathbf{o}(t + \Delta t)$. The time difference Δt is introduced by using suitable delay elements in the feedback path. Therefore, in case of feedback networks the input-output relationship can be expressed as

$$\mathbf{o}(t + \Delta t) = \mathcal{F}(\mathbf{W} \cdot \mathbf{o}(t))$$

20.5 Neural Learning

Neural networks process information by *learning*. A set of training patterns (input patterns) are fed at the input nodes and responses are received at output nodes. Computation of response of the network for a given input pattern is called **recall**. Depending on these responses, a decision is generated regarding the characteristics of an input pattern. When characteristics of all input patterns are determined, the network is said to be *learned*. For neural learning, it is very important that the input training set is complete in all respects.

Whenever a new and unknown input is presented at the input nodes of a learned network, it may associate the new pattern to an already stored similar pattern in the training set. This process is called **autoassociation**. An input pattern may also be associated to one in the training set having different characteristics. This process is called **heteroassociation**.

Due to their learning capability ANNs are the most suitable machines for the task of *classification*. If we store only labelled patterns in the training set, the network can learn about the class characteristics. Hence, after training, they can be employed for classifying unknown patterns of similar types. Basically, classification may be assumed to be a special case of heteroassociation.

In case of non-presence of an exact match in the training set, a different pattern with the nearest match (within a predefined tolerance) with the unknown input may be associated with it. This process is called **recognition**. When the class membership of a pattern in the training set is recalled, recognition becomes identical to classification.

The process of learning is an essential requirement for proper operation of a neural network. Learning can be of two types: *supervised* and *unsupervised*. When the set of training patterns input to a network is complete in all sense, the network can learn in supervised learning mode. In this case, a desired output $\mathbf{d}$, for each training pattern, is provided externally. The difference (error) between $\mathbf{d}$ and the actual output $\mathbf{o}$ is measured and is used to modify the network parameters (weights). A reward-and-punishment scheme is generally used for this purpose. Accurate and inaccurate responses lead to reward and punishment, respectively during modifying weight parameters of the network.

In case of unsupervised learning, a desired output is not available. Therefore, we cannot compute any explicit error for modifying the network parameters. In such a situation, a suitable mechanism for making a decision need to be incorporated in the network. For example, in case of unsupervised classification, a pattern is classified depending on its proximity to a cluster centre already established or assumed.

A third category of learning mechanism, called **reinforced learning** is also used. Here, although a desired output is not available, some information indicating the correctness of the computed output is provided. Based on this information, a reward and punishment system is established within the learning process.

20.6 Perceptron and Learning

Rosenblatt (1962) developed a McCulloch–Pitts neuron based classifier which he called a **perceptron**. A perceptron is a trainable classifier, that one needs to train it with some sample training patterns. More specifically speaking, the perceptron acts as a two class classifier when previously trained with sufficient number of suitable training patterns. This training part is the most time consuming and difficult task for a neural network. And the most advantageous feature of it is that nodes in a layer can operate simultaneously enabling us with a very high degree of parallelism. This parallel execution can be realized only in a true hardware implementation of the underlying neural network.

20.6.1 The Minimum Squared Error Criterion

During training of a perceptron, we want to establish a fixed trained set of weight values by satisfying the minimum squared error criterion. Here, error is the difference between the values of the actual output and the desired output.

We initialize the weights $w_1, w_2, \ldots, w_n$ with arbitrary random values. Then training patterns are fed to the perceptron inputs one by one. The weighted sum is computed and compared with the desired output. The difference between the actual output (y) and the desired output (d) is the error (e) of classification. Our objective is to minimize this error for all possible inputs. This is achieved by updating the weight values during the training phase. Weights can be updated after applying each training pattern, or after applying all the training patterns in one particular iteration. These two updation policies are termed as *onlineupdation* and *epochupdation*, respectively.

Error, as defined above can be written as

$$e = (y - d)^2 \tag{20.6}$$

and,

$$y = w_0x_0 + w_1x_1 + w_2x_2 + \cdots + w_nx_n = \sum_{i=0}^{n} w_ix_i \tag{20.7}$$

Taking partial differentiation of e with respect to w_i, we get

$$\frac{\delta e}{\delta w_i} = (y - d)x_i \tag{20.8}$$

We want to minimize error e. Therefore, weight values are updated according to the following relation:

$$\Delta w_i \leftarrow \beta(y - d)x_i \tag{20.9}$$

and

$$w_i \leftarrow w_i - \Delta w_i \tag{20.10}$$

Here, β is a learning rate factor whose values are kept between 0 and 1.

Perceptron learning algorithm

begin
    for $i \leftarrow 0$ **to** $n-1$ **do**
        initialize weight w_i
    repeat
    for $p \leftarrow 0$ **to** $N-1$ **do**
        begin
            input pattern $\mathbf{x}_p$ along with desired output d_p
            calculate actual output $y_p = \sum_{i=0}^{n} w_i x_{pi}$
            for $i \leftarrow 0$ **to** $n-1$ **do**
                update weight as $w_i \leftarrow w_i - \beta(y_p - d_p)x_{pi}$
        end
    until weights are stable
end

20.6.2 Perceptron and Linearly Separable Tasks

The simple perceptron is able to solve a classification problem when the patterns are linearly separable. Linearly separable patterns on a 2D plane can be separated by a straight line. For multidimensional space we can use a hyperplane to separate such patterns. Linearly and non-linearly separable patters are shown in Figures 20.7(a) and (b), respectively. The above concept is further illustrated by solving simple binary problems in the following subsections.

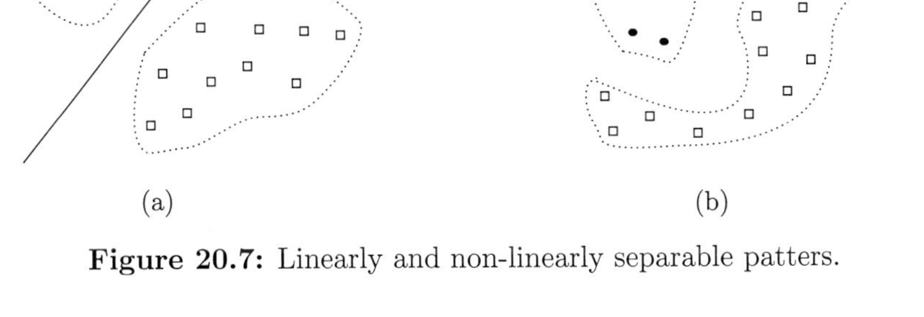

(a) (b)

Figure 20.7: Linearly and non-linearly separable patters.

20.6.3 Modelling AND Gate

The simple perceptron can be used to model an AND gate. Here, we apply known input-output combinations to the perceptron during the training phase and thereby adjust the weight vectors. After training, the perceptron will be able to function as an AND gate. This process of establishing the required weight vector values is called **training** of the perceptron.

Here, the output may be any of the two classes: TRUE or FALSE. If an input combination satisfies logical AND, the corresponding output will be TRUE, otherwise it will be FALSE. Let us consider only two inputs x_1 and x_2. With these two inputs four input patterns are possible (Figure 20.8). The input-output combinations and corresponding classes are shown in Table 20.1. Considering weights w_1 and w_2, the input to the perceptron is $w_1x_1 + w_2x_2$. Our objective is to compute the values of w_1 and w_2 so that the truth table of AND gate is satisfied by the input combination. We start with arbitrarily random values of w_1 and w_2. When, during the learning process, the weights become stable with actual outputs matching the desired outputs, we say that the perceptron is learned or trained.

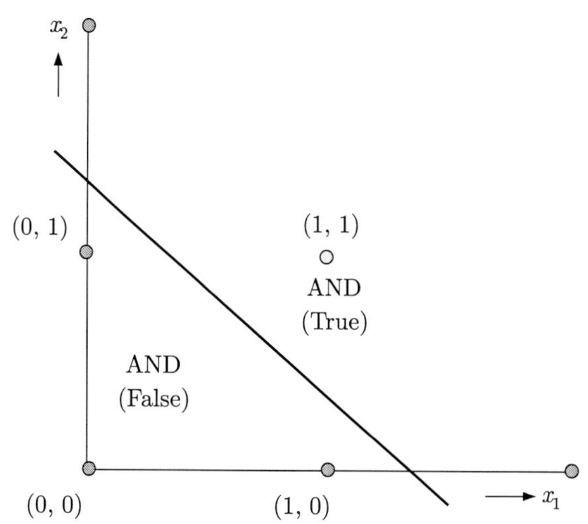

Figure 20.8: Representing AND gate model in $x_1 - x_2$ space.

For applying the perceptron to model the AND gate we apply the perceptron learning algorithm described earlier. The output o for a recall pattern may be defined as follows:

$$o = \begin{cases} 0 & \text{if } w_1x_1 + w_2x_2 < 0.75 \\ 1 & \text{otherwise} \end{cases}$$

Here, the threshold value is considered as $T = 0.75$. However, we might use other values as well. In Table 20.2, we have shown the stepwise execution of the training

Table 20.1: Applying Perceptron to Model AND Gate

Training Pattern	*Attributes* x_1	x_2	*Class*	*Desired Output*
1	1	1	TRUE	1
2	0	1	FALSE	0
3	1	0	FALSE	0
4	0	0	FALSE	0

phase for the AND gate implementation problem. In this table, o and d denote the observed and desired outputs, respectively. Let the learning rate be $\beta = 0.2$.

Table 20.2: Training of Perceptron to Model AND Gate

Iteration	x_1	x_2	*Weights* w_1	w_2	$\sum_i w_i x_i$	o	d	Δw_1	Δw_2
1	1	1	0.2	0.3	0.5	0	1	0.2	0.2
	0	1	0.4	0.5	0.5	0	0	0.0	0.0
	1	0	0.4	0.5	0.4	0	0	0.0	0.0
	0	0	0.4	0.5	0.0	0	0	0.0	0.0
2	1	1	0.4	0.5	0.9	1	1	0.0	0.0
	0	1	0.4	0.5	0.5	0	0	0.0	0.0
	1	0	0.4	0.5	0.4	0	0	0.0	0.0
	0	0	0.4	0.5	0.0	0	0	0.0	0.0

20.6.4 Modelling OR Gate

In a similar manner that is used for the AND gate above, the simple perceptron can be used to model an OR gate also. As before, we apply known input-output combinations to the perceptron during the training phase and thereby adjust the weight vectors. After training, the perceptron will be able to function as an OR gate. This process of establishing the required weight vector values is called **training** of the perceptron.

Here, the output may be any of the two classes: TRUE or FALSE. If an input combination satisfies logical OR, the corresponding output will be TRUE, otherwise it will be FALSE. Let us consider only two inputs x_1 and x_2. With these two inputs four input patterns are possible (Figure 20.9). The input-output combinations and corresponding classes are shown in Table 20.3. Considering weights w_1 and w_2, the input to the perceptron is $w_1x_1 + w_2x_2$. Our objective is to compute the values of w_1 and w_2 so that the truth table of OR gate is satisfied by the input combination. We start with arbitrarily random values of w_1 and w_2. When, during the learning process, the weights become stable with actual outputs matching the desired outputs, we say that the perceptron is learned or trained.

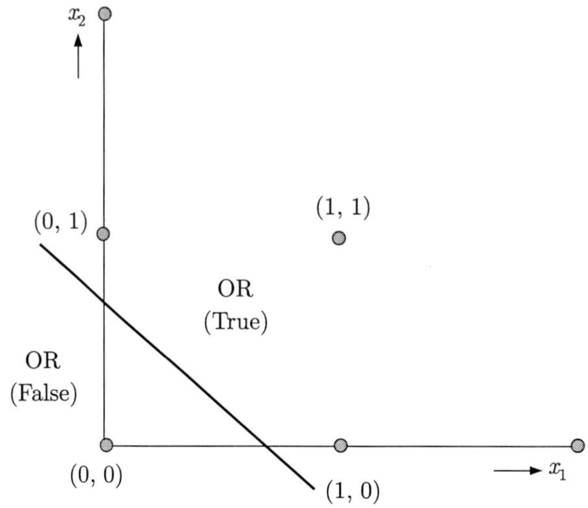

Figure 20.9: Representing OR gate model in $x_1 - x_2$ space.

Table 20.3: Applying Perceptron to Model OR Gate

Training Pattern	*Attributes*		*Class*	*Desired Output*
	x_1	x_2		
1	1	1	TRUE	1
2	0	1	TRUE	1
3	1	0	TRUE	1
4	0	0	FALSE	0

For applying the perceptron to model the OR gate we apply the perceptron learning algorithm described earlier. The output o for a recall pattern may be defined as follows:

$$o = \begin{cases} 0 & \text{if } w_1x_1 + w_2x_2 < 0.6 \\ 1 & \text{otherwise} \end{cases}$$

Here, the threshold is $T = 0.6$ and learning rate $\beta = 0.2$, respectively. However, we might use other values as well. In Table 20.4, we have shown the stepwise execution of the training phase for the OR gate implementation problem. In this table, o and d denote the observed and desired outputs, respectively.

20.6.5 Problems in Modelling XOR Gate

In the earlier subsections, we have seen how AND and OR gates can be modelled using simple perceptrons. Since the outputs of either AND or OR gates forms linearly separable classes only, we could use a simple perceptron for these purposes. The XOR problem, however, is one of the simplest problems that cannot be solved by a

Table 20.4: Training of Perceptron to Model OR Gate

Iteration	x_1	x_2	*Weights*		$\sum_i w_i x_i$	o	d	Δw_1	Δw_2
			w_1	w_2					
1	1	1	0.2	0.3	0.5	0	1	0.2	0.2
	0	1	0.4	0.5	0.5	0	1	0.0	0.2
	1	0	0.4	0.7	0.4	0	1	0.2	0.0
	0	0	0.6	0.7	0.0	0	0	0.0	0.0
2	1	1	0.6	0.7	1.3	1	1	0.0	0.0
	0	1	0.6	0.7	0.7	1	1	0.0	0.0
	1	0	0.6	0.7	0.6	1	1	0.0	0.0
	0	0	0.6	0.7	0.0	0	0	0.0	0.0

simple perceptron. If we plot the XOR inputs in the (x_1, x_2) plane, we see that no straight line can properly classify into proper output classes. This situation is shown in Figure 20.10.

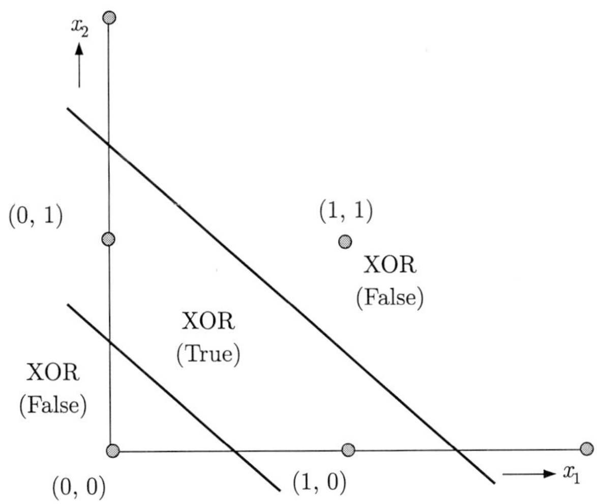

Figure 20.10: Representing XOR gate model in $x_1 - x_2$ space.

The XOR output may be any of the two classes: TRUE or FALSE. If an input combination satisfies logical XOR, the corresponding output will be TRUE, otherwise it will be FALSE. Let us consider only two inputs x_1 and x_2. With these two inputs four input patterns are possible. The input-output combinations and corresponding classes are shown in Table 20.5. From Figure 20.10, it is clear that the XOR inputs cannot be categorized into TRUE and FALSE classes using a single straight line.

If we apply the conventional training for a perceptron then the following situations will arise. Considering weights w_1 and w_2, the input to the perceptron is $w_1x_1 + w_2x_2$.

Table 20.5: Applying Perceptron to Model XOR Gate

Training Pattern	*Attributes* x_1	x_2	*Class*	*Desired Output*
1	1	1	FALSE	0
2	0	1	TRUE	1
3	1	0	TRUE	1
4	0	0	FALSE	0

If the threshold is T, then the perceptron output becomes

$$o = \begin{cases} 0 & \text{if } w_1x_1 + w_2x_2 < T \\ 1 & \text{otherwise} \end{cases}$$

For the first and the fourth input, the value of o should be 0, hence, $y < T$, i.e.

$$w_1x_1 + w_2x_2 < T$$

And for the second and the third input, the value of o should be 1, hence, $y \geq T$, i.e.

$$w_1x_1 + w_2x_2 \geq T$$

Therefore, applying actual input values in above relations, we get the following inequalities.

$$\begin{aligned} w_1 \times 1 + w_2 \times 1 < T \\ w_1 \times 0 + w_2 \times 1 \geq T \\ w_1 \times 1 + w_2 \times 0 \geq T \\ w_1 \times 0 + w_2 \times 0 < T \end{aligned}$$

upon simplification, we arrive at relations

$$\begin{aligned} w_1 + w_2 < T \\ w_1, w_2 \geq T \end{aligned}$$

which are contradictory to each other. Hence, we conclude that XOR cannot be implemented using a perceptron (one neurode).

Actually, the XOR outputs are separable by a pair of *hyperplanes*. If we consider an n-dimensional *hyperspace* then we can assume n one-dimensional hyperplanes; just as we get 2D planes in a 3D space. It should be clear that one or more hyperplanes can suitably partition the corresponding hyperspace into distinct regions. Therefore, we need a non-linear discriminant function for the XOR.

Now, we shall see that how multiple perceptrons can be used to model an XOR gate also. The underlying trick here is to use two layers of neurodes in between the input and output. Incorporation of such a second layer allows the network to solve the XOR problem. Specifically here we need 3 neurodes: two at the input layer and one at the second layer. The underlying network structure is shown in Figure 20.11.

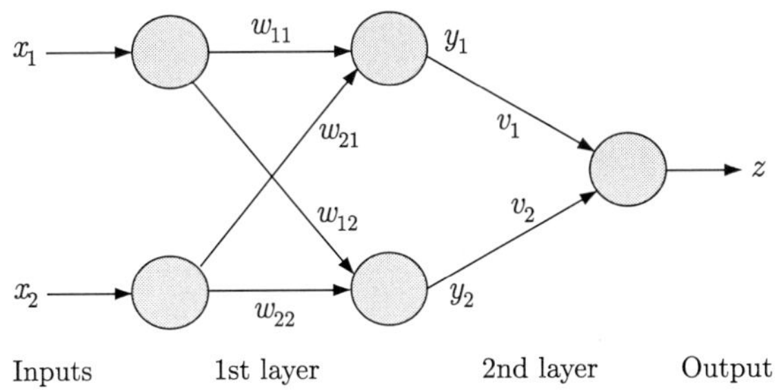

Figure 20.11: Network for modelling XOR gate in $x_1 - x_2$ space.

We apply known input-output combinations to the network during the training phase and thereby adjust the weight vectors at the two layers. When the training is completed, the network becomes able to function as an XOR gate. Here, inputs x_1 and x_2 are applied at the input nodes, their weighted sums are computed at the two neurodes, and thresholded. From knowledge of the input-output relations, let us set the first layer weights as

$$w_{1,1} = 1, w_{1,2} = -1, w_{2,1} = -1 \text{ and } w_{2,2} = 1$$

Therefore, for the first layer we have the following input-output relation

$$\begin{bmatrix} y_1 \\ y_2 \end{bmatrix} = \begin{bmatrix} w_{1,1} & w_{1,2} \\ w_{2,1} & w_{2,2} \end{bmatrix} \times \begin{bmatrix} x_1 \\ x_2 \end{bmatrix}$$

or

$$\begin{bmatrix} y_1 \\ y_2 \end{bmatrix} = \begin{bmatrix} 1 & -1 \\ -1 & 1 \end{bmatrix} \times \begin{bmatrix} x_1 \\ x_2 \end{bmatrix}$$

The outputs from the first layer neurodes enter into the second layer. Hence, for the second layer node, y_1 and y_2 are inputs, and let z denotes the second layer activation and o is the second layer thresholded output. Also, let us denote the second layer weights as v_1 and v_2, respectively. For both the layers we consider a threshold of 0.1. Therefore, the input-output relation for the two layers can be written as

$$o_j = \begin{cases} 0 & \text{if } w_{1j}x_1 + w_{2j}x_2 < 0.1 \\ 1 & \text{otherwise} \end{cases}$$

and

$$o = \begin{cases} 0 & \text{if } v_1y_1 + v_2y_2 < 0.1 \\ 1 & \text{otherwise} \end{cases}$$

In the above relations, we have denoted the thresholded outputs from the first layer by o_1 and o_2, and that from the second layer by o. By using suitable weight vectors and thresholds, we can show that this two layer network can solve the XOR problem. Our example situation is shown in Tables 20.6 and 20.7.

Table 20.6: Execution of the First Layer of a Two Layer XOR Gate

x_1	x_2	w_{11}/w_{22}	w_{12}/w_{21}	y_1	y_2	o_1	o_2
1	1	1	–1	0	0	0	0
0	1	1	–1	–1	1	0	1
1	0	1	–1	1	–1	1	0
0	0	1	–1	0	0	0	0

Table 20.7: Execution of the Second Layer of a Two Layer XOR Gate

o_1	o_2	v_1	v_2	z	o
0	0	1	1	0	0
0	1	1	1	1	1
1	0	1	1	1	1
0	0	1	1	0	0

It may be noted here that using suitable threshold, the XOR simulation shown above is not a general treatment of the concerned problem. Actually, we need to develop a proper technique for training a multilayer network. Also, for different kinds of problems we may need different types of multilayer networks. The underlying theory and problem solving techniques will be discussed in some of the subsequent sections.

Example 1: Let us consider a pattern classification problem. Let the training pattern set contains the labelled patterns given in the Table 20.8. After learning, classify the unknown pattern $p = (0.5 \ \ 0.7)$. Consider a learning factor of 0.1. Initial weights may be assumed as 0.2 and 0.3, respectively. Consider a threshold of 0.6.

Table 20.8: Applying Perceptron to Classify Patterns

Training Pattern	*Attributes*		*Class*
	x_1	x_2	
1	0.1	0.2	0
2	0.2	0.3	0
3	0.6	0.6	1
4	0.8	0.5	1

Solution: After initialization as instructed, the variation of weight parameters during a number of iterations of the perceptron algorithm has been presented in Table 20.9.

Table 20.9: Training of Perceptron to Classify Patterns

Iteration	x_1	x_2	*Weights*		$\sum_i w_i x_i$	o	d	Δw_1	Δw_2
			w_1	w_2					
1	0.1	0.2	0.2	0.3	0.08	0	0	0.0	0.0
	0.2	0.3	0.2	0.3	0.13	0	0	0.0	0.0
	0.6	0.6	0.2	0.3	0.30	0	1	0.06	0.06
	0.8	0.5	0.26	0.36	0.388	0	1	0.08	0.05
2	0.1	0.2	0.34	0.41	0.116	0	0	0.0	0.0
	0.2	0.3	0.34	0.41	0.191	0	0	0.0	0.0
	0.6	0.6	0.34	0.41	0.450	0	1	0.06	0.06
	0.8	0.5	0.40	0.47	0.555	0	1	0.08	0.05
3	0.1	0.2	0.48	0.52	0.152	0	0	0.0	0.0
	0.2	0.3	0.48	0.52	0.252	0	0	0.0	0.0
	0.6	0.6	0.48	0.52	0.60	1	1	0.0	0.0
	0.8	0.5	0.48	0.52	0.644	1	1	0.0	0.0

It is observed that the network has been completely trained after the 3rd iteration (as indicated by non-variation of weights throughout the iteration). The final weight values turned out to be $w_1 = 0.48$ and $w_2 = 0.52$, respectively. For the new (unknown) pattern $p = (0.5\ 0.7)$, the response is

$$y = w_1 x_1 + w_2 x_2 = 0.48 \times 0.5 + 0.52 \times 0.5 = 0.50$$

Therefore, p belongs to category 0.

♣

20.6.6 Limitations of a Perceptron

A simple perceptron is very limited in its capacity. It can classify a set of patterns into two linearly separable classes only. But, in general, many classification problems deal with patterns which are not linearly separable. Let us consider the problems of modelling AND get presented in the earlier subsection. Here, there are two inputs and one output node. The output node activation is, therefore,

$$y = w_1 x_1 + w_2 x_2 \tag{20.11}$$

And the output is

$$o = \begin{cases} 1; & \text{if } w_1 x_1 + w_2 x_2 \geq T \\ 0; & \text{if } w_1 x_1 + w_2 x_2 < T \end{cases} \tag{20.12}$$

Clearly, the threshold value T separates the input patterns by a straight line

$$w_1 x_1 + w_2 x_2 = T \tag{20.13}$$

in the (x_1, x_2) plane.

The two-class restriction can be removed by using multiple output nodes which is described in the following subsection.

20.6.7 The MSE Learning for Multiple Outputs

The learning algorithm given in Section 20.6.1 works only when the output layer contains a single node. With a little modification the MSE learning algorithm may be accommodated for multiple output nodes also. In this case, each input pattern may have different desired outputs $\{d_1, d_2, \ldots, d_m\}$ corresponding m output nodes. Thus, the desired outputs form a vector as $\mathbf{d} = \{d_1, d_2, \ldots, d_m\}$. Similarly, the obtained outputs can be expressed as $\mathbf{o} = \{o_1, o_2, \ldots, o_m\}$. Weight values from input node i to output node j may be represented by w_{ij}. Therefore, the error criterion function becomes

$$e = \sum_{j=1}^{m} (y_j - d_j)^2 \tag{20.14}$$

For the pth input pattern $\mathbf{x}_p$, the error can be computed as

$$e_p = \sum_{j=1}^{m} (y_{pj} - d_{pj})^2 = ||\mathbf{y}_p - \mathbf{d}_p|| \tag{20.15}$$

where, $||.||$ is the squared Euclidean norm.

Now, as in the case of a single output node, each y_j can be evaluated as

$$y_j = w_{0j}x_0 + w_{1j}x_1 + w_{2j}x_2 + \cdots + w_{nj}x_n = \sum_{i=0}^{n} w_{ij}x_i \tag{20.16}$$

In vector notation

$$\mathbf{y} = \mathbf{W}\mathbf{x} \tag{20.17}$$

where,

$$\mathbf{y} = \begin{bmatrix} y_1 \\ y_2 \\ \vdots \\ y_m \end{bmatrix}, \quad \mathbf{W} = \begin{bmatrix} w_{01} & w_{11} & \cdots & w_{n1} \\ w_{02} & w_{12} & \cdots & w_{n2} \\ \vdots & \vdots & \ddots & \vdots \\ w_{0m} & w_{1m} & \cdots & w_{nm} \end{bmatrix} \quad \text{and} \quad \mathbf{x} = \begin{bmatrix} x_0 \\ x_1 \\ \vdots \\ x_n \end{bmatrix}$$

Taking partial differentiation of e with respect to w_{ij} [Eqs. (20.14) and (20.16)], we get

$$\frac{\delta e}{\delta w_{ij}} = (y_j - d_j)x_i \tag{20.18}$$

To minimize error e, weight values are updated according to the following relations

$$\Delta w_{ij} \leftarrow -\beta(y_j - d_j)x_i \tag{20.19}$$

and

$$w_{ij} \leftarrow w_{ij} + \Delta w_{ij} \tag{20.20}$$

MSE learning algorithm for multiple outputs

begin
  for $i \leftarrow 0$ **to** $n-1$ **do**
    for $j \leftarrow 0$ **to** $m-1$ **do**
      initialize weight w_{ij}
  repeat
  for $p \leftarrow 0$ **to** $N-1$ **do**
    begin
      input pattern $\mathbf{x}_p$ along with desired output $\mathbf{d}_p$
      for $i \leftarrow 0$ **to** $n-1$ **do**
        for $j \leftarrow 0$ **to** $m-1$ **do**
          calculate $y_{ij} = \sum_{i=0}^{n} w_{ij} x_{pi}$
      for $i \leftarrow 0$ **to** $n-1$ **do**
          update weight as $w_{ij} \leftarrow w_{ij} - \beta(y_{ij} - d_j)x_{pi}$
    end
  until weights are stable
end

20.7 Multilayer Neural Networks

Single layer networks (perceptrons) are found to be insufficient in many of the situations. They are able to classify patterns into two classes separated by a single hyperplane only. That is, it can determine which of the two half-planes is containing a particular sample pattern. But, there are situations where the underlying classes are not linearly separable. For example, one class boundary may be convex and the other is its complement. Moreover, we may wish to classify patterns into more than two classes. In such situations, we need to use more than one layers of neurons or nodes. The extra layer(s) that lie between the inputs and the output nodes are called **hidden layer(s)**, as they are transparent to the user.

One major problem with the above types of neural network is that it is not very easy to determine the exact number of nodes needed at the hidden layer. This is because the total possible number of feature combinations may be very many. However, the MLPs (Multi Layer Perceptrons) are the most commonly used category of ANNs for pattern classification. This type of networks are also called BPNs (Back Propagation Networks). Basic configuration of an MLP is depicted in Figure 20.12.

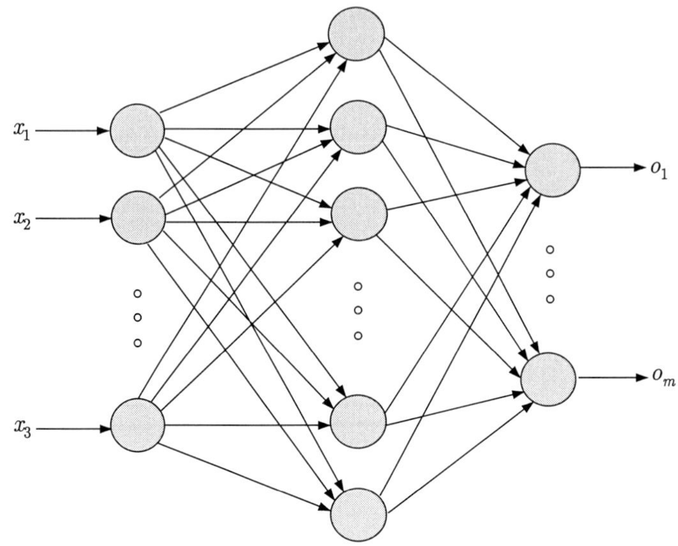

Figure 20.12: Configuration of a Multi Layer Perceptron.

20.7.1 Learning in Multi Layer Perceptrons (MLP)

The MLP network is trained by an algorithm developed by Rumelhart *et al.* (1986), called the **back propagation algorithm**. This training algorithm is an iterative gradient descent algorithm that works by minimizing the Minimum Squared Error (MSE) between the observed output and the desired output. Here, we require a non-linear threshold function. As mentioned earlier threshold may be discrete (step) or continuous (linear). In case of a simple perceptron, we have seen the use of a step function for thresholding. A special case of step thresholding is to use binary threshold, where outputs can be only of two types: one represented by a zero (0) and the other by a one (1). In case of continuous outputs, no thresholding is needed at all. However, in case of multilayer networks the binary **sigmoid function**, is very popular. It is a non-linear S-shaped function having output in range $(0, 1)$ and is given by

$$\mathcal{F}(y) = \frac{1}{1 + e^{-y}} \tag{20.21}$$

where, y is the weighted sum computed at the output node. It is now clear that the thresholded output $\mathcal{F}(y)$ varies from 0 to 1, as y varies from $-\infty$ to $+\infty$, and attains a value of 0.5 at $y = 0$.

In multilayer networks, there exists more than one levels of nodes, and hence, more than one set of weight vectors. Learning in case of multilayer networks is somewhat complicated because of the existence of multiple layers. The algorithm used, in this case, is called the **back propagation algorithm**. The algorithm is outlined below. We have used the following notations for symbols and variables:

- Layers are numbers from $k = 0, 1, \ldots, K$, with $k = 0$ being the input layer and $k = K$ is the output layer.
- The output of a node j at layer k is denoted as $x_j^{(k)}$ for $j = 1, 2, \ldots, n_k$, where, n_k is the number of nodes at layer k, excluding the node with the bias weight.
- For the input layer, inputs and outputs are the same, i.e. $x_j = x_j^{(0)}$ for $j = 1, 2, \ldots, n_0$.
- For $k = 0, 1, \ldots, K-1$ the bias node output is 1 (i.e. $x_0 = 1$). The output layer does not have a bias node.
- Connection weights from node i at layer $k-1$ to node j at layer k is $w_{ij}^{(k)}$.

The MLPs can learn map a set of inputs to a set of outputs. The back propagation learning algorithm for the MLP is given below.

The MLP learning algorithm

begin
  for $k \leftarrow 1$ **to** $K-1$ **do**
    for $i \leftarrow 0$ **to** n_k **do**
      for $j \leftarrow 0$ **to** n_{k+1} **do**
        initialize weight $w_{ij}^{(k)}$
  repeat
  for $t \leftarrow 0$ **to** $N-1$ **do**
    begin
      input pattern $\mathbf{x}_p$ along with desired outputs $\mathbf{d}_p$
      feed forward step:
      for $k \leftarrow 0$ **to** $K-1$ **do**
        for $j \leftarrow 1$ **to** n_{k+1} **do**
          begin
            calculate layer k response $y_j^{(k+1)} = \sum_{i=0}^{n_k} w_{ij}^{(k+1)} x_i^{(k)}$
            calculate layer k output $x_j^{(k+1)} = \mathcal{F}\left(\frac{1}{1+e^{-\left(y_j^{(k+1)}\right)}}\right)$
          end
      feed back step:
      for $j \leftarrow 1$ **to** n_K **do**
          compute error as $\delta_j^{(K)} \leftarrow x_j^{(K)}\left(1 - x_j^{(K)}\right)\left(x_j^{(K)} - d_j\right)$
      for $k \leftarrow K-1$ **down to** 1 **do**
        for $i \leftarrow 1$ **to** n_k **do**
            compute error as $\delta_i^{(k)} \leftarrow x_i^{(k)}\left(1 - x_i^{(k)}\right)\sum_{j=1}^{(n_{k+1})}\left(\delta_j^{(k+1)} w_{ij}^{(k+1)}\right)$
      for $k \leftarrow K$ **down to** 1 **do**
      begin
        for $j \leftarrow 1$ **to** n_k **do**
          begin

for $i \leftarrow 1$ **to** n_{k-1} **do**
update weight as $w_{ij}^{(k)} \leftarrow w_{ij}^{(k)} - \beta\delta_j^{(k)} x_i^{(k-1)}$
end
end
until weights are stable
end

Here, error, for the Kth layers, can be defined as

$$e = \sum_{j=1}^{n_K} \left(x_j^{(K)} - d_j\right)^2 \tag{20.22}$$

Taking partial differentiation of e with respect to $w_{ij}^{(K)}$, we get

$$\frac{\delta e}{\delta w_{ij}^{(K)}} = \left(x_j^{(K)} - d_j\right) \frac{\delta x_j^{(K)}}{\delta w_{ij}^{(K)}} \tag{20.23}$$

Let us considered the partial derivative of the sigmoid function, i.e.

$$\frac{\delta \mathcal{F}(y)}{\delta w} = \frac{\delta \mathcal{F}(y)}{\delta y} \frac{\delta y}{\delta w} \tag{20.24}$$

Now,

$$\frac{\delta(\mathcal{F}(y))}{\delta y} = \frac{\delta}{\delta y}\left(\frac{1}{1+\exp(-y)}\right) = (\mathcal{F}(y))(1 - \mathcal{F}(y)) \tag{20.25}$$

and

$$\frac{\delta y_j^{(K)}}{\delta w_{ij}^{(K)}} = \frac{\delta}{\delta w_{ij}^{(K)}} \mathcal{F}\left(\sum_{i=0}^{n_{K-1}} w_{ij}^{(K)} x_i^{(K-1)}\right) = x_j^{(K)}\left(1 - x_j^{(K)}\right) x_i^{(K-1)} \tag{20.26}$$

Therefore,

$$\frac{\delta e}{\delta w_{ij}^{(K)}} = \left(x_j^{(K)} - d_j\right) x_j^{(K)}\left(1 - x_j^{(K)}\right) x_i^{(K-1)} \tag{20.27}$$

To minimize error e, weight values are updated according to the following relation:

$$\Delta w_{ij}^{(K)} \leftarrow \beta\left(x_j^{(K)} - d_j\right) x_j^{(K)}\left(1 - x_j^{(K)}\right) x_i^{(K-1)} \tag{20.28}$$

and

$$w_{ij}^{(K)} \leftarrow w_{ij}^{(K)} + \Delta w_{ij}^{(K)} \tag{20.29}$$

or

$$w_{ij}^{(K)} \leftarrow w_{ij}^{(K)} + \beta\delta_j^{(K)} x_i^{(K-1)} \tag{20.30}$$

where

$$\delta_j^{(K)} = x_j^{(K)} \left(1 - x_j^{(K)}\right) \left(x_j^{(K)} - d_j\right) \tag{20.31}$$

For the hidden layers ($k = 1, 2, \ldots, K - 1$), the error term is computed in a similar fashion. The weighted error sum from the next layer is used for minimization. Hence, the error term becomes

$$\delta_j^{(k)} = x_j^{(k)} \left(1 - x_j^{(k)}\right) \sum_{i=0}^{n_{k+1}} \left(\delta_j^{(k+1)} w_j^{(k+1)}\right) \tag{20.32}$$

The above learning procedure of the BPN is called the **delta learning rule**.

Example 2: Train the back propagation network shown in Figure 20.13 for a single input pattern (0.5 0.1). Consider a learning rate of $\beta = 0.2$ and target output of 0.8. Use binary sigmoid function as the activation function.

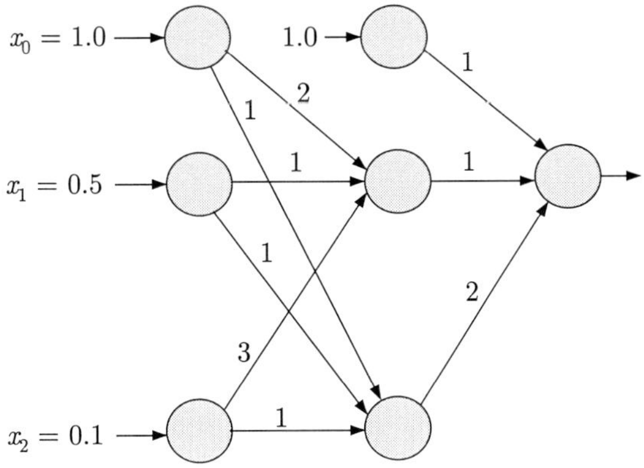

Figure 20.13: Multi layer network for Example 2.

Solution: A stepwise solution of the above problem is given below.

Initialization: Initialize the weights and the bias as

$$\mathbf{w}^{(1)} = \begin{bmatrix} 2 & 1 \\ 1 & 1 \\ 3 & 1 \end{bmatrix} \quad \text{and} \quad \mathbf{w}^{(2)} = \begin{bmatrix} 1 \\ 1 \\ 2 \end{bmatrix}$$

Feed Forward Stage: Compute outputs of nodes in forward direction as

$$\begin{aligned} y_1^{(1)} &= w_{01}^{(1)} x_0^{(0)} + w_{11}^{(1)} x_1^{(0)} + w_{21}^{(1)} x_2^{(0)} \\ &= 2 \times 1 + 1 \times 0.5 + 3 \times 0.1 \\ &= 2 + 0.5 + 0.3 = 2.8 \\ y_2^{(1)} &= w_{02}^{(1)} x_0^{(0)} + w_{12}^{(1)} x_1^{(0)} + w_{22}^{(1)} x_2^{(0)} \\ &= 1 \times 1 + 1 \times 0.5 + 1 \times 0.1 \\ &= 1 + 0.5 + 0.1 = 1.6 \end{aligned}$$

Therefore, layer two inputs are

$$x_1^{(1)} = \mathcal{F}(y_1^{(1)}) = \frac{1}{1 + \exp\{-2.8\}} = 0.9427$$

$$x_2^{(1)} = \mathcal{F}(y_2^{(1)}) = \frac{1}{1 + \exp\{-1.6\}} = 0.8320$$

The second layer output is

$$\begin{aligned} y_1^{(2)} &= w_{01}^{(2)} x_0^{(1)} + w_{11}^{(2)} x_1^{(1)} + w_{21}^{(2)} x_2^{(1)} \\ &= 1 \times 1 + 1 \times 0.9427 + 2 \times 0.8320 \\ &= 1 + 0.9427 + 1.6640 = 3.6067 \end{aligned}$$

Thus, the output from the second layer is

$$o = \mathcal{F}(y_1^{(2)}) = \frac{1}{1 + \exp(-3.6067)} = 0.9736$$

Backward propagation stage: Error propagation to adjust weight values is done as follows:

Error factors for weight updation from the output node to the hidden layer nodes are given by

$$\delta_j^{(K)} \leftarrow x_j^{(K)} \left(1 - x_j^{(K)}\right) \left(x_j^{(K)} - d_j\right)$$

In our example,

$$\begin{aligned} \delta_1^{(2)} &= x_1^{(2)} \left(1 - x_1^{(2)}\right) \left(x_1^{(2)} - 0.8\right) \\ &= 0.9736\,(1 - 0.9736)\,(0.9736 - 0.8) \\ &= 0.9736 \times 0.0264 \times 0.1736 = 0.0045 \end{aligned}$$

And error factors from the hidden layer nodes to the input layer nodes are given by

$$\delta_i^{(k)} \leftarrow x_i^{(k)} \left(1 - x_i^{(k)}\right) \sum_{j=1}^{(n_{k+1})} \left(\delta_j^{(k+1)} w_{ij}^{(k+1)}\right)$$

Therefore,

$$\begin{aligned}\delta_1^{(1)} &= x_1^{(1)} \left(1 - x_1^{(1)}\right) \left(\delta_1^{(2)} w_{11}^{(2)}\right)\\ &= 0.9427 \times (1 - 0.9427) \times (0.0045 \times 1)\\ &= 0.9427 \times 0.0573 \times 0.0045 = 0.00024\\ \delta_2^{(1)} &= x_2^{(1)} \left(1 - x_2^{(1)}\right) \left(\delta_1^{(2)} w_{21}^{(2)}\right)\\ &= 0.8320 \times (1 - 0.8320) \times (0.0045 \times 2)\\ &= 0.8320 \times 0.1680 \times 0.0090 = 0.00125\end{aligned}$$

Weight updation: Weights vectors at different layers are updated according to relation

$$w_{ij}^{(k)} \leftarrow w_{ij}^{(k)} - \beta \delta_j^{(k)} x_i^{(k-1)}$$

Here, we get

$$\begin{aligned}w_{01}^{(2)} &= 1.0 - 0.3 \times 0.0045 \times 1.0\\ &= 1.0 - 0.00135 = 0.99865\end{aligned}$$

$$\begin{aligned}w_{11}^{(2)} &= 1.0 - 0.3 \times 0.0045 \times 0.9427\\ &= 1.0 - 0.00127 = 0.99873\end{aligned}$$

$$\begin{aligned}w_{21}^{(2)} &= 2.0 - 0.3 \times 0.0045 \times 0.8320\\ &= 2.0 - 0.00112 = 1.99888\end{aligned}$$

$$\begin{aligned}w_{01}^{(1)} &= 2.0 - 0.3 \times 0.00024 \times 1.0\\ &= 2.0 - 0.000072 = 1.999928\end{aligned}$$

$$\begin{aligned}w_{02}^{(1)} &= 1.0 - 0.3 \times 0.00024 \times 1.0\\ &= 1.0 - 0.000072 = 0.999928\end{aligned}$$

$$\begin{aligned}w_{11}^{(1)} &= 1.0 - 0.3 \times 0.00024 \times 0.5\\ &= 1.0 - 0.000036 = 0.999964\end{aligned}$$

$$
\begin{aligned}
w_{12}^{(1)} &= 1.0 - 0.3 \times 0.00024 \times 0.5 \\
&= 1.0 - 0.000036 = 0.999964 \\
w_{21}^{(1)} &= 3.0 - 0.3 \times 0.00125 \times 0.1 \\
&= 3.0 - 0.0000375 = 2.9999725 \\
w_{22}^{(1)} &= 1.0 - 0.3 \times 0.00125 \times 0.1 \\
&= 1.0 - 0.0000375 = 0.9999725
\end{aligned}
$$

Therefore, new weight vectors are computed after the first iteration.

♣

20.8 Implementation Parameters

In the earlier sections, we have discussed the working principle of simple neuron, i.e. perceptron and the multilayer network with back propagation learning. To physically implement a practical neural network for problem solving, we need to consider some other aspects, basically some implementation parameters, in details.

20.8.1 Training Data

It is known that to solve a problem using an ANN we need to train it through a learning process. The learning process needs a set of finely collected training data which must belong to the category of the actual input data. Now, a major question in many situations is how to select or prepare the training data sets. In the following, a few strategies are outlined:

We can select a subset of the actual input data as a training set. The complete data set may also be used. But, in many cases, it is unnecessary and undesirable. Only a proper subset can work fine almost always. Reducing the training set size can significantly reduce the learning time. This is important, because, in an ANN, the time complexity is mainly due to the training phase. After the training is complete, the remaining data from the original input data set may be used for verifying the performance of the ANN.

If we wish to train the ANN for a noisy environment, i.e. where the input data is assumed to contain sufficient amount of noise elements, then we must include a few noisy input data elements within the training set. For example, in case of pixel based image segmentation, pixels near object boundaries, whose category is not very clear, may be assumed to be noise data. But, in this case, one must be careful about not to include a large number of noisy training data, because in that case the purpose of training may not be successful.

20.8.2 Network Size

It is always worthy to ask how many layers and how many nodes are needed to solve a particular problem. Generally this depends on the problem concerned. For some problems, only one hidden layer is sufficient, while for some others we need more than one. It is always easier to use lesser number of hidden layers, because then training will be significantly faster.

The number of nodes in the input layer depends on the problem to be solved and the types of inputs we apply at the input layer. Number of output nodes can be simply determined by the true number of different output categories we expect.

But determining the number of nodes in the hidden layers is not so simple. A general idea is to use as few hidden layers as possible. Regarding number of nodes at a hidden layer, we must decide on from experience. We have to execute the process as a test run to check which of the hidden layer nodes are very less sensitive to variations at the input layer. This can be determined by looking at the rate of variation of the concerned weight values. The less sensitive nodes can then be eliminated. Of course, initially we need to start with a fairly large number of hidden layer nodes. There exist different propositions regarding this number of hidden nodes. In general for a binary valued function, the number of hidden nodes may be $N-1$ where N is size of the training set. And for other problems, one may assume $2n$ number of hidden nodes, where n is the number of input nodes. However, all these are crude estimates only.

20.8.3 Wcights and Learning Rate

Weight parameters are generally set as random values in $(-1, 1)$, i.e. weights can be positive or negative. The learning parameter should always be a positive value. A zero value will cause no learning as then the weights will remain unchanged through iterations. Negative values of learning parameters may direct the weight parameters in the reverse direction which is not desirable. Large values of the learning factor may lead to abrupt jump of the weight values and prohibit convergence to the optimum solution. Hence, this value should be kept in the range of $(0, 1)$.

20.9 Self Organizing Map

The self organizing map is one specific category of neural network that mimics the physiological behaviour of the cerebral cortex of human being. The cerebral cortex has a consistently regular structure (it may be thought of a number of collection of brain cells) arranged in different groups. A number of different activities, like speech, thought, vision, hearing, moving of hands and legs (motor actions), etc. are controlled by one of these area of the cortex. Regions with such tonotopic and somatotopic map can be referred to as ordered feature maps. T. Cohonen studied this inherent structure of brain cells and tried to develop a procedure that can organize the nodes of a neural network by learning. If one such self organization is made possible, then we can employ a neural network for unsupervised learning also.

Kohonen's self organizing map algorithm creates a vector quantizer by adjusting weights from a single common input node to M output nodes arranged as one or two-dimensional grids as shown in Figures 20.14 and 20.15. Output nodes are extensively interconnected with their neighbours. Here, unlabelled input vectors are presented to the input one at a time, without specifying a desired output. After a sufficient number of inputs are presented, input-output connection-weight values would specify the cluster centres representing the input space regions such that the point density function of the vector centres tend to approximate the probability density function of the input vectors. Moreover, weights are arranged in such a fashion that topologically closer nodes are sensitive to inputs which are physically similar. Output nodes will thus be ordered naturally.

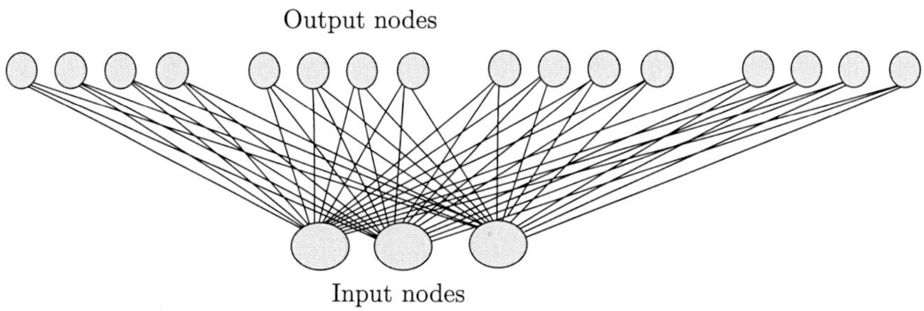

Figure 20.14: Linear array of output nodes in SOM.

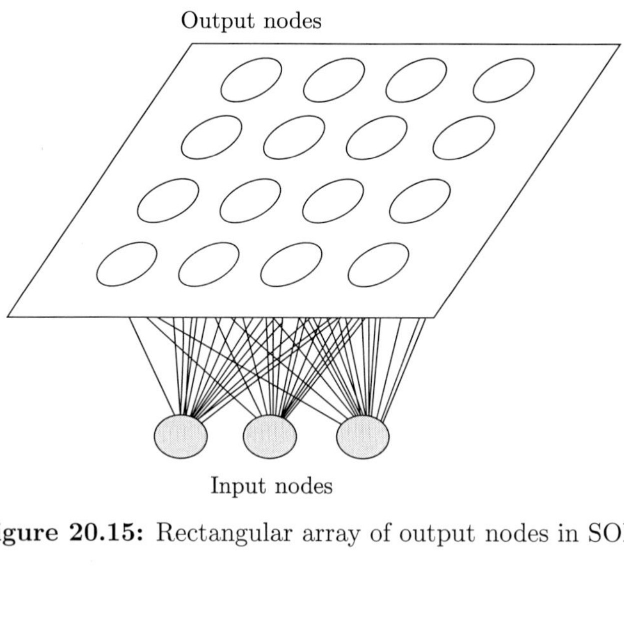

Figure 20.15: Rectangular array of output nodes in SOM.

Kohonen's feature mapping algorithm requires a neighbourhood to be defined around each output node as shown in Figures 20.16 and 20.17. This neighbourhood reduces slowly in size with number of iterations or time.

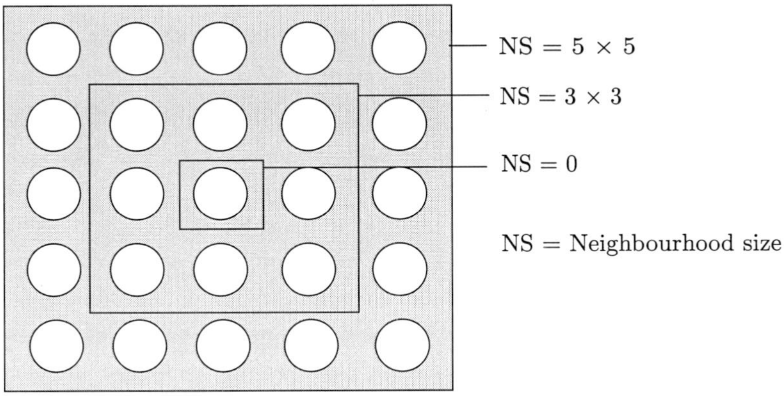

Figure 20.16: Rectangular neighbourhood in SOM.

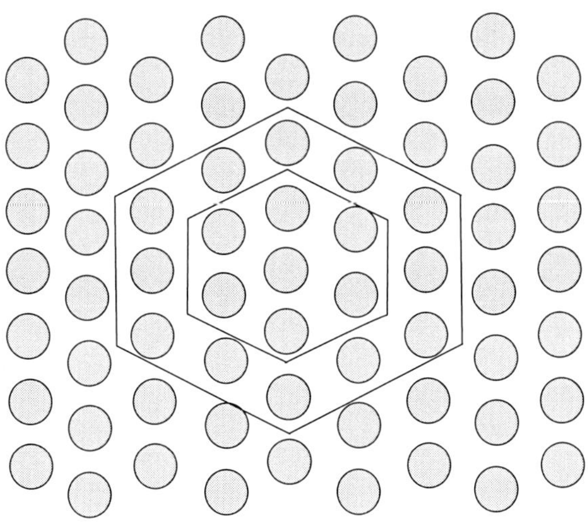

Figure 20.17: Hexagonal neighbourhood in SOM.

20.9.1 Learning in SOM

In a self organized map network, one of the many output nodes will respond to a particular input. The mechanism by which we determine which of the output node responds is called **competition**. The most widely used competition mechanism is *winner-takes-all*. Here, the winner node will have a non-zero output when competition is complete.

When the SOM is employed for clustering, in the training phase, each input pattern tries to update weight vectors in an input to output link while choosing the most suitable output node. Similar input patterns will find a best match weight vector along a particular input to output path. This output node will become the winner of the concerned input vector. The winner then updates the weight vector leading to a learning of the network.

Two methods are basically used to determine a winner. These are:

- Choose an output node for which the squared Euclidean distance between the input vector and the weight vector is the smallest.
- Choose an output node for which the dot product of the input vector and the weight vector is the largest. Larger dot product values indicate smaller angular displacement between the concerned vectors.

In the learning process, all the neighbours of a winning node will receive a positive feedback from the winner, and they also update their weights even if the input does not closely match with these node's weight vectors. Thus, training takes place on an extended region surrounding the winner node. Because of connections among the neighbour output nodes, they can compete for each input pattern.

The SOM algorithm

begin
    for $i \leftarrow 0$ **to** $n-1$ **do**
    for $j \leftarrow 0$ **to** $M-1$ **do**
        initialize weight w_{ij}
    repeat
    present a new input
    for $i \leftarrow 0$ **to** $n-1$ **do**
        begin
            compute distance between input pattern $\mathbf{x}_i$ and each output j
                as $d_j = \sum_{i=0}^{n-1}(x_i - w_{ij})^2$
            determine output node j^* with minimum d_j
            for $j \in j^*$ and its neighbours NE_{j^*} **do**
                update weight as $w_{ij} \leftarrow w_{ij} + \beta(x_i - w_{ij})$
        end
    until weights are stable
end

Algorithm for finding a winner

Algorithm *find_winner*()

begin
    for $j \leftarrow 0$ **to** $M-1$ **do**

```
    present an input
    for i ← 0 to n − 1 do
        begin
            compute distance between input pattern x and each output j
                        as d_j = Σ_{i=0}^{n-1} (x_i − w_ij)^2
            determine output node j* with minimum d_j
            winner ← j*
        end
    return(winner)
end
```

Algorithm for finding a neighbour

Algorithm *check_neighbour*$(R, C, winner)$

```
begin
    row ← (winner − 1) / COL
    col ← (winner − 1) % COL
    δR1 ← max(1, (row − ΔR)
    δR2 ← min(ROWS, (row + ΔR)
    δC1 ← max(1, (col − ΔC)
    δC2 ← min(COLS, (col + ΔR)
    if (δR_1 ≤ R) AND (R ≤ δR_2) AND (δC_1 ≤ C) AND (C ≤ δC_2)
    return(1)
end
```

Algorithm for updating weights

Algorithm *update_weight*()

```
begin
    update_count = 0
    for i ← 0 to ROW − 1 do
    for j ← 0 to COL − 1 do
    begin
        if (check_neighbour(i, j, winner) then
        begin
            update weight as w_ij ← w_ij + β(x_i − w_ij)
            update_count = update_count + 1
        end
    end
    return(update_count)
end
```

Algorithm for SOM Training

begin
  for $i \leftarrow 0$ **to** $N-1$ **do**
  begin
    $\Delta R \leftarrow ROWS/2$
    $\Delta C \leftarrow COLS/2$
    while $(update\_weight() > 1)$ **do**
      $time = time + 1$
      if $(time\%10) = 0$ **then**
      begin
        $\Delta R = max(0,\ \Delta R -\ 1)$
        $\Delta C = max(0,\ \Delta C -\ 1)$
      end
    end while
  end
  for $i \leftarrow 0$ **to** $ITER$ **do**
  for $j \leftarrow 0$ **to** $N-1$ **do**
  begin
    $get\_input()$
    $dummy = update\_weight()$
  end
end

Example 3: A Kohonen's SOM is shown in Figure 20.18 along with weight values. Use this network to classify input pattern (0.3 0.4) to the appropriate category. Use a learning rate of 0.3. Adjust the weight values for the winning node and its immediate neighbours.

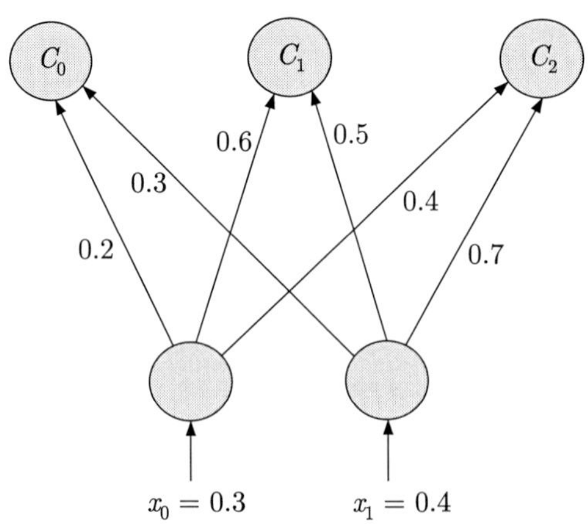

Figure 20.18: SOM network for Example 2.

Solution: The solution steps are shown below.

Initialization: Initialize the weight vectors as

$$\mathbf{w} = \begin{bmatrix} 0.2 & 0.6 & 0.4 \\ 0.3 & 0.5 & 0.7 \end{bmatrix}$$

Initial radius is set to $R = 0$. Initial learning is set to $\beta = 0.3$.

Training phase: Euclidean distance between input pattern $\mathbf{x}_i$ and weight vectors corresponding to output node j are computed as $d_j = \sum_{i=0}^{n-1}(x_i - w_{ij})^2$. Here, $n = 1$.

$$\begin{aligned} d_0 &= (0.3 - 0.2)^2 + (0.4 - 0.3)^2 = 0.02 \\ d_1 &= (0.3 - 0.6)^2 + (0.4 - 0.5)^2 = 0.10 \\ d_2 &= (0.3 - 0.4)^2 + (0.4 - 0.7)^2 = 0.10 \end{aligned}$$

Therefore, the input vector is most similar to output node 1, and we set $j^* = 0$.

Weight updation: Weights of the winning node are updated using relation

$$w_{ij}^{(\text{new})} = w_{ij}^{(\text{old})} + \beta \times (x_i - w_{ij}^{(\text{old})})$$

Therefore, we have

$$\begin{aligned} w_{00}^{(\text{new})} &= w_{00}^{(\text{old})} + 0.3 \times (x_0 - w_{00}^{(\text{old})}) \\ &= 0.2 + 0.3 \times (0.3 - 0.2) = 0.23 \\ w_{10}^{(\text{new})} &= w_{10}^{(\text{old})} + 0.3 \times (x_1 - w_{10}^{(\text{old})}) \\ &= 0.3 + 0.3 \times (0.4 - 0.3) = 0.33 \end{aligned}$$

Weight updation of neighbour nodes: Weights of the neighbouring nodes are updated as follows:

Here, $j^* = 0$, therefore, there is no left neighbour. For the immediate right neighbour, we have

$$\begin{aligned} w_{01}^{(\text{new})} &= w_{01}^{(\text{old})} + 0.3 \times (x_0 - w_{01}^{(\text{old})}) \\ &= 0.6 + 0.3 \times (0.3 - 0.6) = 0.51 \\ w_{11}^{(\text{new})} &= w_{11}^{(\text{old})} + 0.3 \times (x_1 - w_{11}^{(\text{old})}) \\ &= 0.5 + 0.3 \times (0.4 - 0.5) = 0.47 \end{aligned}$$

Therefore, new weight vectors become,

$$\mathbf{w} = \begin{bmatrix} 0.23 & 0.51 & 0.4 \\ 0.33 & 0.47 & 0.7 \end{bmatrix}$$

♣

20.9.2 Learning Vector Quantization (LVQ)

Kohonen's Learning Vector Quantization (LVQ) is a SOM based clustering technique where input vectors are divided into separate areas that are assigned as *code book vectors*. In LVQ the network is initially made to learn, in a supervised fashion, using a set of training patterns. The network has n inputs where n is the dimension of each pattern. N input patterns are grouped by the network into m classes, where m is the number of output nodes of the network. Each of the output nodes represent a *code word*. Combination of all m code words is called a *code book*. After training, the LVQ net is able to classify input vectors to their nearest match prototypes in the code book (formed in the learning phase).

The goal of the LVQ process is to classify a set of input patterns (vectors) into different classes. By learning the network prepares a set of *code book vectors*. Each of the code book vectors represents a particular class.

Voronoi quantizer: A vector quantizer that yields the minimum encoding distortion is called a *Voronoi* or nearest neighbour quantizer. The Voronoi cell about a set of points in an input space corresponds to a partition on that space according to the nearest neighbour rule based on Euclidean distance metric.

In LVQ the SOM algorithm provides an approximate method for computing the Voronoi vectors in an unsupervised manner, with approximation being specified by the synaptic weight vectors of the neurons in the feature map. The vector quantization process requires the size of the code book.

In case of image compression application, the code book size is set to 256, in general. Thus, 256 nodes in the competitive layer compete for the input vector. The weights of the nodes in the competitive layer are taken as outputs of the LVQ network. Weight initialization generally depends on the patterns to be classified. For image segmentation, input image values (in general vectors having component values between 0 and 255) are used randomly for weight initialization.

A 4×4 image block is presented as input to the input nodes. The competitive layer nodes are arranged as square array of 16×16 nodes. Grey values from 16 pixels are input to 16 input nodes. Each of the Kohonen layer nodes are connected to each of the input nodes by connection weights. An input vector is compared with all the connection weights and finds a nearest match. The corresponding Kohonen layer node becomes the winner of that input. The winner activates its spatial neighbours to react to the same input. The weights of the winner and its neighbours undergo adaptation at each learning step, according to SOM rules. All other weights remain unchanged. After training, weights of each neuron form the code book. The LVQ network is shown in Figure 20.19.

In brief, the LVQ based image encoding and decoding processes can be enumerated as follows:

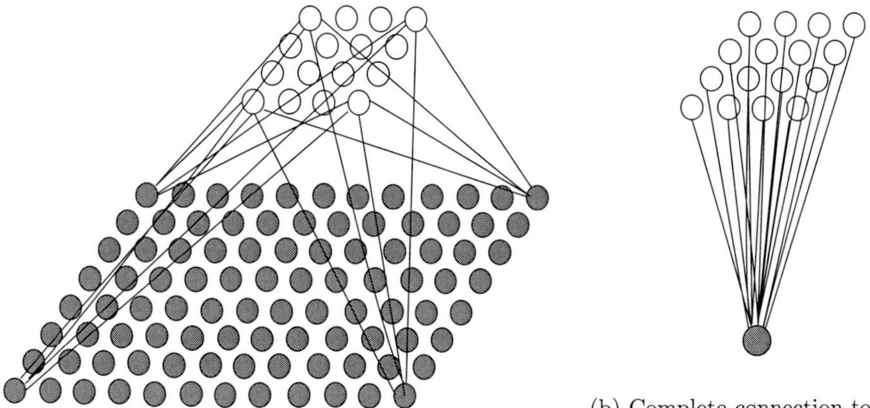

(a) Partial connections

(b) Complete connection to a single Kohonen layer node

Figure 20.19: LVQ network.

Code book based encoding

1. Input image is divided into 4×4 blocks.
2. Image blocks are input to the SOM one by one.
3. Winner neuron is selected based on minimum Euclidean distance.
4. Index of winner neurons for each input block are stored.
5. The index set of all winner neurons for blocks along with the code book gives the encoded image.

Code book based decoding

1. For each index value find the neuron in the SOM.
2. Generate weight vector corresponding to the winner neuron.
3. 16 values of the neuron weights represent the grey levels for the block.
4. Display the grey level values thus obtained as pixels.

Image encoding is, therfore, a very important application of LVQ using SOM.

From the above discussions it is clear that while the perceptrons (single and multilayer) are used for supervised classification, the SOM performs unsupervised classification. All the above mentioned networks are able to map continuous valued inputs into discrete valued output categories. There exist many other types of networks and associated learning techniques in literature. Many of them are fuzzy versions of the networks mentioned here. We have no scope of discussing those various networks in this book.

20.10 Problems

1. What is a neural network? In what ways it is similar to human neural system?
2. What kind of problems can be solved by using an artificial neural network?
3. What are the differences between feedforward and feedback networks?
4. Consider the following set of pattern vectors and desired outputs.

$feature_1$	$feature_2$	$output$
2	2	0
1	−2	1
−2	2	0
−1	1	1

   Find out the weights vectors of a two input-one output perceptron network.

5. Show that the OR function can be solved by a single perceptron. Find out the linear boundary if threshold is considered to 0.7.
6. Why do we consider the Multi Layer Perceptron (MLP) as a feedforward network? For an MLP there are n input nodes, m output nodes and one hidden layer with h nodes. Show the architecture of the network using bias nodes.
7. Show that in absence of hidden layers, MLP learning algorithm reduces to the single layer multi output perceptron algorithm.
8. Write a short note on winner-takes-all strategy.
9. Describe the dot product and Euclidean distance based methods for determining the winner-takes-all strategy.
10. How can one assign the neighbourhood radius in SOM?
11. What are the stopping criteria used in Kohonen's SOM algorithm?
12. How competitions are performed in supervised and unsupervised learning?
13. An MLP contains 3 input nodes, 2 output nodes and one hidden layer with 3 nodes. We need to train the network using the following pattern vectors for two output classes.

$feature_1$	$feature_2$	$feature_3$	$output$
2	1	2	1
1	−2	2	2
1	2	2	1
−1	−2	1	2

   Show a trace of the procedure.

14. Consider a Kohonen network with two output units and three input units. Weight vectors from input to output units are $[0.9\ 0.7\ 0.6]^T$ and $[0.4\ 0.3\ 0.5]^T$, respectively. Use a learning rate of 0.2 to determine the winning unit for input vector $[0.4\ \ 0.2\ \ 0.1]^T$. Also find the new weights associated with the winning node.
15. Consider the following four input vectors and the associated class labels.

$feature_1$	$feature_2$	$feature_3$	$feature_4$	$class$
1	0	1	0	1
0	0	1	1	2
1	1	0	0	1
1	0	0	1	2

Construct a test LVQ to assign these four vectors into two classes. Assume initial learning rate of 0.1 and reduce it upto 0.05.

CHAPTER 21

Clustering

Clustering or unsupervised classification is an important step in many applications like object identification, market analysis, data mining, authentication systems, target detection, and many others. By clustering a set of pattern vectors are classified into a number of groups or classes. Unlike supervised classification processes, here, no *priori* information regarding class membership of patterns are available. Therefore, it is an unsupervised decision making process.

Before the advent of automatic computation systems, human experts were needed for decision making in such situations. Nowadays sophisticated computers are employed for this task, with larger data handling capacity and possibly greater accuracy. Modern computers are highly powerful in sense of processing speed as well as information storage and retrieval capacities. Hence, machines are more suitable for the task of data clustering and decision making. In this chapter, we shall study different techniques of clustering and the corresponding algorithms.

21.1 Basic Concepts

Let us consider how a child learns to recognize. At the very beginning any particular object has no specific meaning to him. The world is then absolutely fuzzy. Gradually a sense of learning arise in him; and then the attempts to categorize objects. Each new object is tried to be associated with one of the already formed statistical populations in the brain. Thus, the problem of pattern clustering may be regarded as one of discriminating the input data, not between individual patterns, but between populations. These populations are searched for a match with the new object with the help of its attributes or features. In pattern recognition terminology, these populations are called clusters and each object is given a machine representation in the form of a feature or pattern vector.

The idea of the learning process mentioned above has been imitated in the field of statistical pattern recognition. Here each pattern consisting of d features is modelled as a vector of dimension d. So each pattern of feature vector is an instance of a point in a d-dimensional space. The objective is to categorize patterns into classes so that patterns belonging to different classes are well separated. The process may start with or without any knowledge of the feature space. Accordingly there are two categories of classification schemes. When we have prior information regarding the class of a subset of the data, the classification scheme is called *supervised classification* or *simply classification*; and when nothing is known *a priori*, the scheme is called **unsupervised classification** or **clustering**. In case of supervised classification, the labelled subset of data is called the **training data**. Given a set of training patterns the objective is to determine the decision boundaries in the feature space which separate patterns belonging to different classes. In some cases, it becomes absolutely impossible to label training data items from ground informations. For example, in land-use classification problem in remote sensing, we need "ground truth" information (category for a subset of pixels) which can be made available by visiting the site or using a geographical information system, if one is available. In such situations, emphasis is given to identify relatively high density regions in the feature space and then trying to minimize the squared-error objective function of clustering by possible rearrangements of patterns between regions.

Being unsupervised in nature, clustering is a very difficult task, because the same data may reveal many different inherent structures depending on the shape and sizes of its distribution. This is often compounded by the fact that the number of clusters depend on the density or resolution of data. So it is very difficult to develop a general technique that is equally applicable to all sorts of data.

21.2 A Brief Overview

The history of development of clustering methodologies take us dates back to the early 1960s. It actually began its journey humbly when the steering has been held by some biologists who were working on numerical taxonomy for nomenclature of animal and plant species. The most important document regarding numerical taxonomy was possibly the book written by Sneath and Sokal in 1973. Blackwelder worked on animal taxonomy in 1966. Within a few years, their developments have been taken up by the statisticians. In his work, Good (1965) classified different classification methods available in those days, upon mathematical basis. Jardine and Sibson (1971) developed different mathematical measures for similarity and dissimilarity of different patterns representing objects. Another earlier work in this regard was by Goodman and Kruskal (1959). The detailed history of early developments may be found in Hartigan (1975).

At present computer scientists, mathematicians and statisticians are using clustering methods in various different fields like machine learning, pattern recognition, image segmentation, marketing analysis and many other fields. Two most important latest additions in this list are bio-informatics and data mining. At present stress is being imposed on clustering very large databases. In this age of the Internet and web, collection of billions of relevant data is a matter of minutes or seconds; computers are processing millions of instructions in seconds; storage volumes touched the high of terabytes. In science, research's, industry's and government's very large databases are frequently being handled using powerful systems. This high need of data and information processing has taken the demand of efficient clustering techniques to a very high level. As a result, newer and newer clustering techniques are also being developed almost everyday.

From the above discussion, it is clear that the new generation clustering methods have to face the challenge of handling very large multidimensional data sets with high degree of accuracy and efficiency. Adjusting performance reasonably with the input load is technically termed as *scalability.* As it is found that the clustering algorithms generally handle data with quadratic processing complexity, their application in areas that need real time response may be devastating and in some cases impossible.

Classically, we can categorize clustering methods into two classes

- Partitional
- Hierarchical

At present many other techniques have been developed. Many of them are hybrid in nature, and hence, it is very difficult to categorize them appropriately. Nevertheless, depending on the basic architecture of clustering techniques they can be classified as *density-based, grid-based, model-based, sample-based, etc.* techniques. Therefore, we get a broader spectrum of methods.

- Partitional clustering methods
- Hierarchical clustering methods
- Density-based clustering methods
- Grid-based clustering methods
- Model-based clustering methods
- Sample-based clustering methods
- High-dimensional clustering methods
- Constraint-based clustering methods

We shall describe some of the above methods which are important in pattern recognition.

21.2.1 Definition of a Cluster

Any classification process attempts to organize data points in multidimensional space (also called feature vectors) into *natural groups* or clusters such that data points within the same cluster are similar in some sense and those belonging to different clusters are dissimilar in the same sense. Thus a cluster may be defined to be a collection of similar objects grouped together. The following definitions of clusters are given by Everitt (1974):

- A cluster is a set of entities which are *alike*, and entities from different clusters are *not alike.*
- A cluster is an aggregation of points in the test space such that the *distance* between any two points in the cluster is less than the *distance* between any point in the cluster and any point not in it.
- Clusters may be described as connected regions of a multidimensional space containing a relatively *high density* of points, separated from other such regions by a region containing a relatively *low density* of points.

The first definition states the general nature of a cluster. In general, the similarity or dissimilarity between data points is measured as a function of the distance between them. The word *distance* in the second definition may be the Euclidean distance or any other distance like Mahalanobis distance (Mahalanobis 1936), Manhattan distance, etc.

It may also be noted that the objects can be grouped into clusters with various purposes of mind. Accordingly, the same data set can reveal clusters of different *shapes* and *sizes.* It is true that, in many situations, we can form more clusters by subdividing an already formed cluster depending on the need of the application.

21.2.2 Defining the Clustering Problem

In clustering we generate some decisions regarding membership of some pattern (information) into a certain class or category. In other words, we perform a mapping from a pattern space (X) to a decision space (D). These two spaces are different in nature.

The pattern space contains multidimensional patterns or data or information. The information content of these patterns may be real valued, i.e. continuous, discrete like binary or integers, or they may have categorical values.

The decision space contains a finite set of discrete class labels. An observation $\mathbf{x} \in X$ is tested for its membership in a class $C \in D$. If the membership condition is satisfied, we assign a label C to the concerned pattern $\mathbf{x}$.

By Fraley and Raftery (1998), the definition of clustering problem is given as

On the basis of quantitative measurements on a set of objects, devise a method that assigns the objects to meaningful subclasses.

In the above definition, the term *quantitative measurements* is representing the values of the components of a pattern vector representing an object. Clearly, this definition signifies unsupervised classification scheme because the algorithm itself needs to determine the class of objects. It is also implied that the algorithm needs to determine the number of classes automatically. However, in practice, in many cases users supply the information regarding the number of classes. If the data is visually realizable then we may identify the value of this parameter. But in case of complex multidimensional it is almost always impossible. Accordingly there are two types of clustering algorithms, algorithms that uses user supplied information regarding number of classes and those that determine it automatically. In most of the cases, a cluster validity measure (index) is used for this purpose.

Clustering is considered to be an important component of *exploratory data analysis.* Many clustering algorithms and their variations exist in the literature. Depending on their speed of execution, reliability and consistency, they can be applicable in areas like data mining, information retrieval, image segmentation, signal compression and coding, machine learning, etc. Most of these algorithms fall under any of the following two categories: *hierarchical* or *partitional.* Hierarchical clustering categorize data in a nested sequence of groups which can be displayed graphically as a dendrogram. Partitional clustering techniques try to optimize a squared-error objective function (a clustering metric). This objective function is commonly either minimum within cluster variation or the maximum between cluster separation.

Some of the common partitional clustering techniques are the k-means algorithm, the Expectation Maximization (EM) algorithm, the *ISODATA* algorithm, the fuzzy c-means algorithm, etc. Common hierarchical methods are single linkage, average linkage and complete linkage methods and minimum spanning tree based techniques. There exist other methods developed using various optimization tools like Simulated Annealing (SA), different kinds of Evolutionary Algorithms (EAs) and Artificial Neural Networks (ANN), etc.

21.2.3 Common Data Structures Used in Clustering

In clustering we deal with a multidimensional data set of a finite cardinality. The data set needs to be partitioned into a number of classes based on some proximity measure. Thus, as a minimum requirement, we need a data matrix and a distance (proximity) matrix for any clustering algorithm, in general.

Data matrix: A data set having n patterns of d-dimension in R^d constitute the data matrix. Each dimension is associated to some attribute or feature of the concerned object (represented by a pattern). The data matrix can be represented as a $n \times d$ matrix

$$\begin{bmatrix} x_{11} & x_{12} & \cdots & x_{1d} \\ x_{21} & x_{22} & \cdots & x_{2d} \\ x_{31} & x_{32} & \cdots & x_{3d} \\ \vdots & \vdots & \ddots & \vdots \\ x_{n1} & x_{n2} & \cdots & x_{nd} \end{bmatrix}$$

Dissimilarity matrix: This matrix stores the proximity measures between any pair of data items (patterns) in the input data set. When there are n patterns, the dissimilarity matrix is of size $n \times n$, and is denoted as

$$\begin{bmatrix} d_{11} & d_{12} & \cdots & d_{1d} \\ d_{21} & d_{22} & \cdots & d_{2d} \\ d_{31} & d_{32} & \cdots & d_{3d} \\ \vdots & \vdots & \ddots & \vdots \\ d_{n1} & d_{n2} & \cdots & d_{nd} \end{bmatrix}$$

where $d(i, j)$ is the distance or dissimilarity between patterns $\mathbf{x}_i$ and $\mathbf{x}_j$. In the above matrix every $d(i, j) \geq 0$ and $d(i, i) = 0$ for all i. Although very commonly the euclidean distance measure is used as the dissimilarity between two patterns, there exist quite a number of different distance measures for different types of data patterns. Some of the commonly used distance measures are Euclidean, Manhattan and Minkowski distance measures.

Since different attributes of a pattern are measured using different scales, we need to standardize them before applying some clustering methods. Otherwise the difference of units may affect the performance of clustering and subsequent analysis. We can standardize the data by applying normalization operation over each attribute separately and thereby producing unitless attribute values. Let, for a given variable v have n different measures denoted by

$$x_{1v}, x_{2v}, x_{3v}, \ldots, x_{nv}$$

then the mean absolute deviation is computed as

$$s_v = \frac{1}{n}\left(|x_{1v} - m_v| + |x_{2v} - m_v| + \cdots + |x_{nv} - m_v|\right) \tag{21.1}$$

where, m_v is the mean value of v, i.e.

$$m_v = \frac{1}{n}\left(x_{1v} + x_{2v} + x_{3v} + \cdots + x_{nv}\right) \tag{21.2}$$

Now, the standardized measure can be computed as

$$z_{iv} = \frac{x_{iv} - m_v}{s_v} \tag{21.3}$$

The mean absolute deviation is found to be more robust than standard deviation. However, other standardization methods can be applied depending on the need of the application.

After standardization, the distance measures are computed. The most common measure is the Euclidean distance defined as

$$d_{ij} = \sqrt{(x_{i1} - x_{j1})^2 + (x_{i2} - x_{j2})^2 + \cdots + (x_{id} - x_{jd})^2} \quad (21.4)$$

Another well known measure is the Manhattan distance defined as

$$d_{ij} = |(x_{i1} - x_{j1})| + |(x_{i2} - x_{j2})| + \cdots + |(x_{id} - x_{jd})| \quad (21.5)$$

The Minkowski distance is a generalization of both Euclidean and Manhattan distance measures. It is defined as

$$d_{ij} = \{|(x_{i1} - x_{j1})|^p + |(x_{i2} - x_{j2})|^p + \cdots + |(x_{id} - x_{jd})|^p\}^{1/p} \quad (21.6)$$

where p is a positive integer. This generalized distance is called L_p **norm distance**. Hence, the Manhattan and the Euclidean distances are of norms L_1 and L_2, respectively.

Individual terms, along each dimension, in all the above distance measures may be weighted.

$$\begin{aligned}
&\text{Euclidean:} && \sqrt{w_1(x_{i1} - x_{j1})^2 + w_2(x_{i2} - x_{j2})^2 + \cdots + w_d(x_{id} - x_{jd})^2}\\
&\text{Manhattan:} && w_1|(x_{i1} - x_{j1})| + w_2|(x_{i2} - x_{j2})| + \cdots + w_d|(x_{id} - x_{jd})|\\
&\text{Minkowski:} && (w_1|(x_{i1} - x_{j1})|^p + w_2|(x_{i2} - x_{j2})|^p + \cdots + w_d|(x_{id} - x_{jd})|^p)^{1/d}
\end{aligned}$$

The Mahalanobis distance is another very important distance measure used in statistics that measures the statistical distance between two populations of Gaussian mixtures having mean μ_i and μ_j, and a common covariance matrix Σ_{ij}. This measure is given by

$$d_{ij} = (\mu_i - \mu_j)^T \sum_{ij} (\mu_i - \mu_j) \quad (21.7)$$

Binary valued patterns: If we apply the above distance measures for binary valued patterns, we may get misleading results. A binary variable may have only two values 0 or 1. In this case, by weighting each binary attribute, we can have a dissimilarity matrix. When all the attributes receive the same weight, the following contingency table (Table 21.1) results.

Table 21.1: Contingency Table for Binary Patterns

		Pattern j		
		1	0	sum
	1	q	r	$q + r$
Pattern i	0	s	t	$s + t$
	sum	$q + s$	$r + t$	p

Here, q is the number of attributes having value 1 for both patterns i and j, r is the number of attributes having value 1 for pattern i and 0 for pattern j, s is the number of attributes having value 0 for pattern i and 1 for pattern j, and t is the number of attributes having value 0 for both patterns i and j. p is the total number of attributes.

Now, the dissimilarity between patterns i and j can be expressed as

$$d(i,j) = \frac{r+s}{q+r+s+t} \tag{21.8}$$

The corresponding similarity measure is defined as

$$\text{sim}(i,j) = 1 - d(i,j) = 1 - \frac{r+s}{q+r+s+t} \tag{21.9}$$

$\text{sim}(i,j)$ is called the **Jacard coefficient**.

Categorical attributes: Categorical attributes are generalization of binary attributes and can assume more than two discrete values. Let the number of values be $M(1, 2, \ldots, M)$. The dissimilarity between patterns i and j can be defined as

$$d(i,j) = \frac{p-m}{p} \tag{21.10}$$

where, m is the number of matches (i.e. number of attributes on which i and j match), and p is the total number of attributes.

21.2.4 Clustering Methods

Unsupervised classification or clustering is a very difficult problem because of the fact that data can reveal clusters with different shapes and sizes. This problem is further compounded by the fact that the number of clusters often depends on the resolution with which we view the data. It is thus a challenge to select an appropriate measure of similarity to define clusters which, in general, is both data (shape) and context (size) dependent.

As a result of its tremendous usefulness in data analysis, hundreds of clustering algorithms have been proposed in the literature and newer algorithms continue to appear. However, most of the clustering algorithms can be categorized into following two classes: iterative partitional clustering and hierarchical clustering. Hierarchical clustering can again be of two types; agglomerative and divisive. Figure 21.1 shows a categorization of different clustering schemes in the form of a tree, as suggested by Lance and Williams (1967).

Another way of classifying the clustering approaches is based on the use of a partition matrix $U = [u_{ik}]_{K \times n}$, where K is the number of clusters, n is the number of

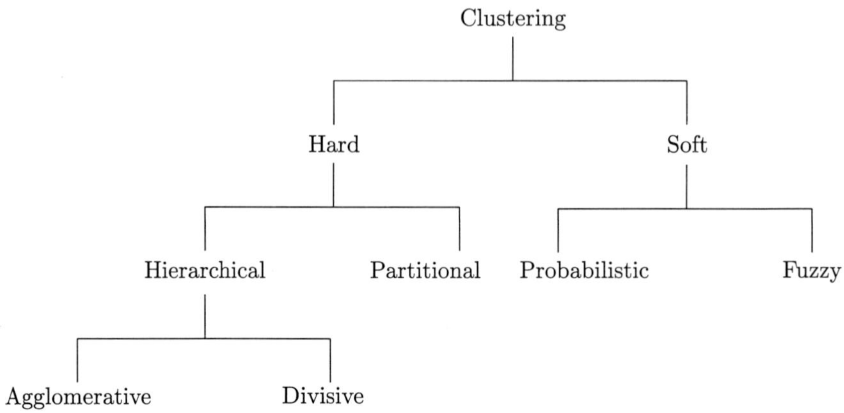

Figure 21.1: Classification schemes.

data points, and $\{u_{ik}\}$ indicates the degree of belongingness of a point x_k to cluster i. Three types of clusterings are possible viz., possibilistic (M_p), fuzzy (M_f) and hard or crisp (M_h) such that

$$M_p = \left\{ U \in R^{Kn} | 0 \leq u_{ij} \leq 1,\ \forall\ i,j;\ \forall j, u_{ij} > 0\ \exists\ i; 0 < \sum_{j=1}^{n} u_{ij} < n\ \forall\ i \right\} \quad (21.11)$$

$$M_f = \left\{ U \in M_p | \sum_{i=1}^{K} u_{ij} = 1\ \forall\ j \right\} \quad (21.12)$$

$$M_h = \{ U \in M_f | u_{ij} = 0 \text{ or } 1\ \forall\ i,j \} \quad (21.13)$$

An interesting example has been provided by Bezdek (1992) to depict the difference of these three matrices. The example is illustrated below. Let $X = \{x_1,\ x_2,\ x_3\} = \{\text{peach, plum, nectarine}\}$, and $K = 2$. One instance of 2-partitions of these three objects in the above three modes are shown in Table 21.2.

Table 21.2: Example of Possibilistic, Fuzzy and Crisp Partitioning

	M_p			M_f			M_h		
Object	x_1	x_2	x_3	x_1	x_2	x_3	x_1	x_2	x_3
Peaches	0.9	0.5	0.5	0.9	0.2	0.4	1	0	0
Plums	0.7	0.8	0.6	0.1	0.8	0.6	0	1	1

The nectarine is a hybrid of peaches and plums. But in the crisp matrix, it is given full membership to the plums class. This is, however, far from reality. So, it is clear that the crisp partitioning may become error prone in such situations. Fuzzy partitioning is capable of avoiding such mistakes. Thus fuzzy models may provide richer and more flexible solution structures which model real objects with a finer degree of physical realism than the harshness the crisp model impose. The possibilistic model relaxes the requirement that for each point, the sum of its membership values to different clusters should be equal to 1.

21.3 Classical Schemes for Clustering

As already mentioned clustering is an important unsupervised classification technique where a set of patterns, usually vectors in a multi-dimensional space, are grouped into clusters in such a way that patterns in the same cluster are similar in some sense and patterns in different clusters are dissimilar in the same sense. For this it is necessary to first define a measure of similarity which establishes a rule for assigning patterns to the domain of a particular cluster centre. One such measure of similarity is the Euclidean distance $\mathbf{D}$ between two patterns $\mathbf{x}$ and $\mathbf{z}$ defined by $\mathbf{D} = ||\mathbf{x} - \mathbf{z}||$. Smaller the distance between $\mathbf{x}$ and $\mathbf{z}$, greater is the similarity between the two and vice versa. Another well known measure that can be found is Mahalanobis distance.

A simple categorization of clustering schemes is hierarchical and partitional clustering. Single linkage, complete linkage and average linkage are some of the widely used schemes in hierarchical clustering. k-means is a very common partitional clustering technique.

21.3.1 Hierarchical Clustering

In hierarchical clustering, we generate a sequence of partitions with different levels of details. This category of clustering methods can again be divided into *agglomerative* and *divisive* approaches. In case of hierarchical clustering, we have to construct a number of cluster configurations before we obtain the desired one. All these cluster configurations constitute a hierarchy of partitions, represented as a *dendrogram* in which each partition is nested within the partition at the next level in the hierarchy.

Agglomerative methods: An agglomerative approach works starting with the individual data elements as isolated single element clusters. Based on the proximity of these clusters, we merge some of these clusters into newer clusters at the next level of hierarchy. We proceed in this way until we are left with a single cluster having all the elements in it. Examples of agglomerative hierarchical clustering algorithms are single-link, complete-link and average-link hierarchical clustering algorithm.

In agglomerative clustering, at each step we proceed by merging the two nearest clusters. A particular distance metric is used for this purpose. Different metrics are used for the three different classes of agglomerative methods. A general class of metrics was given by Lance and Williams. If $d(k, ij)$ be the distance between cluster k and the union of clusters i and j, then $d(k, ij)$ is defined as

$$d(k, ij) = \alpha_i d(k, i) + \alpha_j d(k, j) + \beta d(i, j) + \gamma |d(k, i) - d(k, j)| \tag{21.14}$$

The agglomerative algorithms are illustrated in the following paragraphs.

Single-linkage algorithm: The *single-linkage algorithm* is also known as the *minimum method* and the *nearest neighbour method.* The latter title underscores its close relation to the nearest neighbour classification method. The single linkage algorithm is obtained by defining the distance between two clusters to be the smallest distance between two points such that one point is in each cluster. Formally, if C_i and C_j are clusters, the distance between them is defined as

$$D_{SL}(C_i, C_j) = \min_{a \in C_i, b \in C_j} d(a, b) \tag{21.15}$$

where, $d(a, b)$ denotes the distance between the samples a and b.

Example 1: Consider the data set in Table 21.3 having two attributes and five patterns. Apply the single-linkage algorithm to classify the data set into two clusters.

Table 21.3: Initial unlabelled data for Example 1

Data item	$\mathbf{x}_1$	$\mathbf{x}_2$	$\mathbf{x}_3$	$\mathbf{x}_4$	$\mathbf{x}_5$
Values	(1, 1)	(2, 3)	(3, 1)	(4, 4)	(5, 2)

Solution: The distance matrix (Euclidean distance) for the given data set is shown in Table 21.4.

Table 21.4: Distance Matrix

Patterns	$\mathbf{x}_1$	$\mathbf{x}_2$	$\mathbf{x}_3$	$\mathbf{x}_4$	$\mathbf{x}_5$
$\mathbf{x}_1$	0.0	2.2	2.0	4.2	4.1
$\mathbf{x}_2$	2.2	0.0	2.2	2.2	3.2
$\mathbf{x}_3$	2.0	2.2	0.0	3.2	2.2
$\mathbf{x}_4$	4.2	2.2	3.2	0.0	2.2
$\mathbf{x}_5$	4.1	3.2	2.2	2.2	0.0

In agglomerative methods, we need to start with each individual patterns as a single cluster. Then we proceed via merging of patterns on the basis of their proximity. In this example, the closest two patterns are $\mathbf{x}_1$ and $\mathbf{x}_3$. Therefore, we combine them into a single cluster.

Now, $\{\mathbf{x}_1, \mathbf{x}_3\}$ represent a single cluster. To find its distance from any other cluster $\{\mathbf{x}_4\}$, in single-linkage procedure, we shall consider the minimum of distances between $\mathbf{x}_1$ and $\{\mathbf{x}_4\}$, and $\mathbf{x}_3$ and $\{\mathbf{x}_4\}$. In other words, distance between $\{\mathbf{x}_1, \mathbf{x}_3\}$ and $\{\mathbf{x}_4\}$

= min (distance between $\mathbf{x}_1$ and $\{\mathbf{x}_4\}$, distance between $\mathbf{x}_3$ and $\{\mathbf{x}_4\}$) = min(4.2, 3.2) = 3.2, which is shown in Table 21.5.

In the next step, the two closest clusters are $\{\mathbf{x}_1, \mathbf{x}_3\}$ and $\{\mathbf{x}_2\}$. Of course, we could merge $\{\mathbf{x}_1, \mathbf{x}_3\}$ with $\{\mathbf{x}_5\}$ as well. However, we have selected the former option. Merging results in the following distance matrix.

Table 21.5: Distance Matrix After First Merge

Patterns	$\{\mathbf{x}_1, \mathbf{x}_3\}$	$\{\mathbf{x}_2\}$	$\{\mathbf{x}_4\}$	$\{\mathbf{x}_5\}$
$\{\mathbf{x}_1, \mathbf{x}_3\}$	0.0	2.2	3.2	2.2
$\{\mathbf{x}_2\}$	2.2	0.0	2.2	3.2
$\{\mathbf{x}_4\}$	3.2	2.2	0.0	2.2
$\{\mathbf{x}_5\}$	2.2	3.2	2.2	0.0

In the final step, we will merge clusters $\{\mathbf{x}_1, \mathbf{x}_2, \mathbf{x}_3\}$ and $\{\mathbf{x}_4\}$. (Here also, we could have merged $\{\mathbf{x}_1, \mathbf{x}_2, \mathbf{x}_3\}$ and $\{\mathbf{x}_5\}$.) Therefore, the final clusters are $\{\mathbf{x}_1, \mathbf{x}_2, \mathbf{x}_3, \mathbf{x}_4\}$ and $\{\mathbf{x}_5\}$ (Table 21.6).

♣

Table 21.6: Distance Matrix After Second Merge

Patterns	$\{\mathbf{x}_1, \mathbf{x}_2, \mathbf{x}_3\}$	$\{\mathbf{x}_4\}$	$\{\mathbf{x}_5\}$
$\{\mathbf{x}_1, \mathbf{x}_2, \mathbf{x}_3\}$	0.0	2.2	2.2
$\{\mathbf{x}_4\}$	2.2	0.0	2.2
$\{\mathbf{x}_5\}$	2.2	2.2	0.0

Complete-linkage Algorithm

The *complete-linkage algorithm* is also known as the *maximum method* and the *farthest neighbour method*. The complete linkage algorithm is obtained by defining the distance between two clusters to be the largest distance between two points such that one point is in each cluster. Formally, if C_i and C_j are clusters, the distance between them is defined as

$$D_{CL}(C_i, C_j) = \max_{a \in C_i,\ b \in C_j} d(a, b) \tag{21.16}$$

where, $d(a, b)$ denotes the distance between the samples a and b. The single-linkage algorithm allows clusters to grow long and thin, whereas the complete-linkage algorithm produces more compact clusters. Both clusterings are susceptible to distortion by outliers or deviant observations.

Example 2: Consider the data set given in Table 21.3. Apply the complete-linkage algorithm to classify the data set into two clusters.

Solution: In this case also, we start with five clusters $\{\mathbf{x}_1\}, \{\mathbf{x}_2\}, \{\mathbf{x}_3\}, \{\mathbf{x}_4\}$ and $\{\mathbf{x}_5\}$. Since, the minimum distance is found between $\{\mathbf{x}_1\}$ and $\{\mathbf{x}_3\}$, we merge them into $\{\mathbf{x}_1, \mathbf{x}_3\}$ to get four clusters $\{\mathbf{x}_1, \mathbf{x}_3\}, \{\mathbf{x}_2\}, \{\mathbf{x}_4\}$ and $\{\mathbf{x}_5\}$. In complete-linkage algorithm distance between $\{\mathbf{x}_1, \mathbf{x}_3\}$ and $\{\mathbf{x}_4\}$, say, is the maximum of distances between $\mathbf{x}_1$ and $\mathbf{x}_4$, and $\mathbf{x}_3$ and $\mathbf{x}_4$. Hence, we use distance between $\{\mathbf{x}_1, \mathbf{x}_3\}$ and $\{\mathbf{x}_4\}$ = max (distance between $\mathbf{x}_1$ and $\{\mathbf{x}_4\}$, distance between $\mathbf{x}_3$ and $\{\mathbf{x}_4\}$) $= \min(4.2, 3.2) = 4.2$ in Table 21.7.

Table 21.7: Distance Matrix After First Merge

Patterns	$\{\mathbf{x}_1, \mathbf{x}_3\}$	$\{\mathbf{x}_2\}$	$\{\mathbf{x}_4\}$	$\{\mathbf{x}_5\}$
$\{\mathbf{x}_1, \mathbf{x}_3\}$	0.0	2.2	4.2	2.2
$\{\mathbf{x}_2\}$	2.2	0.0	2.2	3.2
$\{\mathbf{x}_4\}$	4.2	2.2	0.0	2.2
$\{\mathbf{x}_5\}$	2.2	3.2	2.2	0.0

In the next step, the two closest clusters are $\{\mathbf{x}_1, \mathbf{x}_3\}$ and $\{\mathbf{x}_2\}$. (We could have merged $\{\mathbf{x}_4\}$ and $\{\mathbf{x}_5\}$ also.) Merging results in the following distance matrix (Table 21.8).

Table 21.8: Distance Matrix After Second Merge

Patterns	$\{\mathbf{x}_1, \mathbf{x}_2, \mathbf{x}_3\}$	$\{\mathbf{x}_4\}$	$\{\mathbf{x}_5\}$
$\{\mathbf{x}_1, \mathbf{x}_2, \mathbf{x}_3\}$	0.0	4.2	4.1
$\{\mathbf{x}_4\}$	4.2	0.0	2.2
$\{\mathbf{x}_5\}$	4.1	2.2	0.0

In the final step, we will merge clusters $\{\mathbf{x}_4\}$ and $\{\mathbf{x}_5\}$. Therefore, the final clusters are $\{\mathbf{x}_1, \mathbf{x}_2, \mathbf{x}_3\}$ and $\{\mathbf{x}_4, \mathbf{x}_5\}$.

♣

Average-linkage algorithm

The *average-linkage algorithm* is an attempt to compromise between the extremes of the single- and complete-linkage algorithms. This algorithm is also known as **Unweighted Pair-Group Method using Arithmetic Averages(UPGMA)**, and is one of the most widely used hierarchical clustering methods. The average-linkage algorithm is obtained by defining the distance between two clusters to be the average distance between two points such that one point is in each cluster. Formally, if C_i and C_j are clusters with n_i and n_j members, respectively, the distance between them is defined as

$$D_{AL}(C_i, C_j) = \frac{1}{n_i n_j} \sum_{a \in C_i, b \in C_j} d(a, b) \tag{21.17}$$

Example 3: Consider the data set given in Table 21.3. Apply the average-linkage algorithm to classify the data set into two clusters.

Solution: Here also, we start with five clusters $\{\mathbf{x}_1\}, \{\mathbf{x}_2\}, \{\mathbf{x}_3\}, \{\mathbf{x}_4\}$ and $\{\mathbf{x}_5\}$. Since, the minimum distance is found between $\{\mathbf{x}_1\}$ and $\{\mathbf{x}_3\}$, we merge them into $\{\mathbf{x}_1, \mathbf{x}_3\}$ to get four clusters $\{\mathbf{x}_1, \mathbf{x}_3\}, \{\mathbf{x}_2\}, \{\mathbf{x}_4\}$ and $\{\mathbf{x}_5\}$. In average-linkage algorithm distance between $\{\mathbf{x}_1, \mathbf{x}_3\}$ and $\{\mathbf{x}_4\}$, say, is the average of distance between $\mathbf{x}_1$ and $\mathbf{x}_4$, and that between $\mathbf{x}_3$ and $\mathbf{x}_4$. Hence, we use distance between $\{\mathbf{x}_1, \mathbf{x}_3\}$ and $\{\mathbf{x}_4\}$ = avg (distance between $\mathbf{x}_1$ and $\{\mathbf{x}_4\}$, distance between $\mathbf{x}_3$ and $\{\mathbf{x}_4\}$) $= \text{avg}(4.2, 3.2) = \frac{4.2+3.2}{2} = 3.7$ Table 21.9.

Table 21.9: Distance Matrix After First Merge

Patterns	$\{\mathbf{x}_1, \mathbf{x}_3\}$	$\{\mathbf{x}_2\}$	$\{\mathbf{x}_4\}$	$\{\mathbf{x}_5\}$
$\{\mathbf{x}_1, \mathbf{x}_3\}$	0.0	2.2	3.7	3.2
$\{\mathbf{x}_2\}$	2.2	0.0	2.2	3.2
$\{\mathbf{x}_4\}$	3.7	2.2	0.0	2.2
$\{\mathbf{x}_5\}$	3.2	3.2	2.2	0.0

In the next step, the two closest clusters are $\{\mathbf{x}_1, \mathbf{x}_3\}$ and $\{\mathbf{x}_2\}$. (We could have merged $\{\mathbf{x}_2\}$ and $\{\mathbf{x}_4\}$ also.) Merging results in the following distance matrix (Table 21.10).

Table 21.10: Distance Matrix After Second Merge

Patterns	$\{\mathbf{x}_1, \mathbf{x}_2, \mathbf{x}_3\}$	$\{\mathbf{x}_4\}$	$\{\mathbf{x}_5\}$
$\{\mathbf{x}_1, \mathbf{x}_2, \mathbf{x}_3\}$	0.0	3.2	3.2
$\{\mathbf{x}_4\}$	3.2	0.0	2.2
$\{\mathbf{x}_5\}$	3.2	2.2	0.0

In the final step, we will merge clusters $\{\mathbf{x}_4\}$ and $\{\mathbf{x}_5\}$. Therefore, the final clusters are $\{\mathbf{x}_1, \mathbf{x}_2, \mathbf{x}_3\}$ and $\{\mathbf{x}_4, \mathbf{x}_5\}$.

♣

The data set and results for Examples 1, 2 and 3 are depicted in Figure 21.2.

Divisive methods

The divisive approach works in the reverse direction to that of the agglomerative one. Two very commonly used divisive clustering algorithms are briefly outlined below.

Largest diameter algorithm

- An item with the maximum diameter is found.

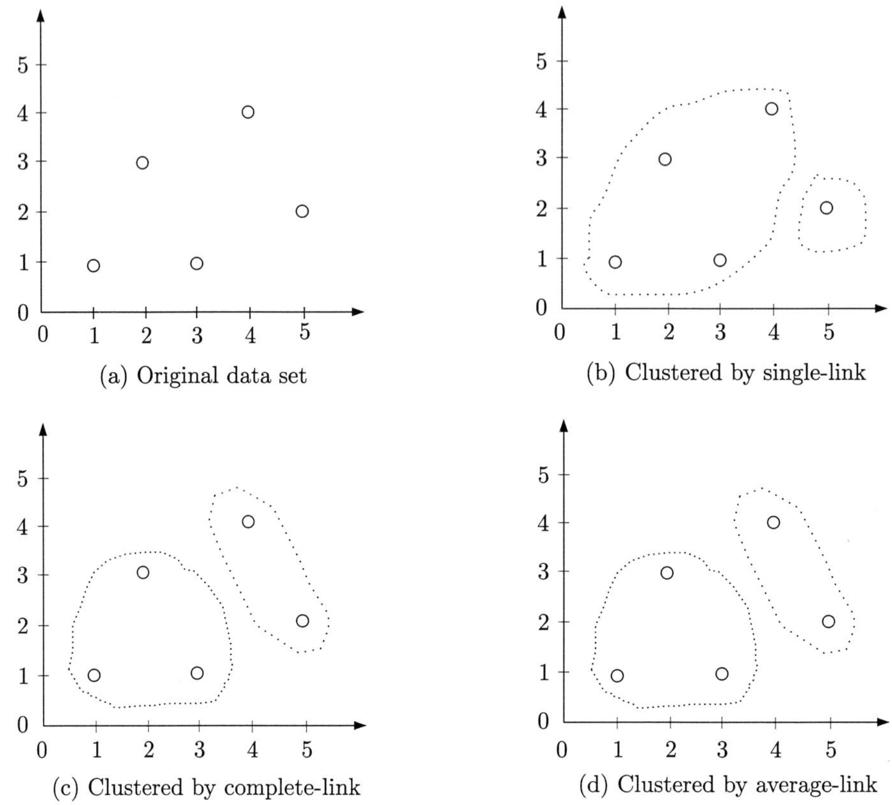

Figure 21.2: Example dataset.

- Maximum diameter means having maximum average distance from all other data items.
- Items are then grouped based on whether they are nearer to this new item or to the centre of the old cluster.
- The above two steps are repeated for the sub-clusters.

Minimum spanning tree algorithm

- An MST is formed using the data items as spatial coordinates.
- This MST forms a single cluster with all items.
- The largest link is removed from the MST to form two clusters.
- The above step is continued to get more clusters.

An example of MST based divisive clustering is shown in Figure 21.3. Here, the initial MST is divided to form two clusters.

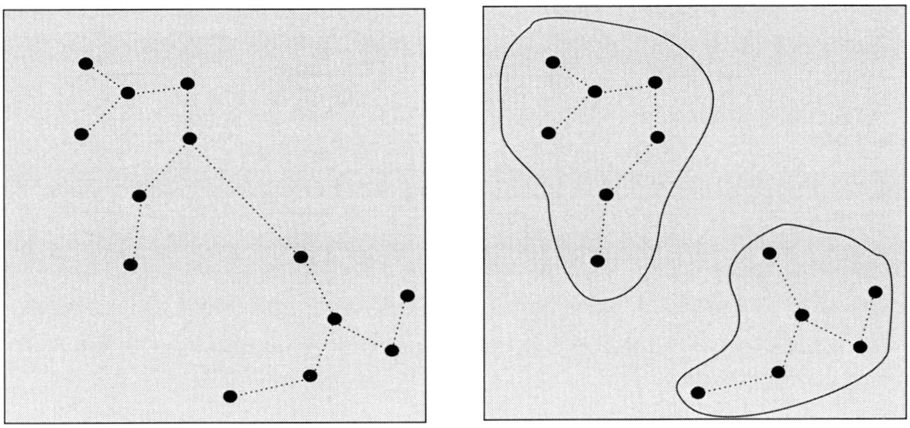

(a) Before clustering (b) After clustering

Figure 21.3: Example of MST based clustering.

21.3.2 Partitional Clustering

The problem of partitional clustering can be formally stated as follows. Given n patterns in an N-dimensional Euclidean space, $I\!R^N$, determine a partition of the patterns into K groups, or clusters, such that the patterns in a cluster are more similar to each other than to patterns in different clusters. The mathematical formulation of the partitional clustering criterion is as follows:

Let the n points $\{\mathbf{x}_1, \mathbf{x}_2, \ldots, \mathbf{x}_n\}$ be represented by S and the K clusters by $\{C_1, C_2, C_3, \ldots, C_K\}$. Then

$$\begin{aligned} &C_i \neq \emptyset && \text{for} \quad i = 1, \ldots, K, \\ &C_i \bigcap C_j = \emptyset && \text{for} \quad i = 1, \ldots, K, \quad j = 1, \ldots, K \text{ and } i \neq j, \text{ and} \\ &\textstyle\bigcup_{i=1}^{K} C_i = S. \end{aligned}$$

Thus in case of partitional clustering, if we know the desired number of clusters, we can start to construct the many numbers of non-overlapping clusters. Such partitions of the data attempt to recover natural groups present in it. One of the most important problems in partitional clustering is to find a partition of the given data , with a specified or estimated number of clusters, that minimizes the sum of within cluster variation. k-means clustering algorithm is one of the most widely used schemes in this category. It attempts to partition the data in such a way that the sum of the squared errors (within cluster variation) is minimized. This criterion is sometimes referred to as *minimum squared-error* criterion. If we have a set of n patterns, $\{\mathbf{x}_1, \mathbf{x}_2, \ldots, \mathbf{x}_n\}$ in d-dimensions, we need to partition it into K clusters $C_1, C_2, \ldots, C_K$ such that cluster C_k has n_k patterns and each pattern is exactly in one cluster, so that $\sum_{k=1}^{K} n_k = n$.

The mean vector or centre, $\mathbf{z}_k$ of cluster C_k is defined as

$$\mathbf{z}_k = \left(\frac{1}{\#C_k}\right) \sum_{\mathbf{x}_i \in C_k} \mathbf{x}_i \tag{21.18}$$

The squared-error for cluster C_k is now defined as the within cluster variation which is given by

$$E_k = \sum_{\mathbf{x}_j \in C_i} ||\mathbf{x}_j - \mathbf{z}_i||^2 \tag{21.19}$$

Thus, squared-error for the entire data set consisting of K clusters become

$$E_K = \sum_{k=1}^{K} E_k \tag{21.20}$$

A general algorithm for iterative partitional clustering algorithm is given below.

Algorithm for iterative partitional clustering

1. Select an initial partition with K clusters. Repeat Steps 2 through 5 until the cluster membership stabilizes.
2. Generate a new partition by assigning each pattern to its closest cluster center.
3. Compute new cluster centres as the centroids of the clusters.
4. Repeat Steps 2 and 3 until an optimum value of the criterion function is found.
5. Adjust the number of clusters by merging and splitting existing clusters or by removing small, or outlier, clusters.

Without Step 5 of the above algorithm, we can work with a fixed number of clusters as is done in well-known crisp partitional clustering algorithms two different versions of which are Forgy's algorithm (1965) and McQueen's k-means algorithm (1967). When Step 5 is included, the algorithm works with variable number of clusters as is done in the ISODATA algorithm (Ball and Hall 1965). In the following, we shall elaborate the steps of McQueen's k-means algorithm (since we have used this algorithm), its fuzzy version and the ISODATA algorithm.

In Forgy's algorithm, besides the data, input consists of k, the number of clusters to be constructed, and k samples called *seed points.* These seed points could be chosen randomly, or some knowledge of the desired cluster structures could be used to guide their selection. The algorithm is given below.

Forgy's algorithm

1. Initialize the cluster centroids to the seed points.
2. For each sample, find the cluster centroid nearest to it. Put the sample in the cluster identified with the nearest cluster centroid.

3. If no samples changed clusters in Step 2, stop.
4. Compute the centroids of the resulting clusters and go to Step 2.

The k-means algorithm differs from Forgy's algorithm in that the centroids of the clusters are recomputed as soon as a sample joins a cluster. Also, unlike Forgy's algorithm which is iterative, the k-means algorithm makes only two passes through the data set. The k-means algorithm is given below.

k-means algorithm

1. Begin with k clusters, each consisting of one of the first k samples. For each of the remaining $n-k$ samples, find the centroid nearest to it. Put the sample in the cluster identified with this nearest centroid. After each sample is assigned, recompute the centroid of the altered cluster.
2. Go through the data a second time. For each sample, find the centroid nearest to it. Put the sample in the cluster identified with this nearest centroid.

An alternative version of the k-means algorithm iterates Step 2. Specifically, Step 2 is replaced by the following Steps 2 through 4:

1. For each sample, find the centroid nearest to it. Put the sample in the cluster identified with this nearest centroid.
2. If no samples changed clusters, stop.
3. Recompute the centroids of altered clusters and go to Step 2.

The goal of Forgy's algorithm and the k-means algorithm is to minimize the squared-error for a fixed number of clusters. Because of greedy nature of these algorithms sometimes they terminate with a clustering that achieves a *local* minimum squared error. Furthermore, clustering depends, in general, on the initial choice of seed points.

Detailed steps of the k-means algorithm

Step 1: Choose K initial cluster centres $\mathbf{z}_1, \mathbf{z}_2, \ldots, \mathbf{z}_K$ randomly from the n points $\{\mathbf{x}_1, \mathbf{x}_2, \ldots, \mathbf{x}_n\}$.

Step 2: Assign point $\mathbf{x}_i$, $i = 1, 2, \ldots, n$ to cluster C_j, $j = 1, 2, \ldots, K$ iff

$$||\mathbf{x}_i - \mathbf{z}_j|| < ||\mathbf{x}_i - \mathbf{z}_p||, \quad p = 1, 2, \ldots, K, \text{ and } j \neq p.$$

Ties are resolved arbitrarily.

Step 3: Compute new cluster centres $\mathbf{z}_1^*, \mathbf{z}_2^*, \ldots, \mathbf{z}_K^*$ as follows:

$$\mathbf{z}_i^* = \frac{1}{n} \sum_{x_j \in C_i} \mathbf{x}_j, \quad i = 1, 2, \ldots, K$$

where n_i is the number of elements belonging to cluster C_i.

Step 4: If $\mathbf{z}_i^* = \mathbf{z}_i$, $i = 1, 2, \ldots, K$ then terminate. Otherwise go to Step 2.

Note that in case the process does not terminate at Step 4 normally, then it is executed for a maximum fixed number of generations.

Example 4: Consider the data set in Tabel 21.11 having two attributes and five patterns. Apply the k-means algorithm to classify the data set into two clusters.

Table 21.11: Initial Unlabelled Data for Example 4

Data Item	$\mathbf{x}_1$	$\mathbf{x}_2$	$\mathbf{x}_3$	$\mathbf{x}_4$	$\mathbf{x}_5$
Values	(1, 1)	(2, 3)	(3, 1)	(4, 4)	(5, 2)

Solution: The k-means randomly selects two patterns to be the initial centre vectors. Let, the first two patterns be selected as initial centre vectors, i.e. $\mathbf{z}_1^{(0)} = \mathbf{x}_1$ and $\mathbf{z}_2^{(0)}$ $= \mathbf{x}_2$.

We now compute the distance the each of the patterns from each centre vectors to determine initial class labels. This is shown in Table 21.12. Iterationwise results are presented in Tables 21.12–21.14.

Table 21.12: Distance Computation and Initial Class Label Assignment

Data Item (Pattern)	$\mathbf{x}_1$	$\mathbf{x}_2$	$\mathbf{x}_3$	$\mathbf{x}_4$	$\mathbf{x}_5$
Distance from $\mathbf{z}_1^{(0)}$	0.00	2.24	2.0	3.00	4.12
Distance from $\mathbf{z}_2^{(0)}$	2.24	0.00	2.24	2.24	3.16
Class label	1	2	1	2	2

Table 21.13: Distance Computation and Assignment During Second Iteration

Data Item (Pattern)	$\mathbf{x}_1$	$\mathbf{x}_2$	$\mathbf{x}_3$	$\mathbf{x}_4$	$\mathbf{x}_5$
Distance from $\mathbf{z}_1^{(1)}$	1.00	2.00	1.0	3.60	3.16
Distance from $\mathbf{z}_2^{(1)}$	5.70	3.81	4.30	1.58	2.55
Class label	1	1	1	2	2

Table 21.14: Distance Computation and Assignment During Third Iteration

Data Item (Pattern)	$\mathbf{x}_1$	$\mathbf{x}_2$	$\mathbf{x}_3$	$\mathbf{x}_4$	$\mathbf{x}_5$
Distance from $\mathbf{z}_1^{(2)}$	2.50	1.12	1.50	2.69	2.50
Distance from $\mathbf{z}_2^{(2)}$	4.03	2.50	2.50	1.12	1.12
Class label	1	1	1	2	2

From Table 21.12 we see that, $\mathbf{x}_1$ and $\mathbf{x}_3$ fall under the first cluster and the others are assigned to the second. The new centre vectors are computed as

$$\mathbf{z}_1^{(1)} = \left(\frac{1+3}{2}, \frac{1+1}{2}\right) = (2.00, 1.00)$$

$$\mathbf{z}_2^{(1)} = \left(\frac{2+4+5}{2}, \frac{3+4+2}{2}\right) = (5.50, 4.50)$$

The centre vectors $\mathbf{z}_1^{(1)}$ and $\mathbf{z}_2^{(1)}$ are not equal to the initial centre vectors. Hence, the process will enter the next iteration.

Therefore, $\mathbf{x}_1, \mathbf{x}_2$ and $\mathbf{x}_3$ fall under the first cluster and the others are assigned to the second. The new centre vectors are computed as

$$\mathbf{z}_1^{(2)} = \left(\frac{1+3+2}{2}, \frac{1+1+3}{2}\right) = (3.00, 2.50)$$

$$\mathbf{z}_2^{(2)} = \left(\frac{4+5}{2}, \frac{4+2}{2}\right) = (4.50, 3.00)$$

The centre vectors $\mathbf{z}_1^{(2)}$ and $\mathbf{z}_2^{(2)}$ are not equal to $\mathbf{z}_1^{(1)}$ and $\mathbf{z}_2^{(1)}$. Hence, the process will entre the next iteration.

Therefore, $\mathbf{x}_1, \mathbf{x}_2$ and $\mathbf{x}_3$ fall under the first cluster and the others are assigned to the second. The new centre vectors are computed as

$$\mathbf{z}_1^{(3)} = \left(\frac{1+3+2}{2}, \frac{1+1+3}{2}\right) = (3.00, 2.50)$$

$$\mathbf{z}_2^{(3)} = \left(\frac{4+5}{2}, \frac{4+2}{2}\right) = (4.50, 3.00)$$

In this iteration, class labels of any of the patterns does not change. Hence, the centre vectors remain unaltered, and the clustering process terminates.

♣

Example 5: Consider the following 2-dimensional data set having 12 elements (Table 21.15). Assume the initial cluster centres as $\mathbf{z}_1 = \mathbf{x}_2$, $\mathbf{z}_2 = \mathbf{x}_5$ and $\mathbf{z}_3 = \mathbf{x}_9$. Trace the k-means algorithm and determine the final clusters.

Table 21.15: Initial Unlabelled Data for Example 5

Data Item	$\mathbf{x}_1$	$\mathbf{x}_2$	$\mathbf{x}_3$	$\mathbf{x}_4$	$\mathbf{x}_5$	$\mathbf{x}_6$	$\mathbf{x}_7$	$\mathbf{x}_8$	$\mathbf{x}_9$	$\mathbf{x}_{10}$	$\mathbf{x}_{11}$	$\mathbf{x}_{12}$
Values	(1, 1)	(1, 2)	(2, 1)	(2, 2)	(3, 1)	(4, 4)	(4, 5)	(5, 1)	(5, 5)	(7, 2)	(7, 3)	(8, 3)

Solution: Results are presented in Tables 21.16–21.21.

After the third iteration the centre vectors reach a stable state. The total within cluster spread is measured to be 16.0.

Table 21.16: Cluster Centres and Distance of Data from Centres During First Iteration

Cluster Number	*Cluster Centre*	*Distance of Data Items*											
		x_1	x_2	x_3	x_4	x_5	x_6	x_7	x_8	x_9	x_{10}	x_{11}	x_{12}
1	(1, 2)	1.00	0.00	1.41	1.00	2.24	3.61	4.24	4.12	5.00	6.00	6.08	7.07
2	(3, 1)	2.00	2.24	1.00	1.41	0.00	3.16	4.12	2.00	4.47	4.12	4.47	5.39
3	(5, 5)	5.66	5.00	5.00	4.24	4.47	1.41	1.00	4.00	0.00	3.61	2.83	3.61

Table 21.17: Class Labels of Data After First Iteration

Data Item	x_1	x_2	x_3	x_4	x_5	x_6	x_7	x_8	x_9	x_{10}	x_{11}	x_{12}
Values	(1, 1)	(1, 2)	(2, 1)	(2, 2)	(3, 1)	(4, 4)	(4, 5)	(5, 1)	(5, 5)	(7, 2)	(7, 3)	(8, 3)
Class labels	1	1	2	1	2	3	3	2	3	3	3	3

Table 21.18: Cluster Centers and Distance of Data from Centres During Second Iteration

Cluster Number	*Cluster Centre*	*Distance of Data Items*											
		x_1	x_2	x_3	x_4	x_5	x_6	x_7	x_8	x_9	x_{10}	x_{11}	x_{12}
1	(1.33, 1.67)	0.75	0.47	0.94	0.75	1.80	3.54	4.27	3.73	4.96	5.68	5.82	6.80
2	(3.33, 1.0)	2.33	2.54	1.33	1.67	0.33	3.07	4.06	1.67	4.33	3.80	4.18	5.08
3	(5.85, 3.67)	5.52	5.11	4.67	4.18	3.89	1.86	2.27	2.79	1.57	2.03	1.34	2.27

Table 21.19: Class Labels of Data After Second Iteration

Data Item	x_1	x_2	x_3	x_4	x_5	x_6	x_7	x_8	x_9	x_{10}	x_{11}	x_{12}
Values	(1, 1)	(1, 2)	(2, 1)	(2, 2)	(3, 1)	(4, 4)	(4, 5)	(5, 1)	(5, 5)	(7, 2)	(7, 3)	(8, 3)
Class labels	1	1	1	1	2	3	3	2	3	3	3	3

Table 21.20: Cluster Centres and Distance of Data from Centres During Third Iteration

Cluster Number	*Cluster Centre*	*Distance of Data Items*											
		x_1	x_2	x_3	x_4	x_5	x_6	x_7	x_8	x_9	x_{10}	x_{11}	x_{12}
1	(1.50, 1.50)	0.71	0.71	0.71	0.71	1.58	3.54	4.30	3.54	4.95	5.52	5.70	6.67
2	(4.00, 1.00)	3.00	3.16	2.00	2.24	1.00	3.00	4.00	1.00	4.12	3.16	3.61	4.47
3	(5.83, 3.67)	5.52	5.11	4.67	4.18	3.89	1.86	2.27	2.79	1.57	2.03	1.34	2.27

Table 21.21: Class Labels of Data After Third Iteration

Data Item	x_1	x_2	x_3	x_4	x_5	x_6	x_7	x_8	x_9	x_{10}	x_{11}	x_{12}
Values	(1, 1)	(1, 2)	(2, 1)	(2, 2)	(3, 1)	(4, 4)	(4, 5)	(5, 1)	(5, 5)	(7, 2)	(7, 3)	(8, 3)
Class labels	1	1	1	1	2	3	3	2	3	3	3	3

♣

Example 6: Consider the 2-dimensional data set of Example 5 with the data (5, 1) changed to (5, 4) and (3, 1) changed to (8, 2). Assume the initial cluster centres as, $\mathbf{z}_1 = \mathbf{x}_2$, $\mathbf{z}_2 = \mathbf{x}_8$ and $\mathbf{z}_3 = \mathbf{x}_9$. Trace the k-means algorithm and determine the final clusters.

Solution: We shall follow a procedure similar to that used in case of Example 5. The results are presented only in tabular forms. For details look at the contents of Tables 21.22–21.26.

Table 21.22: Initial Unlabelled Data

Data Item	x_1	x_2	x_3	x_4	x_5	x_6	x_7	x_8	x_9	x_{10}	x_{11}	x_{12}
Values	(1, 1)	(1, 2)	(2, 1)	(2, 2)	(8, 2)	(4, 4)	(4, 5)	(5, 4)	(5, 5)	(7, 2)	(7, 3)	(8, 3)
Values	(1, 1)	(1, 2)	(2, 1)	(2, 2)	(3, 1)	(4, 4)	(4, 5)	(5, 1)	(5, 5)	(7, 2)	(7, 3)	(8, 3)

Table 21.23: Cluster Centres and Distance of Data from Centres During First Iteration

Cluster Number	*Cluster Centre*	*Distance of Data Items*											
		x_1	x_2	x_3	x_4	x_5	x_6	x_7	x_8	x_9	x_{10}	x_{11}	x_{12}
1	(1.50, 1.50)	0.71	0.71	0.71	0.71	6.52	3.54	4.30	4.30	4.95	5.52	5.70	6.67
2	(6.50, 3.00)	5.85	5.59	4.92	4.61	1.80	2.69	3.20	1.80	2.50	1.12	0.50	1.50
3	(4.50, 5.00)	5.32	4.61	4.72	3.91	4.61	1.12	0.50	1.12	0.50	3.91	3.20	4.03

Table 21.24: Class Labels of Data After First Iteration

Data Item	x_1	x_2	x_3	x_4	x_5	x_6	x_7	x_8	x_9	x_{10}	x_{11}	x_{12}
Values	(1, 1)	(1, 2)	(2, 1)	(2, 2)	(3, 1)	(4, 4)	(4, 5)	(5, 1)	(5, 5)	(7, 2)	(7, 3)	(8, 3)
Class Labels	1	1	1	1	2	3	3	3	3	2	2	2

Table 21.25: Cluster Centres and Distance of Data from Centres During Second Iteration

Cluster Number	*Cluster Centre*	*Distance of Data Items*											
		x_1	x_2	x_3	x_4	x_5	x_6	x_7	x_8	x_9	x_{10}	x_{11}	x_{12}
1	(1.50, 1.50)	0.71	0.71	0.71	0.71	6.52	3.54	4.30	4.30	4.95	5.52	5.70	6.67
2	(7.50, 2.50)	6.67	6.52	5.70	5.52	0.71	3.81	4.30	2.92	3.54	0.71	0.71	0.71
3	(4.50, 4.50)	4.95	4.30	4.30	3.54	4.30	0.71	0.71	0.71	0.71	3.54	2.92	3.81

Table 21.26: Class Labels of Data after Second Iteration

Data Item	x_1	x_2	x_3	x_4	x_5	x_6	x_7	x_8	x_9	x_{10}	x_{11}	x_{12}
Values	(1, 1)	(1, 2)	(2, 1)	(2, 2)	(3, 1)	(4, 4)	(4, 5)	(5, 1)	(5, 5)	(7, 2)	(7, 3)	(8, 3)
Class Labels	1	1	1	1	2	3	3	3	3	2	2	2

After the second iteration the centre vectors reach a stable state. The total within cluster spread is measured to be 8.485280.

♣

Although the k-means algorithm is found to provide very good results, specially when clusters are well separated and hyper spherical in shape, numerous attempts were there to improve the performance of the basic k-means algorithm by absorbing this algorithm within the framework of various optimization algorithms like (i) simulated annealing, genetic algorithm, deterministic annealing, evolutionary programming, tabu search, etc.

21.4 Model Based Methods

Though the k-means algorithm is very effective for many clustering applications, it is solely dependent on distance metrics. It does not derive statistical models of the data and does not allow cluster overlapping. The Expectation Maximization (EM) algorithm, developed by Dempster et al. in 1977, when applied for clustering can produce a proper probabilistic cluster or statistical data model. The problem of clustering can be made fit in the framework of density estimation. Since some combinations of the attribute values are more likely than the others, there exists denser regions in the probability density distribution of a particular data set. The main role of clustering is to identify these denser regions. In EM-Clustering, this probability density function is represented as a mixture of a number of sets of data records (clusters). Thus the data set is a mixture of the clusters and the problem is to identify the data records that constitute a cluster. The EM algorithm is an effective and popular technique for estimating mixture model parameters. The EM algorithm iteratively refines initial mixture model parameter estimates to better fit the data and terminates at a locally optimal solution.

21.4.1 Modelling Clustering as an Estimation of Gaussian Mixture

Theory of Gaussian mixture can provide a suitable framework for clustering. The mixture model approximates the data distribution by fitting a number of density functions f_h, for $h = 1, 2, \ldots, k$ to a data set (S) having n data with d-dimensions or attributes. If $\mathbf{x} \in S$ is any data from S, then the mixture model probability density function at $\mathbf{x}$ can be written as:

$$p(\mathbf{x}) = \sum_{h=1}^{k} w_h \; f_h(\mathbf{x}|\phi_h) \tag{21.21}$$

where, w_h represents the prior probability of any data to belong to cluster C_h. Therefore, for each data item, we have

$$\sum_{h=1}^{k} w_h = 1 \text{ and } w_h \geq 0$$

The functions $f_h(\mathbf{x}|\phi_h)$ for $h = 1, 2, \ldots, k$ are the component density functions modelling distribution of data in cluster C_h, and ϕ_h represents a set of parameters that may be used to compute the value of f_h. In case of a Gaussian mixture, ϕ_h includes the mean (μ_h) and the covariance matrix (Σ_h).

21.4.2 Expectation Maximization (EM) Algorithm

In this approach data and the corresponding clusters are represented as a statistical model. The data are considered to be a collection of random samples from a mixture of several probability distributions. These probability distributions define the clusters also. Each data is generated by one and only one of these distributions, and hence, belongs to one and only one cluster.

Whereas the k-means algorithm partitions a data set into hard clusters, the EM algorithm provides a more general basis and can partition data sets depending on the probability of membership of a data item for all k clusters.

Given observation data set $\mathbf{X} = (\mathbf{x}_i, \mathbf{x}_2, \ldots, \mathbf{x}_n)$, let $f_h(\mathbf{x}|\phi_h)$ be the density of an observation $\mathbf{x}$ from the hth component of the mixture, where ϕ_h are the corresponding parameters. Let K be the total number of components in the mixture. The mixture model for the composite of the clusters is usually formulated in one of the two ways.

In the *classification* approach, the likelihood of the data can be defined as

$$L_C(\phi_1, \ldots, \phi_K; \gamma_1, \ldots, \gamma_K|\mathbf{X}) = \prod_{i=1}^{n} f_{\gamma_i}(\mathbf{x}_i|\phi_{\gamma_i}) \tag{21.22}$$

where, γ_i are the discrete values labelling the classification; $\gamma_i = k$ if $\mathbf{x}_i$ belongs to the kth component.

In the *mixture* approach, the likelihood is

$$L_M(\phi_1, \ldots, \phi_K; \tau_1, \ldots, \tau_K|\mathbf{X}) = \prod_{i=1}^{n} \sum_{k=1}^{K} \tau_k f_k(\mathbf{x}_i|\phi_k) \tag{21.23}$$

where, τ_k are the probabilities that an observation $\mathbf{x}_i$ belongs to the kth component.

Here, we shall consider the mixture model only. Therefore, the probability of membership or weight of data item $\mathbf{x}$ in cluster C_h is

$$w_h(\mathbf{x}) = \frac{f_h(\mathbf{x}|\phi_h)}{\sum_i w_i \; f_i(\mathbf{x}|\phi_i)} \tag{21.24}$$

With the assumption that attributes are independent over data items within a particular cluster, the component density functions can be expressed as a product given below.

$$f_h(\mathbf{x}|\phi_h) = \prod_{j=1}^{d} f_{h,j}(\mathbf{x}_j|\phi_h) \tag{21.25}$$

The multivariate Gaussian for d-dimensional data distribution arranged into k clusters C_h for $h = 1, 2, \ldots, k$, can be expressed, using two parameters, viz. the mean vector μ_h and the $d \times d$ covariance matrix Σ_h, as

$$f_h(\mathbf{x}|\mu_h, \Sigma_h) = \frac{1}{\sqrt{(2\pi)^d|\Sigma_h|}} \exp\left[-\frac{1}{2}(\mathbf{x} - \mu_h)^T (\Sigma_h)^{-1} (\mathbf{x} - \mu_h)\right] \tag{21.26}$$

Here $\mathbf{x}$ and μ_h are column vectors, $|\Sigma_h|$ is determinant of Σ_h.

The Gaussian mixture model for clustering consists of the above two parameters plus the weight w_h associated to cluster C_h for $h = 1, 2, \ldots, k$. If we denote this new set of parameters as $\Phi = \{(w_h, \mu_h, \Sigma_h), h = 1, 2, \ldots, k\}$ then by measuring the quality of a given set of parameters Φ we can get an estimation of the particular mixture model representing the clustering of a data set. This quality can be measured by the log-likelihood of the data, for the particular mixture model, as

$$L(\Phi) = \sum_{x \in S} \log \left[\sum_{h=1}^{k} w_h \; f_h(\mathbf{x}|\mu_h \Sigma_h) \right] \tag{21.27}$$

The EM algorithm iteratively updates an initial estimation of Φ trying to maximize $L(\Phi)$.

We can now switch over to the probability notations and formulate the EM clustering algorithm. As mentioned earlier, each cluster is modelled by a d-dimensional Gaussian probability distribution. The multidimensional Gaussian distribution for cluster C_h, $h = 1, \ldots, k$, is parameterized by a d-dimensional mean vector μ_h and $d \times d$ covariance matrix Σ_h as

$$Pr(\mathbf{x}|h) = \frac{1}{\sqrt{(2\pi)^d |\Sigma_h|}} \exp \left[-\frac{1}{2} (\mathbf{x} - \mu_h)^T (\Sigma_h)^{-1} (\mathbf{x} - \mu_h) \right] \tag{21.28}$$

Here $\mathbf{x}$ and μ^h are column vectors, $|\Sigma^h|$ is determinant of Σ^h. The mixture model probability density function is

$$Pr(\mathbf{x}) = \sum_{h=1}^{k} w_h Pr(\mathbf{x}|h) \tag{21.29}$$

The coefficients w_h (mixture weights) represent the fraction of the database represented by the corresponding cluster. A given data record $\mathbf{x}$ is a member of each of the k clusters with different probabilities of membership. Probability in population (cluster) C_h is given by

$$Pr(h|\mathbf{x}) = \frac{w_h Pr(\mathbf{x}|h)}{Pr(\mathbf{x})} \tag{21.30}$$

EM iteratively computes locally optimal maximum likelihood model parameter values. Steps of the EM algorithm are given below.

The EM clustering algorithm

1. Initialize the mixture model parameters for iteration $j = 0 : w_{0,h}, \mu_{0,h}$ and $\Sigma_{0,h}$, $h = 1, \ldots, k$.

2. Having mixture model parameters at iteration j, update them as follows: For each data item $\mathbf{x} \in S$ (S is the data set):

   Compute the membership probability of $\mathbf{x}$ in each cluster as:

$$Pr(h|\mathbf{x}) = \frac{w_{j,h} Pr^j(\mathbf{x}|h)}{Pr^j(\mathbf{x})}, \text{ for } h = 1, \dots k$$

3. Update mixture model parameters:

$$w_{j+1,h} = \frac{1}{N} \sum_{\mathbf{x} \in D} Pr(h|\mathbf{x})$$

$$\mu_{j+1,h} = \frac{\sum_{\mathbf{x} \in S} \mathbf{x}\; Pr(h|\mathbf{x})}{\sum_{\mathbf{x} \in S} Pr(h|\mathbf{x})}$$

$$\Sigma_{j,h} = \frac{\sum_{\mathbf{x} \in S} Pr(h|\mathbf{x}) \left(\mathbf{x} - \mu_{j+1,h}\right) \left(\mathbf{x} - \mu_{j+1,h}\right)^T}{\sum_{\mathbf{x} \in S} Pr(h|\mathbf{x})}$$

   for $h = 1, \dots, k$.

4. If $|E_j - E_{j+1}| \leq \epsilon$, stop. Else set $j = j + 1$ and go to Step 2. E_j is the log likelihood of the mixture model at iteration j:

$$\begin{aligned} E_j &= \sum_{\mathbf{x} \in S} \log \left[Pr^j(\mathbf{x}) \right] \\ &= \sum_{\mathbf{x} \in S} \log \left[\sum_{h=1}^{k} w_{j,h}\; Pr^j(\mathbf{x}|h) \right] \end{aligned}$$

21.5 Fuzzy Clustering

Hard clustering algorithms work fine in situation where individual clusters are quite isolated and separated from each other. However, in practice we encounter data sets in which elements from different clusters are found to overlap. This problem is very common in large multidimensional data sets. In such situations, hard clustering fails to categorize patterns accurately. Fuzzy decision making is needed to properly resolve any class conflict among overlapped patterns.

The fuzzy version of the k-means algorithm is commonly known as the fuzzy c-means algorithm (Bezdek 1981). Here concepts of fuzzy set theory (Zadeh 1965) has been used. Fuzzy clustering and the fuzzy c-means algorithm are described below.

Fuzzy clustering

In case of fuzzy clustering a pattern may belong to all the classes with certain fuzzy membership grade. So, in this case our purpose is to evolve an appropriate partition matrix $U = [u_{ij}]_{K\times n}$, where $u_{ij} \in [0,\ 1]$, such that u_{ij} denotes the grade of membership of the jth element to the ith cluster. In fuzzy partitioning of the data, the following conditions hold:

$$0 < \sum_{j=1}^{n} u_{ij} < n \quad \text{for} \quad i = 1, \ldots, K,$$

$$\sum_{i=1}^{K} u_{ij} = 1 \qquad \text{for} \quad j = 1, \ldots, n \text{ and,}$$

$$\sum_{i=1}^{K}\sum_{j=1}^{n} u_{ij} = n$$

The Fuzzy c-means algorithm

The well known fuzzy c-means model of clustering uses the weighted within cluster sum of squared error function J_m, which is defined as:

$$J_m = \sum_{j=1}^{n}\sum_{i=1}^{K} u_{ij}^m \|\mathbf{x}_j - \mathbf{z}_i\|_A^{\,2} \tag{21.31}$$

where, $\mathbf{Z} = \mathbf{z}_1, \mathbf{z}_2, \ldots, \mathbf{z}_K$ is the set of cluster centres, $\mathbf{z}_i \in R^p$ for $1 \le i \le K$ and $\|\mathbf{x}\|_A = \sqrt{\mathbf{x}^T A \mathbf{x}}$ is any inner product norm. Minimization of J_m will lead to the optimal cluster structure. This function is exactly similar to the function J_1 [in Eq. (21.20) it is written as E_K], used in hard clustering problems except that there u_{ij} will be either 0 or 1 and $m = 1$.

In Eq. (21.31), the fuzzy membership grade u_{ij} and the fuzzy cluster centre z_i are used. It is observed that a particular assignment of U and Z may minimize the fuzzy objective function J_m only if,

$$u_{ij} = \left[\sum_{k=1}^{K}\left(\frac{D_{ijA}}{D_{kjA}}\right)^{\frac{2}{m-1}}\right]^{-1} \quad \text{for } 1 \le i \le K \text{ and } 1 \le j \le n \tag{21.32}$$

and

$$\mathbf{z}_i = \frac{\sum_{j=1}^{n} (u_{ij})^m \mathbf{x}_j}{\sum_{j=1}^{n} (u_{ij})^m} \quad \text{for } 1 \le i \le K \tag{21.33}$$

when $m > 1$ and $D_{ijA} = \|\mathbf{x}_j - \mathbf{z}_i\|_A > 0\ \forall i, j$.

The fuzzy c-means is a greedy approach to compute the fuzzy membership set $\mathbf{U}$ and the fuzzy centre $\mathbf{Z}$. In every iteration of the algorithm we accept only those changes in $\mathbf{U}$ and $\mathbf{Z}$ that reduce J_m. We stop when there are no more changes or the acceptable error limit has been reached. The algorithm is given below:

- **Step 1:** Select a set of c distinct cluster centres $\mathbf{z}_i$ randomly for $i = 1, 2, \ldots, K$.
- **Step 2:** Calculate U using $\mathbf{z}^{\text{old}}$. Calculate $\mathbf{z}^{\text{new}}$ using U. If $|\mathbf{z}^{\text{new}} - \mathbf{z}^{\text{old}}| \leq \epsilon$ then stop else go to Step 2. Here ϵ is a predefined tolerance limit.
- **Step 3:** Repeat Step 2 until there is no more change in $\mathbf{Z}$ or $|\mathbf{z}^{\text{new}} - \mathbf{z}^{\text{old}}| \leq \epsilon$ for a fixed tolerance ϵ.

21.6 New Approaches for Partitional Clustering

Methods of clustering are now being heavily used for data mining applications. In data mining we are basically interested in finding out different structural informations present in the data set. These structures may be defined by the distribution of data items or by some association rule that correlate them. In other words, we stress on finding out groups of similar data or information as different categories. One of the classical and fundamental methods for determining correlated data is clustering. Of course, in data mining, we can use various other statistical methods like principal component analysis, multivariate analysis, factor analysis, multidimensional scaling, correspondence analysis, etc. But, clustering has a very broad spectrum of application areas in statistics, pattern recognition, image segmentation, codebook design, machine learning, etc. Data mining is possibly the newest addition in this list. The basic difference between classical clustering methods and the data mining approaches is that, in the latter, we use very large sets of data as input to the concerned procedure and expect acceptable outputs within practical time constraints. Accordingly, scientists and researchers try to modify existing classical algorithms suitably or to develop newer methods that satisfy all practical considerations. In this section, we shall describe some of the most commonly used methods in this regard.

21.6.1 The PAM or k-mediod Algorithm

As mentioned earlier, in order to apply partitional clustering methods for large databases several different methods have been developed. The oldest of these approaches is the PAM (Partitioning Around Mediods) algorithm. This algorithm has been developed by Kaufmann and Rousseeuw in 1990. It has an inherent similarity with the classical k-means algorithm for clustering.

The PAM algorithm is also known as the k-mediod method because of its similarity with the classical k-means. However, the PAM is different from the k-means in that

- It uses mediods instead of cluster means to represent cluster prototype.
- It is very robust to the existence of outlier points.

- Unlike k-means, clusters found by PAM do not depend on the order of data items in which they are examined, i.e. independent of the initial cluster configuration.
- PAM is invariant to translations and orthogonal transformations of data items.
- It is found experimentally that PAM can handle large amount of data relatively efficiently.
- While in k-means we need to compute the distance of each element from the corresponding cluster centroid in each iteration, in PAM we compute these distances only once at the beginning of the process.

To find K clusters consider that $\mathbf{x}_i$ is a mediod and $\mathbf{x}_j$ is a non-mediod. $\mathbf{x}_j$ belongs to the cluster represented by $\mathbf{x}_i$, if $d(\mathbf{x}_i, \mathbf{x}_j) = min_k\{d(\mathbf{x}_i, \mathbf{x}_k)\}$ for all mediods $k = 1, \ldots, K$. Here, $d(\mathbf{x}_i, \mathbf{x}_j)$ is the dissimilarity between objects $\mathbf{x}_i$ and $\mathbf{x}_j$. All these dissimilarity values are made input to PAM. Finally, the quality of solution is determined by the average dissimilarity between an object and the mediod of its cluster.

PAM begins with an arbitrary random selection of K mediods from the data set. At each step a non-mediod object is swapped with a mediod with an objective to improve the quality of clustering. This process is continued for each mediod separately. In particular, to calculate the effect of each swap between a pair of a mediod and a non-mediod object, PAM computes a distance measure D_{ijh} for all non-mediod objects $\mathbf{x}_j$. Depending on the situation of $\mathbf{x}_j$, D_{ijh} can be calculated by one of the following equations:

Case 1: $\mathbf{x}_j$ belongs to the cluster represented by $\mathbf{x}_i$. Let, $\mathbf{x}_j$ is more similar to $\mathbf{x}_l$ than $\mathbf{x}_h$, i.e. $d(\mathbf{x}_j, \mathbf{x}_h) \geq d(\mathbf{x}_j, \mathbf{x}_l)$, where $\mathbf{x}_l$ is the second most similar mediod to $\mathbf{x}_j$. Therefore, if $\mathbf{x}_i$ be replaced by $\mathbf{x}_h$ as a mediod, $\mathbf{x}_j$ would belong to the cluster represented by $\mathbf{x}_l$. Hence, the cost of the concerned swap is

$$D_{ijh} = d(\mathbf{x}_j, \mathbf{x}_l) - d(\mathbf{x}_j, \mathbf{x}_i)$$

The above equation always gives a non-negative result, indicating that a non-negative cost is associated to the swap between $\mathbf{x}_i$ and $\mathbf{x}_h$.

Case 2: $\mathbf{x}_j$ currently belongs to the cluster represented by $\mathbf{x}_i$. But, at the same time, $\mathbf{x}_j$ is less similar to $\mathbf{x}_l$ than $\mathbf{x}_h$, i.e. $d(\mathbf{x}_j, \mathbf{x}_h) < d(\mathbf{x}_j, \mathbf{x}_l)$, where $\mathbf{x}_l$ is the second most similar mediod to $\mathbf{x}_j$. Therefore, if $\mathbf{x}_i$ be replaced by $\mathbf{x}_h$ as a mediod, $\mathbf{x}_j$ would belong to the cluster represented by $\mathbf{x}_h$. Thus, the cost of the concerned swap is

$$D_{ijh} = d(\mathbf{x}_j, \mathbf{x}_h) - d(\mathbf{x}_j, \mathbf{x}_i)$$

The above equation may attain positive or negative values, depending on whether $\mathbf{x}_j$ is more similar to $\mathbf{x}_i$ or to $\mathbf{x}_h$.

Case 3: Let, $\mathbf{x}_j$ currently belongs to the cluster represented by $\mathbf{x}_i$. And $\mathbf{x}_l$ is a representative object of that cluster. Furthermore, $\mathbf{x}_j$ is more similar to $\mathbf{x}_l$ than

$\mathbf{x}_h$. Therefore, if $\mathbf{x}_i$ be replaced by $\mathbf{x}_h$ as a mediod, $\mathbf{x}_j$ would belong to the cluster represented by $\mathbf{x}_l$. Thus, the cost of the concerned swap is

$$D_{ijh} = 0$$

The above equation may attain positive or negative values, depending on whether $\mathbf{x}_j$ is more similar to $\mathbf{x}_i$ or to $\mathbf{x}_h$.

Case 4: $\mathbf{x}_j$ currently belongs to the cluster represented by $\mathbf{x}_i$. But, $\mathbf{x}_j$ is less similar to $\mathbf{x}_l$ than $\mathbf{x}_h$. Therefore, if $\mathbf{x}_i$ be replaced by $\mathbf{x}_h$ as a mediod, would cause $\mathbf{x}_j$ to jump to the cluster represented by $\mathbf{x}_h$ from that represented by $\mathbf{x}_l$. Thus, the cost of the concerned swap is

$$D_{ijh} = d(\mathbf{x}_j, \mathbf{x}_h) - d(\mathbf{x}_j, \mathbf{x}_l)$$

The above equation always gives negative values.

Now, combining the four different costs of all the above cases, for replacing $\mathbf{x}_i$ with $\mathbf{x}_h$, we get the total cost as

$$TC_{ih} = \sum_j D_{ijh}$$

The PAM algorithm is presented below.

The PAM Algorithm

- **Step 1:** Select K mediods from the data set arbitrarily.
- **Step 2:** Compute TC_{ih} for all pairs of objects $\mathbf{x}_i, \mathbf{x}_h$, where $\mathbf{x}_i$ is currently a mediod and $\mathbf{x}_h$ is a non-mediod.
- **Step 3:** Select the pair $\mathbf{x}_i, \mathbf{x}_h$ which corresponds to $\min_{i,h} TC_{ih}$.
- **Step 4:** If the minimum TC_{ih} is negative, replace $\mathbf{x}_i$ with $\mathbf{x}_h$ and go back to Step 2.
- **Step 5:** Otherwise, for each non-mediod, find the most similar representative. Stop.

Although, the PAM algorithm is presented by its developers in the above form using different types of cost notations, we can present it in another form that is essentially similar to the k-means algorithm. This new form is given along with its k-means counterpart.

The PAM or k-mediod algorithm

begin
 initialize K mediods
 distribute $N - K$ elements to the mediods upon minimum distance basis
 compute *cost* as the sum of within cluster spread

```
    repeat
        for each of the mediods do
        begin
            for each of the non-mediods do
            begin
                exchange a mediod with a non-mediod
                distribute N − K elements to the mediods upon minimum distance basis
                compute cost as the sum of within cluster spread
                if (cost < old_cost) accept new mediod
                else cancel exchange
            end
        end
    until mediods become stable
end
```

The k-means algorithm can be put in a very similar framework as that of the PAM algorithm. The algorithm is provided below.

The k-means algorithm

```
begin
    initialize K centers
    distribute N elements to the mediods upon minimum distance basis
    compute the Euclidean metric as sum of within cluster spread
    repeat
        compute cluster centers by averaging
        distribute N elements to the centers upon minimum distance basis
        compute the Euclidean metric as the sum of within cluster spread
        if (metric < old_metric) accept new centers
        else do nothing
    until centers become stable
end
```

In the above, we put the PAM and the k-means algorithms in a similar framework for making a comparison between the two. In PAM, there are two nested for loops, one for the mediods and another for the non-mediods. Therefore, we need to check for $K(N-K)$ pairs of mediods and non-mediods in each iteration. For each pair, computing the cost factor involves examination of all $(N-K)$ non-mediods. Thus, complexity of each iteration becomes $\mathcal{O}[K(N-K)^2]$. This should be multiplied by the number of iterations. Therefore, PAM is very costly algorithm for large values of N and K.

The k-means, on the other hand, distributes all the N elements to the K clusters in every iteration. Therefore, complexity of each iteration is NK. However, it is found that for large values of N, the number of iterations is proportional to N. Therefore, the overall complexity becomes $\mathcal{O}\left(KN^2\right)$.

Example 7: Consider the following 2-dimensional data set having 12 elements (Table 21.27). Assume the initial mediods as $\mathbf{z}_1 = \mathbf{x}_4$, $\mathbf{z}_2 = \mathbf{x}_6$ and $\mathbf{z}_3 = \mathbf{x}_8$. Trace the PAM algorithm and determine the final clusters and mediods.

Solution: The results of tracing the PAM algorithm are presented in Tables 21.28–21.30.

Table 21.27: Initial Unlabelled Data

Data Item	x_1	x_2	x_3	x_4	x_5	x_6	x_7	x_8	x_9	x_{10}	x_{11}	x_{12}
Values	(1, 1)	(1, 2)	(2, 1)	(2, 2)	(3, 1)	(4, 4)	(4, 5)	(5, 1)	(5, 5)	(7, 2)	(7, 3)	(8, 3)

Table 21.28: Distance Matrix for the Data Set

Item No.	1	2	3	4	5	6	7	8	9	10	11	12
1	0.00	1.00	1.00	2.00	50.00	18.00	25.00	25.00	32.00	37.00	40.00	53.00
2	1.00	0.00	2.00	1.00	49.00	13.00	18.00	20.00	25.00	36.00	37.00	50.00
3	1.00	2.00	0.00	1.00	37.00	13.00	20.00	18.00	25.00	26.00	29.00	40.00
4	2.00	1.00	1.00	0.00	36.00	8.00	13.00	13.00	18.00	25.00	26.00	37.00
5	50.00	49.00	37.00	36.00	0.00	20.00	25.00	13.00	18.00	1.00	2.00	1.00
6	18.00	13.00	13.00	8.00	20.00	0.00	1.00	1.00	2.00	13.00	10.00	17.00
7	25.00	18.00	20.00	13.00	25.00	1.00	0.00	2.00	1.00	18.00	13.00	20.00
8	25.00	20.00	18.00	13.00	13.00	1.00	2.00	0.00	1.00	8.00	5.00	10.00
9	32.00	25.00	25.00	18.00	18.00	2.00	1.00	1.00	0.00	13.00	8.00	13.00
10	37.00	36.00	26.00	25.00	1.00	13.00	18.00	8.00	13.00	0.00	1.00	2.00
11	40.00	37.00	29.00	26.00	2.00	10.00	13.00	5.00	8.00	1.00	0.00	1.00
12	53.00	50.00	40.00	37.00	1.00	17.00	20.00	10.00	13.00	2.00	1.00	0.00

Table 21.29: Class Labels of Data After First Iteration

Data Item	x_1	x_2	x_3	x_4	x_5	x_6	x_7	x_8	x_9	x_{10}	x_{11}	x_{12}
Values	(1, 1)	(1, 2)	(2, 1)	(2, 2)	(3, 1)	(4, 4)	(4, 5)	(5, 1)	(5, 5)	(7, 2)	(7, 3)	(8, 3)
Class Labels	1	1	1	1	2	1	1	3	3	2	3	3

Table 21.30: Class Labels of Data After Second Iteration

Data Item	x_1	x_2	x_3	x_4	x_5	x_6	x_7	x_8	x_9	x_{10}	x_{11}	x_{12}
Values	(1, 1)	(1, 2)	(2, 1)	(2, 2)	(3, 1)	(4, 4)	(4, 5)	(5, 1)	(5, 5)	(7, 2)	(7, 3)	(8, 3)
Class Labels	1	1	1	1	2	3	3	3	3	2	2	2

After the first iteration mediods are $\mathbf{z}_1 = \mathbf{x}_4$, $\mathbf{z}_2 = \mathbf{x}_5$ and $\mathbf{z}_3 = \mathbf{x}_8$.
After the second iteration mediods are $\mathbf{z}_1 = \mathbf{x}_4$, $\mathbf{z}_2 = \mathbf{x}_5$ and $\mathbf{z}_3 = \mathbf{x}_8$. ♣

21.6.2 The CLARA Algorithm

Observing the high running time complexity of the PAM algorithm, Kauffman and Rousseeuw (1990) have developed a sample based version of it for handling large data sets, and named it as algorithm for Clustering LARge Applications (CLARA). Here, initially a subset of data items are randomly selected from the original data set. And then applied the PAM over this subset. For better approximation, they have used executed multiple instances of the CLARA algorithm and reported the best clustering output. Here, for accuracy, the quality of a clustering is measured based on the average dissimilarity of all data items in the original data set, and not only on the selected samples. Although they have performed experiments on relatively smaller data subsets, it is clear that this new sample based version will be much faster than the original PAM algorithm.

The CLARA algorithm

begin
  for $i = 1$ to 5 repeat the following
  begin
    draw a sample of size $40 + 2K$ randomly from the entire data set
    execute the PAM algorithm over this sampled subset to find mediods
    assign each object in the original data set to its nearest mediod
    calculate the average distance between data items and their respective mediods
    save the best result obtained so far
  end end

21.6.3 The CLARANS Algorithm

This modification of CLARA has been proposed by Ng and Han in 1994. CLARANS stands for Clustering Large Applications based on RANdomized Search. It is supposed to produce better results than CLARA with a smaller number of searches.

As in the case of PAM or CLARA, here also a solution S is a set of K mediods $S = \{\mathbf{x}_{m_1}, \mathbf{x}_{m_2}, \ldots, \mathbf{x}_{m_K}\}$. Two solutions S_1 and S_2 are said to be neighbours if they have $K - 1$ mediods out of the total of K in common. If

$$S_1 = \{\mathbf{x}_{m_1}, \mathbf{x}_{m_2}, \ldots, \mathbf{x}_{m_K}\}$$

and

$$S_2 = \{\mathbf{x}_{n_1}, \mathbf{x}_{n_2}, \ldots, \mathbf{x}_{n_K}\}$$

are two solutions, then S_1 and S_2 are neighbours if and only if $|S_1 \bigcup S_2| = K - 1$.

In CLARANS, all possible candidate solutions are viewed to form a graph $G_{N,K}$, each node of which represents a candidate solution. Two neighbour solutions or nodes in this graph (that are connected by an arc) differ by only one mediod out of K in total. So, each solution may have $K(N - K)$ neighbours, where N is the size of the sampled subset of the original data set. Since each node represents a solution with K mediods, each node represents a corresponding clustering also. Therefore, each node can be assigned a cost that is determined by the total dissimilarity between every non-mediod and the mediod of its cluster. Therefore, if mediods $\mathbf{x}_{m_i}$ and $\mathbf{x}_{n_i}$ are the only different mediods in neighbour solutions S_1 and S_2, the cost difference between S_1 and S_2 is exactly given by $TC_{m_i n_i}$.

Now, we can make a comparison of the PAM, CLARA and CLARANS algorithms using the graph notation. PAM can be viewed as a search for the minimum cost node in $G_{N,K}$. At each steps all the neighbours of the current node are examined. Then the current node is replaced by the lowest cost neighbour. The search is continued until the minimum cost solution is found.

CLARA tries to examine fewer neighbours and restrict the search on a smaller subgraph of $G_{N,K}$. But searching any of the subgraph cannot guarantee that the minimum cost is found ultimately; it may remain outside the search paths followed.

CLARANS also does not check every neighbour of a node. But, unlike CLARA, it searches the complete graph $G_{N,K}$. This is because CLARANS samples a set of neighbours at each step in the search process, instead of sampling the subgraph before search like CLARA. Therefore, search of CLARANS is not limited to any localized subgraph of $G_{N,K}$. As a result CLARANS can produce better results than CLARA in spite of making a non-exhaustive search over $G_{N,K}$.

The CLARANS algorithm

```
begin
    input numlocal and maxsoln
    mincost ← LARGE
    for i = 1 to numlocal repeat the following
    begin
        draw a solution S randomly from the graph G_{N,K}
        compute cost of S
        cost ← cost of S
        j = 1
        while (j < maxsoln) do
        begin
            randomply select a neighbour R of S
            find the cost difference between R and S
            if (cost_difference < 0)
            begin
            cost ← cost + cost_difference
                S ← R
                j ← 1
            end
            else j ← j + 1
        end
        if (cost < mincost)
            begin
                mincost ← cost
                best_solution ← S
            end
    end
    output best_solution obtained so far
end
```

In actual experiments CLARANS is found to be more efficient than both PAM and CLARA in terms of run time.

21.7 New Approaches for Hierarchical Clustering

Although the concepts of classical hierarchical clustering algorithms are very simple, their high time complexities restrict them to be applied for large data sets. Hence, newer methods have been developed. Some of these newer methods are described in the following subsections.

21.7.1 Fractionization Algorithm

The fractionization algorithm was proposed by Cutting et al. in 1992. This algorithm can adapt to handle large data sets. The main idea is to divide the original data set into manageable subsets or fractions, and then to apply a hierarchical algorithm to each of the fractions. Clustered data from each fraction are then reclustered using the same algorithm.

Let us consider the case of clustering a data set of size N into K clusters. Let M be the size of each fraction where $M << N$. The algorithm is given below.

Fractionization algorithm

begin
    divide original data set into fractions of size M
    cluster each fraction into αM clusters, where $\alpha < 1$
    form a new set of meta data with the cluster representatives
        (mean or mediods) and treat it as a new data set
    if the number of meta data in the new set is greater than M
        then repeat the above sub-process until the size becomes $\leq M$
    cluster the set of meta data using a desired algorithm
    assign each original data to the representatives of meta clusters
end

The running time complexity of the above can computed as follows. To cluster each fraction, we need $\mathcal{O}(M^2)$ time. In the ith iteration, we need to process $\alpha^{i-1} \times \left(\frac{N}{M}\right)$ number of fractions. Hence, the total running time is linear with N, i.e. complexity is $\mathcal{O}(N)$ and this is decreasing with α.

There are, however, several drawbacks of this approach. These are:

- The number of clusters are to be provided a priori.
- The meta data obtained from fraction clustering are summaries only of a subset of original data set. All such meta data are expected to form suitable clusters.

But due to random fractionization, all meta data forming a cluster may not come from similar data items in the original data set. Thus, resultant cluster representatives may deviate significantly. There is no chance to recover from such error.

21.7.2 Refractionization Algorithm

To avoid the problems of the refractionization algorithm, Tantrum et al., in 2002, suggested the refractionization algorithm. Here, it is observed that if the fractions are more pure, i.e. predominantly containing data items from only one of the groups, the error factors will be significantly reduced.

Refractionization Algorithm

```
begin
    divide original data set into fractions of size M
    cluster each fraction into αM clusters, where α < 1
    form a new set of meta data with the cluster representatives
            (mean or mediods) and treat it as a new data set
    if the number of meta data in the new set is greater than M
            then repeat the above sub-process until the size becomes ≤ M
    cluster the set of meta data using a desired algorithm
    create new fractions of the original data from the fresh means obtained
    repeat all earlier steps until no more changes occur
    assign each original data to the representatives of meta clusters
end
```

Tantrum et al. (2002) have noted some limitation and requirements of the refractionization algorithm. Let us consider that N_g be the number of groups present in the original data, N_f be the number of fractions after division and N_m be the number of meta data after clustering each fraction. The following observations can now be made

- If $N_g \leq N_m$ then fractionization will work fine and there is no requirement of the refractionization. This is because, in such situations, generally, the fractions are more or less pure in the sense of original distribution of data. However, if $N_g \geq N_m$, the meta data items will not reflect the original distribution of data.
- Refractionization will not recover the actual groups in the data when $N_g > N_f N_m$. In this case, there will be a fraction that contains more than N_m groups which leads to incorrect results.

21.7.3 The BIRCH Algorithm

The BIRCH (Balanced Iterative Reducing using Cluster Hierarchies) clustering algorithm has been proposed by Zhang et al. (1996). This algorithm is almost similar to the fractionization algorithm in its functioning. Here, data items are arranged into sub-clusters called **Clustering Features** (CF). The CFs are then clustered into K groups, in the form of a **Clustering Feature Tree** (CFT), using a traditional hierarchical clustering algorithm. CF and CFT structures help to achieve a very high speed and scalable clustering process which is incremental and dynamic in nature.

For any cluster in a d-dimensional set of patterns we define the centroid $\mathbf{z}$, radius R and diameter D as

$$\mathbf{z} = \frac{\sum_{i=0}^{n-1} \mathbf{x}_i}{n}$$

$$R = \sqrt{\frac{\sum_{i=0}^{n-1} (\mathbf{x}_i - \mathbf{z})^2}{n}}$$

$$D = \sqrt{\frac{\sum_{i=0}^{n-1} \sum_{j=0}^{n-1} ((\mathbf{x}_i - \mathbf{x}_j)^2}{n(n-1)}}$$

A *Clustering Feature* (CF) is a 3-tuple that summarizes information regarding a cluster. For a cluster in a d-dimensional set of patterns $\{\mathbf{x}_i\}$ the CF is defined as

$$CF =< n, LS, SS >$$

where, LS is the linear sum of the n patterns and SS is the sum of squares of them. From statistical point of view, a CF, thus, contains the zeroth, first and second moments of the concerned cluster. CFs are additive, i.e. the cluster formed by merging two sub-clusters having features $CF1$ and $CF2$ will have feature $CF1 + CF2$.

CFT is a height balance tree whose leaf nodes hold individual patterns (as a CF), and the non-leaf nodes contain sum of children CFs. A CFT has two characteristic parameters viz., branching factor B and threshold T. B is the maximum number of children per non-leaf node, and T is the maximum diameter of sub-clusters at the leaf nodes

---

The BIRCH Algorithm

begin
  input the data set $D = \{\mathbf{x}_1, \mathbf{x}_2, \cdots, \mathbf{x}_n\}$
  input threshold T for CFT construction
  for each $\mathbf{x}_i \in D$ **do**
  begin
    find the correct leaf node to insert $\mathbf{x}_i$
    if threshold condition is satisfied **then**
      insert $\mathbf{x}_i$ to cluster and update CF-triples
    else

```
        begin
            if room exists for insertion of x_i then
                insert x_i as a single cluster and update CF-triples
            else
                split leaf node and redistribute CF features
        end
    end
end
```

21.8 When Number of Clusters is Unknown

An interesting and enhanced partitional clustering algorithm is the *ISODATA algorithm.* This algorithm automatically determines the number of clusters along with the cluster configurations depending on some user supplied data. Like Forgy's algorithm and the k-means algorithms, it also tries to minimize the squared error by assigning samples to the nearest centroid. Unlike those algorithms, it does not deal with a fixed number of clusters, but rather deals with k clusters where k is allowed to range over an interval that includes the number of clusters requested by the user. It discards clusters with too few elements. Clusters are merged if number of clusters grow too large or clusters are very close to each other. A cluster is split if the number of clusters is too few or if the clusters contain very dissimilar samples. Besides the data and seed points, the following parameters are required by the isodata algorithm:

no_clusters: The desired number of clusters.

min_elements: The minimum number of sample points per cluster.

min_dist: The minimum distance between cluster centroids.

iter_start: Maximum number of iterations in the first part of the algorithm.

max_merge: Maximum number of cluster merges per iteration.

iter_body: Maximum number of iterations within the main part of the algorithm.

The isodata algorithm

1. Initialize the cluster centroids to the seed points.
2. For each sample, find the cluster centroid nearest to it. Put the sample in the cluster identified with the nearest cluster centroid.
3. Compute the centroids of the resulting clusters.
4. If at least one sample changed clusters and the number of iterations is less than iter_start, go to Step 2.
5. Discard clusters with fewer than min_elements samples. Also discard the samples they contain.

6. If the number of clusters is greater than or equal to $2 \times$ no_clusters or the number of this iteration is even, execute Step 7; otherwise go to Step 8.
7. If the distance between two centroids is less than min_dist, merge these clusters and update the centroids; otherwise, go to Step 7. Repeat this step up to max_merge times and then go to Step 8.
8. If the number of clusters is less than or equal to no_clusters/2 or the number of this iteration is odd, execute Step 9; otherwise go to Step 10.
9. Find a cluster that has a standard deviation for some variable, say x, which exceeds split_size $\times \sigma_x$, where, σ_x is the standard deviation of x in the complete original set of samples. If none, go to Step 10. Compute the mean of x within the cluster. Separate the samples in this cluster into two sets, one consisting of those in which x is greater than or equal to the mean, and the other consisting of those in which x is less than the mean. Compute the centroids of these two clusters. If the distance between these centroids is greater than or equal to $1.1 * mindist$, replace the original cluster by these two clusters; otherwise, do not split the cluster.
10. If Step 10 has been executed iter_body times or no changes occurred in the clusters since the last time Step 10 was executed, stop; otherwise, take the centroids of the clusters as new seed points and go to Step 2.

21.8.1 Use of Cluster Validity Indices

Whenever we deal with the problem of classification of unlabelled data, we need to address the following three naturally occurring questions:

- Is there cluster substructures present in the data?
- If substructures are present, how can we determine them?
- Once clusters are found, how can we validate them?

In most of the cases, we can answer the first question by looking at the distribution of the data, specially, if the data is two-dimensional and we have a printed view of it. However, for large and multidimensional data sets, it is not always possible to make a visual guess. For multidimensional data, we may have several two-dimensional views which may help us in answering the question. However, several formal and informal techniques exist in literature.

The second question deals with finding out the appropriate cluster configurations. There are large number of methods to solve this problem. The most well-known of which is the k-means algorithm. The k-means algorithm is used for crisp clustering. There is a fuzzy version of this algorithm called the fuzzy **c-means algorithm**.

The third question is related to cluster validity. This states that once we find out a partition matrix U, can we rely on it? Or, whether there exists better partitions not yet explored?

Whatever conflicting the above questions are, the algorithmic structure that is generally followed to solve the clustering problem involves answering them in some way. The algorithmic structure is shown in Figure 21.4.

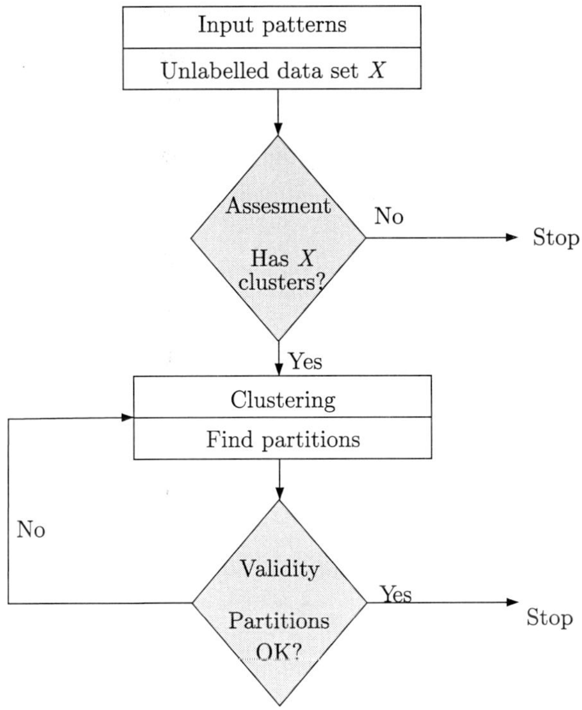

Figure 21.4: Measuring validity of clustering.

A number of attempts were there for finding out a proper cluster validity index, both for crisp and fuzzy clusters. For crisp clustering, the well known indices are the DB-index, the Dunn's index, the Calinski–Harabasz index, the PBM index (Pakhira 2003), etc. A lot of other indices and their descriptions may be found in literature. For fuzzy clustering, we have, the XB-index, the FS-index, Bezdek's PE and PC indices, the PBMF index, etc. All these indices are optimizing indices i.e. either maximum or minimum values of these indices indicate the best cluster configurations. It is worth mention here that generally a cluster validity index serves two purposes. First, it determines the number of clusters, and secondly, it finds out the best cluster configuration. Because of their optimizing nature, the cluster validity indices are best usable in association with any optimization algorithm. Therefore, application of simulated annealing and evolutionary algorithms seem to be appropriate. We have, thus, developed several clustering algorithms based on simulated annealing and evolutionary algorithms. The basic ideas of these optimization techniques are mentioned briefly in the following section.

21.8.2 Use of VAT Algorithm

Very recently a visual technique have been developed (Bezdek 2002), where the clustering tendency of a set of patterns can be displayed on the monitor with a very little effort. This new technique is named as VAT (Visual Assessment of Tendency for clustering). This may be considered as a preprocessing step, i.e before applying a clustering algorithm VAT output may be used as the number of clusters present in the data.

In VAT we work with a pairwise distance matrix of the original object (pattern) set

$$O = o_1, o_2, \ldots, o_N$$

If at the ijth element of the distance matrix pairwise similarities are $S = [S_{ij}]$, then dissimilarities can be obtained by a simple transformation, like

$$R_{ij} = S_{\max} - S_{ij}$$

The VAT algorithm

Input: $N \times N$ pairwise distance matrix

Step 1. *Set* K = {1, 2, ..., N}
Select $(i, j) \in arg\ max(R_{pq})$ where $p, q \in K$
Set $P(1) = i; I = \{i\}$; and $J = K - \{i\}$

Step 2. For $t = 2, 3, \ldots, N$
Select $(i, j) \in arg\ min(R_{pq})$ where $p \in I, q \in J$
Set $P(t) = j$
Replace $I \leftarrow I \cup \{j\}$ and $J \leftarrow J - \{j\}$
Next t.

Step 3. Form the ordered dissimilarity matrix $\tilde{R} = [\tilde{R}_{ij}] = [R_{P(i)P(j)}]$, for $1 \leq i, j \leq N$

Step 4. Display $\tilde{R}$ as an intensity image, scaled so that $max(\tilde{R}_{ij})$ corresponds to white and 0 corresponds to black.

The VAT algorithm rearranges the pairwise distance values in a similar manner to the formation of Minimal Spanning Tree (MST) of a weighted graph following the Prim's algorithm. The difference between Vat and the Prim's algorithm are: VAT does not form a MST, rather it tries to find out the order in which the vertices are added as it is grown, and also it tries to find out the initial vertex which depends on the maximum edge weight in the underlying complete graph. Using this maximum edge weight vertex as the initial point will produce a clear connected graph by avoiding unnecessary zigzagged paths. The permuted indices of the N objects are stored in the array P. Here, no re-computation of distances are done, the reordered graph is obtained by simply rearranging the rows and columns of the original distance matrix. Therefore, the time complexity of the VAT becomes $O(N^2)$. In Table 21.31, a two-dimensional data set with 20 data items is presented. The pairwise distance matrices before and after the application of VAT algorithm are shown in Tables 21.32 and 21.33, respectively.

Table 21.31: Sample 2-dimensional Data

20 2-dimensional Data, Each in a Column																			
2	14	3	14	15	16	3	16	17	4	18	17	17	18	5	6	18	20	10	16
10	6	9	17	4	15	12	8	4	13	6	19	18	20	11	9	16	18	16	6

Table 21.32: Initial Distance Matrix

0	13	1	14	14	15	2	14	16	4	16	17	17	19	3	4	17	20	19	15
13	0	11	11	2	9	13	3	4	12	4	13	12	15	10	9	11	13	12	2
1	11	0	14	13	14	3	13	15	4	15	17	17	19	3	3	17	19	18	13
14	11	14	0	13	3	12	9	13	11	12	4	3	5	11	11	4	6	6	11
14	2	13	13	0	11	14	4	2	14	4	15	14	16	12	10	12	15	13	2
15	9	14	3	11	0	13	7	11	12	9	4	3	5	12	12	2	5	4	9
2	13	3	12	14	13	0	14	16	1	16	16	15	17	2	4	16	18	17	14
14	3	13	9	4	7	14	0	4	13	3	11	10	12	11	10	8	11	9	2
16	4	15	13	2	11	16	4	0	16	2	15	14	16	14	12	12	14	12	2
4	12	4	11	14	12	1	13	16	0	16	14	14	16	2	4	14	17	16	14
16	4	15	12	4	9	16	3	2	16	0	13	12	14	14	12	10	12	10	2
17	13	17	4	15	4	16	11	15	14	13	0	1	1	14	15	3	3	4	13
17	12	17	3	14	3	15	10	14	14	12	1	0	2	14	14	2	3	4	12
19	15	19	5	16	5	17	12	16	16	14	1	2	0	16	16	4	3	4	14
3	10	3	11	12	12	2	11	14	2	14	14	14	16	0	2	14	17	16	12
4	9	3	11	10	12	4	10	12	4	12	15	14	16	2	0	14	17	16	10
17	11	17	4	12	2	16	8	12	14	10	3	2	4	14	14	0	3	2	10
20	13	19	6	15	5	18	11	14	17	12	3	3	3	17	17	3	0	2	13
19	12	18	6	13	4	17	9	12	16	10	4	4	4	16	16	2	2	0	11
15	2	13	11	2	9	14	2	2	14	2	13	12	14	12	10	10	13	11	0

Table 21.33: Distance Matrix After Rearrangement

0	1	2	4	3	4	13	15	16	16	14	14	15	17	19	20	17	17	19	14
1	0	3	4	3	3	11	13	15	15	13	13	14	17	18	19	17	17	19	14
2	3	0	1	2	4	13	14	16	16	14	14	13	16	17	18	15	16	17	12
4	4	1	0	2	4	12	14	16	16	14	13	12	14	16	17	14	14	16	11
3	3	2	2	0	2	10	12	14	14	12	11	12	14	16	17	14	14	16	11
4	3	4	4	2	0	9	10	12	12	10	10	12	14	16	17	14	15	16	11
13	11	13	12	10	9	0	2	4	4	2	3	9	11	12	13	12	13	15	11
15	13	14	14	12	10	2	0	2	2	2	2	9	10	11	13	12	13	14	11
16	15	16	16	14	12	4	2	0	2	4	3	9	10	10	12	12	13	14	12
16	15	16	16	14	12	4	2	2	0	2	4	11	12	12	14	14	15	16	13
14	13	14	14	12	10	2	2	4	2	0	4	11	12	13	15	14	15	16	13
14	13	14	13	11	10	3	2	3	4	4	0	7	8	9	11	10	11	12	9
15	14	13	12	12	12	9	9	9	11	11	7	0	2	4	5	3	4	5	3
17	17	16	14	14	14	11	10	10	12	12	8	2	0	2	3	2	3	4	4
19	18	17	16	16	16	12	11	10	12	13	9	4	2	0	2	4	4	4	6
20	19	18	17	17	17	13	13	12	14	15	11	5	3	2	0	3	3	3	6
17	17	15	14	14	14	12	12	12	14	14	10	3	2	4	3	0	1	2	3
17	17	16	14	14	15	13	13	13	15	15	11	4	3	4	3	1	0	1	4
19	19	17	16	16	16	15	14	14	16	16	12	5	4	4	3	2	1	0	5
14	14	12	11	11	11	11	11	12	13	13	9	3	4	6	6	3	4	5	0

We have executed the VAT algorithm on this small 2-dimensional data set having 3 clusters. The data set and results of VAT are shown in Figures 21.5, 21.6 and 21.7, respectively. The VAT algorithm rearranges the patterns in the set according to their smallest pairwise distance following a procedure similar to the Prim's algorithm for

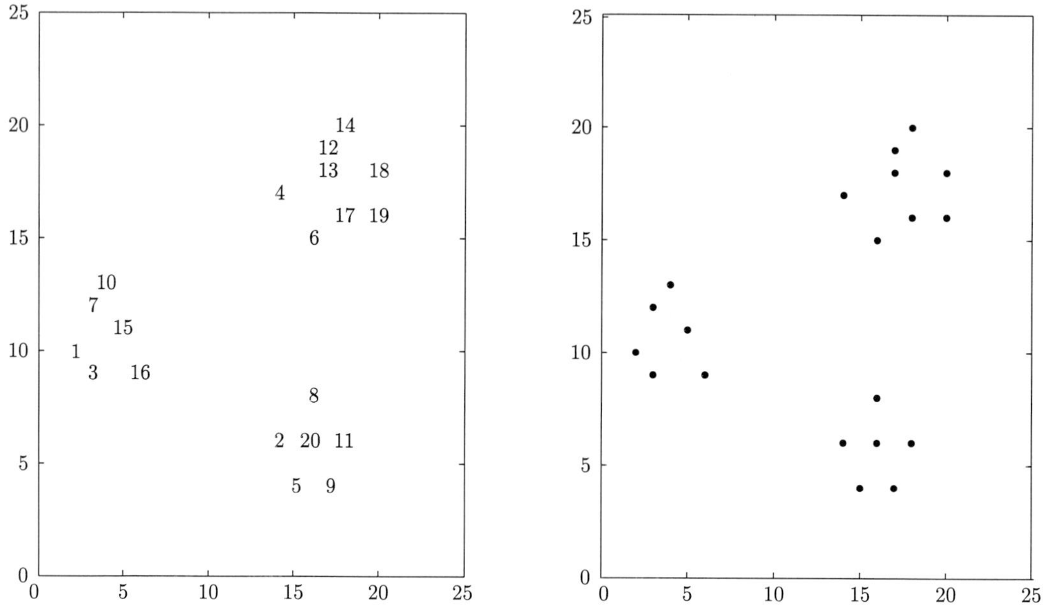

Figure 21.5: A sample data and its plots.

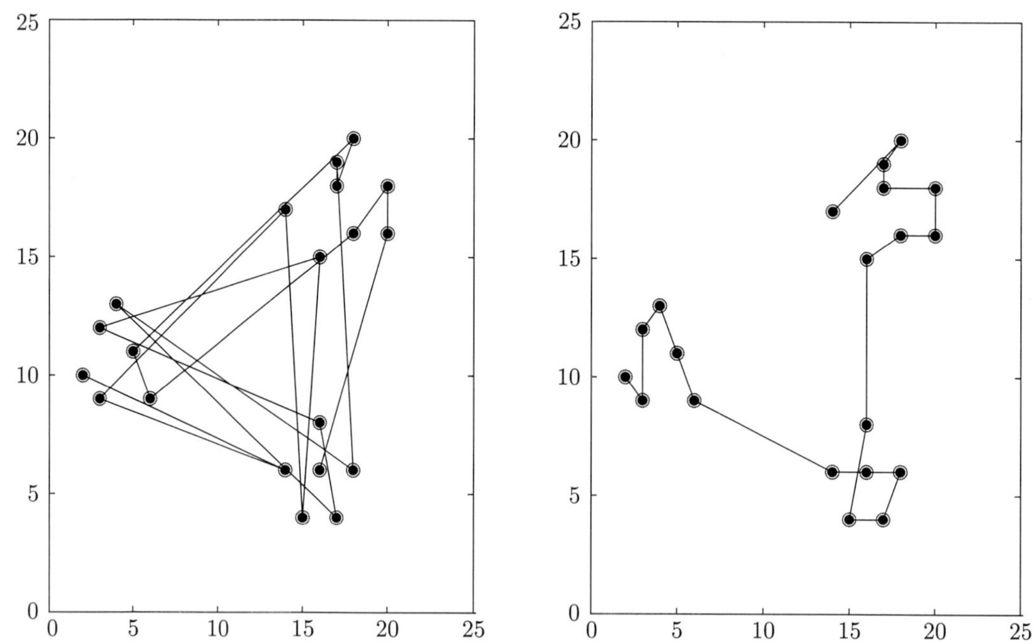

(a) Before rearrangement

(b) After rearrangement

Figure 21.6: Plotted data items are connected.

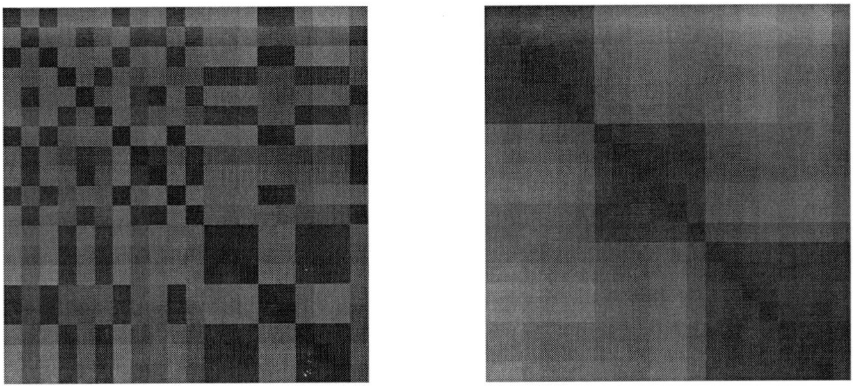

(a) Before rearrangement (b) After rearrangement

Figure 21.7: VAT images.

minimum spanning tree. The rearranged distance matrix is then plotted as a VAT image. From the VAT image the possible number of clusters may be determined as the number of darker squares along the diagonal.

21.9 Optimization Methods Used in Clustering

Optimization techniques are very commonly used for the purpose of clustering. A general optimization algorithm can be used along with some clustering metrics for this purpose. In an earlier chapter we have discussed some of the general optimization techniques like simulated annealing, genetic algorithm, evolutionary programming, annealing evolution, etc. We shall describe how these methods can be used for clustering.

21.9.1 Clustering Using Simulated Annealing

The searching capability of simulated annealing may be used appropriately determining a fixed number K of cluster centres in $\mathbb{R}^N$; thereby suitably clustering the set X of n unlabelled points $\mathbf{x}_1, \mathbf{x}_2, \ldots, \mathbf{x}_n$. The clustering metric that has been adopted is the sum of the Euclidean distances of the points from their respective cluster centres. Thus, like k-means algorithm the simulated annealing tries to minimize the intra cluster spread.

Mathematically, the clustering metric $\mathcal{M}$ for the K clusters $C_1, C_2, \ldots, C_k$ is given by

$$\mathcal{M}(C_1, C_2, \ldots, C_k) = \sum_{i=1}^{K} \sum_{\mathbf{x}_j \in C_i} ||\mathbf{x}_j - \mathbf{z}_i|| \tag{21.34}$$

The goal of the method is to search for the appropriate cluster centres $\mathbf{z}_1, \mathbf{z}_2, \ldots, \mathbf{z}_K$ such that the clustering metric $\mathcal{M}$ is minimized. Let us consider $\mathcal{M}$ as the energy

E associated with a particular configuration, i.e. a partition of the n points in K clusters.

SA-clustering algorithm

In SA-clustering algorithm (Selim and Alsultan 1991), the SA procedure is superimposed on a k-means based clustering algorithm. Here, an initial solution is formed as a concatenation of individual centre vectors, and can be described as

$$\mathbf{Z} = \mathbf{z_1} \ \mathbf{z_2} \ \ldots \ \mathbf{z_K} \tag{21.35}$$

Data points are distributed among corresponding clusters and the metric $\mathcal{M}$ is computed. Now, a small perturbation to the solution vector is made and the new value for $\mathcal{M}(\mathbf{Z})$, i.e. $\mathcal{M}(\mathbf{Z})'$, is computed. The new cluster configuration is accepted according to Boltzmann probability at the current temperature. The above step is done for N_T number of times at each temperature. After this the temperature is reduced following a temperature schedule described below.

The temperature schedule

The asymptotic convergence (i.e. at $t \to \infty$) of the SA is guaranteed for a logarithmic annealing schedule of the form $T_t = T_{\max}/(1 + \ln t)$, where $t \geq 0$ and $T_{\max}$ is the initial temperature. However, in practice, the logarithmic annealing is far too slow, and hence, we may follow a geometric schedule of the form $T_t = (1-\alpha)^t \times T_{\max}$, where α is a positive real number close to zero. As $T_t \to 0(T_{\min})$, no more perturbation of the cluster configuration is possible, and hence, termination condition is assumed to be reached. In practice, the state of the system configuration is found to be frozen well before this.

The SA-clustering algorithm

begin
    initialize temperature $T = T_{max}$
    generate a solution vector $\mathbf{Z}$ consisting of all cluster centres
    compute the value of the clustering metric $\mathcal{M}(\mathbf{Z})$
    while $(T > T_{min})$ **do**
    for *iter* $= 0$ to N_T **do**
        begin
            perturb the centre vector $\mathbf{Z}$ slightly, creating the new vector $\mathbf{Z}'$
            evaluate $\mathcal{M}(\mathbf{Z}')$
            generate a random number $r \in (0, 1)$ from a uniform distribution
                in the interval $(0, 1)$
            if $r < \exp\left[-\frac{\mathcal{M}(\mathbf{Z}')-\mathcal{M}(\mathbf{Z})}{T}\right]$ **then**
                begin

```
                        assign Z = Z'
                        assign M(Z) = M(Z')
                    end
        lower T
      end
   end
end
```

The power of annealing procedure for providing stable minimum energy configuration has been integrated in the above procedure with the simplicity of the classical k-means algorithm to search for appropriate clusters which minimizes a clustering metric $\mathcal{M}$. The conventional k-means algorithm is sometimes found to get stuck at sub optimal values, even for very simple data, while SA-clustering technique has the ability to overcome this. Moreover, since the proposed method is inherently very simple, it may be used as an initial analysis tool for a wide variety of data sets in different domains.

We can modify the above mentioned SA-clustering algorithm by incorporation of a probabilistic redistribution strategy. The new algorithm is termed as the SAKM-clustering algorithm (Bandyopadhyay 2001). Here, no direct perturbation of the solution vector is needed. The perturbation will be incorporated as a result of redistribution.

SAKM-clustering algorithm

In the SAKM-clustering algorithm, K data points are randomly selected to represent centres of K clusters (where K is known *a priori*) as in k-means algorithm. Elements in the data set are then distributed upon minimum distance basis. Each element in a cluster has a certain degree of membership to it which is inversely proportional to its Euclidean distance from the cluster centre. So elements that are at a larger distance from the centre are the fittest candidates for redistribution to another cluster. We have redistributed an element x_i in cluster C_j to cluster C_k with probability

$$\exp\left(\frac{-[D_{ik} - D_{ij}]_+}{T_t}\right) \tag{21.36}$$

where $[x]_+ = \max(x, 0)$, and $D_{ik} = ||\mathbf{x}_i - \mathbf{z}_k||$ and $k \neq j$. T is a temperature schedule, which is a sequence of strictly positive numbers such that $T_1 \geq T_2 \geq \ldots, T_t = 0$, $(\lim t \to \infty)$. The suffix t of T indicates the number of generations through the annealing process.

The SAKM-clustering algorithm

begin
   initialize temperature $T = T_{max}$

```
    generate a solution vector Z consisting of all cluster centres
    compute the value of the clustering metric M(Z)
    while (T > T_min) do
    begin
        for iter = 0 to N_T do
        begin
            evolve a new centre vector Z' with metric M(Z') from
                the old centre vector Z with metric M(Z) by redistributing
                    elements among clusters in the old configuration
            if (M(Z') ≤ M(Z)) then assign Z = Z'
            else assign Z = Z' with probability exp{-(M(Z')-M(Z))/T}
        end
    lower T
    end
end
```

The SAKM-clustering has some advantage over the earlier SA-clustering algorithm. Generally SA is a very time consuming process as it stays at a particular temperature for a fairly long time. In SAKM, one may redistribute only a small percentage of clustered elements to other clusters at each iteration. Hence, depending on the percentage used, the execution time can be made to vary. For large and complex data sets the SAKM is found to perform better compared to the SA-clustering algorithm.

21.9.2 Clustering Using Genetic Algorithm

GAs possess natural evolution mechanisms to search for the maximum or minimum of an objective function. GA can be used for clustering by optimizing a suitable clustering metric. GAs maintain a pool of candidate solutions (called **chromosomes**), and at each generation these chromosomes are evaluated and evolved using genetic operators. For solving the clustering problem, we need to store the solutions (chromosomes) in a form as shown in Eq. (21.35). Each candidate solution is represented in this manner forming a population.

As discussed in Chapter 15, the reproduction operator is responsible for the survival of the fittest and the death of the poor solution strings based on a probabilistic treatment. Different selection mechanisms are there. Some commonly used techniques are the proportionate selection or the roulette-wheel selection, the tournament selection, etc. This process results in a set of solution strings where some strings of higher fitness may be copied more than once into the next population. The total number of strings in any population usually remains unchanged.

The crossover operation can be performed in a number of ways. The crossover may be single point or multipoint one. Also the position of crossover may be fixed or variable. However, its aim is to generate diversity in the pool of solution strings.

The crossover is done with a probability p_c. For a chromosome of length l, a random integer, called the **crossover point**, is generated in the range $[1,\ l-1]$. The portions of the chromosomes lying to the right of the crossover point are exchanged to produce two offsprings.

The mutation operator plays only a secondary role in GAs. Its principle is randomly to change the character of some string of the population from time to time. The rate of mutation is generally kept very low, for example one bit out of one thousand bits may be mutated during some execution. The main reason for mutation is the fact that some local configurations of characters in strings of the population can be totally lost as a result of reproduction and crossover operations Mutation protects GAs against such irrecoverable loss of good solution features.

For binary representation of chromosomes, a bit position is mutated by simply flipping its value (bit complementation). In case of real coded genetic clustering algorithm, we can perform mutation as follows. A number δ in the range $[0,\ 1]$ is generated with uniform distribution. If the value at a gene position is z, after mutation it becomes (Maulik 2000)

$$\begin{aligned} z &\leftarrow z \pm 2 \times \delta \times z \quad &\text{if } z \neq 0 \\ z &\leftarrow z \pm 2 \times \delta \quad &\text{if } z = 0 \end{aligned}$$

The '+' or '−' sign arises with equal probability. The above mutation could be represented as

$$z \leftarrow z \pm \delta \times z$$

But, in that case, if the values at a particular position in all the chromosomes of a population become positive (or negative), we could not generate a new chromosome having a negative (or positive) value at that position. This is why the factor 2 is incorporated.

The basic form of the genetic algorithm is given below.

Genetic algorithm for clustering

```
begin
    g = 0
    initialize P(g) with random centre vectors Z
    evaluate P(g) for clustering metric M(Z)
    termination_condition = false
    while (NOT termination_condition) do
        begin
            g = g + 1
            select parents from P(g)
            perform crossover using pairs of solutions in P(g)
            perform mutation by perturbing centre vector Z
            evaluate P(g + 1) for clustering metric M(Z)
        end
end
```

In the above algorithm, g stands for *generation number* and $P(g)$ represents population at generation g. The genetic algorithm based clustering technique works with multiple initial solutions (sets of centre vectors) as opposed to only one used in the SA based algorithms. Hence, GA-clustering performs a better search at the cost of more computational overhead. The performance of the algorithm depends on efficient encoding of chromosomes, use of proper selection, crossover and mutation methodologies.

21.9.3 Clustering Using Annealing-evolution

The searching capabilities of simulated annealing and evolutionary programming have been used here for appropriately determining a fixed number K of clusters by properly classifying n unlabelled patterns. In our algorithm, we have used the evolution program to guide the search of simulated annealing by providing information regarding a better search area. The criterion function that has been adopted is the sum of within cluster Euclidean distances of the patterns from their respective cluster centres.

Basic principle

Like k-means algorithm the Annealing-Evolution (ANEV) process tries to minimize the intra cluster spread. Mathematically, the criterion function $\mathcal{M}$ for the K clusters $C_1, C_2, \ldots, C_k$ is already given by Eq. (21.34). The goal of the method is to search for the appropriate cluster centres $\mathbf{z}_1, \mathbf{z}_2, \ldots, \mathbf{z}_K$ and the partition matrix such that the criterion function $\mathcal{M}$ is minimized. Here we have used $\mathcal{M}$ as the energy E associated with a particular configuration, i.e. a partition of the n points in K clusters. In this algorithm, the data points are initially assigned to K clusters of a solution string (where K is known *a priori*) randomly, and the cluster centres are computed using Eq. (21.37)

$$\mathbf{z}_i = \frac{1}{n_i} \sum_{\mathbf{x}_j \in C_i} \mathbf{x}_j \qquad i = 1, \ldots, K \tag{21.37}$$

where, n_i is the number of patterns in the ith cluster. This is analogous to the way the centres are computed in the k-means algorithm. The set $\mathbf{z}_1, \mathbf{z}_2, \ldots, \mathbf{z}_K$ constitute a configuration. Once the cluster centres are computed, $\mathcal{M}$ is calculated using Eq. (21.34).

Each element in a cluster has a certain degree of membership to it which is inversely proportional to its Euclidean distance from the cluster centre. So elements that are at a larger distance from the centre are the fittest candidates for redistribution to another cluster. As in the case of the SAKM algorithm, in ANEV-clustering (Pakhira et al. 2004), we have to redistribute an element x_i in cluster C_j to cluster C_k with probability

$$\exp\left(\frac{-[D_{ik} - D_{ij}]_+}{T_g}\right) \tag{21.38}$$

where $[x]_+ = \max(x, 0)$, and $D_{ik} = ||\mathbf{x}_i - \mathbf{z}_k||$ and $k \neq j$. T is a temperature schedule, which is a sequence of strictly positive numbers such that $T_0 \geq T_1 \geq \ldots \geq T_g$. The suffix g of T indicates the number of generations through the annealing process. Note that, $T_g \rightarrow 0$ as $\lim g \rightarrow \infty$.

The ANEV clustering algorithm

In ANEV clustering algorithm, a pool P, of probable solutions are maintained. Each member of the pool (also called **population**) encodes a string of K vectors each identifying a cluster centre. For each member of the pool, the data points are initially assigned to K clusters, known *a priori*, randomly, and the cluster centres are computed as in the k-means algorithm. Thus, we get a number of clustering solutions equal to the POPulation SIZE (POPSIZE). For each configuration (solution string) S_i, we compute its fitness value or energy E_i as the criterion function $\mathcal{M}$ which is to be minimized. The solutions which are potentially strong are selected as the survivor set and used in the mutation phase. At each temperature, T, a new pool is generated for the next generation $(g+1)$ from the current generation (g) pool by the processes of selection and mutation. The annealing-evolution algorithm is shown below.

The annealing-evolution clustering algorithm

begin
  $g = 0$ /*g is generation number */
  $T = T_0$
  initialize $P(g)$
  evaluate $P(g)$
  $termination\_condition = false$
  while (NOT $termination\_condition$) **do**
    begin
      $g = g + 1$
      select $P(g)$ from $P(g-1)$
      for $i = 1$ to POPSIZE **do**
      begin
        evolve configuration $S_i^{'}$ with energy $E^{'}$ from S_i with energy E
          by applying mutation (redistributing elements in S_i
            following equation 21.38)
        if $(E^{'} - E \leq 0)$ **then**
            begin
              $S_i \leftarrow S_i^{'}$
              flag = true
            end
        else if $\exp\left[-\frac{E^{'}-E}{T}\right] \geq$ random (0,1) **then**
            begin

```
                    S_i ← S_i'
                    flag = true
                end
        end for
            if flag then
                begin
                    replace old S_i in P(g) by new S_i
                    flag = false
                end
        T = T(1 − α) /* 0 < α < 1 */
    end
end
```

Selection

Selection is the process where the chromosomes with relatively higher merit (in sense of optimization) are reproduced to form a pool for the next generation. A number of commonly used strategies are there. Two of them are the *roulette − wheel* selection scheme (also called the **proportionate selection scheme**) and the *tournament* selection scheme. In both the cases, the strings are selected with probabilities proportional to their fitness values. We have used the tournament selection scheme with a tournament size of 10. Here, for selection of a single string, a set of 10 randomly identified strings is picked up from $P(g)$, of which the best string is placed in $P(g+1)$.

In addition, the annealing-evolution algorithm uses the *elitist strategy*, which ensures that the best solution string of $P(g)$ survives to $P(g+1)$.

Mutation

The mutation operation may assume many different forms. Here, we have shown three variations corresponding to three different evolution programs for clustering. Two of them are conventional EPs that uses Gauss and Cauchy mutation strategies, and the third one is using a novel mutation strategy based on probabilistic redistribution. We describe these mutation strategies in the following subsections.

Gauss and Cauchy mutation strategies: As mentioned earlier, chromosomes are considered to contain cluster centres. In the mutation phase of the evolution process, these cluster centres are altered by adding small quantities generated by either Gaussian or Cauchy distribution function. These mutation schemes (Xin Yao et al. 1999) are mentioned briefly in the following paragraph.

When a floating point representation of the chromosome is maintained, the non-uniform mutation is used. In our implementation of clustering using conventional EPs, we have coded the chromosomes as a sequence of cluster centres. Let

$\{\mathbf{z}_1, \mathbf{z}_2, \ldots, \mathbf{z}_i, \ldots, \mathbf{z}_K\}$ be a chromosome of dimension $L = d \times K$ (since each component vector is of dimension d), and in the ith cluster centre $\mathbf{z}_i$, the element $z_i(j)$ has been selected for mutation. The result of mutation in $\mathbf{z}_i$ will be a vector $\{z_i(1), z_i(2), \ldots, z_i^{'}(j), \ldots, z_i(d)\}$. In Classical Evolutionary Programming (CEP) Gaussian mutation is commonly used. Gaussian mutation requires two parameters: a mean value and a standard deviation. Generally, mutation in this approach was achieved by transforming the component $z_i(j)$ of a vector $\mathbf{z}_i$ into $z_i^{'}(j)$ by the following relation:

$$z_i^{'}(j) = z_i(j) + \eta_i(j) N_j(0,1) \tag{21.39}$$

$$\eta_i^{'}(j) = \eta_i(j) \exp\left(\tau^{'} N(0,1) + \tau N_j(0,1)\right) \tag{21.40}$$

where η_i's are standard deviations for Gaussian mutations. The suffix j is used to indicate the jth component of the corresponding vectors. Whether mutation would be applied at a gene position is determined by the mutation probability. $N(0,1)$ denotes a normally distributed one-dimensional random number with mean zero and standard deviation one. $N_j(0,1)$ indicates that the random number is generated anew for each value of j. The factors τ and $\tau^{'}$ are usually set to $\left(\sqrt{2\sqrt{L}}\right)^{-1}$ and $\left(\sqrt{2L}\right)^{-1}$, respectively, where L represents the length of a chromosome.

It is shown (Xin Yao, et al. 1999) that the Cauchy mutation function performs better than the Gaussian mutation function for most of the benchmark problems used for EPs. Cauchy mutation can perform longer jumps at a high probability, and hence, its search step size is considerably larger than the Gaussian one.

The Cauchy distribution function is given by $F_t(z) = \frac{1}{2} + \frac{1}{\pi}\text{arc tan}\left(\frac{z}{t}\right)$. where $t > 0$ is a scale parameter.

The Cauchy mutation follows the following relation

$$z_i^{'}(j) = z_i(j) + \eta_i(j)\delta_j \tag{21.41}$$

where, $\delta_j = t \times \tan\left[\pi\left(F_t(z_i(j)) - \frac{1}{2}\right)\right]$. Generally t is taken to be 1. δ_j is computed for each j anew. The relation for changing η remains same as in the case of Gaussian mutation and is given by Eq. 21.40.

Mutation using probabilistic redistribution: Given a string encoding K cluster centres, the associated partitioning of the data can be computed based on the distance of the points from the centres. In order to generate a new partitioning, we redistribute the elements to different clusters. Elements that are at a larger distance from the centre are the fittest candidates for redistribution to another cluster. We have redistributed an element x_i in cluster C_j to cluster C_k with probability given by Eq. (21.38). In this way, a new cluster configuration $S^{'}$ with energy $E^{'}$ is generated from an existing configuration S with energy E. Thus, at each generation a number of alternative solution strings are generated which are accepted or rejected according to probability $\exp\left[-\frac{E'-E}{T_g}\right]$ as shown in the algorithm. In the mutation phase, we have decided whether elements from a cluster will be redistributed to others depending on mutation probability P_m.

The temperature schedule

In the proposed clustering algorithm, we have used a mutation strategy which uses the Boltzmann distribution function like SA. The asymptotic convergence (i.e. at $g \to \infty$) of the SA is guaranteed for a logarithmic annealing schedule of the form $T_g = T_0/(1 + \ln g)$, where $g \geq 0$ and T_0 is the initial temperature. However, in practice, the logarithmic annealing is far too slow, and hence, a geometric schedule may be used. It can be expressed as $T_g = (1 - \alpha)^g * T_0$, where α is a positive real number close to zero. As $T_g \to 0$, no more perturbation of the cluster configuration is possible, and hence, termination condition is assumed to be reached. In practice, the state of the system configuration is found to be frozen well before this.

An annealing-evolution clustering algorithm, called **ANEV-clustering**, has been demonstrated in this section. The power of annealing procedure for providing stable minimum energy configuration has been integrated with the principles of k-means algorithm and conventional evolutionary programming to search for appropriate clusters which minimize a given criterion function $\mathcal{M}$.

21.10 Conclusion

A large number of clustering algorithms exist in literature which can organize large amounts of data with different speed, reliability and consistency. Many of these techniques are thus, useful for applications such as data mining, information retrieval, image segmentation, signal compression and coding, and machine learning. A good deal of literature exists regarding cluster analysis or exploratory data analysis. Clustering or exploratory data analysis is sometimes referred to as partitioning. The essential idea is to properly partition a data set into appropriate partitions or clusters. These clusters should be the natural subgroups as perceived by a human being in visual sense. This automatic partitioning has found applications in many areas of applied sciences. Although it began with the well-known numerical taxonomy (Sneath and Sokal 1973), it soon became popular in various unrelated fields, including psychology, sociology, geology, medicine, clinical diagnosis, agriculture, defense, etc. Good general overviews can be found regarding clustering methods and applications in literature.

In previous sections, we have discussed different types of commonly used clustering algorithms. These algorithms belong to the classes of deterministic and stochastic processes. Hard, fuzzy and model based probabilistic approaches form another type of categorization of clustering algorithms. Classical algorithms were found to be suitable for relatively smaller data sets. To cope with the present day need for handling large data sets efficiently, many new algorithms including density based, grid based spatial clustering algorithms have been developed. Artificial Neural Networks have also been used for solving the clustering problems. Among the well known neural network architectures, Kohonen's self-organizing network and Learning Vector Quantization (LVQ) method are important in this regard.

Although there exists a broad spectrum of clustering algorithms, newer methods are being developed regularly and frequently to suit to specific application areas. It is now necessary to build some form of generalization of all such algorithms.

21.11 Problems

1. What are the major differences between hierarchical and partitional clustering algorithms?
2. Name some real life situations where application of clustering algorithms will be useful.
3. Why do the single link and complete link algorithms are termed as minimum and maximum algorithms also?
4. What do you mean by a partition of a data set? Can you say whether the k-means algorithm produce optimum partitions always?
5. List some advantages and disadvantages of the k-means algorithm.
6. Do you consider that the PAM algorithm is efficient in some way than the k-means algorithm? Explain your answer.
7. Consider the following 2D data set.

Item No.	*Feature 1*	*Feature 2*
1	1.0	1.0
2	2.0	3.0
3	0.5	1.5
4	2.5	5.0
5	5.0	6.0

   Compute average link distance between two clusters $\{5.0, 6.0\}$ and $\{2.0, 3.0\}$.

8. Compute the Euclidean and Manhattan distances between data items $\{5.0, 6.0\}$ and $\{2.0, 3.0\}$.
9. Write down advantages and disadvantages of hard and fuzzy clustering techniques. Show that hard clustering is a special case of fuzzy clustering.

10. Consider the pattern set $S = \{(1,2),(3,2),(2,4),(4,1),(3,4)\}$. Do the following for this set:

    - Apply single-linkage algorithm to classify S into two clusters. Compute the Euclidean distance between the two centres.
    - Apply average-linkage algorithm to classify S into two clusters. Compute the city-block distance between the two centres.
    - Apply complete-linkage algorithm to classify S into two clusters. Compute the Manhattan distance between the two centres.
    - Illustrate the differences between single-linkage, average linkage and complete-linkage clustering algorithms and the obtained cluster structures.

11. What is the stopping criteria for the k-means clustering algorithm? Write down the advantages and disadvantages of this algorithm.
12. Trace the steps of the k-means algorithm for finding out two clusters of the above data set considering $\{5.0, 6.0\}$ and $\{2.0, 3.0\}$ as initial centres.
13. How can one determine the clustering tendency present in a data set? Briefly describe one such method you know.
14. What are the roles of a cluster validity index in clustering? Name some commonly used validity indices and write down their analytic expressions with explanation for the symbols.
15. What are the major drawbacks of the ISODATA algorithm? What other techniques for determining the number of clusters in a data set?
16. What is meant by fuzzy clustering? Write down the relations used for fuzzy membership grade and fuzzy centre vectors used in fuzzy c-means algorithm.
17. What may be the problems of the fuzzy c-means algorithm when applied for large data sets? Can you suggest any method to eliminate such problems?
18. What, in your opinion is the importance of clustering in pattern recognition?
19. What are the advantages of GA based partitional clustering algorithms over k-means?
20. Write down a simulated annealing based clustering algorithm where centre vectors are represented as problem variables which are updated during each iteration.
21. What are the reasons that simulated annealing and genetic algorithm based clustering algorithms are time consuming.
22. Write a short note on annealing-evolution procedure for clustering.

APPENDIX

Edge Detection Using Simulated Annealing

n Chapter 10, it is told that the edge detection process simplifies analysis and repre-entation of images by drastically reducing the amount of data to be processed, while t the same time preserving useful structural information about object boundaries. lassically this problem was tried to be solved by considering image grey level differ-nces. First order, second order differences and their various combinations had been pplied by Sobel, Canny, etc. But all these techniques have their limitations. Later n, with development of stochastic optimization algorithms like simulated annealing, enetic algorithms, etc. the edge detection problem has been modelled as an opti-nization problem, and better solutions were found. We shall describe a simulated nnealing based edge detection algorithm. Here, the edge is defined to be a statistical ost function, whose minimization will lead to a good edge structure for the input mage. This approach involves use of different masks for convolution as well as corre-ation operations needed to find out an approximate edge structure initially and then o find out a better local edge structure by means of correlation, respectively.

A.1 Simulated Annealing

imulated Annealing (SA) is a stochastic optimization technique, belongs to a class f local search algorithms. It utilizes the principles of statistical machines, regarding he behaviour of a large number of atoms at low temperature or low energy states, or finding minimal cost solutions to large optimization problems by minimizing the ssociated energy. However, it is not sufficient to lower the temperature alone, since his results in unstable states. In the annealing process, the temperature is first raised o a high value ($T_{\max}$), then decreases gradually to a very low value ($T_{\min}$), while nsuring that one spends sufficient time at each temperature. This process yields table low energy states. This annealing procedure can be applied in many image rocessing tasks where the concerned problem can be formulated as an optimization unction. Here, a particular use of SA for edge detection is described.

In the present implementation of edge detection using SA, we assume that the initial edge structures are obtained from an image enhancement process. Subsequently, at each pixel site we need to apply the annealing process considering lattice (mask) structure of size 3×3 and compute the response of the mask (lattice). A number of alternative edge structures for each lattice configuration are previously defined and stored for future use. The edge detection problem has been formulated as a cost minimization one. At each edge pixel a local cost can be computed using desired edge characteristics. If an alternative edge structure is found to yield a lower cost at any site, it is used to replace the old one. The candidate edge structures are selected from a pool by applying a certain strategy.

The edge detectors using finite difference operators are found to display many false, thick and improper edge structures. However, it is better to mention that we cannot avoid the use of difference of some kind over the image data, as a basis of any edge detection procedure. Here also, initially a crude edge structure of the image is detected by applying an enhancement procedure. This crude edge pattern passes through a refinement procedure to produce nearly desired edge patterns.

A.1.1 Edge Detection as an Optimization Problem

In many search problems, the search criteria can be formulated as a function, the optimum value of which provides the solution to the problem. The function to be optimized is called the objective function or the cost function or the energy function. The energy defines some kind of goodness of the function with the help of a set of values assigned to the variables of the function (problem variables). Recently, stochastic algorithms like simulated annealing are being widely used to successfully solve various search and optimization problems.

To cast the problem of edge detection as one of the category of optimization problem, we must define the goodness of the edge pattern with the help of variables that represent the desired characteristic properties of the edge pattern. The initial edge structure may be generated randomly or by using some approximate gradient based technique, and then the variables are assigned a different set of values by making a random search or some kind of guided search in the search space, to find a better edge structure.

An edge pattern may be characterized by its thinness, continuity, curvature, regional dissimilarity measure, number of edge points, etc. We use the definition of edge, the energy function and the strategy as proposed by Tan et al. in 1992. They defined the cost function associated with the goodness of an edge at a point with reference to a local edge structure of a certain width around the point. The point cost of an edge configuration S at a pixel site l is defined as

$$F(S,l) = \sum_i w_i C_i(S,l) \tag{A.1}$$

The total cost $F(S)$ of an edge pattern S is the sum of the point costs at each pixel site in the image, defined as

$$F(S) = \sum_{l} F(S, l) = \sum_{l} \sum_{i} w_i C_i(S, l)$$

At every pixel site l, a window $W(l)$ is considered to be replaced by an alternative. If the old pattern at site l be S_i and the new pattern be S_j, then the comparative cost function becomes

$$\Delta F(S_i, S_j, l) = \sum_{w(l)} \sum_{i} w_i [C_k(S_i, l) - C_k(S_j, l)]$$

$$= \sum_{w(l)} \sum_{i} \Delta C_k(S_i, S_j, l)$$

where, $0 \leq C_k \leq 1$ and $w_k \geq 0$. The C_ks are the cost factors and the w_ks are the associated weights. The window $W(l)$ is considered to be a 3×3 window centred at site l. In case of finite difference edge detectors the edges were detected using a pointwise dissimilarity measure, and the local edge structure was not taken into consideration in any way. However, the local edge structure can provide important information regarding the actual edge pattern. This local edge information is considered in the simulated annealing based approach presented here.

A.2 Finding Approximate Edges

Before applying the annealing procedure, we need to find out an approximate edge structure of the image. This process may be termed as an image enhancement process. This is done by measuring region dissimilarities on two sides of some local edge structures. Examples of such local edge structures are shown in Figure A.1. Finding out average grey values on both sides of a local edge structure, computing their difference followed by a thresholding technique we can find out an approximate edge structure for the input image.

A.3 Evaluation of the Parameters Defining the Edge

The edge parameters used in the energy functions $F(S, l)$ or in function $\Delta F(S_i, S_j, l)$ are computed by examining the local edge structure of the edge image and also the image data. The five parameters or cost factors to be considered are:

1. $C_d(S, l)$ based on region dissimilarity
2. $C_t(S, l)$ based on edge thickness.

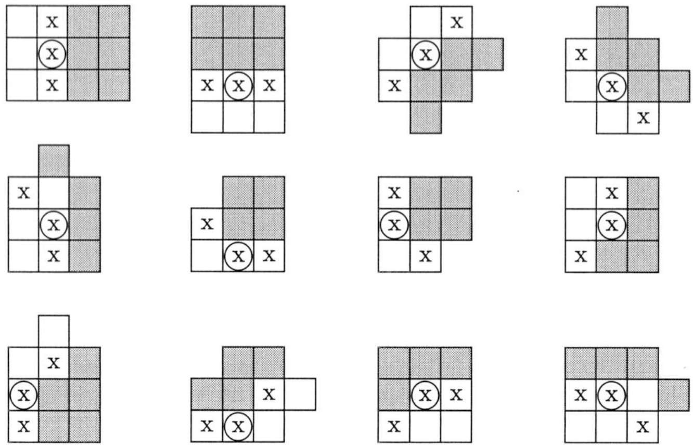

Figure A.1: Enhancement strategy using region dissimilarity.

3. $C_c(S, l)$ based on edge curvature
4. $C_f(S, l)$ based on edge fragmentation
5. $C_e(S, l)$ based on number of edge pixels

Techniques to measure these factors are given in the following subsections.

A.3.1 Region Dissimilarity

The fundamental property of an edge is that it separates regions of dissimilar grey level values. So, we are to find out an approximate edge structure by using a method called **dissimilarity enhancement**. The output of this process is the enhanced image. The enhanced image may be defined as

$$D = D(i, j); \quad 1 \leq i, j \leq N$$

which is a collection of $N \times N$ pixels where each pixel value is proportional to the degree of region dissimilarity that exists at that pixel site. The pixel value lie in the range $0 \leq D(i, j) \leq 1$. Pixels with large values, closer to 1, are considered good candidates for edge points. Two things are considered in the enhancement procedure:

1. Well defined regions of interest on either side of an edge, and
2. A function that measures the dissimilarity between the regions of interest.

The regions of interest are defined with reference to a set of selected edge structures. This set is called the basis set. Actually twelve basic edge structures contained in a 3×3 window are used. These edge configurations of basic edged and corresponding regions of interest are described by Tan et al. (1992). The function that measures the dissimilarity between regions R_1 and R_2 is denoted by $f(R_1, R_2)$. This measure used here is a simple difference of grey value averages in regions R_1 and R_2. The procedure to obtain the enhanced image D from the original image G is given in Figure A.1.

1. Initially, all the pixels in $D(l)$ are set equal to zero
2. At each pixel site l, perform the following steps:
   - Each of the edge structures in the basis set is fitted onto the site l by centering it at location l in G. The corresponding paired regions R_1 and R_2 in G are determined for each structure, and the value of $f(R_1, R_2)$ is computed. The structure giving the maximum value is considered to be the best fitted edge structure. The edge pixels in the best fitted edge structure are named as l, l_1, l_2.
   - Next, the non-maximal supression is performed by shifting the location of the best edge structure in a direction determined by the edge structure. For vertical, horizontal and diagonal edge structures, the shifting is done in the directions perpendicular to the edge structure by one pixel position. For all other edge structures, the shifting is done by moving the edge pattern in each of the four directions: up, down, right and left. For each shifted edge, we determine the new regions for R_1 and R_2 and evaluate the value of $f(R_1, R_2)$. One of the following two cases are then considered:
     - If no larger value of $f(R_1, R_2)$ results from shifting the best fitted edge structure, we set
$$\delta = \frac{f(R_1, R_2)}{3}$$
       where $f(R_1, R_2)$ is determined by using the best fitted edge structure. We then increment the value of each of the pixels $D(l), D(l_1)$ and $D(l_2)$ by δ.
     - If there is a larger value of $f(R_1, R_2)$ from one of the shifted edge structures, we do not alter any pixel value.
3. Finally, the value of the pixel in $D(l)$ at all sites are truncated to a maximum of one.

The last step is performed to ensure that the dissimilarity values lie in the assumed range $0 \leq D(l) \leq 1$. The cost factor $C_d(S, l)$ is computed using the enhanced image $D(l)$ and the edge image $S(l)$. The cost factor $C_d(S, l)$ may be computed by considering a local edge structure around the site l. The local edge structure may be confined within a $3\times$ or $5\times$ or a larger window surrounding the site l.

A.3.2 Edge Thickness

The cost factor $C_t(S, l)$ determines the thickness of an edge pattern and its reduction will improve the desired thinness. If an edge pixel causes multiple links with any of its nearest neighbour pixels then that pixel is a thick pixel and the cost factor $C_t(S, l)$ at that pixel will be equal to 1, otherwise $C_t(S, l) = 0$.

A.3.3 Edge Curvature

The high curvatures at edge corners are not desired in most of the situations. Thus, the cost factor $C_c(S,l)$ is defined, whose value may be 0.0, 0.5 or 1.0 when the curvature at any pixel (edge corner) is zero, less than 45 deg and greater than 45 deg, respectively.

A.3.4 Edge Fragmentation

The fragmented edges are highly undesired. The cost factor $C_f(S,l)$ determines the degree of fragmentation at any particular pixel position. If the pixel at site l is not having any neighbour pixel then $C_f(S,l) = 1$. If the site l has only one neighbour pixel then $C_f(S,l) = 0.5$, otherwise it is 0.

A.3.5 Number of Edge Pixels

The cost factor $C_e(S,l)$ favours the detection of an edge pixel at positions having a non-zero value of $f(R_1, R_2)$, thus, leading to the detection of an excessive number of edge pixels. So, to control the selection of edge points the measure $C_e(S,l)$ is used. If site l is an edge pixel then $C_e(S,l) = 1$, otherwise it is 0.

A.3.6 Weight Factors

Now, as seen from Eq. (A.1), the cost factor at a particular site l is an weighted average of all the above component cost factors. The requirements of the components are conflicting. Thus, the edge detection process using the combined cost factor may be treated as a combinatorial optimization problem.

A decision table for the determination of the values of component cost factors at any site l is illustrated in Table A.1. The values of the weights of the corresponding cost factors are presently determined heuristically. As recommended by Tan et al., (1992) the values may be chosen from

$$w_d(S,l) = 2.00$$

$$w_e(S,l) = 1.00$$

$$w_c(S,l) = 0.25, 0.50, 0.75$$

$$w_f(S,l) = 2.00, 3.00, 4.00$$

$$w_t(S,l) = 2 \times w_f(S,l) - w_e(S,l) + w_d(S,l) - w_e(S,l) + 1.00$$

Table A.1: Decision Table for Computing the Component Cost Factors at Site l (d : Do not Care Values)

Whether Edge or Non-edge	Edge								Non-edge
No. of edge pixels	0	1	2				3		d
Thin or thick pixel	d	d	Thin			Thick	Thin	Thick	d
Curvature at site l	d	d	0°	45°	$\geq 90°$	d	d	d	d
C_c	0	0	0	0.5	1	1	1	1	0
C_d	0	0	0	0	0	0	0	0	$D(l)$
C_e	1	1	1	1	1	1	1	1	0
C_f	1	0.5	0	0	0	0	0	0	0
C_t	0	0	0	0	0	1	0	1	0

A.4 Simulated Annealing Algorithm

The optimization problem can be formulated as a pair (S, E), where $S \in R^n$ and E is an n-dimensional real valued function called the **energy function** providing the mapping $S \to R$. The problem is to find an assignment $x_{\min} \in S$ such that $E(x_{\min})$ is globally minimal on S. In other words, we are to find out an $x_{\min} \in S$, such that

$$\forall x_i \in S : E(x_{\min}) \leq E(x_i)$$

At a given temperature T, the metropolis method is a way to sample states of the physical system with the Boltzmann distribution function

$$f = \exp\left(\frac{-E}{T}\right)$$

which is the probability of the system being in energy state E at temperature T. If a particular state S be represented by the configuration x_i, one small perturbation Δx_i will cause the system to reach the configuration $x_i + \Delta x_i$ and the corresponding change in energy is

$$\Delta E = E(x_i + \Delta x_i) - E(x_i)$$

If $\Delta E \leq 0$, then the perturbation is accepted, for this means the new state is energetically favourable; otherwise, it is accepted with a probability of

$$P = \exp\left(\frac{-\Delta E}{T}\right)$$

The SA algorithm is outlined below

begin
$T = T_{max}$

```
        initialize (T, E)
        while (T > T_min)
        begin
            for i = 1 to N_T do
            begin
                compute E' from E : E' ← E + ΔE
                if (ΔE ≤ 0)
                    then accept the new state and the corresponding energy E'
                    else if (exp(−ΔE/T) > random[0, 1))
                        then accept the new state and the corresponding energy E'
                        else retain the earlier state corresponding to energy E
            end
            decrement T
        end
    end
```

A.5 Implementation of Edge Detector

To implement the simulated annealing based edge detection algorithm, we need to find out an enhanced image. This enhanced edge image is found by applying a set of specific masks of varying sizes (as suggested by Tan et al. 1992). Twelve such masks are used and depending on the maximum response a particular edge structure is selected at each location. Now, this edge image is refined by applying the cost minimization procedure using SA. At each pixel position, either a 3×3 or a 5×5 window is considered around the concerned site l, and then SA based purturbation is applied at different temperatures.

A.5.1 Method of Generating Candidate States

The following five strategies are followed for this purpose. Here, we assume that the site $l \in L$ is given. L is the 3×3 or a 5×5 lattice of pixels under consideration. l is the central pixel site within L.

1. Strategy 1: Complementation of pixel at site l.
2. Strategy 2: Complementation of pixel at sites l and l', where l' is a neighbour of l.
3. Strategy 3: Single pixel shift. A pixel at site $l_1 \in L$ is shifted to one of its neighbouring locations.
4. Strategy 4: pixel shift. More than one pixels within L are shifted to one of their neighbouring locations.
5. Strategy 5: Complementation of pixel value at any arbitrary location within L.

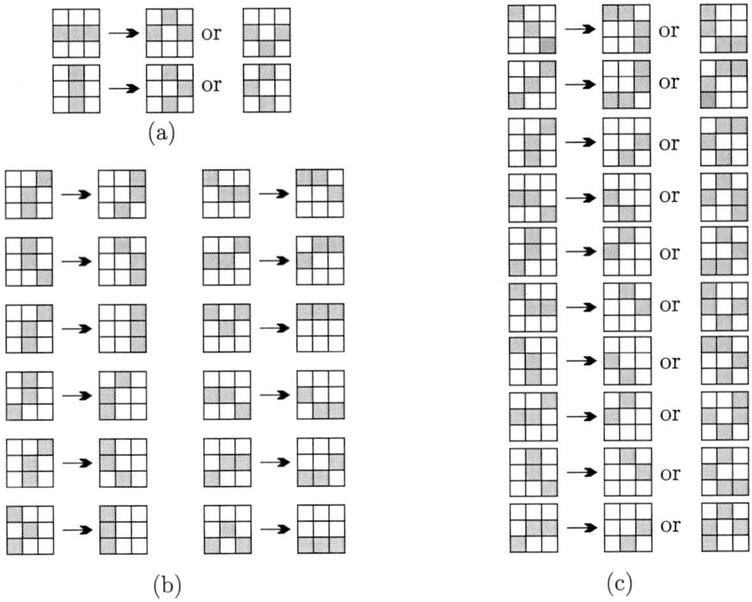

Figure A.2: Different types of alternative edge structure selection strategy.

A candidate is selected from a pool of states applying a certain strategy selected from a transformation distribution $R : \{p_1, p_2, p_3, p_4, p_5\}$ where p_i is the probability of selecting the ith transformation strategy. In Bhanderkar, it is suggested that $p_1 = 200/1024, p_2 = 300/1024, p_3 = 200/1024, p_4 = 200/1024, p_5 = 124/1024$.

The temperature schedule $T = \{T_k\}$ is a sequence of strictly monotonically decrementing non-negative values, which tends to zero as k tends to infinity. Since logarithmic annealing schedule is too slow, a geometric annealing schedule of the form $T_k = T_0 \times (1 - \alpha)^k$ may be very useful in this regard. In the above expression, α may be set to a fraction, say, 0.05 and T_0 may assume any value in $[5, 100]$. With this annealing schedule, most of the applications are found to freeze after 100 to 200 iterations. Since no further changes are possible after this stage, it is assumed that the ground energy state is reached and the best edge configuration is obtained.

A.5.2 Observed Results

The above technique of SA-based edge detector has been applied on the *keys* image. During each scan over the enhanced image of size $N \times N$, the annealing procedure is iterated N^2 times. By applying the annealing procedure, local cost at each site l is computed by using window size of 3×3. One may use a larger window size like 5×5. The logic behind this strategy is that with an enlarged window more local information will be included and the resulting edge structure will be more correct. However, increasing window size by a large value may degrade the process as in that case the differences between cost values rendered by the competing alternative patterns will be significantly less.

In Figure A.3, results of applications of SA based edge detection are shown. Here, the key's image is used as input. After applying the enhancement procedure, we get a relatively thick approximate edge structure. Applications of the annealing process refines this edge image and outputs thin and well formed edge structures. It must be noted in this connection that the results may vary depending on user selected threshold values and other weighing parameters. In the present implementation, a constant annealing temperature schedule of 0.01 is used only. By using more suitable schedules the process may produce better results. It may be noted that by using a proper threshold value the dissimilarity matrix and the approximate edge pattern, in the enhancement phase, can be given more suitable shapes.

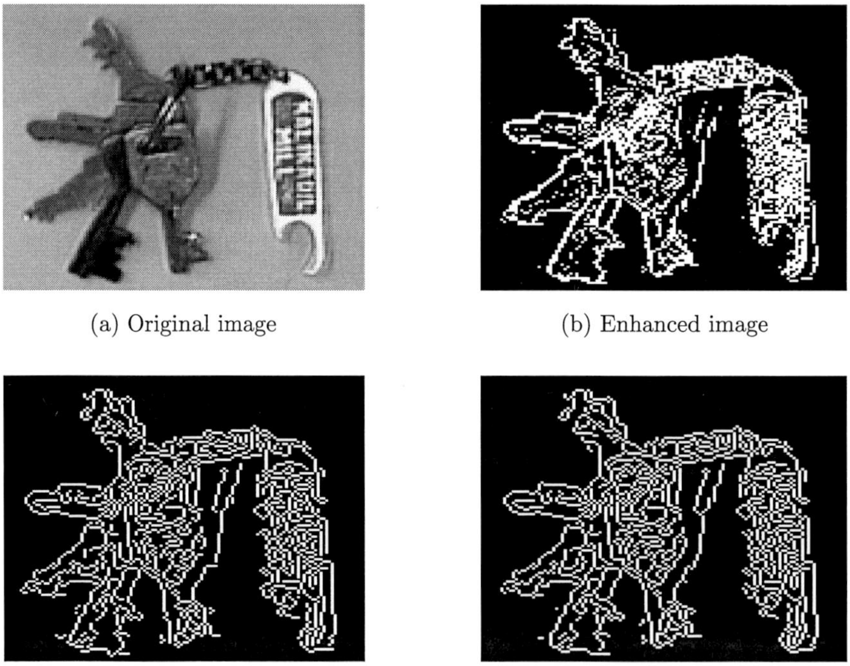

(a) Original image

(b) Enhanced image

(c) After 100 annealing iterations

(d) After 200 annealing iterations

Figure A.3: Edge detection using SA.

Bibliography

Ahmed, N., T. Natarajan and K.R. Rao, "On image processing and discrete cosine transform," *IEEE Transaction on Computers*, vol. C: 23, pp. 90–93, 1974.

Ahuja, N., L. Davis, D.L. Milgram and A. Rosenfeld, "Piecewise approximation of pictures using maximal neighborhood", *IEEE Transaction on Computer*, C-27, pp. 375–379, 1978.

Anderberg, M.R., *Cluster Analysis for Application.* Academic Press, 1973.

Anderson, T.W., *An Introduction to Multivariate Statistical Analysis.* New York: Wiley, 1958.

Ando, S., "Consistent gradient operators," *IEEE Trans. on PAMI*, vol. 22, pp. 252–265, 2000.

Andrews, H.C., *Computer Techniques in Image Processing.* New York: Academic Press, 1977.

Andrews, H.C., *Mathematical Techniques in Pattern Recognition.* New York: Wiley Interscience, 1972.

Ang, P.H., P.A. Ruetz and D. Auld, "Video compression makes big gains," *IEEE Spectrum*, vol. 28, pp. 16–19, 1991.

Ankerbrandt, C.A., B.P. Buckles and F.E. Petry, "Scene recognition using genetic algorithm with semantic nets," *Pattern Recognition Letters*, vol. 11, pp. 285–293, 1990.

Annadurai, S. and R. Shanmugalakshmi, *Fundamentals of Digital Image Processing.* New Delhi: Pearson Education, 2007.

Arcelli, C., L. Cordella and S. Lavialdi, "Parallel thinning of binary pictures", *Electronic Letters*, vol. 11, pp. 148–149, 1975.

Bäck, T., *Evolutionary Algorithms in Theory and Practice.* New York: Oxford University Press, 1996.

Baker, F.B. and L.J. Hubert, "Measuring the power of hierarchical cluster analysis," *J. Am. Statis. Ass.*, vol. 70, pp. 31–38, 1975.

Ball, G.H. and D. Hall, "Isodata: A novel method of data analysis and pattern classification," tech. rep., Stanford Research Institute, Menlo Park, California, 1965.

Bandyopadhyay, S., C.A. Murthy and S.K. Pal, "Pattern classification using genetic algorithms," *Pattern Recog. Lett.*, vol. 16, pp. 801–808, 1995.

Bandyopadhyay, S., U. Maulik and M.K. Pakhira, "Clustering using simulated annealing with probabilistic redistribution," *International Journal of Pattern Recognition and Artificial Intelligence*, vol. 15, pp. 269–285, 2001.

Basak, J., N.R. Pal and P.S. Patel, "Thinning in binary and gray images: A connectionist approach", *J. Inst. Electronics and Tele-Comm. Engrs.*, vol. 42, pp. 305–313, 1996.

Baxes, G.A., *Digital Image Processing: Principles and Applications.* New York: John Wiley & Sons, 1994.

Bezdek, J.C. and N.R. Pal, "Some new indexes of cluster validity," *IEEE Trans. Systs., Man Cyberns. (Part-B)*, vol. 28, pp. 301–315, 1998.

Bezdek, J.C. and R.H. Hathaway, "Vat: A tool for visual assessment of (cluster) tendency," *Proceedings of IJCNN,* Piscataway, NJ: IEEE Press, pp. 2225–2230, 2002.

Bezdek, J.C., R.H. Hathaway and J.M. Huband, "Visual assessment of clustering tendency for rectangular dissimilarity matrices," *IEEE Transaction on Fuzzy Systems*, 2002.

Bezdek, J.C., "Cluster validity with fuzzy sets," *Journal of Cybernetics*, vol. 3, pp. 58–73, 1974.

Bezdek, J.C., "Computing with uncertainty," *IEEE Communications Magazine*, pp. 24–36, September 1992.

Bezdek, J.C., *Pattern Recognition with Fuzzy Objective Function Algorithms.* New York: Plenum Press, 1981.

Bhandari, D., C.A. Murthy and S.K. Pal, "Genetic algorithm with elitist" model and its convergence," *Intl. J. Pattern Recog. Art. Intell.*, vol. 10, pp. 731–747, 1996.

Bhaskaran, V. and K. Konstantinos, *Image and Video Compression Standards: Algorithms and Architectures.* Boston, USA: Kluwer, 1997.

Biberman, L.M., *In Perception of Displayed Information.* New York: Plenum Press, 1973.

Blackwelder, R.E., *Taxonomy.* New York: John Wiley & Sons, 1966.

Boie, R.A. and I.J. Cox, "An analysis of camera noise," *IEEE Trans. on PAMI*, vol. 14, pp. 671–674, 1992.

Borgefors, G., "Distance transformation in arbitrary dimensions," *Computer Vision, Graphics and Image Processing*, vol. 27, pp. 321–345, 1984.

Bracewell, R.N., *The Fourier Transform and its Applications.* New York: McGraw-Hill, 2000.

Bradley, P.S., U. Fayyad and C. Reina, "Scaling clustering algorithms to large databases," in *Proceedings of the 4th ACM SIGKDD,* New York, pp. 9–15, 1998.

Bradley, P.S., U. Fayyad and C. Reina, "Scaling EM (expectation-maximization) clustering to large databases," tech. rep., Microsoft Research, Redmond, USA, 1999.

Brigham, E.O., *The Fast Fourier Transform and its Applications.* Upper Saddle River, NJ: Prentice Hall, 1988.

Canny, J., "A computational approach to edge detection," *IEEE Transaction on PAMI*, vol. 8, no. 679–698, 1986.

Carlson, A.B., *Communication System: An Introduction to Signal and Noise in Electrical Communication.* New York: McGraw-Hill, 1986.

Carnevali, P., L. Coletti and S. Paternello, "Image processing using simulated annealing," *IBM Journal for Research and Development*, vol. 29, no. 6, pp. 569–579, 1985.

Carpenter, G.A. and S. Grossberg, "A massively parallel architecture for a self-organizing neural pattern recognition machine," *Computer Vision, Graphics, Image Processing*, vol. 37, pp. 54–115, 1983.

Carpenter, G.A. and S. Grossberg, "The art of adaptive pattern recognition by self-organizing neural network," *IEEE Computer Magazine*, vol. 21, pp. 77–88, 1988.

Castleman, K.R., *Digital Image Processing.* Upper Saddle River, NJ: Prentice-Hall, 1996.

Centeno, J.A.S. and V. Haertel, "An adaptive image enhancement algorithm," *Pattern Recognition*, vol. 30, pp. 1183–1189, 1997.

Chanda, B. and D.D. Majumder, "A note on use of graylevel cooccurrence matrix in threshold selection," *Signal Processing*, vol. 15, pp. 149–167, 1988.

Chanda, B. and D.D. Majumder, *Digital Image Processing and Analysis.* New Delhi: PHI Learning, 2001.

Chaudhury, B.B., "A note on fast algorithms for spatial domain techniques in image processing," *IEEE Trans. on SMC*, vol. 13, pp. 1166–1169, 1983.

Chen, C.H., "On information and distance measures, error bounds and feature selection," *Information Sciences*, vol. 10, pp. 159–173, 1976.

Cheriet, M., J.N. Said and C.Y. Suen, "A recursive thresholding technique for image segmantation," *IEEE Trans. on Image Processing*, vol. 7, pp. 918–921, 1998.

Clarke, R.J., *Transform Coding of Images.* New York: Academic Press, 1985.

Cooley, J.W. and W.J. Tukey, "An algorithm for machine calculation of complex fourier series," *Mathematics of Computing*, vol. 19, pp. 297–301, 1969.

Cooley, J.W., P.A.W. Lewis and P.D. Welch, "The fast fourier transfor and its applications," *IEEE Trans. on Education*, vol. 12, pp. 27–34, 1969.

Cutting, D.R., D.R. Karger, J.O. Pederson and J.W. Tukey, "Scatter/gather: A cluster-based approach to browsing large document collections," in *Proc. of 15th Annual Intl. conf. SIGIR, 1992*, (Denmark), pp. 318–329, 1992.

Danielsson, P.E., Euclidean distance mapping, *Computer Vision, Graphics and Image Processing*, vol. 14, pp. 227–248, 1980.

Davies, D.L. and D.W. Bouldin, "A cluster separation measure," *IEEE Trans. Patt. Anal. Machine Intell.*, vol. 1, pp. 224–227, 1979.

Davis, L.S., "Hierarchical generalized hough transforms and line segment based generalized hough transform," *Pattern Recognition,* vol. 15, pp. 277–285, 1982.

DeJong, K.A., "Learning with genetic algorithms," *Machine Learning*, vol. 3, pp. 121–138, 1988.

Dempster, A.P., N.M. Laird and D.B. Rubin, "Maximum likelihood from incomplete data via the EM algorithm," *Journal of the Royal Statistical Society, Series B*, vol. 39(1), pp. 1–38, 1977.

Devijver, P.A. and J. Kittler, *Pattern Recognition: A Statistical Approach.* London: Prentice-Hall, 1982.

Dougherty, E.R., *Random Processes for Image and Signal Processing.* New York: IEEE Press, 2000.

Duda, R.O. and P.E. Hart, "Use of the hough transform to detect lines and curves in pictures," *ACM Communications*, vol. 15, pp. 11–15, 1972.

Duda, R.O. and P.E. Hart, *Pattern Classification and Scene Analysis.* New York: Wiley, 1973.

Duda, R.O. and P.E. Hart, *Pattern Classification.* New York: John Wiley & Sons, 2001.

Dunn, J.C., "A fuzzy relative of the isodata process and its use in detecting compact well-separated clusters," *Journal of Cybernetics*, vol. 3, pp. 32–57, 1973.

Equitz, W.H., "A new vector quantization clustering algorithm," *IEEE Trans. on ASSP*, vol. 37, pp. 1568–1575, 1989.

Eshelman, L.J., Ed., *Proc. of 6th Intl. Conf. Genetic Algorithms.* San Mateo: Morgan Kaufmann, 1995.

Everitt, B.S., *Cluster Analysis*, New York: John Wiley & Sons Inc., 1974.

Fleck, M.M., "Some defects in finite difference edge detectors," *IEEE Transaction on PAMI*, vol. 14, no. 3, pp. 337–344, 1992.

Foley, J., A.V. Daam, S. Feiner and J. Hughes, *Computer Graphics: Principles and Practice.* Reading, Massachusetts: Addison-Wesley, 1992.

Forgy, E.W., "Cluster analysis of multivariate data: Efficiency versus interpretability of classifications," *Biometric Soc. Meetings*, vol. 21, p. 768, 1965.

Forrest, S., Ed., *Proc of 5th Intl. Conf. Genetic Algorithms*, San Mateo: Morgan Kaufmann, 1993.

Fraley, C. and A.E. Raftery, "How many clusters? which clustering method? answer via model-based cluster analysis," Tech. Rep., Department of Statistics, University of Washington, Seattle, USA, 1998.

Freeman, H., "Computer processing of line drawing images", *ACM Computing Survey*, vol. 6, pp. 57–97, 1974.

Freeman, H., and R. Shapira, "Determining the minimum-area encasing rectangle for an arbitrary closed curve", *Communications of the ACM*, vol. 18, pp. 409–413, 1975.

Fu, K.S., *Syntactic Pattern Recognition and Applications.* London: Academic Press, 1982.

Fukunaga, K., *Introduction to Statistical Pattern Recognition.* New York: Academic Press, 1972.

Geman, D., S. Geman, C. Graffigne and P. Dong, "Boundary detection by constrained optimization," *IEEE Trans. on Pattern Analysis and Machine Intelligence*, vol. 12, pp. 609–628, 1990.

Goldberg, D.E., *Genetic Algorithms in {S}earch, Optimization and Machine Learning.* New York: Addison-Wesley, 1989.

Gonzalez R.C. and R.E. Woods, *Digital Image Processing.* Reading, Massachusetts: Addison-Wesley, 1992.

Gonzalez, R.C. and P. Wintz, *Digital Image Processing.* Massachusetts: Addison-Wesley, 1977.

Good, I.J., "Categorization of classification," *Mathematics and Computer Science in Biology and Medecine*, 1965.

Goodman, L.P. and W.H. Kruskal, "Measure of association for cross classification," *J. of American Statistical Association*, vol. 49, pp. 732–764, 1954.

Goodman, L.P. and W.H. Kruskal, "Measure of association for cross classification: Further discussion in references," *J. of American Statistical Association*, vol. 54, pp. 123–163, 1959.

Gose, E., R. Johnsonbrugh and S, Jost, *Pattern Recognition and Image Analysis*, New Delhi: PHI Learning, 2005.

Gray, R.M., "Vector quantization," *IEEE Trans. on ASSP*, vol. 1, pp. 4–29, 1984.

Grefenstette, J.J., Ed., *Proc. of 1st Intl. Conf. Genetic Algorithms.* Hillsdale: Lawrence Erlbaum Associates, 1985.

Gunn, S.R., "Edge detection error in the discrete Laplacian of Gaussian," *Proc. of Intl. Conf. on Image Processing*, vol. 2, pp. 515–519, 1998.

Hall, E.L., *Computer Image Processing and Recognition.* New York: Academic Press, 1979.

Hamming, R.W., "Error detecting and error correcting codes," *Bell Systems Technical Journal*, vol. 29, pp. 147–160, 1950.

Haralick, R.M. and J.S.J. Lee, "Context dependent edge detection and evaluation," *Pattern Recognition*, vol. 23, pp. 1–20, 1985.

Haralick, R.M. and L.G. Shapiro, "Survey: Image segmentation," *Computer Vision, Graphics, Image Processing*, vol. 29, pp. 100–132, 1992.

Haralick R.M. and K. Sanmugam, "Combined spectral and spatial processing of ERTS image data", *J. Remote Sensing Environment*, vol. 3, pp. 3–13, 1974.

Haralick, R.M., "Some neighborhood operators", in M. Onoe, K. Jr. Preston and A. Rosenfeld (Eds.), *Real Time Parallel Computing Image Analysis*, New York: Plenum, 1981.

Haralick, R.M., "Statistical image texture analysis", in T.Y. Young and K.S. Fu (Eds.), *Handbook of Pattern Recognition and Image Processing*, San Diego, California: Academic Press, 1986.

Haralick, R.M., K. Sanmugam and I. Dinstein, "Textural features for image classification", *IEEE Transaction on Systems, Man and Cybernetics*, SNC-3, pp. 610–621, 1973.

Hartigan, J.A., *Clustering Algorithms.* Wiley, 1975.

Hathaway, R.J. and J.C. Bezdek, "Optimization of clustering criteria by reformulation," *IEEE Trans. on Fuzzy systems,* vol. 3, pp. 241–245, 1995.

Haykin, Simon S., *Neural Networks*, Macmillan, 1994.

Hill, A. and C.J. Taylor, "Model-based image interpretation using genetic algorithms," *Image and Vision Comput.*, vol. 10, pp. 295–300, 1992.

Holland, J., *Adaptation in Neural and Artificial Systems.* Ann. Arbor, MI: University of Michigan, 1975.

Hubert, L., "Approximate evaluation techniques for the single link and complete link hierarchical clustering procedures," *J. Am. Statis. Ass.*, vol. 69, pp. 698–704, 1974.

Jain, A.K. and R.C. Dubes, *Algorithms for Clustering Data.* Englewood Cliffs, NJ: Prentice-Hall, 1988.

Jain, A.K. and R.P. Duin, "Statistical pattern recognition: A review," *IEEE Transaction on PAMI*, vol. 22, no. 1, pp. 4–37, 1988.

Jain, A.K., "A sinusoidal family of unitary transforms," *IEEE" Transaction on PAMI*, vol. 1, pp. 356–365, 1979.

Jain, A.K., R.P. Duin and J. Mao, "Statistical pattern recognition: A review," *IEEE Transaction on PAMI*, vol. 22, pp. 4–37, 2000.

Janakiraman, V.S., K. Sarukesi and P. Gopalakrishnan, *Artificial Intelligence and Expert Systems.* Delhi: Macmillan India, 2002.

Jardine, N. and R. Sibson, *Mathematical Taxonomy.* London: Wiley, 1971.

Kaufman, L. and P.J. Rousseeuw, Eds., *Finding Groups in Data: an" Introduction to Cluster Analysis.* John Wiley & Sons, 1990.

Kirkpatrick, S., "Optimization by simulated annealing: Quantitative studies," *J. Statist. Phys.*, vol. 34, p. 975, 1984.

Kirkpatrik, S., C. Gellat and M.P. Vecchi, "Optimization by simulated annealing," *Science*, vol. 220, pp. 671–680, 1983.

Kohonen, T., "The self-organizing map," *Proceedings of the IEEE*, vol. 78, no. 9, pp. 1464–1480, 1990.

Kohonen, T., *Self-Organization and Associative Memory.* New York: Springer-Verlag, 1988.

Lance, G.N. and W.T. Williams, "A general theory of classificatory sorting strategies: II. Clustering systems," *Computer Journal*, vol. 10, pp. 271–277, 1967.

Ling, R.F., "A probability theory of cluster analysis," *J. Am. Statis. Ass.,* vol. 68, pp. 159–169, 1973.

Lippmann, R.P., "An introduction to computing with neural networks, *IEEE ASSP Magazine*, pp. 4–22, 1987.

Lisboa, P.G.J., *Neural Networks: Current Applications.* London: Chapman & Hall, 1992.

Mahalanobis, P.C., "On the generalized distance in statistics," *J. of the Indian National Institution of Science*, vol. 2, pp. 49–55, 1936.

Mandal, D.P., C.A. Murthy and S.K. Pal, "Analysis of IRS imagery for detecting man-made objects with a multivalued recognition system," *IEEE Trans. on Syst., Man, Cybern.,* Part A, vol. 26, pp. 241–247, 1996.

Maragos, P., "Pattern spectrum and multiscale shape representation", IEEE Trans. on Pattern Recognition and Machine Intelligence, *PAMI-11*, pp. 701–716, 1989.

Maulik, U. and S. Bandyopadhyay, "Fuzzy partitioning using a real-coded variable length genetic algorithm for pixel classification," *IEEE Trans. on Geoscience and Remote Sensing*, vol. 41, no. 5, pp. 1075–1081, 2003.

Maulik, U. and S. Bandyopadhyay, "Genetic algorithms based clustering technique," *Pattern Recognition*, vol. 33, pp. 1455–1465, 2000.

McCulloch W.S. and W.H. Pitts, "A logical calculus of the ideas imminent in nervous activity," *Bulletin of Mathematical Biophysics*, vol. 5, pp. 115–133, 1943.

McQueen, J.B., "Some methods of classification and analysis of multivariate observations," in *Proc. of 5th Berkeley Symposium on Mathematical Statistics and Probability*, pp. 281–297, 1967.

Metropolis, N., A. Rosenbluth, M. Rosenbluth, A. Teller and E. Teller, "Equation of state calculation by fast computing machines," *Journal of Chemical Physics*, vol. 21, pp. 1087–1092, 1953.

Michalewicz, Z., *Genetic Algorithms + Data Structures = Evolution" Programs.* New York: Springer-Verlag, 1992.

Milligan, G.W. and M.C. Cooper, "An examination of procedures for determining the number of clusters in a data set," *Psychometrika*, vol. 50, pp. 159–179, 1985.

Murthy, C.A. and N. Chowdhury, "In search of optimal clusters using genetic algorithms," *Pattern Recog. Lett.*, vol. 17, pp. 825–832, 1996.

Narayanan, K.A., D. O'Learly and A. Rosenfeld, "Image smoothing and segmentation by cost minimization," *IEEE Trans. on Syst., Man, Cybern,* vol. 12, p. 91, 1982.

Ng, R.T. and J. Han, "Efficient and effective clustering methods for spatial data mining," in *Proceedings of the 20th VLDB Conference,* Santiago, Chile, pp. 144–155, 1994.

Pakhira, M.K., "A hybrid genetic algorithm using probabilistic selection," *Journal of the Institution of Engineers (India)*, vol. 84, pp. 23–30, 2003.

Pakhira, M.K., *Computer Graphics, Multimedia and Animation.* New Delhi: PHI Learning, 2008.

Pakhira, M.K., R.K. De, S. Bandyopadhyay, and U. Maulik, "Pipelined processing of genetic clustering," in *Proc. of Intl. Conference on Intelligent Sensing and Information Processing* (Channai), pp. 23–28, 2004.

Pakhira, M.K., S. Bandyopadhyay and U. Maulik "A study of some fuzzy cluster validity indices, genetic clustering and application to pixel classification," *Fuzzy Sets and Systems*, vol. 155, no. 2, pp. 191–214, 2003.

Pakhira, M.K., S. Bandyopadhyay and U. Maulik, "Validity index for crisp and fuzzy clusters," *Pattern Recognition*, vol. 37, pp. 487–501, 2003.

Pakhira, M.K., S. Bandyopadhyay, and U. Maulik, "An annealing-evolution technique for clustering," *Foundations of Computing and Decision Sciences*, vol. 29, pp. 345–372, 2004.

Pal, N.R. and J.C. Bezdek, "On cluster validity for the fuzzy c-means model," *IEEE Transaction on Fuzzy Systems*, vol. 3, no. 3, pp. 370–379, 1995.

Pal, N.R. and S.K. Pal, "A review of image segmentation," *Pattern Segmentation*, vol. 26, pp. 1277–1294, 1993.

Pal, N.R., J.C. Bezdek, and E.C.K. Tsao, "Generalized clustering networks and Kohonen's self-organizing scheme," *IEEE Trans. on Neural Networks*, vol. 4, pp. 549–557, 1993.

Pal, S.K. and P.P. Wang, Eds., *Genetic Algorithms for Pattern Recognition.* Boca Raton: CRC Press, 1996.

Pal, S.K. and S. Mitra, "Multilayer perceptron, fuzzy sets and classification," *IEEE Trans. Neural Networks,* vol. 3, pp. 683–697, 1992.

Pal, S.K. and S. Mitra, *Neuro-fuzzy Pattern recognition.* New York: John Wiley, 1999.

Pal, S.K., A. Ghosh and B. Umashankar, "Segmentation with remotely sensed images with fuzzy thresholding, and quantitative evaluation," *International Journal of Remote Sensing*, vol. 21, pp. 2269–2300, 2000.

Pal, S.K., D. Bhandari and M.K. Kundu, "Genetic algorithms for optimal image enhancement," *Pattern Recognition Letters*, vol. 15, pp. 261–271, 1994.

Papoulis, A., *Probability, Random Variables, and Stochastic Processes.* New York: McGraw-Hill, 1984.

Pavlidis, T., *Algorithms for Graphics and Image Processing.* Rockville, Maryland: Computer Science Press, 1982.

Pavlidis, T., *Structural Pattern Recognition.* New York: Springer-Verlag, 1977.

Pratt, W.K., *Digital Image Processing.* New York: McGraw-Hill, 1991.

Quinlan, J.R., *C4.5 Programs for Machine Learning.* New Jersey, USA: Morgan Kaufmann, 1993.

Rajasekaran, S. and G.A.V. Pai, *Neural Networks, Fuzzy Logic and Genetic Algorithms.* New Delhi: PHI Learning, 2007.

Rechenberg, I., *Evolutions Strategie: Optimierung Technischer systeme nach Prinzipien der Biologischen Evolution.* Ph.D. thesis, Frommann-Holzboog, Stuttgart, germany, 1973.

Revankar, P.S. and P.R. Patil, "The application of data mining for direct marketing, *CSI Communications*, vol. 33, no. 4, pp. 10–13, 2009.

Richards, J.A., *Remote Sensing Digital Image Analysis: An Introduction.* New York: Springer-Verlag, 1993.

Rosenblatt, F., The perceptron: a probabilistic model for information storage and organization of the brain, *Psychology Review*, vol. 65, pp. 386–408, 1958.

Rosenfeld, A. and A.C. Kak, *Digital Picture Processing.* New York: Academic Press, 1982.

Rosenfeld, A. and J.L. Pfaltj, "Distance function on digital features," *Pattern Recognition*, vol. 1, pp. 33–61, 1968.

Rumelhart, D.E., J. McClelland and the PDP Research Group, *Parallel Distributed Processing*, vol. 2, Cambridge: MIT Press, 1986.

Scheunders, P., "A genetic *c*-means clustering algorithm applied to color image quantization," *Pattern Recognition*, vol. 30, no. 6, pp. 859–866, 1997.

Schwefel, H.P., *Numerical Optimization of Computer Models.* New York: Wiley, 1981.

Selim, S.Z. and K. Alsultan, "A simulated annealing algorithm for the clustering problem," *Pattern Recognition*, vol. 24, no. 10, pp. 1003–1008, 1991.

Singh, J., *Great Ideas in Information Theory, Language, and Genetics*, New York: Dover, 1966,

Shinghal, R., *Pattern Recognition: Techniques and Applications.* New Delhi: Oxford University Press, 2006.

Sneath, P.H.A. and R.R. Sokal, *Numerical Taxonomy.* San Francisco: W.H. Freeman, 1973.

Sonka, M., V. Hlavac and R. Boyle, *Image Processing, Analysis and Machine Vision.* Singapore: PWS Publishing Company, Thomson Learning, 2001.

Tan, H.L., S.B. Gelfand and E.J. Delp, "A cost minimization approach to edge detection using simulated annealing," *IEEE Trans. Pattern Analysis and Machine Intelligence*, vol. 14, pp. 3–18, 1992.

Tantrum, J.M., A. Murua and W. Stuetzle, "Hierarchical model-based clustering of large datasets through fractioning and refractioning," in *Proc. of 8th Intl. conf. on Knowledge Discovery and Data Mining*, pp. 183–190, 2002.

Taub, H., D.L. Schilling and G. Saha, *Taub's Principles of Communication Systems.* New Delhi: Tata McGraw-Hill, 2008.

Torre, V. and T.A. Poggio, "On edge detection," *IEEE Transaction on PAMI*, vol. 8, 1986.

Tou, J.T. and R.C. Gonzalez, *Pattern Recognition Principles.* Reading: Addison-Wesley, 1974.

Wang, Z., K.R. Raom and J. Ben-Arie, "Optimal ramp edge detection using expansion matching," *IEEE Transaction on PAMI*, vol. 18, pp. 1092–1097, 1996.

Weszka, J.S., "A survey of threshold selection techniques," *Computer Graphics and Image Processing*, vol. 7, pp. 259–265, 1978.

Widro, B., R.G. Winter and R. Baxter, "Learning phenomena in neural networks," *Proc. of first IEEE conf. on Neural Networks,* vol. 2, pp. 411–429, 1987.

Xie X.L. and A. Beni, "Validity measure for fuzzy clustering," *IEEE Trans. Pattern Anal. Machine Intell.,* vol. 3, pp. 841–846, 1991.

Yamartihita, M. and T. Ibaraki, "Distance defined by neighborhood sequences," *Pattern Recognition*, vol. 19, pp. 337–346, 1989.

Yao, X., Y. Liu and G. Lin, "Evolutionary programming made faster," *IEEE Transaction on Evolutionary Computation*, vol. 3, no. 2, pp. 82–102, 1999.

Zadeh, L.A., "Fuzzy sets," *Information and Control*, vol. 8, pp. 338–353, 1965.

Zhang, T., R. Ramkrishnan and M. Livny; "Birch: A new data clustering algorithm and its applications," *Data Mining and Knowledge Discovery,* vol. 1, pp. 141–182, 1996.

Ziv, J. and A. Lempel, "A universal algorithm for sequential data compression," *IEEE Trans. on Information Theory*, vol. 23, pp. 337–343, 1977.

Index